W9-BYD-308

Frommer's Ireland

2nd Edition

By Jack Jewers

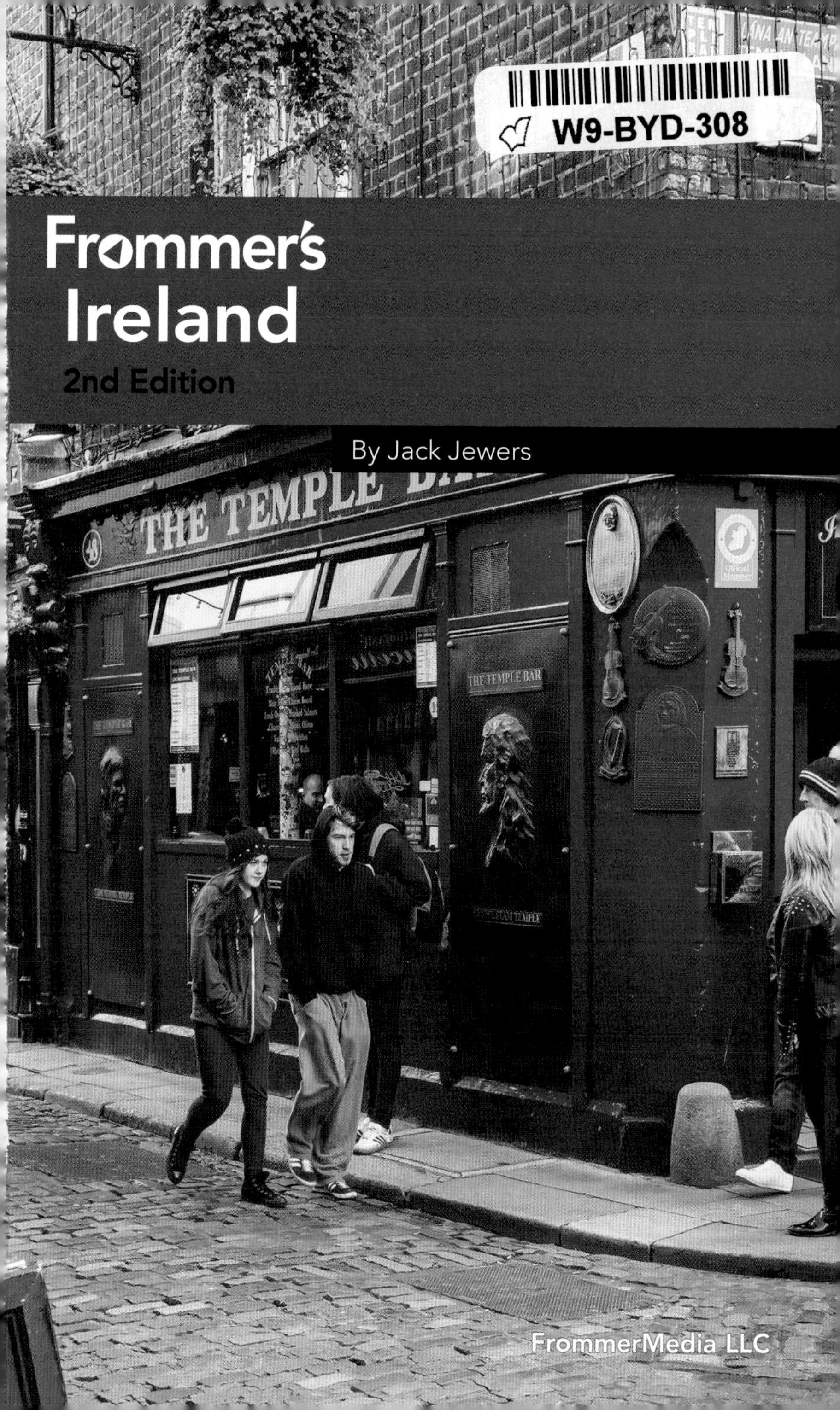

FrommerMedia LLC

Published by:
Frommer Media LLC

Copyright © 2015 by Frommer Media LLC. All rights reserved. No part of this publication may be reproduced, stored in a retrieval system, or transmitted in any form or by any means, electronic, mechanical, photocopying, recording, scanning or otherwise, except as permitted under Sections 107 or 108 of the 1976 United States Copyright Act, without the prior written permission of the Publisher. Requests to the Publisher for permission should be addressed to Support@FrommerMedia.com.

Frommer's is a registered trademark of Arthur Frommer. Frommer Media LLC is not associated with any product or vendor mentioned in this book.

ISBN 978-1-62887-144-9 (paper), 978-62887-145-6 (e-book)

Editorial Director: Pauline Frommer
Development Editor: Melinda Quintero
Production Editor: Donna Wright
Cartographer: Roberta Stockwell

For information on our other products or services, see www.frommers.com.

Frommer Media LLC also publishes its books in a variety of electronic formats. Some content that appears in print may not be available in electronic formats.

Manufactured in China

5 4 3 2 1

CONTENTS

LIST OF MAPS

ABOUT THE AUTHOR

Jack Jewers has written about Ireland for Frommer's since 2006. Born and raised in England, he loved listening to his great aunt's tales about life in Dublin during the civil war. Jack proposed to his Irish-American wife at a spa on the Ring of Kerry. It gets a great review in this book.

ABOUT THE FROMMER TRAVEL GUIDES

For most of the past 50 years, Frommer's has been the leading series of travel guides in North America, accounting for as many as 24% of all guidebooks sold. I think I know why.

Though we hope our books are entertaining, we nevertheless deal with travel in a serious fashion. Our guidebooks have never looked on such journeys as a mere recreation, but as a far more important human function, a time of learning and introspection, an essential part of a civilized life. We stress the culture, lifestyle, history, and beliefs of the destinations we cover, and urge our readers to seek out people and new ideas as the chief rewards of travel.

We have never shied from controversy. We have, from the beginning, encouraged our authors to be intensely judgmental, critical—both pro and con—in their comments, and wholly independent. Our only clients are our readers, and we have triggered the ire of countless prominent sorts, from a tourist newspaper we called "practically worthless" (it unsuccessfully sued us) to the many rip-offs we've condemned.

And because we believe that travel should be available to everyone regardless of their incomes, we have always been cost-conscious at every level of expenditure. Though we have broadened our recommendations beyond the budget category, we insist that every lodging we include be sensibly priced. We use every form of media to assist our readers, and are particularly proud of our feisty daily website, the award-winning Frommers.com.

I have high hopes for the future of Frommer's. May these guidebooks, in all the years ahead, continue to reflect the joy of travel and the freedom that travel represents. May they always pursue a cost-conscious path, so that people of all incomes can enjoy the rewards of travel. And may they create, for both the traveler and the persons among whom we travel, a community of friends, where all human beings live in harmony and peace.

Arthur Frommer

1

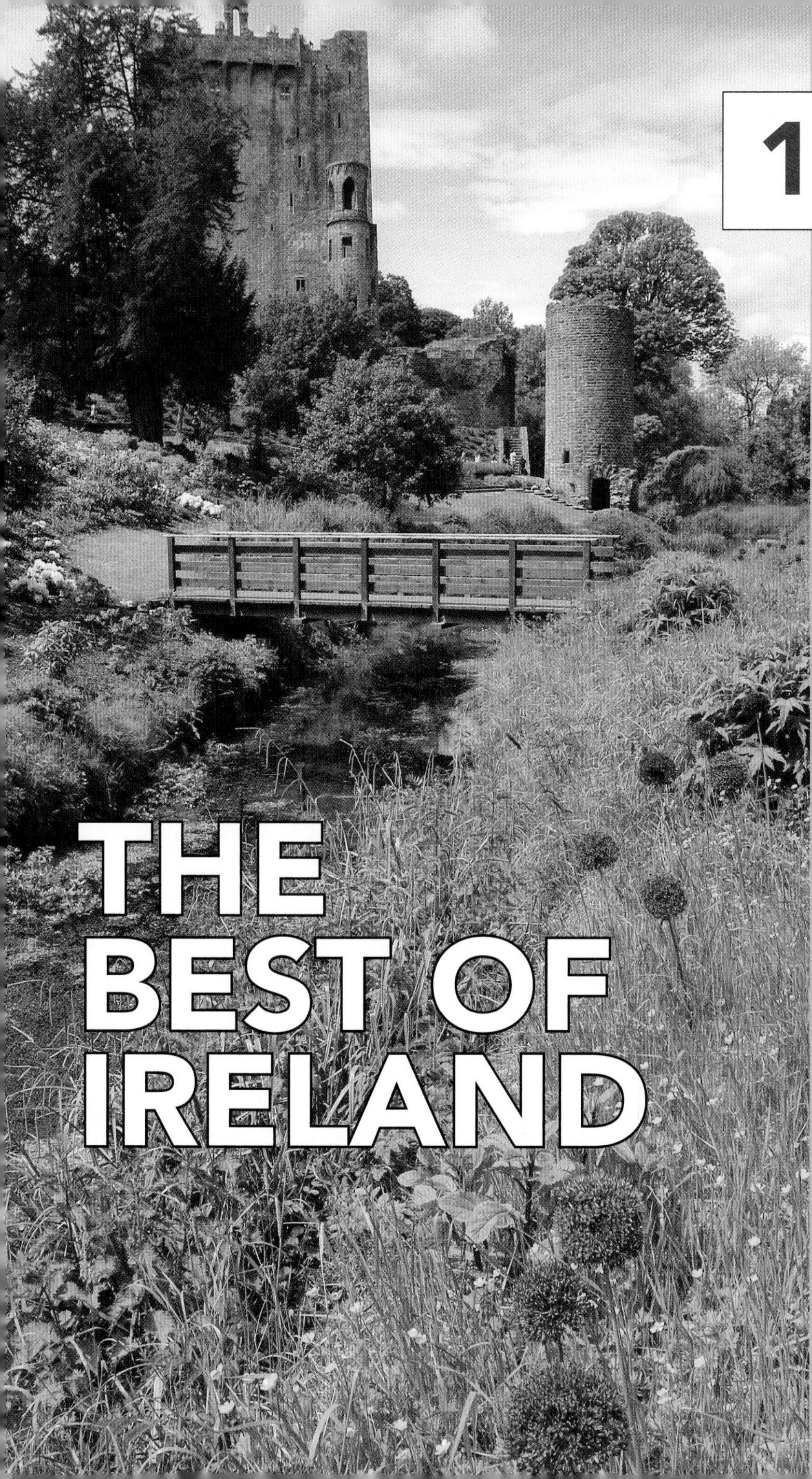

THE BEST OF IRELAND

PREVIOUS PAGE: **Blarney Castle.** ABOVE: **Flagstaff Post near Warrenpoint Town in Northern Ireland.**

Tiny, and with ever-changing scenery, Ireland is an addictive place to explore. Within a few miles you can travel from plunging cliffs and flat pastureland to towering mountains and gloomy peat bogs. You can spend the night in ancient castles or state-of-the-art spa hotels, dine on fine Irish cuisine or snack on crispy fish and chips served in a paper bag. The sheer number of sights, little villages, charming pubs, and adorable restaurants and shops is overwhelming—you always feel that you might be missing something. So it's nice to have somebody to help you focus, and that's why we've put together this list of some of our favorite places and things to do in Ireland. We hope that while you're exploring this magical country, you'll find a few of your own.

THE best AUTHENTIC EXPERIENCES

- **Seeing a traditional music session at a proper Irish pub:** It's not hard to track down live music in Irish pubs, and while plenty of shows are for the tourist crowd, nothing beats the energy, atmosphere, and authenticity of a genuine small-town traditional music session. We've listed some of the best places in this book, including pubs such as the Long Valley in Cork or Gus O'Connor's and McGann's in little Doolin, County Clare. The instructions for getting the most out of a session are simple: Buy a pint, grab a seat (preferably one near a smoldering peat fire), and wait for the action to begin. See p. 237 and p. 330.

- **Getting lost down the back roads of County Kerry:** This is Ireland's most visited county by far, and it's impossible to escape the tourist throng in the summer, especially if you stick to the beaten path. When it all gets too much, you can just veer off onto the winding back roads and allow yourself to get gloriously, hopelessly lost. Forget the clock and embrace a sense of fatalism. New discoveries are always waiting down its breathtaking byways. See chapter 9.
- **Touching the bullet holes in the walls of the General Post Office** (Dublin, County Dublin): It's hard to overstate what a potent national symbol this humble mail hub is. Patrick Pearse read his independence proclamation from its front steps in 1916, and the original document is now displayed inside. The post office was also the scene of fierce fighting during the civil war of 1922, which left the bullet scars that pock the facade. See p. 111.
- **Poking around the shops in Temple Bar** (Dublin, County Dublin): Modern Dublin is a cosmopolitan place, and nowhere is this more so than its trendiest neighborhood, Temple Bar. The name actually has a rather obscure, 17th-century origin, although it's curiously appropriate today given the preponderance of hip watering holes full of beautiful, style-worshiping young things. Daytime offers its own brand of discover, as seemingly around every corner is another trendy boutique, funky store, or art gallery. See p. 108.
- **Walking down the long stone passage at Newgrange** (County Meath): Sacred to the ancients, this passage tomb is more than 5,000 years old—that's older than the Egyptian pyramids or Stonehenge. Walking down the long, atmospheric central tunnel, trying to visualize just how many generations have passed since it was built is mind-blowing. A bit of perspective: the dawn of the Roman Empire is closer in time to us today than the building of Newgrange was to the dawn of the Roman Empire. See p. 180.
- **Checking out what's new in Kinsale's restaurant scene** (County Cork): Kinsale has gone from sleepy fishing port to the food capital of Ireland. On every return trip

Ross Castle in Killarney National Park.

Ireland

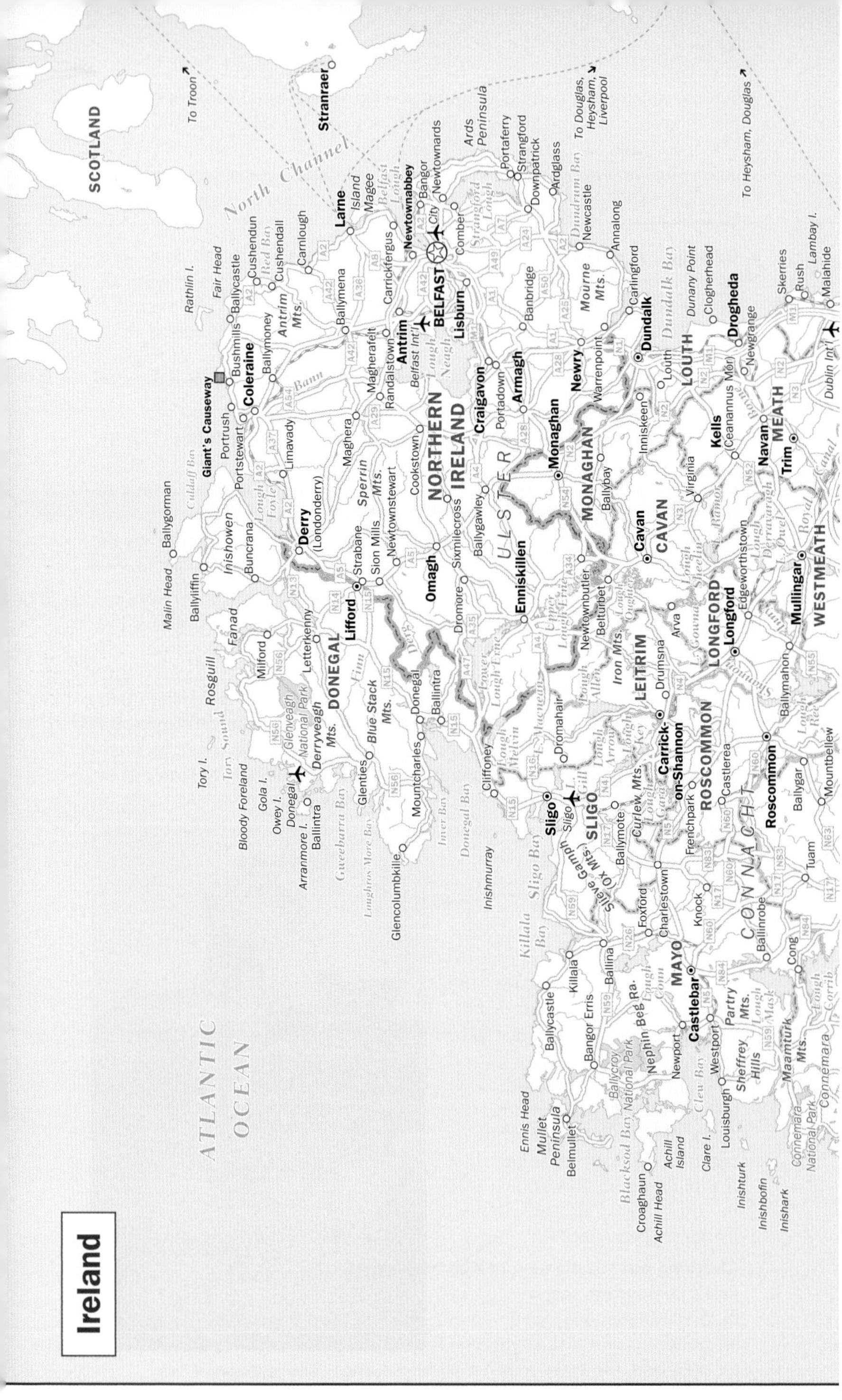

SCOTLAND
To Troon
Stranraer
North Channel
To Douglas, Heysham, Liverpool
To Heysham, Douglas
ATLANTIC OCEAN
Rathlin I.
Fair Head
Ballycastle
Cushendun
Red Bay
Cushendall
Carnlough
Larne
Island Magee
Belfast Lough
Giant's Causeway
Bushmills
Coleraine
Portrush
Portstewart
Ballymoney
Antrim Mts.
Ballymena
Carrickfergus
Newtownabbey
Bangor
Newtownards
City
BELFAST
Belfast Int'l
Antrim
Lisburn
Comber
Ards Peninsula
Strangford Lough
Portaferry
Strangford
Downpatrick
Ardglass
Dundrum Bay
Newcastle
Annalong
Mourne Mts.
Banbridge
Carlingford
Dundalk Bay
Dundalk
Dunany Point
Clogherhead
Drogheda
Newgrange
Skerries
Rush
Lambay I.
Malahide
Dublin Int'l
Bann
Magherafelt
Randalstown
Lough Neagh
Craigavon
Portadown
Armagh
Newry
Warrenpoint
Louth
LOUTH
Ceanannus Mór
Kells
Navan
MEATH
Trim
Boyne
Culdaff Bay
Ballygorman
Malin Head
Inishowen
Ballyliffin
Buncrana
Lough Foyle
Limavady
Derry (Londonderry)
Maghera
Sperrin Mts.
Cookstown
NORTHERN IRELAND
ULSTER
Strabane
Sion Mills
Newtownstewart
Omagh
Sixmilecross
Ballygawley
Monaghan
MONAGHAN
Ballybay
Inniskeen
Lifford
Fanad
Rosguill
Milford
Letterkenny
DONEGAL
Finn
Derg
Tory I.
Tory Sound
Bloody Foreland
Gola I.
Owey I.
Donegal
Arranmore I.
Ballintra
Glenveagh National Park
Derryveagh Mts.
Gweebarra Bay
Glenties
Blue Stack Mts.
Donegal
Ballintra
Mountcharles
Loughros More Bay
Glencolumbkille
Inver Bay
Donegal Bay
Dromore
Enniskillen
Lower Lough Erne
Upper Lough Erne
Newtownbutler
Belturbet
Cavan
CAVAN
Virginia
Lough Sheelin
Lough Ramor
Cliffoney
Lough Melvin
Lough Macnean
Dromahair
Lough Allen
Iron Mts.
LEITRIM
Drumsna
Arva
Lough Gowna
LONGFORD
Longford
Edgeworthstown
Lough Derravaragh
Lough Owel
Mullingar
WESTMEATH
Royal Canal
Inishmurray
Sligo
Sligo Bay
Lough Gill
Lough Arrow
Lough Key
SLIGO
Curlew Mts.
Lough Gara
Ballymote
Carrick-on-Shannon
Frenchpark
Castlerea
ROSCOMMON
Roscommon
Ballymahon
Lough Ree
Shannon
Ballygar
Mountbellew
CONNACHT
Tuam
Slieve Gamph (Ox Mts.)
Killala Bay
Killala
Ballina
Foxford
Charlestown
Knock
Ballinrobe
Cong
Lough Corrib
Lough Mask
Lough Conn
Ballycastle
Bangor Erris
Ballycroy National Park
Nephin Beg Ra.
Newport
Castlebar
MAYO
Westport
Castlebar
Partry Mts.
Clew Bay
Louisburgh
Sheffrey Hills
Maamturk Mts.
Connemara
Connemara National Park
Ennis Head
Mullet Peninsula
Belmullet
Blacksod Bay
Achill Island
Croaghaun
Achill Head
Clare I.
Inishturk
Inishbofin
Inishark

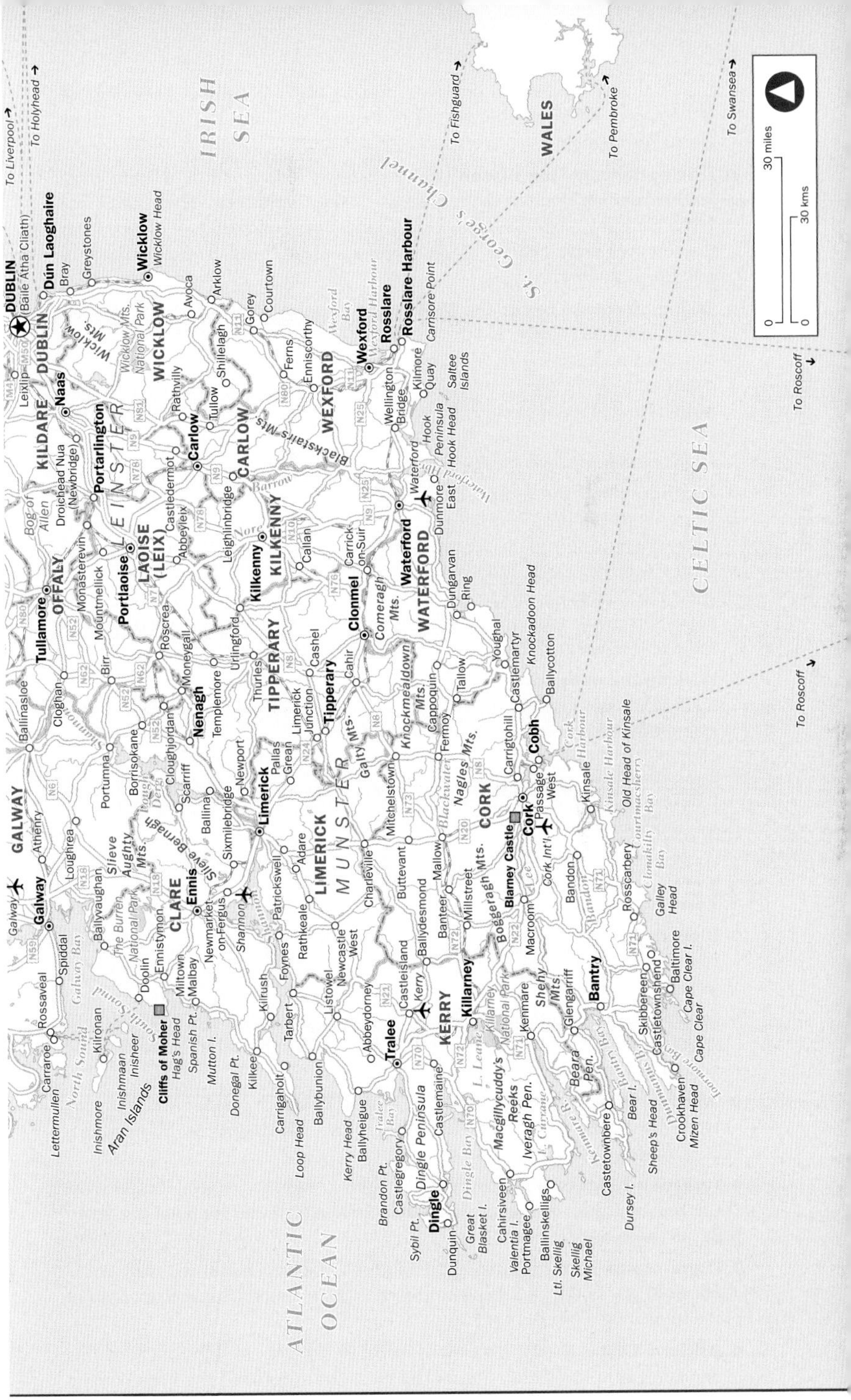
IRISH SEA
To Liverpool
To Holyhead
DUBLIN
Baile Átha Cliath
Dún Laoghaire
Bray
Greystones
Wicklow
Wicklow Head
Arklow
Courtown
Gorey
Avoca
WICKLOW
Wicklow Mts. National Park
Wicklow Mts.
DUBLIN
Leixlip
KILDARE
Naas
Droichead Nua (Newbridge)
Portarlington
Bog of Allen
Monasterevin
OFFALY
Tullamore
Portlaoise
LAOISE (LEIX)
Abbeyleix
Castledermot
Carlow
CARLOW
Rathvilly
Tullow
Shillelagh
LEINSTER
Leighlinbridge
Mountmellick
Kilkenny
KILKENNY
Callan
Carrick-on-Suir
Clonmel
Comeragh Mts.
Waterford
WATERFORD
Dungarvan
Ring
Dunmore East
Waterford Harbour
Hook Peninsula
Hook Head
Wellington Bridge
Kilmore Quay
Saltee Islands
Wexford
WEXFORD
Wexford Bay
Wexford Harbour
Rosslare
Rosslare Harbour
Carnsore Point
Enniscorthy
Ferns
Blackstairs Mts.
Barrow
Nore
St. George's Channel
To Fishguard
To Pembroke
WALES
To Swansea
To Roscoff
CELTIC SEA
0 30 miles
0 30 kms
Ballinasloe
Clogan
Birr
Roscrea
Moneygall
Urlingford
Templemore
Thurles
TIPPERARY
Cashel
Cahir
Tipperary
Limerick Junction
Galty Mts.
Knockmealdown Mts.
Cappoquin
Tallow
Youghal
Knockadoon Head
Ballycotton
Castlemartyr
Fermoy
Nagles Mts.
Blackwater
Mitchelstown
Cobh
Carrigtohill
Cork Harbour
Passage West
Cork
CORK
Cork Int'l
Blarney Castle
Kinsale
Kinsale Harbour
Old Head of Kinsale
Courtmacsherry Bay
Clonakilty Bay
Bandon
Rosscarbery
Galley Head
Skibbereen
Castletownshend
Baltimore
Cape Clear I.
Cape Clear
Crookhaven
Mizen Head
Sheep's Head
Bantry
Bantry Bay
Glengarriff
Shehy Mts.
Kenmare
Beara Pen.
Castletownbere
Bear I.
Dursey I.
Ballinskelligs
Portmagee
Valentia I.
Cahirsiveen
Iveragh Pen.
Macgillycuddy's Reeks
Killarney National Park
Killarney
KERRY
Kerry
Castleisland
Tralee
Castlemaine
Dingle Peninsula
Dingle Bay
Dingle
Dunquin
Great Blasket I.
Sybil Pt.
Brandon Pt.
Castlegregory
Tralee Bay
Ballyheigue
Kerry Head
Ballybunion
Listowel
Abbeydorney
Tarbert
Foynes
Newcastle West
Rathkeale
Ballydesmond
Banteer
Millstreet
Boggeragh Mts.
Macroom
Mallow
Buttevant
Charleville
MUNSTER
LIMERICK
Adare
Patrickswell
Limerick
Pallas Grean
Newport
Nenagh
Cloughjordan
Borrisokane
Portumna
Lough Derg
Scarriff
Ballina
Sixmilebridge
Slieve Bernagh
Shannon
Ennis
CLARE
Newmarket-on-Fergus
Kilrush
Kilkee
Carrigaholt
Loop Head
Mutton I.
Donegal Pt.
Spanish Pt.
Miltown Malbay
Ennistymon
Doolin
Cliffs of Moher
Hag's Head
The Burren National Park
Ballyvaughan
Slieve Aughty Mts.
Galway
GALWAY
Athenry
Loughrea
Galway Bay
Spiddal
Rossaveal
Carraroe
Lettermullen
North Sound
Kilronan
Inishmore
Inishmaan
Inisheer
Aran Islands
South Sound
ATLANTIC OCEAN
Ltl. Skellig
Skellig Michael
Kenmare R.
L. Leane
Shannon

there's almost inevitably a hot new, must-try place to sample. They don't all last forever, but those that do are in themselves worth the trip to County Cork. See chapter 8.

- **Driving through the Burren** (County Clare): Ireland is full of memorable landscapes, but none of them quite as unique as this one. The countryside has a haunting, alien feel, although it's strikingly beautiful too, especially as the sun goes down and the craggy limestone planes turn an evening shade of red. See chapter 10.
- **Taking afternoon tea at The Shelbourne** (Dublin, County Dublin): It's easy to feel like an overgrown kid in the fanciest candy store at The Shelbourne, as you sink into huge leather armchairs while demolishing a tower of cakes and daintily cut sandwiches. If you're in the mood for a history fix afterward, sneak upstairs to find room no. 112. This is where the Irish Constitution was written in 1922. If nobody's staying there—and the concierge is in a good mood—you might even get to look inside. See p. 133.
- **Photographing the murals in Belfast and Derry** (County Antrim/County Derry, Northern Ireland): Half a generation has grown up in Northern Ireland without knowing full-on sectarian bloodshed firsthand. Yet the long, ugly "peace wall" dividing Catholic neighborhoods from near-identical Protestant streets in Belfast is still covered in political street art, much of it preaching nonviolence. Likewise, the so-called "People's Gallery" in Derry will guarantee some of the most striking photos of your trip. See chapter 15.
- **Walking the path down to the Giant's Causeway** (County Antrim): It's like hiking through a fantasy landscape to take the half-mile walk down to this extraordinary natural wonder—37,000 columns of basalt sitting at the base of cliffs along the Antrim Coast. Geologists claim these mystical rocks were formed millions of years ago by cooling volcanoes. But don't you prefer to believe they were really made by giants, as the ancient belief would hold? See p. 482.

THE best HOTELS

- **Monart Spa** (Enniscorthy, County Wexford): A sumptuous countryside retreat, this pampering paradise is consistently rated among the top spas in Ireland. It's a serene, adults-only zone in a beautiful setting. See p. 214.
- **Lawcus Farm Guesthouse** (Stonyford, County Kilkenny): You can help out with feeding the animals at this idyllic B&B in Kilkenny, before relaxing in the beautifully converted farmhouse. See p. 221.
- **Wicklow Way Lodge** (Oldbridge, County Wicklow): It's hard to fault this lovely B&B with spectacular views of the Wicklow Mountains. So we won't. It's just gorgeous. See p. 175.
- **Aghadoe Heights** (Killarney, County Kerry): Another of Ireland's top spas, this one overlooks the Lakes of Killarney from a high vantage point just north of the town. See p. 281.
- **Powerscourt Hotel** (Enniskerry, County Wicklow): One of the truly grand places to stay in the Dublin penumbra, this opulent hotel is on the grounds of the impressive Powerscourt House. See p. 176.
- **Ashford Castle** (Cong, County Mayo): Live like royalty for a night at this fairytale castle in County Mayo. The great and the good have been coming

here for decades to see what the fuss is about. The fuss, it turns out, is justified. See p. 397.

- **Temple House** (Ballymote, County Sligo): Proving that not all the best overnight stays are to be found in luxury hotels, Temple House is an historic countryside B&B that feels like it's in a world of its own. See p. 409.
- **The Bervie** (Keel, County Mayo): Overlooking the Atlantic Ocean on an island off the Mayo coast, the Bervie is a haven of magnificent views and gourmet food. See p. 397.
- **Two Rooms in Dublin** (County Dublin): This exceptionally welcoming townhouse B&B in Dublin has just two rooms, but try as hard as you can to get one. You'll feel better taken care of here than in many of the capital's most upscale hotels. See p. 132.
- **Dolphin Beach House** (Clifden, County Galway): This incredibly special B&B on the Galway coast is a converted, early-20th-century homestead. It adds up to amazing views, gorgeous food, and gregarious hosts. See p. 365.
- **Gregan's Castle Hotel** (Ballyvaughn, County Clare): J. R. R. Tolkein took inspiration for *The Lord of the Rings* while staying at this elegant country house surrounded by the lunar landscape of Burren. See p. 334.
- **Rathmullan House** (Rathmullan, County Donegal): Remote and windswept, County Donegal attracts a fraction of the visitors of Dublin or Kerry. That's good news for those that make the journey to enjoy a night at this incredible 18th-century mansion. See p. 430.
- **Dunnanelly Country House** (Downpatrick, County Down, Northern Ireland): A Regency mansion surrounded by 80 rolling acres of countryside, Dunnanelly is a captivating hideaway just 29km (18 miles) from Belfast. See p. 458.
- **Wineport Lodge** (Athlone, County Westmeath): Calling this place a getaway isn't mere hyperbole; overlooking Lough Rea, Wineport Lodge is a retreat to relax the body and soul. See p. 380.
- **The Merchant Hotel** (Belfast, Northern Ireland): Once a Victorian bank, this trendy hotel in Belfast has been utterly transformed into one of Ireland's most handsome city retreats. See p. 460.

THE best RESTAURANTS

- **Chapter One** (Dublin, County Dublin): In the vaulted basement of the Dublin Writers Museum, this is one of the capital's very best restaurants. It's quite a splurge, but come at lunchtime to experience the same wonderful food at almost half the price. See p. 143.
- **Sabor Brazil** (Dublin, County Dublin): We've deliberately kept the restaurant choices for this book focused on unique, local Irish experiences. But this tiny place in Dublin makes the cut, because where else would you find such an extraordinary fusion of Brazilian and Irish flavors? See p. 145.
- **Fishy Fishy Café** (Kinsale, County Cork): Kinsale is Ireland's unofficial gourmet capital, and the delightful Fishy Fishy is among its best restaurants. The seafood is so local that the menu tells you who caught it—and we're talking dish by dish, name by name. See p. 247.
- **Crackpots** (Kinsale, County Cork): Another Kinsale favorite, Crackpots is a charming combination of designer pottery shop and outstandingly

good restaurant. It's one of the very best places to eat in a town where the competition is stiff. See p. 246.

- **The Strawberry Tree** (Macreddin Village, County Wicklow): Ireland's first fully organic certified restaurant is still at the top of its game for delicious, innovative cooking, prepared from avowedly local ingredients. See p. 177.
- **The Posh Nosh Club at Durhamstown Castle** (Navan, County Meath): A wonderful meal is made even more special by unique surroundings, and dinner here feels like you're at a super-fun dinner party thrown by true *bon viveurs*. See p. 186.
- **Aniar** (Galway, County Galway): Galway City's most sought-after table has a tiny but impeccably judged menu of innovative, modern Irish cuisine. Aniar is one of just a handful of Michelin-starred restaurants in Ireland. See p. 352.

The pours are as perfect as the seafood in County Galway.

- **Wilde's at Lisloughrey Lodge** (Cong, County Mayo): On the grounds of Ashford Castle, Wilde's is a joyous restaurant run by a real star in the making. The dining room has an amazing view of Lough Corrib. See p. 399.
- **Richmond House** (Cappoquin, County Waterford): One of the real destination restaurants of the southeast, the Richmond House is a converted 18th-century mansion. They serve exquisite, seasonal meals, and many of the ingredients come from their own garden. See p. 206.
- **The Wild Geese** (Adare, County Limerick): Adare is one of the prettiest villages in Ireland, and at its heart is one of the region's best restaurants. The Wild Geese has won legions of fans for its modern Irish cooking. See p. 316.
- **The Lime Tree** (Kenmare, County Kerry): This has long been one of the most respected restaurants in County Kerry, and with good reason—the sophisticated modern Irish menu, full of local flavors, is impressive but still surprisingly affordable. See p. 271.
- **Thyme** (Athlone, County Westmeath): Upscale, innovative cooking in a completely relaxed environment, this delightful bistro is one of the very best places to eat in the Midlands. See p. 382
- **Doyle's Seafood Bar** (Dingle, County Kerry): Dingle isn't short of places offering super-fresh, local seafood, and it's hard to pick between them, but

this is probably the best. What you find on the menu will depend on the catch of the day, and it's all impeccably done. See p. 301.

- **Gallagher's Boxty House** (Dublin, County Dublin): Think again if you assume that the best meals always require the deepest pockets. A local man who wanted to preserve the culinary traditions of his childhood started this hugely popular restaurant in Dublin's Temple Bar. The result is captivating. See p. 139.
- **Deane's Seafood Bar** (Belfast, County Antrim, Northern Ireland): The flagship restaurant in Belfast, chef Michael Deane's eponymous mini-chain, Deane's, serves outstanding Irish-French cuisine. The attached seafood bar is just as good—and much cheaper. See p. 463.

THE best PICTURE-POSTCARD TOWNS

- **Adare** (County Limerick): This really is a picture-postcard town, its image having been reproduced alongside a hundred thousand "Wish You Were Heres." Unfortunately the secret is very much out, but if you manage to visit when the roads aren't clogged with tour buses, you'll leave with a memory card full of photos. See p. 310.
- **Athlone** (County Westmeath): Sitting at the edge of the River Shannon, its streets curving around a sturdy, fortress-like castle, Athlone is a charmer. Houses are painted in bright hues, and with its small, funky boutiques and spirit of fun, it has the feel of a busy university town. Good restaurants and lively pubs add to its charms. See chapter 12.
- **Dalkey** (County Dublin): The cutest of a number of upscale seaside towns unfurling south from Dublin like a string of pearls. Dalkey is both a short drive and a million miles away from the busy city. With a castle, a mountaintop folly, lovely beaches, and some fine restaurants, this is a town that tempts you to settle into its comfortable affluence. See p. 119.
- **Kinsale** (County Cork): Kinsale's narrow streets all lead to the sea, dropping steeply from the hills around the harbor. The walk from Kinsale through Scilly to Charles Fort and Frower Point is breathtaking. Kinsale has the added benefit of being a foodie town with no shortage of good restaurants. See p. 238.
- **Kenmare** (County Kerry): It's easy to fall in love with Kenmare, with its stone cottages, colorful gardens, and flowers overflowing from window boxes. It's also home to several elegant hotels, so it makes an enchanting base when exploring the Ring of Kerry. See p. 268.
- **Dingle (*An Daingean*)** (County Kerry): Dingle is a charming hilltop medieval town. Stone buildings ramble up and down hills, and the small population is relaxed about visitors. It has lots of little diners and picturesque pubs, plus a lovely, historic church. See p. 296.
- **Ardara** (County Donegal): On the southwest coast of County Donegal, the tiny town of Ardara looks as if it were carved out of a solid block of granite. Its streets undulate up and down the rocky hills and are lined with little boutiques and charming arts shops, many selling clothes made of the famed Donegal wool. You can wander its entirety in a few minutes. It's a bite-sized place. See p. 425.

THE best NATURAL WONDERS

- **Giant's Causeway** (County Antrim): At the foot of a cliff by the sea, this mysterious mass of tightly packed, naturally occurring hexagonal basalt columns are nothing short of astonishing. This volcanic wonder, formed 60 million years ago, looks marvelous from above, and even better when negotiated (cautiously) on foot. See p. 482.
- **The Burren** (County Clare): We can guarantee this: The Burren is one of the strangest landscapes you're likely to see anywhere in the world. Its vast limestone grassland is spread with a quilt of wildflowers from as far afield as the Alps, all softening the stark stones jutting out of the ground. Its inhabitants include nearly every species of butterfly found in Ireland. See chapter 10.
- **Cliffs of Moher** (County Clare): Rising from Hag's Head to the south, these magnificent sea cliffs reach their full height of 214m (702 ft.) just north of O'Brien's Tower. The views of the open sea, of the Aran Islands, and of the Twelve Bens mountains of Connemara (see below) are spectacular. A walk south along the cliff edge at sunset makes a perfect end to any day. See p. 329.
- **The Twelve Bens** (County Galway): Amid Connemara's central mountains, bogs, and lakes, the rugged Twelve Bens range crowns a spectacular landscape. Some of the peaks are bare and rocky, others clothed in peat. The loftiest, Benbaun in Connemara National Park, reaches a height of 729m (2,392 ft.). See p. 361.
- **Slieve League** (County Donegal): The Slieve League peninsula stretches for 48km (30 miles) into the Atlantic. Its pigmented bluffs rise to startlingly high sea cliffs. They can also be walked along, if you dare. See p. 421.

Giant's Causeway

Hikers on the Slieve League coastal walk in County Donegal.

- **MacGillycuddy's Reeks** (County Kerry): A mountain range on the Iveragh Peninsula, MacGillycuddy's Reeks not only has the best name of any mountain range in Ireland, it also has the highest mountain on the island, Carrantuohill (1,041m/3,414 ft.). The Reeks are among Ireland's greatest spectacles. See p. 275.

THE best CASTLES

- **Kilkenny Castle** (County Kilkenny): Although parts of the castle date from the 13th century, the existing structure has the feel of an 18th-century palace. There have been many modifications since medieval times, including the addition of colorful landscaping, and the old stables now hold numerous art galleries and shops. See p. 216.
- **Blarney Castle** (County Cork): Despite the mobs of tourists who besiege it daily, this majestic tower house is worth a visit. While you're there, check out the Badger Cave and dungeons at the tower's base, as well as the serpentine paths that wind through the castle gardens. Need we mention the Blarney Stone? You sidle in under the upper wall with your head hanging over a 10-story drop. You kiss it. It's a thing people do. See p. 228.
- **Bunratty Castle & Folk Park** (County Clare): This grand old castle has been well restored and filled with a curious assortment of medieval furnishings, offering a glimpse into the life of its past inhabitants. This is the first stop for many arrivals from Shannon, so expect crowds. See p. 328.
- **Charleville Castle** (County Offaly): Sometimes the castles that leave the biggest impressions aren't those in the most impressive states of repair. Not only is Charleville one of the most atmospheric castles in Ireland, it is also reputed to be among its most haunted. See p. 372.

- **Carrickfergus Castle** (County Antrim): This well-preserved Norman fortress on the bank of Belfast Lough is huge and impressive, complete with an imposing tower house and a high wall punctuated by corner towers. See p. 456.
- **Dunluce Castle** (County Antrim): These castle ruins surmount a razor-sharp promontory jutting into the sea. This was a highly defensible setting, and the castle wasn't abandoned until a large section collapsed and fell into the breakers. See p. 482.

THE best PREHISTORIC SITES

- **Hill of Tara** (County Meath): Of ritual significance from the Stone Age to the early Christian period, Tara has seen it all and kept it a secret. This was the traditional center and seat of Ireland's high kings. Although the hill is only 154m (512 ft.) above sea level, from here you can see each of Ireland's four Celtic provinces on a clear day. The site is mostly unexcavated and tells its story in whispers. It's a place to be walked slowly. See p. 178.
- **Newgrange** (County Meath): One of the archaeological wonders of Western Europe, Newgrange is the centerpiece of a megalithic cemetery dating back 5,000 years. Its massive mound and passage tomb are amazing feats of engineering. But the question remains: What was it all for? See p. 180.
- **Knowth** (County Meath): Another great passage tomb, Knowth's awesome presence is matched only by its inscrutability. Hundreds of prehistoric carvings were discovered here when the site was first excavated in the 1960s. And yet, nobody seems to quite understand it to this day. See p. 179.
- **Dún Aengus** (County Galway): No one knows who built this massive stone fort or what year it was constructed. The eminent archaeologist George Petrie called Dún Aengus "the most magnificent barbaric monument in Europe." Facing the sea, where its three stone rings meet steep 90m (295-ft.) cliffs, Dún Aengus still stands guard today over the southern coast of the island of Inishmore, the largest of the Aran Islands. See p. 343.
- **Carrowmore & Carrowkeel** (County Sligo): These two megalithic cities of the dead (Europe's largest) may have once contained more than 200 passage tombs. The two together—one in the valley and the other atop a nearby mountain—convey an unequaled sense of the scale and wonder of the ancient peoples' reverence for the dead. Carrowmore is well presented and interpreted, while Carrowkeel is left to itself for those who seek it out. See p. 399.
- **Corlea Trackway** (County Longford): This place doesn't impress for its grandeur or inscrutability; rather, the amazing thing about this simple wooden trackway in a remote bog is just how unbelievably old it is—people were walking its well-preserved planks well over 2,000 years ago. See p. 373.

THE best EARLY CHRISTIAN RUINS

- **Glendalough** (County Wicklow): Nestled in "the glen of the two lakes," this atmospheric monastic settlement was founded in the 6th century by St.

Kevin, who was looking for seclusion and certainly found it here. The setting is endlessly scenic with lakes and forests surrounding it. Although quite remote, Glendalough suffered assaults from the Vikings and English forces and eventually faded away. Today its stone ruins collude with the countryside to create one of the loveliest spots in Ireland. See p. 168.

Stone stairway of Skellig Michael, County Kerry.

- **The Rock of Cashel** (County Tipperary): In name and appearance, "the Rock" suggests a citadel, a place designed more for power than prayer. In fact, Cashel (or *Caiseal*) means "fortress." The rock is a huge outcropping—or an *up*cropping—of limestone topped with spectacularly beautiful ruins, including what was formerly the country's finest Romanesque chapel. This was the seat of clerics and kings, a power center to rival Tara. Now, however, the two sites vie only for the attention of tourists. See p. 319.
- **Jerpoint Abbey** (County Kilkenny): Jerpoint is the finest representative of the many Cistercian abbeys whose ruins dot the Irish landscape. Somehow, hundreds of years of rain and wind have failed to completely wipe away medieval carvings, leaving us a rare chance for a glimpse of how magnificent these abbeys once were. The splendid, richly carved cloister is the best place to spot the engravings, particularly at the top of the columns. See p. 219.
- **Skellig Michael** (County Kerry): Thirteen kilometers (8 miles) offshore of the Iveragh Peninsula, rising sharply 214m (702 ft.) out of the Atlantic, this is a remote, rocky crag dedicated to the archangel Michael. In flight from the world, early Irish monks in pursuit of "white martyrdom" (meaning martyrdom without bloodshed) chose this spot to build their austere hermitage. Today both the journey to Skellig across choppy seas and the arduous climb to the island's summit are challenging and unforgettable. See p. 289.
- **Clonmacnoise** (County Offaly): The old Irish high kings came to this place to find spiritual solace, and it's still a profound and thought-provoking place to visit. Don't leave without checking out the ancient monumental slabs, inscribed with personal messages in ancient Celtic script. See p. 373.
- **Inishmurray** (County Sligo): This uninhabited island off the Sligo coast holds another striking monastic ruin, this one surrounded by what appears to be the walls of an even more ancient stone fort. Despite its remoteness, the Vikings sought out this outpost of peace-seeking monks for destruction in 807 A.D. Today its circular walls and the surrounding sea create a stunning view, well worth the effort required to reach it. See p. 406.

Glenveagh National Park, on the banks of Lough Veagh in County Donegal.

THE best LITERARY SPOTS

- **Dublin Writers Museum** (Dublin, County Dublin): Filled with letters, personal possessions, and other eclectic ephemera, this great museum in Dublin will be like a pilgrimage for lovers of Irish literature. Bibliophiles of all kinds will learn more about Ireland's masters of the printed word than they ever imagined while basking in their collective glow. See p. 101.
- **Davy Byrnes pub** (Dublin, County Dublin): This place crops up in *Ulysses* when the hero, Leopold Bloom, famously orders a lunch of burgundy and a Gorgonzola sandwich here. The pub is acutely aware of its heritage, but happily knows better than to ruin the appeal by being too touristy. See p. 159.
- **St. Patrick's Cathedral** (Dublin, County Dublin): Jonathan Swift tickled and horrified the world with his vicious wit. He shook up political establishments with his sarcasm and nauseated the English-speaking world with his suggestion that people should dine on Irish babies. While kicking up such a stir, he was dean of St. Patrick's Cathedral, which sponsored and supported him through it all. He is buried here alongside his longtime companion Stella Johnson. See p. 107.
- **County Sligo:** With its many connections to the beloved poet W. B. Yeats, this county is a pilgrimage destination for true fans. The landscape shaped the poet's writing, and many of the monuments—Lough Gill, Glencar Lake, Ben Bulben Mountain, and Maeve's tomb—appear in his words. Several museums house first editions, photographs, and other memorabilia, and Yeats's dark and somber grave is in Drumcliff. See chapter 13.

THE best FAMILY ACTIVITIES

- **Dublin Zoo in Phoenix Park** (Dublin, County Dublin): Kids love this sympathetically designed zoo featuring wild creatures, animal-petting corners, and a train ride. The surrounding park has room to run, picnic, and explore. See p. 117.
- **Irish National Heritage Park** (Ferrycarrig, County Wexford): Millennia of history are made painlessly educational for children and adults at this engaging "living history" museum. It's a fascinating, informative way to while away a couple of hours or more. See p. 207.
- **Fota Island & Wildlife Park** (Carrigtwohill, County Cork): In this wildlife park, rare and endangered animals roam freely. You'll see everything from giraffes and zebras to kangaroos, flamingos, penguins, and monkeys wandering the grassland. Add in a small amusement park for toddlers, a tour train, picnic tables, and a gift shop and you have the makings of a wonderful family outing. See p. 249.
- **Muckross House & Gardens** (Killarney, County Kerry): This impressive mansion acts as the gateway to Killarney National Park today, but the interior has been preserved in all its Victorian splendor. Nearby, people on the Muckross Historic Farms engage in traditional farm activities while dressed in authentic period clothes. See p. 276.
- **Fungie the Dingle Dolphin Tours** (Dingle, County Kerry): Everyday, fishing boats ferry visitors out into the nearby waters to see Fungie, the friendliest dolphin you're ever likely to meet. Fungie swims right up to the boat, and the

Conor Pass in County Kerry on the Dingle Peninsula Drive.

boatmen stay out long enough for ample sightings. You can also arrange an early-morning dolphin swim. See p. 298.

- **Bunratty Castle & Folk Park** (Bunratty, County Clare): Kids love Bunratty, which looks every bit as satisfyingly medieval as an old castle should. The grounds have been turned over to a replica 19th-century village—complete with actors playing Victorian residents going about their daily lives. It's great fun to walk through. See p. 328.
- **Galway Atlantaquaria** (Galway, County Galway): Known more formally as the National Aquarium of Ireland, this is the place that your kids will remember long after memories of the hundredth dolmen you saw by the side of a windswept road have faded. Highlights include a tank full of small sharks and pools where kids can touch curious rays. See p. 356.

THE best MUSEUMS

- **The Chester Beatty Library** (Dublin, County Dublin): This is not just one of Ireland's best museums, but the collection of indescribably rare and precious religious manuscripts here is among the most unique in the world. See p. 97.
- **National Museum of Ireland: Archaeology** (Dublin, County Dublin): Ireland's National Museum is split into four separate sites, of which this is far and away the best. The collection dates back to the earliest settlers, but it's the relics from the Viking invasion and the early Christian period that dazzle the most. See p. 105.
- **Irish National Famine Museum** (Strokestown Park, County Roscommon): This somber and reflective museum, part of a grand and historic estate, does a brilliant job of making the darkest period in Irish history seem immediate and real, including a collection of heartbreaking letters from destitute tenants to their callous landlords. See p. 375.
- **Ulster Folk & Transport Museum** (Cultra, County Antrim): Ireland has several so-called "living history" museums, where stories of people and times past are told through reconstructions of everyday life. This one, just outside Belfast, is one of the liveliest and most engaging. See p. 456.
- **Titanic Belfast** (Belfast, County Antrim): Belfast is incredibly proud of having built the most famous ocean liner in history, despite its ultimate fate—though as they're fond of saying, "she was alright when she left here." This gleaming, high-tech new museum is the best of several attractions in Belfast that tell that story. See p. 453.

Dunguaire Castle in County Galway.

THE best DRIVING TOURS

- **The Ring of Kerry** (County Kerry): It's by far the most well-traveled of Ireland's great routes, but there's no denying the Ring of Kerry's appeal—it's a seductive combination of beautiful countryside, gorgeous villages, and enticing historical sites. The road gets quite busy in summer, but come in the spring or autumn, and it's a much more peaceful experience. See chapter 9.
- **Antrim Coast:** The Antrim Coast is 97km (60 miles) long, stretching north of Larne and west past Bushmills and the Giant's Causeway to Portrush. If you start in gorgeous Glenarm with its castle walls and barbican gate, then head north along the coast from there, the route takes in sweeping views of midnight-blue sea against gray unforgiving cliffs and deep-green hillsides. You often have the road mostly to yourself. See chapter 15.
- **Slea Head Drive** (Dingle Peninsula): This drive, starting from Dingle Town and heading down the Ventry road, follows the sea past a series of ancient ruins such as the Dunbeg Fort. Taking in deep-blue ocean views along the way, it brings you to Dunquin, where you can embark on boats to the Blasket Islands, famous for their ancient remains. From there you continue on to Gallarus Oratory and then back to Dingle Town. See chapter 9.
- **Inishowen Peninsula** (County Donegal): This far-flung promontory in the northern outreaches of Ireland stretches out from Lough Foyle to the east and Lough Swilly to the west toward Malin Head, its farthest point. Around the edges are ancient sites, charming villages, and beautiful beaches surrounded by intimidating rocky coves attacked by crashing waves. At its center are gorgeous views, mountains, and quiet, vivid-green pastures. If you are looking to get lost, this is a great place to do it. See chapter 14.

2

SUGGESTED IRELAND ITINERARIES

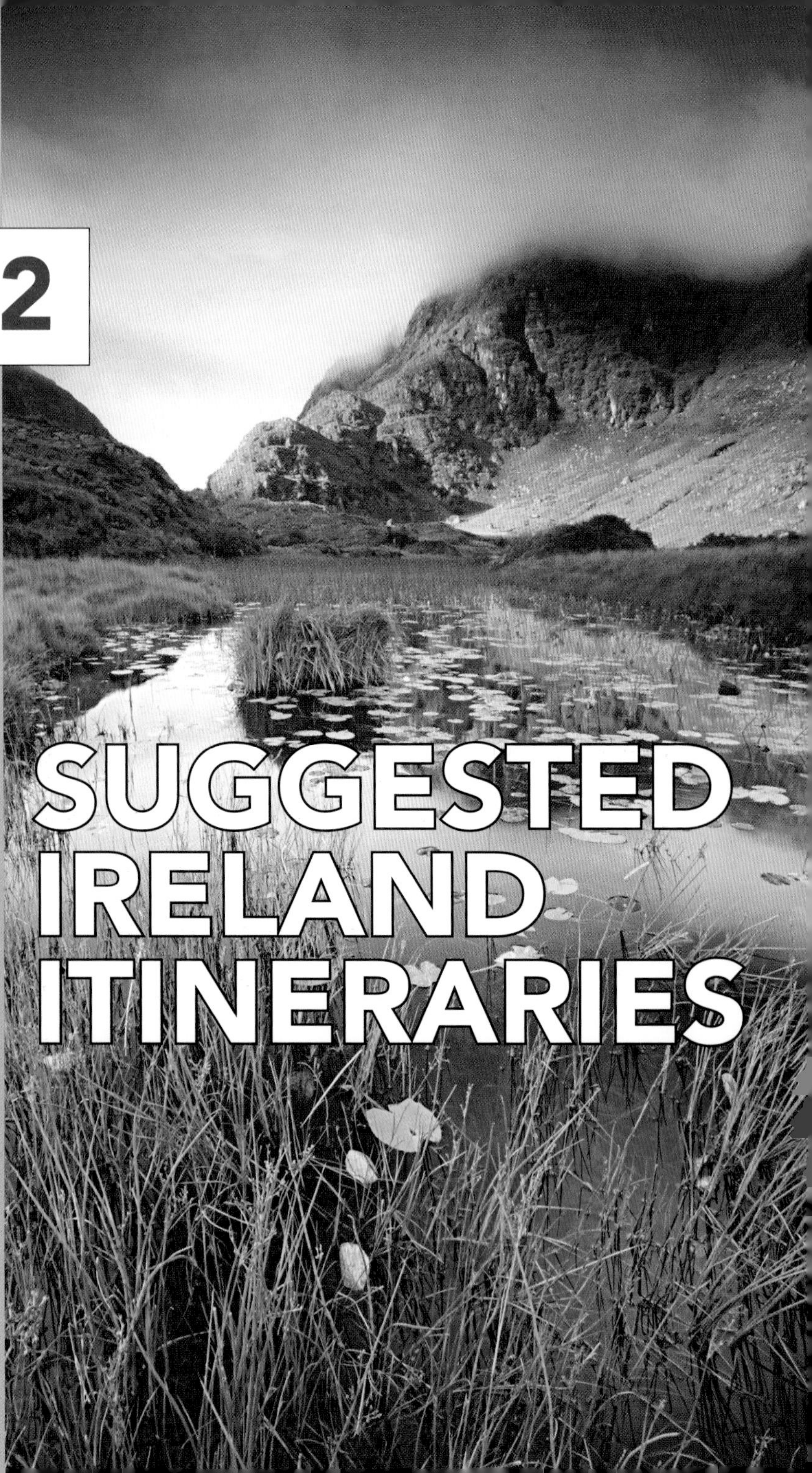

Ireland is such a small island that you can cover a lot of ground in a week and feel quite at home within two. But even with the best of intentions and all the energy in the world, you'll never see it all on a short visit.

However, with a few long days and a savvy attitude, it is possible to see a sizable chunk of the island in just a week. The suggested itineraries over the next few pages will help you get the most out of this extraordinary and varied country—no matter how long you have to see it. If you've only got a week to spend here, the southern regions probably have more to offer. They're generally easier to get around, and the major sights are somewhat closer together. If you're traveling with kids, Dublin and County Kerry have particularly rich pickings when it comes to kid-friendly attractions. However, those in search of the road less traveled will be drawn northwards, especially to places such as Mayo, Sligo, and the wilds of Donegal beyond.

THE REGIONS IN BRIEF

The island of Ireland is divided into two political units: the **Republic of Ireland,** which makes up the vast majority of the country, and **Northern Ireland,** which along with England, Scotland, and Wales is part of the United Kingdom. Of Ireland's 32 counties, all but six are in the Republic.

The ancient Gaelic regions that once divided Ireland are still used in conversation and directions: Ulster is north, Munster is south, Leinster is east, and Connaught is west. Each region is divided into counties:

In Ulster (to the north) Cavan, Donegal, and Monaghan in the Republic; Antrim, Armagh, Derry, Down, Fermanagh, and Tyrone in Northern Ireland.

In Munster (to the south) Clare, Cork, Kerry, Limerick, Tipperary, and Waterford.

In Leinster (to the east) Dublin, Carlow, Kildare, Kilkenny, Laois, Longford, Louth, Meath, Offaly, Westmeath, Wexford, and Wicklow.

In Connaught (to the west) Sligo, Mayo, Galway, Roscommon, and Leitrim.

DUBLIN & ENVIRONS With 40 percent of the Republic's population living within 97km (60 miles) of Dublin, the capital is the center of the profound, high-speed changes that have transformed Ireland into a prosperous and increasingly European country. Within an hour's drive of Dublin are Dalkey, Dún Laoghaire, and many more engaging coastal towns, as well as the rural beauty of the Wicklow Mountains and the prehistoric ruins in County Meath.

THE SOUTHEAST The southeast offers sandy beaches, Wexford's lush and mountainous countryside, Waterford's famous Crystal Factory, Kilkenny and Cahir's ancient castles, the Rock of Cashel, and the Irish National Heritage Park at Ferrycarrig.

CORK & ENVIRONS Cork, Ireland's second largest city, feels like a buzzy university town and provides a congenial gateway to the south and west of the island.

PREVIOUS PAGE: **Clouds over the Gap of Dunloe.**

The bustling Temple Bar district, on the banks of the Liffey in Dublin.

Within arm's reach are Blarney Castle (and its famous stone), the culinary and scenic delights of Kinsale, the Drombeg Stone Circle, Cape Clear Island, and Mizen Head. Also in this region is the dazzling landscape of West Cork.

THE SOUTHWEST The once remote splendor of County Kerry has long ceased to be a secret, so at least during the high season, be prepared to share the view in this gorgeous section. The Ring of Kerry (less glamorously known as hwys. N70 and N71) encircling the Iveragh Peninsula is the most visited attraction in Ireland after the Book of Kells. That's both a recommendation and a warning. Killarney National Park provides a stunning haven from buses. Killarney is surrounded by natural beauty but is filled with souvenir shops and tour groups. Marginally less visited highlights include the rugged Dingle Peninsula and two sets of islands with rich histories: the Skelligs and the Blaskets.

THE WEST The west of Ireland offers a first taste of Ireland's wild beauty and striking diversity for those who fly into Shannon Airport. County Limerick has an array of impressive castles: Knappogue, Bunratty, and (just over the county line in Galway) Dunguaire. County Clare's natural offerings—particularly the unique landscapes of the Burren—are unforgettable. Farther up the coast to the north, past Galway, County Mayo is the home of the sweet town of Westport on Clew Bay. Achill Island (accessible by car) has beaches and stunning cliff views.

GALWAY & ENVIRONS Galway Town is busy, colorful, and funky—a youthful, prospering port and university town and the self-proclaimed arts capital of Ireland with theater, music, dance, and an exciting street life. County Galway is the gateway to Connemara's moody, magical landscapes. Here are the Twelve Bens Mountains, Kylemore Abbey, and the charming seaside town of Clifden. Offshore lie the mysterious Aran Islands—Inishmore, Inishmaan, and Inisheer—with their irresistible desolation.

THE MIDLANDS The lush center of Ireland, bisected by the lazy River Shannon, is a land of pastures, rivers, lakes, woods, and gentle mountain slopes, a verdant antidote to the barren beauty of Connemara and a retreat, in high season, from the throngs of tourists who crowd the coasts. The shores and waters of the Shannon and Lough Derg and of their many lesser cousins provide much of the allure. The Midlands also hold remarkable sites—Birr Castle and its splendid gardens, for example, and Clonmacnois, the evocative ruins of a famous Irish monastic center.

THE NORTHWEST In Ireland it's easy to become convinced that isolated austerity is beautiful, and nowhere is this more evident than Donegal, with its jagged, desolate coastline that, if you don't mind the cold, offers some fine surfing. Inland, Glenveagh National Park has as much wilderness as you could want. County Sligo inspired the poetry of W. B. Yeats with its dense collection of megalithic sites such as the stone circles, passage tombs, dolmens, and cairns at Carrowmore, Knocknarea, and Carrowkeel.

NORTHERN IRELAND Across the border, Northern Ireland's six counties are a decade-and-a-half into a period of intense change. Still one of the most underrated parts of Ireland, the stunning Antrim Coast (particularly Ballycastle and Cushendun), the extraordinary, octagonal basalt columns of the Giant's Causeway, and the Glens of Antrim are unforgettable. The old city walls of Derry, the past glory of Carrickfergus Castle, and Belfast's elaborate political murals make a trip across the border worthwhile.

HOW TO SEE IRELAND

To Drive or Not to Drive?

To get the most out of Ireland, you need to know at least in part what you want to see. You don't *have* to rent a car. However, if your ideal Ireland involves wandering through the countryside, visiting small villages, climbing castle walls, hailing history from a ruined abbey, or finding yourself alone on a rocky beach—you simply cannot do those things without one.

Out of the main towns, public transportation exists, but it's slow and limiting. Every major town has car-rental agencies, so give strong consideration to renting a car. (Just remember: they drive on the ***left.***)

Be Smart Where You Start

The next step is deciding where to start. That decision can be made for you by where your flight terminates. If you're flying into Shannon Airport, then it makes good geographic sense to start out on the west coast. If you're flying into Dublin, you might as well explore that city first, then either head up to the North and the ruggedly beautiful Antrim Coast, or south down to the Wicklow Mountains, Kilkenny, and the rolling green hills of Wexford and Waterford.

Still, if you fly into Dublin but your heart is in Galway, no worries. You can traverse the width of the country in a few hours (once you get out of Dublin's stultifying sprawl), so if you start early enough, it's doable. Just bear in mind that rural roads are not well lit or well signposted, so driving at night should be avoided. It's too stressful, and being lost in unfamiliar territory (where it can be many miles between villages) is no fun at all. This is more of an issue in the winter, when it can get dark as early as 4pm. During summer time, the driving is a little easier, as it often stays light until after 10pm.

So . . . Where to Go?

So taking all of these factors into consideration, the question remains: *Where do you want to go?* We can't answer that question for you, but we can give you some itineraries that we have used ourselves. They might help you focus on ways in which you can orchestrate your journey so that you can get the most out of it with the fewest scheduling worries—the last thing you want to do on vacation is to spend the whole time looking at your watch.

If you've never visited Ireland, Dublin is a great place to start, and the surrounding area holds plenty to keep you busy. If you have been here before, and Dublin and Galway are old hat, you might consider heading north through County Mayo, County Sligo, and on to the exotic wilds of Donegal and the Antrim Coast.

All of these tours (bar one) assume you have a week to see the country. Where there's potential for a longer trip, we've given some alternatives for an extended version. Pick and choose the parts that appeal to you, add in your own favorite shopping or scenic drives, and turn it all into a custom-made holiday for yourself.

THE BEST OF IRELAND IN 1 WEEK

There's something terribly romantic about flying into Dublin. The compact, laid-back city awaits a few miles down the road, packed with old-fashioned pubs, modern restaurants, and absorbing sights all laid out for walking. If you've never been here, a couple of days in Dublin make for a quick primer on Ireland. It's just enough time to do some shopping on **Grafton Street,** head up O'Connell Street to the **General Post Office,** and discover the Georgian beauty of **St. Stephen's Green** and **Merrion Square.** It's not nearly enough time, but you can give the surface of the city a good brush in a couple of days, and then head south to **Kilkenny** and **Wicklow,** on to **Waterford, Cork,** and **Kerry,** and up to **Clare** for a quick glance before the clock runs out. It is only hitting the high points but, as high points go, they're hard to beat.

DAYS 1 & 2: Arrive in Dublin

If it happens that you're arriving from North America, you start with an advantage: Most flights arrive early in the morning, which effectively gives you an extra day's sightseeing. Check into your hotel, say yes to any tea and scones offered, take a minute to relax, and then head out on foot. Get a map from your concierge and then just start walking.

Stay south of the River Liffey and head down Dame Street to **Dublin Castle** (p. 100), home of the magical **Chester Beatty Library** (p. 97) with its vast collection of gorgeous illuminated manuscripts. Later, take in **St. Patrick's Cathedral** (p. 107) and the vibrant green quadrangles of **Trinity College** (p. 108), before heading down to Merrion Square, with its impressive granite architecture and two of the main sites of Ireland's **National Museum** (the third is on the west side of the city; the final one is in County Mayo—see p. 390). **Archaeology** has an extraordinary hoard of ancient gold, while the recently refurbished **Natural History** building contains an array of objects from the ancient past. It's a short stroll from here down to **St. Stephen's Green.** Rest your weary toes and soak up the floral view here, before strolling up **Grafton Street** for a last bit of shopping before collapsing in your hotel.

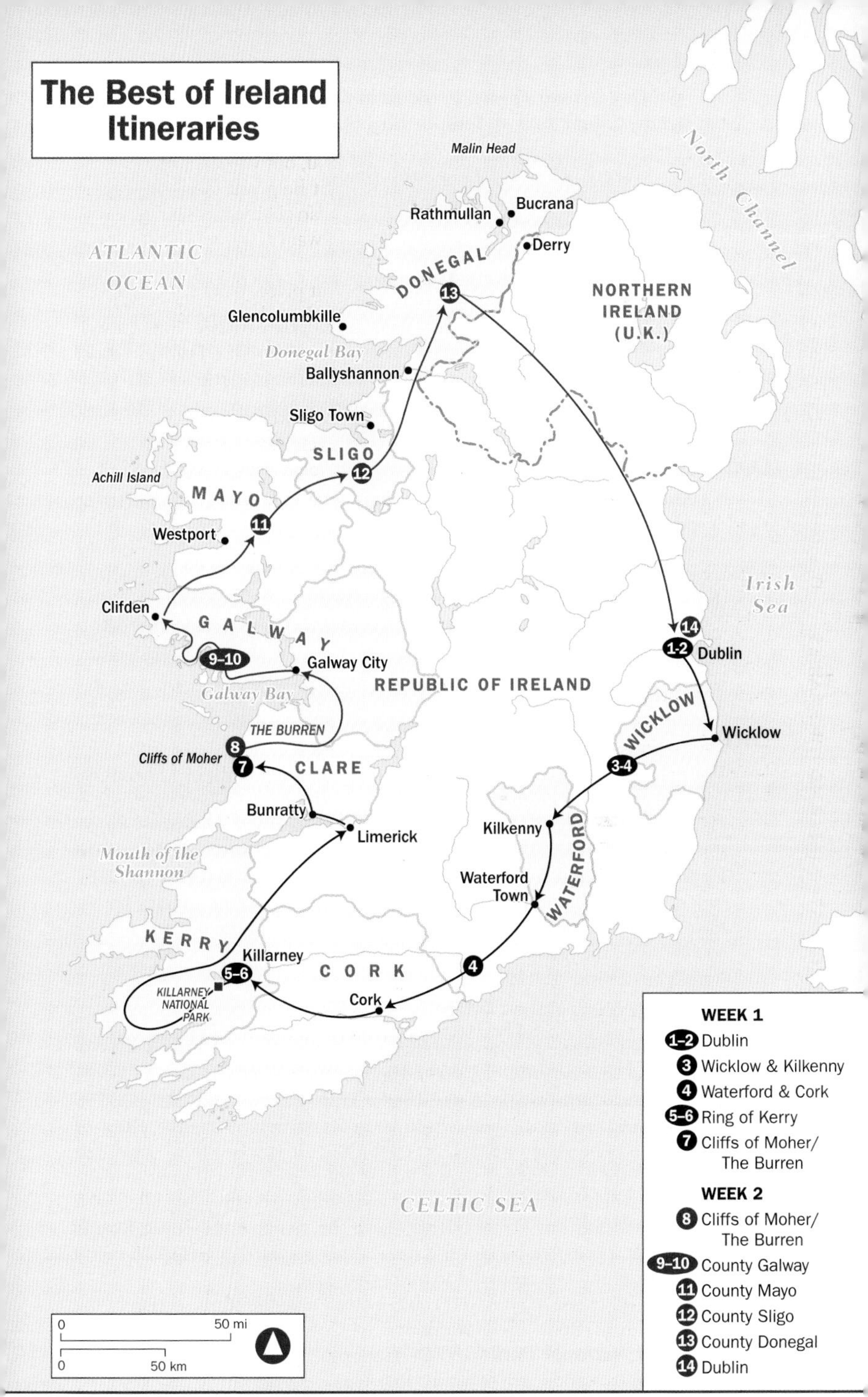
The Best of Ireland Itineraries
Malin Head
Rathmullan
Bucrana
Derry
North Channel
ATLANTIC OCEAN
DONEGAL
NORTHERN IRELAND (U.K.)
Glencolumbkille
Donegal Bay
Ballyshannon
Sligo Town
SLIGO
Achill Island
MAYO
Westport
Irish Sea
Clifden
GALWAY
Galway City
Galway Bay
REPUBLIC OF IRELAND
Dublin
WICKLOW
Wicklow
THE BURREN
Cliffs of Moher
CLARE
Bunratty
Limerick
Kilkenny
Mouth of the Shannon
Waterford Town
WATERFORD
KERRY
Killarney
CORK
KILLARNEY NATIONAL PARK
Cork
CELTIC SEA
WEEK 1
1-2 Dublin
3 Wicklow & Kilkenny
4 Waterford & Cork
5-6 Ring of Kerry
7 Cliffs of Moher/ The Burren
WEEK 2
8 Cliffs of Moher/ The Burren
9-10 County Galway
11 County Mayo
12 County Sligo
13 County Donegal
14 Dublin
0 50 mi
0 50 km

On **Day 2,** have a hearty breakfast in your hotel before striking out for the trendy cultural hub of **Temple Bar.** Stroll down Parliament Street to the river, then take a right, and walk along the noisy, vibrant waterfront to the effervescent arc of the **Ha'penny Bridge.** Head across and down to O'Connell Street and walk on up past its many statues to the bullet-ridden columns of the **General Post Office** (p. 111). This is where the 1916 Easter Rising was based. After exploring its displays, head farther up O'Connell Street to the **Dublin Writers Museum** (p. 101), which bookish types love for its extensive display of memorabilia. Let someone else do the work in the evening, either on a walking tour—such as the **Irish Music Pub Crawl,** perhaps (p. 107)—or some good-natured scares aboard the **Dublin Ghost Bus** (p. 122). However, those in search of something a little less like organized fun will fall in love with the simple, atmospheric pleasure of **An Evening of Food, Folklore & Fairies** (p. 160).

DAY 3: South to Wicklow & Kilkenny

It takes less than 2 hours to drive from the hustle and traffic of Dublin to the peace and quiet of the **Wicklow Mountains** (p. 173). Drive through the town of Enniskerry to the great estate of **Powerscourt** (p. 176) on the south end of the village. After lunching in its Avoca Café, head on to **Glendalough** (p. 168) and feel your soul relax in the pastoral mountain setting of this ancient monastic retreat. From there drive on to the colorful village of **Kilkenny** where you can spend the rest of the day shopping in its pottery and crafts shops and exploring noble **Kilkenny Castle** (p. 216). This is a good place to spend your first night outside of Dublin.

DAY 4: West to Waterford & Cork

Waterford, Ireland's oldest city, is less than an hour south of Kilkenny, so you'll be able to get there with plenty of time to fit in a half-day's sightseeing. Have a quick look around some or all of the **Waterford Treasures** museums (p. 200), before dropping in for a tour of the **House of Waterford Crystal.** After lunch, you have a choice—either head to **Cork** (p. 226), Ireland's busy second city, or **Kinsale** (p. 238), a smaller, quieter harbor town. Both have plenty to keep you busy for the rest of the day and make a good base for the night. But they're very different places, so it depends if you want a bustling or peaceful experience.

DAYS 5 & 6: The Ring of Kerry

If you're not allergic to touristy things, you could stop at **Blarney Castle** (p. 228) on your way out of Cork in the morning; otherwise, on to County Kerry at the southwest tip of the island. Here the most popular place to explore—and one of the busiest tourist spots in Ireland—is the **Ring of Kerry** (see "The Ring of Kerry," in chapter 9). It is a beautiful drive, but because of the frequency of tourist buses, not everybody will want to make it. Others will brave the masses to see extraordinary countryside filled with historic sites and tiny villages. If you have the stamina, the entire Ring is doable at a reasonable pace over 2 days, although you'd have to skip pretty much everything else around it to make that goal.

If it's quiet you're after, you could instead take the short section of the Ring that runs from lovely **Kenmare** (p. 268) to the bucolic peace of **Killarney National Park** (p. 276). Here you can indulge in a buggy ride around the lake and leave only your footsteps.

DAY 7: County Clare

Time is short now, so you won't be able to see as much of Clare as it deserves. But make a promise to yourself to come back someday and head for the perilously tall **Cliffs of Moher** (p. 329) where the view seems to stretch all the way to America (although the price to park will make you shiver). Then you've another choice: Spend the rest of the day exploring **Bunratty Castle** (p. 328)—where medieval fortress meets historical theme park—or marveling at the otherworldly landscape of the **Burren** (see "The Burren," in chapter 10). If it's the latter, strike out for the R480 road that offers the best immediate gratification, as it winds its way through the extraordinary limestone landscape. What a way to end your trip!

THE BEST OF IRELAND IN 2 WEEKS

With 2 weeks, your visit to Ireland will be much more relaxed. You can stretch out a bit more in your travels, heading to less crowded counties with more time to meet the locals. In your second week, head up to Galway, Mayo, and Donegal, taking time to smell the heather along the way.

DAYS 1–7

Follow "The Best of Ireland in 1 Week" itinerary, as outlined above.

DAY 8

After spending Day 7 exploring Clare, you'll discover that you need more time to really get the most out of this big, varied place. If you didn't make it to the Burren, spend most of your day here. Otherwise, you could visit another of the county's great medieval buildings such as **Knappogue Castle** (p. 330) or the exquisite ruins of **Corcomroe Abbey** (p. 327). In a different vein, lovers of live music will want to spend the evening in **Doolin** (p. 329). It's one of the very best places in the country to catch proper, traditional music.

DAYS 9 & 10: County Galway

Start the day with a drive up from Clare to Galway City (it will take around an hour). You could spend a relaxing day walking the delightful streets of this artsy, vibrant town, take a cruise out to the misty **Aran Islands** (see "The Aran Islands," in chapter 11), or, if you've got kids to keep amused, take them to the fabulous **Galway Atlantaquaria** (p. 356). You could go east or west on the following day; either to explore **Connemara National Park** (p. 361), where it's time to get out

A busker entertains passerby in Galway.

from behind the wheel, and maybe even see this lovely park by horseback if you're feeling brave; or you could head inland for a whistle-stop tour of what the Irish Midlands have to offer (chapter 12). You could either head back to Galway City for a second night or pick a B&B in the countryside.

DAY 11: County Mayo

Driving up from Galway, the scenery is also spectacular in Mayo. Here the rocky shoreline plunges into the cobalt sea in glorious fashion. Head to the south Mayo town of **Westport.** It sits at the edge of a picturesque river and is a delightful, peaceful place to wander. Probably depending on whether or not you've got a family to entertain, you could either spend a couple of hours at **Westport House and Pirate Adventure Park** (p. 390) or visit the **National Museum of Ireland: Country Life** (p. 390) near Castlebar. Ancient history buffs will probably want to press right ahead to County Sligo at this point (see below), but if it's quiet retreat you're after, drive across the strangely empty flatlands to **Achill Island** (p. 394). The route along the coast and out across the bridge to the island is slow and windy, but the views are fantastic. If you do make it out to Achill, consider an overnight stay at the **Bervie** (p. 397), where the sea is right outside the door.

DAY 12: County Sligo

Depending on where you based yourself for the night, you may be in for a long drive, so start early. **Sligo Town** (p. 400) has a few worthwhile attractions, but mostly it will be useful as a stop for lunch. The real reason to come this far lies in the surrounding countryside. There is an astonishing concentration of ancient burial sites here, including **Carrowkeel** and **Carrowmore** that contain the world's oldest piece of freestanding architecture. Our favorite place to stay the night in these parts is the extraordinary **Temple House** (p. 409).

Rough surf on Tullan Strand-Bundoran, in County Donegal.

DAY 13: North to Donegal

You're really entering the wilds of Ireland now. Head up the coast past Donegal Town until you catch the N15 road. Then follow it around the breathtaking coastline to the busy hill town of **Ballyshannon** (p. 417), an excellent spot for crafts shops and glorious views from the top of the hill. The adventurous can explore the **Catsby Cave** (p. 417), a picturesque grotto at the edge of the Abbey River. But here the drive is really the thing, so head on to the darling town of **Glencolumbkille** (p. 420). The excellent folk park here is well worth an hour of your time before you head on to the stone-cut town of Ardara at the foot of a steep hill—it's wall-to-wall arts-and-crafts shops and is a pleasure to explore. Art lovers won't want to miss the revelatory gallery at

Glebe House (p. 427). You've spent a lot of time in the car today, but if you can face another 40 minutes or so to the wonderful **Rathmullan House** (p. 430), you'll find a beautiful, elegant seaside retreat waiting for you on your last night.

DAY 14: Heading Home

If your flight leaves late, you could rise early and spend the morning driving up to **Malin Head** (p. 433), the northernmost tip of Ireland. It's a wild and wooly place just a couple of hours' drive from Rathmullan. From there, expect the journey to the airport to take at least 4 hours, but allow plenty of time in case of traffic backups around Dublin—they're virtually constant.

IRELAND FOR FREE OR DIRT CHEAP

Ireland is no longer a cheap country to visit—and hasn't been for some time. The economic crash of the late 2000s drove prices down a bit, but hotels and restaurants are still pricey, and in recent years the euro/dollar exchange rate has not been favorable to travelers from the U.S. And that's not even taking into account the global economic conditions that make these uncertain financial times. But here's the good news: You can visit a lot of great sites for free in Ireland, including some of the biggest tourist attractions in the country. You can also save a lot of money by sticking mainly to places that can be reached by public transport, rather than hiring a car (every place we list is easily accessible by train or bus). You'd be surprised by how much of Ireland you can see without blowing the budget. We're starting this tour in Northern Ireland (maybe you got a great deal on a flight to Belfast!), because it's one of the more budget-friendly regions. For more information on train and bus timetables, see **www.irishrail.ie** and **www.buseireann.ie**.

DAY 1: Belfast

Belfast is rich with free attractions. The excellent **Ulster Museum** (p. 456) displays artifacts from across 9,000 years of Irish history. Exhibitions also explore Belfast and the capital's more recent industrial past. Right next door is the **Belfast Botanic Gardens & Palm House** (p. 450) that's also a short walk from the campus of **Queen's University** (p. 452). Belfast **City Hall** (p. 451) runs free guided tours. Another exceptional Victorian landmark, **Belfast Cathedral** (p. 447), is also free, and **Cave Hill Country Park** (p. 450) is a tranquil place with good walking trails and incredible views of the city. Last but not least, Belfast is still most famous for the violence and hardship it endured in the mid- to late-20th century. The epicenter of the conflict was the **Falls and Shankill roads area** (p. 449). Political murals are still a salient feature of these neighborhoods, though they are now safe for visitors to explore. To get the most out of them, you may want to spend some of that cash you've saved so far on a **Black Taxi Tour** (p. 449).

Catch a train from Belfast to Dublin (Connolly Station). Time: 2 hr. 10 min. Fares start at about €22 for adults.

DAYS 2 & 3: Dublin

Ireland's capital is also the number one destination in the country for free sites. The **Chester Beatty Library** (p. 97) is, for our money, one of the

SAVING MONEY ON trains & buses

The cost of rail travel can quickly mount up, but there are ways to save money. Whenever you can, *book in advance*. The example fares listed in this itinerary are all pre-booked; walk-up fares can be higher. The downside for booking that way is that you have to specify times of travel—but Irish Rail has a handy policy of letting you upgrade a pre-booked ticket into something more flexible for just €10.

If you're going to be spending a lot of time on public transportation, you should also strongly consider buying a money-saving pass. In the Irish Republic, the **Eurail Pass** is good for travel on trains, Expressway coaches, and the Irish Continental Lines ferries between France and Ireland. They cost around €155 for a 3-day pass and €235 for a 5-day pass. Youth passes (ages 16–25), family, and first-class passes are also available. For further details, or for purchase, visit www.eurail.com.

BritRail Pass + Ireland: Includes all rail travel throughout the United Kingdom and Ireland, including a round-trip ferry crossing on Stena Line. Available from **BritRail** (✆ **866/938-RAIL** in the U.S. and Canada; www.britrail.com). Prices for a 5-day pass start at £389 adults, £289 children. The BritRail pass is not available to British citizens.

Either of these can add up to significant savings, but there are a couple bits of small print to be aware of. First, it's still advisable to make seat reservations to guarantee a space—this may cost a few extra euro or pounds each time in booking fees. Also, not everybody can buy a pass. E.U. citizens aren't allowed to buy Eurail passes, and likewise, British citizens can't buy BritRail passes.

Both passes can also be purchased from **Railpass** (www.railpass.com), **STA Travel** (✆ **800/781-4040** in the U.S.; www.sta.com) and other travel agents.

A classic corner pub in Dublin.

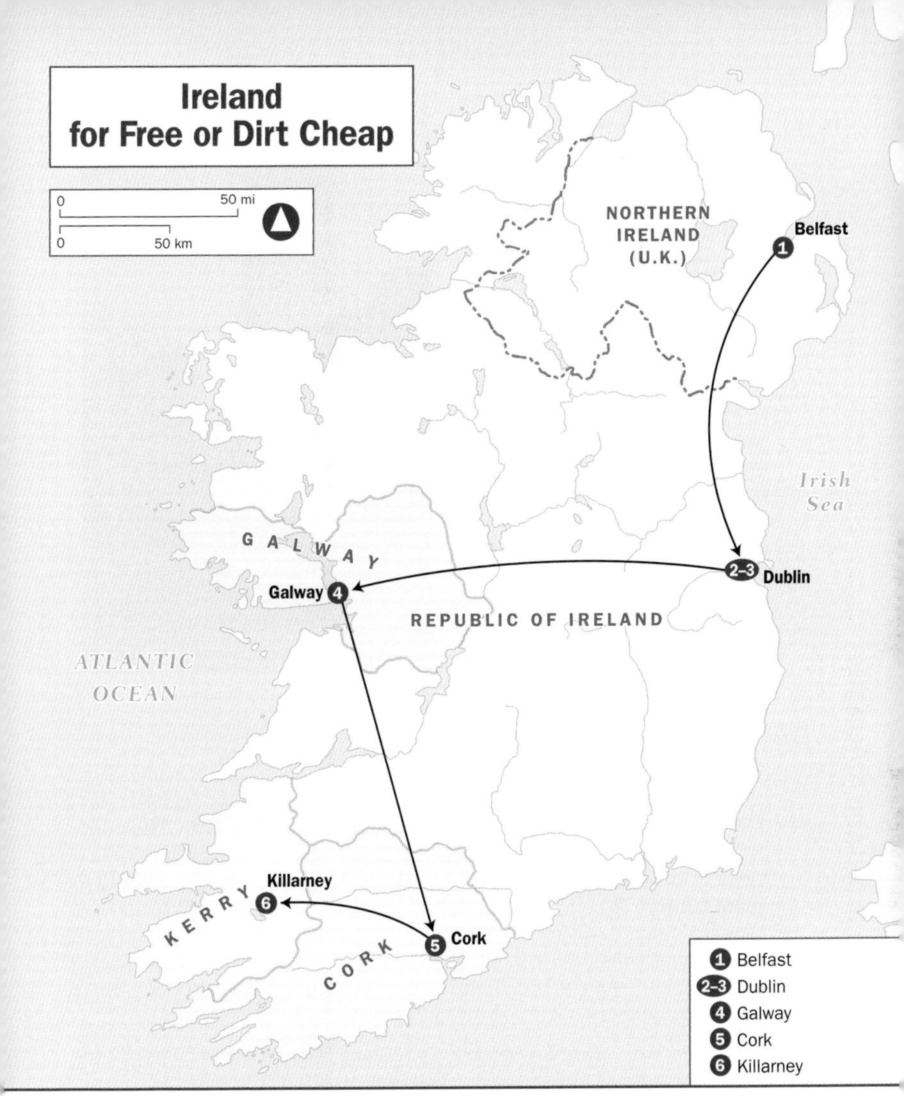

best museums in Europe. The collection of illuminated gospels and early copies of the Bible, Torah, and Koran would justify a steep entrance fee, but it won't cost you a cent. Three of the four separate museums constituting the **National Museum of Ireland** are in Dublin— **Archaeology, Natural History,** and **Decorative Arts and History**—and all are free. Each contains some incredible treasures, and collectively have enough to keep you occupied for a day or more. All of Dublin's best major art galleries are free. The collection at the **National Gallery of Ireland,** though relatively small, includes works by Titian, Vermeer, Monet, and Picasso. Also complimentary are the **Irish Museum of Modern Art** (p. 114), the **Temple Bar Gallery** (p. 116), and the excellent **Hugh Lane Gallery** (p. 103). Many of Dublin's most historic public buildings don't charge admission. **The Irish President's House** (Áras an Uachtaráin, p. 103) is accessible only by tour on a first-come, first-served basis; the queue forms at the visitor center in Phoenix Park. The **Bank of Ireland/Parliament House** (p. 113) and the **Four Courts** (p. 110) are also free. The **General Post Office** on O'Connell Street (p. 111) is still a working post office but has a small number of exhibits devoted to the Easter Rising, including the original Declaration of Independence. Add to this the great public spaces such as **Phoenix Park** (p. 118), **St. Stephen's Green** (p. 108), and **Trinity College** (p. 108), and you'll see it's possible to spend a full 2 days here without spending a penny on sightseeing.

Wellington Monument in Phoenix Park, Dublin.

Catch a train from Dublin (Heuston Station) to Galway. Time: 2 hr. 40 min. Fares start at about €33 for adults.

DAY 4: Galway

Ireland's artsy, seductive west coast city offers plenty of free pursuits. The **Galway Arts Centre** (p. 344) usually has good exhibitions, and you can often score cheap tickets for performances. The **Galway City Museum** (p. 344) makes for a stellar introduction to the region, with its fine collection of artifacts from the medieval period onward. **St. Nicholas' Collegiate Church** (p. 346), the oldest church in the city, contains a 12th-century crusader's tomb and other extraordinary historic pieces. Make sure you devote some time to just wandering the streets of this eminently walkable town too; its central medieval district is a tiny, tangled area featuring plenty of interesting shops. Getting lost is half the fun.

Catch a bus from Galway Bus Station to Cork (Parnell Place Bus Station). Time: 3½ hr. with one change or 4 hr. 20 min. direct. Fares start at about €27 for adults.

DAY 5: Galway to Cork

This busy, youthful city doesn't have a great deal of free attractions, but if you're up for a large dose of culture, you'll find plenty to do without paying a cent. You'll have enough here to keep you busy for the day if you hit the ground running. Start with a trip to the **Old English Market** (p. 232) for a browse and a cheap lunch. Afterward, head to the **Crawford Art Gallery** (p. 231)—it's one of the very best in Ireland and completely free. More excellent free art is to be found at the **Lewis Glucksman Gallery** (p. 234) on the campus of **University College Cork.** In the evening, check out a few of Cork's exceptional pubs. They have a reputation for being among the best in the country for traditional music (see "A Tuneful Pint" on p. 237).

Catch a train from Cork to Killarney. Most change at Mallow. Time: 1 hr. 20 min. direct, or 2 hr. with change. Fares start at about €29 for adults.

DAY 6: Cork to Killarney

It's not exactly difficult to reach **Killarney National Park** (p. 276) from Killarney Town; you just walk toward the cathedral and turn left. This 65sq. km (25-sq. mile) expanse of forest, lakes, and mountains is crisscrossed with several well-conceived nature trails, plus more challenging routes for serious hikers. Formerly the grounds of a great mansion, the **Knockreer Estate** (p. 276) still has lovely gardens and beautiful views. Free sites in Killarney Town itself include the rather grand neo-Gothic **St. Mary's Cathedral** (p. 278). For dinner, the frugal traveler will be drawn to **Pay as You Please** (p. 285)—a solid restaurant with no prices on the menu. You pay what you feel the food is worth.

Catch a train Killarney to Dublin—again, nearly all change at Mallow. Time: 3½ hr. Fares start at about €44 for adults.

DAY 7: Homeward Bound . . .

Assuming your airline will let you fly out of Dublin, an early-ish train back to the capital should allow you some time to pick up any of the free sites you didn't manage to cover earlier in the tour. Otherwise, you'll have to catch a train straight on to Belfast for your flight home (about 7½ hr. with up to three changes; fares from Killarney start at about €38 adults). And that's it! You've done a fair bit of Ireland without breaking the bank. Pick your accommodations early and wisely to save the most. Plenty of inexpensive B&Bs are listed in this book for all of these cities. Your other main expense on this itinerary will be rail fares, but you can save money on those too (see "Saving Money on Trains & Buses" on p. 28).

THE BEST OF IRELAND FOR FAMILIES

Traveling with children is always a bit of an adventure, and you'll want all the help you can get. Luckily Ireland—with its vast open countryside, farm hotels, and castles—is a fairy-tale playground for kids. You may have trouble finding babysitters outside major towns, so just take the kids with you. Most restaurants, sights, and even pubs (during the day) welcome children. The best part of the country for those traveling with kids is arguably Cork and Kerry, where everything seems to be set up for families. Here's a sample itinerary to give you some ideas.

DAYS 1 & 2: Dublin

The sprawling greens of **Phoenix Park** (p. 118) are a great place for little ones to let off steam (it's the best place in the city for a picnic too, if the weather's good). Within the park, **Dublin Zoo** (p. 117) is thoughtfully designed to cater to the younger ones (you can take a train ride around the zoo, for instance). Inquisitive young minds will be inspired by the cabinets of curiosity at the **National Museum of Ireland: Natural History** (p. 106), and have their interest piqued by **Number Twenty-Nine: Georgian House Museum** (p. 112), a house which has been kept exactly as it would have been at the turn of the 19th century. The guides at another museum, the **Little Museum of Dublin**

(p. 112), do a great job of putting the ordinary lives of Dubliners in the last hundred years into context for younger visitors. But if their attention spans demand something a little flashier, try a **Viking Splash Tour** (p. 122), a historical whirl around the city in a World War II amphibious vehicle, complete with headlong splash into the River Liffey. Parents who don't mind indulging a junior fascination with all the ghoulish may want to take their kids to see the creepy crypts at **St. Michan's Church** (p. 120); but if that's too much like real scares, parents with younger kids are all but guaranteed to love an evening aboard the **Dublin Ghost Bus** (p. 122).

DAY 2: County Cork

Okay, so it's not exactly untouched by the tourism fairy, but kids find plenty to love about **Blarney Castle** (p. 228), just outside Cork City. They can kiss the famous stone if they don't mind an attendant holding them upside down. A few miles away, the **Fota Island & Wildlife Park** (p. 249) is a well-designed zoo where the docile animals (those that don't bite, kick, or stomp) roam among the visitors.

DAYS 3–5: County Kerry

Kerry is probably Ireland's most kid-friendly county, so there's enough to keep you busy here for at least a couple of days. Fungie, star of the **Dingle Dolphin Boat Tours** (p. 298) has been entertaining kids and grown-ups alike for the last 30 years. In Kenmare, **Seafari** cruises and seal-watching trips (p. 269) teach kids about conservation issues by putting them in touch with the underwater residents of Kenmare Bay. **Blueberry Hill Farm** (p. 288), in Sneem, is a working, old-fashioned farmstead where kids can help milk cows, make butter, and take part in a treasure hunt. Meanwhile, an underground tour of the atmospheric **Crag Cave** (p. 288) is a surefire winner—as is a stop for high-energy playtime at the **Crazy Cave** (p. 288) adventure playground. And don't overlook what **Killarney National Park** (p. 276) has to offer little ones. A ride around the park in a horse-drawn "jarvey" is bound to meet with their approval.

DAY 6: Bunratty Folk Park

You could spend most of the day at **Bunratty Castle & Folk Park** (p. 298), an attraction that combines one of Ireland's best medieval castles with a living history museum. It's a brilliant recreation of a 19th-century village, complete with costumed actors strolling down the street, chatting to passersby, and even working in the shops. Bunratty is also the setting for a lively (and hugely popular) **Medieval Banquet.** It's raucous, but surprisingly good fun; book an early evening sitting to suit young bedtimes.

DAY 7: Heading Home

If you have time before the drive back to the airport, head into the **Burren** (see "The Burren" in chapter 10). Young imaginations will be fired up by the dolmens and other ancient sites that litter the otherworldly landscape. It's also where you'll find the **Burren Birds of Prey Centre** at Aillwee Cave (p. 327); you can see buzzards, falcons, eagles, and owls in flight at this working aviary.

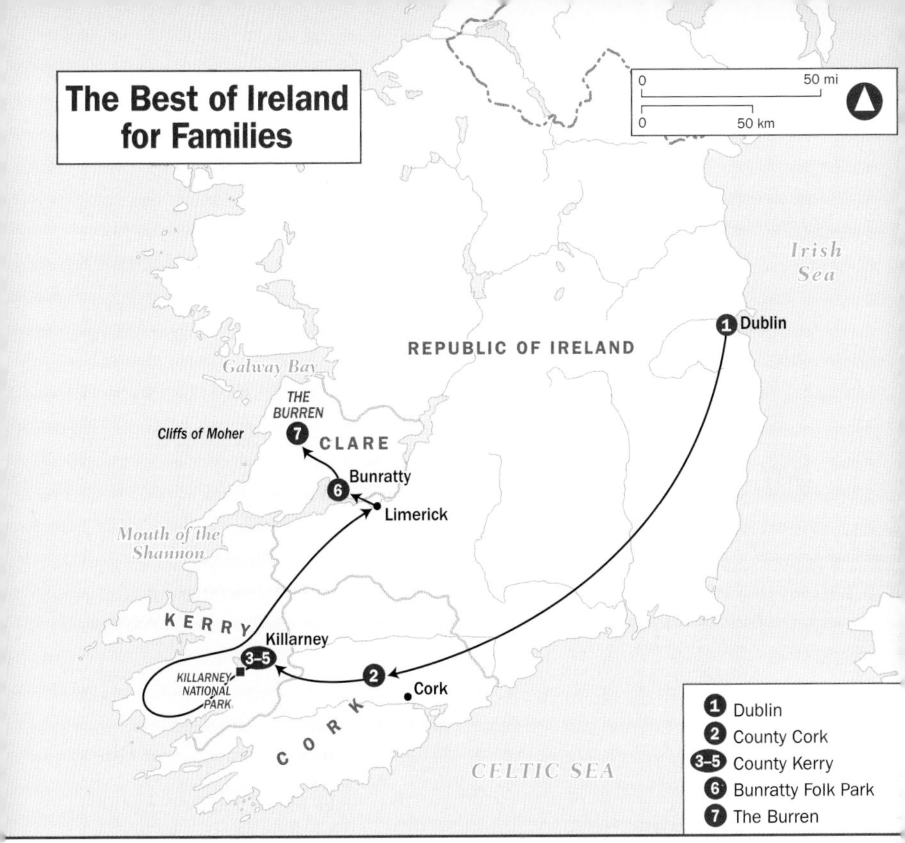

BEYOND A WEEK . . .

If your trip extends beyond a week, your family will find plenty of standout attractions for kids further north.

The **Atlantaquaria** (p. 356), just outside Galway City, is a new, state-of-the-art aquarium, while pony trekking across **Connemara National Park** (p. 361) is a unique way to see this beautiful, windswept landscape.

In Mayo, **Westport House and Pirate Adventure Park** (p. 390) has all the components necessary for high-activity fun, and young ones are bound to enjoy learning all about the region's real-life pirate hero, **Grace O'Malley** (see p. 392).

If you're going as far as Belfast, the attractions around the new Titanic Quarter hold plenty of kid-friendly appeal. Try the hands-on science center, **W5** (p. 455), and the state-of-the-art **Titanic Belfast** museum (p. 453).

And the **Antrim Coast Drive** (see p. 480) has two key highlights that children will adore: the perilous (but fun) **Carrick-a-Rede Rope Bridge** (p. 481) and the awe-inspiring alien shapes of the **Giant's Causeway** (p. 482).

EXPLORING ANCIENT IRELAND

Ireland has treasured and protected its ancient past, and its mysterious stone circles, cairns, and huge stone tables called *dolmens* can still be found perfectly preserved in pastures and on hillsides all over the island. These are precious connections to our own long-lost pasts, as they provide a window through which we can catch a hazy glimpse of what life was like very long ago. You'll need to be intrepid and cover a lot of ground in the car, but it'll be worth it. Some of the oldest tombs predate the Egyptian pyramids by centuries, and, in many cases, the sites are preserved but their meaning has long since disappeared, making them intriguing and elusive in equal measures. Exploring these rocky symbols can be the most memorable part of any trip to Ireland.

DAY 1: Knowth & the Boyne Valley

After an early breakfast, head north to the rich rolling Boyne Valley (about an hour's drive north of Dublin off the N2) to the Brú na Bóinne Visitor Centre and this extensive Neolithic burial ground. This huge necropolis holds numerous sites, with three open to visitors—**Newgrange** (p. 180), **Knowth** (p. 179), and **Dowth.** Register at the center to tour Newgrange first. A tour here, early in the day before it gets crowded, is spectacular. Next tour the burial ground at Knowth with its extensive collection of passage-grave art. In the afternoon, head down the N3 to the **Hill of Tara** (p. 178). Here mounds and passage graves date from the Bronze Age.

DAY 2: Céide Fields

It will take a couple of hours to drive to the remote location in north County Mayo, but your efforts will be rewarded. This extraordinary ancient site

One of many ancient tombs at Carrowmore, a Megalithic burial ground in County Sligo.

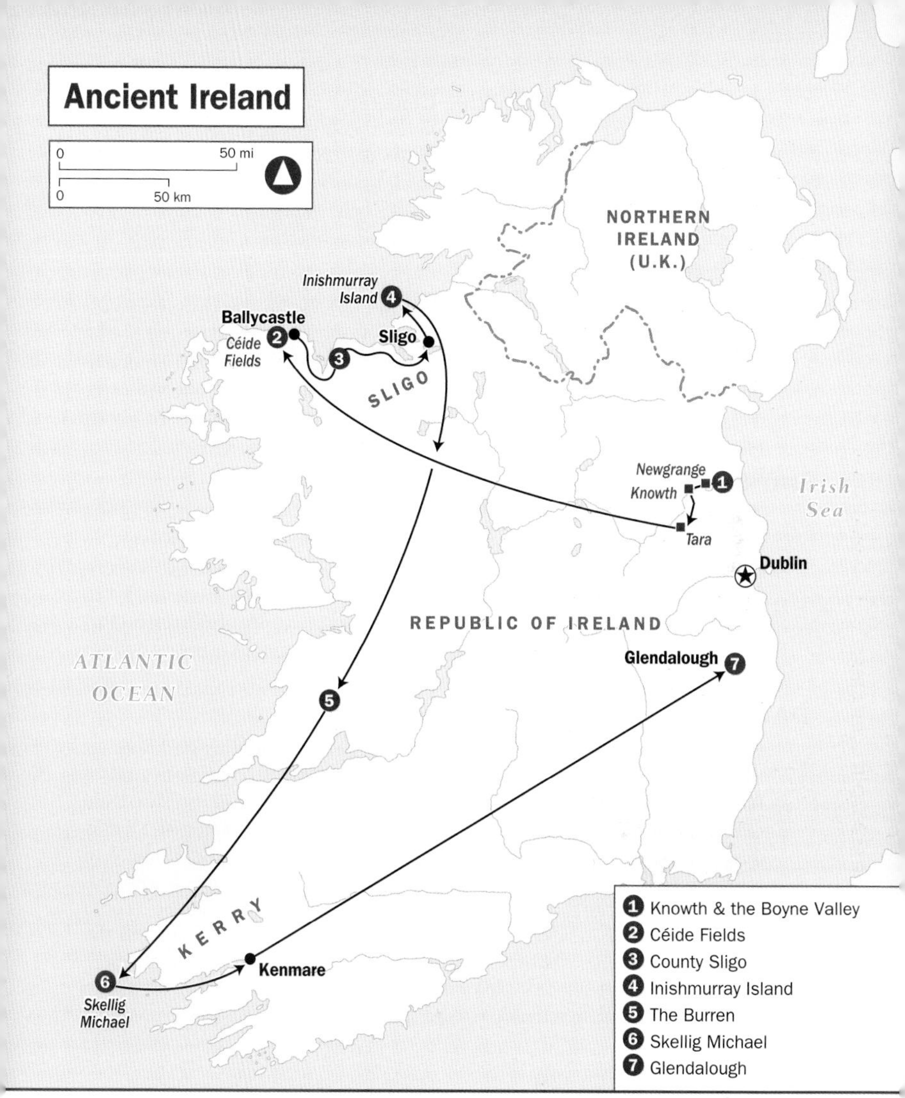

(p. 393) holds the stony remains of an entire prehistoric farming village on top of a cliff and has breathtaking views of the sea and surrounding countryside. Spend the day exploring the 5,000-year-old site, and lunch in the excellent visitor center.

DAY 3: County Sligo

In the morning, drive east to County Sligo. On the N4, south of Sligo Town, visit the **Carrowkeel Passage Tomb Cemetery** (p. 405) perched on a hilltop overlooking Lough Arrow. It has wide, sweeping views, and the 14 cairns and dolmens are often very quiet early in the day—with luck you might have them all to yourself. Then head on to Sligo Town and follow signs to **Carrowmore Megalithic Cemetery** (p. 405). This extraordinary site has 60 stone circles, passage tombs, and dolmens scattered across acres of green pastures. They are believed to predate Newgrange by nearly a millennium. In the afternoon, if you're feeling energetic, climb to the hilltop cairn of **Knocknarea** located nearby—it's believed to be the grave of folklore fairy Queen Maeve.

DAY 4: Inishmurray Island

After a relaxing morning, travel by boat to the island of **Inishmurray** (see p. 406) off the coast of Sligo. There you can spend the day wandering the impressively complete remains of the early monastic settlement founded in the 6th century. You can still make out its ancient chapels, beehive cells, and altars. If the weather is fine, pack a picnic lunch and eat on the sunny beach. Return to Sligo for the night.

DAY 5: The Burren

Today begins with another long drive, but you'll pass through some of the most beautiful parts of Galway and Mayo along the way. **The Burren,** in County Clare, is one of the richest areas of the country for ancient remains from the Neolithic period through medieval times. There are around 120 dolmens and wedge tombs—including the impressive **Poulnabrone Dolmen** (p. 328)—and as many as 500 ring forts. For more on this extraordinary region see "The Burren" in chapter 10.

DAY 6: Skellig Michael

Right after breakfast, head south to County Kerry, where this starkly beautiful island sits 13km (8 miles) offshore, standing sternly as a kind of memorial to the hardy souls who once eked out a living amid its formidable cliffs and stony mountains (see "The Ring of Kerry" in chapter 9). Deeply observant early Christian monks punished their bodies by living here in miserable conditions and spent their days carving 600 steps into the unyielding stone, so their walk up to the beehive huts and icy chapels could be made somewhat safer. Today it is an unforgettable landscape, and the ruins of their homes are evocative and profoundly moving. A trip out here by boat and an afternoon's exploration will take up much of the day. Once you return to the mainland, reward yourself with a relaxing evening in Kenmare.

DAY 7: Glendalough

Drive east today to County Wicklow, where the evocative ruins of the monastery at **Glendalough** (p. 168) are sprawled around two peaceful lakes nestled on the side of a mountain. Get a map from the visitor center before beginning your exploration of the round towers, chapels, and huts dotted around the wooded site. Don't miss the ancient chapel known as **St. Kevin's Kitchen.** If the weather is warm, bring your lunch and picnic by the lake. You can easily spend a day here.

IRELAND OFF THE BEATEN PATH

We start this tour in Belfast, a city in the midst of an immense transformation since the 1998 Good Friday Agreement that finally established a detente in

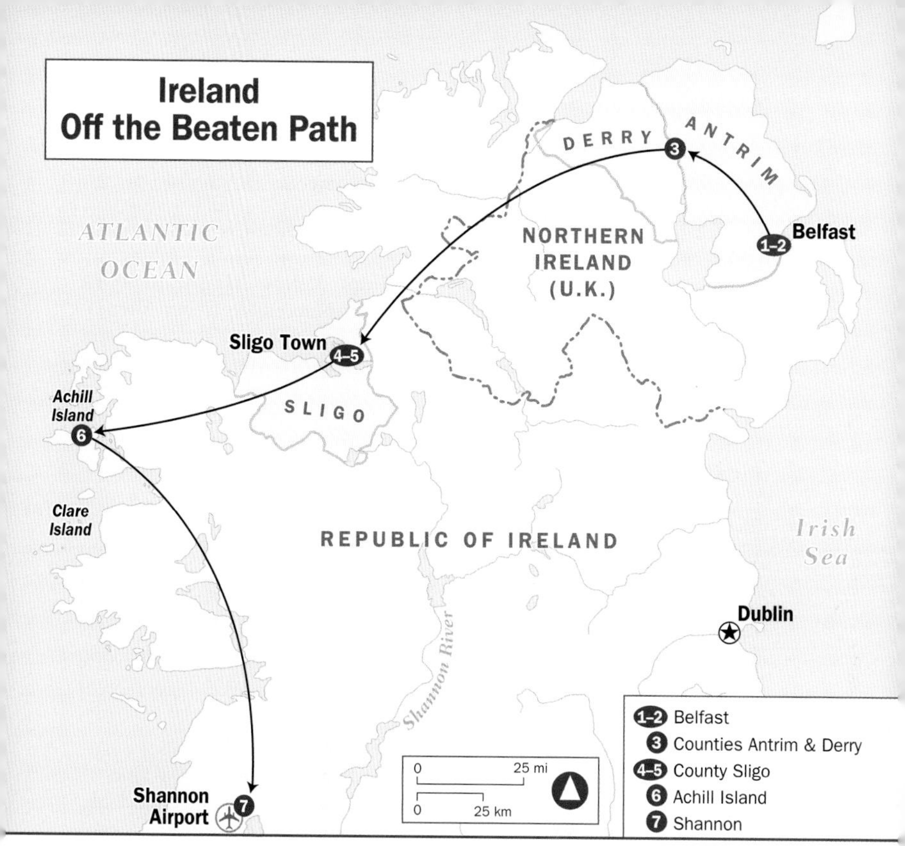

Northern Ireland. Tourism has steadily increased in this region over the last decade, but the crowds still have yet to arrive en masse. If the best sites of the Antrim Coast were in County Cork or Kerry, they'd be overrun with tourists; as it is, one can still visit a spectacular setting such as the Giant's Causeway and find oneself alone with nature. This tour then heads west to take a couple of Sligo's prehistoric sites and continues south for a visit to Achill Island, a peaceful retreat off the coast of County Mayo.

DAYS 1 & 2: Belfast

Northern Ireland's capital—and the island of Ireland's second largest city—is a historic, vibrant town. Start with a visit to the **Ulster Museum** (p. 456) and experience some of the city's more recent past firsthand with a **Black Taxi Tour** (p. 449). The new museums in the Titanic Quarter, such as the immense **Titanic Belfast** (p. 453), provide a more high-tech dose of history; alternatively, you could immerse yourself in the city's present by exploring its busy shopping districts. The **Belfast Botanic Gardens & Palm House** (p. 450) and **Queen's University** (p. 452) are also worth a look. Round off the day with a pint at one of

Belfast's extraordinarily pretty pubs like the **Crown Liquor Saloon** (p. 451) and a meal at one of the small but growing number of world-class restaurants.

DAY 3: County Antrim

One of the North's loveliest counties, Antrim is home to two gorgeous parks: the **Castlewellan Forest Park** (p. 473) with formal gardens and gorgeous woodland walks, and the **Silent Valley Mountain Park** (p. 474) with beautiful walks and even more incredible views. Alternatively, the Antrim Coast road is one of Ireland's great coastal drives—and one of the least spoiled. Few tourists ever venture this far north; those who do will reap spectacular rewards. Start in **Carrickfergus,** with a brief stop to look around its medieval castle (p. 455), before heading north along the coast road. For the best views take the **Torr Head Scenic Road** (p. 484) located just after the village of **Cushendun** (p. 481). It's an alternative, signposted road running parallel to the main route, ideal for those with a good head for heights. From up here on a clear day, you can see all the way to the Mull of Kintyre in Scotland. The Antrim Coast's most remarkable asset is the **Giant's Causeway** (p. 482), an uncanny natural rock formation comprised of thousands of tightly packed basalt columns. You could do the drive in about 2 hours, but you'll want to allow considerably longer than that to give yourself time to stop along the way. There are places along the coast to spend the night, or you could go straight on into **Derry** (p. 487). It's about another hour on from the Giant's Causeway.

DAY 4: Derry to Sligo

Straddling the border between Northern Ireland and the Republic, this vibrant town was synonymous with political strife. Though it's peaceful these days, it's still a divided place—the residents can't even agree on what to call it. Road signs from the Republic point to Derry; those in the North point to Londonderry. How can a place like that not be full of character and history? Check out the award-winning **Tower Museum** (p. 492) and the Gothic, 17th-century **Cathedral of St. Columb** (p. 491) before recharging for a long drive to County Sligo in the afternoon.

DAY 5: County Sligo

Nestled within the gentle, verdant hills of this underrated county are some dramatic archaeological sites. Within a short drive from Sligo Town are two of the most incredible: **Carrowkeel Passage Tomb Cemetery** (p. 405) packed with 14 cairns, dolmens, and stone circles, and the impossibly ancient **Carrowmore Megalithic Cemetery** (p. 405). Here's a thought to ponder while clambering around the latter: The innocuously named tomb 52A is thought to be 7,400 years old, making it the earliest known piece of freestanding stone architecture in the world.

DAY 6: Sligo to Achill Island

This is a wild and beautiful place of unspoiled beaches and spectacular scenery. But you'll also find a handful of excellent little hotels and B&Bs, mostly in the vicinity of **Keel,** the island's most attractive village. This is also major outdoor sports territory, as the constant wind off the Atlantic Ocean is ideal for windsurfing, hang gliding, and any other sport that depends on a breeze. One of the best (and least known) discoveries on Achill Island is a deserted village on the slopes of **Mount Slievemore** (p. 394). Not too many people venture up there, making it an even more extraordinary and moving place to visit.

DAY 7: Achill Island to Shannon

It's a long drive to whichever airport you're flying home from, but a flight out of Shannon will give you the most spectacular route. If you can extend your trip a little, **Clare Island** (p. 391) is a lovely place to spend a day. Even more peaceful and isolated than its near neighbor, Achill, Clare's permanent population amounts to just 150 people, and you can go a long way without bumping into any of them.

3

IRELAND IN CONTEXT

This is a difficult time for Ireland, as it reels from an ongoing economic crisis and struggles to find political and financial equilibrium. In 2011, the country's government collapsed and a new government was elected quickly, but the Irish are clearly worried about where they're headed. A complex, small country with a deeply troubled past, Ireland is rich with history, beauty, and life. Troubled though these days are, this is a fascinating time to visit and see Ireland in transition.

IRELAND TODAY

The Irish boom economy of the late 1990s changed the country monumentally—resulting in an unprecedented spread of unbelievable wealth and a huge amount of property development. The excess associated with the boom—business executives flying from Dublin to Galway in their private helicopters for lunch at a particularly good oyster bar, for example, and small apartments in Dublin selling for millions of euro—always seemed unsustainable. And so it was. As suddenly as the boom started, it ended. Over the course of a few weeks in 2008, the economy crashed, sending the country into an economic and political tailspin. Ireland's banks were faced catastrophic levels of bad debt. As the devastating wave of economic disaster crashed down across Europe, Ireland found itself among the very worst affected.

This all came as a shock to the Irish, who, after more than 15 years of European investment, had begun to believe their newfound affluence would last forever. The chatter of jackhammers formed a constant aural background in nearly every town in the Republic, and the dump truck seemed to be the national symbol of Ireland, as the huge vehicles trundled along by the dozen, carrying tons of gravel and sand to be used laying new roads and building new neighborhoods. But construction far outpaced demand. Entire subdivisions were built with nobody to live in them—thousands of new homes sat empty. Developers gambling on future growth built shining new ghost towns.

Now, it seems, birdsong is returning to Ireland. The worst years of the crash are over, and the economy is slowly turning a corner. But it is a changed country. Experts think this gradual process of recovery could take years, possibly decades. But Ireland will bounce back. It has been through worse.

THE MAKING OF IRELAND

THE FIRST SETTLERS With some degree of confidence, we can place the date of the first human habitation of the island somewhere after the end of the last ice age, around the late 8000s B.C. Ireland's first colonizers, Mesolithic Homo sapiens, walked, waded, or floated across the narrow strait from what is now Britain in search of flint and, of course, food.

The next momentous prehistoric event was the arrival of Neolithic farmers and herders, sometime around 3500 B.C. Unlike Ireland's Mesolithic hunters,

PREVIOUS PAGE: **The grounds of St. Dubhan's Church, on the Hook Peninsula in County Cork.**

who barely left a trace, this second wave of colonizers began to transform the island at once.

They came with stone axes that could fell a good-sized elm in less than an hour. Ireland's hardwood forests receded to make room for tilled fields and pastureland. Villages sprang up, and more permanent homes, planked with split oak, appeared at this time.

Far more striking, though, was the appearance of massive megalithic monuments, including court cairns, dolmens (stone tables), round subterranean passage tombs, and wedge tombs. Thousands of these tombs are scattered around Ireland, and to this day only a small percentage of them have been excavated. These megalithic monuments speak volumes about the early Irish. To visit **Newgrange** (p. 180) and **Knowth** (see p. 179) in the Boyne Valley and **Carrowmore** (see p. 404) in County Sligo is to marvel at the mystical practices of the early Irish. Even today little is known about the meaning of these mysterious stone remnants of their lives.

Early Celtic inhabitants of the island assumed that the tremendous stones and mounds were raised by giants. They called them the people of the sí, who eventually became the *Tuatha Dé Danann*, and, finally, *fairies*. Over many generations of oral tradition, the mythical people were downsized into "little people," who were believed to have led a magical life, mostly underground, in the thousands of raths (earthwork structures) coursing the island like giant mole tunnels. All of these sites were believed to be protected by fairies. To tamper with them was believed to bring great bad luck, so nobody ever touched them. Thus, they have lasted to this day—ungraffitied, undamaged, unprotected by any visible fences or wires, but utterly safe.

THE CELTS Of all the successive waves of outsiders who have, over the years, shaped, cajoled, and pockmarked the timeline of Irish history, none have made quite such a deep-seated impact as that of the Celts. They came in waves, the first perhaps as early as the 6th century B.C. and continuing until the end of the first millennium. They fled from the Roman invasion and clung to the edge of Europe—Ireland being, at the time, about as far as you could go to elude a Roman force. In time, they controlled the island and absorbed into their culture everyone they found there.

DATELINE

ca. 8000 B.C. Earliest known human settlers arrive in Ireland.

ca. 700 B.C. Celtic settlement of Ireland begins.

ca. A.D. 100 The Gaels arrive in Ireland, naming one of their biggest settlements *Dubhlinn*.

A.D. 432 Traditional date of St. Patrick's return to Ireland as a Christian missionary.

500–800 Ireland becomes one of the largest centers of Christianity in Europe—often referred to as the "Golden Age."

795 First Viking invasion.

841 Vikings build a sea fort in the area of modern-day Dublin.

1014 Battle of Clontarf. High king of Ireland, Brian Boru, defeats the Vikings.

1167–71 Forces of English King Henry II seize Dublin and surrounding areas.

1204 Dublin Castle becomes center of English power.

1300s First great plague kills a third of the population of Dublin.

Despite their cultural potency, however, the Celts developed little in the way of centralized government, existing instead in a near-perpetual state of division and conflict with one another. The island was divided among as many as 150 tribes, grouped under alliances to five provincial kings. The provinces of Munster, Leinster, Ulster, and Connaught date from this period. They fought fiercely among themselves over cattle (their "currency" and standard of wealth), land, and women. None among them ever ruled the entire island, though not for lack of trying. One of the most impressive monuments from the time of the warring Celts is the stone fortress of **Dún Aengus,** on the wind-swept hills of the Aran Islands (see p. 343).

THE COMING OF CHRISTIANITY The Celtic chiefs neither warmly welcomed nor violently resisted the Christians who came ashore beginning in the 5th century A.D. Although threatened, the pagan Celts settled for a bloodless rivalry with this new religion. In retrospect, this may have been a mistake.

Not the first, but eventually the most famous, of these Christian newcomers was a man called Maewyn Succat, a young Roman citizen torn from his Welsh homeland in a Celtic raid and brought to Ireland as a slave, where he was forced to work in a place called the Forest of Foclut (thought to be around modern County Antrim). He escaped on a ship bound for France, where he spent several years as a priest before returning to Ireland as a missionary. He began preaching at sacred Celtic festivals, a tactic that frequently led to confrontations with religious and political leaders, but eventually he became such a popular figure with the people of Ireland that after his death in 461, a dozen clan chiefs fought over the right to bury him. His lasting legacy was, of course, the establishment in Ireland of one of the strongest Christian orthodoxies in Europe—an achievement for which he was later beatified as St. Patrick.

Ireland's conversion to Christianity was a somewhat negotiated process. The church at the time of St. Patrick was, like the man who brought it, Roman. To Ireland, an island then still without a single proper town, the Roman system of dioceses and archdioceses didn't apply to the way they lived. So the Irish adapted the church to their own situation. They built isolated monasteries with extended monastic "families," each more or less autonomous. The pope, like an

1500s	English rule consolidated across Ireland. Henry VIII proclaims himself king of Ireland.
1534–52	Henry VIII begins suppression of Catholic Church in Ireland.
1558–1603	Reign of Elizabeth I. Ireland proclaimed an Anglican country. The "plantation" of Munster divides Ireland into counties.
1591	Trinity College founded.
1601–02	Spanish forces, in consort with Irish rebels, attempt to stage an invasion of Ireland. They are defeated by the English after a 3-month siege.
1607	The flight of the Irish earls, marking the demise of the old Gaelic order.
1641	Irish Catholic revolt in Ulster led by Sir Phelim O'Neill ends in defeat.
1649	Oliver Cromwell invades and begins the reconquest of Ireland.
1690	The forces of King James II, a Catholic, are defeated at the Battle of the Boyne, consolidating Protestant order in England.

continues

Trinity College, Dublin, home of the Book of Kells.

Irish high king, was to them like an ordained prizefighter—he was expected to defend his title, one challenge after another, or lose it.

Ireland flourished in this fashion for several centuries, and became a center of monastic learning and culture. Monks and scholars were drawn to it in droves, and they were sent out in great numbers as well, to Britain and the Continent as emissaries for the island's way of thinking and praying.

Like their megalithic ancestors, these monks left traces of their lives behind, and these have become enduring monuments to their spirituality.

1704 Enactment of first anti-Catholic "Penal Laws." Apartheid comes to Ireland.

1778 The Penal Laws are progressively repealed.

1782 The Irish Parliament is granted independence.

1791 Wolfe Tone founds the Society of the United Irishmen.

1796–97 Wolfe Tone launches an invasion from France, fails, is taken captive, and commits suicide.

1798 "The Year of the French." A French invasion force is defeated at Killala Bay. General Humbert surrenders to Cornwallis.

1801 The Irish Parliament is induced to dissolve itself. Ireland becomes part of the United Kingdom.

1803 Twenty-five-year-old Robert Emmet is hanged after his uprising of fewer than 100 men is a tragic failure.

1829 Daniel O'Connell secures passage of the Catholic Emancipation Act. He is later named lord mayor of Dublin.

monk-y BUSINESS

The Iliad and *The Odyssey* may have taken place on the turquoise deeps of the Aegean, but it was on the dark waters of the Irish Sea that many classics of Roman and Greek literature survived the sack of Rome and the ensuing Dark Ages. But how did it happen? How did—in the words of bestselling author and historian Thomas Cahill—the Irish save civilization?

The year is 464 A.D. The mighty Roman Empire is on its knees. The Eternal City is under eternal siege, and its great libraries and universities are about to be looted and burned. The world order is quite literally falling apart. Meanwhile, the far-flung backwater of Ireland is undergoing a spiritual revolution. The pagan Gaels are being converted to Christianity by an escaped Roman slave from Wales with a good line in stubbornness. They call him Patricio—known today as St. Patrick.

The Irish wholeheartedly embrace monastic life. Centers of Christian learning pop up across the island, including the remote **Skellig Islands** (see p. 289), where monks copy the Bible and other works. Masters of calligraphic arts, they produce beautiful illuminated texts such as the **Book of Kells** (see p. 96) and *the Book of Durrow.* Gaeilge becomes the first vernacular language (slang, effectively) in Europe to have been written down. Some of Europe's finest minds flee the continental anarchy for Ireland, bringing books and learning with them. Knowledge-hungry monks duplicate great Latin and Greek works of literature. After St. Patrick, missionaries such as Columcille and Columbanus began to look abroad. With the end the Roman Empire in the West, Europe had become a fragmented patchwork of fiefdoms. The hardy Celtic monks set up new monasteries in France, Germany, Switzerland, and Italy—and they took their skills with them. Beautifully decorated Irish manuscripts from this period have been found as far away as Russia, where the monks continued to advance the art of bookmaking.

1845–ca.52 The Great Famine. An estimated two million Irish either die or emigrate, mostly to the U.S.

1858 The Irish Republican Brotherhood, a secret society known as the Fenians, is founded in New York.

1866 In an imaginative publicity stunt, a minuscule army of Fenians attempts to invade Canada.

1879 Michael Davitt founds the National Land League to support the claims of tenant farmers.

1879–82 The "land war" forces the enactment of reform. The tenant system unravels; land returns to those who work it.

1886 & 1894 Bills for Home Rule are defeated in Parliament.

1893 The Gaelic League is founded to revive the Irish language.

1905–08 Founding of *Sinn Féin* ("We Ourselves") with close links to the Irish Republican Brotherhood.

continues

Early monastic sites such as gorgeous **Glendalough** in County Wicklow (see p. 168), wind-swept **Clonmacnoise** in County Offaly (see p. 373), and isolated **Skellig Michael** off the Kerry coast (see p. 289) give you an idea of how they lived, while striking examples of their work can be seen at Trinity College (which houses the Book of Kells) and at the Chester Beatty museum at Dublin Castle.

THE VIKING INVASIONS The monastic city-states of early medieval Ireland might have continued to lead the world's intellectual development, but the Vikings came along and ruined everything. After centuries of relative peace, the first wave of Viking invaders arrived in A.D. 795. The wealthy nonviolent Irish monasteries were among their first targets. Unprepared and unprotected, the monasteries, which had amassed collections of gold, jewels, and art from followers and thinkers around the world, were decimated. The round towers to which the monks retreated for safety were neither high enough nor strong enough to protect them and their treasures from the onslaught.

Once word spread of the wealth to be had on the small island, the Scandinavian invaders just kept on coming, but much as they were experts in the arts of pillage and plunder, one thing of which they had no knowledge was literature. They didn't know how to read. Therefore, they paid scant attention to the magnificent books they came across, passing them over for more obvious riches. This fortunate quirk of history allowed the monks some means of preserving their dying culture—and their immeasurably valuable work—for the benefit of future generations.

After the Vikings left, Ireland enjoyed something of a renewal in the 11th and 12th centuries. Its towns grew, its regional kings made successive unsuccessful bids to unite the country under a single high kingship, and its church came under increased pressure to conform to the Vatican's rules. All of these factors would play a part in ripening Ireland for the next invasion.

The Vikings may have been gone, but prosperous and factionalized Ireland made attractive prey to other nations, and it was, tragically, an Irish king who opened the door to the next predator. Diarmait Mac Murchada, king of

1912 Third Home Rule bill passes in the House of Commons and is defeated by the House of Lords.

1916 Patrick Pearse and James Connolly lead an armed uprising on Easter Monday to proclaim the Irish Republic. Defeat is followed by the execution of 15 leaders of the revolt.

1919 Sinn Féin, led by Eamon de Valera, constitutes itself as the first Irish Dáil and declares independence.

1919–21 The Irish War of Independence. Michael Collins commands the Irish forces.

1921 Anglo-Irish Treaty. Ireland is partitioned. Twenty-six counties form the Free State; the other six remain a part of the U.K. The Free State adopts its first constitution a year later.

1922–23 The Irish civil war, between the government of the Free State and those who opposed the Anglo-Irish treaty. Michael Collins is assassinated by the IRA, who saw the treaty as a sellout.

Leinster, whose ambition was to be king of all of Ireland, decided he could do it, with a little help. So he called on Henry II, the Norman king of England. Diarmait offered Henry a series of incentives in return for military aid: Not only did he bequeath his eldest daughter to whoever led the army, but he also offered them overlordship of the Kingdom of Leinster. To put it bluntly, he made Henry an offer he couldn't refuse. So it was that an expeditionary force, led by the Earl of Pembroke, Richard de Clare—better known as Strongbow—was sent to Diarmait's aid. After the successful invasion and subsequent battles in which Strongbow emerged victorious, he remained in Ireland as governor, and thus gave the English their first foothold in Ireland. What Diarmait did not realize, of course, was that they would never leave.

THE NORMAN INVASION In successive expeditions from 1167 to 1169, the Normans, who had already conquered England, crossed the Irish Sea with crushing force. During the next century, the Norman-English settled in, consolidating their power in new towns and cities. Indeed, many settlers grew attached to the island, and did their best to integrate with the local culture. Marriages between the native Irish and the invaders became commonplace. Over the next couple of centuries, they became more Irish and less English in their loyalties.

Over the next two centuries, attempts to rid Ireland of its English overlords fell short. Independent Gaelic lords in the North and West continued to maintain their territories. By the close of the 15th century, English control of the island was effectively limited to the Pale, a walled and fortified cordon around what is now greater Dublin. (The phrase "beyond the pale" comes from this—meaning anything that is uncontrollable or unacceptable.)

ENGLISH POWER & THE FLIGHT OF THE EARLS During the reign of the Tudor monarchs in England (1485–1603), the brutal reconquest of Ireland was set in motion. Henry VIII was the first to proclaim himself king of all Ireland—something even his warlike ancestors had stopped short of doing—but it wasn't until later that century that the claim was backed up by force. Elizabeth I, Henry's daughter, declared that all Gaelic lords in Ireland must surrender

1932 Eamon de Valera leads Fianna Fáil to victory and becomes head of government.

1937 The Free State adopts a new constitution, abandoning membership of the British Commonwealth and changing the country's official name to Eire.

1939 Dublin is bombed by Germany at start of World War II, but Ireland remains neutral.

1948 The Republic of Ireland Act. Ireland severs its last constitutional links with Britain.

1955 Ireland is admitted into the United Nations.

1963 U.S. President John F. Kennedy visits Ireland.

1969 Violence breaks out in Northern Ireland. British troops are called in.

1972 In Derry a peaceful rally turns into "Bloody Sunday." The Northern Irish Parliament is dissolved, and direct rule is imposed from Britain.

1973 Ireland joins the European Community.

continues

their lands to her, with the dubious promise that she would immediately grant them all back again—unsurprisingly, the proposition was hardly welcomed in Ireland, and a rebel army was raised by Hugh O'Neill and "Red" Hugh O'Donnell, two Irish chieftains. Despite significant victories early on in their decade-long campaign, most notably over a force led by the Earl of Essex, whom Elizabeth had personally sent to subdue them, by 1603 O'Neill was left with few allies and no option but to surrender, which he did on March 23rd, the day before Elizabeth died.

THE COMING OF CROMWELL By the 1640s, Ireland was effectively an English plantation. Family estates had been seized and foreign (Scottish) labor brought in to work them. A systematic persecution of Catholics, which began with Henry VIII's split from Rome but did not die with him, barred Catholics from practicing their faith. Resentment against the English and their punitive laws led to fierce uprisings in Ulster and Leinster in 1641, and by early 1642 most of Ireland was again under Irish control. Unfortunately for the rebels, any hope of extending the victories was destroyed by internal disunion and by the eventual decision to support the Royalist side in the English civil war. In 1648 King Charles I of England was beheaded, and the victorious commander of the parliamentary forces, Oliver Cromwell, was installed as ruler. Soon his supporters were taking on his enemies in Ireland. A year later, the Royalists' stand collapsed in defeat at Rathmines, just south of Dublin.

Defeat for the Royalist cause did not, however, mean the end of the war. Cromwell became paranoid that Ireland would be used to launch a French-backed insurgency if it was not brought to heel, and he detested the country's Catholic beliefs. So it was that as the hot, sticky summer of 1649 drew to a close, Cromwell set sail for Dublin, bringing with him an army of 12,000 men, and a battle plan so ruthless that it remains notorious to this day.

In the town of Drogheda, more than 3,552 Irish soldiers were slaughtered in a single night. When a group of men sought sanctuary in the local church, Cromwell ordered the church burned down with them locked inside—an act of such monstrosity that some of his own men risked a charge of mutiny and

1986 The Anglo-Irish Agreement gives the Republic a say in the government of Northern Ireland.

1990 Mary Robinson is elected Ireland's first female president.

1994 The IRA announces a cease-fire, and the Protestant paramilitaries follow suit. Commencement of peace talks.

1995 Unprecedented economic growth in Ireland hails the start of the so-called "Celtic Tiger". The boom years would last for over a decade.

1995 U.S. President Bill Clinton makes an historic visit to Ireland, speaking to large crowds in Belfast and Derry, and becoming directly involved with the peace process. He is received with enthusiasm in the Republic.

1996 The IRA breaks its cease-fire. The North sees the worst rioting in 15 years.

1997 The IRA declares a new cease-fire. Sinn Féin enters inclusive all-party peace talks designed to bring about a comprehensive settlement.

The Oliver Cromwell mural on a gable in Belfast.

refused the order. On another day, in Wexford, more than 2,000 were murdered, many of them civilians. The trail of destruction rolled on, devastating counties Galway and Waterford. When asked where the Irish citizens could go to be safe from him, Cromwell famously suggested they could go "to hell or Connaught"—the latter being the most far-flung, rocky, and unfarmable part of Ireland.

After a rampage that lasted 7 months, killing thousands and leaving churches, monasteries, and castles in ruins, Cromwell finally left Ireland in the

---

1998 Peace talks conclude in April with the so-called Good Friday Agreement, later strongly supported in referendums held on the same day in the Republic and the North. The agreement establishes self-government in Northern Ireland. In August, an IRA bomb in Omagh kills 29, the bloodiest incident of the entire conflict.

2001 After 3 further years of political wrangling over the terms of power sharing, the IRA finally begins to decommission its weapons. It officially ceases to exist as a paramilitary organization 4 years later—though splinter groups persist to this day.

2004 The Irish government bans smoking in public places.

2007 A new power-sharing executive is put into place in Northern Ireland, bringing together lifelong enemies DUP leader Ian Paisley and Sinn Féin leader Gerry Adams.

2008 Ireland's economy begins to crash as the country becomes the first in the European Union to officially enter recession.

continues

care of his lieutenants and returned to England. Hundreds of years later, the memory and lore of his extraordinary violence lingers painfully in Ireland. In certain parts of the country, people still spit at the mention of his name.

THE ANTI-CATHOLIC LAWS Cromwell died in 1658, and 2 years later the English monarchy was restored, but the anti-Catholic oppression continued. In 1685, though, something quite remarkable happened. Contrary to the efforts of the English establishment, the new king, James II, refused to relinquish his Catholic faith after ascending to the throne. It looked for a while as if things could change in Ireland, and that the Catholics might have found a new ally in the unlikeliest of quarters. However, such hopes were dashed 3 years later, when James was ousted from power, and the Protestant William of Orange installed in his place.

James fled to France to raise support for a rebellion, and then sailed to Ireland to launch his attack. He struck first at Derry, to which he laid siege for 15 weeks before finally being defeated by William's forces at the Battle of the Boyne. The battle effectively ended James's cause, and with it, the hopes of Catholic Ireland for the best part of a century.

After James's defeat, English power was once more consolidated across Ireland. Protestant landowners were granted full political power, while laws were enacted to effectively immobilize the Catholic population. Being a Catholic in late-17th-century Ireland was not exactly illegal per se, but in practice life was all but impossible for those who refused to convert to Protestantism. Catholics could not purchase land, and existing landholdings were split up unless the families who owned them became Protestants; Catholic schools were banned, as were priests and all forms of public worship. Catholics were barred from holding any office of state, practicing law, or joining the army. Those who still refused to relinquish their faith were forced to pay a tax to the Anglican Church. And by virtue of not being able to own land, the few who previously had been allowed to vote were not allowed to anymore.

The new British landlords settled in, planted crops, made laws, and sowed their own seeds. Inevitably, over time, the "Anglos" became the Anglo-Irish.

2009 The Irish government issues a damning report into child sex abuse in the Catholic church—part of the wide-ranging scandal that eventually leads to the resignation of Pope Benedict XVI in 2012.

2010 British Prime Minister David Cameron apologizes for "Bloody Sunday," when British soldiers killed 14 Irish protesters in Bogside, a Catholic neighborhood in Derry, Northern Ireland in 1972.

2011 Longtime ruling party Fianna Fáil is swept out of office on a wave of voter anger, replaced by Fine Gael. New *Taoiseach* (Prime Minister), Enda Kenny, vows to restore Irish economic stability.

2011 Queen Elizabeth II becomes the first British monarch to visit the Republic of Ireland. The following year, in Belfast, she shakes hands with Sinn Féin's Martin McGuinness—a former IRA

Hyphenated or not, they were Irish, and their loyalties were increasingly unpredictable. After all, an immigrant is only an immigrant for a generation; whatever the birthright of the colonists, their children would be Irish-born and bred. And so it was that an uncomfortable sort of stability set in for a generation or three, albeit of a kind that was very much separate and unequal. There were the haves, the wealthy Protestants, and the have-nots, the deprived and disenfranchised Catholics.

A kind of unhappy peace held for some time. But by the end of the 18th century, the appetite for rebellion was whetted again. To understand why, one need look no further than the intellectual hotbed that flourished among the coffee shops and lecture halls of Europe's newest boomtown: Dublin.

THE UNITED IRISHMEN & THE 1798 REBELLION By the 1770s, Dublin was thriving as never before. As a center for culture and learning, it was rivaled only by Paris and London; thanks to the work of such architects as Henry Gratton (who designed Custom House, the Kings Inns, and the Four Courts), its very streets were being remodeled in a grand, neoclassical style that was more akin to the great cities of southern Italy than of southern Ireland.

However, while the urban classes reveled in their newfound wealth, the stringent Penal Laws that had effectively cut off the Catholic workers from their own countryside forced many of them to turn to the city for work. In Dublin's buzzing intellectual scene political dissent soon brewed, and even after a campaign by Irish politicians led to many of the Penal Laws being repealed in 1783, Dublin was a breeding ground for radicals and political activists. The results were explosive.

When war broke out between Britain and France in the 1790s, the United Irishmen—a nonviolent society formed to lobby for admission of Catholic Irishmen to the Irish Parliament—sent a secret delegation to persuade the French to intervene on Ireland's behalf against the British. Their emissary in this venture was a Dublin lawyer named Wolfe Tone. In 1796 Tone sailed with a French force bound for Ireland and determined to defeat forces loyal to the English crown, but they were turned back by storms.

commander, now deputy First Minister of Northern Ireland.

2011 Michael Higgins, who was once a professor at the University of Southern Illinois, is elected the 9th president of the Republic of Ireland.

2012 The death of Savita Halappanavar, an Indian national who was working as a dentist in Galway, sparks renewed debate about the country's abortion laws. Halappanavar died after being admitted to hospital while suffering a miscarriage, only to have doctors refuse her a life-saving abortion.

2013 Enda Kenny issues an emotional public apology for the so-called "Magdalene Laundries"—government-backed religious workhouses that effectively kept women in slave labor, until as recently as the 1990s.

2013 Seamus Heaney, widely acclaimed as one of the greatest poets of the modern age, dies in Dublin at the age of 74.

In 1798, though, full-scale insurrection led by the United Irishmen did spread across much of Ireland, particularly the southwestern counties of Kilkenny and Wexford, where a tiny republic was briefly declared in June. But it was crushed by Loyalist forces, which then went on a murderous spree, killing tens of thousands of men, women, and children, and burning towns to the ground. The nadir of the rebellion came when Wolfe Tone, having raised another French invasion force, sailed into Lough Swilley in Donegal, but was promptly captured by the British. At his trial, wearing a French uniform, Tone requested that he be shot, in accordance with the rights of a foreign soldier, but when the request was refused, he suffered a more gruesome end. While waiting for the gallows, he slit his own throat in jail; however, he missed the jugular vein, instead severing his windpipe, leading to a slow and painful death 8 days later. His last words were reputed to have been: "It appears, sir, that I am but a bad anatomist."

The rebellion was over. In the space of three weeks, more than 30,000 Irish had been killed. As a final indignity in what became known as "The Year of the French," the British tricked the Irish Parliament into dissolving itself, and Ireland reverted to strict British rule.

A CONFLICT OF CONFLICTS In 1828 a Catholic lawyer named Daniel O'Connell, who had earlier formed the Catholic Association to represent the interests of tenant farmers, was elected to the British Parliament as Member of Parliament for Dublin. Public opinion was so solidly behind him that he was able to persuade the British prime minister that the only way to avoid a civil war in Ireland was to force the Catholic Emancipation Act through Parliament. He remained an MP until 1841, when he was elected Lord Mayor of Dublin, a platform he used to push for repeal of the direct rule imposed from London after the 1798 rebellion.

O'Connell organized enormous rallies (nicknamed "monster meetings") attended by hundreds of thousands, and provoked an unresponsive conservative government to such an extent that it eventually arrested him on charges of seditious conspiracy. The charges were dropped, but the incident—coupled with growing impatience toward his nonviolent approach of protest and reform—led to the breakdown of his power base. "The Liberator," as he had been known, faded, his health failed, and he died on a trip to Rome.

THE GREAT FAMINE Even after the anti-Catholic legislation began to recede, the vast majority of farmland available to the poor, mostly Catholic population of the countryside was harsh, and difficult to cultivate. One of the few crops that could be grown reliably was the potato, which effectively became the staple diet of the rural poor. So when, in 1845, a fungus destroyed much of the potato crop of Ireland, it is not difficult to understand the scale of the devastation this caused. However, to label the Great Irish Famine of the 1840s and 50s as merely a "tragedy" would be an incomplete description. It was, of course, tragic—but at the same time, the word implies a randomness to the whole sorry, sickening affair that fails to capture its true awfulness. The fact is that what started out as a disaster was turned into a devastating crisis by the callous response of an uninterested British establishment.

As the potato blight worsened, it became apparent to many landlords that their farm tenants would be unable to pay rent. In order to offset their financial losses, they continued to ship grain overseas, in lieu of rent from their now-starving tenants. The British Parliament, meanwhile, was reluctant to send aid, putting the reports of a crisis down to, in the words of Prime Minister Robert Peel, "the Irish tendency to exaggerate."

Of course, as people started to die by the thousands, it became clear to the government that something had to be done, and emergency relief was sent to Ireland in the form of cheap, imported Indian cornmeal. However, this contained virtually no nutrients, and ultimately contributed to the spread of such diseases as typhus and cholera, which were to claim more victims than starvation itself.

To make matters worse, the cornmeal was not simply given to those in need of it. Fearful that handouts would encourage laziness among a population they viewed as prone to that malaise, the British government forced people to work for their food. Entirely pointless make-work projects were initiated, just to give the starving men something to do for their cornmeal; roads were built that led nowhere, for instance, and elaborate follies constructed that served no discernible purpose, some of which still litter the countryside today, memorials to cruelty and ignorance.

One of the most difficult things to comprehend, more than a century and a half later, is the sheer futility of it all. For behind the statistics, the memorials, and the endless personal anguish, lies perhaps the most painful truth of all: that the famine was easily preventable. Enormous cargoes of imported corn sat in Irish ports for months, until the British government felt that releasing them to the people would not adversely affect market rates. Meanwhile, huge quantities of meat and grain were exported from Ireland. (Indeed, in 1847, cattle exports went up 33 percent from the previous year.)

Given the circumstances, it is easy to understand why so many chose to leave Ireland. More than a million emigrated over the next decade, about three-quarters of them to America, the rest to Britain or Europe. They drained the country. In 1841, Ireland's population was 8 million; by 1851 it was 6.5 million.

THE STRUGGLE FOR HOME RULE As the famine waned and life returned to something like normality, the Irish independence movement gained new momentum. New fronts opened up in the struggle for Home Rule, both violent and nonviolent, and, significantly, the Republicans now drew considerable support from overseas—particularly from America. There, groups such as the Fenians fundraised and published newspapers in support of the Irish cause, while more audacious schemes, such as an 1866 "invasion" of Canada with fewer than 100 men, amounted to little more than publicity stunts, designed to raise awareness for the cause.

Back home in Ireland, partial concessions were won in Parliament, and by the 1880s, nationalists such as the MP for Meath, Charles Stewart Parnell, were able to unite various factions of Irish nationalists (including the Fenian Brotherhood in America) to fight for Home Rule. In a tumultuous decade of legislation, he came close, but revelations about his long affair with Kitty O'Shea, the wife of a supporter, brought about his downfall as a politician.

By 1912, a bill to give Ireland Home Rule was passed through the British House of Commons, but was defeated in the House of Lords. Many felt that the political process was still all but unstoppable, and that it was only a matter of time before the bill passed fully into law and effective political independence for Ireland would be secured. However, when the onset of World War I in 1914 forced the issue onto the back burner once again, many in the Home Rule movement grew tired of the political process.

THE EASTER REBELLION On Easter Monday 1916, a group of nationalists occupied the **General Post Office** (see p. 111) in the heart of Dublin, from which they proclaimed the foundation of an Irish Republic. Inside were 1,500

The general post office in Dublin.

fighters, led by schoolteacher and Gaelic League member Patrick Pearse and Socialist leader James Connolly.

The British, nervous at an armed uprising on its doorstep while it fought a massive war in Europe, responded with overwhelming force. Soldiers were sent in, and a battle raged in the streets of Dublin for 6 days before the leaders of the rebellion were captured and imprisoned. The walls of the post office and other buildings, and statues up and down O'Connell Street still have bullet holes in them. Pearse, Connolly, and 12 other leaders were imprisoned, secretly tried, and speedily executed.

Ultimately, though, the British reaction was as counterproductive as it was harsh. The totality with which those involved in organizing the rebellion were pursued and dispatched acted as a lightning rod for many of those who had been undecided about the effectiveness of a purely political struggle. Indeed, a fact that has become somewhat lost in the ensuing hundred or so years since Patrick Pearse stood on the steps of the post office early on that cold Monday morning, reading a treatise on Irish independence, is that a great many Irish didn't support the rebellion at the time. Many either believed that the best course of action was to lay low until the war had ended, when concessions would be won as a result, or that it was simply the wrong thing to do, as long as sons of Ireland were sacrificing their lives in the trenches of Europe.

The aftermath of 1916 all but guaranteed, for better or for worse, that Ireland's future would be decided by the gun.

REBELLION A power vacuum was left at the heart of the nationalist movement after the Easter Rising, and it was filled by two men: Michael Collins and Eamon de Valera. On the surface, both men had much in common; Collins was a Cork man who had returned from Britain in order to join the Irish Volunteers (later to become the Irish Republican Army, or IRA), while de Valera was an

Irish-American math teacher who came back to Ireland to set up a new political party, *Sinn Féin*.

When de Valera's party won a landslide victory in the general election of 1918, its MPs refused to sit in London, instead proclaiming the first Dáil, or independent parliament, in Dublin. De Valera went to rally support for the cause in America, while Collins stayed to concentrate on his work as head of the Irish Volunteers. Tensions escalated into violence, and for the next 2 years, Irish nationalists fought a tit-for-tat military campaign against the British in Ireland.

The low point of the struggle came in 1920, when Collins ordered 14 British operatives to be murdered in their beds, in response to which British troops opened fire on the audience at a football game at Croke Park in Dublin, randomly killing 12 innocent people. A truce was eventually declared on July 9, 1921, and 6 months later, the Anglo-Irish treaty was signed in London, granting legislative independence to 26 Irish counties (known together as the Irish Free State). The compromise through which that freedom was won, though, was that six counties in the north would remain part of the United Kingdom. Collins knew that compromise would not be accepted by the more strident members of his rebel group. He also knew they would blame him for agreeing to it in the first place. When he signed the treaty he told the people present, "I am signing my own death warrant."

As he feared, nationalists were split between those who accepted the treaty as a platform on which to build, and those, led by the nationalist de Valera, who saw it as a betrayal, and would accept nothing less than immediate and full independence at any cost. Even the withdrawal of British troops from Dublin for the first time in nearly 800 years did not quell their anger. The result was an inexorable slide into civil war. The flashpoint came in April 1922, when violence erupted around the streets of the capital, and rolled on for 8 days until de Valera's supporters were forced to surrender.

The government of the fledgling free state ordered that Republicans be shot on sight, leading to the deaths of 77 people. And Collins had been right about his own fate: Four months later he was assassinated while on a visit to his childhood home.

The fallout from the civil war dominated Irish politics for the next decade. De Valera split from the Republicans to form another party, Fianna Fáil ("the Warriors of Ireland"), which won the election of 1932 and governed for 17 years. Despite his continuing dedication to the Republican ideal, however, de Valera was not to be the one who finally declared Ireland a republic, in 1948; ironically, that distinction went to a coalition led by de Valera's opponent, Douglas Hyde, whose victory in the election of 1947 was attributed to the fact that de Valera had become too obsessed with abstract Republican ideals to govern effectively.

STUCK IN NEUTRAL One of the more controversial, not to say morally ambiguous, decisions that Eamon de Valera made while in office was to stay neutral during World War II, despite the best efforts of Winston Churchill and Franklin Roosevelt to persuade him otherwise. The basis for his decision—a combination of Ireland's size and economic weakness, and the British presence in Northern Ireland—may have made sense to some extent, but it left Ireland in the peculiar position of tacitly favoring one side in the war, but refusing to help it. After the death of Adolf Hitler in April 1945, de Valera alienated the Allies further by sending his personal sympathies to the German ambassador.

His reticence didn't find much favor among the Irish population either. During the war, as many as 300,000 Irish men found ways to enlist in the British or

U.S. armies. In the end, more than 50,000 Irish soldiers perished in a war their country had refused to join.

TROUBLE ON THE WAY After the war, 2 decades passed without violence in Ireland, until the late 1960s, when the outbreak of sectarian conflict in the North erupted. What started out as a civil rights movement to demand greater equality for Catholics within Northern Ireland, soon escalated into a cycle of violence that lasted for 30 years.

It would be a terrible oversimplification to say that the Troubles were merely a clear-cut struggle between those who wanted to complete the process of Irish unification and those who wanted to remain part of the United Kingdom—although that was, of course, the crux of the conflict. Factors such as organized crime and terrorism, together with centuries-old conflicts over religious, land, and social issues, make the conflict even harder for outsiders to understand.

The worst of the Troubles came in the 1970s. In 1972, British troops inexplicably opened fire on a peaceful demonstration in Derry, killing 12 people—many of whom were shot while they tended to the wounds of the first people injured. The IRA took advantage of the mood of public outrage to begin a civilian bombing campaign on the British mainland. The cycle of violence continued for 20 years, inexorably and depressingly, all the while none of the myriad sides in the conflict would talk to each other. Finally, in the early 1990s, secret talks were opened between the British and the IRA, leading to an IRA cease-fire in 1994 (although the cease-fire held only shakily—an IRA bomb in Omagh 4 years later killed 29, the most to die in any single incident of the Troubles).

The peace process continued throughout the 1990s, helped significantly by the mediation efforts of U.S. President Bill Clinton, who arguably became more involved in Irish affairs than any president before him until, eventually, on Good Friday 1998, a peace accord was finally signed in Belfast. The agreement committed all sides to a peaceful resolution of the conflict in Northern Ireland, and included the reinstatement of full self-government for the region in a power-sharing administration. It stopped short of resolving the territorial issue once and for all—in other words, Northern Ireland is still part of the U.K., and will be for the foreseeable future. On the contrary, to some extent the conflicts rage more bitterly and more divisively than ever before, the difference being that, with notable exceptions, they are fought through the ballot box, rather than the barrel of a gun. In 2005 the IRA fully decommissioned its weapons, and officially dissolved itself as a paramilitary unit.

REBIRTH While Northern Ireland still struggled to find peace, the Republic of Ireland flourished. The 1990s brought unprecedented wealth and prosperity to the country, thanks in part to European Union subsidies, and partly to a thriving economy, which acquired the nickname "the Celtic Tiger" for its new global strength. Ireland became a rich country, widely seen as one of the best places in the world to live and work.

However, that boom came crashing down after the banking crisis of 2008. The Irish government was forced to seek financial aid from the European Union, worth more than 50 percent of the whole economy, to save the country from bankruptcy. The op-ed pages of any Irish newspaper were filled with real feelings of betrayal and a deep sense of opportunity lost.

Since then, things have once more begun to look up for the Irish economy—although the recovery will be a slow one. And there is something to be said for the Irish spirit. For the ability to find humor in the darkest of places. Every new crisis brings fresh jokes alongside the rage. Every new leader is a target for

A harbinger of Northern Ireland's progress, the renovation of the Merchant Hotel transformed a bank building in downtown Belfast.

general hilarity. And while nobody in the country would tell you there is not work to be done, you get the distinct impression that the people—if not the politicians and the bankers who got them into this mess—are ready to do that work.

IRELAND IN CULTURE

LITERATURE For more than 100 years, Ireland has had a place in literature disproportionate to its small size and modest population. Four writers from this tiny country have won the Nobel Prize for literature. Inspired by the country's unique beauty, the unfairness they perceived in its political system, and its cruel legacy of poverty and struggle, the country's authors, poets, and playwrights wrote about the Irish for the Irish, and to raise awareness in the rest of the world. No matter where you live, you've probably been reading about Ireland all your life.

One of the country's best-known early writers was satirist **Jonathan Swift,** who was born in Dublin in 1667. Educated at Trinity College, he left Ireland for England in 1688 to avoid the Glorious Revolution. He spent much of his adult life in London, returning to Ireland when he was over 50 years old, at which point he began to write his most famous works. The suffering of the poor in Ireland greatly affected him, but he translated his anger into dark, vicious humor. His tract *A Modest Proposal* is widely credited with inventing satire as we now know it. His best-known works have political undertones—even *Gulliver's Travels* is a political allegory.

Best known for his novel *Dracula*, the novelist and theater promoter **Bram Stoker** was born in Clontarf, a coastal suburb of Dublin, in 1847. As a young man fresh out of Trinity College, he began reviewing theater productions for local newspapers, which is how he met the actor Henry Irving. He spent much of his time promoting and working for Irving and wrote novels on the side for extra money. He spent most of his life in England, which largely inspired his work, although it is said that **St. Michan's Church** in Dublin (see p. 120), with its ghostly crypt, and St. Mary's in Killarney (see p. 278) helped to contribute to *Dracula*'s creepy feel.

Born in Dublin in 1854, **Oscar Wilde** was a popular and successful student at Trinity College, winning a scholarship to continue his studies in England at Oxford. After a flamboyant time there, he graduated with top honors and returned to Ireland, only to lose his girlfriend to Bram Stoker in 1878, after which he left Ireland forever. His writing—including the novel *The Picture of Dorian Gray,* plays including *The Importance of Being Earnest,* and books of poetry—were forever overshadowed by his personal life. While a statue of him stands in Dublin, his works were largely inspired by British and French writers, and he spent the majority of his life abroad.

George Bernard Shaw was born in Dublin in 1856 and attended school in the city, but never went to college, as he came to loathe the organized education system. His literary style was, therefore, self-taught, and he spent his life studying and writing. He moved to England as a young man and lived much of his life in a village in Hertfordshire in England. As a result, many of his works have a distinctly English feel. His plays are known both for their sharp wit and for their sense of outrage over unfairness in society and the absurdity of the British class system. He is the only person ever to have won both the Nobel Prize and an Oscar (for *Pygmalion*).

William Butler Yeats was born in Sandy Mount outside Dublin in 1865, and attended the Metropolitan School of Art in Dublin, but his poetry and prose were heavily inspired by County Sligo, where he spent much of his time, and where he is buried. One of the leading figures of the Irish literary revival in the early 20th century, he won the Nobel Prize in 1923.

James Joyce was born in the Dublin suburb of Rathgar in 1882 and educated at Jesuit boarding schools, and later at Trinity College. He wrote vividly—and sometimes impenetrably—about Dublin, despite spending much of his life as an expat living nomadically in Europe. His controversial and hugely complex novels *Ulysses* and *Finnegan's Wake* are his most celebrated (and least understood) works. They and his collection of short stories, *Dubliners*, are seen as touching deeply on the character of the people of Dublin.

The poet and playwright **Samuel Beckett** was born in 1906 in the Dublin suburb of Foxrock and educated at Trinity College. His work, however, was heavily influenced by German and French postmodernists, and he spent much of his life abroad, even serving with the Resistance in France during World War II. Best known for his complex absurdist play *Waiting for Godot,* he won the Nobel Prize in 1969.

The controversial writer, erstwhile terrorist, and all-round bon vivant **Brendan Behan** was born in Dublin in 1923. His father fought in the Easter Rising and read revolutionary literature to his children as bedtime stories. His mother was a close friend of Michael Collins. When he was 14, Behan joined Fianna Éireann, the youth organization of the IRA. A terrible terrorist, he was arrested on his first solo mission to blow up England's Liverpool Docks when he was 16 years old. His autobiographical book, *Borstal Boy,* describes this period in his life in exquisite detail. His play *The Quare Fellow* made him an international literary star, and he would spend the rest of his life as a jolly, hopeless alcoholic, drinking his way through London, Dublin, and New York, better known for his quick wit and bons mots than for his plays.

Among modern Irish writers, the best known is arguably the poet **Seamus Heaney.** He was born in 1939 near a small town called Castledawson in Northern Ireland, where as a child he won scholarships to boarding school in Derry and later to Queen's University in Belfast. His years studying classic ancient Greek and Latin literature and Anglo-Saxon writing heavily influenced his poetry, but all of his writing is marked by his life in the troubled region where he grew up. His works, including *The Cure at Troy* (based on the works of Sophocles), *The Haw Lantern,* and *The Government of the Tongue,* ultimately earned him the Nobel Prize in 1995. Heaney's death in the summer of 2013 brought an outpouring of affection from fans across the world.

Other Irish writers who have been burning up the book charts in recent years include **Marian Keyes** (whose hugely popular novels include *Lucy Sullivan is Getting Married* and *This Charming Man*); **Roddy Doyle** (*The Commitments, Paddy Clarke Ha Ha Ha*), and the late **Maeve Binchy** (*A Week in Winter, Circle of Friends*).

NONFICTION Nonfiction works about Ireland are less well-known than the country's fiction, but if you want to know about Ireland and the Irish, plenty of talented writers in and out of the country are willing to tell you.

Jonathan Bardon's *A History of Ireland in 250 Episodes* is a good general introduction to Irish history. The book is broken up into 250 short chapters—learned without being too dense, and a very useful primer.

To understand more about the famine, try the British author **Cecil Woodham-Smith's** *The Great Hunger.* Written in 1962, it's still viewed as the definitive, dispassionate examination of this dark period in Irish history.

The author **Tim Pat Coogan** is the son of an IRA volunteer, and he has written two excellent books, *The Irish Civil War* (2001) and *The Troubles: Ireland's Ordeal 1966–1996* (1997), both of which are essential reading for anyone wanting to understand the complexities of 21st-century Ireland. He also wrote a controversial biography, *Eamon de Valera,* criticizing the former Irish president's actions and legacy.

For a look at Ireland in recent history, try **John Ardagh's** *Ireland and the Irish* (1995) or **F. S. Lyons's** *Ireland Since the Famine* (1973).

The late Dublin-born journalist **Nuala O'Faolain** wrote two top-selling memoirs, *Are You Somebody?* (1996) and *Almost There* (2003), which give the reader an insider's view of living and growing up in modern Ireland.

The late Irish-born American writer **Frank McCourt** earned acclaim and won the Pulitzer Prize for *Angela's Ashes* (1996), his grim memoir of a childhood spent partly in Limerick and partly in Brooklyn. But it has been bitterly disputed by many in Limerick who claim it is not an accurate representation of the city during that time, and the book is very controversial in Ireland.

FILM Many controversial, complex, and difficult Irish subjects have been tackled by an international array of directors and actors. Here are a few of the better known ones—and a few obscure gems worth seeking out. ***Man of Aran*** (directed by Robert Flaherty, 1934) is a "docufiction" about life on the Aran Islands. Long respected as a documentary, it's now known that much of it was staged by its American director. Still, it's an interesting look at what the islands looked like in the early-20th century.

Virtually unknown today, ***Maeve*** (directed by John Davis/Pat Murphy, 1982) is a fascinating piece of Irish independent film from the early 1980s. Starring the American actress Mary Jackson, it follows an Irish expat in England who decides to return to strife-torn Northern Ireland.

The Commitments (directed by Alan Parker, 1991) may be the most famous Irish musical ever made. With its cast of young, largely inexperienced Irish actors playing musicians dedicated to American soul music, it's a delightful piece of filmmaking.

Michael Collins (directed by Neil Jordan, 1996) is a fine biopic about the Irish rebel, filmed largely on location and starring the Irish actor Liam Neeson.

Veronica Guerin (directed by Joel Schumacher, 2003) is a dark, fact-based film (with the Australian actress Cate Blanchett doing an excellent Irish accent) about a troubled Irish investigative reporter on the trail of a drug boss.

Intermission (directed by Jim Crowley, 2003) is a lively urban romance filmed on location in Dublin, featuring the Irish actor Colin Farrell (talking in his real accent for a change). A great look at Dublin right in the middle of its economic boom.

The Wind That Shakes the Barley (directed by Ken Loach, 2006), with a mostly Irish cast and English director, won the Palme d'Or at Cannes for its depiction of Ireland's early 20th-century fight for independence.

Once (directed by John Carney, 2007) is a touching, Oscar-nominated portrait of two struggling young musicians—an Irish singer (played by the Irish actor Glen Hansard) and a Czech piano player trying to make it big in Dublin. The film was subsequently turned into a hit stage musical.

In Bruges (directed by Martin McDonagh, 2008), is an inventive, jet-black comedy-drama about two Irish hitmen sent to carry out a job in the Belgian city of Bruges. Only the intended target is a big surprise to both of them. A U.K.-U.S. co-production, with an Irish writer-director and stars, the film won many awards and has become a cult favorite.

The little-seen, low budget ***Wake Wood*** (directed by David Keating, 2011) is a slice of pure Gothic horror fun. A young Irish couple move to a new village when their daughter is tragically killed. Turns out the villagers can bring the girl back from the dead—but only for 3 days. When time's up, they refuse to let her go. What could possibly go wrong?

On the other end of the genre scale, ***Silence*** (directed by Pat Collins, 2012) is a meditative, dreamlike art film about a sound recordist who travels deep into the Irish countryside in search of places completely free of manmade sound. (Spoiler alert: he has a hard time finding any.)

Shadow Dancer (directed by James Marsh, 2012) is an exciting spy thriller set in early 1990s Belfast. The film, which was a hit at the Sundance Film Festival, pulls off the rare trick of being about the Troubles without getting bogged down in politics.

MUSIC Music is inescapable in Ireland, and if you hear a band play in a bar and you like them, we strongly advise you to buy a CD from them. In the days of Internet radio, the best way to discover new sounds is to tune in to Irish radio stations online. An excellent list of stations that stream live (including links) can be found at www.radiofeeds.co.uk/irish.asp. Good places to start are the stations run by **RTÉ,** the national broadcaster, particularly the music and entertainment-oriented **2FM,** (www.rte.ie/2fm); **Today FM** (www.todayfm.com), a national station that's extremely popular with a young demographic; and **TXFM** (www.txfm.ie), a Dublin-based station that specializes in the latest indie and alternative sounds.

Some cool, quintessentially Irish names to check out, both in and out of the mainstream: **Villagers,** a young indie-folk duo who were nominated for the prestigious Mercury Prize in 2013; **Lisa Hannigan,** a singer-songwriter with a line in infectiously romantic indie-pop; **Damien Rice,** another soloist who has risen to huge chart success over the past decade; Cork-based electro-pop duo **Young**

Wonder, who mix brash big beats with beautiful vocals; **Rejjie Snow,** an Irish hip-hop artist who has been compared to Kanye West; and **Soak,** an absurdly talented 17-year-old Derry native who has been wowing the music world with her simple but enchantingly beautiful ballads.

Obviously, traditional music is still alive and well in Ireland, particularly in close association with Irish step dancing. The folk culture is primarily found outside of Dublin, although some pubs in the city do still showcase traditional music. There's also Cultúrlann na hÉireann, which offers much in the way of traditional Irish performances. In County Kerry, Siamsa Ti offers a mixture of Irish music, dance, and mime. For a less formal atmosphere, check out local pubs in small towns, which almost always can be counted on to host Irish music and sometimes dancing, too.

SOCIAL MEDIA Users of social media, particularly Twitter, are uniquely placed to absorb a sense of what modern-day Ireland is really like through the eyes of its journalists, thinkers—and just ordinary folk with something to say. Some excellent suggestions for where to start can be found at **www.irishexaminer.com/lifestyle/the-twitter-feeds-you-need-202990.html** and www.dailyedge.ie/funniest-irish-twitter-accounts-1216927-Dec2013.

EATING & DRINKING IN IRELAND

Restaurants

Restaurants in Ireland have become surprisingly expensive in recent years, and even with the economic crash the cost of eating out here is still well above the European average. On the plus side, restaurants are varied and interesting in Ireland—settings range from old-world hotel dining rooms, country mansions,

A session of traditional Irish music in Dublin.

Dining Bargains

Despite the economic bust, restaurant prices are still generally high, largely because of taxes, but partly for reasons of hubris. Nobody is more aware of this than the Irish. Here are some strategies they use (and you can too) to keep meal costs down.

If you want to try a top-rated restaurant but can't afford dinner, have your main meal there in the middle of the day by trying the set-lunch menu. You'll experience the same great cuisine at half the price of a nighttime meal. The latest economic troubles have seen restaurants competing for customers by offering more set-price meals, early-bird specials (sometimes through the whole evening, or every night early in the week), and other discount enticements. Keep an eye out for them.

Alternatively, try an inexpensive lunch in a cafe or a pub. Pub food is usually a lot better than its name suggests; the menu usually includes a mix of sandwiches and traditional Irish food, including stews and meat pies. In recent years, many pubs have converted or expanded into restaurants, serving excellent, unpretentious meals at (somewhat) reasonable prices. Check the menu before you sit down at a table (most places post them by their doors).

Supermarkets and grocery stores in Ireland sell good premade sandwiches (these are much better than similar supermarket sandwiches in the U.S.) for a few euro. These can make a good, cheap lunch or dinner. Coffee shops also sell sandwiches for a few euro, and muffins for even less (for a quick, cheap breakfast).

and castles to sky-lit terraces, shop-front bistros, riverside cottages, thatched-roof pubs, and converted houses. Lately, appreciation has grown for creative cooking here, with an emphasis on locally grown produce and meat.

Before you book a table, here are a few things you should know.

RESERVATIONS Except for self-service eateries, informal cafes, and some popular seafood spots, most restaurants encourage reservations; most expensive restaurants require them. In the most popular eateries, Friday and Saturday nights are often booked up a week or more in advance, so have a few options in mind if you're booking at the last minute and want to try out the hot spots.

Tip: If you stop into or phone a restaurant and find that it is booked from 8 or 8:30pm onward, ask if you can dine early (at 6:30 or 7pm), with a promise to leave by 8pm. It works sometimes.

PRICES Meal prices at restaurants include national sales taxes (universally referred to as "VAT" which stands for Value Added Tax), at the rate of 13.5% in the Republic of Ireland and 20% in Northern Ireland. Many restaurants include the tip as a service charge added automatically to the bill (it's usually listed at the bottom, just before the bill's total). It usually ranges from 10% to 15%. When no service charge is added, tip around 12% or so, depending on the quality of the service. But do check your bill, as some unscrupulous restaurants do not make it clear that you have already tipped, thus encouraging you to accidentally do so twice.

The price categories used in this book are based on the price of a complete dinner (or lunch, if dinner is not served) for one person, including tax and tip, but not wine or alcoholic beverages:

Very Expensive €50 and up

Expensive €305 to €50

Moderate €157 to €304

Inexpensive Under €157

DINING TIPS Don't be surprised if you are not ushered to your table as soon as you arrive at some upscale restaurants. This is not a delaying tactic—many of the better dining rooms carry on the old custom of seating you in a lounge while you sip an aperitif and peruse the menu. Your waiter then comes to discuss the choices and to take your order. You are not called to the table until the first course is about to be served. You are not under an obligation to have a cocktail, of course. It's perfectly fine to order a soft drink or just a glass of water.

Pubs

The pub continues to be a mainstay of Irish social life. Every city, town, and hamlet has a pub. Most people have a "local"—a favorite pub near home—where they go for a drink and some conversation with neighbors, family, and friends. Pubs are not bars—they are more about socializing than drinking, and many people you see in the pub are just having a soft drink (lime cordial and soda water is a particular favorite, or orange juice and lemon soda). So feel free to go to the pub, even if you don't drink alcohol. It's a good way to meet locals.

PUB HOURS Pubs in the Republic set their own hours, although closing times are bound by the type of alcohol license they have. Those with a regular license must shut by 11:30pm, Monday to Thursday and Sunday, and 12:30am on Saturday. Those with late licenses can stay open until 2:30am, Monday to

Two pints of beer served at the Guinness Brewery.

Saturday, and 2am Sunday. In Northern Ireland (which is goverened by different laws), hours are slightly more restrictive, although this is currently the subject of some debate. On Friday and Saturday nights, many pubs stay open until midnight or 1am, and a few even later than that—particularly in large towns and cities. It should also be noted that legal closing times can be hard to police in rural areas.

You'll notice that when the dreaded "closing time" comes, nobody clears out of the pub. That's because the term is a misnomer. The "closing time" is actually the time when the barmen must stop serving alcohol, so expect to hear a shout for "Last orders!" or, occasionally, the marvelous if antiquated "Time, gentlemen, please!" Anyone who wants to order his or her last drink does so at that point. The pubs don't actually shut their doors for another 20 to 30 minutes. When the time comes to really close, the bartenders will shout "Time to leave!" lights will be turned up brightly, and people make their way to the doors.

WHEN TO GO

A visit to Ireland in the summer is very different from a trip in the winter. Apart from climatic considerations are the issues of cost, closures, and crowds. Generally speaking, in summer, airfares, car-rental rates, and hotel prices are highest and crowds at their most intense. But the days are long (6am sunrises and 10pm sunsets), the weather is warm, and every sightseeing attraction and B&B is open. In winter, you can get rock-bottom prices on airfare and hotels. But it will rain and the wind will blow, and many rural sights and a fair proportion of the rural B&Bs and restaurants will be closed.

All things considered, we think the best time to visit is in spring and fall when the weather falls in between seasons, but you get lower-than-high-season prices and the crowds have yet to descend.

Weather

Rain is the one constant in Irish weather, although a bit of sunshine is usually just around the corner. The best of times and the worst of times are often only hours, or even minutes, apart. It can be chilly in Ireland at any time of year, so think *layers* when you pack.

Winters can be brutal, as the wind blows in off the Atlantic with numbing constancy, and strong gales are common. But deep snow is rare and temperatures rarely drop much below freezing. In fact, Ireland is a fairly temperate place: January and February bring frosts but seldom snow, and July and August are very warm but rarely hot. The Irish consider any temperature over 68°F (20°C) to be "roasting" and below 34°F (1°C) as bone chilling. For a complete online guide to Irish weather, consult **www.ireland.com/weather**.

Average Monthly Temperatures in Dublin

	JAN	FEB	MAR	APR	MAY	JUNE	JULY	AUG	SEPT	OCT	NOV	DEC
TEMP (°F)	36–46	37–48	37–49	38–52	42–57	46–62	51–66	50–65	48–62	44–56	39–49	38–47
TEMP (°C)	2–8	3–9	3–9	3–11	6–14	8–17	11–19	10–18	9–17	7–13	4–9	3–8

HOLIDAYS

The Republic observes the following national holidays, also known as "Bank Holidays": New Year's Day (January 1); St. Patrick's Day (March 17); Easter Monday (variable); May Day (May 1); first Mondays in June and August (summer Bank Holidays); last Monday in October (autumn Bank Holiday); Christmas (December 25); and St. Stephen's Day (December 26). Good Friday (the Fri before Easter) is mostly observed but is not statutory. All pubs must close on Good Friday, although this archaic (and famously detested) law is the subject of hot debate. In the North, the schedule of holidays is the same as in the Republic, with some exceptions: the North's summer Bank Holidays fall on the last Monday of May and August; the Battle of the Boyne is celebrated on Orangeman's Day (July 12); and Boxing Day (December 26) follows Christmas.

In both Ireland and Northern Ireland, holidays that fall on weekends are celebrated the following Monday.

Ireland Calendar of Events

This sampling of events is drawn from 2011 schedules. Many events had not set their 2012 dates at the time this book was being written. The most up-to-date listings of events can be found at **www.discoverireland.ie** and www.entertainment.ie.

JANUARY

Funderland. Royal Dublin Society, Ballsbridge, Dublin 4. An annual indoor fun fair, complete with white-knuckle rides, carnival stalls, and family entertainment (✆ **01/283-8188;** www.funderland.com). December/January. (Also smaller events in Cork, Limerick, and Belfast later in the year; check the website for details.)

FEBRUARY

Dublin International Film Festival. Irish Film Centre, Temple Bar, Dublin 2, and various cinemas in Dublin. More than 100 films are featured, with screenings of the best in Irish and world cinema, plus seminars and lectures on filmmaking, currently sponsored by Jameson whiskey (✆ **01/662-4620;** www.jdiff.com). Late February.

MARCH

St. Patrick's Dublin Festival. Held around St. Patrick's Day itself, this massive 4-day festival is open, free, and accessible to everyone. Street theater, carnival acts, sports, music, fireworks, and other festivities culminate in Ireland's grandest parade, with marching bands, drill teams, floats, and delegations from around the world (✆ **www.stpatricksday.ie**). On and around March 17.

St. Patrick's Day Parades. Held all over Ireland and Northern Ireland, celebrating Ireland's patron saint. March 17.

APRIL

Dublin Writers Festival. Dublin, County Dublin. One of the biggest events in the Irish literary calendar, this nine-day festival draws high-profile authors from across the world. Events take place at venues across the city, including Dublin Castle. (✆ **01/222-5455;** www.dublin writersfestival.com). Mid-May.

Pan Celtic Festival. County Donegal. For 5 days, the wider Celtic family (including Cornwall, Isle of Man, Scotland, Wales, and Brittany) unites for culture, song, dance, sports, and parades with marching bands and pipers. Fringe events range from nature walks to poetry readings (✆ **028/7126-4132;** www.panceltic.ie). March/April.

World Irish Dancing Championships. Gleneagle Hotel, Killarney. The premier international competition in Irish dancing features more than 4,000 contenders from as far away as New Zealand (✆ **01/814-6298;** www.clrg.ie). April.

MAY

Belfast City Marathon. An epic 42km (26-mile) race of 6,000 international runners through the city. It starts and finishes at Maysfield Leisure Centre (✆ **028/9060-5944;** www.belfastcity marathon.com). Early May.

May Day Races. Down Royal Racecourse, Maze, Lisburn, County Antrim. One of the major events on the horse-racing calendar (✆ **028/9262-1256;** www.downroyal.com). Early May.

Wicklow Arts Festival. This is Wicklow's big spring event, held over 5 days in Wicklow Town. Many of the dozens of music, theater, art, and literary events are free (**www.wicklowartsfestival.ie**). Early May.

JUNE

Sky Cat Laughs Comedy Festival. Various venues in Kilkenny Town. Past performers at this international festival of stand-up comedy include American comics Bill Murray, George Wendt, and Emo Phillips, and Ireland's Dara O'Briain (✆ **www.thecatlaughs.com**). Early June.

Taste of Dublin. Dublin, County Dublin. Held over 4 days in Iveagh Gardens, this is one of Ireland's biggest and most high-profile food festivals. Visitors can sample dishes prepared by some of the country's top chefs, and over 100 artisan producers, The event is usually a sellout, so booking is advisable. (✆ **www.tasteofdublin.ie**). Mid-June.

Bloomsday Festival. Various Dublin venues. This unique day of festivity celebrates Leopold Bloom, the central character of James Joyce's *Ulysses*. Every aspect of the city, including the menus at restaurants and pubs, duplicates the aromas, sights, sounds, and tastes of Joyce's fictitious Dublin on June 16, 1904, the day when all of the action in *Ulysses* takes place. Ceremonies are held at the James Joyce Tower and Museum; guided walks visit Joycean sights. Contact the James Joyce Centre, 35 N. Great George's St., Dublin 1 (✆ **01/878-8547;** www.jamesjoyce.ie). June 16.

Cork Midsummer Arts Festival. Emmet Place, Cork City. The program includes musical performances and traditional Irish *céilí* bands, and always has a strong literary content. Bonfire nights are particularly popular (✆ **021/421-5131;** www.corkmidsummer.com). Mid- to late June.

Irish Derby. The Curragh, County Kildare. This is Ireland's version of the Kentucky Derby or Royal Ascot and is a fashionable gathering (***hint:*** jackets for men, posh hats for women) of racing fans from all over the world. It's one of the richest and most definitive middle-distance horse races in Europe. Booking recommended (✆ **045/441205;** www.curragh.ie). Late June.

Oxegen. Punchestown Racecourse, County Kildare. This (mainly rock) music festival is now one of Europe's premier summer music fests, with nearly 100 acts playing on five stages during one weekend. Previous headliners have included Coldplay and David Guetta. For tickets, contact **www.ticketmaster.ie** or **www.oxegen.ie**. Early July.

Battle of the Boyne Commemoration. Belfast and other cities. This annual event, often called Orangeman's Day, recalls the historic battle between two 17th-century kings. It's a national day of parades by Protestants all over Northern Ireland— but the event is contentious, and there's a weary inevitability to how some parades in urban Belfast and Derry always turn nasty. This may be one better viewed from afar. July 12.

Galway Arts Festival & Races. Galway City and Racecourse. This 2-week fest is a shining star on the Irish arts scene, featuring international theater, concerts, literary evenings, street shows, arts, parades, music, and more. (✆ **091/509700;** www.galwayartsfestival.ie). The famous Galway Races follow, with 5 more days of racing and merriment, music, and song. See p. 347 for more details. Mid- to late July.

Lughnasa Fair. Carrickfergus Castle, County Antrim. A spectacular revival with a 12th-century Norman castle and its grounds, this event features people in period costumes, medieval games, traditional food, entertainment, and crafts (✆ **028/9335-8049;** www.carrickfergus.org). Late July/early August.

AUGUST

Fáilte Ireland Horse Show. RDS Showgrounds, Ballsbridge, Dublin 4. This is the most important equestrian and social event on the Irish national calendar. Aside from the daily dressage and jumping competitions, highlights include a fashionable ladies' day, nightly formal hunt balls, and the awarding of the Aga Khan Trophy and the Nation's Cup (✆ **081/871-9300;** www.dublinhorseshow.ie or www.rds.ie). Early August.

Kilkenny Arts Festival. Kilkenny Town. This weeklong event has it all, from classical and traditional music to plays, one-person shows, readings, films, poetry, and art exhibitions (✆ **056/ 775-2175;** www.kilkennyarts.ie). August.

Puck Fair. Killorglin, County Kerry. This is one of Ireland's oldest festivals. Each year the residents of this tiny Ring of Kerry town capture a wild goat and enthrone it as "king" over 3 days of merrymaking that include open-air concerts, horse fairs, parades, and fireworks. And yes, the goat does get to wear a crown (✆ **066/976-2366;** www.puckfair.ie). August 10–12.

Electric Picnic. Stradbally, County Laois. This midsize music festival, held on the grounds of Stradbally Hall, County Laois, is known for its eclectic lineup. Recent acts to have played here include Sonic Youth, Björk, Fatboy Slim, and Sigur Rós. (**www.electricpicnic.ie**). Late August.

Rose of Tralee International Festival. Tralee, County Kerry. A gala atmosphere prevails at this 5-day event, with a full program of concerts, street entertainment, horse races, and a beauty-and-talent pageant leading up to the televised selection of the "Rose of Tralee" (✆ **066/712-1322;** www.roseoftralee.ie). Late August.

National Heritage Week. More than 400 events are held throughout the country—walks, lectures, exhibitions, music recitals, and more (✆ **185/020-0878;** www.heritageweek.ie). Late August.

Fleadh Cheoil na hÉireann. Sligo, County Sligo. This has been Ireland's premier summer festival of traditional music since 1951, with competitions held to select the all-Ireland champions in all categories of instruments and singing. The host city changes every year; for 2015, Sligo is expected to take the honor for the second year running (✆ **www.fleadhcheoil.ie**). Late August/early September.

SEPTEMBER

Lisdoonvarna Matchmaking Festival. Lisdoonvarna, County Clare. Still the biggest and best singles' event after all these years, this traditional "bachelor" festival carries on in the lovely spa town of Lisdoonvarna, with lots of wonderful music and dance (✆ **065/707-4005;** www.matchmakerireland.com). September/October.

All-Ireland Hurling & Gaelic Football Finals. Croke Park, Dublin 3. The finals of Ireland's most beloved sports, hurling and Gaelic football, are Ireland's equivalent of the Super Bowl. If you can't be at Croke Park, experience this in the full bonhomie of a pub. You can find information at **www.gaa.ie**, or obtain tickets through Ticketmaster (✆ **081/871-9300;** www.ticketmaster.ie). September.

Irish Antique Dealers' Fair. RDS Showgrounds, Ballsbridge, Dublin 4. Ireland's premier annual antiques fair, with hundreds of dealers from all over the island (✆ **01/679-4147;** www.iada.ie). Late September/early October.

Galway International Oyster Festival. A haven for oyster aficionados from across the globe, the highlights of this festival include the World Oyster Opening Championship, a grand opening parade, a yacht race, an art exhibition, a gala banquet, traditional music, and, of course, lots of oyster eating (✆ **091/575875;** www.galwayoysterfest.com). Late September.

Dublin Theatre Festival. Theaters throughout Dublin. Showcases for new plays by every major Irish company (including the Abbey and the Gate), plus a range of productions from abroad (✆ **01/677-8439;** www.dublintheatre festival.com). Late September/ mid-October.

OCTOBER

Kinsale International Gourmet Festival. Kinsale, County Cork. The foodie capital of Ireland hosts this well-respected annual fest, featuring special menus in all the restaurants and plenty of star chefs in town from abroad (✆ **021/477-3571;** www.kinsalerestaurants.com). October.

Baboró International Arts Festival for Children. Galway. A fun-filled, educational festival geared to kids 3 to 12 years of age, with theater, music, dance, museum exhibitions, and literary events (✆ **091/562667;** www.baboro.ie). Late October.

Guinness Cork Jazz Festival. Cork City. Ireland's second city stages a first-rate festival of jazz, with an international lineup of live acts playing in hotels, concert halls, and pubs (✆ **021/427-8979**). Late October.

Dublin City Marathon. On the last Monday in October, more than 5,000 runners from both sides of the Atlantic and the Irish Sea participate in this popular run through the streets of the capital (✆ **01/623-2250;** www.dublinmarathon.ie). Late October.

Wexford Festival Opera. Wexford, County Wexford. This is not your average stuffy opera festival. Famous as much for the jubilant, informal atmosphere as for the acclaimed productions of lesser known 18th- and 19th-century operatic masterpieces, the festival also offers classical music concerts, recitals, and more.(✆ **053/912-2144;** www.wexford opera.com). Late October/early November.

Belfast Festival at Queen's. Queen's University, Belfast. Ireland's largest arts festival attracts enormous crowds each year for its stellar program of drama, opera, music, and film (**www.belfast festival.com**). October/November.

NOVEMBER

Murphy's Cork International Film Festival. Cinemas throughout Cork. Ireland's oldest film festival offers a plethora of international features, documentaries, short films, and special programs (✆ **021/427-1711;** www.corkfilmfest.org). Mid-November.

DECEMBER

Killarney Christmas Market. Fair Hill, Killarney, County Kerry. Killarney gets very enthusiastic indeed about the festive season, so it's unsurprising that it should host some of the region's best Christmas markets, devoted mainly to quality local crafts and food (✆ **064/663-7928;** www.christmasinkillarney.com). Various dates in December.

Dublin Docklands Christmas Festival. Now part of the traditional run-up to Christmas in Dublin, this huge event all but takes over Docklands. Mostly it's an opportunity to shop (there are over 100 different traders), but there's also a traditional-style fairground, and festive food and drink aplenty (✆ **01/496-9883;** www.docklands.ie). Mid-December until Christmas.

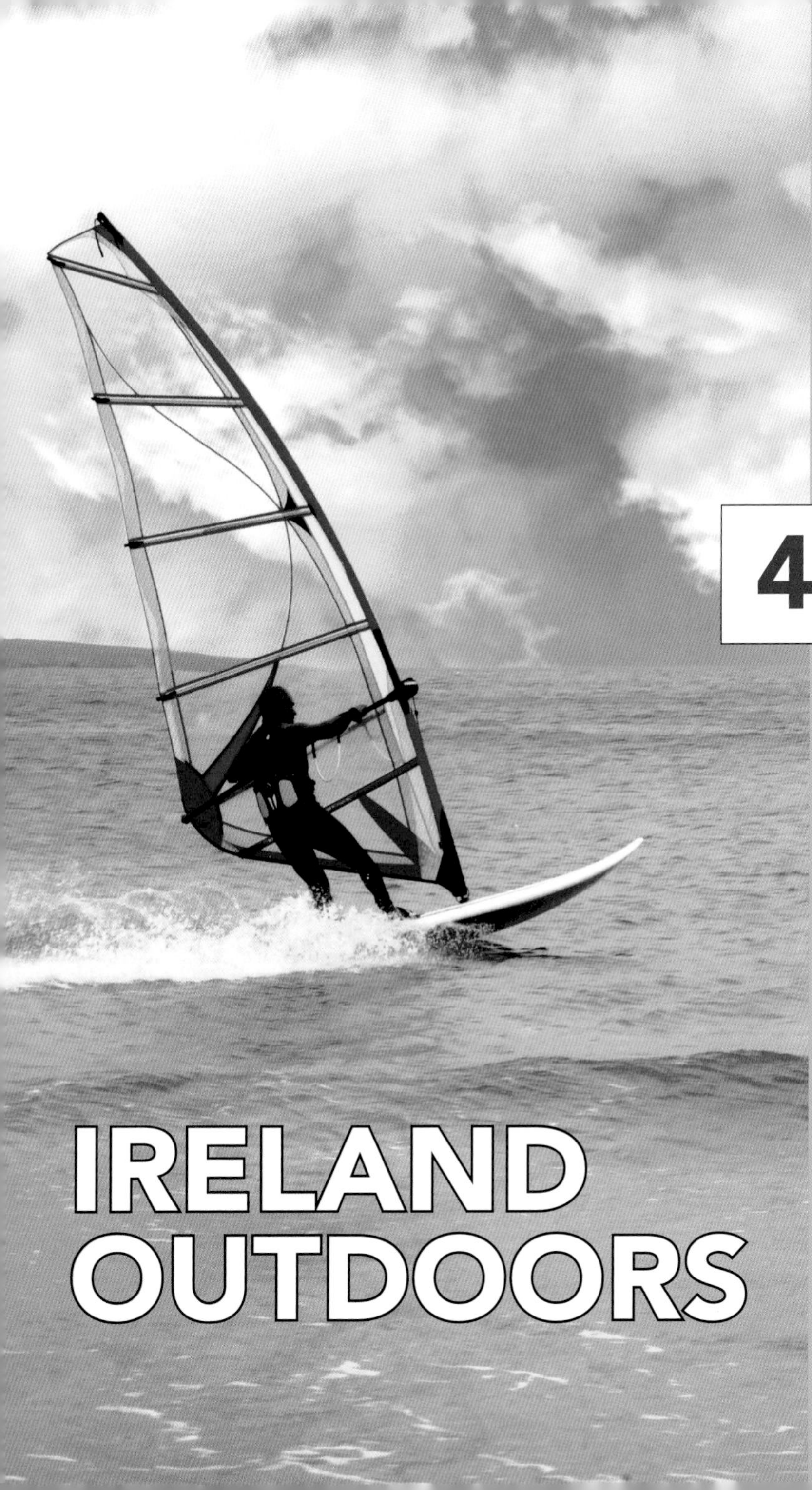

4

IRELAND OUTDOORS

Ireland is a satisfyingly wild place, where foxes and hares wander in and out of city limits, otters frolic in the rivers, seals bark on the beaches, and wildflowers blanket the countryside so thoroughly it looks like someone spilled the paint. It has spaces of extreme isolation—in Donegal and County Mayo you can drive for long stretches on empty highways and walk for hours along a coastal headland without meeting another human. It can almost be unnerving. But you have to get out of the city to do it.

About a third of Ireland's 4.5 million residents live in Dublin and its sprawling suburbs—and almost half its entire population lives within 97km (60 miles). Apart from a few other small cities, the remaining population spreads thinly across the rest of the island, putting very few demands on the environment. As a result, Ireland has remarkably intact bird and wildlife habitats.

That's the way the locals like it—they love the outdoors and spend as much of their time in it as possible. So what if it rains? That doesn't stop the Irish from golfing, hiking, fishing, and cycling. You're not made of sugar—get outside.

BIRD-WATCHING

Ireland is of great interest to birders because of its position on the migration routes of many passerines and seabirds, which find the isle a convenient stopping point on their Atlantic journeys. Opportunities for birding abound, particularly in the 71 **National Nature Reserves.** The network of reserves covers woodlands, bog lands, grasslands, sand dune systems, bird sanctuaries, coastal heath lands, and marine areas.

Most of the important nesting colonies for seabirds are on the west coast, the westernmost promontory of Europe; exceptions are Lambey Island, near Dublin, and Great Saltee in County Wexford. Sandy beaches and tidal flats on the east and west coasts are nesting grounds for large populations of winter waders and smaller, isolated tern colonies. In the North, the largest seabird colony is on Rathlin Island, off the North Antrim Coast (see chapter 15).

Until recently, rural Ireland was home to large numbers of a small bird known as the **corncrake** *(Crex crex),* whose unusual cry during breeding season was a common feature of the early summer night. Sadly, the introduction of heavy machinery for cutting silage has destroyed the protective high-grass environment in which the mother corncrake lays her eggs. (The period for cutting silage coincides with the corncrake breeding period.) Ireland now has only a few areas where the corncrake still breeds. One is the **Shannon Callows,** around Athlone and Lough Derg in County Westmeath (chapter 14). where the bird's cry, which now seems quite mournful, can often be heard in the quiet of nightfall.

Ireland's lakes and wetlands also serve as a **wintering ground** for great numbers of wildfowl from the Arctic and northern Europe. From Greenland,

REVIOUS PAGE: **Windsurfing in Maharees in County Kerry.**

Cliffs of Moher

Iceland, and Canada come waders such as knot, golden plover, and black-tailed godwit; flocks of brent, barnacle, and white-fronted geese; and thousands of whooper swans. Every year, as many as 10,000 Greenland white-fronted geese winter on the north shores of Wexford Harbor, making it a mecca for birders. Flooded fields, or "callows," provide habitats for wigeons, whooping swans, and plover; the callows of the Shannon and the Blackwater are especially popular with birders. One of the best winter bird-watching sites is the Wexford Wildfowl Reserve (see chapter 7).

From March onward, mild **spring** weather invites Irish birds to begin nesting early, and their songs fill the woods and hedgerows. The arrival of migrants from Africa can be observed in April and May all along the south coast. Rathlin Island reserve (chapter 15), home to Northern Ireland's largest seabird colony, is best visited in May and June.

Summer is the time to head to the west of Ireland, where seaside cliffs are an ideal place for large seabird colonies such as puffins and gannets. Some of the best summer birding sites are Great Saltee Island in County Wexford (see chapter 7), Cape Clear Island in County Cork (chapter 8), the Skellig Islands in County Kerry (chapter 9), and Loop Head in County Clare (chapter 10).

Autumn is a particularly attractive time for bird-watchers in Ireland, when many rare American waders—mainly sandpipers and plovers—arrive when blown across the Atlantic. A spectacular avian event is the annual fall migration of brent geese. On the shores of Strangford Lough in County Down—Europe's premier brent-watching site—you might see as many as 3,000 on a single day.

Bird-Watching Resources

One of the best sources of information is the **Irish Birding** website (**www.irishbirding.com**), which features links on birding events, sites, and news. Another excellent resource is **BirdWatch Ireland** (✆ **01/281-9878;** www.birdwatchireland.ie), an organization devoted to bird conservation in the Republic of Ireland. An equivalent organization in Northern Ireland is the **Royal Society for the Protection of Birds** (✆ **028/9049-1547;** www.rspb.org.uk/northernireland).

CYCLING

Cycling is an ideal way to explore the Irish landscape. The distances are quite manageable, and in a week or two on a bike, you can travel through several of the regions described in this guide or explore one in greater detail. Hostels, B&Bs, and hotels are abundantly available for touring cyclists who don't want to deal with the extra weight of a tent and sleeping bag. Even if you're not game to undertake a full-fledged bike tour, day trips on two wheels are a great way to stretch your legs after spending too much time in the car.

Roads in Ireland are categorized as **M** (Motorway), **N** (National), or **R** (Regional); a few still bear the older **T** (Trunk) and **L** (Link) designations. For reasons of scenery as well as safety, you probably want to avoid national roads. It is illegal to cycle on motorways. The R and L are always suitable for cycling, as are the N roads in outlying areas with little traffic. The biggest disadvantage of the smaller roads in remote areas is that they often are not signposted, so you should have a good map and compass. In some areas of the west and northwest, *only* the N roads are consistently signposted. Smaller roads are quite narrow and winding, however, which can be somewhat hair-raising.

If you're going to hook up with a cycling outfitter (see below), you probably won't need to bring your own gear. But if you're planning on going it alone, ask your airline how much it will cost to stow your bike in the baggage hold. Be forewarned that airlines are increasingly charging additional fees for "oddly" shaped and bulky items, such as golf bags and bicycles.

Even if you'll be renting a bike, you'll still want to consider bringing a few of your own items. Rental panniers (saddlebags) are often on the flimsy side. If you have cycling shoes and good pedals, you can easily attach them to the rental bike and make your trip immeasurably more enjoyable. With advance notice, most rental shops can outfit a bike with toe clips, bar ends, and water-bottle holders; an advance booking can also improve your chances of reserving the right size bike. Many rental outfits can also arrange a one-way rental over a short distance (up to 161km/100 miles or so). The national companies, such as **Raleigh** and **Ireland Rent-A-Bike** (see below), are set up for one-way rentals throughout the country.

Anyone cycling in Ireland should be prepared for two inevitable obstacles: wind and hills. Outside the Midlands, hills are just about everywhere, and those on the back roads can have thigh-burning grades. Road engineering is often, well, not very engineered—instead of having switchbacks on a steep slope, roads often climb by the most direct route.

Cyclists have long favored the coastal roads of the southwest, west, and northwest. The quiet roads and rugged scenery of the Beara Peninsula (see chapter chapter 8) make it perfect for a cycling tour, along with the nearby Dingle Peninsula (chapter 9). The spectacular Causeway Coast and the Glens of Antrim in the North (chapter 15) are just made for cycling, with quiet roads and dazzling views. Donegal (chapter 14) is one of the hilliest regions and rewards the energetic cyclist with some of the country's most spectacular coastal and mountain scenery. ***Tip:*** if you'll be biking in the west, plan your route from south to north—the same direction as the prevailing winds.

Ireland's many islands provide further cycling options—you can bring your bike on all passenger ferries, often for no extra charge, and roads out on the islands have little or no traffic. Some of the best islands with accommodations are Cape Clear, County Cork (see chapter 8); the Aran Islands and County Galway (chapter 11); and Achill and Clare islands, County Mayo (chapter 13). Wonderful cycling can also be had on Great Blasket Island, County Kerry (chapter 9), although you'll have to find accommodations on the mainland.

Just one more thing: Remember to cycle on the ***left!***

Cycling Outfitters & Resources

If you're booking from the United States, **Backroads** (✆ **800/462-2848** or 510/527-1555; www.backroads.com) and **VBT** (✆ **800/245-3868;** www.vbt.com) are both well-regarded companies offering all-inclusive bicycle trips in Ireland. Included are bikes, gear, luggage transportation via a support van, good food, and rooms in local inns and hotels of character—everything bundled into one price.

If you want to design your own itinerary and bike independently, several rental agencies with depots nationwide permit one-way rental. They include **Raleigh** (✆ **01/465-9659;** www.raleigh.ie); and **Emerald Cycles/Ireland Rent-A-Bike** (✆ **061/416983;** www.irelandrentabike.com). Mountain and cross-country bike-rental rates average around €20 per day, €80 per week. You can also rent a car bike carrier for €40 per week (good for up to three bikes). On top of the hire price, you'll also have to fork up a refundable deposit of about €50 per bike.

Tip: Don't wait until you arrive in Ireland to reserve your bike. Places do get booked up, and several outfitters have gone out of business in the past few years due to skyrocketing insurance costs and the recession. The only way to guarantee you'll have a bike is to prebook.

If you want your cycling trip orchestrated and outfitted by affable local experts, consider **Irish Cycling Safaris,** Belfield Bike Shop, Belfield House, University College Dublin, Dublin 4 (✆ **01/260-0749;** www.cyclingsafaris.com). It offers trips to practically every part of Ireland suitable for two wheels, including packages that cover B&B and some meals.

DIVING

With visibility averaging 15m (49 ft.) and occasionally reaching 29m (95 ft.), and many wrecks to explore, the west coast of Ireland may be cold, but it's still a pretty good place for divers.

The Irish dive season generally starts in March and ends in October, although specific dates depend on your comfort zone. Outside these months, weather and ocean conditions could make jumping into the sea unappealing. The PADI open-water diver certification is the minimum requirement for all dives; most schools also offer introductory dives for novices.

The rocky coast of West Cork and Kerry is great for diving, with centers in Baltimore (see chapter 8) and Dingle (chapter 9). On the west coast are many great locations, one of which is the deep, sheltered Killary Harbour. Northern Ireland offers many interesting dives, with more than 400 named wrecks off the coast and many in the Irish Sea and in Belfast Lough.

Diving Resources

The **Irish Underwater Council** (**CFT,** or **Comhairle Fo-Thuinn**), (✆ **01/284-4601;** www.cft.ie), is an association of more than 70 Irish diving clubs. Its website lists information on diving and snorkeling, dive centers, and other information on exploring the Emerald Isle's emerald waters. The CFT operates under the aegis of the CMAS (Confédération Mondiale des Activités Subaquatiques), the world diving federation.

Sign up for certified level-one and level-two instruction and equipment rental for kayaking, sailing, and windsurfing at the **Surfdock Centre,** Grand

Canal Dock Yard, Ringsend, Dublin 4 (✆ **01/668-3945;** www.surfdock.ie). Dublin Bay is filled with sea life and old wrecks, making it ideal for cold-water diving. To try it out, get in touch with **Oceantec Adventures** in Dún Laoghaire (toll-free within Ireland at ✆ **1800/272-822**). It offers a five-star PADI diving school and arranges dive vacations on the west coast.

The **U.K. Diving** website, **www.ukdiving.co.uk**, features information on diving in Northern Ireland, including an excellent wreck database you can access either through a conventional listing or by pinpointing on a map.

Irish dive centers and schools include **Discover Scuba,** 20 Terenure Park, Dublin 6 (✆ **01/492-7392;** www.discoverscuba.ie); **Oceantec Adventures,** Dún Laoghaire, County Dublin (✆ **1800/272-822**); **Baltimore Diving Centre,** Baltimore, County Cork (✆/fax **028/20300;** www.baltimorediving.com); and **Scubadive West,** Renvyle, County Galway (✆ **095/43922;** www.scubadivewest.com).

FISHING

What makes Ireland such a great fishing destination? A coastline of more than 5,603km (3,472 miles), thousands of lakes and ponds, countless creeks, rills, streams, and rivers—those certainly don't hurt. Ireland's temperate climate and low pollution also encourage a high fish population, and low human density has put little pressure on that. It all adds up to fairly ideal fishing conditions.

The sport of fishing—referred to by the Irish as **angling**—is a cherished tradition. Festivals and competitions celebrate the many forms of this sport; for dates and locations, contact Tourism Ireland; you have to sign up well in advance to participate in most of the competitions. Among the festivals are **Killybegs International Sea Angling Festival** in July, the **Baltimore Deep Sea Angling Festival** (www.baltimoreseaangling.com) in August, and the **Cobh International Deep Sea Angling Festival** in September.

In the west and northwest, Killybegs (see chapter 14) is a center for sea angling, while Lough Corrib (see chapter 11) offers much to entice the fresh-water angler. The Killarney area (see chapter 9) is a popular angling destination, as are the Blackwater River near Cork and Kinsale (see chapter 8) for sea angling. Also consider the Shannon River and its lakes.

Fishing Resources

The best all-round online resource for fishing in Ireland is the prosaically named **Fishing in Ireland** (**www.fishinginireland.info**). In addition to up-to-date details on licenses and permits (see below), it also has a wealth of information on everything from local regulations, weather, and tides to locations suitable for disabled anglers. Tourism Ireland devotes a section of its website to fishing. Visit **www.discoverireland.com**, click on "Things to see & do," then "Activities," and then "Fishing."

A helpful brochure, *Angling in Ireland,* detailing what fish can be caught where, is available from the Angling Information Office at the **Central Fisheries Board,** Swords Business Campus, Swords, County Dublin (✆ **01/884-2600;** fax 01/836-0060; www.cfb.ie). Another helpful resource, *The Angler's Guide,* is published by Tourism Ireland. Permits, licenses, and specific information can also be obtained from local outfitters or the Central Fisheries Board.

Fishing seasons are as follows: salmon, January 1 to September 30; brown trout, February 15 to October 12; sea trout, June 1 to September 30; coarse fishing and sea angling, all year. A license is required only for salmon and sea trout angling; the cost is €20 for a day, €46 for 21 days, or €120 annually. For information about permits, visit the Central Fisheries Boards website (www.cfb.ie). You can purchase fishing licenses at most bait and tackle shops. For all private salmon and sea trout fisheries, a permit is required in addition to the license, and it can be considerably more expensive. Prices vary greatly, from €10 to €200 per rod per day (depending on the venue and provider), although most permits run €30 to €40.

Many hotels have exclusive access to lakes and ponds, and will rent boats, gear, and *ghillies* (fishing guides) to their guests. Over a dozen such hotels have formed the **Great Fishing Houses of Ireland** (**www.irelandfishing.com**). Examples include Adare Manor in Limerick (p. 314); the Delphi Lodge in County Galway; and Newport House Hotel and Enniscoe House (p. 397), both in Mayo.

In Northern Ireland, you must get a rod license from the **Department for Culture, Arts and Leisure (DCNI),** 1–7 Bedford St., Belfast, County Antrim (✆ **028/9025-8825;** www.dcalni.gov.uk), or in the Derry area from the **Foyle Carlingford Irish Lights Commission,** 22 Victoria Rd., Derry (✆ **028/7134-2100;** www.loughs-agency.org). A permit may also be required; you can obtain information from local outfitters or the DCNI. A rod license costs £3.50 to £24, depending on the license provider and duration of license; day permits cost around £10. You can find a wealth of information in *An Information Guide to Game Fishing,* available from any office of the Northern Ireland Tourist Board.

GOLF

Golf is the single biggest sporting attraction in Ireland, with nearly a quarter of a million visitors traveling here specifically to play. The Irish landscape and climate, like those of Scotland, seem almost custom-designed for scenic links, fair

Dromoland Golf Course, County Clare.

fairways, green greens, and dramatic traps—and there is never a shortage of 19th holes. In short, Ireland is a place of golfing pilgrimage.

Best of all, golfing is not confined to those with an Olympian income. Membership fees do not require mortgages, and greens fees for walk-ins are often quite modest, especially on weekdays and at off-peak hours.

See "Sports & Outdoor Pursuits" in each of the sightseeing chapters for a recommended selection of each region's top courses.

Golf Resources

Tourism Ireland has a dedicated golf website with numerous contacts and links (no pun intended) at **www.golf.discoverireland.ie/Home.aspx**.

A host of U.S. companies offer package golf tours. Among them are **Golf International** (**© 800/833-1389** or 212/986-9176; www.golfinternational.com) and **Wide World of Golf** (**© 800/214-4653;** www.wideworldofgolf.com).

HIKING

Hiking is an increasingly popular activity in Ireland. Since 1982, the network of long-distance, marked trails has grown from 1 to 25, and now stretches across more than 2,414km (1,500 miles). The first to open was the **Wicklow Way,** which begins just outside Dublin and proceeds through rugged hills and serene pastures on its 132km (82-mile) course. Others include the **Beara**

Hiking the Slieve League in Donegal.

IRELAND'S NATIONAL parks

Ireland's six **national parks** offer some of the most spectacular scenery and best walking in the country, and all have free admission.

- The **Burren National Park,** Mullaghmore, County Clare (**www.burrennationalpark.ie**), holds fascinating landscapes—a series of limestone beds eroded during the Ice Age to form a barren, lunarlike landscape. The Burren is of particular interest to botanists, since it's the only place in the world where Arctic, Mediterranean, and Alpine species of wildflowers grow side by side in the fissures of the rock.
- **Connemara National Park,** Letterfrack, County Galway (**www.connemaranationalpark.ie**), is a rugged, heather-clad landscape of blanket bog and wet heath, encompassing some of the Twelve Bens mountain range. The nature trails have accompanying map/booklets (guided walks are available in summer); a visitor center is in Letterfrack.
- **Glenveagh National Park,** near Gweedore, County Donegal (**www.glenveaghnationalpark.ie**), is Ireland's largest national park and also its remotest wilderness—103,600 sq. km (40,000 sq. miles) of mountains, lakes, and natural woodlands that are home to a large red deer population. From the visitor center, you can grab a ride on a minibus along the shores of Lough Veagh to Glenveagh Castle, notable for its outstanding gardens. There are also a self-guided nature trail and a summer program of guided walks.
- **Killarney National Park,** Killarney, County Kerry (**www.killarneynationalpark.ie**), contains nearly 64,750 sq. km (25,000 sq. miles) of spectacular lake and mountain scenery. There are four self-guided trails, a visitor center with a restaurant, and two small lodges with tearooms.
- **Ballycroy National Park,** Ballycroy, County Mayo (**www.ballycroynationalpark.ie**), is the newest of the parks, centered in the Owenduff-Nephinbeg area. It features gorgeous bog landscapes. Along with a visitor center in Ballycroy, there are nature trails galore.
- **Wicklow Mountains National Park,** Glendalough, County Wicklow (**www.wicklowmountainsnationalpark.ie**), is the only park of the six that's not on the west coast. At over 129,500 sq. km (50,000 sq. miles), it contains picturesque woodlands, moors, and mountains, and includes the atmospheric Glendalough monastic site and the Glenealo Valley. A park information office is at the Upper Lake, near the Glendalough car park.

In addition to national parks are 12 **forest reserve parks,** several of which were former private estates. Among the most enchanting is **Lough Key Forest Park (www.loughkey.ie),** in County Roscommon, which features a bog-garden, fairy bridge, and archaeological monuments.

Peninsula (see chapter 8), the **Kerry Way** and the **Dingle Way** (chapter 9), and the **Ulster Way** (chapter 15). Most trails are routed so that meals and accommodations—B&Bs, hostels, or hotels—are never more than a day's walk apart. Routes are generally uncrowded, and lots of people tend to walk just part of the trails' lengths.

Walking the Nano Nagle Footbridge in Cork.

For inland hillwalking, try Glenveagh National Park (chapter 14). For coastal walks, the best-known kind in this island country, try also the Inishowen Peninsula and the Donegal Bay Coast (chapter 14), and the Western Way in Connemara (chapter 11).

Though long-distance routes are the best-marked trails in Ireland, the signposting is surprisingly random and inadequate, and a good terrain map is an absolute necessity. Don't expect the kind of close management you'd find on trails in National Parks in the U.S., however; the countryside here may be awe-inspiring, but it can get to feel very wild indeed once you're a few miles off the beaten path.

Markers are frequently miles apart and often seem to be lacking at crucial crossroads. Look for a post or cairn on each summit, which usually indicates the way between two peaks. Trees on Irish hillsides rarely impede visibility but a compass becomes crucial when a fog blows in and all landmarks quickly disappear. ***Be warned:*** This can happen quite unexpectedly, and the safest strategy when you can't see your way is to stay exactly where you are until the fog clears.

The walks listed in this guide are on clearly marked trails whenever possible, and otherwise indicated if sections are without markings. We can't give you all the information you need for the walks, so you should consult the local tourist office for advice before setting out. Visitors from Britain—or those who are familiar with their fiercely upheld "rambling" laws—should note that the laws are not the same in Ireland. In parts of the U.K. (*not* including Northern Ireland), walkers have the right of way across most private property when the land is rural and uncultivated, and fences that cross public paths must have places for walkers to pass through. By contrast, in Ireland the laws favor property owners, and farmers are passionate about the privacy of their land. Basically, stay on marked paths, or face the unmitigated wrath of a territorial Irish sheep farmer.

Hiking Resources

Start your research with two excellent online resources with plenty of recommended walks: **www.gowalkingireland.com** and **www.walkni.com**. The **Mountaineering Council of Ireland,** which oversees hillwalking on the island, can be visited at **www.mountaineering.ie**.

You can buy maps and guidebooks in local bookshops and outdoor-gear shops across Ireland. Guides can also be obtained from **AnÓige,** the Irish Youth Hostel Association (© **01/830-4555;** www.anoige.ie), or in the North from **Hostelling International Northern Ireland,** 22–32 Donegall Rd., Belfast BT12 5JN (© **028/9032-4733;** www.hini.org.uk).

In the west of Ireland is a wide selection of guided walks in the Burren, from 1 day to a week or more. Contact **Guided Walks and Hikes** (© **065/707-6100;** www.burrenguidedwalks.com) for guided walks and hikes of varying lengths. In the southwest, contact **SouthWestWalks Ireland** (© **066/718-6181;** www.southwestwalksireland.com). For a full walking holiday package to County Kerry or County Clare and Connemara, the U.S.-based **Backroads** (© **800/462-2848;** www.backroads.com) is one highly recommended operator.

On the Northern Ireland Tourist Board's website (**www.discovernorthernireland.com/walking**), a walking and hiking page lists self-guided tours, short hikes along the Ulster Way, and names and addresses of organizations offering guided walks throughout the North.

A WALK ON THE wild SIDE

One hazard you won't encounter in the Irish countryside: dangerous wildlife. Fearsome beasts once common around these parts—including brown bears, wolves, and wildcats—are long since extinct, and we all know the story about St. Patrick banishing the snakes. You may, however, meet European foxes (more the size of large dogs than their American cousins) or badgers, but both are notoriously timid creatures; leave them alone and they'll quite happily follow suit. In fact, if the experience of your Frommer's authors is anything to go by, the worst you have to fear is an attack of the heebie-jeebies from encountering large spiders (up to 8cm/3 in. in length); although these, too, are entirely harmless.

Nope, nothing to fear in the countryside—that is, unless you believe in monsters. **Doyar-Chú** are creatures said to live in the lakes of County Galway. Half-dog, half-fish, and about the size of a crocodile, they supposedly lie in wait for unsuspecting hikers and dog walkers, ready to drag them underwater with their terrifying jaws. Meanwhile, **Muckie** is a Loch Ness monster–type beastie (allegedly) spotted in the Lakes of Killarney. Descriptions range from your average terrifying sea monster to, well, a scary giant black aquatic hog that rises out of the depths of Lough Leane. (That's right. Hog.) Muckie was given an unexpected boost a few years ago when a sonar survey of the lakes showed a large unidentified object that could conceivably have been a living creature, although it vanished instantly. A Japanese TV crew went searching for the beast in 2004, but failed to find anything.

Our advice? Bring a camera. That seems to ensure the monsters will leave you alone given that nobody's ever managed to photograph anything.

Four people riding horses on the beach in County Donegal.

HORSEBACK RIDING

Ireland is a horse-loving country, with a plethora of stables and equestrian centers offering trail rides and instruction. The **Association of Irish Riding Establishments** (✆ **045/854518;** www.aire.ie) is the regulatory body that accredits stables, ensuring adequate safety standards and instructor competence. Riding prices range from about €20 to €50 per hour; expect to pay €25 on average. A list of accredited stables throughout the country is available from Tourism Ireland.

Choose your trek or horse ride based on your interests and experience. Pony trekking caters primarily to beginners, and you don't need experience. Long-distance trail riding requires you to trot for extended periods, which can be exhausting (and painful) for a novice. Some horse-riding tours offer meals and lodging as well as riding. Post-to-post trail riding allows a rider to stay at different lodgings each night, riding on trails all day.

Horseback Riding Resources

Tourism Ireland has an informative section on its website about horse riding. Visit **www.discoverireland.com**, click on "Things to see & do," then "Activities," and then select "Equestrian."

Two good riding establishments on the west coast are **Dingle Horse Riding,** Ballinaboula, Dingle, County Kerry (✆ **066/915-2199;** www.dinglehorseriding.com), and **Drummindoo Stud & Equestrian Centre,** Knockranny, Westport, County Mayo (✆ **098/25616;** www.drummindoo.com).

In Dublin, you can go trail riding through Phoenix Park with **Ashtown Riding Stables** (✆ **01/838-3807**). They're in the village of Ashtown adjoining the park and only 10 minutes by car or bus (no. 37, 38, 39, or 70) from the city center. Among the other riding centers within easy reach of downtown Dublin are **Carrickmines Equestrian Centre,** Glenamuck Road, Foxrock, Dublin 18 (✆ **01/295-5990;** www.carrickminesequestrian.ie), and **Brennanstown Riding School,** Hollybrook, County Wicklow (✆ **01/286-3778;** www.brennanstownrs.ie). You can see the beaches of Connemara from horseback on a trek with the **Cleggan Riding Centre,** Cleggan, County Galway (✆ **095/44746;** www.clegganridingcentre.com). The center offers beach and mountain treks, and the most popular is a 3-hour ride to Omey Island at low tide.

Hidden Trails (✆ **888/9-TRAILS** [987-2457]; www.hiddentrails.com) offers 7-day guided riding tours in several regions in Ireland, including the Wicklow Mountains, West Cork, and Connemara. The tours are graded easy, moderate, or challenging, and include lodging and meals (breakfast, picnic lunch, and dinner).

KAYAKING

This sport has always been popular with the natives—and no wonder, considering the island's 5,603km (3,472 miles) of coastline, plus its numerous lakes and rivers.

In particular, the coastline provides year-round superb sea-kayaking waters, some of which are remote, with spectacular scenery. In a sea kayak, the wonders of the Irish coast can be investigated up close. You'll find caves, tiny inlets, out-of-the-way cliffs, and reefs inhabited by abundant seabirds, colorful crustaceans, seals, and the occasional dolphin. Many islands are within easy reach of the mainland, and with experience and good conditions, a sea kayaker can reach any of Ireland's island outposts.

A number of adventure centers offer kayaking lessons, and a few schools are devoted solely to kayaking. For those new to the sport or unfamiliar with the Irish coast, a guided excursion is the best option.

Kayaking around Virgin Rock in Ballybunion.

Kayaking Resources

For a rich source of information about kayaking in Ireland, visit the **Irish Canoe Union** website at **www.canoe.ie**.

Courses and day trips for all levels of experience are available from **Deep Blue Sea Kayaking** (✆ **086/820-5627;** www.deepblueseakayaking.com) and **Shearwater Sea Kayaking** (✆ **086/836-8736** or 087/988-5658; www.shearwaterseakayaking.ie). Although kayaking is mainly a summer activity, the latter also runs special winter excursions to the Skerries and Lambay Island in Dublin Bay. Kayaking vacations are also available at **Delphi Mountain Resort,** Leenane, County Galway (✆ **095/42208;** www.delphimountainresort.com).

SAILING

Whether cruising from port to port or dinghy sailing on the lakes, you can experience many regions of Ireland from the water. The craggy and indented coastline has plenty of safe havens for overnight stops—there are more than 140 between Cork Harbor and the Dingle Peninsula alone. This region of West Cork and Kerry is the most popular coastline for cruising, and several companies offer yacht charters.

Some of the harbors in the southwest that are most popular with sailors include Cork, Kinsale, Glandore, Baltimore, and Bantry. On the **west coast,** Killary Harbour, Westport, and Sligo have sailing clubs and are in areas of great beauty. There are also several sailing clubs and yacht-charter companies in the Dublin area.

Sailing Resources

Sailing schools hold courses for sailors at all levels of experience, and sometimes offer day sailing as well. Ireland also has more than 120 yacht and sailing clubs along the coast and lakes. The best sources for information are Tourism Ireland; the **Irish Sailing Association,** 3 Park Rd., Dún Laoghaire, County Dublin

A yellow yacht on the Donegal coast.

A BIT OF adventure

If you're looking for more from your Ireland trip than just a bit of golf or hiking, you might want to try one of the country's adventure centers. These lively, youthful facilities offer a range of guided activities—from rappelling to kite surfing—in some of the country's most remote and beautiful settings, along with accommodations, food, and all you need for a holiday with like-minded folk.

The **Delphi Mountain Resort,** Leenane, County Galway (✆ **095/42208;** www.delphimountainresort.com), is a popular option deep in the mountains of County Galway. There is almost nothing you can't do here; the resort offers courses in kayaking, windsurfing, and raft building, as well as mountaineering, abseiling, hiking, and archery. Everything is reasonably priced, and the atmosphere is laid-back and friendly.

Another option is **Little Killary Adventure Company,** Leenane, County Galway (✆ **095/43411;** www.killaryadventure.com), which will take you on Hobie Cat sailing trips, or guide you through an exploration of the countryside by kayak, water skis, or on foot on hill- and coastal walking tours, straight up on rock-climbing expeditions, and more.

On the southern shores of Carlingford Lough, an hour's drive north of Dublin, the **Carlingford Adventure Centre** (✆ **042/937-3100;** www.carlingfordadventure.com) offers residential and day courses in canoeing, kayaking, sailing, and windsurfing, as well as land-based activities such as rock climbing, archery, zip wire, and the ominously titled "Leap of Faith."

(✆ **01/280-0239;** www.sailing.ie); and *East and North Coasts of Ireland Sailing Directions* and *South and West Coasts of Ireland Sailing Directions* (both published by Imray, Laurie, Norie & Wilson Ltd. of Wych House) from the Irish Cruising Club (**www.irishcruisingclub.com**). The guides give information on harbors, port facilities, tides, and other topics of interest. They are available in bookshops in Ireland or online at www.imray.com.

The **International Sailing Schools Association** is an excellent resource for finding a sailing school; you can find links to members at www.sailingschools.org. **Sailing Ireland** (✆ **053/913-9163;** www.sailingireland.ie) runs a variety of sailing courses, and also offers yacht charters from its base in Bridgetown, County Wexford.

Kinsale Yacht Charters, 2 Castlepark Marina Centre, Kinsale, County Cork (✆ **087/271-0371;** www.kinsaleyachtcharter.com; see chapter 8), is one of the largest charter firms in Ireland and also offers package deals. A full range of yacht sailing options is available from **Sovereign Sailing** (✆ **021/477-4145;** www.sovereignsailing.com). They also offer racing charter packages if money is no object. Yacht charters are also available from **Shannon Sailing Ltd.,** New Harbour, Dromineer, Nenagh, County Tipperary (✆ **067/24499;** www.shannonsailing.com).

WINDSURFING

Windsurfing is increasingly popular in Ireland, and some spots play host to vast flotillas of colorful sails and wet-suited windsurfers when conditions are good.

Some of the best locations are in remote areas of the west coast, and those spots are rarely crowded. Windsurfing schools with boards for rent can be found in most regions of the country, with the greatest concentration on the southeast and southwest coasts.

In Dublin the most popular spot is Dollymount Beach; Salthill, behind Dún Laoghaire Harbour, is another good choice. In the southeast, try Brittas Bay (County Wicklow), Cahore (County Wexford), and Rosslare (County Wexford). Dunmore East (County Waterford), Dungarvan (County Waterford), and Cobh (County Cork) are good in the south. The most challenging waves and winds are in the west, at Brandon Bay on the Dingle Peninsula, Roundstone in Galway, Achill Island in Mayo, and Magheroarty and Rossnowlagh in Donegal.

Because even skilled windsurfers spend a sizable portion of their time in the water, the water quality is surely a concern. The Republic of Ireland has 27 designated European Union Blue Flag beaches and marinas, and Northern Ireland has 12. To find a complete listing or to check out a particular beach in advance, go to **www.blueflag.org**.

Windsurfing Resources

Equipment rental and lessons are widely available on Ireland's coasts and lakes. Try the following centers: the **Surfdock Centre,** Grand Canal Dock Yard, Ringsend, Dublin 4 (✆ **01/668-3945;** www.surfdock.ie); the **Dunmore East Adventure Centre,** Stoney Cove, Dunmore East, County Waterford (✆ **051/383783;** www.dunmoreadventure.com); the **Oysterhaven Centre,** Oysterhaven, Kinsale, County Cork (✆ **021/477-0738;** www.oysterhaven.com); and, in the North, **Craigavon Watersports Centre,** 1 Lake Rd., Craigavon, County Armagh, BT64 1AS (✆ **028/3834-2669;** www.craigavonactivity.org).

If kite surfing is your thing, check out the website **www.kitesurfing.ie**. It offers advice on where to buy or rent boards, the best locations, and weather conditions, and it also hooks you up with other kite surfers.

DUBLIN

5

Teach Tábhairne
Pub
HE TEMPLE BAR
WM. FLANNERY
LIVE
MUSIC
DAILY
EST WHISKY
D.W.D.
ISKY DISTILLERY

For such an ancient town, Dublin is doing a pretty good job of not showing its age. Despite its stony gray appearance, the Irish capital is actually one of Europe's most youthful cities. Around half of its residents are under the age of 28—and almost a full third of Ireland's entire population live in the greater Dublin area. Dublin's oldest landmarks are still among its most interesting, but they're enlivened now by a new wealth of modern attractions: Edgy bars and cafes buzz alongside pubs that have stood for centuries, while chic boutiques are snuggled into the medieval precincts of Old City. It's yours to discover afresh—and even if you think you know what to expect, you're almost certain to be surprised by what you find.

ESSENTIALS

Arriving

BY PLANE **Aer Lingus** (✆ **01/814-1111;** www.aerlingus.com)**,** Ireland's national airline, operates regular, direct scheduled flights between Dublin International Airport and numerous cities worldwide. From the U.S., direct routes are Boston, Chicago (O'Hare), and New York (J.F.K). **American Airlines** (✆ **1800/433-7300;** www.aa.com), **Delta** (✆ **800/221-1212;** www.delta.com) and **United** (✆ **1800/864-8331;** www.united.com) all fly direct to Dublin from at least one of those same cities. From Canada, direct flights are operated by **Air Canada** (✆ **1888/247-2262;** www.aircanada.com). Most of the major European airlines have direct flights to Dublin.

Dublin International Airport (✆ **01/814-1111;** www.dublinairport.com) is 11km (6¾ miles) north of the city center. A travel information desk in the arrivals concourse provides information on public bus and rail services throughout the country.

An excellent airport-to-city shuttle bus service called **AirCoach** operates 24 hours a day, making runs at 15-minute intervals. Its buses go direct from the airport to Dublin's city center and south side. Not all the major stops are covered on every service, so do check that you've got the right one before you board. City center fares are €6–€7 one-way, depending on where you are going; and to Ballsbridge, Dún Laoghaire or Dalkey, around €10. Children aged 5 to 12 are €2–€5; children 13 and over are counted as adults. You buy your ticket from the driver. Although AirCoach is slightly more expensive than the Dublin Bus (see below), it makes fewer stops, so it is faster (the journey to the city center takes about 45 min.), and it brings you into the hotel districts. To confirm AirCoach departures and arrivals, call ✆ **01/844-7118** or find it online at **www.aircoach.ie**.

PREVIOUS PAGE: **Temple Bar in Dublin, known for lively nightlife.**

If you need to connect with the Irish bus or rail service, Dublin Bus's route 747, otherwise known as the **Airlink** (✆ **01/844-4265;** www.dublinbus.ie), provides express coach services from the airport into central Dublin and beyond. Buses go to the city's central bus station, **Busáras,** on Store Street and on to **Connolly** and **Heuston** railway stations. Service runs daily from 6am until 11:30pm (Sun 7am–11:20pm), with departures every 15 to 20 minutes. One-way fare is €6 for adults and €3 for children 11 and under.

Finally, **Dublin Bus** (✆ **01/873-4222;** www.dublinbus.ie) has regular daily connections between the airport and the city center from 6am to 11:30pm. The one-way trip takes about 30 minutes, and the one-way fare is €6 adults, €3 children. Consult the travel information desk in the arrivals concourse to figure out which bus takes you closest to your hotel.

For speed and ease—especially if you have a lot of luggage—a **taxi** is the best way to get directly to your hotel or guesthouse. Depending on your destination, fares average between €20 and €35. A tip of a couple of euro is standard. Taxis are lined up at a first-come, first-served taxi stand outside the arrivals terminal.

Major international and local car-rental companies operate desks at Dublin Airport.

BY FERRY Passenger and car ferries from Britain arrive at the Dublin Ferryport, on the eastern end of the North Docks, and at the Dún Laoghaire Ferryport, in the city's southeastern suburbs. Call **Irish Ferries** (✆ **0818/300-400;** www.irishferries.ie), **P&O Irish Sea** (✆ **01/407-3434;** www.poirishsea.com), or **Stena Line** (✆ **01/204-7777;** www.stenaline.com) for bookings and information. Buses and taxis service both ports.

BY TRAIN **Irish Rail** (✆ **1890/77-88-99** for timetables, ✆ **1850/366-222** to prebook tickets; www.irishrail.ie), Iarnród Éireann in Gaelic, operates daily train service to Dublin from Belfast, Northern Ireland, and all major cities in the Irish Republic, including Cork, Galway, Limerick, Killarney, Sligo, Wexford, and Waterford. Trains from the south, west, and southwest arrive at **Heuston Station,** Kingsbridge, off St. John's Road; from the north and northwest at **Connolly Station,** Amiens Street; and from the southeast at **Pearse Station,** Westland Row, Tara Street.

BY BUS **Bus Éireann** (✆ **01/836-6111;** www.buseireann.ie) operates daily express coach and local bus service from all major cities and towns in Ireland into Dublin's central bus station, **Busáras,** Store Street.

BY CAR If you are arriving by car from other parts of Ireland or on a car ferry from Britain, all main roads lead into the heart of Dublin and are well signposted to **An Lar** (City Centre). To bypass the city center, the East Link toll bridge (€2) and West Link are signposted, and M50 circuits the city on three sides. From Wexford Town, Galway, or Belfast the drive takes around 2 hours; from Cork, 2½ hours.

Visitor Information

Dublin Tourism operates several walk-in visitor centers in greater Dublin that are open every day except Christmas. The principal center is on Suffolk Street, Dublin 2, open from Monday to Saturday from 9am to 8:30pm, Sunday and bank holidays 10:30am to 3pm. The Suffolk Street office has a currency exchange counter, a car-rental counter, an accommodations-reservations service, bus and

Dublin Orientation

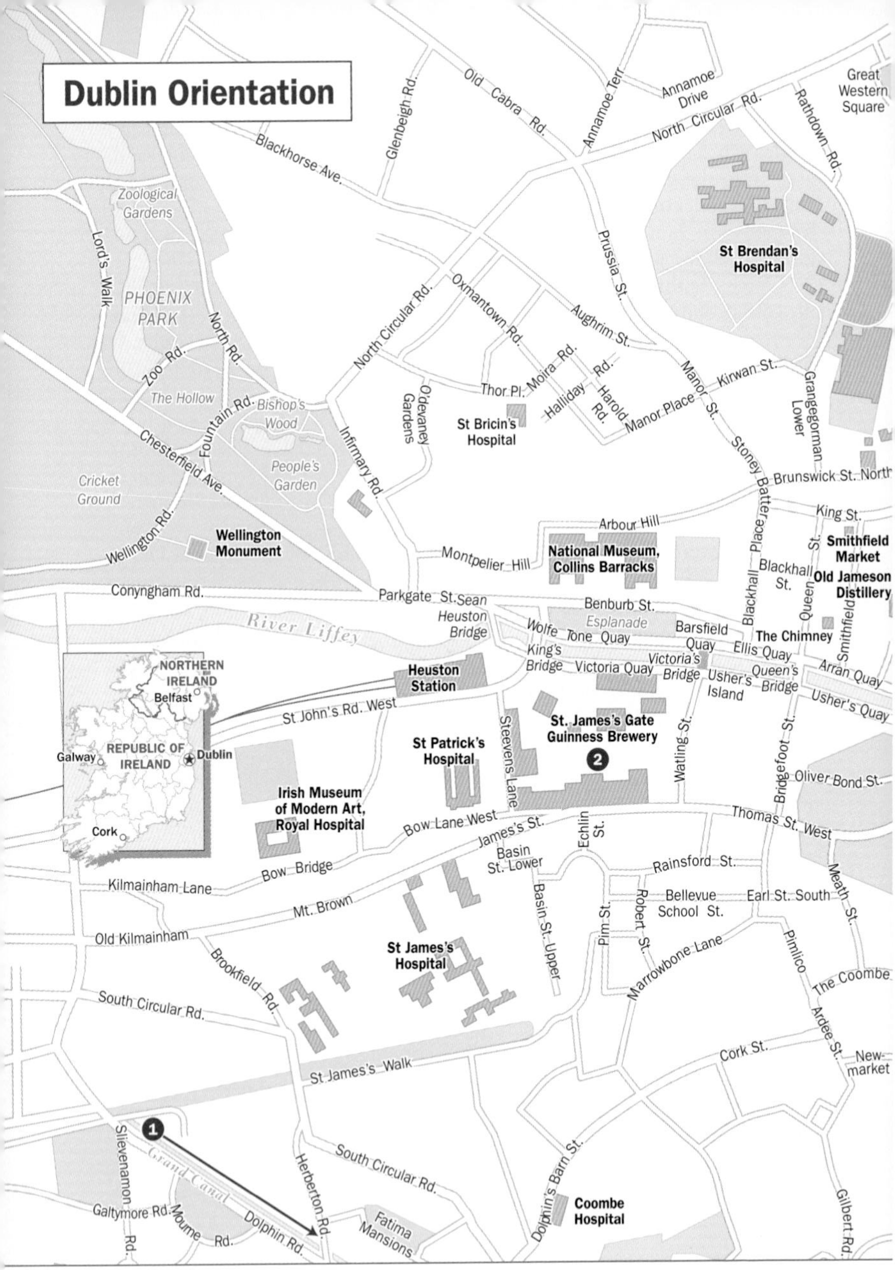

Busáras/Central Bus Station **5**
Connolly DART Station **4**
Dublin Castle/City Hall **9**
Dublin Tourism Office **10**
Fitzwilliam Square **17**
Grafton Street **15**
Grand Canal **1**
Guinness Brewery **2**
Leinster House **14**
Merrion Square **13**
O'Connell Street **3**
Old City/Historic Area **8**
Pearse DART Station **12**
St. Stephen's Green **16**
Tara Street DART Station **6**
Temple Bar **7**
Trinity College **11**

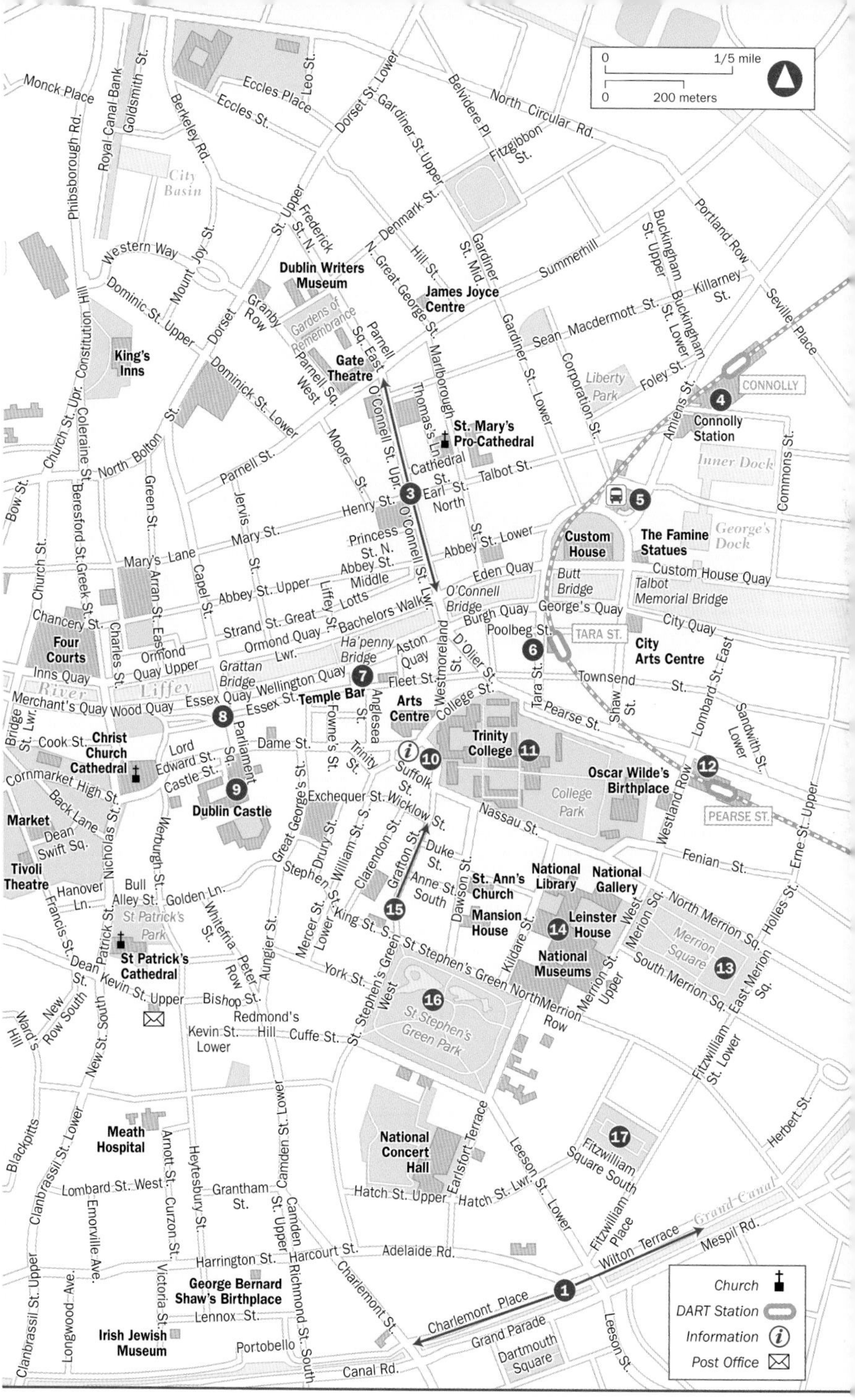
0
1/5 mile
0
200 meters
Monck Place
Phibsborough Rd.
Royal Canal Bank
Goldsmith St.
Berkeley Rd.
Eccles St.
Eccles Place
Leo St.
Dorset St. Lower
Gardiner St. Upper
Belvidere Pl.
North Circular Rd.
Fitzgibbon St.
City Basin
St. Upper Frederick St. N.
Denmark St.
Western Way
Mount Joy St.
Dominic St. Upper
Dorset St.
Granby Row
Dublin Writers Museum
Gardens of Remembrance
Parnell Sq. East
Parnell Sq. West
Gate Theatre
N. Great George St.
Hill St.
James Joyce Centre
Gardiner St. Mid.
Summerhill
Buckingham St. Upper
Buckingham St. Lower
Portland Row
Killarney St.
Seville Place
Sean Macdermott St.
Gardiner St. Lower
Corporation St.
Liberty Park
Foley St.
Amiens St.
CONNOLLY
Connolly Station
King's Inns
Constitution Hill
Church St. Upr.
Coleraine St.
Dominick St. Lower
North Bolton St.
Parnell St.
O'Connell St. Upr.
Moore St.
Thomas's Ln.
Marlborough St.
St. Mary's Pro-Cathedral
Cathedral St.
Talbot St.
Earl St. North
Inner Dock
Commons St.
Bow St.
Beresford St.
Green St.
Jervis St.
Henry St.
Mary St.
Mary's Lane
Princess St. N.
Abbey St. Middle
Abbey St. Lower
Abbey St. Upper
O'Connell St. Lwr.
Custom House
The Famine Statues
George's Dock
Custom House Quay
Eden Quay
Butt Bridge
Talbot Memorial Bridge
Church St.
Greek St.
Arran St. East
Capel St.
Liffey St.
Lotts
Bachelors Walk
O'Connell Bridge
Burgh Quay
George's Quay
City Quay
Chancery St.
Four Courts
Charles St.
Ormond Quay Upper
Strand St. Great
Ormond Quay Lwr.
Ha'penny Bridge
Aston Quay
Westmoreland St.
D'Olier St.
Poolbeg St.
TARA ST.
City Arts Centre
Inns Quay
River Liffey
Grattan Bridge
Wellington Quay
Fleet St.
Townsend St.
Merchant's Quay
Wood Quay
Essex Quay
Essex St.
Temple Bar
Anglesea St.
Arts Centre
College St.
Tara St.
Pearse St.
Shaw St.
Lombard St. East
Sandwith St. Lower
Bridge St. Lwr.
Cook St.
Christ Church Cathedral
Lord Edward St.
Parliament Sq.
Dame St.
Fowne's St.
Trinity St.
Trinity College
Oscar Wilde's Birthplace
Westland Row
Cornmarket
High St.
Castle St.
Dublin Castle
Great George's St. S.
Exchequer St.
Suffolk St.
Wicklow St.
College Park
Nassau St.
PEARSE ST.
Erne St. Upper
Back Lane
Market
Dean Swift Sq.
Nicholas St.
Drury St.
William St. S.
Clarendon St.
Grafton St.
Duke St.
Fenian St.
Tivoli Theatre
Hanover Ln.
Francis St.
Bull Alley St.
Werburgh St.
Golden Ln.
Stephen St. Lower
Anne St. South
Dawson St.
St. Ann's Church
National Library
National Gallery
North Merrion Sq.
Holles St.
St Patrick's Park
Whitefriar St.
Mercer St. Lower
King St. S.
Mansion House
Kildare St.
Leinster House
Merrion Sq. West
Merrion Square
Patrick St.
St Patrick's Cathedral
Dean St.
Kevin St. Upper
Peter Row
Aungier St.
York St.
St Stephen's Green West
St Stephen's Green North
National Museums
Merrion St. Upper
Merrion Row
South Merrion Sq.
East Merion Sq.
Ward's Hill
New Row South
New St. South
Bishop St.
Redmond's Hill
Kevin St. Lower
Cuffe St.
St Stephen's Green Park
Fitzwilliam St. Lower
Herbert St.
Blackpitts
Clanbrassil St. Lower
Meath Hospital
Arnott St.
Heytesbury St.
Camden St. Lower
National Concert Hall
Earlsfort Terrace
Leeson St. Lower
Fitzwilliam Square South
Lombard St. West
Emorville Ave.
Curzon St.
Grantham St.
St. Upper
Camden
Hatch St. Upper
Hatch St. Lwr.
Grand Canal
Fitzwilliam Place
Wilton Terrace
Mespil Rd.
Harrington St.
Harcourt St.
Adelaide Rd.
Charlemont St.
Clanbrassil St. Upper
Longwood Ave.
Victoria St.
George Bernard Shaw's Birthplace
Lennox St.
Richmond St. South
Charlemont Place
Grand Parade
Leeson St.
Irish Jewish Museum
Portobello
Dartmouth Square
Canal Rd.
Church
DART Station
Information
Post Office

Grafton Street is bustling with shoppers, buskers, and curious passerby.

rail information desks, a gift shop, and a cafe. For accommodation reservations throughout Ireland by credit card (including some good last-minute deals on Dublin hotels), contact Dublin Tourism at ✆ **1890/324-583** or **www.visitdublin.com**. A tourism center is also in the arrivals concourse of Dublin Airport and the ferry terminal at Dún Laoghaire Harbor.

At any of these centers you can pick up the free **Totally Dublin,** a monthly entertainment guide. Alternatively, the website **In Dublin** (www.indublin.ie), has a comprehensive what's-on section.

City Layout

Dublin is divided down the middle by the curves of the River Liffey, which empties into the sea at the city's farthest edge. To the north and south, canals encircle the city center: The Royal Canal arcs across the north and the Grand Canal through the south. Traditionally, the area south of the river has been Dublin's buzzing, prosperous hub. It still holds most of the best hotels, restaurants, shops, and sights, but the Northside is on the upswing, and hip new bars and hotels give it a trendy edge. Dublin is compact and easily walked in an hour. In fact, a 45-minute walk from the bucolic peace of St. Stephen's Green, up Grafton Street, and across the Liffey to the top of O'Connell Street offers a good overview of the city's prosperous present and troubled past.

MAIN STREETS & SQUARES In the town center just south of the river, **Dame Street,** which changes its name to College Green, Westmoreland Street, and Lord Edward Street at various points, is the main east-west artery connecting **Trinity College** with **Dublin Castle** and **Christ Church Cathedral.** On one

Murky Origins

For most visitors, the very word "Dublin" may bring to mind a heady, romantic mix of history and good times to come, but it actually has a more prosaic origin. The name comes from the ancient Celtic words *"dubh linn,"* meaning "the black pool." Specifically, it refers to a natural inlet where the River Liffey met the River Poddle, and the waters were dark and murky. Long since buried, the inlet is thought to be somewhere around Dublin Castle.

However, an allusion to these watery origins still survives in the city's Gaelic name, *Baile Átha Cliath.* It means "the town of the hurdled ford"—a ford being a point where a stream or river crosses a road. When fords were "hurdled" in medieval times, it meant that they were covered at low tide with woven sheets of willow, making them easier to cross.

side of Dame Street are the winding medieval lanes of **Temple Bar,** Dublin's party central thanks to plenty of pubs. On the other side of Dame Street are tributary streets lined with shops and cafes. Where Dame Street turns into College Green, the sturdy gray stone walls of Trinity College make an excellent landmark to get your bearings. At the southwest corner is the top of **Grafton Street**—a lively pedestrianized shopping lane crowded with tourists, musicians, and artists, which leads to the bucolic, statue-filled peace of **St. Stephen's Green.** From there, heading back up via **Kildare Street** will take you past

St. Stephens Green Park is serene despite the crowds passing through en route to shops and restaurants.

Leinster House, where the Irish Parliament meets, and a turn to the right brings you to **Merrion Square,** another of Dublin's extraordinarily well-preserved Georgian squares.

To get to the Northside, most visitors choose to walk across the photogenic arch of the **Ha'penny Bridge** (see p. 111), but most locals take the less attractive **O'Connell Bridge** nearby. You can be different and cross via the Ha'penny's sleekly modern neighbor, the **Millennium Bridge,** which is beautifully illuminated after dark. The O'Connell Bridge leads directly onto **O'Connell Street,** a wide, statue-lined boulevard that is the north's main thoroughfare. O'Connell Street runs north to **Parnell Square,** which holds a couple of marvelous museums and marks the edge of central Dublin. From the bottom to the top, O'Connell Street is lined with statues, starting with an absurdly ornate representation of the titular politician Daniel O'Connell surrounded by angels (which still have bullet holes left from the Easter Rising). The street running along the Liffey's embankment is called the **North Quays** by all, though its name changes on virtually every block, reflecting the long-gone docks that once lined it.

In the older section of the city, **High Street** is the gateway to medieval and Viking Dublin, from the city's two medieval cathedrals to the old city walls and nearby Dublin Castle.

Dublin Neighborhoods in Brief

TRINITY COLLEGE AREA On the south side of the River Liffey, is Trinity College with its shady quadrangles and atmospheric stone buildings. It's virtually the dead center of the city and is surrounded by bookstores, shops, and noisy traffic. This area lies in the Dublin 2 postal code.

TEMPLE BAR Wedged between Trinity College and the Old City, this is Dublin's party hub, and it's packed with bars, discos, and pubs. During the day, it's quieter and more refined thanks to good shops, two worthwhile art galleries, recording studios, and theaters. But at night, this is largely the stamping ground of young tourists looking for lots of alcohol, and it's easy to feel over the hill here if you're over 25. This area is in the Dublin 2 and Dublin 8 postal codes.

OLD CITY Dating from Viking and medieval times, the cobblestone enclave of the historic Old City includes Dublin Castle, the remnants of the city's original walls, and Christ Church and St. Patrick's cathedrals. It encompasses the Dublin 2 and 8 zones.

LIBERTIES Adjacent to Old City, the Liberties district takes its name from the fact that it was once just outside the city walls, and, therefore, exempt from Dublin's jurisdiction. Although it prospered in its early days, Liberties fell on hard times in the 17th and 18th centuries and has only felt the touch of urban renewal in the last decade or so. Its main claim to fame is the Guinness Brewery. Most of this area is in the Dublin 8 zone.

ST. STEPHEN'S GREEN/GRAFTON STREET AREA The biggest tourist draw in town, this district is home to Dublin's finest hotels, restaurants, and shops. The neighborhood is filled with impressive Georgian architecture and is primarily a business and shopping zone. It is part of Dublin 2.

FITZWILLIAM & MERRION SQUARES These two little square parks between Trinity College and St. Stephen's Green are surrounded by grand Georgian town houses. Some of Dublin's most famous citizens once lived here; today many of the houses are offices for doctors, lawyers, and government agencies. This area is part of the Dublin 2 zone.

O'CONNELL STREET (NORTH OF THE LIFFEY) The epicenter of Dublin's stormy political struggles, the north was once a fashionable area, but it lost much of its charm as it declined in the 20th century. It has experienced something of a resurgence in recent years, and now is home to some high-profile hotels, shops, and restaurants. But it still feels a little more down-at-heel than the Southside. With four theaters in walking distance of O'Connell Street, this is also Dublin's theater district. It is mostly in Dublin 1.

NORTH QUAYS (the Liffey Riverbanks on the Northside) Once the center of Dublin's shipping industry, this is now a trendy address for hotels, bars, and clubs. The quays are actually a series of streets named after the wharves that once stood at water's edge. The quays start near the mouth of the Liffey and end in the green peace of Phoenix Park. This area is mostly in Dublin 1.

BALLSBRIDGE/EMBASSY ROW Immediately south of the Grand Canal, this upscale suburb is just barely within walking distance of the city center. Primarily a prestigious residential area, it is also home to hotels, restaurants, and embassies. This area is part of the Dublin 4 zone.

Getting Around

If your stay in Dublin is short, geography is on your side. The vast majority of the capital's best sites are concentrated in the city center, an area of no more than a few square kilometers. This leads to your first, most important (and quite frankly, easiest) decision: If you have a car, leave it behind at your hotel (or as close as you can get—parking is notoriously difficult). Dublin's roads are crowded and confusing. Baffling one-way streets, bad signage, and terrible traffic are all common problems.

However, cars aside, Dublin is a very easy and convenient city to get around. Public transportation is good and getting better, taxis are plentiful and reasonably priced, and your own two feet can easily carry you from one end of town to the other. In fact, with its perennial traffic and parking problems, it's a city where the foot is mightier than the wheel.

BY BUS After walking, buses are the most convenient and practical way to get between the city center sights. Dublin Bus operates a fleet of double-deckers, single-deckers, and minibuses (the latter charmingly called "imps"). Most originate on or near O'Connell Street, Abbey Street, and Eden Quay on the Northside, and at Aston Quay, College Street, and Fleet Street on the south side. Bus stops resembling big blue or green lollipops are every few blocks on main thoroughfares. To tell where the bus is going, look at the destination street and bus number above its front window; those heading for the city center indicate that with an odd mix of Latin and Gaelic: via an lar.

Bus service runs daily throughout the city, starting at 6am (10am on Sun), with the last bus at about 11:30pm. On Friday and Saturday nights, **Nitelink** service runs from the city center to the suburbs from midnight to 4am. Buses operate every 30 minutes for most runs; schedules are posted on revolving notice boards at bus stops.

Inner-city fares are based on distances traveled. Daytime journeys that take place entirely within the designated "City Centre Zone" cost €0.70. This stretches

leap CARDS

If you're likely to use public transport a lot while in Dublin, consider getting a **Leap Card.** They allow you to pre-pay for reduced-cost travel on all Dublin buses (including Airlink and Nightlink), DART, Luas, and commuter trains. You can buy them at around 400 shops in and around the city—look out for the distinctive green logo depicting a rather over-excited looking frog in mid-leap—including the small **Easons, Kiosk,** and **Spa** shops within Dublin Airport. You can also get them from ticket machines in some city center DART and railway stations, or order them online at **www.leapcard.ie**. They're free, but you have to pay a refundable deposit of €5 adults, €3 children, and buy at least €5 worth of credit up-front.

from Parnell Square in the north, to Connolly Station and Merrion Square in the east, St. Stephen's Green in the south, and Ormond Quay in the west. Longer journeys cost anything from €1.65 all the way up to around €4.50 if you're going as far as the outer suburbs.

You pay on board the bus, using an automatic fare machine located in front of the driver. **No Dublin bus accepts notes or gives change.** If you don't have the exact money in coins, the driver will issue you with a "change receipt." You must then take this to the Dublin Bus headquarters on O'Connell Street to collect your change (a process not designed to encourage refunds). The sole exception to this rule is route 747 ("Airlink"), which runs between the airport and the city center. It accepts notes and gives change normally.

BY DART An acronym for Dublin Area Rapid Transit, the electric DART trains travel above ground, linking the city center stations at **Connolly Station, Tara Street,** and **Pearse Street** with suburbs and seaside communities as far as Malahide to the north and Greystones to the south. Service operates roughly every 10 to 20 minutes Monday to Saturday from around 6am to midnight and Sunday from 9:30am to 11pm. For further information, contact DART, Dublin Pearse Station (✆ **01/703-3592;** www.dart.ie).

BY TRAM The sleek, modern (and wheelchair accessible) light rail tram system known as **Luas** runs from around 5:30am to 12:30am Monday to Friday, 6:30am to 12:30am Saturday, and 7am to 11:30pm on Sunday. (The last trams to certain stations are earlier—be sure to check the timetable). There are two lines, Red and Green: The Green Line links St. Stephen's Green with Sandyford in the south; the Red Line runs between the Point, near the O2 in Dublin Docklands, and Connolly Railway Station, down to the southwestern suburbs of Saggart and Tallaght. For further information, contact Luas (✆ **01/800-300-604** or 01/461-4910; www.luas.ie).

ON FOOT Marvelously compact, Dublin is ideal for walking. Just remember to look right and then left (and in the direction opposite your instincts if you're from North America) before crossing the street. Pedestrians have the right of way at specially marked, zebra-striped crossings (these intersections usually have two flashing lights).

BY TAXI It's very difficult to hail a taxi on the street; instead, they line up at taxi stands (called "ranks") outside major hotels, at bus and train stations, and on

learning the lingo: "BANK HOLIDAYS"

No, they don't give banks extra vacation in Ireland. Though you can expect to see this sign a lot, especially on lists of opening times, the phrase simply means a public holiday. Many shops are either closed or run on reduced hours on Bank Holidays.

There are currently nine regular Bank Holidays in Ireland: New Year's Day (January 1st); St. Patrick's Day (March 17th); Easter Monday; the first Mondays in every month from May to August, except July; the final Monday in October; Christmas Day (December 25th) and St. Stephen's Day (December 26th).

prime thoroughfares such as Upper O'Connell Street, College Green, and the north side of St. Stephen's Green. You can also phone for a taxi; see the numbers listed in the "Fast Facts" section below.

[FastFACTS] DUBLIN

ATMs/Banks Nearly all banks are open Monday to Friday 10am to 4pm (to 5pm Thurs). Convenient locations include the **Bank of Ireland,** at 2 College Green, Dublin 2, 88 Camden St. Lower, Dublin 1, and at Trinity College; and the **Allied Irish Bank (AIB),** at 100 Grafton St., Dublin 2, and 37 O'Connell St., Dublin 1.

Currency Exchange Currency-exchange services, signposted as **Bureau de Change,** are in most Dublin banks and at many branches of the Irish post office system, known as **An Post.** A bureau de change operates daily during flight arrival and departure times at Dublin Airport. Some hotels and travel agencies offer bureau de change services. ***Tip:*** The best rate of exchange is almost always when you use your bank card at an ATM.

Dentists For dental emergencies, your hotel will usually contact a dentist for you; otherwise, try **Smiles Dental,** 28 O'Connell St. (✆ **1850/323-323**); **Molesworth Dental Surgery,** 2 Molesworth Place (✆ **01/661-5544**).

Doctors & Hospitals For emergencies, dial ✆ **999.** If you need a doctor, your hotel should be able to contact one for you. Otherwise you could try **Dame Street Medical Center,** 16 Dame St. (✆ **01/679-0754**), or the **Suffolk Street Surgery,** 107 Grafton St. (✆ **01/679-8181**).

Emergencies For police, fire, or other emergencies, dial ✆ **999.**

Luggage Storage If check-out at your hotel is in the morning and your flight in the evening (or you arrive too early to check in), many hotels will look after your baggage. Alternatively, **Global Internet Café,** 8 Lower O'Connell St. (✆ **01/878-0295**) can store bags securely. There's also a "Left Luggage" facility at the Terminal 1 parking lot at Dublin Airport.

Pharmacies **City Pharmacy,** 14 Dame St. (✆ **01/670-4523**) stays open until 10pm weekdays, 9pm Sat; **Boots the Chemist,** 20 Henry St. (✆ **01/873-0209**) or 12 Grafton St. (✆ **01/677-3000**), stays open until 9pm Thursday and Friday, 7pm Saturday and Sunday, and 8pm Monday to Wednesday. Dublin does not have 24-hr. pharmacies.

Mail and Postage **General Post Office,** O'Connell St. (✆ **01/705-8833**) is open Monday through Saturday, 8:30am–6pm. Postage for a letter or postcard costs €0.65 within Ireland and Northern Ireland; €0.90 to the rest of the world.

Newspapers & Magazines Look out for **Totally Dublin,** a free monthly entertainment guide, at tourism offices. One of the best online magazines is **In Dublin** (www.indublin.ie), which has comprehensive event listings. The monthly **Gay Community News** (www.theoutmost.com), another free magazine, is also full of entertainment listings; there's a print edition, but the online version is completely free.

Taxis Taxi ranks are outside major hotels, at bus and train stations, and on Upper O'Connell Street, College Green, and the north side of St. Stephen's Green. To call a cab try **Co-Op** (✆ **01/677-7777**), **Trinity** (✆ **01/708-2222**), and **VIP/ACE Taxis** (✆ **01/478-3333**).

EXPLORING DUBLIN

Wandering Dublin—just walking down its Georgian streets with a map only in case you get *really* lost—is one of the great pleasures of a visit here. The city center, where the vast majority of the sights are to be found, is small enough that there's almost no way you can go wrong. One minute, you're walking along a quiet leafy street and suddenly the Irish Parliament appears before you. A few minutes later, it's gorgeous Merrion Square. Then, you're upon the granite buildings of Trinity College—and on and on. So pack a sturdy pair of shoes, have your umbrella at the ready, and head out to discover how rewarding this wonderful old town can be.

Top Attractions

Book of Kells and Old Library

★ This hand-drawn manuscript of the four gospels, dating to the year 800, is one of Ireland's national treasures. The elaborate scripting and colorful illumination drawn by Irish monks is undeniably magnificent. Unfortunately, you'll find it hard to see past the hordes of onlookers into the dim glass box where it is kept, and you're handsomely charged for the privilege. However, the Library's **Long Room** goes a long way toward making up for that. The grand, chained library holds many rare works on Irish history and presents frequently changing displays of classic works. The Book of Kells is located in the Old Library building, on the south side of Library Square, inside the main campus.

The Library Building, Trinity College, College Green, Dublin 2. ✆ **01/896-2320.** www.tcd.ie/Library/bookofkells. Admission €9; €10 including campus tour. May–Sept Mon–Sat 9:30am–5pm; Sun 9:30am–4:30pm; Oct–Apr

Trinity College in Dublin, home of the Book of Kells.

LOCAL hero: SIR ALFRED CHESTER BEATTY

Few people embody the term "citizen of the world" as much as Sir Alfred Chester Beatty. Born in New York in 1875, Beatty's American mining business earned him the nickname "the King of Copper"—and a multimillion-dollar fortune to boot. This fabulous wealth gave him the means to pursue his passion for ancient manuscripts and works of art, and by the time he was an old man, his collection rivaled some of the world's greatest museums. Beatty became a British citizen in the 1930s and was knighted by Queen Elizabeth in 1954, after he made a generous bequest to the British Museum. However, he left the vast majority of his collection to Ireland—his ancestral home and a place he always loved. In return Beatty was made an honorary citizen in 1957. He died 11 years later in Monaco, but was brought back to Dublin for a state funeral—to date the only civilian to be given this honor. However, despite all this, Beatty is a surprisingly little-known figure in his adoptive home today. Many Dublin tourist guides don't list the Chester Beatty Museum among the city's top attractions, and we've even spoken to locals who had never heard of the museum—or the man himself—at all.

Mon–Sat 9:30am–5pm; Sun noon–4:30pm. DART: Pearse St., Connolly St. Luas: Lower Abbey St., St. Stephen's Green. Bus: College Green entrance: 7N, 15N, 15X, 44N, 46N, 48N, 49N, 51D, 51X, 54N, 56A, 70B, 70X, 77A, 77N, 92. Nassau St. entrance (for Old Library/Book of Kells): 25X, 32X, 33X, 41X, 51D, 51X, 58X, 67X, 84X, 92.

Chester Beatty Library ★★★ This dazzling collection of early religious texts and other priceless artifacts is named in honor of Sir Alfred Chester Beatty, an Anglo-American industrialist who bequeathed his unique private collection to the Irish nation when he died in 1968. And what a collection it is! Beatty was one of the great 20th-century adventurer-collectors, of the kind that simply could not exist today. Highlights of the bequest include breathtaking illuminated gospels; 8th and 9th century Qurans; sacred Buddhist texts from Burma and Tibet; nearly 1,000 Japanese prints from the Edo era; jade and snuff bottles from China; and cuneiform writing tablets dating back nearly 5,000 years. If there's a better museum of this size in Ireland, we have yet to find it. Why queue and pay €9 to see two pages from the Book of Kells when you can lose yourself in this wonderful place for free?

On the grounds of Dublin Castle, Dame St., Dublin 2. ✆ **01/407-0750.** www.cbl.ie. Free admission. May–Sept Mon–Fri 10am–5:30pm; Sat 11am–5:30pm; Sun 1pm–5pm; Oct–Apr Tues–Fri 10am–5:30pm; Sat 11am–5:30pm; Sun 1pm–5pm. Luas: Jervis. Bus: 37, 39, 39A, 39B, 39C, 49, 49A, 49X, 50, 50X, 56A, 65X, 70, 70A, 70X, 77, 77A, 77X, 123.

Christ Church Cathedral ★★ This magnificent cathedral was designed to be seen from the river, so walk to it from the riverside in order to truly appreciate its size. It dates from 1038, when Sitric, Danish king of Dublin, built the first wooden Christ Church here. In 1171, the original foundation was extended into a cruciform and rebuilt in stone by the Norman warrior Strongbow. The present structure dates mainly from 1871 to 1878, when a huge restoration took place—the work done then remains controversial to this day, as much of the building's

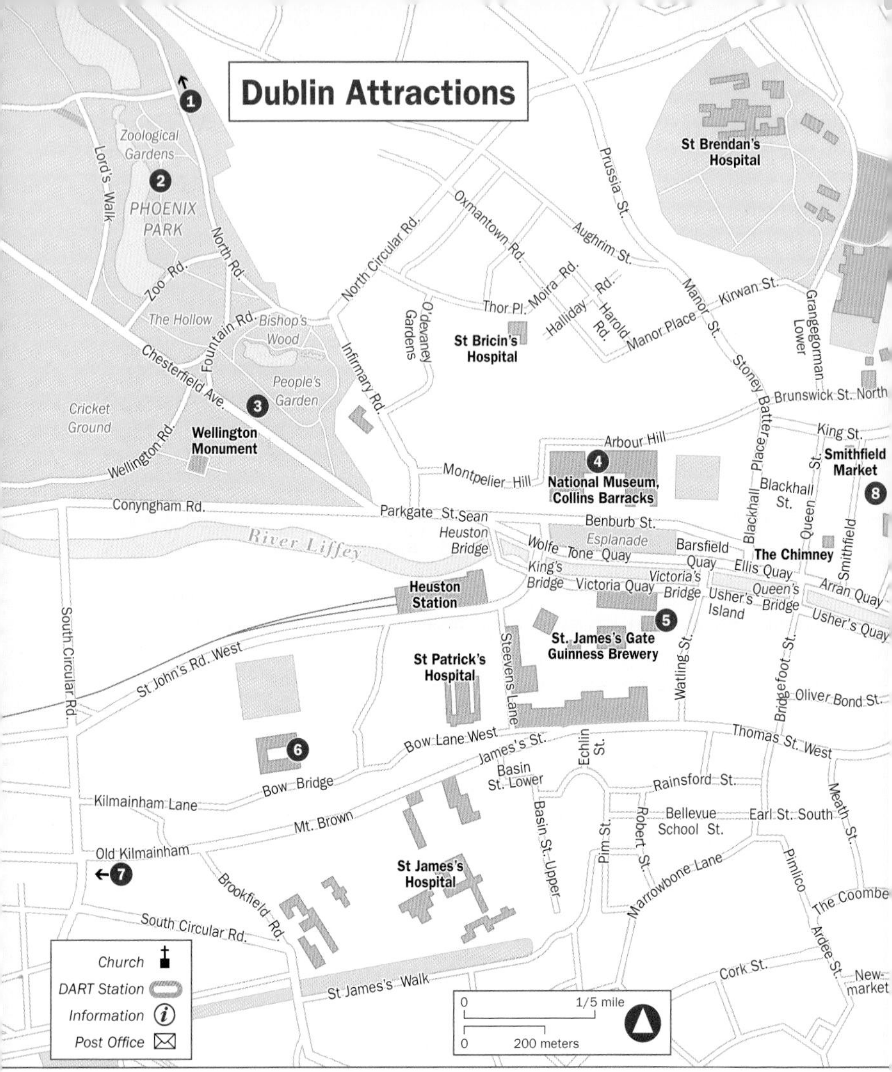

Abbey Theatre **18**
The Ark **28**
Avoca **36**
Book of Kells/Old Library **37**
Brown Thomas **39**
Casino Marino **9**
Chester Beatty Library **32**
Christ Church Cathedral **27**
Claddagh Records **17**
Croke Park Stadium & GAA Museum **20**
Custom House **21**
Dalkey **55**
The Design Tower **38**
Dublinia **26**
Dublin Castle **31**
Dublin Writers Museum **10**
Dublin Zoo **2**
Dún Laoghaire **54**
An Evening of Food, Folklore & Fairies **24**
The Four Courts **15**
Gaiety Theatre **44**
The Gate Theatre **13**
General Post Office **16**
Grafton Street **45**
Guinness Storehouse **5**
Ha'Penny Bridge **23**
Hugh Lane Gallery **11**
Irish Film Institute **30**
Irish Museum of Modern Art **6**
The Irish President's House (Áras an Uachtaráin) **1**
James Joyce Centre **12**
Kilmainham Gaol **7**
Leinster House **48**
The Little Museum of Dublin **49**
Marsh's Library **41**
National Gallery of Ireland **47**
National Library of Ireland **46**
National Museum of Ireland; Archaeology **51**

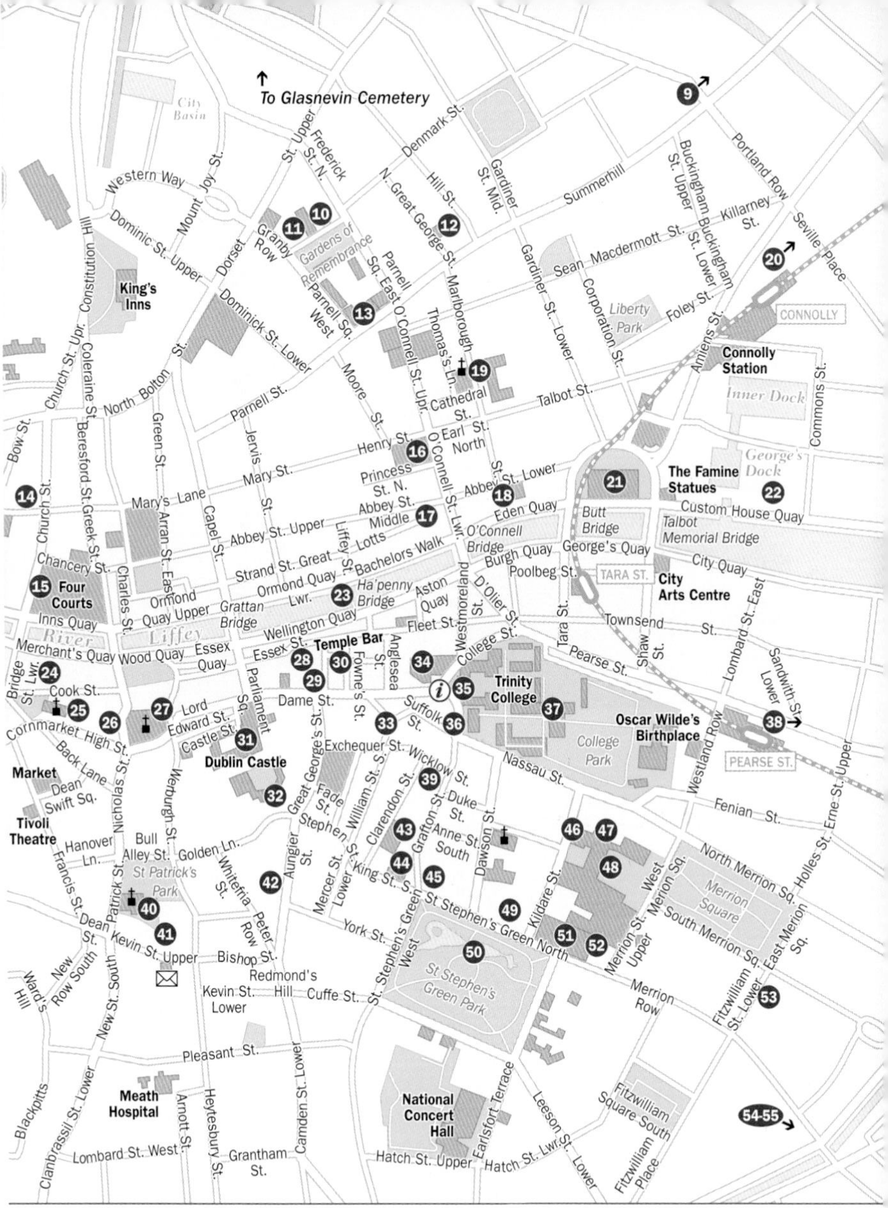

National Museum of Ireland; Decorative Arts & History, Collins Barracks **4**
National Museum of Ireland; Natural History **52**
Number Tweny-Nine: Georgian House Museum **53**
Old Jameson Distillery **8**
The O2 **22**
Parliament House **34**
Phoenix Park **3**
Powerscourt Townhouse Centre **33**
St. Audeon's Church **25**
St. Mary's Pro Cathedral **19**
St. Michan's Church **14**
St. Patrick's Cathedral **40**
St. Stephen's Green **50**
St. Teresa's Church **43**
Temple Bar Gallery **29**
Trinity College **35**
Whitefriar St. Carmelite Church **42**

Christ Church Cathedral

old detail was destroyed in the process. Still, magnificent stonework and graceful pointed arches survive. (There's also a statue of Strongbow inside, and some believe his tomb is here as well, although historians are not convinced). The best way to get a glimpse of what the original building must have been like is to visit the 12th-century crypt, which has been kept untouched. An intriguing side note: Christ Church once displayed what was believed to be the preserved heart of St. Laurence O'Toole (1128–80). However, in early 2012, the holy relic was stolen in an audacious nighttime raid. Nothing else was taken, including items of much higher value. Other, similar thefts have taken place across Ireland in recent years, leading police to surmise that a collector may be having relics stolen to order. As of this writing, the heart is still missing.

Christchurch Place, Dublin 8. ✆ **01/677-8099.** www.christchurchdublin.ie. Admission €6 adults; €4.50 seniors and students; €2 children € (15 and under); €15 families. Mar–May Mon–Sat 9am–6pm; Sun 12:30–2:30pm, 4:30–6pm. June–Sept Mon–Sat 9am–7pm; Sun 12:30–2:30pm, 4:30–6pm. Oct Mon–Sat 9am–5pm; Sun 12:30–2:30pm, 4:30–6pm. Nov–Feb Mon–Sat 9am–5pm; Sun 12:30–2:30pm. Mar–Apr Mon–Sat 9am–5pm; Sun 12:30–2:20pm, 4:30–6pm. Last entry 45 min. before closing (Mon–Sat). Bus: 37, 39, 39A, 39B, 39C, 39X, 49, 49A, 49X, 50X, 54A, 56A, 70, 70A, 70X, 78A.

Dublin Castle ★ This 13th-century structure was the center of British power in Ireland for more than 700 years, until the new Irish government took it over in 1922. You can wander the grounds for free, but they're disappointingly plain; the official tour takes in the much more impressive State Apartments, the early-18th-century Treasury, and the Gothic style Chapel Royal chapel building that boasts fine plaster decoration and a carved-oak gallery. The castle's only extant tower

Monumental Wit

Few cities have such a love-hate relationship with their statues as Dublin. Locals have an acerbic nickname for each one, many of them unprintable. The statue of Molly Malone on Grafton Street is, variously, "the Tart with the Cart," "the Trollope with the Scallop," or "the Flirt in the Skirt"; the James Joyce statue on O'Connell Street is "the Prick with a Stick"; the statue of Anna Livia (a character in *Finnegan's Wake* who symbolized the Liffey), rising from an ornamental pond in Croppies Park, is "the Floozie in the Jacuzzi"; and, depending on whom you talk to, the Spire of Dublin on O'Connell Street is either "the Stiletto in the Ghetto," "the Skewer in the Sewer," "the Stiffy by the Liffey," or "the Nail in the Pale."

now holds a small museum dedicated to the Garda (Irish police). The 13th century structure was once used as a dungeon for those suspected of treason. The castle's Upper Yard is dominated by an impressive Georgian structure called the Bedford Tower, which used to contain the Irish crown jewels. The treasures were stolen in 1907 and have never been found. The yard was also the scene of the last trial by mortal combat to take place in Ireland in 1583. If it's open, check out the Medieval Undercroft, an excavated site on the grounds where an early Viking fortress once stood. ***Note:*** This is a government building, so areas are may be closed for state events.

Dame St., Dublin 2. ✆ **01/645-8813.** www.dublincastle.ie. Admission €4.50 adults; €3.50 seniors and students; €2 children (11 and under). Mon–Sat 10am–4:45pm; Sun and public holidays noon–4:45pm. Luas: Jervis. Bus: 37, 39, 39A, 39B, 39C, 49, 49A, 49X, 50, 50X, 56A, 65X, 70, 70A, 70X, 77, 77A, 77X, 123.

Dublin Writers Museum ★★ Manuscripts, early editions, personal possessions, and other pieces of ephemera relating to Ireland's most famous writers are on display at this great museum in Parnell Square. The exhibits are laid out across two rooms, tracing the development of Irish literature up to the present day. Lovers of Behan, Joyce, Shaw, Stoker, Wilde, Yeats, and the other greats of the canon will find plenty to love here—from the trivial (knickknacks such as Brendan Behan's postcard from Los Angeles extolling its virtues as a place to get drunk) to the profound (a first

The personal correspondence and effects of Ireland's greatest writers are on public display at the Dublin Writers Museum.

edition of Patrick Kavanagh's *The Great Hunger*, complete with a handwritten extra section that his publisher refused to publish, fearing it too controversial). You can take a self-guided audio tour, and there's a suitably excellent bookshop. Talks, readings, and other special events are occasionally held here; call or check the website for details.

18 Parnell Sq., Dublin 1. ✆ **01/872-2077.** www.writersmuseum.com. Admission €7.50 adults; €6.50 seniors and students; €5 children; €18 families. Mon–Sat 10am–5pm; Sun and public holidays 11am–5pm. Last admission 45 min. before closing. Bus: 1, 2, 8, 14, 14A, 16, 16A, 19, 19A, 33X, 39X, 40, 40A, 40B, 40C, 41X, 48A, 58X, 70B, 70X, 116, 120, 123, 145.

Dublinia ★ This museum presents history of Dublin from the Viking age through medieval times. It's very much aimed at children, although there are a few interesting displays and exhibits. Mostly, this is fun size history, presented as a series of interactive tableaux—complete with sound effects, smells, and audio "reconstructions" of *olde worlde* Dublin that are such effective earworms that you might find yourself thinking about them for years after. But kids enjoy trying on clothes like the ones their ancestors may have worn, or even find themselves placed in the Dublin stocks as "felons." Check the website for details of special tours, with costumed guides, and other family-friendly activities. Dublinia is right across from Christ Church Cathedral, making this an excellent payoff for any little ones who patiently trudged around that historic but austere building; combined tickets for the two offer big savings.

St. Michael's Hill, Christ Church, Dublin 8. ✆ **01/679-4611.** www.dublinia.ie. Admission €7.50 adults; €6.50 seniors and students; €5 children; €23 families. Mar–Sept daily 10am–5pm; Oct–Feb daily 10am–4:30pm. Luas: Four Courts. Bus: 49, 49A, 54A, 123.

Grafton Street ★ Dublin's most famous shopping street is a combination of big chains, chichi department stores, and little shops. It's as pricey as in any big city—although bargains can be found. It's also a popular site for street performers, so you're almost guaranteed an impromptu show on a sunny day. There's an irresistible photo op to be found at the junction with Sloane Street, in the form of a life-sized bronze statue of poor, doomed Molly Malone. Unveiled in 1987, it raised a few eyebrows due to Molly's somewhat revealing décolletage. With typical dryness, locals swiftly nicknamed it "the Tart with the Cart."

Dublin 2. Bus: 11, 11A, 11B, 14, 14A, 15A, 15C, 15X, 20B, 27C, 32X, 33X, 39B, 41X, 46B, 46C, 51X, 58X, 70X, 84X.

Guinness Storehouse ★ Opened in 1759, the Guinness Storehouse is one of the world's most famous breweries, producing the distinctive dark stout, known and loved the world over. You can explore the Guinness Hopstore, tour a converted 19th-century building housing the World of Guinness Exhibition, and view a film showing how the stout is made; then move on to the Gilroy Gallery that's dedicated to the graphic design work of John Gilroy (whose work you will have seen if you've ever been in an Irish pub); and last but not least, stop in at the breathtaking Gravity Bar. Here you can sample a glass of the famous brew in the glass-enclosed bar 61m (200 ft.) above the ground, complete with 360-degree views of the city.

St. James's Gate, off Robert St., Dublin 8. ✆ **01/408-4800.** www.guinness-storehouse.com. Admission €16.50 adults; €13 seniors and students over 18; €10.50 student under 18; €6.50 children; €40 families. Sept–May daily 9:30am–5pm; July–Aug daily 9:30am–7pm. Bus: 123.

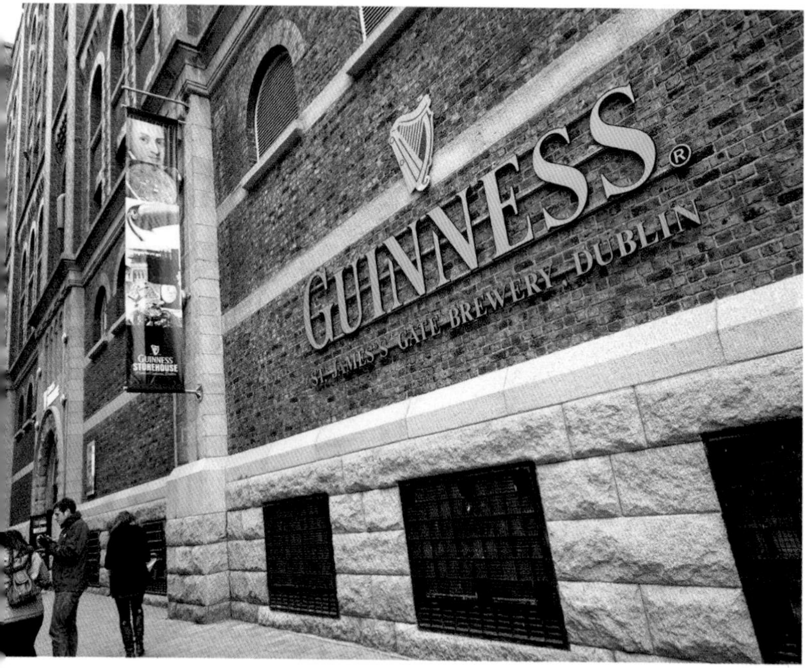

The Guinness Storehouse in Dublin.

Hugh Lane Gallery ★★ This small art gallery punches above its weight with a strong collection of Impressionist works. Highlights of the collection include Degas's *Sur la Plage* and Manet's *La Musique aux Tuileries*. There are also sculptures by Rodin, a marvelous collection of Harry Clarke stained glass, and numerous works by modern Irish artists. One room holds the maddeningly cluttered studio of the Irish painter Francis Bacon that the gallery purchased from London and moved to Dublin, where it has been reconstructed behind glass. They moved everything—right down to the dust. It's an excellent, compact art museum, and a great place to spend an afternoon.

Parnell Sq. North, Dublin 1. ✆ **01/222-5550.** www.hughlane.ie. Free admission. Tues–Thurs 10am–6pm; Fri–Sat 10am–5pm; Sun 11am–5pm. Bus: 1, 2, 8, 10A, 14, 14A, 16, 16A, 19, 19A, 33X, 39X, 40, 41X, 46A, 46B, 46X, 48A, 58C, 58X, 70B, 70X, 116, 145.

The Irish President's House (Áras an Uachtaráin) ★★ Áras an Uachtaráin was once the Viceregal Lodge, the summer retreat of the British viceroy, whose main digs were in Dublin Castle. From what were never humble beginnings, the original 1751 country house was expanded several times, gradually accumulating splendor. Guided tours leave from the Phoenix Park Visitors Centre every Saturday. After an introductory historical film, a bus brings visitors to and from the house. The focus of the tour is the state reception rooms. The entire tour lasts about an hour (a little longer in summer, when the gardens are included on the itinerary, weather permitting). A strictly limited number of tickets are given out, on a first-come, first-served basis. The house

THE tortured TALE OF THE HUGH LANE GALLERY

Hugh Lane was a millionaire and exuberant collector of art. In the early 20th century, he opened his own gallery in Dublin on Harcourt Street, but he soon tired of running it, and offered to donate the whole thing—millions of pounds worth of Impressionist paintings—to the city. His only condition was that the city should build an appropriate structure to hold it all. Dublin agreed, and all seemed well. However, months later, having failed to find a suitable structure, and caught up in wrangling over the cost, the city withdrew from the deal. Lane was furious and, in a temper, made an agreement with the National Gallery in London to give that vast art museum his collection instead.

To the rescue came W. B. Yeats, who was so infuriated by the government's ineptitude that he wrote a series of angry poems lambasting it for its failure to find a place to house such magnificent works. Inspired in part by Yeats's fervor, Lane changed his mind, and decided to leave his collection to Dublin after all. He ordered his will changed, but had not yet had it signed and witnessed when he was killed in 1915 aboard the ocean liner *Lusitania* when it was torpedoed by a German U-boat.

So began a legal stalemate in which the National Gallery and the city of Dublin struggled for the ownerships of the Monets, Courbets, and Manets that a few months earlier Dublin wasn't even sure it wanted.

To an extent, the issue is still unresolved 90 years later, but luckily an agreement is in place by which the main works in the collection are displayed at different times by both galleries. The Hugh Lane Gallery now has a gorgeous home in the classical Charlemont House on Parnell Square.

Mr. Lane would surely approve.

may occasionally be closed for state events, so it's wise to call ahead. ***Note:*** For security reasons, no backpacks, travel bags, strollers, cameras, or mobile phones are allowed on the tour.

Tour departs from Phoenix Park Visitor Centre, Dublin 8. ✆ **01/677-0095** (Phoenix Park visitor center). www.president.ie. Free admission. Sat 10:30am–3:30pm. Bus: 37.

Kilmainham Gaol ★★★ This is a key sight for anyone interested in Ireland's struggle for independence from British rule. Within these walls, political prisoners were incarcerated, tortured, and killed from 1796 until 1924. The leaders of the 1916 Easter Uprising were executed here, along with many others. Future president Eamon de Valera was its final prisoner. There is an exhibition devoted to the brutal history of the Irish penal system and a historical film. It's extremely well presented, even if it is hard not to feel overwhelmed at times by the awfulness of it all. To walk along these corridors through the grim exercise yard or into the walled compound is a moving experience that will linger in your memory.

Inchicore Rd., Kilmainham, Dublin 8. ✆ **01/453-5984.** www.heritageireland.ie/en/Dublin/KilmainhamGaol. Admission €6 adults; €4 seniors; €2 students and children; €14 families. Apr–Sept daily 9:30am–6pm; Oct–Mar Mon–Sat 9:30am–5:30pm; Sun 10am–6pm. Last admission 1 hr. before closing. Bus: 51B, 51C, 63, 69, 78A, 123, 206.

For more than a century, Irish revolutionaries were imprisoned and punished in Kilmainham Gaol.

National Gallery of Ireland ★★ George Bernard Shaw loved this place so much that he left it a sizeable chunk of his royalties after he died. He saw it as paying a debt, so important was the gallery to his education. It is still a place to wander, wonder, and just be in thrall to so much beautiful art. Highlights of the permanent collection include paintings by Caravaggio, Gainsborough, Rubens, Goya, Rembrandt, Monet, and Picasso. The Irish national portrait collection is housed in one wing, while another area is devoted to the career of Jack B. Yeats (brother of W. B. Yeats), an Irish painter of some note. Major exhibitions change regularly, and the subjects are often more imaginative than just the usual run of retrospectives and national landscapes (although those appear too); recent shows have included an exhibition devoted to painting without color. In keeping with the "art for all" ethos that so enamored Bernard Shaw, entry to the permanent collection and many of the temporary shows is free.

Merrion Sq. West, Dublin 2. ✆ **01/661-5133.** www.nationalgallery.ie. Free admission. Mon–Wed, Fri–Sat 9:30am–5:30pm; Thurs 9:30am–8:30pm; Sun noon–5:30pm; public holidays 10am–5:30pm. DART: Pearse. Luas: St. Stephen's Green, Grafton St. Bus: 4, 5, 7, 7A, 8, 13, 13A, 39, 39A, 44, 45, 46A, 48A.

National Museum of Ireland: Archaeology ★★★ The most impressive of the four sites that collectively make up the National Museum of Ireland, this excellent museum is devoted to the ancient history of Ireland and beyond. The collections cover the Stone Age up to the Early Modern period. Highlights include a stunning collection of Viking artifacts from the archaeological digs that took place in Dublin from the 1960s to the early 1980s—a haul so important that in one fell swoop they rewrote the history of Viking settlement in Ireland. There is also an enormous range of Bronze Age gold and metalwork and iconic Christian treasures from the Dark Ages and early medieval periods, including the Ardagh Chalice, the Molylough Belt Shrine and the Tara Brooch. Smaller galleries cover artifacts from the Classical world, including 2nd-century Roman figurines and homewares, and an extraordinary granite table made in Egypt circa 1870 B.C. The other sites of the NMI are the Natural History Museum on nearby Kildare Street; Decorative Arts and History, Collins Barracks, in Benburb, just west of the city center; and Country Life in Castlebar, County Mayo (see p. 390).

Kildare St., Dublin 2. ✆ **01/677-7444.** www.museum.ie. Free admission. Tues–Sat 10am–5pm; Sun 2–5pm. Bus: 7B, 7D, 10, 10A, 11, 11A, 11B, 14, 14A, 15, 15A, 15B, 15C, 20B, 25X, 32X.

National Museum of Ireland: Decorative Arts & History, Collins Barracks ★★ As the name of this branch of the National Museum of Ireland suggests, this museum is unusually located in a converted 18th-century army building. The collection tells the story of Irish history through fashion, jewelry, furniture, and other decorative arts, with the bulk of the collection spanning the 1760s to the 1960s. One gallery is devoted to the work of Eileen Gray (1878–1976), an Irish architect and furniture designer who became one of the most important figures of the Modernist movement; another showcases the extraordinary collection of Asian art bequeathed to the Irish nation in the 1930s by Irish-American philanthropist Albert Bender. This branch of the National Museum isn't entirely devoted to the arts, however; eight galleries are devoted to Irish military history from the 16th century to the present day, including a fascinating section about the Easter Rising of 1916.

Collins Barracks, Benburb St., Dublin 7. ✆ **01/677-7444.** www.museum.ie. Free admission. Tues–Sat 10am–5pm; Sun 2–5pm. Luas: Museum. Rail: Heuston. Bus: 39B, 70N.

National Museum of Ireland: Natural History ★★ Before it underwent a huge renovation in the late 2000s, this vast museum was a venerable, but rather moth eaten institution. Today the building has never looked better—right down to the grand Victorian staircase, closed for years, that takes visitors to the upper floors. The core collection itself has changed little since the museum was founded in the mid-19th century—from small stuffed native Irish animals and primates to the skeletons of enormous sea creatures. Recent additions include the new Discovery Zone, in which visitors can open a series of drawers, like cabinets of curiosity, to discover the unusual specimens within. Sadly, however, the much-trumpeted restoration was barely over when new problems were identified with safety on the balcony levels, which, at this writing, were closed pending a review. This means that some of the most unique parts of the collection are temporarily inaccessible. These include the avian galleries, and the "crystal jellies" collection—beautiful oversize glass models of microscopic sea creatures, made in the 19th century by the eccentric and brilliant Blaschka brothers of Dresden, whose work is now highly prized by collectors.

Merrion St., Dublin 2. ✆ **01/677-7444.** www.museum.ie. Free admission. Tues–Sat 10am–5pm; Sun 2–5pm. Bus: 4, 5, 7A, 8, 15X, 44, 44B, 44C, 48A, 49X, 50X, 51X, 63, 65X, 77X, 84.

DUBLIN walking tours

Small and compact, Dublin was made for walking. Some of the best experiences the city has to offer involve taking it at your own pace, with a map and an open mind, preparing to get a little lost along the way. However, if you'd like more guidance, historical background, or just some company, you might want to consider one of the following.

You could hardly be in better or more learned hands for the **Historical Walking Tours of Dublin** (✆ **087/688-9412;** www.historicaltours.ie), whose guides are all post-grad students at Trinity College, Dublin. Established for nearly 30 years, the tours are engaging and peerless in their historical insight. In addition to the general tour, you can choose from a variety of intriguing themes, from Medieval and Revolutionary Dublin to Irish Food and even a Running Tour for those who like their history combined with a workout. Meet outside the front gates to Trinity College, College Green, Dublin 2. The cost is €12 adults, €10 seniors and students.

If you prefer to take in the sights at a more leisurely pace, with a bit of liquid refreshment to keep things lively, try the **Literary Pub Crawl** (✆ **01/670-5602;** www.dublinpubcrawl.com). Walking in the footsteps of Joyce, Behan, Beckett, Shaw, Kavanagh, and other Irish literary greats, this tour visits Dublin's most famous pubs and explores their deep literary connections. Actors provide humorous performances and commentary between stops. Tickets cost €12 adults, €10 students. No children are allowed, for obvious reasons.

Another fine example of sightseeing for the thirsty is the **Traditional Irish Music Pub Crawl** (✆ **01/475-3313;** www.discoverdublin.ie/musical-pub-crawl). Two professional musicians, who sing as you make your way from one famous musical pub to another in Temple Bar, lead the tour. The evening is touristy, but the music is good. The cost is €12 adults, €10 students. Again, no children.

Dublin was profoundly changed by the rebellion early in the 20th century that became known as the Easter Rising. The **1916 Rebellion Walking Tour** (✆ **086/858-3847;** www.1916rising.com) takes you into the heat of the action at the General Post Office, explaining how the anger rose until the rebellion exploded on Easter Sunday in 1916. The tour is well thought out and run by local historians who wrote a book on the events of that year. Tickets cost €12.

St. Patrick's Cathedral ★★ The largest church in Ireland, and one of the most beloved places of worship in the world, St. Patrick's is one of two Anglican Cathedrals in Dublin. Most of what you can see dates from the 14th century, but religious buildings stood here nearly a thousand years before that. It is mainly early English in style, with a square medieval tower that houses the largest ringing peal bells in Ireland, and an 18th-century spire. A moving collection of war memorials is tucked away at the very back of the cavernous nave, including a very low-key tribute to the Irish dead of World War II. (Ireland was neutral in that war, but around 300,000 men volunteered to fight with the Allies.) Admission includes an irregular program of lunchtime classical music recitals at the Cathedral. Dates vary; call or check the website for details.

St. Patrick's Close, Dublin 8. ✆ **01/453-9472.** www.stpatrickscathedral.ie. Admission €5.50 adults; €4.50 seniors and students; €15 families. Mar–Oct Mon–Fri 9am (9:20 in school term time)–5pm; Sat 9am–6pm; Sun 9–10:30am, 12:30–2:30pm, 4:30–6pm. Nov–Feb Mon–Fri 9am (9:20 in school term time)–5pm; Sat 9am–5pm; Sun 9am–10:30am, 12:30–2:30pm. Last admission 30 min. before closing. Bus: 49, 49A, 49X, 50X, 54A, 56A, 77, 77A, 77X, 150, 151.

Sections of St. Patrick's foundation date to the 12th century.

St. Stephen's Green ★ This lovely urban park is filled with public art, and there always seems to be something new and imaginative hidden amid its leafy walkways. Among them is a beautiful statue commemorating the Irish rebel Wolfe Tone (beside an affecting monument to the Great Famine) and a garden of scented plants for blind visitors. This is a great place for a summer picnic. If the weather's fine, you can take a buggy ride through the park; rides leave from the Grafton Street side and cost around €20 to €50 for one to four passengers.

Dublin 2. Luas: St. Stephen's Green. Bus: 20B, 32X, 33X, 39X, 40A, 40C, 41X, 46B, 46N, 46X, 51X, 58X, 70B, 70X, 84X, 92.

Temple Bar ★★ There are really two Temple Bars, depending on when you visit. During the day, Temple Bar is an artsy, cultured district full of trendy shops and modern art galleries, such as the excellent **Temple Bar Gallery** (see p. 116). But such refinement gives way to an altogether more raucous atmosphere at night, when things can get pretty lively. With its myriad selection of pubs, bars, and hip clubs, this is definitely where it's at in Dublin after dark.

Dublin 2. DART: Tara St. Luas: Jervis. Bus: 37, 39, 39A, 39B, 39C, 49X, 50X, 51, 51B, 51C, 51D, 51X, 65X, 68, 69, 69X, 70, 70A, 77X, 78, 78A, 79, 79A, 90, 92, 206.

Trinity College ★★ The oldest university in Ireland, Trinity was founded in 1592 by Queen Elizabeth I to offer an education to the children of the upper classes and protect them from the "malign" Catholic influences elsewhere in Europe. Now it is simply the most well-respected university in Ireland. Among its alumni are Bram Stoker, Jonathan Swift, Oscar Wilde, and Samuel Beckett, as well as an array of rebels and revolutionaries who helped create the Republic of Ireland. The campus spreads across central Dublin just south of the River Liffey, with cobbled squares, gardens, a picturesque quadrangle, and buildings dating from the 17th to the 20th centuries. You can wander the campus for free; alternatively, between May and September, tours take in all of the main

A TOUR OF trinity college

The Trinity campus is open to the public year-round, although there might be some access restrictions during the exam periods. It's a beautiful, grand, romantic place to wander around—and free.

The most striking and famous monument inside the Trinity grounds, the white **Campanile,** or bell tower, grabs your attention as soon as you enter through the main archway. Dating from the mid-19th century, it stands on the site of the college's original foundations, from 300 years earlier.

The **Old Library Building** is the only section of the campus that you have to pay to see. It's where you'll find the **Book of Kells,** although the library's magnificent **Long Room** is almost as great an attraction (see p. 96).

Part of the 1970s **Arts Building,** the **Douglas Hyde Gallery** displays a regularly changing program of modern art. Exhibitions switch out about every three months and admission is always free.

Home to the geography and geology departments, the **Museum Building** is one of Trinity's hidden gems. It was built in the mid-19th century with a combination of Byzantine and Moorish influences. Walk through and look up to the domed ceiling and the green marbled banisters.

One of the more benign remnants of English rule, the **College Park Cricket Pitch** is a small park where you'll often find a cricket match in progress on summer weekends. The rules are notoriously arcane for the uninitiated, so instead just enjoy the uniquely picturesque sight of the players in their white uniforms and move on.

The **Berkley Library** sharply divides opinion for its austere modernism. The library's position between two architectural masterpieces—the Museum Building and Thomas Burgh's Library—caused controversy from the start. Designer Paul Koralek's library honors Bishop George Berkeley, famed for his philosophical theory of "immaterialism" (things that can't be proved cannot exist), which went against the theories of both Isaac Newton and the Catholic Church. The gleaming sculpture outside the library is ***Sphere with Sphere*** by Arnaldo Pomodoro (1983). Others in the same series can be found at the Vatican and the United Nations building in New York.

Tucked away in the far northeastern corner of the campus is the excellent **Science Gallery.** A combination of art space, science museum and debating forum, it has fun and thought-provoking exhibitions, workshops, public lectures, and even shows. Entry is free, except to certain special events. See **www.sciencegallery.com** for more details.

sights, plus a ticket for the Book of Kells (see p. 96) and the Old Library included in the price.

College Green, Dublin 2. ✆ **01/896-1000.** www.tcd.ie. Campus tours €5; including Old Library €10 (half-price for students, Oct–Mar) Library and Book of Kells only €9. Campus tours: May–Sept 10:15, 10:35, 10:55, 11:20, 11:45am, 12:10, 12:40, 1:05, 1:30, 2, 2:25, 2:50, 3:15, 3:40pm (no 3:40pm tour Sun and public holidays). DART: Pearse St., Connolly St. Luas: Lower Abbey St., St. Stephen's Green. Bus: College Green entrance (for tours): 7N, 15N, 15X, 44N, 46N, 48N, 49N, 51D, 51X, 54N, 56A, 70B, 70X, 77A, 77N, 92. Nassau St. entrance (for Old Library/Book of Kells): 25X, 32X, 33X, 41X, 51D, 51X, 58X, 67X, 84X, 92.

The Old Library Long Room at Trinity College.

More Attractions

HISTORIC ARCHITECTURE & BUILDINGS

Custom House ★ Completed in 1791, this beautifully proportioned Georgian building has a long classical facade of graceful pavilions, arcades, and a central dome topped by a statue of Commerce. The 14 keystones over the doors and windows are known as the Riverine Heads, because they represent the Atlantic Ocean and the 13 principal rivers of Ireland. Although it burned to a shell in 1921, the building has been masterfully restored. The exterior is the main attraction here, and most of the interior is closed to the public; but in case you're keen on learning more, the visitor center has exhibitions and an audiovisual presentation telling the story of its reconstruction.

Custom House Quay, Dublin 1. ✆ **01/888-2000.** Admission €1 adults; €3 families; students free. Visitor center: mid-Mar–Oct Mon–Fri 10am–12:30pm, 2–5pm; Sat–Sun and public holidays 2–5pm. Nov–mid-Mar Wed–Fri 10am–12:30pm, 2–5pm; Sun 2–5pm. Luas: Busáras. Bus: 27C, 41X, 90, 92, 151, 747, 748.

The Four Courts ★ Home to the Irish legal courts since 1796, this fine 18th-century building was designed by James Gandon (who also designed the Custom House; see above). It is distinguished by its graceful Corinthian columns, massive dome, and exterior statues of Justice, Mercy, Wisdom, and Moses. The building was at the center of the fighting during the civil war of 1922 and was badly damaged in the battle. It was later artfully restored, although some details, such as the statues of famous Irish lawyers that used to adorn the niches of the Round Hall, were lost. Tours are available, but frustratingly only for law students (who must book as part of a group). The only way to see the interior is usually to watch a trial in progress.

Inns Quay, Dublin 8. ✆ **01/888-6000.** www.courts.ie. Luas: Four Courts. Bus: 25, 25A, 51D, 51X, 68, 69, 78, 79, 79A, 83, 151, 172.

Dublin PASS

If you're planning a lot of sightseeing in Dublin, the tourism board would like you to consider purchasing its **Dublin Pass,** which offers free admission to most of the city's major sights, as well as free travel from the airport on the AirCoach shuttle, and discounts at a number of shops, bars, and restaurants.

Unfortunately, the pass is a bit pricey, given that so many of Dublin's sights are free, and the Dublin Pass website muddies the water by including free museums (such as the Chester Beatty Library and the national museums) among fee-charging sights. Our advice is this: Buy the pass, but plan carefully how best to use it. For example, consider buying a pass good for 1 or 2 days, and then see all of the city's most expensive sights (the Guinness Storehouse, Kilmainham Gaol, and so forth) on those days. On the other days of your trip, you can devote your time to the museums, parks, and galleries that charge no entrance fee.

An adult pass costs €39 for 1 day, €61 for 2 days, €71 for 3 days, and €105 for 6 days. A child's pass costs €21 for 1 day, €35 for 2 days, €42 for 3 days, and €54 for 6 days.

You can purchase a pass at any Dublin Tourism office, or online at **www.dublinpass.ie**. There are sometimes discounts available if you buy one in advance.

General Post Office ★ Don't be fooled by the nondescript name: With a facade of Ionic columns and Greco-Roman pilasters 60m long (197 ft.) and 17m high (56 ft.), this is more than a post office—it is the symbol of Irish freedom. Built between 1815 and 1818, it was the main stronghold of the Irish Volunteers during the Easter Rising. On Easter Sunday, 1916, Patrick Pearse stood on its steps and read a proclamation declaring a free Irish Republic. It began, "In every generation the Irish people have asserted their right to national freedom and sovereignty." Then he and an army of supporters barricaded themselves inside. A siege ensued that ultimately involved much of the north of the city, and before it was over, the building was all but destroyed. It had barely been restored before the civil war broke out in 1922, and it was heavily damaged again. It's still a working post office today, although it does house a few exhibits, including the original Declaration of Independence. That's all very much a secondary attraction, though; touching the bullet holes in the walls out front is a far more powerful way to experience a sense of this building's history.

O'Connell St., Dublin 1. ✆ **01/705-8833.** www.anpost.ie. Free admission (museum €2). Post Office building: Mon–Sat 8:30am–6:00pm. Closed public holidays. Museum: Mon–Sat 10am–5pm. Luas: Abbey St. Bus: 10, 10A, 32X, 33X, 39X, 40A, 40C, 41X, 46A, 46B, 46C, 46D, 46E, 116, 123, 145, 747.

Ha'penny Bridge ★ Built in 1816, and one of the earliest cast-iron bridges in Europe, the graceful, pedestrian-only Ha'penny Bridge (pronounced Haypenny) is the still the most attractive of Dublin's bridges. Officially named the Liffey Bridge, it's universally known by the toll it once charged to cross it: half a penny. The turnstiles were removed in 1919 when passage was made free. The bridge is at its prettiest after sundown, when the old lamps atop its three filigreed arches are lit, and the underside at each end is illuminated in green. During the

2000s it became traditional for couples to leave padlocks latched onto the bridge, with their names inscribed, before throwing the keys into the water. Dublin's city government now forbids the practice, seeing them more as an eyesore than a symbol of eternal love.

Connects Wellington Quay and Lower Ormond Quay, Dublin 2. Luas: Jervis. Bus: 39B, 51, 51B, 51C, 51D, 51X, 68, 69, 69X, 78, 78A, 79, 79A, 90, 92, 206.

Leinster House ★ The home of the Dáil (Irish House of Representatives) and Seanad (Irish Senate), this is the modern center of Irish government. Dating from 1745, it was originally known as Kildare House and was the seat of the Dukes of Leinster. Like the Parliament House building (see p. 113), it is said to have been a major influence on the architects of Washington, D.C.; the resemblance to Irish-born James Hoban's design for the White House, built 78 years later, is certainly clear enough. Tickets are available for guided tours 2 to 4 days per week. When the Dáil is in session you may also be able to watch part of a debate in the public gallery. For tickets, call the events desk (✆ **01/618-3271** or 3781 email event.desk@oireachtas.ie), or contact your country's embassy in Dublin, and they can arrange a tour on your behalf. ***Note:*** You need to bring I.D. (such as a driver's license, bank card, or passport) to gain admission.

Kildare St. and Merrion Sq., Dublin 2. ✆ **01/618-3271** or 3781. www.oireachtas.ie. Free admission. Entry by tour only, Mon and Fri 10:30am, 2:30, 3:30pm. (Additional tours when Dáil and Seanad in session, Tues and Wed 7, 8pm). Bus: 4, 5, 7A, 8, 7B, 7D, 10, 10A, 11, 11A, 11B, 14, 14A, 15, 15A, 15B, 15C, 15X, 20B, 25X, 32X, 44, 44B, 44C, 48A, 49X, 50X, 51X, 63, 65X, 77X, 84.

The Little Museum of Dublin ★★ Stuffed full of ephemera relating to the lives of ordinary Dubliners—art, toys, photographs, newspapers, prints, and other artifacts of the everyday—this delightful little museum forms a remarkably absorbing chronicle of what it was like to live in the city during the 20th century. Thoughtfully laid out inside a beautifully preserved Georgian townhouse, the vast majority of the items on display were donated by the people of Dublin, and the collection is being added to all the time. In among the curios are genuine documents of social history, including items relating to the First World War, the struggle for independence, and the suffrage movement. Several of the objects on display have little tales of their own—such as the music stand that, in June 1963, was hurriedly borrowed from the home of a local antique dealer by visiting U.S. President John F. Kennedy, when he realized he had nowhere to put his papers during a speech. Tours are lively and informative, and guides are good at engaging younger visitors in what all this really means.

15 St. Stephen's Green, Dublin 2. ✆ **01/661-1000.** www.littlemuseum.ie. Admission €6 adults; €5 seniors; €4 students and children; €13 families. Deluxe ticket (includes private guided tour) €10. Fri–Wed 9:30am–5pm; Thurs 9:30am–8pm. Luas: St. Stephen's Green. Bus: 15X, 32X, 39X, 41X, 46X, 51X,

Number Twenty-Nine: Georgian House Museum ★★ A little time capsule of family life in Georgian Dublin, Number 29 is a fascinating curiosity. Rooms are kept as close as possible to how they would have looked in the period from 1790 to about 1820. The differences between family living spaces and the basement servants' quarters are, unsurprisingly, stark. The two elegant drawing rooms, richly carpeted with expensive blue wallpaper and crystal chandeliers, stand in sharp relief to the sparse housekeeper's bedroom, or the simple, homely

The Custom House at night.

kitchen. At the same time, however, the industriousness of the kitchen is quite a revelation—medicines and cosmetics were made here from scratch by the servants, in addition to all the family's meals. The self-guided audio tour is informative, or if you can't bear to be in a place like this without being able to ask questions, there's a full tour daily at 3pm.

Corner of Fitzwilliam St. Lower and Mount St. Upper, Dublin 2. ✆ **01/702-6165.** www.esb.ie/no29. Admission €6 adults; €3 seniors and students; children 15 and under free. Tues–Sat 10am–5pm. Last admission 30 min. before closing. Tours: 3pm. DART: Pearse. Bus: 15X, 49X, 50X, 65X, 77X.

Parliament House ★ This impressive, colonnaded facade of this building was allegedly the model for the Capitol building in Washington, D.C.—with one key difference: It's completely devoid of windows. When Parliament House was built in the 1730s, a vicious window tax was in force, so not having any was a neat way to save money. The Irish Parliament met here until 1801, when, by an extraordinary quirk of history, it voted for its own abolition. William Pitt the Younger, then Prime Minister of Britain, had promised sweeping reform of the anti-Catholic laws if Ireland agreed to a formal union with Britain. They did so, but Pitt was deposed by King George III, the reforms never happened, and the Irish lost what little self-government they had. Today the building is owned by the Bank of Ireland, but you can see parts of the magnificent interior featuring oak woodwork, 18th-century tapestries, and a sparkling crystal chandelier. Friendly porters are on hand to fill you in on the history and are known to give informal tours of rooms you can't normally see, if you ask nicely.

2 College Green, Dublin 2. ✆ **01/661-5933.** Free admission. Mon, Tues, Fri 10am–4pm; Wed 10:30am–4pm; Thurs 10am–5pm. Bus: 7N, 15N, 15X, 44N, 46N, 48N, 49N, 51D, 51X, 54N, 56A, 70B, 70X, 77A, 77N, 92.

The harp-like Samuel Beckett Bridge, named after the famed Irish playwright.

ART MUSEUMS & LIBRARIES

Irish Film Institute ★ This art-house film institute is a hip hangout for cinephiles in Dublin's artsy Temple Bar district. It houses three cinemas, the Irish Film Archive, a library, a small but comprehensive bookshop, and a cafe that makes a good place for a cup of coffee on a cold afternoon. There's also a busy bar that does banner business. The cinemas show arty, groundbreaking films, with a good mixture of new titles and classics. There are also special film-related events, many of which are free. The IFI isn't just a place for hip young things; "Wild Strawberries" is the IFI's excellent seniors club, which is open to all. You can see a movie for €4, including tea and coffee. It usually runs on twice monthly; call the box office for details.

6 Eustace St., Dublin 2. ✆ **01/679-3477.** www.irishfilm.ie. Free admission. Cinema tickets €7–€10. Mon–Thurs 10am–11:30pm; Fri–Sun 10am–11pm. Bus: 27, 40, 49, 54A, 56A, 65, 65B, 68, 68A, 69, 69X, 77A, 77X, 79, 79A.

Irish Museum of Modern Art ★ This small but handsome museum, located in a beautiful 17th-century former hospital building, has a strong collection of modern art dating from the 1940s to the present day. Highlights include a striking series of mid-1970s photographs by Serbian conceptual artist Marina Abramovic; etchings and lithographs by Alice Maher, Louis le Brocquy, and Marcel Duchamp; and the Madden Arnholz Collection that's made up of around 2,000 old master prints, including works by Hogarth and Rembrandt. The beautifully restored grounds are also used as an exhibition space, with a number of changing pieces set among the formal lawns and clipped box hedges.

Royal Hospital, Military Rd., Kilmainham, Dublin 8. ✆ **01/612-9900.** www.imma.ie. Free admission. Thurs–Fri, Mon–Tues 10am–5:30pm; Wed 10:30am–5:30pm; Sun and public holidays noon–5:30pm. Last admission 45 min. before closing. Luas: Heuston. Bus: 26, 51, 51B, 78A, 79, 90, 123.

The James Joyce Centre ★ This idiosyncratic museum is set in a handsome Georgian house that once belonged to the Earl of Kenmare. Joyce himself never lived here; however, he was rather taken with a former owner of the house named Denis Maginni. An eccentric man, who was Irish but added the "i" to give himself an air of Italian sophistication, Maginni appears as a character in *Ulysses*. Today the center functions as both a small museum and a cultural center devoted to Joyce and his work. Actual exhibits are a little thin on the ground, but they hold interesting (at least for Joyce fans) lectures and special events, and also organize a Joyce-themed walking tour of Dublin. Unsurprisingly, this place becomes an explosion of activity around Bloomsday (June 16th); unlike the rest of Dublin, which makes do with a single day of celebrating its most famous 20th century literary hero, the James Joyce Centre turns it into a week-long festival.

35 North Great George's St., Dublin 1. ✆ **01/878-8547.** www.jamesjoyce.ie. Admission €5 adults; €4 seniors and students. Mon–Sat 10am–5pm; Sun noon–5pm. Bus: 1, 2, 8, 14, 14A, 16, 16A, 19, 19A, 33X, 39X, 41X, 48A, 58X, 70B, 70X, 116, 145.

Marsh's Library ★★ This caged library was founded by Narcissus Marsh, the Archbishop of Dublin, in 1701. Unlike Trinity College's Long Room, which is largely for show these days, Marsh's Library is still functioning. The walls are lined with scholarly volumes, chiefly focused on theology, medicine, ancient history, and maps, along with Hebrew, Greek, Latin, and French literature. Wire cages, in which readers would be locked in with the more valuable tomes, still stand anachronistically. The interior—a magnificent example of a 17th-century scholar's library—has remained much the same for 3 centuries. The excellent collection of books by and about Jonathan Swift includes volumes with his editing comments in the margins—ironically, perhaps, given that Swift himself said of Archbishop Marsh, "He is the first of human race, that with great advantages of learning, piety, and station ever escaped being a great man."

St Patrick's Close, Dublin 8. ✆ **01/454-3511.** www.marshlibrary.ie. Admission €2.50 adults; €1.50 seniors and students; children 15 and under free. Wed–Sat, Mon 9:30am–1pm, 2–5pm; Sat 10am–1pm. Closed public holidays and last week in Dec. Bus: 49, 49A, 50X, 54A, 56A, 77A, 77X, 150, 151.

National Library of Ireland ★ If you're coming to Ireland to research your roots, this library should be one of your first stops. It has thousands of volumes and records that yield ancestral information. Open at this location since 1890, this is the principal library of Irish studies. It's particularly noted for its collection of first editions and the papers of Irish writers and political figures, such as W. B. Yeats, Daniel O'Connell, and Patrick Pearse. It also has an unrivaled collection of maps of Ireland. A specialist **Genealogy Advisory Service** is open Monday to Friday, 9:30am to 12:30pm and 2 to 5pm (closes 4:35pm, Thurs and Fri). It's free of charge and you don't have to book an appointment.

Kildare St., Dublin 2. ✆ **01/603-0200.** www.nli.ie. Free admission. Mon–Wed 9:30am–7:45pm; Thurs–Fri 9:30am–4:45pm; Sat 9:30am–4:45pm; Sun 1–4:45pm. Exhibitions close 4:30pm Sat. DART: Pearse. Bus: 7B, 7D, 10, 10A, 11, 11A, 11B, 14, 14A, 15, 15A, 15B, 15C, 20B, 25X, 32X.

Temple Bar Gallery ★★ This big, rambling art gallery sums up all that is good about Temple Bar. Founded in 1983 in the heart of Dublin's "Left Bank," this is one of the largest studio and gallery complexes of its kind in Europe. It's filled with innovative work by contemporary Irish artists—more than 30 of them, in a variety of disciplines, including sculpture, painting, printing, and photography. The colors and creativity are dazzling, and it's run by helpful, friendly people. Only the gallery section is open to the public, but you can make an appointment in advance to view individual artists at work. The Studios hosts free talks and discussion panels, featuring the great and the good of the Irish arts scene. Call or go online for details.

5–9 Temple Bar, Dublin 2. ✆ **01/671-0073.** www.templebargallery.com. Free admission. Tues–Sat 11am–6pm. Bus: 26, 37, 39, 39A, 39B, 39C, 49X, 50X, 65X, 66, 66A, 66B, 66D, 67, 67A, 69X, 70, 70A, 77X.

PARKS & GARDENS

Croke Park Stadium & GAA Museum ★ Croke Park is the headquarters, and main sports ground, of the Gaelic Athletic Association (GAA). They oversee most of the traditional Irish sports—including hurling, rounders, and Gaelic football. The on-site museum does a good job of setting out the history of these games and putting them into the wider historical context of the importance of sport to the Irish way of life. The interactive exhibits include a large video archive, and you can take a tour of the stadium too. But the most excitement is, of course, to be had on match days—check the website for fixtures if you want to come and hear the roar of the crowd for real.

Jones Rd., Dublin 3. ✆ **01/819-2300.** www.crokepark.ie. Tour and museum: €12 adults; €9 seniors and students; €8 children 11 and under; €32 families. Museum only: €6 adults; €5 seniors

Grattan Bridge over the River Liffey.

and students; €4 children 11 and under; €16 families. Jan–May, Sept–Dec Mon–Sat 9:30am–5pm; Sun and public holidays 10:30am–5pm. June–Aug Mon–Sat 9:30am–6pm; Sun and public holidays 10:30am–5pm. Closed on match days (unless you have a ticket to the game). Tours: Jan–May, Sept–Dec Mon–Fri 11am, 1, 3pm; Sat 10, 11am, noon, 1, 2, 3pm; Sun and public holidays 11am, noon, 1, 2, 3pm. June Mon–Fri 11am, 1, 3, 4pm; Sat 10, 11am, noon, 1, 2, 3, 4pm; Sun and public holidays 11am, noon, 1, 2, 3pm. July–Aug Mon–Sat 10, 11am, noon, 1, 2, 3, 4pm; Sun and public holidays 11am, noon, 1, 2, 3pm. No tours on match days. Bus: 1, 11, 13, 16, 33, 41, 41B, 41C, 44.

Dublin Zoo ★★ If you've got kids and they're in need of a change from castles, churches and history, here's the antidote. This modern, humane zoo provides a naturally landscaped habitat for more than 235 species of wild animals and tropical birds. The animals live inside a series of realistically created habitats such as "African Savanna," home to giraffes, rhinos, and ostriches; "Gorilla Rainforest," a 12,000 square meter (7½ sq. mile) enclosure that currently houses five lowland gorillas; "Asian Forest," home to Sumatran tigers and a growing pack of lions, thanks to the recent arrival of two female cubs; and the "the South American House" with an eclectic range of almost unbearably cute species, including golden lion tamarins, tiny pygmy marmosets, and two-toed sloths. Further amusements for youngsters include a train ride around the zoo and the unfailingly cute Children's Pets Corner. There are playgrounds and gift shops scattered throughout. Feeding times and scheduled talks are posted on the zoo's website (several times daily from March to September, weekends only from October to February). A restaurant is on site, as well as plenty of picnic areas for those who prefer to bring their own meals.

Phoenix Park, Dublin 8. ✆ **01/474-8900.** www.dublinzoo.ie. Admission €16 adults; €12.50 seniors; €12.50 students; €11.50 children 3–15; €5.50 special needs child; €8.70 special needs adult; €45.50–€54 families. Mar–Sept daily 9:30am–6pm; Oct 9:30am–5:30pm; Nov–Dec 9:30am–4pm; Jan 9:30am–4:30pm; Feb 9:30am–5pm. Last admission to zoo 1 hr. before closing; last admission to African Plains 30 min. before closing. Luas: Heuston (15-min. walk). Bus: 25, 26, 46A, 66, 66A, 66B, 67, 69.

HORSE-DRAWN carriage tours

You can tour Dublin in true old-fashioned style in a horse-drawn carriage, with a driver who will comment on the sights as you travel the city's streets and squares. To arrange a ride, consult one of the drivers stationed with carriages at the Grafton Street side of St. Stephen's Green. Rides range from a short swing around the green to a half-hour Georgian tour or an hour-long Old City tour.

Rides are available on a first-come, first-served basis from April to October (weather permitting) and will run you about €20 to €60 for one to four passengers.

Alternatively, to book a tour in advance, **Bernard Fagan Horse Drawn Carriages** (✆ **086/874-8691;** www.bernardfagancarriages.com) is one recommended company. They build their tours around what you're interested in seeing; prices vary accordingly, but expect to pay upwards of €20 per person for an hour-long tour.

Phoenix Park ★ The vast green expanses of Phoenix Park are Dublin's playground, and it's easy to see why. This is a well-designed, user-friendly park crisscrossed by a network of roads and quiet pedestrian walkways that make its 704 hectares (1,739 acres) easily accessible. Avenues of oaks, beech trees, pines, and chestnut trees are shady hideaways, or you can sun yourself in broad expanses of grassland. It's a relaxing place to spend a restful afternoon, but there's plenty to do here should you feel active. The home of the Irish president (see p. 103) is in the park, as is the Dublin Zoo (see p. 117). Livestock graze peacefully on pasturelands, deer roam the forested areas, and horses romp on polo fields. The visitor center, adjacent to Ashtown Castle, has information about all the park has to offer. The cafe/restaurant is open 10am to 5pm weekdays, 10am to 6pm weekends. Free parking is adjacent to the center. Also next to the center is the **Victorian Tea Kiosk,** which serves snacks and light lunches, and has toilets. It's open from 10am to 4:30pm daily. The park is 3km (2 miles) west of the city center on the north bank of the River Liffey.

Phoenix Park, Dublin 8. ✆ **01/677-0095.** www.phoenixpark.ie. Free admission. Park: 24 hr. Visitor center: Apr–Dec daily 10am–6pm; Jan–Mar Wed–Sun 9:30am–5:30pm. Last admission 45 min. before closing. Bus: Castleknock Road entrance: 37. Navan Road entrance: 37, 38, 39, 70. North Circular Road entrance: 46A.

FOR KIDS

The Ark: A Cultural Centre for Children ★ This is a great option for children who are makers, thinkers, doers, listeners, and watchers. Age-specific programs are geared to small groups of kids from 2 to 12 years old. There are organized mini-courses (1–2 hr. long) designed around themes in music, visual arts, and theater, as well as workshops in photography, instrument making, and the art of architecture. The custom-designed arts center has three modern floors that house a theater, a gallery, and a workshop for hands-on learning sessions. Tickets include one child and one adult; prices vary, but expect to pay around €5-€12 for most events. Check the current themes and schedule on the Ark's very helpful website and book well ahead.

11a Eustace St., Dublin 2. ✆ **01/670--7788.** www.ark.ie. Ticket prices vary. Event times vary; call ahead. DART: Tara St. Luas: Jervis. Bus: 27, 40, 49, 54A, 56A, 65, 65B, 68, 68A, 69, 69X, 77A, 77X, 79, 79A.

CHURCHES & CATHEDRALS

St. Audeon's Church ★ Near the only remaining gate of the Old City walls (dating from 1214), this church is said to be the only surviving medieval parish in Dublin. Although it is partly in ruins, significant parts have survived, including the west doorway, which dates from 1190, and the 13th-century nave. It's a Church of Ireland property, but nearby is another St. Audeon's Church, this one Catholic and dating from 1846. It was in the latter church that Father "Flash" Kavanagh used to say the world's fastest Mass so that his congregation was out in time for the football matches. Entrance to the ancient church is through a visitor center. The center's exhibition, relating the history of St. Audeon's, is self-guided; visits to the church itself are by guided tour, and it is only open in high season.

14 High St., Dublin 8. ✆ **01/677-0088.** www.heritageireland.ie. Free admission. Daily 9:30am–5:30pm. Bus: 49X, 50X, 51B, 51C, 51N, 54A, 78A, 206.

FAMILY favorites

As with any big(ish) city, Dublin can seem a little kid-unfriendly, but never fear—there's more than enough to do here to keep the little ones happy.

If the weather's fine, Dublin's many parks give families on the go a respite from the city's ruckus. Right in the center at **Merrion Square** and **St. Stephen's Green,** are lawns for picnicking, ducks for feeding, playgrounds for swinging, and gardens for dashing around madly. If you feel like splurging, the whole family can take a carriage ride around the parks.

West of Dublin's city center, the vast **Phoenix Park** is paradise for children on a sunny day (see on previous page). It holds the **Dublin Zoo** (see p. 117) as well as sports fields, playgrounds, and herds of free-roaming deer. Ice cream vendors and teahouses are on hand.

For a lively tour of Dublin's Viking history (well, it's a gentle brush across the surface of Dublin's Viking history, to be honest), the **Viking Splash Tour,** in a reconditioned World War II amphibious "duck" vehicle (see "Dublin Bus Tours," p. 122), is more about fun than history.

If they need a little artistic stimulation, the **Ark** (see on previous page) offers arts classes and cultural experiences ranging from painting and drawing to theater.

At the edge of town in the suburbs, fresh air, ocean breezes, and castles await their wondering eyes. North of the city is the Malahide Castle, with a grand, rambling old stone castle, acres of parks and playgrounds.

The towns south of Dublin are best explored by DART light rail from the city center. Something wonderful is usually going on at the **Lambert Puppet Theatre** (Clifton Lane; ✆ **01/280-0974;** www.lambertpuppettheatre.com), which has a full program of shows running all year; or, if the kids need a little seaside adventure, go on a few more stops to the heritage village of **Dalkey**. At Coliemore Harbour, just a 10-minute walk from the train, you can take a ferry out to explore **Dalkey Island** and return a few hours later. After your adventure, reward yourself with a soft-scoop ice cream cone in the village. The park at the top of **Dalkey Hill** offers a memorable view of the town and bay beyond, but it's a very steep climb.

One stop after Dalkey on the DART lies the long pebbled beach of **Killiney.** This is just the place to find the perfect stone for your family collection while taking a beachcombing stroll along the strand. Farther on down the line is the seaside resort town of **Bray,** where Irish water creatures, from starfish to sharks, can be found in the **National Sea Life Centre** (Strand Rd.; ✆ **01/286-6939;** www.visitsealife.com/bray). Along with the aquarium, Bray has arcades, games, and other family amusements along its boardwalk. If you get to Bray with energy and daylight to spare, the hike up **Bray Head** will give you a spectacular view of the Dublin coastline; in summer, it's covered in purple heather and yellow gorse.

Even with so much out there for families to do together, there may be some events—a romantic dinner, perhaps?—to which you'd rather not bring the kids. Dublin parents swear by **Minder Finders** (www.minderfinders.ie), a clued-in agency that uses certified babysitters (many are former nannies or teachers) who arrive armed with a bag full of kid-friendly activities. Each sitter is matched with your kids' ages and interests in mind, to alleviate any "new babysitter" jitters.

St. Mary's Pro Cathedral ★ No, there's no pro and amateur league for Cathedrals in Ireland—"pro" simply means "temporary." And therein lies a fascinating piece of historical trivia. Contrary to popular belief, Dublin has no Roman Catholic Cathedral (St. Patrick's and Christ Church have been part of the Anglican Church of Ireland since the 16th century.) But the Vatican views Christ Church as Dublin's "true" Catholic Cathedral. Therefore, St. Mary's has been designated the "temporary" official Catholic cathedral in Dublin since 1820. It's tucked away on a rather unimpressive back street, but it's nonetheless the heart of the city's Northside. It was built between 1815 and 1825 in Greek Revival Doric style. The exterior portico is modeled on the Temple of Theseus in Athens, with six Doric columns, while the Renaissance-style interior is patterned after the Church of Saint-Philippe du Roule of Paris. The church is noted for its awe-inspiring Palestrina Choir, which sings a Latin Mass every Sunday at 11am (during term times).

83 Marlborough St., Dublin 1. ✆ **01/874-5441.** www.procathedral.ie. Free admission. Mon–Fri 7:30am–6:45pm; Sat 7:30am–7:15pm; Sun 9am–1:45pm, 5:30–7:45pm; public holidays 10am–1:30pm. DART: Connolly, Tara St. Luas: Abbey St. Bus: 2, 3, 4, 5, 7, 7A, 7B, 7D, 8, 10, 10A, 11, 11A, 11B, 13, 20B, 27, 32X, 33X, 39X, 40A, 40C, 41, 41A, 41B, 41C, 41X, 42, 42A, 42B, 43, 51A, 116, 123, 130, 142, 747.

St. Michan's Church ★★ Built on the site of an early Danish chapel (1095), this 17th-century edifice has fine interior woodwork and an organ (dated 1724) on which Handel is said to have played his *Messiah*. A unique (and, let it be noted, macabre) feature of this church is the underground burial vault. Because of the dry atmosphere, mummified bodies have lain for centuries in an extraordinary state of preservation. A few still have their hair and fingernails; on others you can see desiccated internal organs under the skin. The tallest mummy is known as "the Crusader"; his legs were broken in order to fit him into the coffin. Others in residence include "the Nun" and "the Thief"—although their true identities were lost when the church records were destroyed during the civil war in 1922. It is said that Bram Stoker was inspired to write *Dracula* in part by having visited the vaults as a child. ***Note:*** The church is wheelchair accessible, but the vaults are not.

Church St., Dublin 7. ✆ **01/872-4154.** www.stmichans.com. Admission €5 adults; €4 seniors and students; €3.50 children; €15 families. Crypt: Mid-Mar–Oct Mon–Fri 10am–12:45pm, 2–4:45pm; Sat 10am–12:45pm. Nov–mid-Mar Mon–Fri 12:30–3:30pm; Sat 10am–12:45pm. No crypt tours Sun. Luas: Four Courts, Smithfield. Bus: 51D, 51X.

St. Teresa's Church The foundation stone was laid for this building in 1793, and the church was opened in 1810 by the Discalced Carmelite Fathers. After continuous enlargement, it reached its present form in 1876. After years of anti-Catholic legislation, this was the first Catholic church to be legally and openly erected in Dublin, following the Catholic Relief Act of 1793. Among the artistic highlights are John Hogan's *Dead Christ*, a sculpture displayed beneath the altar, and Phyllis Burke's seven beautiful stained glass windows.

Clarendon St., Dublin 2. ✆ **01/671-8466.** www.clarendonstreet.com. Free admission; donations welcome. Daily 8am–8pm or longer. Bus: 15A, 15B, 44, 61, 100X, 101X, 109, 111, 133, 140.

Whitefriar Street Carmelite Church This 19th-century Byzantine-style church is unexpectedly one of the city's most romantic spots. Lovers are drawn here because the church holds the relics of St. Valentine. The pieces of bone are

HARD TO love: JONATHAN SWIFT

For all his cynicism, the sardonic writer Jonathan Swift loved Dublin and its residents. While dean of St. Patrick's Cathedral from 1713 to 1745, he wrote many of his most controversial works, and he knew that he owed the church and the city a great deal for supporting him when, given that they were often the targets of his barbed wit, they could hardly have been blamed for throwing him out. Heaven knows the English wouldn't have wanted him—he'd already written such sharp polemics about English governmental corruption that he was infamous in that country. In his own way, Swift understood the Irish and the English a bit too well for their comfort. But the Irish kept him on, even after he published his infamous essay "A Modest Proposal," in which he advocated (sarcastically) that the English should eat Irish babies in order to solve Ireland's famine problems.

One of Swift's biggest causes was humane treatment for the mentally ill, which in his time was unheard of. When he died, he bequeathed much of his estate to found St. Patrick's Hospital for the mentally ill.

Typically, though, he couldn't just leave it at that. Instead, he wrote one last caustic verse, as if seeking to guarantee that no Irish person would ever leave flowers on his grave:

"He left the little wealth he had
To build a house for fools and mad;
Showing in one satiric touch
No nation needed it so much."

believed to be authentic, and they were given to the church by Pope Gregory XVI in 1836. They're kept in a casket on an altar to the right of the main altar, but once a year (on St. Valentine's Day, of course) are carried out in procession for a special Mass. The church also holds an icon known as **Our Lady of Dublin,** a 15th-century woodcarving that was rescued from a nearby farm where it had been used as a pig trough.

56 Aungier St., Dublin 2. ✆ **01/475-8821.** Free admission. Mon and Wed–Fri 8am–6:30pm; Tues 8am–9:30pm; Sat 8am–7pm; Sun 8am–7:30pm. Bus: 16, 16A, 19, 19A, 83, 122, or 155.

A CEMETERY

Glasnevin Cemetery & Museum ★ North of the city center, the Irish national cemetery was founded in 1832 and covers more than 50 hectares (124 acres). Most people buried here were ordinary citizens, but there are also many famous names on the headstones, ranging from former Irish Taoiseach (prime minister) Eamon de Valera to other political heroes and rebels including Michael Collins, Daniel O'Connell, Countess Constance Markievicz, and Charles Stewart Parnell. Literary figures also have their place here, and you can find writers Christy Brown (immortalized in the film *My Left Foot*) and Brendan Behan. There's a small museum devoted to the cemetery and its famous occupants. Guided tours run daily, or you can download a self-guided tour app for your smartphone for €10 via the cemetery's website. Maps showing who is buried where are also for sale in the flower shop at the entrance.

Finglas Rd., Glasnevin, Dublin 11. ✆ **01/882-6550.** www.glasnevintrust.ie. Museum and tour €12 seniors and adults, €8 students and children, €25 families; museum only €6 adults, €4 seniors, students and children, €15 families; self-guided audio tour €10. Mon–Fri 10am–5pm;

Sat–Sun and public holidays 11am–5pm. Tours: Sept–June daily 11:30am, 2:30pm; early to mid–July daily 11:30am, 1, 2:30pm; mid-July–Aug Mon–Wed 11:30am, 1, 2:30pm, Thurs–Sun daily 11:30am, 2:30pm. Bus: 4, 9, 83, 140. 58X, 66X, 67X, 70X, 84X, 92.

A DISTILLERY

The Old Jameson Distillery ★ Learn as much as you can bear about one of Ireland's most famous whiskies from the right-in-front-of-your-eyes demonstrations at this working distillery, near St. Michan's Church (see p. 120) on the north side of the city. At the conclusion of the tour, you can sip a little firewater and see what you think. A couple of lucky people on each tour are selected to be "tasters" and sample different Irish, Scotch, and American whiskeys. Tours run throughout the day, about every 30 minutes, and last an hour.

DUBLIN bus tours

Convenient, comfortable, and—remember this when the heavens open in June—relatively immune to inclement weather, bus tours are a great way to pack a lot of sightseeing into a little time. And while Dublin has more than its fair share of standard tourist buses, a few are slightly more original.

For a lively tour of Dublin's Viking history, the **Viking Splash Tour** (**✆ 01/707-6000;** www.vikingsplash.ie) in a reconditioned World War II amphibious "duck" vehicle starts on land and eventually splashes into the Grand Canal. Viking helmets, though supplied, are optional. Tickets are €20 adults, €18 seniors and students, €16 teenagers and €12 children.

Of the many "hop on, hop off" style bus tours of the city, one of the best is the **Dublin Sightseeing** tour, run by **Dublin Bus** (**✆ 01/703-3028;** www.dublinsightseeing.ie). The 24-stop tour takes you all around the city center and out as far as Kilmainham Gaol (see p. 104). You can leave and rejoin the tours as many times as you like in a day. Buses run all day, every 10 minutes from 9am to 3:30pm, every 15 minutes until 5:30pm, and every 30 minutes until the last bus at around 6:30pm. Tickets cost €18 adults, €16 seniors and students, €8 children.

The **North Coast and Castle Tour** and the **South Coast and Gardens Tour,** also run by Dublin Bus, take you on all-day excursions to the picturesque coastal regions on the far fringes of Dublin. Tickets for both tours include entry to a separate attraction; the medieval Malahide Castle and its landscaped park to the north and **Powerscourt House and Gardens** (see p. 171) to the south. The cost is €24 adults, €12 children.

A spooky evening tour in a bus decked out in, um . . . spooky wallpaper, **Dublin Ghost Bus** (**✆ 01/703-3028;** www.dublinsightseeing.ie/ghostbus) addresses Dublin's history of felons, fiends, and phantoms. You'll see haunted houses, learn of Dracula's Dublin origins, and even get a crash course in body snatching. It's all ghoulish fun but actually quite scary in places, so it's not recommended for pre-teens. Tickets cost €28.

Likewise, the entertaining **Gravediggers Tour** (**✆ 086/411-3326;** www.thegravedigger.ie) takes you in pursuit of a few ghoulish and well-intentioned scares. Just when it all seems like too much for the faint hearted, the bus stops at the Gravediggers Pub by Glasnevin Cemetery (see p. 121) for a fortifying drink—included in the ticket price of €25. Live actors and 4D technology help bring the whole experience to life. Or should that be . . .

Bow St., Smithfield Village, Dublin 7. ✆ **01/807-2348.** www.jamesonwhiskey.com. Admission €14 adults; €10 seniors; €11 students; €8 children; €35 families. Mon–Sat 9am–6pm (last tour at 5:15pm); Sun 10am–6pm (last tour 5:15pm). Closed Good Friday and Christmas holidays. Bus: 67, 67A, 68, 69, 79, 90.

Outlying Attractions

Casino Marino ★★ This unique and unexpected little architectural gem in the middle of a suburban park has nothing at all to do with gambling; "casino" simply means "little house." Built in around 1770, the tiny neoclassical exterior is exquisitely proportioned, with Corinthian columns and elaborate detail around the white stone cornices. Inside the are, unlikely though it seems from the compactness of the exterior, a full 16 rooms—decorated with rich 18th-century architectural details, such as beautiful plasterwork ceilings and subtly curved windows. Entry is by tour only, but the cheerful guides help put it all into context.

Casino Park (signposted from R107, Malahide Road), Dublin. ✆ **01/833-1618.** www.heritage ireland.ie. Admission €3 adults; €2 seniors; €1 families €8 children and students. Mid-Mar–Oct daily 10am–5pm. Last admission 45 min. before closing. Closed Nov–mid-Mar except to prebooked groups. Bus: 20B, 27, 27B, 27C, 127, 129.

Dalkey Castle & Heritage Centre ★ Housed in a 15th-century tower house, this center tells the history of venerable Dalkey town in a few sweet, if unsophisticated, displays. Tours run by costumed guides tell the tale of the building (complete with live performance), or you can duck out of the tour and take in the view from the battlements instead. Adjoining the center is a medieval graveyard and the Church of St. Begnet (Dalkey's patron saint), whose foundations date back to Ireland's early Christian period. Dalkey itself is worth a wander; a heritage town with plenty of historic buildings, it also has lots of charming pubs, restaurants, and pricey little boutiques.

Castle St., Dalkey (16km/10 miles southeast of Dublin on R119). ✆ **01/285-8366.** www.dalkey castle.com. Admission €8 adults; €7 seniors and students; €6 children; €23 families. Mon, Wed–Fri 10am–6pm; Sat–Sun 11am–6pm. DART: Dalkey. Bus: 7D, 59.

Dún Laoghaire ★ The bustling harbor town of Dún Laoghaire (pronounced Dun *Lear*-y) is one of a string of Dublin commuter towns that, in the 2000s, became known as "Bel Eire" for their beauty and for the density of Irish celebrity residents. You could spend an afternoon wandering here; there are plenty of interesting shops, a bucolic park, and the long promenade alongside the harbor is a beautiful spot.

13km (8 miles) southeast of Dublin on R118. Rail: Dún Laoghaire. DART: Sandycove and Glasthule. Bus: 7, 7N, 46A, 46N, 59, 63, 75, 111.

SPORTS & OUTDOOR PURSUITS

BEACHES Plenty of fine beaches are accessible by city bus or DART, which follows the coast from Howth, north of the city, to Bray, south of the city in County Wicklow. Some popular beaches include **Dollymount,** 5km (3 miles) away; **Sutton,** 11km (6¾ miles) away; **Howth,** 15km (9⅓ miles) away; and **Portmarnock** and **Malahide,** each 11km (6¾ miles) away. In addition, the southern suburb of **Dún Laoghaire,** 11km (6¾ miles) away, offers a beach (at Sandycove) and a long bayfront promenade ideal for strolling in the sea air. For more details, inquire at the Dublin Tourism office.

BIRD-WATCHING The many estuaries, salt marshes, sand flats, and islands near Dublin Bay provide a varied habitat for a number of species. **Rockabill Island,** off the coast at Skerries, is home to an important colony of roseate terns; there is no public access to the island, but the birds can be seen from the shore. **Rogerstown and Malahide estuaries,** on the Northside of Dublin, are wintering grounds for large numbers of brent geese, ducks, and waders. **Sandymount Strand,** on Dublin's south side, has a vast intertidal zone; around dusk in July and August, you can often see large numbers of terns, including visiting roseate terns from Rockabill Island.

Your all-around best bet is a bird sanctuary called Bull Island, also known as the **North Bull,** just north of Dublin city harbor at the suburb of Clontarf. It's not an island at all, but a 3km (2-mile) spit of marshland connected to the mainland by a bridge. It was created by Captain William Bligh, of *Mutiny on the Bounty* fame. Early in the 19th century, he was head of the Port and Docks Board, and he ordered the construction of a harbor wall at the mouth of the River Liffey, in an effort to stop the bay from silting up. In fairly short order, the shifting sands created this small landmass. Its dunes, salt marsh, and extensive intertidal flats provide a unique environment that attracts thousands of seabirds. Hundreds of species have been recorded and 40,000 birds shelter and nest here. In winter, these figures are boosted by tens of thousands of migrants from the Arctic Circle, and North American spoonbills, little egrets, and sandpipers. Together, they all make a deafening racket. A visitor center is open daily 10am to 4:30pm; admission is free.

FISHING Local rivers, reservoirs, and fisheries offer plenty of opportunities for freshwater angling. A day's catch might include perch, rudd, pike, salmon, sea trout, brown trout, or freshwater eel. **Inland Fisheries Ireland (IFI),** a governmental agency, runs a great website dedicated to fishing in Ireland—the prosaically-named **Fishing in Ireland** (**www.fishinginireland.info**). In addition to handy run-downs of rules, regulations, and license details for pike, salmon, trout and other forms of fishing, they also have a contact list for local angling clubs. The Dublin regional office is **IFI Blackrock** at 15 Main Street, Blackrock, Co. Dublin (**✆01/278-7022;** email blackrock@fisheriesireland.ie.)

GOLF Dublin is one of the world's great golfing capitals. A quarter of Ireland's courses—including 5 of the top 10—lie within an hour's drive of the city. Visitors are welcome, but phone ahead and make a reservation. The following four courses—two parkland and two links—are among the best 18-hole courses in the Dublin area.

Elm Park Golf & Sports Club ★, Nutley Lane, Donnybrook, Dublin 4 (**✆ 01/269-3438;** www.elmparkgolfclub.ie), is in the residential, privileged south side of Dublin. The beautifully manicured parkland, par-69 course is especially popular with visitors because it is within 6km (3¾ miles) of the city center and close to the Jurys, Berkeley Court, and Four Seasons hotels. Greens fees are €50 weekends, €45 weekends, or €45 before 10am. (Non-members are not allowed after midday on weekends.)

Portmarnock Golf Club ★, Portmarnock, County Dublin (**✆ 01/846-2968;** www.portmarnockgolfclub.ie), is a respected links course. About 16km (10 miles) from the city center on Dublin's Northside, on a spit of land between the Irish Sea and a tidal inlet, this course opened in 1894. Over the years, the par-72 championship course has been the scene of leading tournaments, including the Dunlop Masters (1959, 1965), Canada Cup (1960), Alcan (1970), St. Andrews Trophy (1968), and many an Irish Open. You won't be surprised, then, to find out that fees are a bit pricey. Greens fees are around €180, or €150 before 9am or after 4pm (3pm September and April) on weekdays.

Royal Dublin Golf Club ★, Bull Island, Dollymount, Dublin 3 (✆ **01/833-6346;** www.theroyaldublingolfclub.com), is often compared to St. Andrews. The century-old, par-73 championship seaside links is on an island in Dublin Bay, 4.8km (3 miles) northeast of the city center. Like Portmarnock, it has been rated among the world's top courses and has played host to several Irish Opens. The home base of Ireland's legendary champion Christy O'Connor, Sr., the Royal Dublin is well known for its fine bunkers, close lies, and subtle trappings. Visitors can play on weekdays except Wednesday, and they hold a few slots for guests on Saturday 4am to 5:30pm and Sunday 10am to noon. Greens fees are €120; a second round may be played at half price if there's space available.

St. Margaret's Golf & Country Club ★, Skephubble, St. Margaret's, County Dublin (✆ **01/864-0400;** www.stmargaretsgolf.com), is a stunning, par-72 parkland course 4.8km (3 miles) west of Dublin Airport. Greens fees are around €50 Monday to Thursday, €65 Friday to Sunday.

HORSEBACK RIDING Plenty of riding stables are within easy reach of central Dublin, and prices average about €25 to €50 an hour, with or without instruction. Many stables offer guided trail riding, as well as courses in show jumping, dressage, prehunting, eventing, and cross-country riding. For trail riding through Phoenix Park, **Ashtown Riding Stables** (✆ **01/838-3807;** www.ashtownstables.com) is ideal. They're in the village of Ashtown, adjoining the park and only 10 minutes by car or bus (no. 37, 38, 39, 70, or 120) from the city center. You can also get there by train from Dublin Connolly station in about 15 minutes; Ashtown station is directly opposite the stables. Among the other riding centers within easy reach of downtown Dublin is **Carrickmines Equestrian Centre,** Glenamuck Road, Foxrock, Dublin 18 (✆ **01/295-5990;** www.carrickminesequestrian.ie), and **Brennanstown Riding School,** Hollybrook, Kilmacanogue, County Dublin (✆ **01/286-3778;** www.brennanstownrs.ie).

WALKING For casual walking, the Royal Canal and Grand Canal, which skirt the north and south city centers, respectively, are ideal for seeing the area. Both are marked trails, so you can't get lost, and because they stick to the towpaths of the canals, the paths are flat and easy. Both routes pass a range of small towns and villages that can be used as starting or stopping points.

The walk from Bray (the southern terminus of the DART) to Greystones along the rocky promontory of **Bray Head** is a great excursion, with beautiful views back toward Killiney Bay, Dalkey Island, and Bray. Follow the beachside promenade south through Bray; at the outskirts of town, the promenade turns left and up, beginning the ascent of Bray Head. Shortly after the ascent begins, a trail branches to the left—this is the cliffside walk, which continues another 5km (3 miles) along the coast to Greystones. From the center of Greystones, a train will take you back to Bray. This is an easy walk, about 2 hours each way. Don't attempt this walk in bad weather or strong winds, as the cliffside path will be quite treacherous.

Dalkey Hill and **Killiney Hill** drop steeply into the sea and command great views of Killiney Bay, Bray Head, and Sugarloaf Mountain. To get there, leave the Dalkey DART station, head into the center of Dalkey and then south on Dalkey Avenue (at the post office). About 1km (½ mile) from the post office, you'll pass a road ascending through fields on your left—this is the entrance to the Dalkey Hill Park. From the parking lot, climb a series of steps to the top of Dalkey Hill; from here you can see the expanse of the bay, the Wicklow Hills in the distance, and the obelisk topping nearby Killiney Hill. If you continue on to the obelisk, there is a trail leading from there down the seaward side to Vico Road, another lovely place for a seaside walk. It's about 1km (½ mile) from the parking lot to Killiney Hill.

WATERSPORTS Certified level-one and level-two instruction and equipment rental for three watersports—kayaking, sailing, and windsurfing—are available at the **Surfdock Centre,** Grand Canal Dock Yard, Ringsend, Dublin 4 (✆ **01/668-3945;** www.surfdock.ie). The center has 17 hectares (42 acres) of enclosed fresh water for its courses.

SPECTATOR SPORTS

GAELIC SPORTS If your schedule permits, try to get to a **Gaelic football** or **hurling** match—the only indigenously Irish games and two of the fastest-moving sports around. Gaelic football is vaguely a cross between soccer and American football; you can move the ball with either your hands or feet. **Hurling** is a lightning-speed game in which 30 men use heavy sticks to fling a hard leather ball called a *sliotar*—think field hockey meets lacrosse. Both amateur sports are played every weekend throughout the summer at local fields, culminating in September with the **All-Ireland Finals,** the Irish version of the Super Bowl. For schedules and admission fees, phone the **Gaelic Athletic Association,** Croke Park, Jones Road, Dublin 3 (✆ **01/836-3222;** www.gaa.ie).

RUGBY & SOCCER The **Aviva Stadium,** 62 Lansdowne Rd., Dublin 4 (✆ **01/238-2300;** www.avivastadium.ie) is, depending on your perspective, either a gleaming new monument to modern Irish sports, or Dublin's newest eyesore. Either way you really can't miss it. This is the official home of both the national rugby and football (soccer) teams.

GREYHOUND RACING Races are held throughout the year at **Shelbourne Park Greyhound Stadium,** South Lotts Road, Dublin 4 (✆ **01/668-3502**), and **Harold's Cross Stadium,** 151 Harold's Cross Rd., Dublin 6 (✆ **01/497-1081;** www.igb.ie/harolds-cross). For a complete schedule and details for races throughout Ireland, contact **Irish Greyhound Board,** Limerick (✆ **061/448000;** www.igb.ie).

HORSE RACING The closest racecourse to the city center is the **Leopardstown Race Course,** off the Stillorgan road (N11), Foxrock, Dublin 18 (✆ **01/289-0500;** www.leopardstown.com). This modern facility with all-weather, glass-enclosed spectator stands is 9.7km (6 miles) south of the city center. Racing meets—mainly steeplechases, but also a few flats—are scheduled throughout the year, two or three times a month.

WHERE TO STAY IN DUBLIN

With a healthy mix of plush hotels and grand old guesthouses, Dublin excels in providing a place to rest your head at the end of a day. Unfortunately, finding a really great, *affordable* place to stay is a tougher prospect. In this book we have tried to list as many of these "finds" as we can. However, if you're prepared to stay slightly outside of the city center, your options open up quite a bit (remember that public transportation, including taxis, is relatively cheap). This is particularly true in the leafy suburb of Ballsbridge (just south of the city center) that is fast becoming a center for affordable accommodations.

The Octagon Bar in the Clarence hotel draws celebrities, not to the exclusion of regular folk.

Wherever you're staying, try to book as far in advance as possible. The most sought-after places fill up fast. Always try to book online in the first instance—many hotels offer web-only special deals that can amount to massive savings on the rack rate. Remember, the fact that times are tough in the global economy right now cuts both ways: Hotels are at greater risk of closure, but they will also be more eager to secure your business. There are some truly amazing deals out there, if you know where to look. Don't be shy about asking about any available discounts or special offers.

If you arrive in Ireland without a reservation, don't despair. One of the best sources of last-minute rooms (often at a discount) is **www.visitdublin.com**. The website lets you view hotels and guesthouses with immediate availability. However, you will face tough questions at immigration if you arrive in Ireland without a place to stay at least for your first night.

Historic Old City & Temple Bar/Trinity College Area

Temple Bar is the youngest, most vibrant niche in a young, vibrant town. Stay here and you'll be on the doorstep of practically anywhere you'd want to go. That said, it can get *very* noisy at night, so request a room on a top floor or at the rear of the establishment if you want some shut eye.

EXPENSIVE

The Clarence ★★ Back in the 1990s, when the Celtic Tiger was starting to roar, the Clarence became something of a symbol of the "new" Dublin. Chic, fashionable, and with megastar owners to boot (Bono and the Edge from U2, who can still occasionally be spotted here), it spoke of Dublin's revival as a modern and cultured capital city. These days the economy may be skulking along at more of a purr, and the Clarence has lost some of its original luster (a refurbishment is overdue in places); however, it remains a quintessential part of on-trend Temple Bar. The decent-sized guestrooms are done in contemporary tones (chocolate and cream or white with accents of scarlet and black). Most of the furniture is the work of Irish designers, and beds are luxuriously

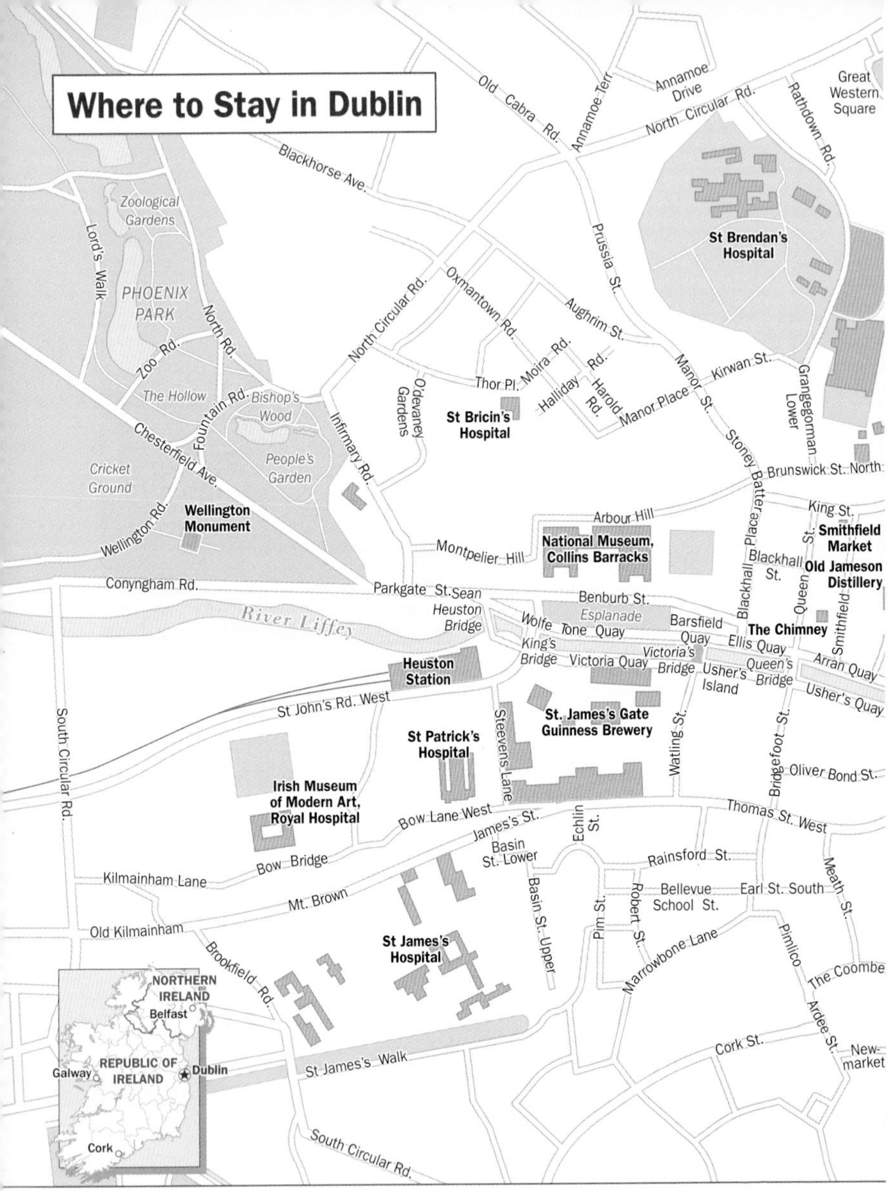

Aberdeen Lodge **19**
Ariel House **16**
Buswells **13**
Camden Court Hotel **18**
The Clarence **5**
The Conrad **17**
Eliza Lodge **6**
Grand Canal Hotel **15**
The Gresham **2**
Harding Hotel **4**
The Merchant House **7**
Mespil Hotel **8**
The Morrison **3**
Quince Cottage **20**
The Shelbourne **14**
Temple Bar Hotel **9**
Trinity Lodge **11**
Two Rooms in Dublin **1**
The Westbury **12**
The Westin **10**

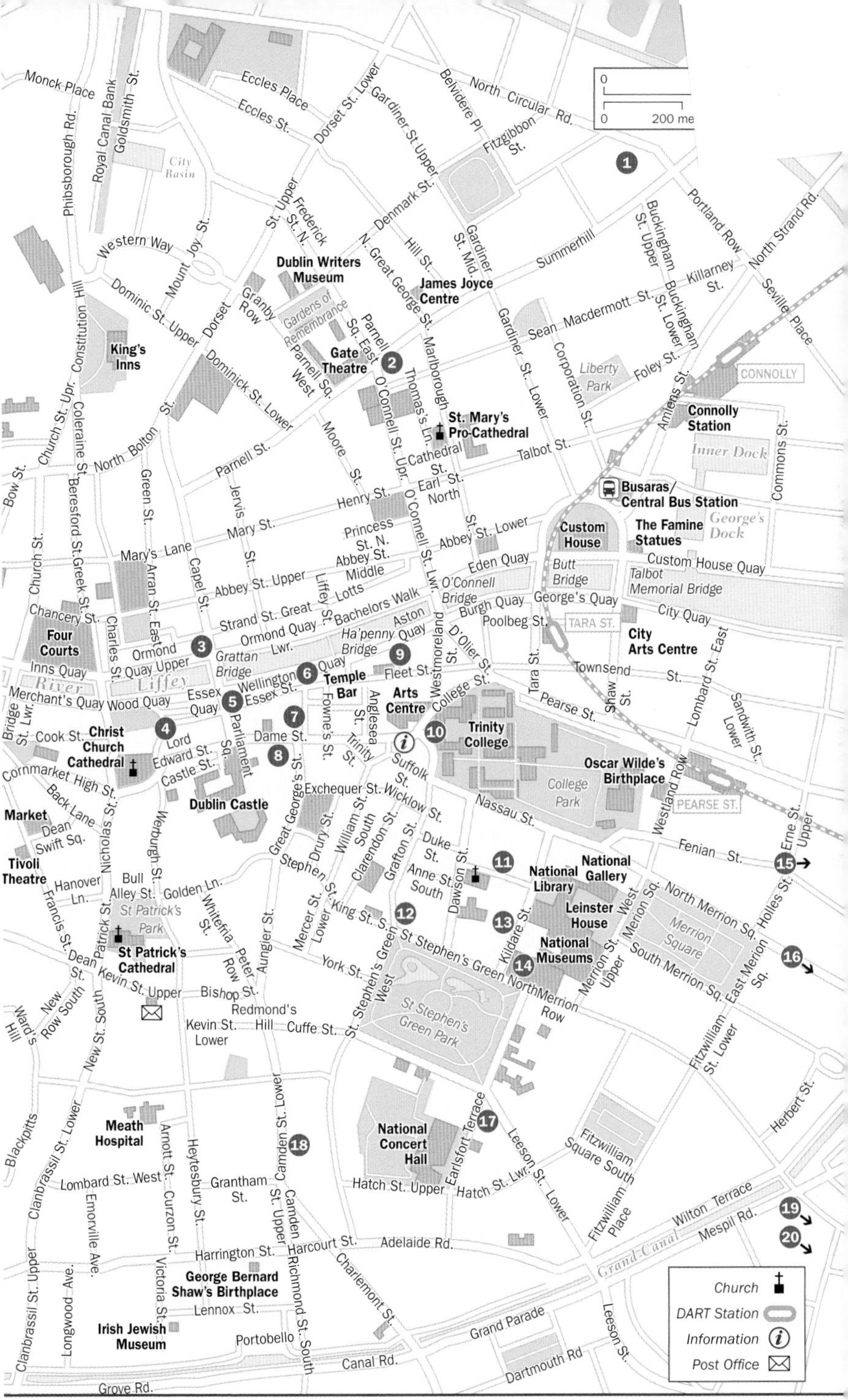

0
0
200 me
Monck Place
Eccles Place
Eccles St.
Dorset St. Lower
Gardiner St Upper
Belvidere Pl
North Circular Rd.
Fitzgibbon St.
Phibsborough Rd.
Royal Canal Bank
Goldsmith St.
City Basin
Denmark St.
St. Upper
Frederick St. N.
Western Way
Mount Joy St.
Dominic St. Upper
Dorset
Granby Row
Dublin Writers Museum
Gardens of Remembrance
N. Great George's St.
Hill St.
James Joyce Centre
Gardiner St. Mid.
Summerhill
Buckingham St. Upper
Portland Row
North Strand Rd.
Killarney St.
Buckingham St. Lower
Seville Place
Constitution Hill
King's Inns
Parnell Sq. East
Parnell Sq. West
Gate Theatre
Sean Macdermott St.
Gardiner St. Lower
Corporation St.
Liberty Park
Foley St.
CONNOLLY
Amiens St.
Connolly Station
Dominick St. Lower
Marlborough
Thomas's Ln.
O'Connell St. Upr.
St. Mary's Pro-Cathedral
Moore St.
Church St. Upr.
Coleraine St.
North Bolton St.
Parnell St.
Cathedral St.
Talbot St.
Inner Dock
Commons St.
Bow St.
Beresford St.
Green St.
Jervis St.
Henry St.
Earl St. North
Busaras/ Central Bus Station
Custom House
The Famine Statues
George's Dock
Mary St.
Princess St. N.
Abbey St. Lower
Church St.
Greek St.
Mary's Lane
Arran St. East
Capel St.
Abbey St. Middle
Abbey St. Upper
O'Connell St. Lwr.
Eden Quay
Butt Bridge
Custom House Quay
Talbot Memorial Bridge
Chancery St.
Liffey St.
Lotts
Bachelors Walk
O'Connell Bridge
Burgh Quay
George's Quay
City Quay
Strand St. Great
Ormond Quay Lwr.
Aston Quay
Westmoreland St.
D'Olier St.
Poolbeg St.
TARA ST.
Four Courts
Charles St.
Ormond Quay Upper
Ha'penny Bridge
City Arts Centre
Inns Quay
Grattan Bridge
Wellington Quay
Fleet St.
Tara St.
Townsend St.
Lombard St. East
River Liffey
Temple Bar
Essex Quay
Essex St.
Arts Centre
College St.
Merchant's Quay
Wood Quay
Fowne's St.
Anglesea St.
Pearse St.
Shaw St.
Sandwith St. Lower
Bridge St. Lwr.
Cook St.
Christ Church Cathedral
Lord Edward St.
Parliament Sq.
Dame St.
Trinity St.
Trinity College
Castle St.
Suffolk St.
Oscar Wilde's Birthplace
Cornmarket High St.
Dublin Castle
Great George's St.
Exchequer St.
Wicklow St.
College Park
Westland Row
PEARSE ST.
Back Lane
Nicholas St.
Drury St.
William St. South
Clarendon St.
Grafton St.
Nassau St.
Market
Dean Swift Sq.
Werburgh St.
Stephen St.
Duke St.
Dawson St.
National Gallery
National Library
Fenian St.
Erne St. Upper
Tivoli Theatre
Hanover Ln.
Bull Alley St.
Golden Ln.
Anne St. South
North Merrion Sq.
Holles St.
Francis St.
St Patrick's Park
Whitefriar St.
Mercer St. Lower
King St. S.
Leinster House
Merrion Sq. West
Merrion Square
Patrick St.
St Patrick's Cathedral
Peter Row
Aungier St.
St Stephen's Green North
Kildare St.
National Museums
Merrion St. Upper
South Merrion Sq.
East Merrion Sq.
Dean St.
Kevin St. Upper
York St.
St. Stephen's Green West
Merrion Row
Ward's Hill
New Row South
Bishop St.
Redmond's Hill
St Stephen's Green Park
Kevin St. Lower
Cuffe St.
St. Stephen's Green
Fitzwilliam St. Lower
New St. South
Herbert St.
Blackpitts
Clanbrassil St. Lower
Meath Hospital
National Concert Hall
Earlsfort Terrace
Leeson St. Lower
Camden St. Lower
Fitzwilliam Square South
Arnott St.
Heytesbury St.
Lombard St. West
Grantham St.
Hatch St. Upper
Hatch St. Lwr.
Fitzwilliam Place
Emorville Ave.
Curzon St.
Camden St. Upper
Wilton Terrace
Mespil Rd.
Harrington St.
Harcourt St.
Adelaide Rd.
Grand Canal
Clanbrassil St. Upper
Longwood Ave.
Victoria St.
George Bernard Shaw's Birthplace
Richmond St. South
Charlemont St.
Lennox St.
Irish Jewish Museum
Portobello
Grand Parade
Leeson St.
Canal Rd.
Dartmouth Rd
Grove Rd.
Church
DART Station
Information
Post Office
1
2
3
4
5
6
7
8
9
10
11
12
13
14
15
16
17
18
19
20

comfortable. The **Tea Room** restaurant serves ultra-contemporary Irish cuisine, and dropping in at the **Octagon Bar** for a pint of Guinness is a must even if you're not staying.

6-8 Wellington Quay, Dublin 2. ✆ **01/407-0800.** www.theclarence.ie. 49 units. €165–€270 double; €250–€550 suite. Breakfast €18–€24. Dinner, bed and breakfast packages available. Valet parking €5 per hour. **Amenities:** Wi-Fi; bar; restaurant; gym; room service; spa. Bus: 26, 66, 66A, 66B, 66D, 67, 67A.

The Westin ★★ The grand, imposing façade of this hotel is down to its former incarnation as a bank. Original 19th century features pervade throughout the interior—and those parts that feel more modern have an impeccably well-maintained elegance to them all the same. Guestrooms are large and with an appropriately traditional air to the modern decor, with subtly distressed wood furniture and wide leather headboards on the outrageously comfortable beds. The Mint Bar remains a fashionable hangout for the Dublin glitterati, and the basement **Exchange** restaurant serves excellent, modern European food. The only thing missing is a spa, but you can book pampering treatments in your room.

Westmoreland St., Dublin 2. ✆ **01/645-1000.** www.thewestindublin.com. 163 units. €230–€310 double; €350–€520 suite. Rates include breakfast. Dinner, bed and breakfast packages available. Valet parking €25 per day. **Amenities:** Wi-Fi; bar; restaurant; gym; room service. Bus: 1, 7B, 7D, 9, 11, 13, 16, 16C, 25N, 26, 33N, 39N, 40, 41N, 44, 100, 133.

MODERATE

Buswells ★★ This midprice hotel in central Dublin has the pleasing air of a gentleman's club. Decor in the public areas remains traditional, from the original, intricately detailed cornices of the 19th-century plasterwork to the polished marble fireplaces and heavy curtains. However, the small but decently furnished guestrooms are wholly contemporary in style (rather bland, even, after the lovely Georgian spaces one walks through to get to them). Visitors with mobility problems should be certain to ask for a room on a lower floor, as the old building (actually three townhouses merged together), is full of stairs to climb. Pleasant though it is, Buswell's real selling point is the location—just a few minutes' walk to Trinity College in one direction and St. Stephen's Green in the other. You're in the very heart of the action here.

23–25 Molesworth St., Dublin 2. ✆ **01/614-6500.** www.buswells.ie. 69 units. €98–€168 double. Hotel covers cost of parking at nearby lot (overnight only). Cheaper rates do not include breakfast. **Amenities:** Wi-Fi (free); restaurant; bar; room service. DART: Pearse. Bus: 7B, 7D, 10, 10A, 11, 11A, 11B, 13, 14, 14A, 15, 15A, 15B, 15C, 15X, 20B, 25X, 32X, 27C, 33X, 39B, 40A, 40C, 41X, 46A, 46B, 46C, 51D, 51X, 58X, 67X, 84X, 92.

Eliza Lodge ★ Right in the middle of Temple Bar, above a popular Italian restaurant, and overlooking the River Liffey, this smart hotel is smack dab in the thick of the action. Guestrooms are simple and compact, with large windows letting in plenty of natural light, although the modern bathrooms can verge on shoebox size. The only real drawback to this place is the flipside of its greatest asset: the location. Temple Bar is the liveliest part of a busy capital city, and the fact that Eliza Lodge is also on a major traffic intersection hardly acts as an aid to restful sleep. Even without the enticement of a better view of the river, that's good enough reason to fork over extra for an upper floor room. One useful tip for travelers arriving on the redeye: You can check in (very) early for just €20 extra, although this must be pre-booked.

23–24 Wellington Quay, Dublin 2. ✆ **01/671-8044.** www.elizalodge.com. 18 units. €99–€159 double. Discount parking at nearby lot (€7 overnight, €14 for 24 hr.). Rates include breakfast. Dinner, bed and breakfast packages available. **Amenities:** Wi-Fi (free); restaurant. Bus: 26, 39B, 51, 51B, 51C, 51D, 51X, 66, 66A, 66B, 66D, 67, 67A, 68, 69, 69X, 78, 78A, 79, 79A, 90, 92, 206, 748.

Harding Hotel ★★ Just central enough not to feel like a trek to the main tourist sites, but just far enough to escape the inevitable nighttime crowds that descend on nearby Temple Bar, this is an excellent, low-cost option on the western edge of the city center. The polished wood and bright, floor-to-ceiling windows of the cheerful lobby give off a pleasantly old-fashioned vibe, even though most of the hotel is quite modern. The comfortable guestrooms are a terrific value. Even in high season, you can usually find a double room for well under €100, and triple rooms typically cost just a little bit more than standard doubles. This makes the Harding a particularly stand-out option for families. It's not overly fancy, but it's pleasant, clean, and has everything you need. All in all, this is one of the best finds for budget travelers the city has to offer.

Copper Alley, Fishamble St., Dublin 2. ✆ **01/679-6500.** www.hardinghotel.ie. 52 units. €79–€139 double. No parking. Breakfast not included in lower rates. **Amenities:** Wi-Fi (free); restaurant; bar; accessible rooms. Bus: 37, 39, 39A, 39B, 39C, 39X, 49, 49A, 49X, 50, 50X, 56A, 70, 70A, 70X.

The Merchant House ★ One of a relatively new breed of accommodations geared towards business travelers and couples, the concept here is different from a conventional guesthouse. The Merchant House is a series of swanky guest suites, with various services attached but no dedicated reception area. The upside to this is a greater degree of privacy and freedom. The downside is that, while the entrance is secure and private, the building isn't staffed all the time. (Travelers who prefer their local color not too, well, colorful, should also be warned that it's next door to a fetish shop—albeit a discreet one). The suites themselves are extremely well designed; features of the original 18th-century building were beautifully retained when the place was renovated in 2006. Nicely modern touches include flatscreen TVs and elegant contemporary furnishings, and fancy optional extras include a dedicated chauffeur. The bed-and-breakfast rate includes daily housekeeping service and breakfast at a nearby café.

8 Eustace St., Dublin 2. ✆ **01/633-4447.** www.themerchanthouse.eu. 4 units. €113–€152 double. No children. No parking. Breakfast not included in lower rates. **Amenities:** Wi-Fi (free). Bus: 39B, 49X, 50X, 65X, 77X.

Temple Bar Hotel ★ This cheerful, well-run hotel certainly wins in the location stakes, being slap bang in the middle of trendy Temple Bar. Guestrooms are surprisingly large, and decorated in a clean, modern style, albeit with slightly cheap furnishings. Executive rooms offer plenty of extra space for a small premium. The bar downstairs has live music, although if it's not to your fancy, you can hardly strike a plectrum in this area without hitting a dozen lively pubs. The amenities are somewhat lacking for the price, but then again this *is* Temple Bar—around here, a room in the region of €100 per night counts as budget.

10 Fleet St., Dublin 2. ✆ **01/612-9200.** www.templebarhotel.com. 129 units. €100–€140 double. Rates include breakfast. **Amenities:** Wi-Fi (free); bar; room service. DART: Pearse. Bus: 100X, 133.

O'Connell Street Area/North of the Liffey

The Northside has some good offerings in the way of hotels. Though in some respects a less sought-after area, it's still very central and within walking distance of all the major sights and shops. Hotel rates tend to be lower than they are just across the bridge.

EXPENSIVE

The Morrison ★★ Rooms at this chic hotel on the north bank of the Liffey verge on futuristic, with ultra-modern furniture, moody uplighting, and a host of flashy extras, such 40-inch HDTVs. It's all very straight lines and fancy gizmos (they even have in-house tech support), although song lyrics painted onto the walls here and there add an edge of Irish literary romance. There are two good in-house restaurants–the well-regarded **Halo,** and the more casual **Morrison Grill**—and a funky cocktail lounge. Sometimes it all verges on form over function, but the helpful staff make everything run smoothly.

Lower Ormond Quay, Dublin 1. ✆ **01/874-6881.** www.morrisonhotel.ie. 138 units. €179–€242 double; €224–€379 suite. No children under 3. Discount parking at nearby lot (€12 per day). Rates include breakfast. **Amenities:** Wi-Fi (free); 2 restaurants; bar; room service; gym. Bus: 25, 25A, 25B, 25N, 25X, 26, 66, 66A, 66B, 66N, 66X, 67, 67N, 67X, 69N.

MODERATE

The Gresham ★★ One of Dublin's most historic hotels, the Gresham is also one of the oldest—it opened in 1817, though it was almost destroyed during the Easter Rising of 1916. Most of the current building dates from the 1920s; the public areas retain a wonderfully glamorous art deco feel, despite a big modernization in the mid-2000s. The result can be a little bland (in the cheaper rooms at least; the suites are nothing short of opulent), but it's comfortable, well equipped, and most importantly, surprisingly affordable for a hotel with this kind of pedigree. The **Writer's Lounge,** a beautiful remnant of its Jazz Age heyday, is a popular spot for afternoon tea. Overlooking both the hotel lobby and busy O'Connell Street, it's also one of the best perches in the city for some unashamed people watching.

23 Upper O'Connell St., Dublin 1. ✆ **01/874-6881.** www.gresham-hotels.com. 298 units. €85–€200 double. No children under 3. Discount parking at nearby lot (€15 overnight). Breakfast not included in lower rates. Dinner, bed and breakfast packages available. **Amenities:** Wi-Fi (free); 2 restaurants; 2 bars; room service; discounted use of nearby gym and pool (€10). Luas: Abbey St. Bus: 2, 3, 4, 5, 7, 7A, 7B, 7D, 8, 10, 10A, 11, 11A, 11B, 13.

INEXPENSIVE

Two Rooms in Dublin ★★★ This exceptionally sweet and welcoming little B&B on the Northside of Dublin is run by two of the most cultured and well-travelled hoteliers you're likely to meet. Kevin, a filmmaker, and Garvan, a photographer, seem always to be campaigning to preserve some part of historic Dublin or other. That love for heritage shines through in the chic and beautiful restoration of their 1834 townhouse. The eponymous two guestrooms are spacious and filled with light, featuring antique brass beds and sunken baths. The Garden Room opens out onto a private patio, where breakfast can be taken if the sun's out; or, in gloomier weather, you can light a fire in the original Victorian grate. TVs are banished to preserve the peaceful atmosphere, but each bedroom does have its own antique radio set. Delicious, home-cooked breakfasts make excellent use of seasonal produce and ethically sourced ingredients. This is simply one of the most charming and intimate B&Bs in Dublin.

18 Summer St. North, Dublin 1. ✆ **086/822-5572.** www.tworoomsindublin.com. 2 units. €100 double. Two-night minimum. On-street parking nearby. Rates include breakfast. **Amenities:** Wi-Fi (free). Bus: 7, 8, 14, 15 51A, 123. Rail: Connolly (10-min. walk).

St. Stephen's Green/Grafton Street Area

St. Stephen's Green may be only a 10-minute walk from the hustle and bustle of Temple Bar and Trinity College, but it's infinitely calmer and less harried. This is a good area if you're looking for a little peace and quiet.

EXPENSIVE

The Conrad ★★ The Dublin outpost of Hilton's high-end brand is all about the luxury. Beds in the spacious, modern guestrooms are sumptuously comfortable (and refreshingly large for a European hotel, even in the cheapest rooms). Color schemes of chocolate and cream, or oatmeal and royal blue, help convey an air of elegance without feeling too fussy. Thoughtful touches, such as Nespresso machines in every room, are welcome—although charging steeply for something as basic as Wi-Fi, when almost every good B&B in the city now provides it for free, is parsimonious. Despite all the luxury, this place certainly feels geared more towards business travelers than anyone else. The excellent **Alex** restaurant, specializing in seafood, is well worth a splurge.

Earlsfort Terrace, Dublin 2. ✆ **01/602-8900.** conradhotels3.hilton.com. 191 units. €126–€350 double; €289–€439 suite. Valet parking €19 per day. Rates include breakfast. **Amenities:** Wi-Fi; bar; restaurant; room service; gym. Bus: 126.

The Shelbourne ★★★ Dublin hotels simply don't come with a better historic pedigree than this—the Irish constitution was written in this very building (room 112, to be precise). The Shelbourne was acquired by the Marriott group a few years ago, but traditionalists need not fear, because the hotel is still its grand old self. Most of the old wrinkles were ironed out courtesy of a major refurbishment in 2007. A feeling of *fin de siècle* elegance pervades throughout the public areas, with high plaster ceilings, crystal chandeliers, and a winding iron staircase. Guestrooms have a much more discreet, contemporary elegance, with extremely luxurious beds and a host of modern extras. There's also an excellent spa, and you can even book a session with a Genealogy Butler if you need a little expert help in tracing your Irish roots. Afternoon tea at the Shelbourne is a true Dublin institution; consider splurging on a booking, even if you can't spring for a night here.

27 St. Stephen's Green, Dublin 2. ✆ **01/663-4500.** www.marriott.co.uk. 190 units. €279–€409 double; €650–€800 suite. Valet parking €25 per day. Breakfast €21–€29. Dinner, bed and breakfast packages available. **Amenities:** Wi-Fi (free); 3 restaurants; 3 bars; afternoon tea; gym; spa; accessible rooms. Luas: St. Stephen's Green. Bus: 7B, 7D, 10, 10A, 11, 11A, 11B, 14, 14A, 15, 15A, 15B, 15C, 15X, 20B, 25X, 32X, 39X, 40A, 40C, 41X, 51X, 70B, 84X.

The Westbury ★★★ Virtually made for well-heeled shopaholics, this top-end hotel on Grafton Street is a luxurious and stylish retreat. Bedrooms are huge and modern, with subtle floral wallpaper, handmade furniture, and soothing beige and cream tones. Beds are comfortable (although with so much space to spare, they could be bigger) and a few are modern-style four posters. **Wilde,** the excellent Modern Irish restaurant, is a beautiful space overlooking Grafton Street; it also serves one of the city's finest afternoon teas. There's also a more relaxed bar and bistro. Check the website for some enticing package deals, including dinner-bed-and-breakfast and theater options.

Grafton St., Dublin 2. ✆ **01/602-8900.** www.doylecollection.com. 205 units. €230–€310 double; €300–€1700 suite. Parking €20 per day. Rates include breakfast. **Amenities:** Wi-fi (free); bar; 2 restaurants; room service; gym. Bus: 11, 11a, 11b, 14, 14a, 15a, 15c, 15x, 20b, 27c, 33x, 39b, 41x, 46b, 46c.

MODERATE

Camden Court Hotel ★ Although perhaps not quite making budget status, this large hotel just south of St. Stephen's Green is still a great value for what you get. Guestrooms are basic but good-sized and modern. Family rooms are especially a bargain. A practical standard hotel, rather than one overflowing with character and charm, the Camden Court is nonetheless well equipped. Guests can enjoy a pool and massage salon to sooth away a few of those sightseeing aches and pains. You'd probably pay significantly more if this place was just a few blocks north; as it is, the only real drawback is that you're a 10 to 20 minute walk from the center.

Camden St. Lower (near junction with Charlotte Way), Dublin 2. ✆ **01/475-9666.** www.camdencourthotel.com. 246 units. €100–€135 double. Parking (free). Breakfast not included in lower rates. **Amenities:** Wi-Fi (free); bar; restaurant; gym; pool; beauty salon; room service; accessible rooms. Luas: Harcourt St. Bus: 15X, 16, 16A, 19, 19A, 65, 65B, 65X, 83, 122.

Trinity Lodge ★ This small hotel is full of quirks—not all of them convenient (there's no elevator and plenty of stairs, for instance), but the bedrooms are comfortable, contemporary, and surprisingly large for a place in this price range. A converted townhouse, the hotel was built in 1785, and some of the bedrooms retain a historic feel to the design. Quadruple rooms offer outstanding value for families. South Frederick Street is little more than a stone's throw from Trinity College; however, it's also a comparative rarity in the city center—it's generally quite peaceful at night. Breakfast is Continental and "express style" (translation: basic), but the neighborhood has plenty of other options.

12 South Frederick St., Dublin 2. ✆ **01/617-0900.** www.trinitylodge.com. 16 units. €130–€170 double. Two-night minimum on some summer weekends. Discounted parking at nearby lot (€3 overnight, €12.50 24 hr.). Rates include continental breakfast; 10% discount on cooked breakfasts at nearby cafes. **Amenities:** Wi-Fi; restaurant; room service (7am–11pm). Rail: Connolly. Luas: St. Stephen's Green. DART: Pearse. Bus: 7B, 7D, 10, 10A, 11, 11A, 11B, 14, 14A, 15, 15A, 15B, 15C, 15X, 20B, 25X, 27C, 32X, 33X, 39B, 41X, 46B, 46C, 51D, 51X, 58X, 67X, 84X, 92.

Ballsbridge & the Southern Suburbs

This is a prestigious Dublin residential neighborhood, south of the canal. Half the foreign embassies in Dublin are located in this district, coveted for its leafy streets and historic buildings. It's also growing as a hotel quarter—the distance from the city center means that you'll get so much more for your money by staying here.

EXPENSIVE

The Four Seasons ★★★ It's not hard to see how his luxurious hotel in Dublin's southern suburbs has won so many dedicated fans. From the

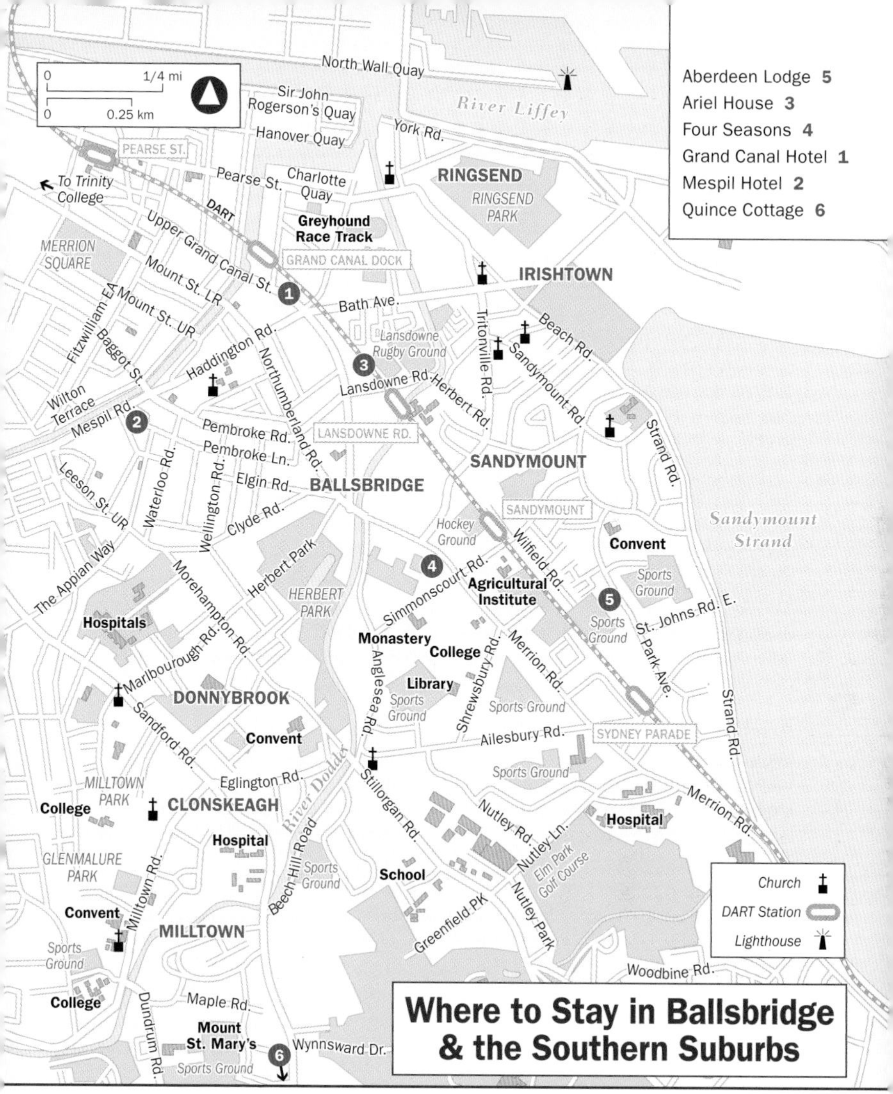

elegantly simple guestrooms, with their sumptuously comfortable beds, to the outstanding, full service spa, this is the kind of place where nothing is too much trouble—but a host of thoughtful touches mean you rarely find anything much to ask for. The only downside is the location—views over the rooftops of Ballsbridge are never going to appeal as much as the kind of vista you get at high-end establishments in the city center—but the payoff is greater peace and quiet. (It's only a short train or taxi ride into the center anyway). Parents will welcome the above-average childcare facilities too; in addition to children's welcome packs (complete with adorable miniature bathrobe), the hotel offers babysitting, and will arrange a host of family activities, from the loan of video games, to city tours, and even puppet shows.

Simmonscourt Rd., Ballsbridge, Dublin 4. ✆ **01/665-4676.** www.fourseasons.com/dublin. 197 units. €300–€375 double; €400–€700 suite. Valet parking (free). Breakfast not included in lower rates. **Amenities:** Wi-Fi; restaurant; bar; spa; pool. DART: Sandymount. Bus: 4, 7, 7N, 8, 27X.

MODERATE

Aberdeen Lodge ★★ Drive up to this elegant Regency building in the springtime, and its front can be so covered in ivy as to resemble a vertical lawn with spaces cut for the windows. Inside, the decor is rather endearingly old fashioned; the neat-as-a-pin public spaces are decorated in heritage tones, and the heavy, antique-style furnishings are scattered with embroidered pillows. Guestrooms are comfortable and quiet, albeit somewhat plain, but modern bathrooms are a big plus. Some have views of the large garden, where guests can take tea—often in the company of the hotel's friendly cat. Aberdeen Lodge is a short walk to the nearest DART station, and from here it's a short hop to the city center. Alternatively, a 5-minute stroll takes you to a pleasant walking path through a park beside the coast. If you do come this way, look out for the grey stone tower, now stuck rather ignominiously between a public toilet and a payphone—it's an example of a Martello Tower, a small defensive fortification that was built by the British to ward off a feared invasion from France in the early 19th century.

53–55 Park Avenue, Ballsbridge, Dublin 4. ✆ **01/283-8155.** www.aberdeen-lodge.com. 11 units. €119–€169 double. Parking (free). Rates include breakfast. **Amenities:** Wi-Fi; restaurant; bar; use of nearby spa. DART: Sydney Parade, Sandymount. Bus: 2, 3, 18, 84N.

Ariel House ★★★ This charming guesthouse in Ballsbridge has won several plaudits over the last few years. And rightly so—it's a smoothly run, good value-for-the-money operation. Situated on a quiet Victorian street, the most obvious landmark is, depending on your point of view, either a hideous blot on a heritage landscape or just a great day out. The Aviva Stadium, one of Ireland's major sports grounds, is literally a block away. Inside the hotel, the vibe is decidedly more old school, with a subtle contemporary flourish. The small, simple guestrooms are tastefully decorated in earthy oatmeal or cream with brocade-pattern bedspreads. The lounge is a pleasant space with an honesty bar; musically inclined guests are even free to tickle the ivories of the lovely old piano. The breakfast menu doesn't veer too far from the traditional Irish staples, but it's exceptionally well done. So long as you're not staying on a match day, the neighborhood is quiet enough to make you feel cosseted away from the crowds, but with good transport links to central Dublin.

50–54 Lansdowne Road, Ballsbridge, Dublin 4. ✆ **01/668-5512.** www.ariel-house.net. 37 units. €90–€140 double. Parking (free). Rates include breakfast. **Amenities:** Wi-Fi (free); honesty bar; afternoon tea; room service. DART: Lansdowne Road Bus: 4, 7, 8, 84.

Grand Canal Hotel ★ Overlooking the 18th-century Grand Canal—a major part of Dublin's industrial heritage, long since abandoned as anything but a picturesque waterway—this large hotel is a strikingly modern place. The Aviva Stadium is a stone's throw away, making this a popular choice for people in town for a game, as well as business travelers and tourists looking for a no-frills place to stay. Usually rooms go for under €100 per night. It wins no awards for style, but it's cheerful, spotlessly clean, and the bedrooms are huge by Dublin standards. The neighborhood is nothing too exciting, but the center is a just short journey by public transport. You could even walk if you wanted to work off one of the hearty hotel breakfasts—Trinity College is about 25 minutes on foot.

Grand Canal St. Upper, Ballsbridge, Dublin 4. ✆ **01/646-1000.** www.grandcanalhotel.ie. 142 units. €69–€153 double. Theater and O2 Arena packages available. Parking (free). Breakfast not included in lower rates. **Amenities:** Wi-Fi (free); restaurant; bar; room service; accessible rooms. DART: Grand Canal Dock. Bus: 4, 5, 7, 7A, 8, 45, 63, 84.

Mespil Hotel ★ Another good budget option in Ballsbridge, the Mespil is within walking distance of the city center—St. Stephen's Green is about a 15-minute stroll. But of course, most visitors pick the south side for the bargain rates (by Dublin standards), rather than the height of convenience, and the accommodations here are certainly of a higher standard than what you're likely to find uptown for the same price. The guestrooms are spacious and feature modern decor and comfortable beds. In common with most hotels of this type, breakfast is served buffet style—tasty and excellent fuel, although you may want a break from all that fried meat and eggs after a couple of days. One nice little bonus: Although not run by the hotel, an excellent gourmet food market is alongside the canal, just outside, every Thursday from 11am to 2pm. See www.irishvillage markets.com for more details.

50–60 Mespil Road, Dublin 4. ✆ **01/448-4600.** www.mespilhotel.com. 255 units. €85–€136 double. Parking (limited). Breakfast €12. **Amenities:** Wi-Fi (free); restaurant; bar; gym; room service; accessible rooms. Bus: 10, 10A, 15X, 49X, 50X, 66D, 92.

INEXPENSIVE

Quince Cottage ★★ This place isn't the most convenient location—it's in Sandyford, a southern suburb about 20 minutes by Luas (tram) from central Dublin—but what Quince Cottage lacks in convenience, it more than makes up for in authenticity. Owners Paula and Brandon have converted their century-old suburban home into a bright and modern B&B. Bedrooms are perfectly pleasant, albeit basic, with modern furnishings and decent-sized beds. Breakfasts are hearty—try the American-style pancakes served with fresh fruit. The spacious, buttercream-colored guest lounge adds to the feeling that you are a guest in a pleasant Dublin home, rather than a number in an impersonal hotel. For those seeking even more privacy, there is also a two-room apartment (the oldest part of the house) that can be rented on a self-catering basis or with breakfast included. Sandyford is about 12km (7½ miles) south of Dublin city center.

Quince Cottage, Kilgobbin Rd., Sandyford, Dublin 18. ✆ **01/295-8488.** www.quince cottage.ie. 4 units. €90 double; €80 for 2 or more nights. Parking (free). Rates include breakfast. **Amenities:** Wi-Fi (free). Luas: Glencairn Bus: 44.

North of Dublin

Skerries is a pleasant seaside commuter town, north of Dublin. It's most definitely outside of the city—about 30km (18½ miles) from Temple Bar—but transport links are reasonably good. Of course, those seeking peace and quiet at the end of the day will see this as a selling point.

INEXPENSIVE

The White Cottages ★★★ The sea is an ever-present feature at this pleasant, whitewashed little B&B in Skerries, a small and pretty commuter town just north of Dublin. The coastline is literally feet away from the wooden terrace at the back, and the sound of the waves can help sooth you to a restful sleep at night. Guestrooms are decorated in summery tones of white and blue with jaunty, candy-striped motifs. The owners are welcoming and extremely helpful—Joe, the co-owner, is a mine of information about the local area, and his wife Jackie displays some of her art around the house. Breakfasts are good, but you have to fend for yourself at dinnertime (Joe is always on hand with an exhaustive list of places to eat nearby). The only major snag is that Skerries is far outside of the city; the train journey to the center takes about 40 minutes, and the bus over an hour. Still, it's nothing more than local commuters do every day, and you'll be hard pressed to find a more tranquil and welcoming retreat after a long day's sightseeing.

Balbriggan Rd., Skerries, Co. Dublin. © **01/849-2231.** www.thewhitecottages.com. 4 units. €80 double. Parking (free). Rates include breakfast. **Amenities:** Wi-Fi; picnic lunches. Rail: Skerries. Bus: 33.

WHERE TO DINE IN DUBLIN

The economic boom years of the early 2000s in Dublin brought with it a new generation of international, sophisticated restaurants. Ireland embraced foodie culture in a way that it never really had before. However, as the economy crashed, so too came a minor resurgence in the popularity of traditional Irish fare, even in expensive restaurants. That's not to say that the food in Dublin is on the downswing—far from it—it's just become easier to find traditional-style Irish food in the city than it was a decade ago. In other words, Ireland is both re-embracing and re-inventing its food heritage.

However, Dublin is still a notoriously expensive city in which to eat out. Prices have certainly come down in recent years, but you're still likely to pay much more for a meal here than in a comparable U.S. city; maybe about the same as you'd expect in Paris or London. But when the food here is good, it's very good, so if you can afford to splurge once or twice while you're in town, do so—you're in for a treat.

Temple Bar/Trinity College Area

Avoca Café ★★ CAFE So much better than just another department store cafe, this is a great place for breakfast, lunch, or a mid-shopping snack. The morning menu is more varied and interesting than at most hotels; free range scrambled eggs with arugula salad, several types of pancakes, French toast, and even the ubiquitous "full Irish" with (rarely found in Ireland) American-style bacon. Lunches are healthy and delicious—think crab salad with home-baked bread or a plate of Middle Eastern style mezze made with Wicklow lamb and served with baba ghanouj and hummus. The delicious soups are somewhat famous with the locals. Or you could just drop in for a tempting slice of cake and a restorative cup of tea.

11–13 Suffolk St., Dublin 2. © **01/677-4215.** www.avoca.ie. Breakfast €3–€12. Lunch €13–€20. Mon–Wed 9:30am–4:30pm; Thurs–Sat 9:30am–5:30pm; Sun 11am–4:30pm. Bus: 15X, 32X, 33X, 39X, 41X, 51D, 51X, 58X, 70X, 84X.

The Bank on College Green ★ PUB Undoubtedly one of Dublin's most jaw-droppingly handsome interiors, this place would be worth visiting even if it didn't serve great pub food. Built in 1892, at the height of Victorian opulence, several remnants of the original bank building were kept when it was converted into a pub (including the wonderful old-style safes that you can still see downstairs). A small and fairly traditional lunch menu of burgers, fish and chips, sandwiches, and salads gives way to a more extensive selection in the evening, including steaks, pasta, and a handy sharing plate. It's all very informal but hugely satisfying. Come on Sunday for a leisurely brunch or a traditional roast at lunchtime.

20 College Green, Dublin 2. ✆ **01/677-0677.** www.bankoncollegegreen.com. Main courses €13–€29. Mon–Fri noon–4pm, 6–10pm; Sat–Sun noon–5pm, 6–10pm. Bus: 15X, 32X, 33X, 39B, 39X, 41X, 49X, 50X, 51X, 58X, 65X, 70X, 77X, 84X.

Brasserie Sixty6 ★★ IRISH/INTERNATIONAL This cheerful, well-run bistro near Trinity College is a popular choice with locals for special occasions. Roast meats cooked rotisserie style are a specialty. Try the garlic and lemon chicken served with herb stuffing and a bunch of sides, or dig into citrus glazed duck with duck fat–roasted potatoes and salad. The rest of the menu is made up of modern bistro fare like roast monkfish with artichokes or a simple, juicy steak with fondant potatoes and peppercorn sauce. Vegetarians are well catered for too, with choices such as vegetable tagine and haloumi Caesar salad. Service is stellar and the portions generous. It's not cheap, although the pre-theater menu is an excellent value (€22 for 2 courses, served until 7pm/6:30pm on Fridays and Saturdays). There's also a popular brunch served until 4pm on Sundays, accompanied by a live jazz band.

66 South Great Georges St., Dublin 2. ✆ **01/400-5878.** www.brasseriesixty6.com. Main courses €24–€31. Mon–Thurs noon–10pm; Fri noon–11pm; Sat 10am–11pm; Sun 10am–10pm. Bus: 15E, 15F, 16, 16A, 19, 19A, 65, 65B, 65X, 83, 122.

Fallon & Byrne ★★★ MODERN EUROPEAN A top-floor adjunct to the wonderful food and wine store, Fallon & Byrne (p. 152), this food hall serves delicious, seasonal Irish fare sourced from artisan producers. Nothing seems to have come very far—crab from the tiny port of Castletownbere, County Cork; lamb from Lough Erne; or oysters from Carlingford. The menu strikes a nice balance between ambitious dishes and more down-to-earth options, so while you may find turbot served with pink grapefruit and crushed new potatoes, you could just as easily opt for a simple burger topped with Cashel blue cheese and smoked bacon. And if you prefer to fend for yourselves, an enormous selection of deli items is downstairs, available to go.

11–17 Exchequer St., Dublin 2. ✆ **01/472-1010.** www.fallonandbyrne.com. Main courses €11–€33. Wed–Thurs noon–3pm, 6–10pm; Fri–Sat noon–3pm, 6–11pm; Sun noon–4pm, 6–9pm; Mon–Tues 12–3pm, 6–9pm. Bus: 15E, 15F, 16, 16A, 19, 19A, 65, 65B, 65X, 83, 122.

Gallagher's Boxty House ★★★ IRISH There's a great story behind this captivating and hugely popular restaurant in Temple Bar. While living in Venezuela as a young man, the owner was struck by the pride his fellow workers took in simple, traditional home cooking. He came home and founded a restaurant to preserve and update some of the Irish traditions in his own style. Boxty—which comes from an old Gaelic term meaning "poor bread"—is a distinctive kind of potato pancake. It's the house signature dish, served with a variety of delicious meat and fish fillings. Also on the menu are steaks, seafood, and a range of Irish stews (try the Spicy Dublin Coddle, a modern variant on an old recipe, made

Where to Dine in Dublin

101 Talbot **4**
Aqua **5**
Arch Bistro **22**
Avoca Café **12**
Bang **18**
The Bank on College Green **11**
Bewley's **16**
Brasserie Sixty6 **15**
Chapter One **3**
Epicurean Food Hall **2**
Fallon & Byrne **14**
Gallagher's Boxty House **9**
Isabel's **19**
Leo Burdock's **7**
The Lord Edward **6**
The Merry Ploughboy **21**
The Old Storehouse **10**
The Pig's Ear **13**
Queen of Tarts **8**
Sabor Brazil **17**
The Sussex **20**
The Winding Stair **1**

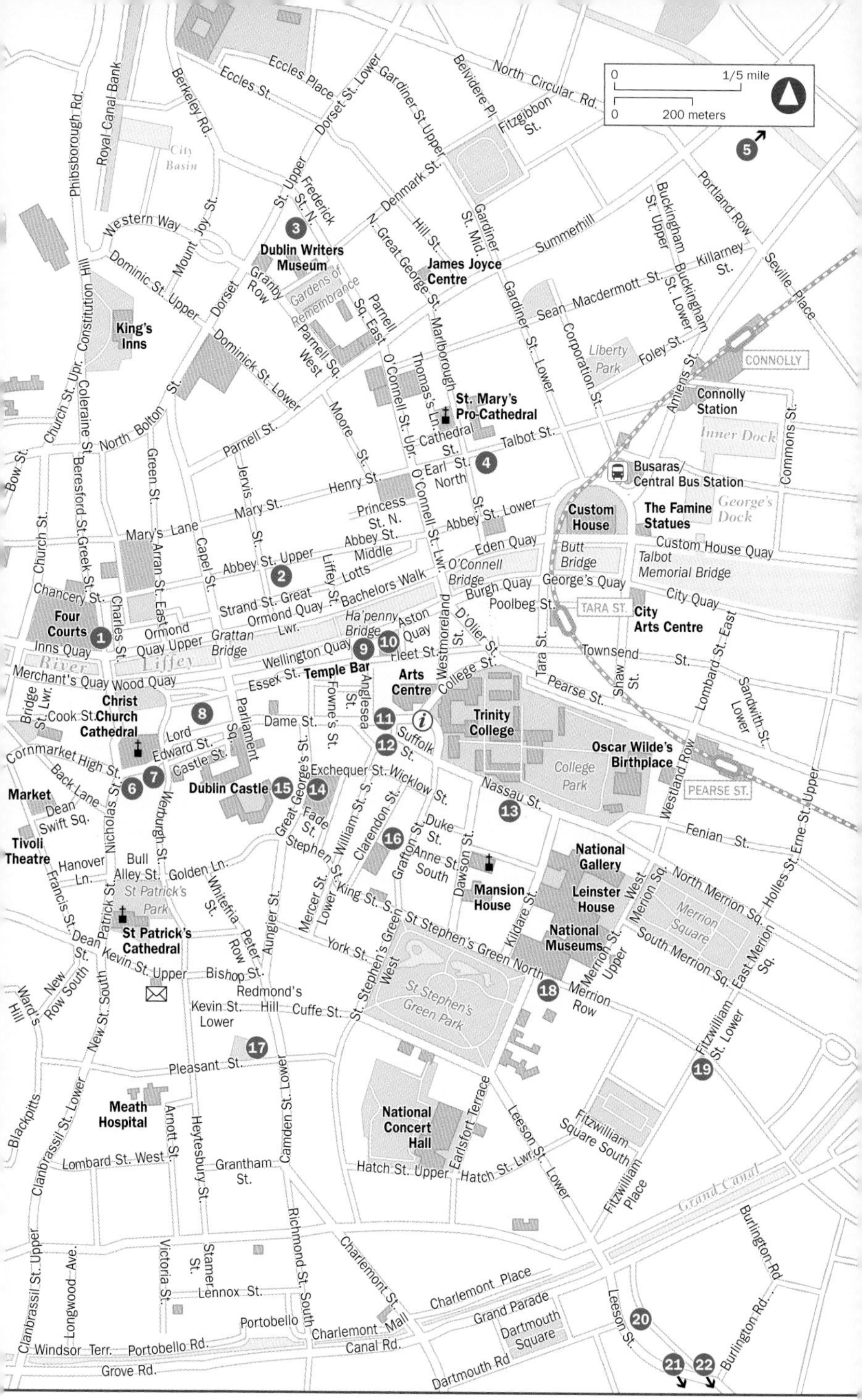
0 1/5 mile
0 200 meters
Eccles Place
Eccles St.
Dorset St. Lower
Gardiner St. Upper
Belvidere Pl.
North Circular Rd.
Fitzgibbon St.
Berkeley Rd.
Royal Canal Bank
Phibsborough Rd.
City Basin
St. Upper Frederick St. N.
Denmark St.
Portland Row
Buckingham St. Upper
Western Way
Mount Joy St.
Dominic St. Upper
Dublin Writers Museum
Granby Row
Gardens of Remembrance
Parnell Sq. West
Parnell Sq. East
N. Great George's St.
Hill St.
Gardiner St. Mid.
James Joyce Centre
Summerhill
Killarney St.
Seville Place
Sean Macdermott St.
Buckingham St. Lower
Constitution Hill
King's Inns
Dorset St.
Dominick St. Lower
Marlborough St.
Thomas's Ln.
Gardiner St. Lower
Corporation St.
Liberty Park
Foley St.
Amiens St.
CONNOLLY
Connolly Station
Coleraine St.
Church St. Upr.
North Bolton St.
O'Connell St. Upr.
St. Mary's Pro-Cathedral
Cathedral St.
Moore St.
Parnell St.
Talbot St.
Earl St. North
Inner Dock
Commons St.
Bow St.
Beresford St.
Green St.
Jervis St.
Henry St.
Busaras/ Central Bus Station
Mary St.
Princess St. N.
O'Connell St. Lwr.
Abbey St. Lower
Custom House
The Famine Statues
George's Dock
Church St.
Mary's Lane
Capel St.
Abbey St. Middle
Eden Quay
Butt Bridge
Custom House Quay
Greek St.
Arran St. East
Abbey St. Upper
Liffey St.
Lotts
O'Connell Bridge
Talbot Memorial Bridge
Chancery St.
Strand St. Great
Bachelors Walk
Burgh Quay
George's Quay
Four Courts
Charles St.
Ormond Quay Upper
Ormond Quay Lwr.
Ha'penny Bridge
Aston Quay
Poolbeg St.
TARA ST.
City Quay
City Arts Centre
Inns Quay
Grattan Bridge
Wellington Quay
Fleet St.
Westmoreland St.
D'Olier St.
Tara St.
Townsend St.
Lombard St. East
River Liffey
Merchant's Quay
Wood Quay
Essex St.
Temple Bar
Arts Centre
College St.
Pearse St.
Shaw St.
Sandwith St. Lower
Bridge St. Lwr.
Christ Church Cathedral
Cook St.
Dame St.
Fowne's St.
Anglesea St.
Trinity College
Oscar Wilde's Birthplace
Lord Edward St.
Parliament Sq.
Suffolk St.
College Park
Westland Row
Cornmarket
High St.
Castle St.
Great George's St.
Exchequer St.
Wicklow St.
PEARSE ST.
Erne St. Upper
Back Lane
Dublin Castle
Nassau St.
Market
Dean Swift Sq.
Nicholas St.
Werburgh St.
Fade St.
William St. S.
Clarendon St.
Duke St.
Fenian St.
Tivoli Theatre
Hanover Ln.
Bull Alley St.
Golden Ln.
Stephen St.
Grafton St.
Anne St. South
Dawson St.
National Gallery
North Merrion Sq.
Holles St.
Francis St.
St Patrick's Park
Whitefriar St.
Aungier St.
Mercer St. Lower
King St. S.
Mansion House
Leinster House
Merrion Sq. West
Merrion Square
Patrick St.
St Patrick's Cathedral
Peter Row
St Stephen's Green North
Kildare St.
National Museums
Merrion St. Upper
South Merrion Sq.
Dean St.
Kevin St. Upper
Bishop St.
York St.
St Stephen's Green West
St Stephen's Green Park
Merrion Row
East Merrion Sq.
Ward's Hill
New Row South
New St. South
Kevin St. Lower
Redmond's Hill
Cuffe St.
Fitzwilliam St. Lower
Pleasant St.
Camden St. Lower
Earlsfort Terrace
Leeson St. Lower
Meath Hospital
Blackpitts
Clanbrassil St. Lower
Arnott St.
Heytesbury St.
National Concert Hall
Fitzwilliam Square South
Lombard St. West
Grantham St.
Hatch St. Upper
Hatch St. Lwr.
Fitzwilliam Place
Grand Canal
Burlington Rd.
Richmond St. South
Charlemont St.
Clanbrassil St. Upper
Longwood Ave.
Victoria St.
Stamer St.
Lennox St.
Charlemont Place
Grand Parade
Portobello
Charlemont Mall
Dartmouth Square
Leeson St.
Windsor Terr.
Portobello Rd.
Canal Rd.
Grove Rd.
Dartmouth Rd.
1
2
3
4
5
6
7
8
9
10
11
12
13
14
15
16
17
18
19
20
21
22

with chorizo and served with soda bread). Modern restaurants don't come with a greater appreciation for culinary heritage than this one.

20–21 Temple Bar, Dublin 2. ✆ **01/677-2762.** www.boxtyhouse.ie. Main courses €15–€17. Mon–Thurs 11am–11:30pm; Fri–Sat 11am–11pm; Sun 11am–10:30pm. Luas: Jervis. Bus: 22, 39B, 49X, 50X, 65X, 66, 66A, 66B, 66D, 67, 67A, 69X, 77X.

The Old Storehouse ★★ IRISH/PUB There isn't much in the way of risk or innovation on the menu of hearty Irish classics at this popular pub in Temple Bar—and that's precisely why it's so popular. What you get is delicious, traditional pub food mixed with just a hint of bistro-style around the edges. Think a fat, juicy burger served with vine tomatoes and cocktail sauce; bangers and mash (sausages and mashed potato) with ale gravy; or perhaps some steamed mussels with garlic bread. There's a small wine list, but the beer selection is better. As much of a draw as the food is the nightly live music; all traditional and all free, they have up to 20 acts a week in the summer. The Old Storehouse doesn't accept reservations, so be prepared to wait for a table when it's busy.

Crown Alley, off Cope St., Dublin 2. ✆ **01/607-4003.** www.theoldstorehouse.ie. Main courses €11–€16. Daily noon–10pm. Bus: 39B, 49X, 50X, 65X, 77X.

The Pig's Ear ★★★ MODERN IRISH A deliciously inventive approach to traditional Irish tastes pervades at this super-cool restaurant overlooking Trinity College. However, this isn't one of those trendy eateries in which the menu is too concerned with being clever to be satisfying. Classic ingredients are offered with modern flair: pan fried cod served with garlic micro potatoes and golden raisins, for example, or pig belly with salted celeriac, burnt pear, and barley. Desserts have a playfully retro edge: Guinness and date pudding (a sweet steamed cake) with vanilla ice cream and candied pecan, or cheesecake served with Hob Nobs, a brand of cookie liable to give local diners a flush of nostalgia. You certainly won't be able to miss this place from the outside—just look out for the shocking pink door with a candy-striped awning.

4 Nassau St., Dublin 2. ✆ **01/670-3865.** www.thepigsear.ie. Main courses €11–€27. Mon–Sat noon–2:45pm, 5:30–10pm. DART: Pearse St. Bus: 25X, 32X, 33X, 41X, 51D, 51X, 58X, 67X, 84X, 92.

Queen of Tarts ★★ CAFE This cheerful little tearoom in the heart of Temple Bar is a delightful pit stop for a pot of tea and some form of sweet, diet-busting snack. Cakes and tarts are the specialty; it's all good, but try the lemon meringue or the old-fashioned Victoria sponge (white cake with a jam filling and a dusting of sugar on top). They also serve breakfast until noon during the week, 1pm on Saturday, and a decadent 2pm on Sunday. At lunchtime you can order soups or sandwiches, but it's the cakes that keep us coming back.

Cows Lane, Dame St., Dublin 2. ✆ **01/633-4681.** www.queenoftarts.ie. Breakfast €4.50–€10. Lunch €6–€10. Mon–Fri 8am–7pm; Sat 9am–7pm; Sun 10am–6pm. Bus: 37, 39, 39A, 39C, 70, 70A.

Historic Old City

Leo Burdock's ★★ FISH & CHIPS Proof that not all great food experiences come with a hefty price tag, Leo Burdock's is probably the most famous fish and chip shop in Ireland. In fact, it's virtually *de rigueur* for passing celebrities to pop in; the photographic "wall of fame" includes Sandra Bullock,

Russell Crowe, and Tom Cruise. But don't come expecting cutting-edge cuisine because Leo Burdock's still trades on the same simple, winning formula that it has since 1913: battered fresh fish (cod, sole, ray or scampi) and thick chips (like very fat steak fries), all cooked the old fashioned way, in beef drippings. There are other options on the menu, including hamburgers, but frankly what's the point of coming to a place like this if you don't order the one thing for which it's world famous?

2 Werburgh St., Dublin 8. ✆ **01/454-0306.** www.leoburdock.com. Main courses €2.50–€7.50. Daily noon–midnight. Bus: 49X, 50X, 54A, 50X, 56A, 77, 77A, 77X, 78A, 150, 151.

The Lord Edward ★★ SEAFOOD With a believable claim to be the oldest seafood restaurant in Dublin, the Lord Edward has been a city staple since 1890. The rather unreconstructed menu contains a huge range of seafood such as sole, prawns, scallops, lobster, and various other fruits of the sea, all served every traditional way you can think of and a few you probably can't. The dining room is avowedly old fashioned. This is certainly not the place to come if you're seeking out what's new and what's hot in the Irish culinary scene. But fans of the Lord Edward (and there are plenty of them) adore coming here for the sense of continuity and old-school charm.

23 Christchurch Place, Dublin 8. ✆ **01/454-2420.** www.lordedward.ie. Main courses €19–€39. Wed–Fri 12:30–2:30pm, 6–10:45pm; Sat 6–10:45pm. Bus: 50X, 56A, 77, 77A, 77X, 150, 151.

O'Connell Street Area/North of the Liffey

101 Talbot ★★ INTERNATIONAL This cheery and informal spot, a 3-minute walk from the G.P.O. on O'Connell Street, is strong on delicious Irish cuisine with global influences and a healthy twist. The bright, airy dining room, lined with modern art, is an appealingly contemporary space. Specials may include roast salmon with asparagus and champ (mashed potato with spring onion and buttermilk); or steamed mussels in white wine, garlic, and cream sauce. The early bird menu (two courses for €20) is a particularly good deal and popular with pre-theater diners attending the Abbey Theatre just around the corner.

101–102 Talbot St., Dublin 1. ✆ **01/874-5011.** www.101talbot.ie. Main courses €16–€22. Tues–Sat noon–3pm, 5–11pm. Luas: Abbey St. Bus: 20B, 32X, 33X, 41, 41A, 41B, 41C, 42, 42A, 42B, 43, 51A, 130, 142.

Chapter One ★★★ MODERN IRISH The vaulted basement of the excellent Dublin Writers Museum (see p. 101) houses one of the city's most feted restaurants. The fixed-price menus make excellent use of local flavors and organic ingredients. Feast on gourmet dishes like poached lobster with smoked haddock mousse or lamb served with fried sweetbreads and garlic sauce. The separate set menu for vegetarians has dishes such as aged Parmesan ravioli with asparagus and wild garlic. Adventurous diners will relish the chef's table: Seated in a little booth right inside the kitchen, guests are served a special 6-course menu (€80 per person) while the culinary theater happens before your eyes. The wine list is excellent; consider splurging on a Meerlust Rubicon 2005, an outstanding and little-seen South African vintage with a sublime, smoky flavor. ***Tip:*** The lunch menu is nearly half the price of dinner.

19 Parnell Sq. North, Dublin 1. ✆ **01/873-2266.** www.chapteronerestaurant.com. 4 course fixed-price menu €65. Tues–Fri 12:30–2pm, 6–10:30pm; Sat 6–10:30pm. Luas: Abbey St. DART: Connolly St. Bus: 1, 2, 14, 14A, 16, 16A, 19, 19A, 33X, 39X, 41X, 48A, 58X, 70B, 70X.

Epicurean Food Hall ★ MEDITERRANEAN An energetic coming together of flavors from disparate corners of the global village, this delightful food hall is a voyage of discovery for the epi-curious. The selection of lunch options changes quite regularly, but long-standing kitchens include **Istanbul,** specializing in Mediterranean dishes and Turkish kebabs; **Saburritos,** which serves a combination of authentic and California-style Mexican street food; **Rafa's Temaki,** which claims to be the first place in Ireland to sell Temaki—a healthful, fast food-style combination of Japanese sushi and sashimi; and a branch of the famous Dublin fish and chip takeaway, **Leo Burdock.** The various stalls share a common seating area, or you can get it to go.

1 Liffey St. Lower, Dublin 1. ✆ **01/283-6077.** www.epicureanfoodhall.com. Main courses €4–€13. Mon–Sat 9am–8pm; Sun noon–7pm. Luas: Jervis. Bus: 39B, 69X.

The Winding Stair ★★ MODERN IRISH A sweet old bookstore downstairs and a chic restaurant upstairs, The Winding Stair is situated a stone's throw from the Ha'penny Bridge. The views of the Liffey are romantic, but of course it's the inventive modern Irish cooking that pulls in the crowds. After a starter of Dingle Bay crab or Connemara ham with Irish mozzarella and rocket (arugula), you could opt for milk-poached smoked haddock with cheddar cheese mash, or perhaps spring lamb with minted courgettes (zucchini). Desserts include pear and ginger cake topped with ice cream from Gathabawn, a small village near Kilkenny. The enormous wine list, which is helpfully arranged by character rather than region, features several decently priced options. Two- and three-course pre-theater menus are a great value at €25 to €30. ***Just note:*** You must be finished by 8:15pm.

40 Lower Ormond Quay, Dublin 1. ✆ **01/872-7320.** www.winding-stair.com. Main courses €23–€27. Fri–Sat noon–3:30pm, 5:30–10:30pm; Sun–Thurs noon–5pm, 5:30–10:30pm. Luas: Jervis. Bus: 39B, 51, 51B, 51C, 51D, 51X, 68, 69, 69X, 78, 78A, 79, 79A, 90, 92, 206.

Fitzwilliam Square/Merrion Square Area

Isabel's ★★★ MODERN IRISH The dining room of this in-vogue modern Irish restaurant, just east of St. Stephen's Green, is arrestingly well designed; expanses of ancient, exposed brickwork give way to (literally) stacks of wine in open crates. The menu infuses modern bistro cuisine with local and seasonal produce. Scallops come with Wicklow nettle risotto and sea vegetables, for example, while the slow-cooked lamb is served with samphire (a little-used vegetable found only in coastal areas that resembles seaweed and has a piquant, salty flavor). Typical desserts include chocolate mousse served with peanut panna cotta and honeycomb. It's all finely judged and beautifully presented. If dinner here is too expensive for you, come for a simpler, cheaper lunch. They also do a small and reasonably priced breakfast menu.

112 Baggot St. Lower, Dublin 2. ✆ **01/661-9000.** www.isabels.ie. Main courses €20–€25. Mon 6–10pm; Tues–Thurs noon–3pm, 6–10pm; Fri noon–3pm, 5:30–10pm; Sat 5:30–10pm. Bus: 10, 10A, 15X, 49X, 50X, 66D.

The Sussex ★★ IRISH The gastropub reinvention of traditional Irish cooking into something chic and fashionable finds one of its best proponents at this rather refined pub (above another popular bar), a 10-minute walk south of St. Stephen's Green. The menu takes classic pub fare, prepares it beautifully, and adds an oh-so-subtle twist—fish and chips with pea and mint puree, perhaps, or linguine served with Dingle Bay prawns, garlic, and lemon.

For dessert try the posset (a syllabub-like concoction containing cream and lemon) served with spiced shortbread. As you'd expect, all the ingredients are sourced as locally as possible, with plenty of attention to what's in season. The wine list is well judged, with plenty of reasonably priced options. ***Tip:*** The lunch menu is an edited version of what's for dinner—but significantly cheaper.

9 Sussex Terrace (at junction of Sussex Road; above M. O'Briens Pub), Dublin 4. ✆ **01/676-2851.** www.thesussex.ie. Main courses €15–€27. Mon noon–3pm; Tues noon–11pm; Sun 5–11pm. Bus: 7B, 7D, 11, 11A, 11B, 27C, 39B, 39X, 46B, 46C, 46D, 46E, 58C, 58X, 70B, 70X, 116.

St. Stephen's Green/Grafton Street Area

Bang ★★ MODERN IRISH The presence of so many Irish place names on the menu indicates how much this place has embraced the slow food ethos. The vast majority of ingredients are regionally sourced from specialist Irish producers. You may find Clare Island salmon served with local radishes and pickled cucumber; John Dory from Kilkeel; or perhaps a rib-eye steak from County Fermanagh. If it all seems too hard to choose from, you could opt for one of the tasting menus (€69–€79, depending on the number of courses). The wine list is expertly chosen, and there's also a small but delightfully put together cocktail menu—try the vodka martini made with sweet County Wexford strawberries.

11 Merrion Row, Dublin 2. ✆ **01/400-4229.** www.bangrestaurant.com. Main courses €22–€32. Mon–Tues 5:30–10pm; Wed 12:30–10pm; Thurs–Sat 12:30–11pm. Luas: St. Stephen's Green. Bus: 25X, 51D, 51X, 65X, 66X, 67X, 77X.

Bewley's ★ CAFE A Dublin landmark since 1927, Bewley's has a literary pedigree as well as an historic one. James Joyce was a regular (it makes an appearance in his book *Dubliners*), and a host of subsequent literary greats made this their regular stop-off for a cup of joe and a slice of cake. It's still hugely popular, and not just for coffee; you can get a pretty good pizza, salad, or burger here at lunch or dinnertime, in addition to a more modest menu of light snacks. Fun fact: the distinctive, ornate faux-Egyptian facade (incongruously framing the rarely used full name, "Bewley's Oriental Café") owes its existence to the fact that, when the place opened, Europe was still in the grip of a craze for all things Ancient Egyptian, following the discovery of Tutankhamen's tomb just 5 years before.

78–79 Grafton St., Dublin 2. ✆ **01/672-7720.** www.bewleys.com. Main courses breakfast €3–€12. Lunch and dinner €8–€15. Mon–Wed 8am–10pm; Thurs–Sat 8am–11pm; Sun 9am–10pm. Bus: 11, 11A, 11B, 14, 14A, 15A, 15C, 15X, 20B, 27C, 33X, 39B, 41X, 46B, 46C.

Sabor Brazil ★★★ BRAZILIAN A good Brazilian restaurant isn't high on the list of things one expects to find in Dublin—even less so, an innovative and wildly fashionable spot in a slightly dicey neighborhood south of the center. And yet Sabor Brazil not only serves outstanding food, but visiting here is half of the fun for a unique and memorable experience. The tiny dining room is decorated in a wry combination of Regency Baroque and Latinate flourishes. The menu (€100 per person for 7 courses, no a la carte) fuses contemporary Brazilian flavors with an Irish inflection; rock salt-coated steak fillet, pan fried in garlic with apricot and walnut sauce, for instance, or a pastel (kind of like South American dim sum) filled with whatever the chef decides is best that day. A vegetarian alternative is always available. Reservations are essential (with a booking deposit, credited to your bill on the night), and the restaurant will generally cater to couples only.

50 Pleasants St., Off Camden St., Dublin 8. ✆ **01/475-0304.** www.saborbrazil.ie. Tasting menu only €100. Tues–Sun 6–11pm. Bus: 65, 65X.

Ballsbridge & the Southern Suburbs

Arch Bistro ★★★ MODERN EUROPEAN One of those places that even locals talk about as a "find," the Arch is an adorable little pub bistro in Churchtown, one of Dublin's southern suburbs. The lovingly crafted vintage vibe of the exterior—all thatched roofs and antique Guinness signs—shines above the urban blandness of the neighborhood. Inside, the space is elegant and cozy. The menu takes contemporary bistro classics and shakes them up with flashes of individuality; pan seared seabass is served with a fennel and citrus salad, and the potato gnocchi comes with aubergine (eggplant) caviar. Even the fish and chips come with a subtle twist—the batter is Japanese tempura style, and the fries are served with mango salsa. The three-course set menu is particularly good discount at just €25.

Landscape Rd., Churchtown, Dublin 14. ✆ **01/296-6340.** www.thearchbistro.com. Main courses €17–€27. Tues–Fri 12:30–2:30pm, 5:30–10pm; Sat 5–10pm; Sun noon–3pm, 5–8pm. Bus: 14.

North of Dublin

Aqua ★★★ SEAFOOD With a jaw-dropping view over Dublin Bay, this has to be one of the most romantic dining spots in the region. Service is excellent—attentive without being overbearing—and the seafood is delicious and fresh-as-can-be. You can start with a half dozen oysters from Carlingford Lough, before moving on to John Dory fillet with sweet potato and celeriac puree, or try the seabass in a Chinese-style dressing. There's also a small range of tasty meat options for those who aren't wowed by the bounty of the sea. Howth is a small commuter suburb of Dublin, about 16km (10 miles) northeast of the city center. The restaurant is about a 10-minute walk from the Howth DART station, while a cab out here from the city should run you about €30. Definitely worth the splurge.

1 West Pier, Howth, Co. Dublin. ✆ **01/832-0690.** www.aqua.ie. Main courses €24–€34. Tues–Sat 12:30–3:30pm, 5:30–10pm; Sun noon–5pm, 5:30–8:30pm; Mon 12:30–9pm (a la carte and specials only). DART: Howth. Bus: 31.

South of Dublin

The Merry Ploughboy ★ IRISH/PUB An exuberant live show of traditional music and dancing accompanies dinner at this hugely popular pub in Rathfarnham, one of Dublin's further-flung southern suburbs. Admittedly it's all very touristy, but you certainly get your money's worth—the show runs for 2 hours, and the food, while limited, is actually pretty good. Expect beef braised in Guinness served with root vegetables and rosemary jus or trout in a dill and lemon crust. The only real drawback is the time it takes to get here (Rathfarnham is about 6km/3¾ miles) from the center), although a dedicated minibus will pick you up and take you back at the end of the night for the bargain price of €5.50 round-trip.

Edmondstown Rd., Rockbrook, Rathfarnham, Dublin 16. ✆ **01/493-1495.** www.mpbpub.com. Dinner and show €49.50. Bar menu €9–€21. Daily dinner 7:30pm sharp; show 8:30–10:30pm. Bar food: Mon–Fri 4:30–9:30pm; Sat 12:30–9:30pm; Sun 12:30–8pm. Special bus leaves from and returns to six locations in central Dublin (€5.50 per person; must be pre-booked).

SHOPPING

Although Dublin took its fair share of pain during Ireland's recent economic woes, it remains a world-class shopping town. Although interesting, small independent shops and boutiques have inevitably struggled more than their big-name chain store rivals, you can still find excellent craftsmanship in the form of handwoven wool blankets and clothes in a vivid array of colors, high-quality crafts and antiques, and chic clothes from the seemingly limitless line of Dublin designers.

The hub of mainstream shopping south of the Liffey is **Grafton Street,** crowned by the city's most fashionable department store, Brown Thomas (known as BT), and the jeweler Weirs, but much better shopping is on the smaller streets radiating out from Grafton, such as **Duke, Dawson, Nassau,** and **Wicklow.** On these streets you'll find small, interesting shops that specialize in books, handicrafts, jewelry, gifts, and clothing. For clothes, look out for tiny **Cow's Lane,** off Lord Edward Street—it is popular with those in the know for its excellent clothing boutiques selling the works of local designers. Also in Grafton's penumbra are **William Street South, Castle Market,** and **Drury Street,** all of which have smart boutiques and irresistible tiny shops. On William Street South, look out for the **Powerscourt Townhouse Centre,** a small, elegant shopping center in a grand Georgian town house. It has relaxing cafes, antiques shops, shoe shops, and the top-floor Design Centre, which sells works by some of Ireland's top designers. Not far away, the **George's Street Arcade** is a marvelous clutter of bohemian jewelry, used books, vintage clothes, and other things appealing to the alternative crowd (they even have a resident fortune teller).

Generally, Dublin shops are open from 9am to 6pm Monday to Saturday, and Thursday until 9pm. Many larger shops have Sunday hours from noon to 6pm.

Major department stores include, on the Northside, **Arnotts,** 12 Henry St., Dublin 1 (✆ **01/805-0400;** www.arnotts.ie), and the marvelously traditional **Clerys,** 18–27 Lower O'Connell St., Dublin 1 (✆ **01/878-6000;** www.clerys.com); and on the south side, **Brown Thomas,** 85–95 Grafton St., Dublin 2 (✆ **01/605-6666;** www.brownthomas.com).

Dublin also has several clusters of shops in **multistory malls** or ground-level **arcades,** ideal for indoor shopping on rainy days. On the Northside, these include the **ILAC Centre,** off Henry Street, Dublin 1 (✆ **01/878-2275;** www.ilac.ie), and the **Jervis Shopping Centre** (✆ **01/878-1323;** www.jervis.ie), at 125 Abbey St., Dublin 1. On the south side, there's the **Royal Hibernian Way,** 49–50 Dawson St., Dublin 2 (✆ **01/679-5919**); the gleaming wrought-iron-and-glass **St. Stephen's Green Centre,** at the top of Grafton Street, Dublin 2 (✆ **01/478-0888;** www.stephensgreen.com); and the aforementioned **Powerscourt Townhouse Centre,** 59 William St. S., Dublin 2 (✆ **01/679-4144;** www.powerscourtcentre.com).

Art & Antiques

Caxton ★★ Antique prints from the 16th, 17th, and 18th centuries are a specialty of this wonderful art store. The prices can be astronomical, but even if you're not buying, browsing here is like being a kid in a candy store for lovers of the antiquarian. 63 Patrick St., Dublin 8. ✆ **01/453-0060.** Bus: 49, 54A.

Christy Bird ★ "Variety is our specialty" proclaims a sign at this appealing antique store, which has been in business since the 1940s. And it certainly lives up to the promise—stocked with a happy jumble of knick-knacks, collectibles, tat and genuine antiques, the joy is that you never quite know what you're going to find. 32 South Richmond St., Dublin 2. ✆ **01/475-4049.** www.christybird.com. Luas: Charlemount, Harcourt St. Bus: 14, 14A, 14B, 15, 15B, 65B, 74, 83, 128.

Danker Antiques ★★ This friendly, approachable dealer, in an arcade just off Dawson Street, has a fine collection of antique silver tableware and jewelry. They specialise in designs from the Celtic Revival period of the early 20th century, and usually have some beautiful Art Deco pieces too. Royal Hibernian Way, Dawson St., Dublin 2. ✆ **01/677-4009.** www.dankerantiques.com. Bus: 15A, 15B, 44, 61, 140

The Doorway Gallery ★★★ A mixture of new and established Irish artists display their work at this cheerful art gallery. There's always something wonderful to discover, and many prices are affordable too. 24 S. Frederick St., Dublin 2. ✆ **01/764-5895.** www.thedoorwaygallery.com. Bus: 4, 7, 8, 7B, 7D, 25, 25A, 25B, 25X, 26, 27X, 46A, 66, 66A, 66A, 66B, 66X, 67, 67X, 120, 145.

Green on Red ★★★ Outstanding contemporary art can be found at this little gallery just northwest of Trinity College. It's a great place for spotting new talent in the Irish art world. 26–28 Lombard St., Dublin 2. ✆ **01/671-3414.** www.greenonredgallery.com. DART: Pearse. Bus: 4, 7, 8, 26, 27X, 44, 61, 66, 66A, 66B, 67, 120.

Books & Stationery

Cathach Books ★★★ When lovers of Irish literature and antiquarian books die, if they've been good, they get to spend eternity at Cathach Books. This is where to come for rare copies of Joyce, Yeats, Wilde, Behan, Stoker, and just about every luminary of the Irish canon you can think of. Prices range from the barely affordable (€375 for a rare 1927 Dracula), to the stratospheric (€35,000 for a first edition Ulysses) but it's simply heaven to browse. 10 Duke St., Dublin 2. ✆ **01/671-8676.** www.rarebooks.ie. DART: Pearse. Bus: 10, 11A, 11B, 13, 20B.

Eason ★ This multi-storey bookstore on O'Connell Street is one of Ireland's oldest—it's been in business since 1819. Pretty much everything you could want is here, from history and local interest titles, to the latest bestsellers. 40 Lower O'Connell St. ✆ **01/858-3800.** www.easons.com. Luas: Abbey St. Bus: 1, 11, 38, 38A, 38B, 39N, 88N, 120, 122, 123, 747.

Hodges Figgis ★ Another enormous *grande dame* Dublin bookshop, this one's even older than Eason's—they've been dealing in the printed page here since 1768. Now owned by the Waterstones chain, Hodges Figgis one of the go-to places in the city for books of all kinds. 56–58 Dawson St., Dublin 2. ✆ **01/677-4754.** Bus: 15A, 15B, 44, 61, 140.

The Pen Corner ★★★ Keeping the flame alive for the dying art of letter writing, this delightfully old-fashioned shop sells exquisite fountain pens, paper, and other writing implements. They also sell notebooks and cards. 12 College Green, Dublin 2. ✆ **01/679-3641.** Luas: Abbey St. Bus: 9, 13, 16, 16C, 19, 49N, 54A, 83, 83A, 122, 123, 150, 747, 869.

Crafts, Design & Homeware

Avoca Handweavers ★★★ This place is a wonderland of vivid colors, soft, intricately woven fabrics, blankets, light woolen sweaters, children's clothes, and

toys, all in a delightful shopping environment spread over three floors near Trinity College. All the fabrics are woven in the Vale of Avoca in the Wicklow Mountains. The store also sells pottery, jewelry, vintage and antique clothing, food, and adorable little things you really don't need, but can't live without. Hands down, this is one of the best stores in Dublin. The top-floor **cafe** is a great place for lunch (see p. 138). 11–13 Suffolk St., Dublin 2. ✆ **01/677-4215.** www.avoca.ie. Bus: All An Lar (cross-city) buses.

The Design Tower ★★ A cutting-edge convocation of hot designers and craftspeople work at this former sugar refinery at the Grand Canal Quay on the eastern side of the city. Occupants include Seamus Gill, who makes extraordinary, almost organic-seeming silverware; conceptual artist and fashion designer Roisin Gartland; and jewelry designer Brenda Haugh, whose work includes interesting modern interpretations of Celtic motifs. Some designers here have walk-in shops, but most prefer appointments, so call ahead if you want to see someone specific. The Design Tower is near Grand Canal Dock DART station, or about a 20-minute walk from Grafton Street. Trinity Centre, Grand Canal Quay, Dublin 2. ✆ **01/677-0107.** www.thedesigntower.com. DART: Grand Canal Dock. Bus: 1, 2, 3, 50, 56A, 77A.

House of Ireland ★ An excellent "one-stop shop" for quality Irish souvenirs, this is the place to come for Waterford and Galway Crystal, Belleek China, jewelry, linens, and clothing by big-name Irish designers such as Eugene and Anke McKernan, John Rocha, and Louise Kennedy. Just one trip here and nobody back home needs to know that you didn't really scour the country for that perfect knick-knack or gift. If you've really left your souvenir shopping until the last minute, two smaller outlet branches are at Dublin Airport. 37–38 Nassau St., Dublin 2. ✆ **01/671-1111.** www.houseofireland.com. Bus: 15X, 25X, 32X, 33X, 39X, 41X, 51D, 51X, 58X, 67X, 70X, 84X, 92.

Mayfly ★★★ You know you're visiting somewhere that's quintessentially Temple Bar when the directions on the website tell you to look out for the cow in the buggy out front. This is a treasure trove for deliciously creative, artsy gifts, jewelry, clothing, and other doodads that are impossible to resist. Artists whose work is for sale include Courtney Tyler, who turns old watch faces into interesting jewelry, and embroiderer Victoria White, who makes misfit toys by hand. 11 Fownes St., Dublin 2. ✆ **086/376-4189.** www.mayfly.ie. Bus: 39B, 49X, 50X, 65X, 77X.

Moss Cottage ★★★ A real one-of-a-kind craft store, Moss Cottage is the kind of place where you go in for a browse and leave with bags full of souvenirs and a mental note to email the lovely owner pictures of all your finds in situ back home. They specialize in "upcycling"—converting old junk into beautiful things—and stock everything from scented candles to vintage homewares. The shop is in the suburb of Dundrum, about 7km (4½ miles) south of the city center. 4 Pembroke Cottages, Main St., Dundrum, Dublin 14. ✆ **01/215-7696.** www.mosscottage.ie. Luas: Dundrum. Bus: 14, 14C, 44, 44B.

Powerscourt Townhouse Centre ★★ In a restored 1774 town house, this four-story complex consists of a central sky-lit courtyard and more than 60 boutiques, craft shops, art galleries, snack bars, wine bars, and restaurants. The wares include all kinds of crafts, antiques, paintings, prints, ceramics, leatherwork, jewelry, clothing, chocolates, and farmhouse cheeses. You can also book a behind-the-scenes tour to learn more about the house's history. You can see the old kitchen and cellars, the former Lord and Lady's bedrooms and dressing rooms, the music room, ballroom, and dining room. For details and booking contact Shireen Gail on ✆ **086/806-5505,** or email shireengail@gmail.com. 59 S. William St., Dublin 2. ✆ **01/679-4144.** www.powerscourtcentre.com. DART: Pearse. Luas: St. Stephen's Green. Bus: 11, 11A, 11B, 14, 14A, 15A, 15C, 15X, 20B, 27C, 32X, 33X, 39B, 39X, 41X, 46B, 46C, 46N, 46X, 51X, 58X, 65X, 70X, 84X.

Department Stores

Arnott's ★★ Ireland's original department store, Arnott's first opened its illustrious doors in 1843. Its selection of womenswear, menswear, gifts and beauty products is enormous. Weary shoppers will also be delighted to find a branch of that most famous of Dublin coffee houses, Bewley's, next to the Abbey Street entrance on the lower ground floor. Arnott's stays open for late shopping until 9:30pm on Thursdays and 8pm on Fridays. Henry St., Dublin 1. ✆ **01/805-0400.** www.arnotts.ie. Luas: Abbey St. Bus: 1, 7, 7B, 7D, 8, 11, 38, 38A, 38B, 39N, 40, 88N, 120, 122, 123, 747.

Brown Thomas ★★★ The top-hatted doorman out front sets a deceptively formal tone for this great old Dublin institution; we've always found it a relaxed and friendly place, even if the credit card seems to take a bit of a beating. Stop by for most of the major fashion labels before getting your nails done, having a one-to-one at the cosmetics counters, and indulging yourself at the bar and cafe or the elegant new restaurant. 88–95 Grafton St., Dublin 2. ✆ **01/605-6666.** www.brownthomas.com. Luas: St. Stephen's Green. Bus: 11, 11A, 11B, 14, 14A, 15A, 15C, 15X, 20B, 27C, 32X, 33X, 39B, 39X, 41X, 46B, 46C, 51X, 58X, 70X, 84X.

Cleary's ★ Another traditional favorite among Dublin's trendy set (this one's been keeping them dressed in the height of fashion since 1941), Cleary's carries a veritable directory of big-name international fashion brands. They also have beauty treatment rooms, a hair salon, and a chiropody center. 18–27 Lower O'Connell St., Dublin 1. ✆ **01/878-0600.** www.clerys.ie. Luas: Abbey St. Bus: 1, 11, 38, 38A, 38B, 39N, 88N, 120, 122, 123, 747.

Harvey Nichol's ★ The only Irish outpost of the famous British department store chain, "Harvey Nicks" is as renowned for its outstanding food court as it is for its high-end fashion and beauty. There's also a good steakhouse and trendy cocktail bar. Harvey Nichol's is in the Dundrum Town Centre mall, 8km (5 miles) south of Dublin city center. Dundrum Town Centre, Sandyford Rd., Dundrum, Dublin 16. ✆ **01/291-0488.** Luas: Dundrum. Bus: 14, 14C, 44, 44B.

Fashion & Clothing

Alias Tom ★★ This has long been one of Dublin's top boutique clothing stores. Alias Tom made its name in menswear, but now sells designer fashions (mostly Italian) for women, too. Prices tend to be high, but the quality is good. Duke House, Duke St., Dublin 2. ✆ **01/671-5443** (menswear) ✆ **01/677-8842.** www.aliastom.com. Bus: 15A, 15B, 44, 61, 100X, 101X, 111, 133, 140.

BT2 ★ A more cutting-edge spin-off from the department store Brown Thomas (see above), BT2 sells youthful designer fashions for men and women. They also have the biggest denim bar in Ireland, full of hip brand names such as Citizens of Humanity and Seven For All Mankind. They also have a branch in the **Dundrum Town Centre** mall (✆ **01/296-8400**). 28–29 Grafton St., Dublin 2. ✆ **01/605-6747.** www.bt2.ie. DART: Pearse. Bus: 10, 11A, 11B, 13, or 20B.

China Blue ★ Shelves upon shelves of women's and men's footwear can be found at this trendy shoe store—including an enticing range of designer Doc Martens. They also sell a good selection of kids' shoes. Merchants Arch, Temple Bar, Dublin 2. ✆ **01/671-8785.** www.chinablueshoes.com. Bus: 25, 25A, 25B, 25N, 37, 39A, 51D, 67N, 69, 69X, 70, 70N, 79, 79A.

Claire Garvey ★★★ One of the top young Irish fashion designers to have emerged in the 21st century so far, Claire Garvey sells beautiful, bold and feminine creations from her boutique on uber-trendy Cow's Lane. Her creations, which are full of elegance and dramatic flair, are true one-of-a-kind items. 6 Cow's Lane, Dublin 8. ✆ **01/671-7287.** www.clairegarvey.com. Bus: 13, 27, 37, 39, 39A, 40, 49, 51D, 69, 69X, 70, 70N, 77A, 77X, 79, 79A, 83, 83A, 123, 145, 747.

Costelloe & Costelloe ★ This sweet clothing and accessories store sells a great range of handbags, pashminas, shrugs, and—delightfully—fascinators and headpieces.Best of all, prices are thoroughly reasonable. 14A Chatham St., Temple Bar, Dublin 2. ✆ **01/671-4209.** www.costelloeandcostelloe.com. DART: Tara St. Bus: 15A, 15B, 44, 61, 140.

Design Centre ★★★ Located in the Powerscourt Townhouse Centre (see p. 149), this is a great showcase for Irish fashion designers, both new and established. A lot of what's on offer is unsurprisingly expensive, but you can sometimes walk away with a bargain—particularly seconds—and score at the sales, too. Powerscourt Townhouse Centre, Dublin 2. ✆ **01/679-5863** or 679-5718. www.designcentre.ie. DART: Pearse. Luas: St. Stephen's Green. Bus: 11, 11A, 11B, 14, 14A, 15A, 15C, 15X, 20B, 27C, 32X, 33X, 39B, 39X, 41X, 46B, 46C, 46N, 46X, 51X, 58X, 65X, 70X, 84X.

Kevin & Howlin ★ There's nothing cutting edge whatsoever about this place—and that's just why people like it. Dublin's go-to store for Donegal tweed, they've been selling hand-woven jackets, coats, hats and other traditional Irish countryware since the 1930s. 31 Nassau St., Dublin 2. ✆ **01/633-4576.** www.kevinandhowlin.com. DART: Pearse. Bus: 7B, 7D, 25, 25A, 25B, 25X, 26, 46A, 66, 66A, 66B, 66X, 67, 67X, 145.

Louise Kennedy ★★★ Undoubtedly one of the biggest names in contemporary Irish fashion—so respected that they put her on a postage stamp a few years ago—Louise Kennedy's illustrious career has seen her dress everyone from heads of state to Hollywood superstars. Her boutique in Merrion Square showcases the best of her current collection. Among the items she's famous for is the gorgeous "Kennedy bag," a limited edition handbag that became the must-have accessory among the Irish *glierrati* in 2013—yours for a mere €1,500. 56 Merrion Sq., Dublin 2. ✆ **01/662-0056.** www.louisekennedy.com. DART: Pearse. Bus: 25, 25A, 25B, 26, 66, 66A, 66B, 67.

Mad Hatter ★ Going for a day at the races? Preparing for that special event? Talented milliner, Nessa Cronin, sells her quirky, original, elegant and fun designs here, alongside hats by other top European designers. She also has a range of handbags, jewelry and other accessories—but the headgear's always the star. 20 Lower Stephen St., Dublin 2. ✆ **01/405-4936.** www.madhatterhat.ie. Bus: 9, 16, 49N, 65, 65B, 68, 68A, 83, 83A, 122.

Om Diva ★★★ Proof that not every designer emporium has to be the kind of place where they check your credit rating at the door, Om Diva is a delightful, cheery place, with a great selection of designer women's fashion, handmade jewelry, vintage clothes and accessories. One of Dublin's real finds. 27 Drury St., Dublin 2. ✆ **01/679-1211.** www.madhatterhat.ie. Bus: 9, 16, 16A, 83.

Gourmet Food

Butlers Chocolate Café ★★ These chocolatiers now sell their delicious wares all over the world, but the business is still owned and run by the same Dublin family who founded it in 1932. Their Chocolate Cafes are all over Dublin, including Grafton Steet, Henry Street and the airport, but the one on Wicklow Street is the flagship. In addition to an enormous selection of gourmet chocolates, they also sell cakes, cookies, flapjacks—and make a mean cup of joe. 24 Wicklow St., Dublin 2. ✆ **01/671-0591.** www butlerschocolates.com. Bus: 9, 16, 49N, 54A, 65, 65B, 68, 68A, 83, 83A, 100X, 101X, 109, 111, 122, 133, 150.

Fallon & Byrne Food Hall ★★★ This exceptional artisan food and wine store is like a high-end deli crossed with an old-fashioned grocer's—albeit a rather posh, modern version. Produce is laid out in open crates and the shelves are stocked with epicurean treats of all kinds, plus cheese, charcuterie, and a great selection of wine. They also have an outstanding restaurant on the top floor (see p. 139). 11–17 Exchequer St., Dublin 2. ✆ **01/472-1010.** www.fallonandbyrne.com. Bus: 9, 16, 16C, 49N, 65, 65B, 68, 68A, 83, 83A, 122, 150.

Sheridan's Cheesemongers ★★★ Serious cheese lovers need look no further for their fix than this wonderful cheesemonger on South Anne Street.

STEP away FROM THE LEPRECHAUN: THREE ALTERNATIVE DUBLIN SOUVENIRS

Sure, you can stop by any of the multitude of souvenir stores in Dublin for a keychain shaped like a shamrock, or a t-shirt with an "amusing" slogan (Irish I were drunk! Fifty Shades of Green! A leprechaun with his pants down? Be still our aching sides!) But unless your friends really *do* want a hat shaped like a pint of Guinness, you might score better points back home with one of these more authentic mementos.

- **A pennywhistle.** At **Waltons** (69 S. Great Georges St., Dublin 2; ✆ **1/475-0661;** www.waltons.ie), which has been in the music business since the 1920s, you'll find sheet music, instructional CDs, and instruments both traditional and modern, ranging from an authentic *bodhrán* (drum) for about €42, to an "absolute beginners" Dublin tin whistle set, complete with DVD tutorial and songbook, for €16.95.
- **Marmalade** at Avoca. **Avoca Handweavers** (11–13 Suffolk St., Dublin 2; ✆ **1/677-4215;** www.avoca.ie) is known for its lovely clothing and accessories, but their Dublin location also has a lot of handmade and local sweets and savories in the lower level dining area (not the rooftop cafe). Get a jar of traditional Irish breakfast marmalade, some whiskey marmalade, or perhaps some delightfully named hedgerow jam—each an Avoca specialty costing €4.95.
- **Flapjacks.** If you ask for a flapjack in Ireland, you won't get a pancake, but a delightful biscuit (cookie to the North Americans) made from rolled oats, butter, brown sugar, and honey, often with fruit, nuts, or yogurt added. The traditional treats can be bought in boxes at food stores, or grab one in a coffee shop for a euro or two—and they stay fresh for a few days.

They stock around 100 different varieties of cheese—French, English, Italian, you name it—but unsurprisingly it's the traditional Irish varieties that are a particular specialty. They also sell other deli items, such as wine and cold meats, and do sandwiches to go. 11 South Anne St., Dublin 2. ✆ **01/679-3143.** www.sheridanscheesemongers.com. Bus: 15A, 15B, 44, 61, 140.

Jewelry

DESIGNyard ★★★ Some of Ireland's leading designers of contemporary jewelry have creations for sale here. Prices tend to be quite high—the cheapest items are around €100 and rise to thousands—but you'll be walking away with something beautiful and unique. They have an especially beautiful range of engagement rings. 25 S. Frederick St., Dublin 2. ✆ **01/474-1011.** www.designyardgallery.com. DART: Pearse. Bus: 7B, 7D, 25, 25A, 25B, 25X, 26, 46A, 66, 66A, 66B, 66X, 67, 67X, 145.

Gollum's Precious ★ Come here for classic vintage and designer jewelry—especially French. They have a particularly good collection of contemporary pearl earrings, bracelets and necklaces. Ground floor, Powerscourt Centre, Dublin 2. ✆ **01/670-5400.** DART: Pearse. Luas: St. Stephen's Green. Bus: 11, 11A, 11B, 14, 14A, 15A, 15C, 15X, 20B, 27C, 32X, 33X, 39B, 39X, 41X, 46B, 46C, 46N, 46X, 51X, 58X, 65X, 70X, 84X.

Rhinestones ★ This small but delightful jewelry store specializes in costume jewelry, contemporary and vintage. The antique pieces go back to the early Victorian age, but the mid-20th century collection has a particular air of glamour. 18 St. Andrews St., Dublin 2. ✆ **01/679-0759.** Bus: 9, 13, 16, 16C, 49N, 54A, 83, 83A, 100X, 101X, 109, 111, 122, 123, 133, 150, 747, 869.

Weir & Sons ★★ Established in 1869, this is the granddaddy of Dublin's fine jewelry shops. It sells new and antique jewelry, as well as silver, china, and crystal. The ground floor of the main branch on Grafton Street also has a section devoted to 17th, 18th, and 19th century antique silver from Ireland and Britain. The shop is located on the corner of Grafton and Wicklow Streets. A second branch can be found in Dundrum, about 7km (4⅓ miles) south of the city center. 96–99 Grafton St. and 1–3 Wicklow St., Dublin 2. ✆ **01/677-9678.** www.weirandsons.ie. Bus: 15X, 32X, 33X, 39X, 41X, 51X, 58X, 70X, 84X.

Specialist

Forbidden Planet ★ Geeks assemble! This treasure trove of comics, books, DVDs, and other assorted memorabilia celebrates everything cult. Their range of comics and graphic novels is enormous. 5–6 Crampton Quay, Dublin 2. ✆ **01/671-0688.** www.forbiddenplanet.co.uk. Luas: Jervis. Bus: 25, 25A, 25B, 25N, 37, 39, 39A, 51D, 67N, 69, 69X, 70, 70N, 79, 79A.

The R.A.G.E. ★★ Imagine the kind of shop where 1980s teenagers hung out in John Hughes movies and you've got this place about right. A combination of vinyl record store and retro video game emporium, everything here is vintage—all the vinyl can be sampled first, and you can even play some of the old video games on an original arcade machine. 16B Fade St., Dublin 2. ✆ **01/677-9594.** www.therage.ie. Bus: 9, 16, 49N, 65, 65B, 68, 68A, 83, 83A, 122.

Traditional Irish Music

The Celtic Note ★★ One of the granddaddies of Dublin music stores, the Celtic Note has a comprehensive range of traditional Irish music CDs. The knowledgeable staff will guide you through what's on offer and let you "try before

TEMPLE BAR street markets

Not all the best shopping in Temple Bar is to be found indoors: It's also home to three of Dublin's finest street markets.

The **Designer Mart** is a great showcase for fashion designers and craftspeople from all over Ireland. It takes place in uber-trendy Cow's Lane every Saturday from 10am until 5pm.

The **Book Market** takes over Temple Bar Square all weekend, from 10am to 6pm. It's relatively small, but there's always some piece of printed treasure or other to be unearthed among its second hand book stalls.

A must for foodies, the **Food Market** makes its presence felt most of all, through the wafts of tempting aromas that hang around Meeting House Square from 10am to 4:30pm on Saturday. Should the weather take a turn for the worse, there's even a fancy retractable roof to keep you dry while you deliberate over which Irish farmhouse cheese to take away, before waiting in line for a freshly cooked snack.

you buy". They also sell books and t-shirts. 12 Nassau St., Dublin 2. ✆ **01/670-4157.** www.celticnote.com. DART: Pearse. Bus: 4, 7, 7B, 8, 25, 25A, 25B, 25X, 26, 27X, 46A, 66, 66A, 66B, 66X, 67X, 120, 145.

Claddagh Records ★★★ Renowned among insiders in traditional Irish music circles, this is where to find "the genuine article" in traditional music and perhaps discover a new favorite. Not only is the staff knowledgeable and enthusiastic about new artists, but they're able to tell you which venues and pubs are hosting the best music sessions that week. 65 Middle Abbey St., Dublin 1. ✆ **01/872-0075.** www.claddaghrecords.com. Luas: Jervis. Bus: 4, 5, 7, 7A, 7B, 7D, 8, 39B, 70B, 70X, 116.

DUBLIN AFTER DARK

Nightlife in Dublin is a mixed bag of traditional old pubs, where the likes of Joyce and Behan once imbibed and where Irish music is often reeling away, and cool modern bars, where the hottest new international sounds fill the air and the crowd knows more about Prada than the Pogues. There's little in the way of crossover, although there are a couple of quieter bars and a few with an alternative angle, so you take your pick. Admission to nightclubs varies from free if you arrive early-ish, to around €20 for the very fanciest places. Aside from the eternal elderly pubs, things change rapidly in the world of Dublin nightlife, so pick up a copy of local listings magazines, such as *Totally Dublin* (p. 96) if you're looking for the very latest in the club scene.

The tourism website **www.ireland.com** offers a "what's on" daily guide to cinema, theater, music, and whatever else you're up for—follow the "Events" link from the front page. The **Dublin Events Guide,** at **www.dublinevents.com,** also provides a comprehensive listing of the week's entertainment possibilities.

As with any big city, ticket prices for shows vary considerably, from around €5 to over €100. Advance bookings for most large concerts, major plays, and so forth can be made through **Ticketmaster Ireland** (✆ **081/890-3001** or 353/1677-9647 internationally, including Northern Ireland; www.

ticketmaster.ie). The best way to arrange tickets is by phone, but if you prefer to speak to a human being in person, you can also drop in at one of their small Ticket Centres—central Dublin locations are at **Ticketron,** Jervis Shopping Centre, Jervis St., Dublin 1, and St. Stephen's Green Shopping Centre, St. Stephen's Green, Dublin 2; **FAI Umbro Store,** the Football Association of Ireland, 15 Westmoreland St., Dublin 2; the Pavillion at **The Hub,** Dublin City University, Glasnevin; **Dublin Institute of Technology Student Union,** Aungier St. or Bolton St. (No individual phone numbers; use the main ticket line).

Of course, foremost in anyone's mind when it comes to Dublin nightlife is bound to be its pubs. These are the secular temples of Ireland, and a cultural export that has conquered the world. The Irish didn't invent the pub, but many would say they perfected it. In *Ulysses,* James Joyce referred to the puzzle of trying to cross Dublin without passing a pub; his characters quickly abandoned the quest as impossible, and stop to sample a few pints instead. You may want to look upon that as a challenge.

Arenas & Concert Venues

The O2 ★ This enormous indoor arena is the biggest venue in Dublin, and the fifth-best attended in the world at this writing. It's the go-to place for major international acts, standup comedy, and other big-ticket entertainment events—all top-of-the-bill stuff. North Wall Quay, Dublin 1. ✆ Box Office: **081/871-9300;** Enquiries: 01/819-8888. www.theo2.ie. Luas: The Point. Bus: 151.

National Concert Hall ★★ This is the place to come if classical music is more your thing. The program also covers opera, world music, jazz, show tunes and musicals. Something is on virtually every night; check the website for full listings. Earlsfort Terrace, Dublin 2. ✆ **01/417-0000.** www.nch.ie. Luas: Harcourt. Bus: 100X, 101, 101X, 109, 111, 126, 133.

Vicar Street ★★ This much-loved venue is definitely not Dublin's largest—its capacity is roughly 1/14th that of the O2 (see above)—but it attracts consistently big names in music and standup comedy. 58–59 Thomas St., Dublin 8. ✆ **01/775-5800.** www.vicarstreet.ie. Bus: 13, 25N, 40, 69N, 123.

Bars & Nightclubs

37 Dawson Street ★★ This sumptuous cocktail bar is crammed with antiques and curios—everything from a stuffed bull's head on a polished wood wall, to old anatomical drawings and ornate vases. Their cocktail list is as extensive and imaginative as the quirky surroundings would suggest, and at the back of the building is a proper, old-style whiskey bar. They also have a good restaurant. 37 Dawson St., Dublin 2. ✆ **01/902-2908.** www.37dawsonstreet.ie. Mon noon–11:30pm; Tues–Sat noon–2:30am; Sun noon–11pm. Luas: St. Stephen's Green. Bus: 15A, 15B, 44, 61, 140.

Café en Seine ★★★ This elegant, 1920s-style café bar is the cat's pajamas. The interior is all terribly Gatsby, with hanging lamps, glass ceilings, faux-baroque furniture and polished brass statuettes. Their cocktail list is straight-up fun, the whiskey menu a page long, and the atmosphere appropriately decadent. They also serve a bistro menu until 9pm, and on Sundays they do a popular jazz brunch from noon to 5pm. 39 Dawson St., Dublin 2. ✆ **01/677-4567.** www.cafeenseine.ie. Mon noon–11:30pm; Mon–Tues noon–12:30am; Wed–Sat noon–2:30am; Sun noon–12:30am. Luas: St. Stephen's Green. Bus: 15A, 15B, 44, 61, 140.

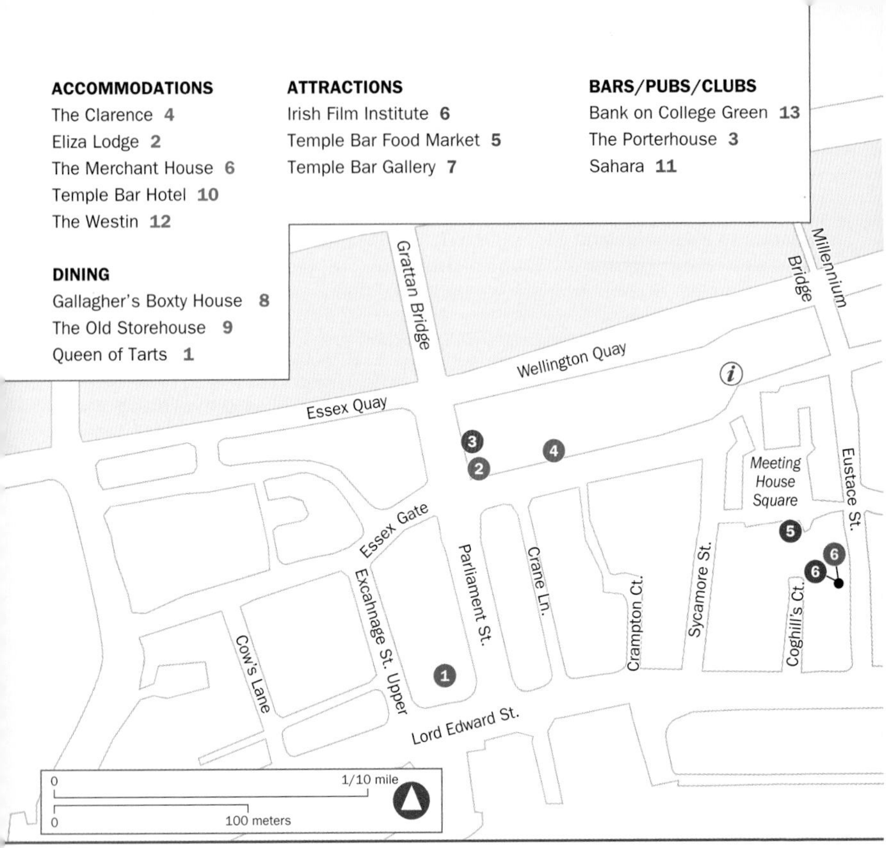

Dakota ★★ This stylish bar on South William Street is small but perfectly curated, with a hip clientele and an outstanding selection of bottled beers and cocktails. The crowd is young and the atmosphere raucously sophisticated. 9 S. William St., Dublin 2. ✆ **01/672-7969.** www.dakotabar.ie. Mon–Wed noon–11:30pm; Thurs noon–12:30am; Fri–Sat noon–2:30am; Sun noon–11:30pm. Bus: 9, 16, 49N, 54A, 65, 65B, 68, 68A, 83, 83A, 122, 150.

Lillie's Bordello ★ This has long been one of Dublin's real "VIP" clubs, with a notoriously snooty door policy and plenty of roped off areas to make you feel excluded from where the real fun is happening. Still, if glamour is your thing, put on your glitziest gear and act like you just *belong* inside. Adam Court, Grafton St., Dublin 2. ✆ **01/679-9204.** www.lilliesbordello.ie. Mon–Sat. 11:30pm–2:30am. Bus: 15A, 15B, 44, 61, 100X, 101, 101X, 111, 140.

Panti Bar ★★ One of Dublin's most famous gay clubs—its full name is "Pantibar Homo Activity Centre"—this place is hugely popular and riotously good fun. Saturday night is cabaret night, hosted by drag queen Panti herself, and there's a "gay ole' tea dance" from 3pm on Sundays. 7–8 Capel St., Dublin 1. ✆ **01/874-0710.** www.pantibar.com. Mon, Wed, and Sun 5–11:30pm; Tues 5pm–2am; Thurs–Sat 5pm–2:30am. Luas: Jervis, Four Courts. Bus: 25, 25A, 25B, 25N, 25X, 26, 66, 66A, 66B, 66N, 66X, 67, 67N, 67X, 69, 69N, 79, 79A.

Sahara ★★ This cool Temple Bar nightclub has a dash of celebrity credo to go along with its Near Eastern theme (try their delicious, Moroccan-style twist

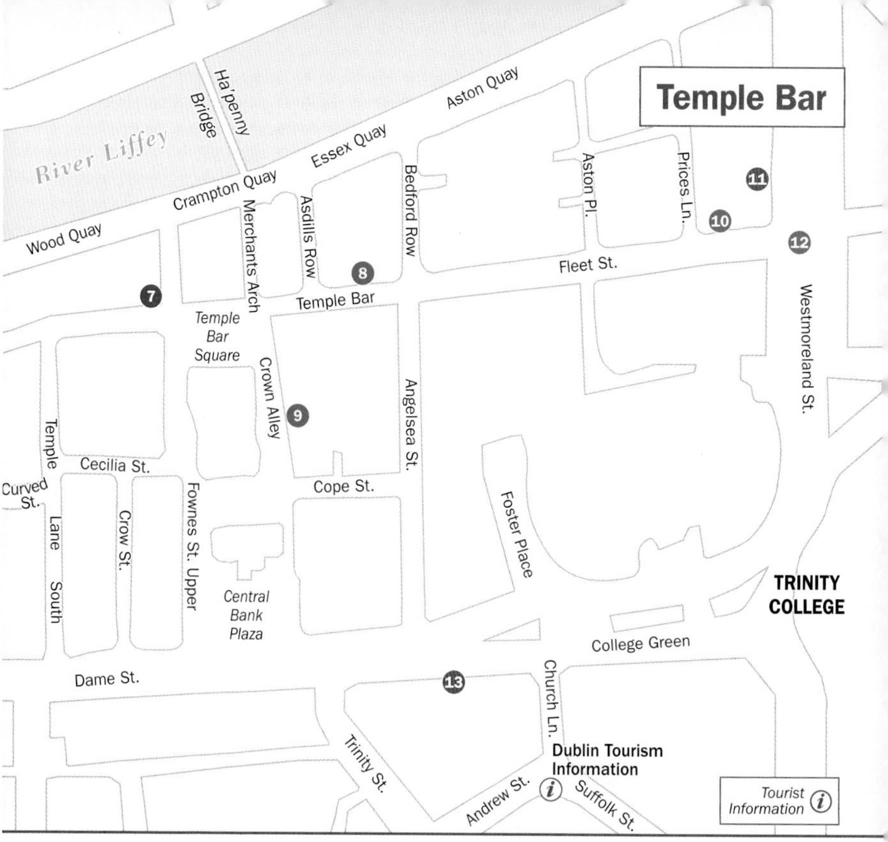

on a Long Island Iced Tea.) The latest sounds are on the turntables, the clientele is young, and the atmosphere suitably laid back. 10 Westmoreland St., Dublin 2. ✆ **01/670-8128.** www.saharadublin.com. Fri and Sat 11pm–3am. Luas: Tara St. Bus: 100X, 133.

Vanilla ★★ A generation ago, this is how everyone thought nightclubs would look in the 21st century. With artfully moulded furniture, bold lighting effects, an illuminated dance floor and flatscreen TVs, the look (and sound) of this place is so trendy it almost hurts. Dress to impress or you won't make it past the door. 19 Morehampton Rd., Ballsbridge, Dublin 4. ✆ **087/417-4877.** www.vanillanightclub.com. Fri and Sat 11pm–3am. Bus: 7B, 7D, 25X, 39, 39A, 41X, 46A, 46E, 66X, 67X, 116, 118, 145, 700.

The Woolshed Baa and Grill ★ If you're looking for somewhere to watch a big game, this is the place to do it. Enormous TV screens flank the bar, showing whatever's hot on in the sporting world—including football (the European kind), rugby, U.S. sports (including football, the American kind), and whatever else happens to be going on. They also serve crowd-pleasing bar food. Parnell St., Dublin 1. ✆ **01/872-4325.** www.woolshedbaa.com. Mon–Tues noon–11:30pm; Wed noon–2:30am; Thurs noon–2am; Fri–Sat. noon–1am; Sun noon–11pm. Luas: Jervis. Bus: 13, 40, 40B, 40D, 140.

Comedy Clubs

The Comedy Cellar ★★ This is one of the country's top comedy clubs, showcasing the best young pretenders in the world of Irish standup. The Comedy Cellar happens once weekly, on Wednesday night, when it takes over the upstairs room of the International Bar on Wicklow Street. Tickets cost €10. The International, 21 Wicklow St., Dublin 2. ✆ **01/677-9250.** www.dublincomedycellar.com. Wed 9:30pm (doors open 9pm). Bus: 16, 49N, 54A, 83, 83A, 100X, 101X, 109, 111, 133, 150.

Laughter Lines ★★ What is it about Dublin on a Wednesday that everybody needs cheering up? Another midweek pub takeover, this one happens at the Duke on Duke Street, every Wednesday night at 8:30pm. The talented company improvises sketches according to whatever the audience suggests. It's chaotic and great fun. Tickets are €5. The Duke, Duke St., Dublin 2. ✆ **01/679-9553.** www.dublincomedycellar.com. Wed 8:30pm. Bus: 11, 11A, 11B, 14, 14A, 15A, 15C, 15X, 20B, 27C, 33X, 39B, 41X, 46B, 46C.

Pubs

The Bank on College Green ★★ Undoubtedly one of Dublin's most jaw-droppingly handsome interiors, this place was built in 1892, at the height of Victorian opulence. No prizes for deducing what the building used to be; several remnants of the original were kept when it was converted into a pub, including the wonderful old-style safes that you can still see downstairs. For full review see p. 138. 20 College Green, Dublin 2. ✆ **01/677-0677.** www.bankoncollegegreen.com. Mon–Fri noon–4pm and 6–10pm; Sat–Sun noon–5pm and 6–10pm. Bus: 15X, 32X, 33X, 39B, 39X, 41X, 49X, 50X, 51X, 58X, 65X, 70X, 77X, 84X.

The Brazen Head ★★★ This is a serious contender for the coveted title of "oldest pub in Ireland," having been serving the locals continually since 1661 (although an alehouse was on the same spot for hundreds of years before that—nobody quite knows for sure whether any of the current building goes back that far). It was once a hangout for Irish revolutionaries, and Joyce mentioned the place in Ulysses, although today it's more famous for its lively traditional music sessions. Every night features a different act, and a popular open session is on Sundays from 3:30 to 6:30pm—join in if you think you've got what it takes! 20 Lower Bridge St., Dublin 8. ✆ **01/677-9549.** Mon–Thurs 10am–midnight; Fri–Sat 10am–12:30am; Sun 11am–midnight. Luas: Smithfield. Bus: 25, 25A, 25B, 25X, 26, 37, 39, 39A, 51D, 51X, 66, 66A, 66B, 66X, 67.

The Cobblestones ★★ This is a real musician's pub, and authentic down to the last note. In fact it's as much a traditional music venue as it is a pub, such is the standard of the music. Free sessions are in the front bar nightly, plus ticketed acts in the Backroom, a dedicated performance space. The

Listen to the Music

When you're out for a night of traditional Irish folk music, you should know that some pubs charge and some do not; if the band is playing informally in the main bar, as often happens, there's no charge, although they will probably pass a hat at some point, and everybody should toss in a few euro. If there is a charge, the music usually happens in a separate room from the main pub, and the charge will be noted on the door; usually it's about €5 to €10, and you pay as you go in, cash only.

And, don't worry. If they're selling CDs they'll make sure you know about it. (They'll probably autograph them too, after the set.).

popularity of The Cobblestones with locals is a testament to how good it all is. The pub is on the Northside of the city center, a 5-minute walk from the Old Jameson Distillery (p. 122). 77 North King St., Smithfield, Dublin 7. ✆ **01/872-1799.** www.cobblestonepub.ie. Mon–Thurs 4–11:30pm; Fri–Sat 4pm–12:30am; Sun 1–11pm. Luas: 37, 39, 39A, 70, 70N.

Davy Byrnes ★★ "He entered Davy Byrnes," wrote Joyce of Leopold Bloom, the hero of *Ulysses*. "Moral pub. He doesn't chat. Stands a drink now and then. But in a leap year once in four. Cashed a cheque for me once." For a place with such impeccable literary connections as this, it's unsurprising that so many writers make this something of a pilgrimage spot when they're in town. Joyce himself was a regular here, although the food has certainly improved since his day—the menu of pub classics and sandwiches is actually pretty good, and reasonably priced too. *Ulysses* fans will be delighted to hear that you can still order a gorgonzola sandwich—Bloom's snack of choice. 21 Duke St., off Grafton St., Dublin 2. ✆ **01/677-5217.** www.davybyrnes.com. Mon–Wed 11am–11:30pm; Thurs–Fri 11am–12:30am; Sat 10:30am–12:30am; Sun 12:30–11pm. Bus: 11, 11A, 11B, 14, 14A, 15A, 15C, 15X, 20B, 27C, 33X, 39B, 41X, 46B, 46C.

Doheny and Nesbitt ★★★ From the outside this pub brings to mind a Victorian medicine cabinet, all polished wood with a rich blue-and-gold sign. Its proximity to the political and economic heart of the capital makes it a perennial hangout for politicos, lawyers, economists, and those who write about them—which can make for some spectacularly good eavesdropping. (Indeed the name spawned a whole political shorthand, "the Doheny and Nesbitt School of Economics" to describe the great and the good who used to shoot the breeze here during Ireland's boom years of the 1990s and 2000s). If you want to spend time admiring the cozy interior, a midweek daytime visit is best—this place gets packed in the evenings (especially on summer weekends) and even more so when a big sports match is on. 5 Baggot St. Lower, Dublin 2. ✆ **01/676-2945.** www.dohenyandnesbitts.ie. Wed–Thurs 10am–12:30am; Fri–Sat 10am–2am; Sun noon–11pm; Mon 10am–11:30pm; Tues 10am–midnight. Bus: 10, 10A, 25X, 51D, 51X, 65X, 66D, 66X, 67X, 77X.

Grogan's Castle Lounge ★★★ There's a friendly, chatty vibe at this satisfyingly old-fashioned place, considered one of Dublin's "quintessential" pubs. There's nothing modern or polished about the dimly lit, atmospheric interior, save for the slightly incongruous art collection on the walls (ask if you like a piece—most of it is for sale). Grogan's reputation rests mostly on its mixed clientele, ranging from grizzled old folks who have been coming here for years to hipsterish, artsy types in search of a low-fi hangout. 15 S. William St., Dublin 2. ✆ **01/677-9320.** www.groganspub.ie. Mon–Thurs 10:30am–11:30pm; Fri–Sat 10:30am–12:30am; Sun 12:30pm–11pm. Bus: 15, 32X, 33X, 39X, 41X, 51X, 58X, 70X, 84X.

Kehoe's ★★ This lovely old pub is virtually sepia toned, with its burned orange walls and acres of polished walnut. That's an appropriate analogy for the atmosphere too—easy-going and frequently packed in the evenings, Kehoe's is best enjoyed in daylight hours, when you can people watch the local characters and soak up the old-school Irish pub atmosphere. A particularly appealing feature of this place is that it's retained its original "snugs"—tiny private rooms, almost like booths. 9 South Anne St., Dublin 2. ✆ **01/677-8312.** Mon–Thurs 10:30am–11:30pm; Fri–Sat 10:30am–12:30am; Sun 12:30pm–11pm. Bus: 15A, 15B, 44, 61, 140.

The Long Hall ★★★ The gorgeous, polished walnut-and-brass interior of this Victorian pub is liable to elicit purrs of delight from thirsty patrons as soon as they walk through the door. Undoubtedly one of Dublin's most gorgeously, seductively . . . well, *Irish* of pubs, the Long Hall is named for the bar that runs the entire length of the interior. Regulars have to fight for space alongside the tourist crowd, but it's more than worth squeezing in for a look at the interior. Not that staying here for a few pints is anything like a chore. 51 South Great George's St., Dublin 2. ✆ **01/475-1590.** Mon–Wed 4–11:30pm; Thurs 1–11:30pm; Fri–Sat 1pm–12:30am; Sun 1–11pm. Bus: 11E, 15F, 16, 16A, 19, 19A, 39X, 65, 65B, 65X, 83, 122.

The Merry Ploughboy ★ In many ways this is sort of the antithesis to The Cobblestones (see above), in that its live music show is very much for tourists. It's cheesy but good fun and hugely popular. They will even ferry you here from the city center and take you back again for just €5.50 round-trip. See p. 146 for full review. Edmondstown Road, Rockbrook, Rathfarnham, Dublin 16. ✆ **01/493-1495.** www.mpbpub.com. Daily dinner 7:30pm sharp; show 8:30–10:30pm. Bar food: Mon–Fri 4:30–9:30pm; Sat 12:30–9:30pm; Sun 12:30–8pm. Special bus leaves from and returns to six locations in central Dublin (€5.50 per person; must be pre-booked).

McDaid's ★★ This was Brendan Behan's favorite pub—and if there ever was a man to be trusted to know a thing or two about such matters, it was surely he. A lively atmosphere always prevails under the high ceilings of this satisfyingly traditional place, well worth dropping in for a slow pint and maybe a browse through one of the antiquarian books on the shelves in the corner. Not that you'll have chance to do much browsing once the evening heats up—ever since Behan spilled the beans, hordes of contented visitors come here to try it for themselves. Still, it's a welcoming, traditional spot. 3 Harry St., off Grafton St. ✆ **01/679-4395.** Mon–Thurs 10:30am–11:30pm; Fri–Sat 10:30am–12:30am; Sun 12:30–11pm. Luas: St. Stephen's Green. Bus: 11, 11A, 11B, 14, 14A, 15A, 15C, 15X, 20B, 27C, 33X, 39B, 40A, 40C, 41X, 46B, 46C, 46N, 46X, 51X, 58X, 67X, 70X, 84X.

Neary's ★ A favorite hangout of Dublin's theatergoers—and actors, stage crews, and just about everyone else from the Gaiety Theatre (p. 161) next door. It's full of Victorian features—such as wonderful globe lanterns out front, which are held aloft by a brass arm, emerging from the brickwork. The upstairs bar can be something of a quiet retreat during the day. 1 Chatham St., Dublin 2. ✆ **01/677-8596.** Mon–Thurs 10:30am–11:30pm; Fri–Sat 10:30am–12:30am; Sun 12:30–11pm. Luas: St. Stephen's Green. Bus: 15A, 15B, 61, 140.

The Porterhouse ★★ This lovely pub in Temple Bar was the first in Dublin to sell only microbrewery beers. Most are produced by the Porterhouse's own mini-chain, and the range is constantly updated, so you never quite know what you're going to get from one visit to the next. The relaxed, jovial vibe, and the hearty pub lunches make it a perfect pit stop on a long day's sightseeing. They also do live music every night. 16–18 Parliament St., Dublin 2. ✆ **01/679-8847.** www.porterhousebrewco.com. Mon–Tues 10:30am–midnight; Wed 10:30am–1:30am; Thurs 10:30am–2am; Fri–Sat. 10:30am–2:30am; Sun noon–midnight. Bus: 13, 27, 37, 39, 39A, 40, 49, 51D, 54A, 56A, 65, 65B, 68, 68A, 69, 69X, 70, 77A, 77X, 79, 79A, 83, 123, 145, 747.

Storytelling

An Evening of Food, Folklore & Fairies ★★★ The concept of this wonderful evening is timeless, yet brilliant in its simplicity. No high tech smoke and mirrors; just compelling tales from Irish folklore, passionately told by masters of the storytelling craft. To be clear, this is storytelling for all ages, not just children, and it's a brilliant revival of an ancient art. The whole thing takes place in an atmospherically lit room inside the Brazen Head, one of the oldest pubs in Dublin. During dinner, the storytellers spin their yarns—not all of them fantastical in nature, but each one hugely absorbing. The meal, which is included in the price, is suitably traditional: beef and Guinness stew or bacon and cabbage with mashed potatoes. If you haven't had your fill of tradition by the end of it all, you can go downstairs and hear some live music in the bar. The Brazen Head Pub, 20 Bridge St Lower., Dublin 8. ✆ **01/218-8555.** www.irishfolktours.com. Tickets €46 adults; €42 seniors and students; €29 children. Mar–Dec nightly 7pm. Jan–Feb Thurs and Sat 7pm. Bus: 25, 25A, 37, 51C, 51D, 51X, 66, 66D, 69X, 70, 70A, 78A, 79, 79A, 90, 92.

Theater

Abbey Theatre ★ Since 1903, the Abbey has been the national theater of Ireland. The original theater, destroyed by fire in 1951, was replaced in 1966 by the current functional, although uninspired, 492-seat house. It remains one of the most respected and prestigious theaters in the country. In addition to its main stage, the theater also has a 127-seat basement studio, the **Peacock,** where it presents newer and more experimental work. 26 Lower Abbey St., Dublin 1. ✆ **01/878-7222.** www.abbeytheatre.ie. Ticket prices vary; generally between about €13–€40. Event times vary; call ahead. Rail: Tara St., Connolly. Luas: Abbey St. Bus: 2, 3, 4, 5, 7, 7A, 7B, 7D, 8, 10, 10A, 15, 15A, 15B, 15C, 15E, 15F, 20B, 27B, 27C, 29A, 31, 31B, 32, 32A, 32B, 32X, 33, 33X, 38, 38A, 38C, 41, 41A, 41B, 41C, 41X, 42, 42A, 42B, 43, 45, 46A, 46B, 46C, 46E, 51A, 70B, 70X, 121, 122, 130, 142, 145.

Cofounded by William Butler Yeats, the Abbey Theatre is still going strong in the 21st century.

Gaiety Theatre ★ The elegant little Gaiety, opened in 1871, hosts a varied array of performances, including everything from opera to classical Irish plays and Broadway-style musicals. And when the thespians leave, the partygoers arrive. On Friday and Saturday from midnight on, the place turns into a nightclub, with four bars hosting live bands and DJs, spinning R&B, indie, blues or hip hop. There are even occasional cult movie showings. Don't forget to check out the ornate decor before you get too tipsy. The Gaiety Theatre, South King St., Dublin 2. ✆ **081/871-9388.** www.gaietytheatre.ie. Ticket prices vary; generally between €15–€50. Event times vary; call ahead. Luas: St. Stephen's Green. Bus: 11, 11A, 11B, 14, 14A, 15A, 15C, 15X, 20B, 27C, 33X, 39B, 40A, 40C, 41X, 46B, 46C, 46N, 46X, 51X, 58X, 67X, 70X, 84X.

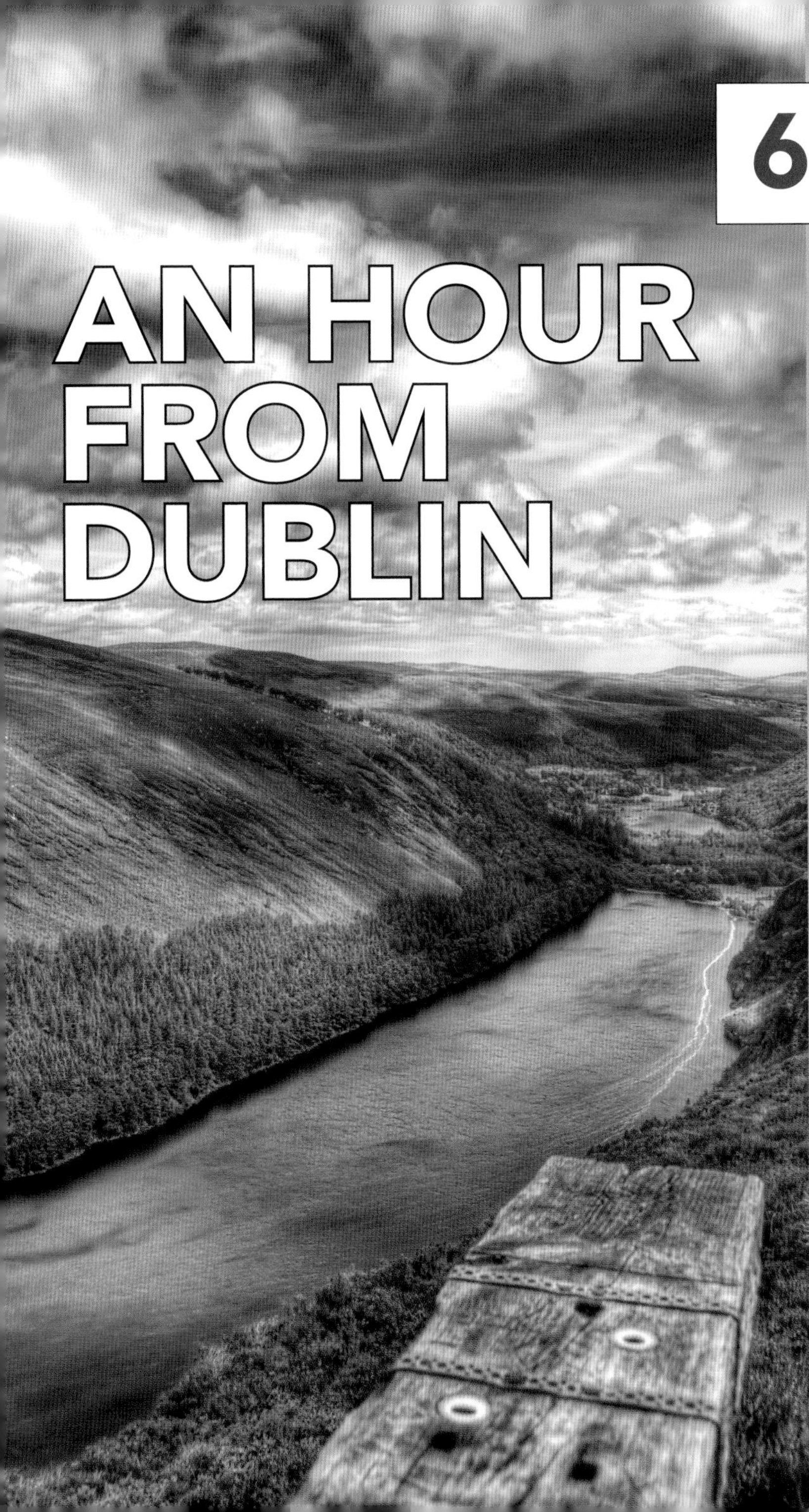

6

AN HOUR FROM DUBLIN

The areas immediately around Dublin are not the most dramatic or beautiful in Ireland, but if you get off the big, bland motorways, you'll find treasures in those hills—all within easy reach from the city. You can discover plenty to do within about a half-hour drive north, south or west of Dublin—so that's exactly how we've split this chapter.

South of Dublin, you have the brooding Wicklow Mountains. Home to early religious sites and peaceful river valleys, these hills are perfect for a day trip from Dublin, and make a good starting point for a driving tour of the south of Ireland.

North of Dublin, you can see the remnants of ancient civilizations at prehistoric sites Newgrange and Knowth. A short distance away, the green hills around the Boyne Valley are where the Irish kings once reigned with a mixture of mysticism and force.

West of Dublin is Kildare, known primarily as Ireland's horse country. Pickings here are a little slimmer than elsewhere if you're not into horseracing, although a couple of good stately homes and other historical sites are well worth checking out.

Although everything listed in this chapter is doable on a day trip from Dublin, the area has enough special places to stay and eat that taking a day or two to explore the regions can yield its own rewards.

ESSENTIALS

Arriving

BY TRAIN **Irish Rail** (✆ **1850/366-222;** www.irishrail.ie) operates several direct trains daily from Dublin Connolly to Wicklow; the journey takes an hour. Trains leave Dublin's Heuston station for Kildare at least once an hour. The journey takes between 25 and 45 minutes.

BY BUS **Bus Éireann** (✆ **01/836-6111;** www.buseireann.ie) operates services from the central bus station (Busáras) out to each of the regions listed in this chapter, although there aren't always practical links to the more remote sites. If you're looking to visit attractions by bus, the best bet is probably to take a tour—see the box on p. 183.

BY CAR Most of the attractions listed in this chapter are easily accessible by car in about an hour from Dublin. The roads are generally good in the regions around the city, although traffic can be a problem—particularly during rush hour, when the Dublin it slows in the hinterland to a crawl. As a guide, in reasonable traffic, Glendalough is about an hour's drive south of the city; Newgrange and Knowth, an hour north; and Kildare Town and its nearby attractions just under an hour to the southwest. The Dublin Tourist Office has excellent road maps.

PREVIOUS PAGE: **Upper Lake in Glendalough, County Wicklow.**

Counties Louth & Meath

Hill of Tara **11**
Knowth **8**
Loughcrew **2**
Monasterboice **4**
Newgrange **7**
Newgrange Farm **9**
Old Mellifont Abbey **5**
Proleek Dolmen **1**
St. Colmcille's House **3**
St. Peter's Church of Ireland **6**
Trim Castle **10**

County Kildare

Castletown **12**
The Curragh Racetrack **16**
Irish National Stud **14**
Irish Pewtermill **22**
Japanese Gardens **15**
Moone High Cross **21**
Newbridge Silverware **18**
St. Brigid's Cathedral **17**
Steam Museum **13**

Counties Wicklow & Carlow

Avoca Handweavers **27**
Browne's Hill Dolmen **29**
Glendalough **24**
Glenmacnass Waterfall **26**
Huntington Castle **30**
Mount Usher Gardens **25**
Powerscourt Gardens, House & Waterfall **20**
Russborough House **19**
St. Mullin's Monastery **31**
Vale of Avoca **28**
Wicklow Mountains National Park **23**

Getting Around

Although tourist buses go from Dublin to several of the major sights, including **Glendalough, Newgrange,** the **Hill of Tara** and **Trim Castle** (see p. 183), you really need a car to explore fully the regions to the north, south and west of the city.

A Note on Listings

All listings in this chapter—*Exploring, Where to Stay*, and *Where to Dine*—have been split by region, rather than town or county. As there are no particularly must-see large towns or population centers, it's generally better to stick to small towns and out-of-the-way retreats as bases in which to stay.

[FastFACTS] OUT FROM DUBLIN

ATMs/Banks Conveniently located ATMs include the **Allied Irish Bank (AIB)** on Abbey St. Wicklow; **Ulster Bank** on High St., Trim, Co. Meath; and **Bank of Ireland** on The Square, Kildare, Co. Kildare.

Dentists For dental emergencies, your hotel will usually contact a dentist for you; otherwise, in Wicklow, try **Wicklow Dental,** Abbey St., Wicklow Town (✆ **040/469977**); in Meath, try Denis Coughlan on Bective Sq., Kells (✆ **046/928-2888**); or in Kildare, try **James and Dolores Walsh,** Fairgreen Court, Kildare Town (✆ **045/530088**).

Doctors In emergencies dial ✆ **999.** For non-emergencies, any good hotel will contact a doctor for you. Otherwise, in Wicklow you could try the **Church Street Clinic,** Church St., Wicklow Town (✆ **01/287-5396**) or the **Bray Medical Centre,** Herbert Rd., Bray (✆ **01/286-2035**). In Meath try **The Surgery,** Finnigans Way, Trim (✆ **046/943-6215**) or the **Abbey House Medical Centre,** Abbey Rd., Navan (✆ **046/905-1500**). In Kildare try the **Naas General Practice Centre,** Dublin Rd., Naas (✆ **045/876129**) or the **Kildare Medical Centre,** Bride St., Kildare Town (✆ **045/521361**).

Emergencies For police, fire, or other emergencies, dial ✆ **999.**

Pharmacies In Wicklow try the **Abbey Pharmacy** on Abbey St., Wicklow Town (✆ **040/467451**); in Meath try **O'Shaughnessys Pharmacy** on Haggard St., Trim (✆ **046/943-1928**) or **Lynch's Pharmacy,** Farrel St., Kells (✆ **046/924-0515**); in Kildare try **Whelan's Pharmacy** in the Kildare Shopping Centre, Clargate St., Kildare (✆ **045/531426**) or **Boots the Chemist** in the Monread Shopping Centre, Monread Rd., Naas (✆ **045/899322**).

Taxis The best way to get a taxi is usually to ask the hotel or restaurant you're in to call you one; otherwise, in Wicklow, try **Church St. Cabs,** Wicklow Town (✆ **040/469500**), or **Cabs Direct,** Bray (✆ **01/286-5555**); in Meath try **Tobins Taxis,** Trim (✆ **046/943-7086**) or **Kells Taxi Hire** (✆ **087/250-4242**); and in Kildare, try **Naas Cabs,** Naas (✆ **045/871414**) or **Hoggy's Taxi,** Kildare Town (✆ **087/613-3280**). South of Dublin: Counties Wicklow and Carlow

Wicklow's northernmost border is just a dozen or so miles south of Dublin, making it one of the easiest day trips from the city. The beauty of the mountains,

An easy day trip from Dublin, Glendalough is a world apart from the bustling capital.

with their peaceful **Vale of Avoca** and isolated, contemplative monastery site, **Glendalough,** makes this landscape one of the most rewarding views.

Bray is a cheerful, upscale town, 12.6km (7¾ miles) further south along the coast from Dún Laoghaire (see p. 123). It's a busy place, however, so many people choose to head to County Wicklow by way of the sweet little harbor town of **Greystones** instead.

Beyond Greystones, a raised granite ridge runs through the county, peaking at two of the highest mountain passes in Ireland—the **Sally Gap** and the **Wicklow Gap.** Hikers will want to strike out on foot on the well-marked **Wicklow Way** walking path, which wanders for miles past mountain tarns and secluded glens. You can pick up a map at any tourism office, and then choose a stretch of the path to explore. If you're staying in the car, you'll want to track down the picturesque villages of **Roundwood, Laragh,** and **Aughrim.**

Just over the border of County Wicklow lies County Carlow, one of Ireland's smallest counties, bordered to the east by the **Blackstairs Mountains** and to the west by the fertile limestone land of the Barrow Valley and the Killeshin Hills. Its most prominent feature is the 5,000-year-old granite formation known as **Browne's Hill Dolmen.** Its capstone is believed to weigh a colossal 100 tons.

Visitor Information

The **Wicklow Tourist Office,** Fitzwilliam Square, Wicklow Town, County Wicklow (✆ **040/469117;** www.visitwicklow.ie), is open Monday to Friday year-round from 9:20am to 1:15pm and 2 to 5:15pm. The **Carlow Tourist Office,** Library Building, College Street, Carlow Town, County Carlow (✆ **059/913-1554;** www.carlowtourism.com), is open Monday to Friday year-round, from 9:30am to 5:30pm. Both are also open selected Saturdays in the summer; call before you visit.

Exploring South of Dublin

Browne's Hill Dolmen ★ The purpose of this megalithic stone table has been the subject of conjecture for centuries, but nobody knows for certain. The tomb is an estimated 5,000 years old, and its massive size led earlier Irish residents to believe it was built by giants. Archaeologists believe the capstone was rolled into place on an earthen ramp constructed for the process and then destroyed. It's likely the dolmen is the burial place of a long-dead king, but it has a rich heritage of myth and legend.

Off Rathvilly Rd., Carlow, Co. Carlow. No phone. Free admission. Daily dawn–dusk. Access via parking lot and enclosed pedestrian pathway.

Glendalough ★★★ Nestled on the edge of dark lakes and surrounded by hills and forests, this evocative, misty glen is a magical place. Within is a 6th century monastery that was once a major center for Christian worship and scholarly learning. The coming of first the Vikings and then the English spelled darker times for those who lived here, but enough survives to make the ruins a striking and evocative sight. The combination of so many years of history and such a beautiful setting means that there's plenty to see here. Stop by the visitor center at the entrance to the ruins to pick up a map. Each of the many walking trails takes in different ruins, as the chapels were scattered over several miles. The oldest ruins, the **Teampall na Skellig,** can be seen across the lake at the foot of towering cliffs, but because there's no boat service, they cannot be visited. The cave known as Kevin's Bed is believed to be where the saint lived when he first arrived at Glendalough. Follow the path from the upper lake to the lower lake and walk through the remains of the monastery complex. Although much of the monastic city is in ruins, there's a nearly

DARKNESS & light: THE RISE & FALL OF GLENDALOUGH

The ruins of Glendalough date from the 6th century, when a monk named Coemgen chose this secluded setting to build a great church. He is thought to have been born in 498, to parents named Coemlog and Coemell, at a place called "the Fort of the White Fountain" in Leinster. However, given that the date of his death is placed by most sources as 618—a highly improbable lifespan for the age—none of this is certain. "Coemgen" was later anglicized to Kevin, the name by which he was eventually canonized in 1903.

Kevin founded his monastery at Glendalough sometime in the 6th century. It is thought the site was chosen for its isolation, although the fact it was the location of a Bronze Age tomb may mean that it had some older religious significance.

Over the next 4 centuries, Kevin's church became a center of religious learning, attracting thousands of students from all over Europe.

Unfortunately, Glendalough's success, as with so many early Irish religious sites, was its downfall. The monastery soon came to the attention of Vikings, who pillaged it repeatedly between A.D. 775 and 1071. On one such raid they stole timbers that were used to construct the biggest Viking ship ever known to have been built.

Despite suffering centuries of attack, the monastery at Glendalough always somehow managed to rebuild and bounce back, stronger than ever. However, the crushing blow came in 1398, when it was virtually destroyed by invading English troops. Attempts were made to resuscitate it once more, and the monastery limped on as just a shadow of all it had been until the 17th century, when it was finally abandoned forever.

perfect round tower, 31m (102 ft.) high and 16m (52 ft.) around the base, as well as hundreds of timeworn Celtic crosses and several chapels. One of these is St. Kevin's Chapel, often called **St. Kevin's Kitchen,** a fine specimen of an early Irish barrel-vaulted oratory with a miniature round belfry rising from a stone roof.

Signposted from R756, 2km (1⅓ miles) west of Laragh, Co. Wicklow. ✆ **040/445-600.** www.glendalough.ie. Admission €3 adults; €2 students; €1 children; €8 families. Mid-Mar–mid-Oct daily 9:30am–6pm; mid-Oct–mid-Mar daily 9:30am–5pm; last admission 45 min. before closing.

Glenmacnass Waterfall ★ The River Glenmacnass flows south across the highest mountain in western Wicklow, Mt. Mullaghcleevaun (848m/2,781 ft.). At one point, it reaches the edge of a plateau and flows off the edge quite spectacularly. A parking lot and a path to the falls is near the top, but take care on the rocks, which can be treacherous.

Laragh, Co. Wicklow. Follow Military Rd., through the Sally Gap and Laragh to the top of Glenmacnass Valley, and then watch for signs to the waterfall. Free admission.

Huntington Castle ★★ On the site of an abbey, which was itself built in the 14th century on the site of a Druid temple (a shrine to the Goddess Isis is in the basement), this rambling, crenelated manor house was originally the home of Lord Esmond. His descendants still occupy the main building. The

Huntington Castle in Clonegal, County Carlow.

gardens here are beautiful and as historic as the house—many of the plants date back to the 18th century—and the 17th century water features have been recently restored to working condition. Don't miss the extraordinary walking path guarded on either side by ancient yew trees. There's also an adventure playground to keep little ones busy. An intriguing side note about this place: Supposedly this is one of the most haunted buildings in Ireland, and there are fireside tales to be told aplenty. By 2015 the castle should be offering bed-and-breakfast and self catering accommodations in the Georgian gatehouse; check the website for details.

Clonegal, County Carlow (off N80, 6.5km/4 miles from Bunclody). ✆ **053/937-7552.** Guided tours: €8 adults; €6 children 12–18; €2.50 children 11 and under. Gardens only: €5 adults; €4 children 12–18; €2.50 children 11 and under. May, Sept Sat–Sun 2–6pm; June–Aug daily 2–6pm; last admission 1 hr. before closing.

Mount Usher Gardens ★★ Spreading out on 8 hectares (20 acres) at the edge of the River Vartry, this peaceful and romantic site was once an ancient lake. These days, it's a riverside garden, designed in a distinctively informal style. Fiery rhododendrons, fragrant eucalyptus trees, giant Tibetan lilies, and snowy camellias compete for your attention. Informal and responsive to their natural setting, these gardens have an almost untended feel—a sort of floral woodland. A spacious cafe, run by the fantastic Avoca chain, overlooks the river and gardens. The courtyard at the entrance to the gardens contains an interesting assortment of shops.

Ashford, County Wicklow (off the N11). ✆ **040/440205.** www.mountushergardens.ie. Admission €7.50 adults; €6 seniors and students; €3 children 5–16; free for children 4 and under. Mar–Oct daily 10am–6pm; last admission 40 min. before closing. Avoca Garden Café: year-round Mon–Fri 9:30am–5pm; Sat–Sun10am–5pm.

The Powerscourt Estate ★★★ The 20th century was not kind to this magnificent estate; abandoned and then gutted by fire, it took more than 30 years to restore the Palladian house to its former glory. The gardens are magnificent, with classical statuary everywhere, a shady grotto made of petrified moss, a Japanese garden, and an over-the-top fountain from which statues of winged horses rise. The landscaper Daniel Robertson designed the gardens between 1745 and 1767. Legend has it that due to terrible gout, he oversaw the work while being carted around in a wheelbarrow, sipping port as he went. When the bottle was dry, work was done for the day. At the garden center you can learn everything

View of Powerscourt House and Gardens, Wicklow.

THE curse OF POWERSCOURT HOUSE

This grand house in Enniskerry has a history of misfortune. It was designed in the 18th century by Richard Cassels, who also designed Russborough House (see below) and Dublin's Parliament building. The same family lived in the building for 350 years until the 1950s, but their fortunes gradually declined. By the time they moved out and donated the once magnificent house to the state, it was in terrible condition, and the country had little money to restore it. Its renovation was a painstaking project plagued with financial problems. In the end, the process took two decades.

Finally, in 1974, the work was done, and a grand reopening was planned. However, it was not meant to be. The day before the event was due to take place a fire broke out, gutting the building. So the slow, painful process of reconstruction began again—this time it was to last more than 30 years.

Today the house has a new lease on life as one of the region's biggest tourist attractions, even though just a small part may currently be seen in its fully restored condition.

there is to know about the plants that thrive here and pick up seeds to take home (although make sure you won't get in trouble at your country's customs for doing so). A few rooms of the house are open to the public, including an exhibition that tells the history of the house and its restoration. There's also a playground and several gift shops. If you feel energetic, follow the well-marked path over 7km (4 miles) to the picturesque **Powerscourt Waterfall**—the highest in Ireland at 121m (397 ft.). Or you can drive, following signs from the estate.

On R760, Enniskerry, Co. Wicklow. ✆ **01/204-6000.** www.powerscourt.ie. Gardens: €8.50 adults; €7.50 seniors and students; €5 children 15 and under; €25 families. Waterfall: €5.50 adults; €5 seniors and students; €2.50 children 15 and under; €16 families. Gardens: daily 9:30am–5:30pm (or at dusk if earlier). Garden Pavilion: Mon–Sat 9:30am–5:30pm; Sun 10am–5:30pm. Ballroom and Garden Rooms: May–Sept Sun–Mon 9:30am–1:30pm; Oct–Apr 9:30am–1:30pm. Powerscourt Waterfall: Jan–Feb, Nov–Dec 10:30am–4:30pm; Mar–Apr, Sept–Oct 10:30am–5:30pm; May–Aug 9:30am–7pm. About 20km (12½ miles) south of Dublin. Bus: 44, 185 (nearest stop is Enniskerry village, approx. 1–2km/⅔–1¼ mile walk).

Russborough House ★★ This impressive villa was built between 1741 and 1751, designed by the great Richard Cassels, who also designed Powerscourt House (see p. 170). In the 1950s, the house was bought by Sir Alfred Beit, a member of the De Beers diamond family. He had inherited a massive collection of art and wanted someplace to keep it. He thought this rural mansion was just the spot. Thus began one of the most exquisite small rural art collections you're likely to find anywhere with paintings by Vermeer, Gainsborough, and Rubens, although most of the paintings have been moved out over the last decade to other museums after a series of robberies. You can see the house only by guided tour, and there is certainly a lot to see—ornate plaster ceilings by the Lafranchini brothers, huge marble mantelpieces, inlaid floors, and lavish use of mahogany in doors and the staircase, as well as fine displays of silver, porcelain, and furniture. Kids will be kept amused by a 3D exhibition and a fiendish maze.

Signposted from N81, 3.2km (2 miles) south of Blessington, Co. Wicklow. ✆ **045/865-239.** www.russboroughhouse.ie. House: €10 adults; €6 seniors and students; €6 children 15 and under; €25 families. 3D exhibition: €6 adults; €4 seniors and students; €4 children 15 and under; €15 families. Combined ticket: €12 adults; €8 seniors and students; €8 children 15 and under; €30 families. Maze: €3. Daily house tours hourly 10am–5pm. 3D exhibition: 10am–5pm. Bus: 65.

St. Mullin's Monastery ★★ This little gem is a well-kept secret. On a sunny day, its idyllic setting—in a sleepy hamlet beside the River Barrow, surrounded by soft carpeted hills—is reason enough for a visit. Besides that, this is a fascinating spot, spanning Irish history from the early Christian period to the present, over the course of a few acres. These are the ruins of a monastery founded by St. Moling (Mullin) in roughly A.D. 614. Plundered again and again by the Vikings in the 9th and 10th centuries, it was annexed in the 12th century by a nearby Augustinian abbey. Here, too, are a steep grassy motte (the mound on which a castle was built) and the outline of a bailey (the outer wall or court of a castle) constructed by the Normans in the 12th century. In the Middle Ages, the monastery ruins were a popular destination, especially during the height of the Black Death in 1348, when pilgrims would cross the river barefoot, circle the burial spot of St. Mullin nine times in prayer, adding small stones to the cairn marking the spot, and drink from the healing waters of the saint's well. These ruins and waters are still the subject of an annual

Wicklow Mountains National Park

pilgrimage on or near July 25th. Adjoining the monastery buildings is an ancient cemetery still in use, where, contrary to common practice, Protestants and Catholics have long lain side by side. A number of rebels from the 1798 Rising are buried here.

On the Barrow Dr., 12km (7½ miles) north of New Ross, St. Mullins, Co. Carlow. Free admission. Daily dawn–dusk.

Vale of Avoca ★ Basically a peaceful riverbank, the Vale of Avoca was immortalized in the writings of 19th-century poet Thomas Moore. It's here at the "Meeting of the Waters" that the Avonmore and Avonbeg rivers join to form the Avoca River. It's said that the poet sat under "Tom Moore's Tree" looking for inspiration and penned the lines, "There is not in the wide world a valley so sweet as the vale in whose bosom the bright waters meet. . . ." The tree itself is a sorry sight—nothing left but a stump—but it's still a beautiful place. Three kilometers (2 miles) away, the charming riverside village of Avoca makes a good stop.

Rte. 755, Avoca, County Wicklow.

Wicklow Mountains National Park ★★★ Nearly 20,000 hectares (49,400 acres) of County Wicklow make up this national park. The core area surrounds Glendalough, including the Glendalough Valley and Glendalough Wood Nature Reserves. Hikers will be drawn here for the most mountainous stretch of the Wicklow Way, which cuts through the park (see below). In the high season, you'll find an information station at the Upper Lake at Glendalough where you can get maps and route guides for hiking in the Glendalough Valley and surrounding hills. Behind the center is a sweet little "sensory garden" (free admission), containing a variety of plants chosen for to their scent, texture, and even the sounds of the wildlife they attract. The closest parking is at Upper Lake, where you'll pay a couple of euro per car; or, just walk up from the Glendalough Visitor Centre, where the parking is free. ***Note:*** The Irish National Parks and Wildlife Service warns that ticks carrying Lyme disease are known to live in the hills. While the risk of contracting the disease is small, you should dress in long sleeves, wear a hat, avoid hiking in shorts, and check for ticks afterwards.

Glendalough, County Wicklow. ✆ **040/445425.** www.wicklowmountainsnationalpark.ie. Free admission. No opening restrictions to park. Information office May–Sept daily 10:30am–5:30pm; Oct, Feb–Apr Sat–Sun 10am–5pm; Nov–Jan Sat–Sun 10am–4pm.

Sports & Outdoor Pursuits

CYCLING To hire a mountain bike, try **Wicklow Adventures,** Hidden Valley Holiday Park, Rathdrum, Co. Wicklow (✆ **086/727-2872**; www.wicklowadventures.ie). They do rentals for €15 per day, including helmet and map. Also, **Cycling Safaris** (✆ **01/260-0749;** www.cyclingsafaris.com) offers a weeklong tour of the area for upward of €730 per person, including bed, breakfast and one night's dinner. They also do shorter 3 and 4 night tours.

GOLF If you're looking for cachet, head to the championship **Druids Glen Golf Club,** Newtonmountkennedy, Co. Wicklow (✆ **01/287-3600;** www.druidsglen.ie), a beauty of a championship course that bears more than a fleeting resemblance to Augusta and has hosted the Irish open four times. Greens fees are €75 midweek, €90 weekends.It also has a partner course nearby, **Druid's Heath.** The **Arklow Golf Club,** Arklow, Co. Wicklow

WALK THIS WAY: hiking IN COUNTY WICKLOW

Loved by hikers and ramblers for its peace, isolation, and sheer beauty, the **Wicklow Way** is a 132km (82-mile) signposted walking path that follows forest trails, sheep paths, and country roads from the suburbs south of Dublin, up into the Wicklow Mountains, and down through country farmland to Clonegal. It takes about 5 to 7 days to walk its entirety, with overnight stops at B&Bs and hostels along the route. Most people choose to walk sections as day trips. You can find more information on the Wicklow Way at **www.irishways.com**.

You can pick up information and maps at the Wicklow National Park center at Glendalough, or at any local tourist office. Leaflets containing maps and route descriptions for less strenuous walks can also be found at tourist offices.

The most spectacular places to walk in Wicklow are in the north and central parts of the county, traversed by the Wicklow Way and numerous short trails. One lovely walk on the Way begins at the **Deerpark parking lot** near the Dargle River and continues to Luggala, passing Djouce Mountain; the next section, between Luggala and Laragh, traverses some wild country around Lough Dan.

St. Kevin's Way, an ancient pilgrims' route more than 1,000 years old, has recently been restored. The path runs for 30km (19 miles) through scenic countryside from Hollywood to Glendalough, following the route taken by pilgrims who visited the ancient monastic site, and winds its way through roads, forest paths, and open mountainside. It takes in many of the historical sites associated with St. Kevin, who traveled the route in search of a mountain hermitage, as well as areas of geological interest and scenic beauty.

Folks who prefer less strenuous walking can follow the paths around the lakes at **Glendalough,** or join the southern section of the **Wicklow Way,** through Tinahely, Shillelagh, and Clonegal. Not as rugged as the terrain in central Wicklow, the gentle hills roll through peaceful glens. Through much of this section, the path follows country roads chosen for their lack of traffic.

(**✆ 0402/32492;** www.arklowgolflinks.com), a seaside par-68 course, charges fees of €25 to €60 depending on the time of day.

HORSEBACK RIDING The hillside paths of Wicklow are perfect for horseback riding. More than a dozen stables and equestrian centers offer horses for hire and instructional programs. Rates for horse hire average around €30 to €50 per hour. **Brennanstown Riding School,** Hollybrook, Kilmacanogue (**✆ 01/286-3778;** www.brennanstownrs.ie), offers beginner's treks up the picturesque Little Sugar Loaf Mountain, which has views across Dublin Bay. Another leading stable in the area is the **Paulbeg Riding School,** Shillelagh (**✆ 053/942-9100**), where experienced riders can explore the surrounding hills, and beginners can receive expert instruction.

WATERSPORTS & ADVENTURE SPORTS Deep in the Wicklow Mountains, the Blessington Lakes are a 2,000-hectare (4,940-acre) playground of tranquil, clean, speedboat-free water. Less than an hour's drive from Dublin center, and signposted on N81, the **Blessington Lakes Leisure,** Blessington, Co. Wicklow (✆ **045/857844**), provides all you need for canoeing, kayaking, sailing, and windsurfing, as well as land-based sports such as archery, orienteering, tennis, and pony trekking. And at the Hidden Valley Holiday Park in Rathdrum, **Wicklow Adventures** (✆ **086/727-2872;** www.wicklowadventures.ie) offer a variety of high-octane outdoor activities, including kayaking and laser tag.

Where to Stay South of Dublin

BrookLodge ★★ A winning combination of top-end hotel, spa, and holiday village, BrookLodge is a luxurious hideaway. Guestrooms are understated and contemporary in design, while suites—which come with a stylish mezzanine level—offer plenty of extra room for not much greater cost. The hotel's award-winning spa, **Wells,** is top-notch, and surprisingly inexpensive—most 1-hour treatments cost just €75. The main restaurant, the excellent **Strawberry Tree** (see p. 177), was the first in Ireland to gain full organic certification—many of the ingredients are so local that there's a good chance your dinner was at least partly foraged by the kitchen staff. The hotel is surrounded by an entire village of activities, from golf, hiking, and horseback riding, to an artisan baker, deli, and craft store. Check the website for special offers, including dinner, and bed-and-breakfast packages.

Macreddin Village (btw. Aughrim and Aghavannagh), Co. Wicklow. ✆ **040/236444.** www.brooklodge.com. 86 units. €170–€225 double; €175–€270 suite. Free parking. Breakfast included. **Amenities:** Wi-Fi (free); 2 restaurant; bar; 2 pub; room service; spa; gym; pool; golf course.

The Lord Bagenal ★ This cheerful hotel on the banks of the River Barrow looks like a traditional Irish country inn from the outside, but the interior is completely modern. The downside is that it loses points for character; however, the bedrooms are spacious and comfortable and the service efficient. Children are well catered for as the staff will help organize family activities, such as kayaking or fishing on the river, and the bar also has a designated family area. The in-house bistro is well-regarded, while the bar serves a more straightforward menu in a more relaxed environment. One downside to this place: It's an extremely popular wedding venue, especially on summer weekends.

Main St., Leighlinbridge, Co. Carlow. ✆ **059/977-4000.** www.lordbagenal.com. 9 units. €90–€130 double. Breakfast included. **Amenities:** Wi-Fi (free); restaurant; bar; room service.

Wicklow Way Lodge ★★★ It's hard to fault this wonderful B&B, just 6km (4 miles) from Glendalough (see p. 168). The views of the Wicklow Mountains are spectacular, especially from the front of the building. Guestrooms are simple but tastefully furnished, with lots of polished wood and cozy underfloor heating. They also have—how could they not?—enormous windows to take advantage of the picture-perfect surroundings. There's one family room (children are charged at a 50% reduction on the adult rate), although because of the split-level design of the house, very young kids aren't allowed. Hosts Marilyn and Seamus are a joy; genuinely kind and helpful, they're full of tips for the best walking paths and other local knowledge. Marilyn makes a mean full Irish breakfast (though you should try the porridge too). A haven of tranquility and charm.

Oldbridge, Roundwood, Co. Wicklow. ✆ **01/281-8489.** www.wicklowwaylodge.com. 5 units. €90 double. Free parking. Breakfast included. **Amenities:** Wi-Fi (free in lounge only).

Powerscourt Hotel ★★★ The grand, sweeping Palladian frontage of this gorgeous hotel is almost as impressive as its namesake, Powerscourt House (see p. 170). Opened to much fanfare as a cornerstone of the Powerscourt Estate's late-2000s renaissance, the hotel was originally a Ritz-Carlton. It's now owned by the Marriott chain, and while the brand name on the gate may not be quite so exclusive, the luxury quotient remains every bit as high. Guestrooms are large and elegantly furnished; some have balconies with views of the Wicklow Mountains. The in-house spa, **Espa,** is positively sci-fi in its sleek, high-tech design—the pool is lit by illuminated Swarovski crystals—and the tempting menu of treatments includes a 90-minute "warming peat ritual" for €145. The **Sika** restaurant serves outstanding modern Irish cuisine, although you'll pay top whack; fortunately there's also a lounge and a pub for more relaxed (and reasonably priced) fare. Needless to say, the service throughout the hotel is impeccable.

Powerscourt Estate, Enniskerry, Co. Wicklow. ✆ **01/274-8888.** www.powerscourthotel.com. 200 units. €180–€275 double; €215-€700 suite. Free parking. Breakfast €22–€28. **Amenities:** Wi-Fi (free); 2 restaurants; bar; pub; room service; gym; pool; spa.

Where to Dine South of Dublin

Brunel ★★ MODERN IRISH This place has won plenty of accolades over the years, and still deserves its reputation for excellent modern Irish cuisine. The menu changes regularly, but you can expect to find such dishes as Wicklow lamb with parsnip and leek crumble and a thyme jus, or perhaps some simple grilled hake with potato gratin. Vegetarians are much better catered for than at many fine dining restaurants, with a full menu on offer, rather than the customary one or two non-meat choices. They also serve a traditional afternoon tea for a thoroughly reasonable €10.50.

At the Tinakilly Country House Hotel, Rathnew, Co. Wicklow (on R750, off the N11). ✆ **040/469274.** www.tinakilly.ie. Reservations recommended. Main courses €18–€32. Mon–Sat 6–10pm; Sun noon–4pm.

Chakra by Jaipur ★★ INDIAN If you need a break from Irish food, or just fancy something a little more adventurous, this outstanding Indian restaurant is an excellent choice. It's not the most idyllic location, in a concrete-and-glass shopping mall down a rather nondescript street in Greystones, but the food is worth it. You might start with a *murgh malai* kebab, made with free-range chicken, saffron mascarpone and beetroot, before following on to the *lahsooni machhi*, a curry made with local monkfish, turmeric, cilantro and rock salt, or the succulent *tawa jhinga kadai*—griddled tiger prawns in a sauce made with caramelized onions.

1st Floor, Meridian Point, Church Rd., Greystones, Co. Wicklow. ✆ **01/201-7222.** Main courses €14–€24. Mon–Sat 5:30–11pm; Sun 1–5pm.

Poppies ★ DELI/IRISH This is a great pit stop for a cheap and cheerful lunch in Enniskerry, a few minutes' drive from Powerscourt House (see p. 170). You shouldn't expect anything fancy, it's all good and freshly made—panini, sandwiches, salads, quiches, and pies. Treat yourself to one of the delicious cakes for dessert. You can also get anything on the menu to go.

The Square, Enniskerry, Co. Wicklow. ✆ **01/282-8869.** www.poppies.ie. Main courses €5.50–€10. Daily 10am–6pm.

Roundwood Inn ★ MODERN IRISH/EUROPEAN This cozy, welcoming inn has been in business since the 1600s, and it still retains a wonderfully traditional atmosphere. An open fire roars in the grate, while the menu doesn't stray far from tradition—and why should it? Roast meats, seafood, game, and hearty stews are all unpretentious and deliciously prepared. But don't be fooled into mistaking comfort food for a lack of sophistication—the owners have won awards for their excellent wine list too. The Roundwood Inn is not far from Glendalough (see p. 168), so the resulting mix of hungry hikers, chatty locals, and passing tourists makes for a cheerful crowd.

Main St., Roundwood, Co. Wicklow. ✆ **01/281-8107.** Main courses €9–€14. Daily noon–9:30pm.

The Strawberry Tree ★★★ MODERN IRISH The main restaurant of the excellent BrookLodge and spa complex (see p. 175) is rightly regarded as one of the best places to dine in the region. It was the first restaurant in Ireland to receive full organic certification. That ethos pervades the outstanding modern Irish menu, which takes localism seriously—alongside each dish, the menu lists the name of whoever raised, produced or otherwise supplied its main ingredient. Depending on the season, you might find wild hake served with rainbow chard and lemon sauce, or beef loin with a celeriac puree and red wine jus. If you're feeling gregarious, book a place on the "big table"—a communal table, that seats up to 40, on which you're served a set menu in the style of a feast.

At the BrookLodge, Macreddin Village (btw. Aughrim and Aghavannagh), Co. Wicklow. ✆ **040/236444.** www.brooklodge.com. Fixed-price menus €65. Tues–Sun 7–9pm.

NORTH OF DUBLIN: COUNTIES MEATH & LOUTH

Less than 48km (30 miles) north of Dublin along Ireland's east coast runs the River Boyne, surrounded by the rich, fertile countryside of counties Meath and Louth. More than any other river in the country, this meandering body of water has been at the center of Irish history. The banks of the Boyne hold reminders of Ireland's ancient past in the extraordinary and mysterious prehistoric passage tombs of Newgrange and the storied Hill of Tara, once the seat of the high kings.

This was also the setting for the infamous Battle of the Boyne, when in July 1690 King William III defeated the exiled King James II for the crown of England. This battle, perhaps more than any other single event, was to shape Irish history over the next three centuries—first through the mass arrival of Protestant settlers, and therefore, indirectly, the division of Ireland and the subsequent "Troubles" that so plagued the North in the 20th century. (For more on this, see chapter 15, "Northern Ireland".)

Today the Boyne Valley is a much more peaceful place, its historic treasures tucked away among miles of farmland, smooth, rolling hills, and the outer fringes of the modern Dublin suburbs.

Visitor Information

The **Dundalk Tourist Office** is on Market Square, Dundalk (✆ **042/935-2111**). It's open Monday to Saturday from 9:30 to 1pm and 2pm to 5pm. The

COUNTY MEATH: ANCIENT wonders UNDERFOOT

An old Irish saying goes that a farm in Meath is worth two in any other county. With sheep grazing peacefully in rich, verdant pastures, the countryside here may look quite ordinary—but those hills are littered with remnants of Dublin's mysterious ancient past.

One of the most iconic of these sites is the **Hill of Tara** (see above)—the Olympus of early Ireland where the kings of Ireland held court. But by Irish standards, even that isn't particularly ancient. People traveled here over great distances to attend the great festivals at which laws were made and judgments were passed; and yet, the ground they trampled underfoot hid the remnants of civilizations thousands of years older than their own.

Meath's rich soil has attracted settlers for more than 8,000 years, and archaeologists have uncovered burial grounds that give fascinating insight into where and how they lived. The most intriguing of these is **Newgrange** (see p. 180), with its mysterious carvings and huge stone passage tombs. Nearby, the Hill of Slane, a lofty 150m (492-ft.) mound, overlooks one of the loveliest parts of the Boyne Valley. On this hill, tradition has it, Patrick lit the Christian paschal fire in direct defiance of the Irish King Laoghaire, throwing down the gauntlet for a confrontation between Ireland's old and new religious orders.

History pops up everywhere in County Meath, even on the beach: The **Tara Brooch** was found at the little beach community of **Bettystown** in 1850. Often copied in modern jewelry designs, the brooch is one of Ireland's finest pieces of early Christian gold-filigree work, embellished with amber and glass. It's on view at the National Museum of Ireland: Archaeology in Dublin (see p. 105).

Drogheda Tourist Office, West St., Drogheda, Co. Louth; ✆ **041/987-2843**) is open Monday to Saturday from 9:30am to 5:30pm (closed Saturdays from December–April). The **Bru na Boinne Center,** the center for Newgrange and Knowth, is at Newgrange, Donore, County Meath (✆ **041/988-0300**). Its opening hours are February to April and October, daily 9:30am to 5:30pm; May and the second half of September, daily 9am to 6:30pm; June to mid-September, daily 9am to 7pm; and November to January, daily 9am to 5pm.

Exploring North of Dublin

Hill of Tara ★★ Legends and folklore place this atmospheric place at the center of early Irish history. Ancient tombs have been discovered on the hill that date back to the Stone Age. Pagans believed that the goddess Queen Maeve lived and reigned from here. By the 3rd century, it was home to the most powerful men in Ireland—the high kings. They had a ceremonial residence on the hill and ruled as much by myth as by military strength. Every 3 years they would hold a *feis* (a kind of giant party-cum-government session), at which more than 1,000 princes, poets, athletes, priests, druids, musicians, and jesters celebrated for a week. A *feis* wasn't all fun and games: Laws were passed, disputes settled, and matters of defense decided. The last *feis* was

A Stone Age burial ground, Knowth contains Europe's largest collection of passage tomb art.

held in A.D. 560. Thereafter, Tara went into a decline as the power and popularity of Christianity rose. Although little is left to see except grassy mounds, some ancient pillar stones, and depressions where the Iron Age ring forts stood, it's still a magnificent spot. A visitor center is in the old church beside the entrance to the archaeological area.

Signposted on N3, about 12km south of Navan, Co. Meath. ✆ **046/902-5903** (summer); **041/988-0300** (winter). www.hilloftara.org. Admission €3 adults; €2 seniors; €1 students and children; €8 families. Mid-May–mid-Sept daily 10am–6pm.

Knowth ★★★ This extraordinary prehistoric burial site contains the longest passage tombs ever discovered in Ireland. Knowth was closed to the public for many years as archaeologists explored its depths, but at last it is now open, at least in part. It is mainly composed of two massively long underground burial chambers, the longest of which stretches for 40m (131 ft.) and was discovered only in 1968. In the mound itself, scientists found the largest collection of passage tomb art uncovered thus far in Europe, as well as a number of underground chambers and 300 carved slabs. The mound is surrounded by 17 satellite graves in a complex pattern. And still, nobody can give a definitive answer to the biggest mystery of all: What was it all for? The meaning of it all remains shadowed in mystery, and even now, all of Knowth's secrets have not been uncovered—excavation work is quite constant here, and you may get a chance to see the archaeologists at work. All tickets for here and Newgrange (see p. 180) are issued at the Brú na Bóinne Visitor

Centre near Donore. As with Newgrange, there is no direct access to the monument; a shuttle bus takes visitors there.

Brú na Bóinne Visitor Centre, on N51, 2km (1¼ miles) west of Donore, Co. Meath. ✆ **041/988-0300.** www.knowth.com. Visitor center and Knowth: €5 adults; €3 seniors; €3 students and children; €13 families. Combined ticket with Newgrange: €11 adults; €8 seniors; €6 students and children; €28 families. Feb–Apr, Oct daily 9:30am–5:30pm; May daily 9am–6pm; June–mid-Sept daily 9–7pm; mid–end Sept daily 9am–6:30pm; Nov–Jan daily 9am–5pm.

Loughcrew Cairns and Gardens ★★ The 30 passage tombs of Loughcrew, also known as *Slieve na Calliaghe*—which translates as "The Hill of the Witch"—crown three hilltops in western Meath. From their summits, the views of the plains of Meath and the lakelands of Cavan are spectacular on a clear day. One of the cairns can be visited with a key; ask at the Loughcrew Coffee Shop in the parking lot. The 2½-hectare (6-acre) Loughcrew Gardens contain two beautiful lakes, a 19th century pleasure garden, a canal, children's playground, sculpture garden, and the family church of St. Oliver Plunkett (1625–81)—whose head, if you're interested, is on display at St. Peter's Church in Drogheda. You don't have to buy a ticket to the gardens to visit the cairns.

Outside Oldcastle, Co. Meath. From N3, take R195 through Oldcastle toward Mullingar; 2.4km (1½ miles) out of Oldcastle, look for signposted left turn. The next left turn into Loughcrew is also signposted. ✆ **049/854-1356.** www.loughcrew.com. Gardens: €6 adults; €5 seniors; €3 children; €20 families. Free admission to cairns. Mid-Mar–Oct Mon–Fri 9:30am–5:30pm, Sat–Sun 11am–5:30pm; Nov–mid-Mar Sat–Sun 11am–4pm.

Monasterboice ★ This ancient monastic site holds a peaceful cemetery, one of the tallest round towers in Ireland, ancient church ruins, and two excellent high crosses. The atmosphere here is dreamy, giving you the sense that it was once a peaceful place of prayer. The original site is said to have been founded in the 4th century by a follower of St. Patrick named St. Buithe. The name "Buithe" was corrupted to Boyne over time, and thus the whole region is named after him. The small monastic community thrived here for centuries, until it was seized and occupied by Vikings in the 10th century, but the Vikings were, in turn, defeated by the Irish high king of Tara, Donal, who is said to have single-handedly killed 300 of them. Today only a little is left, but the Muiredeach's High Cross is worth the trip all on its own. Dating from 922, the near-perfect cross is carved with elaborate scenes from the Old and New Testaments. Two other high crosses are more faded, and one was smashed by Cromwell's forces.

Off the main Dublin rd. (N1), 9.7km (6 miles) northwest of Drogheda, near Collon, Co. Louth. Free admission. Daily dawn–dusk.

Newgrange ★★★ Ireland's best-known prehistoric monument is one of the archaeological wonders of Western Europe. Built as a burial mound more than 5,000 years ago—long before the Egyptian Pyramids or Stonehenge—it sits atop a hill near the Boyne, massive and mysterious. Newgrange is so old, in fact, that when it was being built there were still woolly mammoths living in parts of Europe. The mound is 11m (36 ft.) tall and approximately 78m (256 ft.) in diameter. It consists of 200,000 tons of stone, a 6-ton capstone, and other stones weighing up to 16 tons each, many of which were hauled from as far away as County Wicklow and the Mountains of Mourne. Each

HIGH CROSSES: icons OF IRELAND

You see them all over Ireland, often in the most picturesque rural surroundings, standing alone like sentries, high Celtic crosses with faded stories carved into every inch of space. They are extraordinary—mournful and unforgettable—but when they were created, they served a useful purpose: They were books, of sorts, in the days when books were rare and precious. Think of the carvings, which inevitably explain the stories of the Bible, as illustrations acting sort of like cartoons explaining the Bible to the uneducated population. When they were created, the crosses were probably brightly painted as well, but the paint has long been lost to the wind and rain.

The **Muiredach Cross ★** at Monasterboice has carvings telling, from the bottom up, the stories of Adam and Eve, Cain and Abel, David and Goliath, and Moses, as well as the wise men bringing gifts to the baby Jesus. At the center of the old cross, the carving is thought to be of Revelation, while, at the top, St. Paul stands alone in the desert. The western side of the cross tells the stories of the New Testament, with, from the top down, a figure praying, the Crucifixion, St. Peter, Doubting Thomas, and, below that, Jesus' arrest. On the base of the cross is an inscription of the sort found often carved on stones in ancient Irish monasteries. It reads in Gaelic, "A prayer for Muiredach for whom the cross was made." Muiredach was the abbot at Monasterboice until 922, so the cross was probably made as a memorial shortly after his death.

Another excellent example of a carved high cross is to be found at the monastery of Clonmacnoise near Shannonbridge (see p. 373).

stone fits perfectly in the overall pattern, and the result is a watertight structure, an amazing feat of engineering. The question remains, though: Why? Even as archaeologists found more elaborate carvings in the stones, they deduced no clues as to whether it was built for kings, political leaders, or long-lost rituals. Inside, a passage 18m (59 ft.) long leads to a central burial chamber that sits in pitch-darkness all year, except for 5 days in December. During the winter solstice (December 19–23), a shaft of sunlight travels down the arrow-straight passageway for 17 minutes when it hits the back wall of the burial chamber. You can register for a lottery to be in the tomb for this extraordinary event, although competition is fierce. As part of the daily tour, you can walk down the passage, past elaborately carved stones and into the chamber, which has three sections, each with a basin stone that once held cremated human remains. ***Tip:*** The site has no direct access; you have to come via the Brú na Bóinne Visitor Centre near Donore.

Brú na Bóinne Visitor Centre: on N51, 2km (1¼ miles) west of Donore, Co. Meath. ✆ **041/988-0300.** www.newgrange.com. Visitor center and Newgrange: €6 adults; €5 seniors; €3 students and children; €15 families. Combined ticket with Knowth: €11 adults; €8 seniors; €6 students and children; €28 families. Feb–Apr, Oct daily 9:30am–5:30pm; May daily 9am–6pm; June–mid-Sept daily 9–7pm; mid–end Sept daily 9am–6:30pm; Nov–Jan daily 9am–5pm.

Newgrange Farm ★ After all that history, the kids will thank you for bringing them here to this busy 133-hectare (329-acre) farm where farmer Willie

Redhouse and his family will take them on a 1½-hour tour. You can feed the ducks, groom a calf, and bottle-feed the lambs and kid goats. Children can hold a newborn chick, pet a pony, and play with the pigs. In the aviaries are pheasants and rare birds. You can take a ride on a tractor for an extra €2.50. The high point of the week (for kids, anyway) occurs every Sunday afternoon (and on Bank Holidays), when the sheep take to the track with teddy bear jockeys for the weekly derby—call to check race times. Demonstrations of sheepdogs working, threshing, and horseshoeing are regularly underway. The farm has a coffee shop and plenty of picnic space.

Off N51, 3.2km (2 miles) east of Slane (signposted off N51 and directly west of Newgrange monument), Co. Meath. ✆ **041/982-4119.** www.newgrangefarm.com. Admission €9 adults and children; €15–€42 families. Mid-Mar–early Sept daily 10am–6pm; last admission 1 hr. before closing.

Old Mellifont Abbey ★ Founded in the 12th century, this was the first Cistercian monastery on the island, and ultimately became the most spectacular. Enough is left of the abbey buildings just a few miles north of Drogheda to give you an idea of what Mellifont was like in its day, when it was the center of Cistercian faith in Ireland, with more than 400 monks living and working within its walls. You can see the outline of the cross-shaped nave, as well as the remains of the cloister, refectory, and warming room, which, because the monks lived lives of suffering, would have been the only part of the monastery with heating. Mellifont was closed in the 16th century during the English dissolution, and a manor house was soon built on the site for an English landlord, using the abbey's stones. A century later, that house would be the last place where Hugh O'Neill, the final Irish chief, stayed before surrendering to the English and then fleeing to Europe in 1607, in the "flight of the Earls." At the good visitor center next door you can find out more about the monastery and its complex and lengthy history.

Signposted off R168, 9.7km (6 miles) west of Drogheda, Co. Louth. ✆ **041/982-6459.** www.heritageireland.ie. Admission €3 adults; €2 seniors; €1 students and children; €8 families. June–Aug daily 10am–6pm; last admission 45 min. before closing.

Proleek Dolmen ★ Standing around 3.6m (12 ft.) tall, this huge dolmen is said to resemble a giant's finger when viewed from a distance. That is, to say the least, rather subjective. But finger or not, it's still an impressive sight. The capstone, which looks alarmingly precarious, balanced on top of three smaller stones like a crude, misshapen tripod, weighs a massive 35 tons. The top of the capstone is invariably covered with pebbles, due to a local legend that if you can throw a stone and it stays there, your wish will come true. You can reach the dolmen down a paved footpath from the parking lot of the **Ballymascanlon House Hotel** (✆ **042/935-8200;** www.ballymascanlon.com), about 6km (3¾ miles) outside Dundalk. The Dolmen is about a .4km (¼ mile) walk. To find the hotel from Dublin, take exit 18 for Dundalk North off the M1, then take the N52 off the first roundabout, and the road to Ballymascanlon from the second. The hotel is about 3km (1¾ miles) down this road.

On the grounds of the Ballymascanlon House Hotel, Dundalk, Co. Louth. No phone; hotel ✆ **042/935-8200.** Free admission.

St. Colmcille's House ★ Sitting incongruously near more modern houses in Kells, like a memory of Ireland's past, St. Colmcille's House is all that's left of

bus trips **FROM DUBLIN**

Although you'll need a car to fully explore what the regions around Dublin have to offer, it's possible to see virtually all of the big attractions by taking guided bus tours. Most leave from central Dublin, quite early in the day, and deposit you back around 5 or 6pm. Book tours directly with the operator; Dublin tourist offices can also help. Here are a few of the most popular ones. **Bus Éireann** (✆ **01/836-6111;** www.buseireann.ie) runs day trips from the main bus station in Dublin. The **Glendalough, Powerscourt Garden and Wicklow Panorama** stops at Glendalough, Powerscourt, and the Wicklow Gap. The price includes a guided tour of Glendalough. It runs from about April to September, from Thursday to Saturday at 10am. The **Boyne Valley and Newgrange Tour,** which also stops at the **Hill of Tara,** includes admission to Newgrange. It also runs from about April to September, on Thursday and Saturday at 10am. Both tours cost €34.

Glendalough Bus (✆ **01/281-8119;** www.glendaloughbus.com) runs day trips from the top of Dawson Street, Dublin 2 (opposite the Mansion House), to Glendalough every day at 11:30am. Tickets cost €20 and you buy them from the driver.

Newgrange Tours by Mary Gibbons (✆ **086/355-1355;** www.newgrangetours.com) are among the most respected of the guided tours that visit the ancient burial site. Mary is an excellent guide and her tours have an allocated entry slot at Newgrange, meaning you don't have to wait. They run daily from several pickup points in Dublin, starting at 9:30am Monday to Friday and 7:50am Saturday and Sunday. The cost is €35.

Coach Tours of Ireland (✆ **01/898-0700** or 087/996-6660; www.coachtoursofireland.ie) runs a popular **Day Tour of Wicklow,** including the **Sally Gap** and **Glendalough.** Tours cost €26 adults, €20 children.

The **Wild Wicklow Tour** (✆ **01/280-1899;** www.wildwicklow.ie) takes in Dún Laoghaire Harbour and Dalkey, before heading to Glendalough and the Sally Gap. They even take you to a pub for lunch (not included in the price). The tours—which are perhaps skewed towards youthful travelers—leave from several points in Dublin, starting at 8:50am. Tickets cost €28.

Paddy Wagon Tours (✆ **01/823-0822;** www.paddywagontours.com) run a number of rather touristy trips from Dublin as far as Kilkenny, including ones that cover **Kildare, Trim Castle,** and the **Browne's Hill Dolmen.** Tickets cost €28.

an old monastic settlement that once stood where modern homes are now built. Most of the building is 10th century, although the oldest parts predate that by another 100 years. Precisely what the house was built for is unknown, although some experts believe it was once a scriptorium—where monks wrote and illuminated books. The first-floor room still contains the traces of an ancient fireplace and entryway. A narrow metal staircase ascends 4.5m (15 ft.) to a dark vault just under the roof. The small two-chambered space has both a structural and mythical dimension. It is thought to help reinforce the stone arch of the oratory roof and—though this is more conjectural—is also said to be the place where the Book of Kells was completed.

About 180m (about 590 ft.) northwest of St. Columba's Church, Church Lane, Kells, County Meath. No phone. Free admission. June–Sept 10am–5pm. Ask for key from caretaker, Mrs. Carpenter, who lives next door to the oratory on Church Lane.

St. Peter's Church of Ireland ★ This church dating from the 18th century is the latest in a series of churches on this site. It's a low-key but lovely place, approached through frilly, wrought-iron gates. Inside the simple, peaceful nave are several heavily carved tombs, including one spooky carving featuring skeletons wearing shrouds. Some have associated it with the Black Death. St. Peter's is notorious for an incident that occurred here during the battle of Drogheda in 1649. A group of Irish men, fleeing the losing battle, sought refuge in this Protestant church. When Cromwell's forces invaded the church, the men climbed into the steeple. Cromwell's troops used the pews as timber to start a fire, and the men were burned alive, an act so terrible that some of his own men refused the order, risking a charge of mutiny. This is the second rebuilding of St. Peter's since that infamous event.

William St., Drogheda, Co. Louth. No phone. Free admission. Daily 10am–3pm.

Trim Castle ★ This massive Anglo-Norman edifice is a magnificent sight. The Norman lord Hugh de Lacy occupied the site in 1172 and built the enclosed cruciform keep. In the 13th century, his son Walter enlarged the keep, circled it with a many-towered curtain wall, and added a great hall as an upgraded venue for courts, parliaments, and feasts. After the 17th century, it was abandoned and lay in ruins for centuries. Few paid much attention to it until Mel Gibson chose to use it as a setting for the film *Braveheart*. The Irish Heritage Service restored it as a "preserved ruin," leaving much of its historic integrity. It's a skeletal reminder of the once-great Anglo-Norman clout. Entry to the main part of the castle is by guided tour only, but arrive early if you're visiting in summer—space is limited and the tour can't be booked in advance, so it frequently sells out. ***Note:*** This tour is unsuitable for small or unruly children, and for anyone unable to maneuver steep climbs or afraid of formidable heights.

Castle St., Trim, Co. Meath. ✆ **046/943-8619.** www.heritageireland.ie. Admission €4 adults; €3 seniors; €2 students and children; €10 families. Mid-Mar–Sept daily 10am–6pm; Oct daily 9:30am–5:30pm; last admission 1 hr. before closing.

Sports & Outdoor Pursuits

CYCLING You can rent bikes from the **Boyne Valley Activities,** Trim, Co. Meath (✆ **086/734-2585;** www.boynevalleyactivities.ie). The cost is around €20 per day.

A Gruesome Find at Trim Castle

In 1971, when excavation work was underway at Trim Castle, workers made a macabre discovery: While digging to the south of the central keep, they uncovered the remains of 10 headless men. Historians believe that the bodies date from the 15th century. During a time of high crime in 1465, King Edward IV ordered that all robbers should be beheaded, and their heads displayed on spikes to intimidate those who might be thinking of a career in crime. Presumably, these men had all suffered that fate . . .

GOLF The **Headfort Golf Club,** Kells (✆ **046/924-0146;** www.headfortgolfclub.ie), has two courses and its greens fees are €45 to €70 weekends, depending on the time of year. Even more reasonably priced is the par-73 **County Meath Golf Club,** Trim (✆ **046/943-1463;** www.countymeathgolfclubtrim.ie), with greens fees of €20 to €35. If you prefer links courses, the **Laytown and Bettystown Golf Club,** Bettystown (✆ **041/982-7170;** www.landb.ie), charges greens fees of €40 weekdays, €45 weekends.

HORSEBACK RIDING Visitors can expect to pay an average of €25 per hour for trekking or trail riding in the countryside. To arrange a ride, contact the **Kells Equestrian Centre,** Kells (✆ **046/924-6998;** www.kellsequestrian.com).

WATERSPORTS & ADVENTURE SPORTS The **Boyne Valley Activities,** Trim, Co. Meath (✆**086/734-2585;** www.boynevalleyactivities.ie) has a wealth of outdoorsy activities to keep thrill seekers happily occupied, including whitewater rafting, kayaking, archery and high ropes.

Where to Stay North of Dublin

Ghan House ★★ Overlooking Carlingford Lough, Ghan House is a sweet, old fashioned kind of hotel. Guestrooms are good-sized and traditionally furnished, with antiques and sofas. Most are in the main, 17th century building—though there is also a modern extension—and many have views of the lake or mountains. "Superior" rooms have half tester beds and deep Victorian bathtubs. The award-winning restaurant serves excellent modern Irish menus, and the owners hold cookery and wine tasting classes on site too. Check the website for special offers, including midweek packages that include dinner for two.

2 Ghan Rd., Carlingford, Co. Louth. ✆ **042/937-3682.** www.ghanhouse.com. 12 units. €75–€180 double. Free parking. Breakfast included. **Amenities:** Wi-Fi (free); restaurant; bar.

Durhamstown Castle ★★ This charming and friendly B&B transforms into a foodie's paradise on weekends, when divine suppers are whisked up—although they're open to non-residents and are extremely popular, so you'll have to book (€35 and worth every cent). A real love of the finer things in life is obvious here, and a sense of artistry pervades the beautifully renovated 14th century building (which is really more of a country house than a castle). Playful design flourishes provide a wry sense of fun: an antique rocking horse in the corridor, a cast-iron clawfoot tub painted Cadbury purple, and an old-fashioned easel set up in one of the bedrooms, as if the painter had just nipped out and will be back any minute to finish the job. Full dinners are only provided on Fridays, although they can often cook for you during the week with a bit of notice. Durhamstown Castle is about 7km (4 miles) west of Navan.

Durhamstown, Bohermeen, Navan, Co. Meath. ✆ **046/902-8045.** www.theposhnoshclub.com. 4 units. €130 double. Free parking. Breakfast €15.

Headfort Arms Hotel ★ This pleasant, cheery hotel is a 5-minute walk from St. Colmcille's House (see p. 182) in the center of Kells. The picture-postcard front of the building—all hanging baskets and neat little shutters—gives way to a more modern interior, and bedrooms are simple but clean and tidy. Executive rooms have copper sprung beds. The small spa offers massage and beauty treatments at extremely reasonable prices—several cost just €25 on Wednesdays only—and the restaurant, **Vanilla Pod** (p. 187), is one of the best in the area.

Headfort Place., Kells, Co. Meath. ✆ **046/924-0063.** www.headfortarms.ie. 45 units. €130 double. Free parking. Breakfast included. **Amenities:** Wi-Fi (free); restaurant; bar; room service; spa.

Trim Castle Hotel ★ Were it not for the fact that it's wrong to throw stones at a 900 year-old building, you wouldn't have to throw one very hard to hit Trim Castle from here. This pleasant little hotel is directly opposite the castle (see p. 184), and many of the comfortable, modern bedrooms have direct views of the ruins. Spacious family rooms sleep up to 4. The good bistro-style restaurant offers reasonably priced classic Irish fare (€25 for 3 courses), and a lovely rooftop patio (overlooking the castle, of course) is a fine place to take a coffee or just soak up the view. One downside is that—like so many country hotels within a short drive of Dublin—it can get booked up with wedding parties in the summer.

Castle St., Trim, Co. Meath. ✆ **046/948-3000**. www.trimcastlehotel.com. 68 units. €85–€150 double. Free parking. Breakfast included. **Amenities:** Wi-Fi (free); restaurant; bar; room service.

Where to Dine North of Dublin

The Bay Tree ★★ IRISH The chef at this wonderful little place is a protégée of Michael Deane, Irish celebrity chef and the much-vaunted proprietor of his own illustrious mini-chain of restaurants in Belfast. The cooking is top-notch, allowing the freshest, local ingredients plenty of space to shine without overloading the palate. Start with some grilled oysters with lemon and chili, or perhaps some scallops, before moving on to a plate of organic salmon with potato charlotte, or perhaps a simple sirloin with hand cut chips and pepper sauce. Follow it up with a delightfully retro baked Alaska, or maybe a plate of specialist cheeses from Ireland and Britain. The Bay Tree has an attached B&B, where pleasant, modern bedrooms cost from €90 per night for a double.

Newry St., Carlingford, Co. Louth. ✆ **042/938-3848.** Main courses €18–€30. Wed–Thurs 6–9pm; Fri–Sat 6–9:30pm; Sun 1–4:30pm and 6–8pm.

Java Juice ★ CAFÉ Sometimes all you need is a quick lunch or a caffeinated pick-me-up, in which case this cheerful cafe in the center of Trim is what you need. Good, simple lunches are served with minimal fuss—salads, wraps, sandwiches, or perhaps a burger. The all day breakfasts are popular with locals. Or you could simply drop in for a cup of coffee—as the sign behind the counter reads, "a day without coffee is like a day without sunshine."

Haggard St., Trim, Co. Meath. ✆ **046/943-8771.** www.javajuice.ie. Main courses €5–€9. Mon–Sat 8am–4pm.

The Posh Nosh Club at Durhamstown Castle ★★★ MODERN EUROPEAN The gregarious, *bon viveur* owners of the wonderful B&B near Navan throw open the doors of their 14th century house every Friday evening, when people come from miles off to experience their exquisite cooking. The menu is never very long, with just a couple of choices per course, but what's on offer is beautifully chosen and prepared. You may start with a simple asparagus soup before moving on to some slow cooked pork in a yogurt and paprika sauce, or perhaps a tender daube of beef. (A vegetarian option is always offered too). The excellent wine list, all French, is reasonably priced. The atmosphere here is much more like a country house dinner party than a restaurant, with everybody sitting at one large table. If you love the place so much you don't want to leave—and who could blame you?—rooms cost €130 for a double. Special events are occasionally held here, such as dinner with live opera. Check the website for listings.

Durhamstown, Bohermeen, Navan, Co. Meath. ✆ **046/902-8045.** www.theposhnoshclub.com. Fixed-price menus €35. Booking essential. Fri 7:30pm (seating times can vary; always confirm when booking).

Vanilla Pod ★★ MODERN EUROPEAN Imaginative Irish cooking with international influences and plenty of local ingredients is the focus of this great little restaurant in Kells. The menu is seasonal; think bon-bons made with crab from Clogher Head in County Louth; lemon sole filet served with fennel and chorizo; or perhaps a simple potato and pear tart with blue cheese from the Boyne Valley. Vanilla Pod is in the pleasant Headfort Arms Hotel (see p. 185).

At the Headfort Arms Hotel, John St., Kells, Co. Meath. ✆ **046/924-0084.** Main courses €16–€23. Mon–Thurs 5–10pm; Fri–Sat 5–11pm; Sun 12:30–9:30pm.

WEST OF DUBLIN: COUNTY KILDARE

The flatlands of Kildare are rich in more ways than one. The soil is lush and fertile, producing miles of green pastures perfect for raising horses, and the population is one of the most affluent in the country, with plenty of cash for buying horses. Driving through the smooth rolling hills, home to sleek thoroughbreds, you'll notice a similarity to the green grass of Kentucky—in fact, the county is twinned with Lexington, Kentucky. This is the home of the Curragh, the racetrack where the Irish Derby is held, and of smaller tracks at Naas and Punchestown.

Once the stronghold of the Fitzgerald Clan, Kildare comes from the Irish *cill dara,* or "Church of the Oak Tree," a reference to St. Brigid's monastery, which once sat in the county, surrounded by oak trees. Brigid was a bit ahead of her time as an early exponent for women's equality—she founded her coed monastery in the 5th or 6th century.

Visitor Information

The **Kildare Heritage Centre** is in Market Square, Kildare Town (✆ **045/530672**). It's open Monday to Saturday from 9:30 to 1pm and 2 to 5pm. Top Attractions West of Dublin

Exploring West of Dublin

Castletown ★★ This spectacular Palladian-style mansion has been imitated many times across Ireland over the centuries. Palladian architecture—named for the Italian architect Andrea Palladio (1508–80)—became hugely popular, first in Britain and then Ireland, from the early 18th century onward. Indeed, so great was its impact that the Palladian style virtually *is* upper-class Anglo-Irish architecture from that period, until it was superseded in fashionable circles by the more austere Gothic Revival in the mid-19th century. Castletown was the first flourishing of Palladianism in Ireland. It was built between 1722 and 1729, designed by Italian architect Alessandro Galilei for then-speaker of the Irish House of Commons, William Connolly. Today, it's beautifully maintained and the fully restored interior is worth the price of admission. The two glorious follies on the grounds—both commissioned by William Connolly's wife, Louisa—were built as make-work for the starving population during the famine. One is a graceful obelisk, the other is the extraordinarily playful barn, created as a slightly crooked inverted funnel, around which winds a stone staircase. Its name, appropriately enough, is the "Wonderful Barn."

Signposted from R403, off main Dublin-Galway Rd. (N4), Celbridge, Co. Kildare. ✆ **01/628-8252.** www.castletownhouse.ie. Admission €4.50 adults; €3.50 seniors; students and children; €12.50 families. Tours mid-Mar–Oct Tues–Sun 10am–4:45pm. Call ahead to confirm times.

The Curragh ★★ This is the country's best-known racetrack, majestically placed at the edge of Ireland's central plain, and home to the **Irish Derby,** held every spring. Races are on at least one Saturday a month from March to October. The nearest train station is Kildare Town; trains run direct from Waterford, Cork, Limerick, Galway, and Dublin's Heuston station. Fares start at around €13.50, and there's a free shuttle bus to the track on race days. Dublin Coach (✆ **01/465-9972;** www.dublincoach.ie) runs a "Race Bus" from Westmoreland Street in central Dublin. Fares start at around €10. The Curragh website has full details on all races and tickets, including premium packages. Derby day tickets are inevitably more expensive than for other races; expect to pay upwards of €30 or €40 with transport to and from Dublin (prebooking essential).

Dublin-Limerick Rd. (N7), Curragh, Co. Kildare. ✆ **045/441205.** www.curragh.ie. Standard race days €15 adults; €8 seniors and under 25; children under 16 (accompanied by adult) free. Classic race days €20 adults; €10 seniors and under 25; children under 16 (accompanied by adult) free. Hours vary; 1st race usually 2pm, but check newspaper sports pages.

Irish National Stud with Japanese Gardens & St. Fiachra's Garden ★★ Some of Ireland's fastest horses have been bred on the grounds of this government-sponsored stud farm. Horse lovers and racing fans will be in heaven walking around the 383-hectare (946-acre) grounds watching the well-groomed horses being trained. A converted groom's house has exhibits on racing, steeplechase, hunting, and show jumping, plus a rather macabre display featuring the skeleton of Arkle, one of Ireland's most famous horses. The peaceful **Japanese Garden,** dating from 1906, has pagodas, ponds, and trickling streams and the beautifully designed visitor center has a restaurant and shop. A garden dedicated to St. Fiachra—the patron saint of gardeners—is in a beautiful natural setting of woods and wetlands, and the reconstructed hermitage has a Waterford crystal garden of rocks and delicate glass orchids.

Off the Dublin-Limerick Rd. (N7), Tully, Kildare, Co. Kildare. ✆ **045/522963.** www.irish-national-stud.ie. Admission €12.50 adults; €9.50 seniors and students; €7 children 5–15; €29.50 families. Daily 9am–6pm; last admission 1 hr. before closing. Tours daily noon, 2:30, 4pm.

Irish Pewtermill Centre ★ In an 11th-century mill originally constructed for the nunnery of St. Moling, Ireland's oldest pewter mill makes for a nice diversion. Six skilled craftsmen cast pewter in antique molds, some of which are 300 years old. Casting takes place most days, usually in the morning. The showroom has a wide selection of high-quality, hand-cast pewter gifts for sale, from bowls to brooches, at reasonable prices.

Timolin-Moone Rd. (signposted off N9 in Moone), Co. Kildare. ✆ **087/909-0044.** Free admission. Mon–Fri 10am–4:30pm, Sat–Sun 11am–4pm.

Connemara mare and foal at the Irish National Stud, home of many of Ireland's finest thoroughbred race horses.

Moone High Cross ★ Amid the picturesque ruins of Moone Abbey, this magnificent high cross is nearly 1,200 years old. The abbey, established by St. Columba in the 6th century, is in evocative ruins around it. The cross features finely crafted Celtic designs as well as biblical scenes: the temptation of Adam and Eve, the sacrifice of Isaac, and Daniel in the lions' den. Among the carvings are several surprises, such as a carving of a Near Eastern fish that reproduces when the male feeds the female her own eggs, which eventually hatch from her mouth

Signposted off N9 on southern edge of Moone, Co. Kildare. No phone. Free admission. Daily dawn–dusk.

St. Brigid's Cathedral ★ This 13th-century church stands on the site of St. Brigid's monastery, which was founded in the 5th century. The church, which dominates central Kildare, is a beautiful building with exquisite stained-glass windows portraying Ireland's three great saints: Patrick, Colmcille, and Brigid. The round tower on the grounds dates to the 10th century, and is the second tallest in the country (33m/108 ft.). Somewhere down the line, its pointed roof was replaced by a Norman turret. If the groundskeeper is in, you can climb the stairs to the top for €4. The strange-looking stone with a hole at the top near the tower is known as the "wishing stone"—according to lore, if you put your arm through the hole and touch your shoulder when you make a wish, then your wish will come true. The Cathedral is closed to visitors from October to April.

Market Sq., Kildare Town, Co. Kildare. ✆ **045/521229.** Free admission to Cathedral; round tower €4. May–Sept Mon–Sat 10am–1pm, 2–5pm; Sun 2–5pm. Closed Oct–Apr.

local hero: ST. BRIGID

Feminists have embraced this 5th-century saint for decades. Brigid was a headstrong girl who fought against the oppressive, patriarchal rules of her time. When her father picked a husband for her, she refused to marry him. Legend holds that when her father insisted that the wedding should go forward, she pulled out her own eye to prove she was strong enough to resist his plans. He backed down, and the mutilated girl joined a convent, but when she took her vows the bishop accidentally ordained her as a bishop rather than a nun. It is said that as soon as that happened, she was miraculously made beautiful again.

As she grew older, Brigid remained a rebel. She founded a monastery in Kildare, but insisted that it be open to both nuns and monks—something that was extraordinary at that time. Unsurprisingly, word of the monastery, and of its unusual abbess, soon spread throughout Europe and she became a powerful figure in European Christianity. Her followers marked their homes with a plain cross woven from river reeds, and you'll still find crosses, made in precisely that way, in some Irish homes.

One of Brigid's strangest rules for her monastery was that a fire should always be kept burning, day and night, tended by 20 virgins. Long after she died, the fire at St. Brigid's burned constantly, tended as she said it should be. This continued as late as 1220, when the bishop of Dublin insisted that the tradition, which he viewed as pagan, be stopped. But there is still a fire pit at St. Brigid's Cathedral (see p. 189), and a fire is lit in it every February 1, on St. Brigid's feast day.

Sports & Outdoor Pursuits

CYCLING Kildare's flat-to-rolling landscape is perfect for gentle cycling. Sadly, most organized tours bypass Kildare for regions with more diverse scenery, but you can always plan your own route. Bike rental shops are surprisingly few in County Kildare, but **Cahill Cycles,** Fishery Lane, Naas, Co. Kildare (✆ **045/881-585;** www.cahill.ie) comes highly recommended. Alternatively, you could rent a bike in Dublin.

GOLF The flat plains here create excellent parkland layouts, including two 18-hole championship courses. If your wallet is padded, the Arnold Palmer–designed, par-72 **Kildare Hotel & Country Club** (also known as the **K Club**), Straffan, Co. Kildare (✆ **01/601-7200;** www.kclub.com), has two courses, with greens fees ranging from €95 to €120 for non-residents. For a less costly game, try the par-72 championship course at the **Curragh Golf Club,** Curragh, Co. Kildare (✆ **045/441714;** www.curraghgolf.com), with greens fees of €25 to €35, depending on the time of year.

HORSEBACK RIDING To arrange a trek in the Kildare countryside, contact the **Kill International Equestrian Centre,** Kill (✆ **045/877-333;** www.killinternational.ie). A semi-private lesson costs €45.

WALKING The way-marked **Grand Canal Way** is a long-distance walking path that cuts through part of Kildare. Its flatness makes it ideal for beginners and for walkers with no pretenses of ambition. The canal passes through plenty of scenic towns, such as Sallins, Robertstown, and Edenderry, where you can find a room and stock up on provisions. For more information see **www.irishtrails.ie/Trail/Grand-Canal-Way/18**, or contact the tourist office.

Where to Stay West of Dublin

Griesmount ★★ The ancestors of the great British polar explorer Ernest Shackleton built this charming country manor set amid acres of gently rolling green hills. There must be something in the water here, as current owners Carolyn and Robert have a rather adventurous past of their own, having traveled and lived in Africa for many years before settling down to run Griesmount as a B&B. Guestrooms are traditionally furnished, with famously comfortable beds—the guestbook is full of praise for the heavenly four poster—and two of the rooms have views of the River Griese. Carolyn's delicious, hearty breakfasts are served in a room overlooking an old ruined mill. Dinners can also be arranged with notice. Griesmount has a two-night minimum stay on weekends.

Fullers Court Rd., Ballitore, Co. Kildare. ✆ **059/862-3158.** www.griesemounthouse.com. 3 units. €70–€110 double. Free parking. Breakfast included. **Amenities:** Wi-Fi (free).

Martinstown House ★★ An elegant country house getaway near the famous Curragh racecourse (see p. 188), Martinstown dates mostly from the 1830s. Bedrooms are decorated with more than a few nods to its early Victorian origins, with heritage color schemes and antique-style furniture. Excellent 4-course dinners (€49) are served around a single, long, candlelit table, which gives the appealing sense of an upper-class house party from a bygone age. Expect seasonal fare such as roast duck with sausage and sage stuffing, or grilled sole with lemon and caper butter. ***Note:*** Although the Curragh is just 8km (5 miles) away, a frustrating road layout means driving between the Martinstown and the racecourse takes up to a half-hour each way.

Off L6078 (follow signs for Martinstown), Ballysaxhills, Curragh, Co. Kildare. ✆ **045/441269.** www.martinstownhouse.com. 6 units. €150–€200 double. Free parking. Breakfast included. **Amenities:** Wi-Fi (free).

Barberstown Castle ★★ Although parts of this hotel were built as recently as the early 2000s, enough genuine old castle is still on view as you approach for it to look and feel satisfyingly, well, *castle*-like. The oldest section dates from the 12th century, and even the modern guestrooms have a pleasantly subtle antique feel to them, thanks in part to the four-poster beds in a few. Family rooms are available too. The formal **Barton Rooms** restaurant serves classic Irish bistro fare (although it's very pricey), and there's also a tearoom. The only potential downside is that Barberstown is a very popular wedding venue, particularly in the summer months. One spot of trivia: For what it's worth, Barberstown Castle was the home of Eric Clapton in the 1970s.

On R403, Straffan, Co. Kildare. ✆ **01/628-8157.** www.barberstowncastle.ie. 55 units. €190–€220 double. Free parking. Breakfast included. **Amenities:** Restaurant; room service.

Where to Dine West of Dublin

Cunninghams ★ THAI/PUB FOOD Inside and out, Cunningham's is a fairly traditional, run-of-the-mill Irish pub—which makes it all the more unlikely that it also serves some of the best Thai food in the area. Delicious, authentic style meals are prepared by the Thai chef, Chock, and served in the bar nightly.

local hero: **SILKEN THOMAS**

Nobleman and rebel rolled into one, Silken Thomas was an unlikely revolutionary.

More properly known as Thomas FitzGerald, the 10th Earl of Kildare, he was born in 1513 to illustrious parents—his father was governor of Ireland—and spent much of his childhood at the court of King Henry VIII in England.

Thomas returned to Ireland as a young man, all set to follow in his father's footsteps and rule on behalf of the king. However, when word reached him that his father had fallen out with Henry and been executed, Thomas raised a rebellion.

It began with a blistering attack on Dublin Castle. It failed, but the English were rattled. Thomas and his men retreated to the relative safety of County Kildare, expecting a counter-attack at any moment. And indeed it came . . . but by stealth. While Thomas was temporarily absent from his garrison, a guard was bribed to let in a small group of English soldiers, who massacred everybody inside.

It was a huge blow to the rebellion but Thomas and his remaining men fought on for a while longer. The fight was futile, however, and Thomas eventually agreed to surrender in return for a promise that he and his closest compatriots would be spared. But King Henry wasn't one for keeping his word. Thomas and his men were sentenced to death by hanging, drawing, and quartering. What happened next is enough to make the blood run cold.

On a bleak February morning in 1537, they were dragged through the streets of London to a site of public execution. First Thomas and the others were hanged by the neck, but cut down before they died. Then they were cut open, their bowels and genitals removed and burned in front of their eyes, before finally being killed by beheading. Their bodies were then cut into quarters and placed on spikes. Such was the wrath of kings.

Despite this most chilling end, Thomas remains a folk hero in Ireland. But why the unusual nickname? The sobriquet "Silken Thomas" comes from a wonderful footnote to history. It is recorded that Thomas was a dashing and handsome man, always dressed in the height of fashion. And when his army of 200 men rode into battle, they wore strands of silk, streaming from their helmets.

You could go for a spicy red, green or panang curry, made with coconut and chili, or a classic pad Thai served with crispy wontons. The menu also has a few traditional pub options, such as burgers and steaks, but it's the Thai food that packs in the crowds. Some nights include live music.

Main St., Kildare, Co. Kildare. ✆ **045/521780.** www.cunninghamskildare.com. Main courses €10.50–€21. Mon–Sat 10:30am–10pm.

Silken Thomas ★ INTERNATIONAL Named for a real-life knight and dashing rebel (see below), this atmospheric pub offers simple, tasty, unfussy meals in a jovial atmosphere. The menu is something of a global tour, with Mexican fajitas, Chinese stir-frys, and Indian curries happily served alongside burgers, steaks, fish and chips, and other familiar Irish fare. They do a popular "cavery" (buffet-style roast lunch) on Sundays, and if you're here on a Friday and

Saturday night and just not ready to go home, stick around after 11:30pm when it becomes a nightclub.

The Square, Kildare, Co. Kildare. ✆ **045/522232.** www.silkenthomas.com. Main courses €7–€22. Mon–Sat 10:30am–10pm.

Trax Brasserie ★★ IRISH This laidback but elegant brasserie in tiny Naas, about 22km (13½ miles) northeast of Kildare, is a real find. The 1880s building was originally a railway shed, hence the subtle hints of the industrial in the dining room, such as exposed stone walls and "slabs of slate" serving plates. The fixed-price two-and three-course menus focus on classic Irish flavors with an international flair. You might start with some oak smoked salmon, before moving on to a main of seared scallops served with zucchini tempura, or confit duck leg with an orange glaze.

Friary Rd., Naas, Co. Kildare. ✆ **045/889333.** www.traxbrasserie.ie. Fixed-price menus €24–€28. Mon–Sat 5–10pm; Sun 12:30–2:45pm, 5–8pm.

7

THE SOUTHEAST

Dramatic coastline, misty mountains, and evocative historic monuments characterize the lush counties south of Dublin. The area also has a distinctive, musical dialect, peppered with unique words and phrases—remnants of the ancient Yola language that was once spoken here. The three main tourist centers of the Southeast—**Waterford, Wexford,** and **Kilkenny**—are close enough together that you could use any as a base for exploring the region by car. And make no mistake: It's not long before you really start to feel like you've left the city behind and entered the real countryside. But "city" is a relative term out here; Waterford, the biggest population center in the region, has a population of just 46,000.

ESSENTIALS

Arriving

BY BUS **Bus Éireann** (✆ **01/703-2420;** www.buseireann.ie) operates direct service several times a day from the central bus station (Busáras) on Store Street, Dublin, into Kilkenny, Wexford, and Waterford. The journey to Kilkenny takes upwards of 2 hours; to Wexford and Waterford, closer to three.

BY TRAIN **Irish Rail** (✆ **1850/366-222;** www.irishrail.ie) operates several trains daily between Dublin and Kilkenny, Wexford, and Waterford. The journey to Kilkenny takes about an hour and a half; to Waterford, a little over 2 hours; and to Wexford, 2½ hours.

BY FERRY Ferries from Britain sail to Rosslare Harbour, 19km (12 miles) south of Wexford Town. Call **Irish Ferries** (✆ **0818/300-400;** www.irishferries.ie) or **Stena Line** (✆ **01/204-7777;** www.stenaline.com) for bookings and information. Irish Ferries also sail to Rosslare from northern France.

BY CAR The journey from Dublin to Kilkenny, Waterford, or Wexford is nearly all motorway. For Kilkenny, take E20, then M7 southwest out of Dublin, then split off onto M9. If you're heading to Waterford, stay on M9 for another 50km (31 miles) after the turnoff for Kilkenny. From Dublin to Wexford, take N11 south (you may want to loop around and join it via N81 and M50 if you're starting on the northside), then keep heading south on this road until you reach Wexford. The drive to Kilkenny is about 1½ hours, and to Waterford or Wexford, about 2 hours—but remember traffic can be terrible around Dublin, especially during rush hour.

PREVIOUS PAGE: **Hook Lighthouse at Hook Head, County Wexford.**

BY PLANE Tiny **Waterford Airport** is in Killowen (✆ **051/846-600;** www.waterfordairport.ie), 9km (5⅔ miles) south of Waterford Town. The British budget airline **Flybe** (www.flybe.com) flies here a few times per week from Manchester and Birmingham in the U.K.

Getting Around

Getting from Dublin to the centers of Kilkenny, Wexford, or Waterford by public transport is easy. It's also relatively simple to travel between them; however, as with most rural areas in Ireland, getting *around* the countryside by public transport once you're here is extremely difficult. Unless you're sticking to the big towns, your best option is to rent a car.

BY BUS A handful of buses per day run between Kilkenny and Waterford; the journey takes 1 to 2 hours, depending on if you have to change buses (which you almost always do). No convenient bus routes connect Kilkenny and Wexford. A couple of direct services per day run between Waterford and Kilkenny, plus slightly more if you don't mind changing buses; journey times are also 1 to 2 hours. Direct buses connect Waterford and Wexford every couple of hours; most journeys take an hour.

BY TRAIN A half-dozen or so trains daily go between Kilkenny and Waterford; the journey takes 35 minutes. Getting from Kilkenny or Waterford to Wexford by train is a laborious, all-day process involving multiple changes and should be avoided if at all possible.

BY CAR To rent a car from Dublin, try **Hertz** (www.hertz.ie) at Dublin Airport (✆ **01/844-5466**); 151–157 South Circular Rd., Dublin 8 (✆ **01/709-3060**); or 2 Haddington Rd., Dublin 4 (✆ **01/668-7566**). **Europcar** also has branches at Dublin Airport (✆ **01/812-2800**) and Marks St. (off Pearse St.), Dublin 2 (✆ **01/648-5900**). In Kilkenny, try **Enterprise-Rent-a-Car** at Barlo Nissan, Dublin Rd. (✆ **056/775-3318;** www.enterprise.ie). **Hertz** has a branch in Wexford Town, on Ferrybank (✆ **053/915-2500**), or you can try **Budget Car Rental** at Rosslare Ferryport (✆ **053/913-3318**; www.budget.ie). In Waterford, Enterprise has a branch on Tranmore Rd.

BY FERRY The drive between Waterford and Wexford requires you to take a circuitous route via New Ross that doubles the distance. Unless, that is, you take the handy car ferry from the poetically named **Passage East,** about 12km (7½ miles) east of Waterford (✆ **051/382-480;** www.passageferry.ie). Regular crossings are April to September, Monday to Saturday 7am to 10pm, Sunday and public holidays 9:30am to 10pm; October to March, Monday to Saturday 7am to 8pm, Sunday and public holidays 9:30am to 8pm. Tickets per car are €8 one-way, €12 round-trip.

A Note on Listings

Given that the main attractions in the Southeast are close enough together that you could use either Waterford, Wexford, or Kilkenny as a base to explore the region by car, we have grouped together the hotel and restaurant listings for all three in this chapter. However, to reflect the wealth of attractions in each of those areas, sightseeing listings have been separated out.

Kilkenny, Wexford & Waterford
0 10 miles
0 10 kms
IRISH SEA
St. George's Channel
CELTIC SEA
To Fishguard
To Pembroke
To Roscoff
NORTHERN IRELAND
Belfast
REPUBLIC OF IRELAND
Dublin
Galway
Map Area
Cork
WICKLOW
LAOISE (LEIX)
OFFALY
CARLOW
KILKENNY
WEXFORD
TIPPERARY
WATERFORD
LIMERICK
CLARE
CORK
Arklow
Courtown
Kilmuckridge
Wexford Bay
Curracloe
Wexford Harbour
Wexford
Rosslare
Rosslare Harbour
Lady Island Lake
Carnsore Point
Killinick
Saltee Islands
Kilmore Quay
Hook Peninsula
Hook Head
Waterford Harbour
Baltinglass
Hacketstown
Aughrim
Tinahely
Shillelagh
Gorey
Camolin
Ferns
Bunclody
Clonegal
Tullow
Rathvilly
Slaney
Mt. Leinster
Blackstairs Mts.
Enniscorthy
Oilgate
Adamstown
Clonroche
Wellington Bridge
Castledermot
Carlow
Ballon
Bagenalstown
Borris
Ballymurphy
Graiguenamanagh
Drummin
Inistioge
New Ross
Lukeswell
Cheekpoint
Duncannon
Dunmore East
Graigue
Leighlinbridge
Barrow
Whitehall
Ballinakill
Ballyragget
Durrow
Abbeyleix
Freshford
Nore
Kilkenny
Bennettsbridge
Thomastown
Kells
Knocktopher
Ninemilehouse
Ballyhale
Callan
Mooncoin
Waterford
Tramore
Annestown
Carrick-on-Suir
Portlaw
Suir
Knockanaffrin
Kilmacthomas
Bunmahon
Lemybrien
Dungarvan
Ring
Johnstown
Rathdowney
Roscrea
Templemore
Templetuohy
Urlingford
Littleton
Ballingarry
Fethard
Clonmel
Comeragh Mts.
Thurles
Cashel
Rathkeevin
Ardfinnan
Newinn
Clogheen
Kilcommon
Knockmealdown Mts.
Cappoquin
Lismore
Ballymacmague
Grange
Ardmore
Youghal
Clashmore
Tallow
Ballymacoda
Castlemartyr
Ballycotton
Milestone
Dundrum
Limerick Junction
Tipperary
Bansha
Cahir
Galtymore
Galty Mts.
Mitchelstown
Glanworth
Fermoy
Blackwater
Watergrasshill
Carrigtohill
Midleton
Cobh
Cloyne
Passage West
Cork
Cork Int'l
Blarney
Kilmona
Castletownroche
Doneraile
Kilfinane
Kilmallock
Bruff
Hospital
Lough Gur
Oola
Pallas Grean
Limerick
Castleconnell
Newport
Killaloe
Ballina
Nenagh

local hero: THOMAS FRANCIS MEAGHER

The Granville Hotel on Waterford Quay (see p. 204) was the birthplace of Thomas Francis Meagher, a relatively little-known revolutionary who led a colorful life.

After twice being elected mayor of Waterford—the first Catholic to hold such an office since the 16th century—he was arrested and sentenced to death for his part in an anti-British rebellion in 1848. His sentence was commuted to exile in Australia; however, he escaped and fled to America, where he rose to become a senior Union officer in the Civil War.

Meagher died after falling from a steamboat into the Missouri River in 1867. At the time of his death he was governor of the Montana Territory. Many believed he was pushed overboard by an assassin, possibly in retaliation for military campaigns he had led against the Native American tribes of Idaho.

[FastFACTS] THE SOUTHEAST

ATMs/Banks Convenient locations include the **Allied Irish Bank (AIB)** on Dublin Rd., Kilkenny, and 72 The Quay, Waterford; and **Bank of Ireland** at 29 Parnell St., Waterford, and Custom House Quay, Wexford.

Dentists For dental emergencies, your hotel will usually contact a dentist for you; otherwise, in Kilkenny try **Market Cross Dental Surgery,** James St. (✆ **056/772-1386**); in Waterford, **O'Connell Street Dental Clinic,** 38 O'Connell St. (✆ **051/856-800**); and in Wexford, **Allsmile Dental Practise,** 27 St. John's Gate (✆ **053/912-1748**).

Doctors In emergencies dial ✆ **999.** For non-emergencies, any good hotel will contact a doctor for you. Otherwise, in Kilkenny try **Friary Court Clinic,** Friary St. (✆ **056/776-5613**); in Waterford, **Catherine Street Medical Centre,** 18 Catherine St. (✆ **051/875338**); and in Wexford, **Whiterock Family Practise,** Whiterock Hill (✆ **053/916-0070**).

Emergencies For police, fire, or other emergencies, dial ✆ **999.**

Pharmacies In Kilkenny try **White's Chemist,** 5 High St. (✆ **056/772-1328**); in Waterford, **Gallagher's Late Night Pharmacy,** 29 Barronstrand St. (✆ **051/878103**); and in Wexford, **Boots the Chemist,** 54 North Main St. (✆ **053/914-7851**).

Taxis In Kilkenny, call **Ray Cabs** (✆ **086/888-2777**) or **Town & County Taxi** (✆ **056/776-5714**); in Waterford, **Rapid Cabs** (✆ **051/858-585**) or **Swift Cabs** (✆ **051/898-989**); and in Wexford, **Wexford Cabs** (✆ **053/912-3123**) or **Wexford Taxi Services** (✆ **053/914-6666**).

EXPLORING COUNTY WATERFORD

The main seaport of southeast Ireland, Waterford City's unprotected proximity at the edge of the ferocious Atlantic Ocean makes it Ireland's Windy City, as a sea breeze is always blowing here. Its oceanside location has a lot to

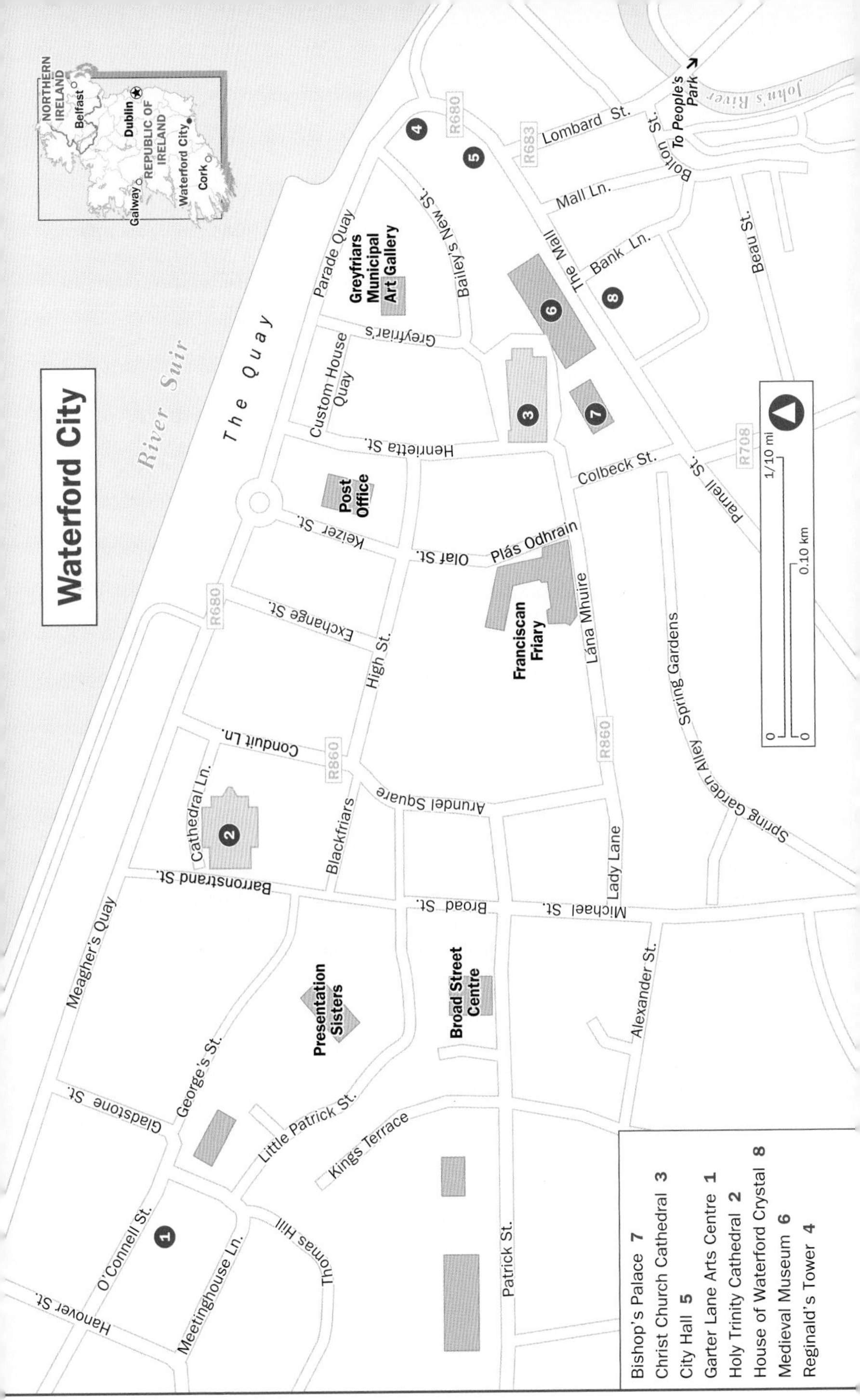
Waterford City
River Suir
The Quay
NORTHERN IRELAND
Belfast
Dublin
REPUBLIC OF IRELAND
Waterford City
Galway
Cork
Parade Quay
Greyfriars Municipal Art Gallery
Bailey's New St.
Greyfriar's
Custom House Quay
Henrietta St.
Post Office
Keizer St.
Olaf St.
Plás Odhrain
Franciscan Friary
Lána Mhuire
Exchange St.
High St.
Conduit Ln.
Cathedral Ln.
Blackfriars
Arundel Square
Barronstrand St.
Broad St.
Michael St.
Lady Lane
Meagher's Quay
Presentation Sisters
Broad Street Centre
George's St.
Gladstone St.
Little Patrick St.
Kings Terrace
O'Connell St.
Meetinghouse Ln.
Thomas Hill
Hanover St.
Patrick St.
Alexander St.
Spring Gardens
Spring Garden Alley
Parnell St.
Colbeck St.
The Mall
Bank Ln.
Mall Ln.
Lombard St.
Bolton St.
Beau St.
To People's Park
John's River
R680
R683
R860
R708
1/10 mi
0.10 km
0
Bishop's Palace 7
Christ Church Cathedral 3
City Hall 5
Garter Lane Arts Centre 1
Holy Trinity Cathedral 2
House of Waterford Crystal 8
Medieval Museum 6
Reginald's Tower 4

do with its status as the oldest city in the country, founded by Viking invaders in the 9th century.

Visitor Information

The **Waterford Tourist Office** is at The Granary, The Quay, Waterford (✆ **051/875788;** www.waterfordtourism.com). In May, June, and September it's open Monday to Saturday 9:30am to 5:30pm; July and August, Monday to Friday 9pm to 6pm, Saturdays 9:30 and to 5:30pm, and also Sundays 11am to 5pm from late July to mid-August; and from October to April, Monday to Saturday 9:15am to 5pm.

Exploring Waterford City

Bishop's Palace ★★ One of three separate museums that are known collectively as ***Waterford Treasures,*** the Bishop's Palace focuses on life in the city from 1700 until the mid-20th century. The collection covering the 18th century is by far the most impressive including furniture, art, fashion, and some exquisite glass and silverwork. Appropriately enough, given the close proximity to the famous factory (see p. 201), it also holds the earliest surviving pieces of Waterford Crystal, a decanter dating from 1789. The Bishop's Palace, itself an elegant example of Georgian architecture, was built by Richard Cassels (1690–1751), who was also the architect of Leinster House in Dublin (see p. 112).

The Mall, Waterford, Co. Waterford. ✆ **051/849650.** www.waterfordtreasures.com/bishops-palace. Admission €5 adults; €4 seniors and students; children 13 and under free. June–Aug Mon–Sat 9am–6pm; Sun and public holidays 11am–6pm. Sept–May Mon–Sat 10am–5pm; Sun and public holidays 11am–5pm.

City Hall ★ Headquarters of the local city government, this late-18th-century building houses a few pieces of interesting local memorabilia, including the city's founding charter, dating from 1205. The main council chamber contains a panoramic landscape of Waterford City painted by the Dutch artist Willem Van der Hagen (?-1745). It is thought to be the earliest landscape painting of an Irish city in existence. There's also a small exhibit on the extraordinary life of Thomas Francis Meagher, a leader in an Irish insurrection in 1848, who went on to be governor of Montana (see p. 198).

The Mall, Waterford, County Waterford. ✆ **051/860856.** Free admission. Mon–Fri 9am–5pm.

Garter Lane Arts Centre ★ One of Ireland's largest arts centers, the Garter Lane occupies two buildings on O'Connell Street. Number 5 holds exhibition rooms and artists' studios, and no. 22a, a former Friends Meeting House, is home of the Garter Lane Theatre along with an art gallery and courtyard. The gallery showcases works by contemporary and local artists, plus a varied program of music, dance, and films.

O'Connell St., Waterford, Co. Waterford. ✆ **051/855038.** www.garterlane.ie. Many events and exhibits free; ticketed events from €5–€20. Tues–Sat 11am–10pm; Sun 7–10pm; individual performance times vary.

Holy Trinity Cathedrals ★ Waterford has two impressive cathedrals, one Catholic and the other Protestant, both built by one equal-opportunity architect, John Roberts. Roberts lived 82 years (1714–96), fathered 22 children with his beloved wife, and built nearly every significant 18th-century building in and around Waterford. Holy Trinity on Barronstrand is the only baroque cathedral in Ireland and has 10 unique Waterford crystal chandeliers. The Anglican or Church of Ireland Holy Trinity Cathedral (conveniently nicknamed Christ Church) on Henrietta Street has a most peculiar spire and only clear glass, because its first bishop and rector disliked stained glass.

Barronstrand and Henrietta sts., Waterford, Co. Waterford. ✆ **051/875166.** www.waterford-cathedral.com. Free admission. Daily, hours can vary but generally 7:30am–7pm.

House of Waterford Crystal ★ One of the best-known Irish brands in the world, Waterford Crystal has been made in the city (with significant periods of hiatus) since 1783. In 2009 the company filed for bankruptcy—perhaps Ireland's most high-profile victim of the financial crisis—but new owners were soon found, and with them came this shiny, purpose-built factory and visitor center, right in the heart of Waterford. You can tour the factory to watch the glittering products being molded, blown, cut, and finished—or just drop in at the enormous shop for some sparkly souvenirs.

The Mall, Waterford, Co. Waterford. ✆ **051/317000.** www.waterfordvisitorcentre.com. Admission €12.50 adults; €9.50 seniors and students; €4.50 children 6–18; children 5 and under free; €32 families. Tour: Apr–Oct Mon–Sat 9am–4:15pm; Sun 9:30am–4:15pm. Nov–Dec Mon–Fri 9:30am–3:15pm. Jan–Feb Mon–Fri 9am–3:15pm. Mar Mon–Sat 9am–3:15pm; Sun 9:30am–3:15pm. Shop stays open 1 hr. 45 min. after start of last tour.

Medieval Museum ★★ The latest addition to the multi-site Waterford Treasures, the Medieval Museum has some beautiful artifacts from the city's medieval period, but they're not the only attraction here. Just as interesting is the 13th-century Choristor's Hall with its vaulted stone ceiling. Closed off for years, it now forms one of the main areas of the museum, together with a 15th century wine vault. Highlights of the permanent collection include medieval art, clothing (including a velvet cap given to the Mayor of Waterford by Henry VIII), and the city's original charter, dating from 1373.

Cathedral Sq., Waterford, Co. Waterford. ✆ **051/849501.** www.waterfordtreasures.com/medieval-museum. Admission €5 adults; €4 seniors and students; children 13 and under free; €10 families. Easter–May daily 10am–5pm; June–mid-Sept daily 10am–6pm; mid-Sept–Easter Wed–Sun 10am–5pm.

Reginald's Tower ★★ Claimed to be Ireland's oldest building that's still in day-to-day use, Reginald's Tower was built around the year 1000 by the Viking invaders who founded the city. Today it houses a museum devoted to that period in Waterford's history; inevitably much of it is interpretive in nature, with displays that tell the story in absorbing detail, but a surprising number of actual items are on display too. Highlights include fragments of Viking pottery, coins, and jewelry—including a stunning ornamental clasp, intricately patterned with fine threads of gold and silver.

The Quay, Waterford, Co. Waterford. ✆ **051/304220.** www.waterfordtreasures.com/reginalds-tower. Admission €3 adults; €2 seniors; €1 students and children; €8 families. Easter–May daily 10am–5pm; June–mid-Sept daily 10am–6pm; mid-Sept–Easter Wed–Sun 10am–5pm.

Waterford City Walking Tours ★★ Local guide Jack Burtchaell is well versed in the history, folklore, and witty anecdotes of his home city. He conducts this engaging hour-long tour of the old city twice daily, leaving from the tourist office at 11:45am and 1:45pm, and the reception area of the Granville Hotel on the Quay at noon and 2pm. You don't have to book—just show up a little before departure time.

The Quay, Waterford, Co. Waterford. ✆ **051/873711.** www.jackswalkingtours.com. Tour €7. Daily 11:45am, 2pm.

Further Afield in County Waterford

Ardmore High Cross ★ Ardmore (Irish for "the great height") is a very ancient Christian site—St. Declan, its founder, is said to have been a bishop in Munster as early as the mid–4th century, well before St. Patrick came to Ireland. Tradition has it that the small stone oratory in a cemetery high above Ardmore marks his burial site. St. Declan's Oratory is one of several stone structures here composing the ancient monastic settlement. The most striking is the perfectly intact 30m-high (98-ft.) round tower. On site are also ruins of a medieval cathedral and, nearby, St. Declan's well and church. Ardmore is near the border with County Cork, about 70km (43 miles) southwest of Waterford City.

On R673, Ardmore, Co. Waterford. R673; from the main N25 road, follow signs to Ardmore. Free admission. Daily dawn–dusk.

Lismore Castle Gardens ★ High above the River Blackwater, this turreted medieval fortress dates from 1185, when Prince John of England established a castle on this site. The grounds, surrounded by thick defensive walls

Lismore Castle

A WALK TO mahon falls

These impressive, 80m (262½ ft.) waterfalls are in the Comeragh Mountains, on R676 between Carrick-on-Suir and Dungarvan. At the tiny village of Mahon Bridge, 26km (16 miles) south of Carrick-on-Suir, turn west on the road marked for Mahon Falls, then follow signs for the falls and the Comeragh Drive. In about 5km (3 miles), you reach a parking lot along the Mahon River (in fact, just a tiny stream). The trail, indicated by two boulders, begins across the road. Follow the stream along the floor of the valley to the base of the falls. From here you can see the fields of Waterford spread out below you, and the sea a glittering mirror beyond. Walking time is about 30 minutes round-trip.

Mahon Falls in the Comeragh Mountains.

dating from 1626, are spread across nearly 3 hectares (7 acres). They're peaceful and quite lovely to wander around, dotted with sculptures and with views of the impressive-looking castle. You're free to wander the whole 3,200-hectare (7,904-acre) estate of gardens, forests, and farmland—but not the castle itself. Lismore is owned by the Duke and Duchess of Devonshire, wealthy British aristocrats, who won't let the general public in. That said, they're not above a spot of entrepreneurism; in fact, if you've got the money, you can see it all, since the castle can be rented, complete with the Duke's personal staff, to private groups, for around €35,000 per week. (See **www.lismorecastle.com** for more details, although, frankly, if you can afford that price, you've probably got a castle of your own.)

Lismore, Co. Waterford. From Cappoquin, take N72 6.5km (4 miles) west. ✆ **058/54061.** www.lismorecastlegardens.com. Admission €8 adults; €4 children 15 and under. Apr–Sept 10:30am–5:30pm. Last admission 1 hr. before closing.

Sports & Outdoor Pursuits

BEACHES Wide sandy beaches are at Tramore, Ardmore, Clonea, or Dunmore East.

CYCLING From Waterford City, you can ride 13km (8 miles) to Passage East and take the ferry to Wexford and the beautiful Hook Peninsula (fare with bicycle €2 one-way, €3 round-trip). Or continue on from Passage East to Dunmore East, a picturesque seaside village with a small beach hemmed in by cliffs. The road from there to Tramore and Dungarvan is quite scenic. For bicycle hire, try **Atltitude Cycle and Outdoor Store** at 22 Ballybricken, Waterford City (✆ **051/970356;** www.altitude.ie), just outside the city center, about a 15-minute walk from the Waterford Treasures museums (see p. 200).

FISHING There is good fishing to be had in County Waterford. Colligan River is excellent for sea trout and salmon. The River Slaney, brimming with salmon and sea trout, can be fished from the old bridge in Enniscorthy. And the River Blackwater has sea trout, brown trout, and wild salmon. **Knockaderry Reservoir** is an enormous, 28-hectare (70-acre) fishery 12km (7½ miles) southwest of Waterford City. Permits (€25) must be purchased from the Centra supermarket on the main R680 road in Kilmeaden. Boats can also be hired for €15 from Pat Smith, the treasurer of the local angling association (✆**051/384428**). Meanwhile, the **Fort William Fishery,** Glencairn, Lismore (✆**087/829-2077;** www.fortwilliamfishing.net) is renowned for wild salmon; permits cost between €15 and €100 per day, depending on the time of year. They also rent a fisherman's cottage for €450 per week during summer, €35 per week in the rest of the year—see the website for more details. If you're seeking a bigger challenge, deep sea angling trips (including reef and wreck dives) can be organized by **Gone Fishing,** 42 Lower Main St., Dungarvan (✆ **058/43514**). They can also rent rods and other fishing gear.

GOLF County Waterford's golf venues include three 18-hole championship courses. **Waterford Castle Golf and Country Club,** The Island, Ballinakill, Waterford (✆ **051/871633;** www.waterfordcastle.com/golf.html), is a par-72 parkland course; greens fees are €15 to €30. **Faithlegg Golf Club,** Faithlegg House (✆ **051/382000;** www.faithlegg.com), a par-72 parkland course beside the River Suir, charges greens fees of €25 to €45. **Dungarvan Golf Club,** Knocknagranagh, Dungarvan (✆ **058/41605;** www.dungarvangolfclub.com), a par-72 parkland course, has greens fees of €20 to €40. In addition, the 18-hole par-71 inland course at **Waterford Golf Club,** Newrath, Waterford (✆ **051/876748**), is 1.6km (1 mile) from the center of the city. Its greens fees are €30 to €40.

HORSEBACK RIDING Arrange to ride at **Killotteran Equitation Centre,** Killotteran, Waterford (✆ **051/384158;** www.kec.ie). Fees average around €25 per hour.

SAILING, WINDSURFING & SEA KAYAKING From May to September, the **Dunmore East Adventure Centre,** Dunmore East (✆ **051/383783;** www.dunmoreadventure.com), offers courses of 1 to 4 days that cost around €45 to €100 per day, including equipment rental. Summer programs for children are also available.

Where to Stay in County Waterford

Granville Hotel ★★ The elegant, Sienna-colored frontage of this welcoming hotel gives a clue to its history. Built in the late 1700s, it has been in business continuously since 1865. The interior retains something of a manor house feel, with elegant color schemes, deep red carpeting, and antique furniture. Guestrooms are comfortable and reasonably spacious—although not all have air conditioning, so make sure you request this when you book if it's important to you. Some rooms overlook Waterford Quay, with its field of gently bobbing yacht masts. The hotel bar is popular with locals, and the modern Irish **Bianconi Restaurant** is excellent. Staff could hardly be friendlier or more helpful. You can book a relaxing (and reasonably priced) massage beauty treatment in the Therapy Room.

Meagher's Quay, Waterford, Co. Waterford. ✆ **051/305-555.** www.granville-hotel.ie. 98 units. €83–€98 double. Parking at nearby lots (no discount) €3.50–€5 overnight; €5–€16 for 24 hr. Breakfast not included in lower rates. Dinner, bed and breakfast packages available. **Amenities:** Wi-Fi (free); restaurant; bar; room service.

Sion Hill House ★★ The liberal scattering of handsome old antiques around this 18th-century house tells you something about its storied past. Ask your host, George, to fill you in—it has enough history to fill a small book. The elegant guestrooms are decorated with tantalizing elements of that history in mind, and it feels like there's a new story to be told around each corner. One room has a large bell outside the window that was used to signal the start and end of the day for the gardeners who once worked the grounds; another has antique French furnishings, to reflect a connection between the house and Princess Letizia Bonaparte, niece of Napoleon. The 2 hectares (5 acres) of gardens are peaceful, with lovely views across the river to Waterford. They're quite famed locally; George and his wife, Antoinette, even run tours for non-residents. Check the website for some excellent off-season deals, including almost half-price room rates.

Dock Road, Ferrybank, Waterford, Co. Waterford. ✆ **051/851-558.** www.sionhillhouse.net. 4 units. Free parking. €80–€96 double. Rates include breakfast. **Amenities:** Wi-Fi (free).

Waterford Marina Hotel ★ This modern, well-run hotel, overlooking the River Suir, isn't particularly characterful—but it's in a great location, a short walk from the center of Waterford. Rooms are clean and have everything you need, with comfortable beds. Family rooms are an exceptionally good value—they sleep up to four, for only €10 or so more than the standard double rates. (You'll pay a €25 supplement for kids between 12 and 16.) Some bedrooms have lovely views over the water. Special offers are often listed on the website, including packages that cover dinner in the excellent restaurant. ***Tip:*** Ask for an upper floor room—the views better and, since there can be street noise at night, particularly on weekends, you're just a bit above the ruckus.

Canada St., Waterford, Co. Waterford. ✆ **051/856-600.** www.waterfordmarinahotel.com. 81 units. €58–€136 double. Parking (free). Breakfast not included in lower rates. **Amenities:** Wi-Fi (free); restaurant; bar; room service; accessible rooms.

Where to Dine in County Waterford

Even in straitened times, Waterford's restaurant scene is impressive for such a small city. Restaurants such as **Rinuccini,** a winning combination of Irish and Italian, really raise the bar—although it's perfectly possible to find a decent meal without stretching the wallet.

Bodega! ★★ MODERN IRISH/EUROPEAN A restaurant with an exclamation point in the name is hardly the sort of place in which one expects to sit up straight, and Bodega! certainly does its best to cultivate an upbeat, funky vibe. The menu is similarly vivacious: smoked salmon cured in gin to start, followed by piri-piri marinated tiger prawns, or maybe an order of chicken wings flavored with honey and a kick of ginger. Subtler, more traditional bistro-style choices are on the menu too, along with plenty of daily specials. The long cocktail list should help maintain the buzz.

54 John's St., Waterford. ✆ **051/844-177.** www.bodegawaterford.com. Main courses €15–€28. Mon–Sat noon–10pm.

The Munster ★ BISTRO This cozy bar, across the street from the House of Waterford Crystal visitor center (see p. 201), serves a smallish menu of unpretentious, traditional pub grub—think sandwiches, Irish stew, seafood pie, and an enormous house burger. The early evening menu has a few slightly more ambitious choices, such as chicken breast with chorizo and parmesan cream, or salmon fishcake served with chili jam. It may lack frills, but everything's well done.

Bailey's New Street, Waterford, Co. Waterford. ✆ **051/874-656.** www.themunsterbar.com. Main courses €12–€14. Mon 12:30am–2:30pm; Tues–Fri 12:30–2:30pm, 5–9pm; Sat 5–9pm; Sun 4–8pm.

Richmond House ★★★ MODERN IRISH The grounds of this 18th-century mansion hideaway an industrious vegetable patch, where the chef gets most of the fruit and vegetables for the restaurant's kitchen. This is something of a dining destination for people in this part of Ireland, and it's easy to see why—the menu is a hugely successful combination of Irish and Continental flavors. Menus change daily, according to what's fresh and in season, but you're likely to find locally sourced lamb, beef, and seafood served with sides like champ (mashed potato and spring onion) or something freshly picked from the garden. The wine list is perfectly judged, with a better than average selection of wines by the glass—a relief, given the price of dinner. Those wanting to sample some of this sumptuous home cooking on a budget may want to check out the €33 early bird menu, served until 7:30pm.

Singposted from N72, Cappoquin, Co. Waterford. ✆ **058/54278.** www.richmondhouse.net. Fixed-price menus: 2 courses €25; 3 courses €55. Daily 6–9pm. Closed Dec 22–Jan 10.

EXPLORING COUNTY WEXFORD

Although it's within easy reach of County Wexford, Dublin might as well be hundreds of miles away—the countryside in this area feels so bucolic and peaceful. Wexford is known for its long stretches of pristine beaches and for the evocative historic monuments in Wexford Town and on the Hook Peninsula. The modern English name of Wexford evolved from *Waesfjord,* which is what the Vikings called it when they invaded in the 9th century. The Normans captured the town at the end of the 12th century, and you can still see remnants of their fort at the Irish National Heritage Park.

Visitor Information

The **Wexford Tourist Office** is on Crescent Quay, Wexford (✆ **053/912-3111;** www.visitwexford.ie). It's open Monday to Friday from 9am to 6pm, and Saturday from 10:30am to 5pm. From late July to mid-August it's also open on Sundays from 10:30am to 5pm.

Exploring Wexford Town

The Bull Ring ★ In 1798, the first declaration of an Irish republic was made here, and a statue memorializes the Irish pikemen who fought for the cause. Earlier, in the 17th century, the town square was a venue for bull baiting, a sport introduced by the butcher's guild. Tradition maintained that after a match, the hide of the ill-fated bull was presented to the mayor and the meat was used to feed the poor. Today, activity at the ring is much tamer: an excellent outdoor market is every Friday and Saturday from 10am to 4:30pm.

Off N. Main St., Wexford, Co. Wexford.

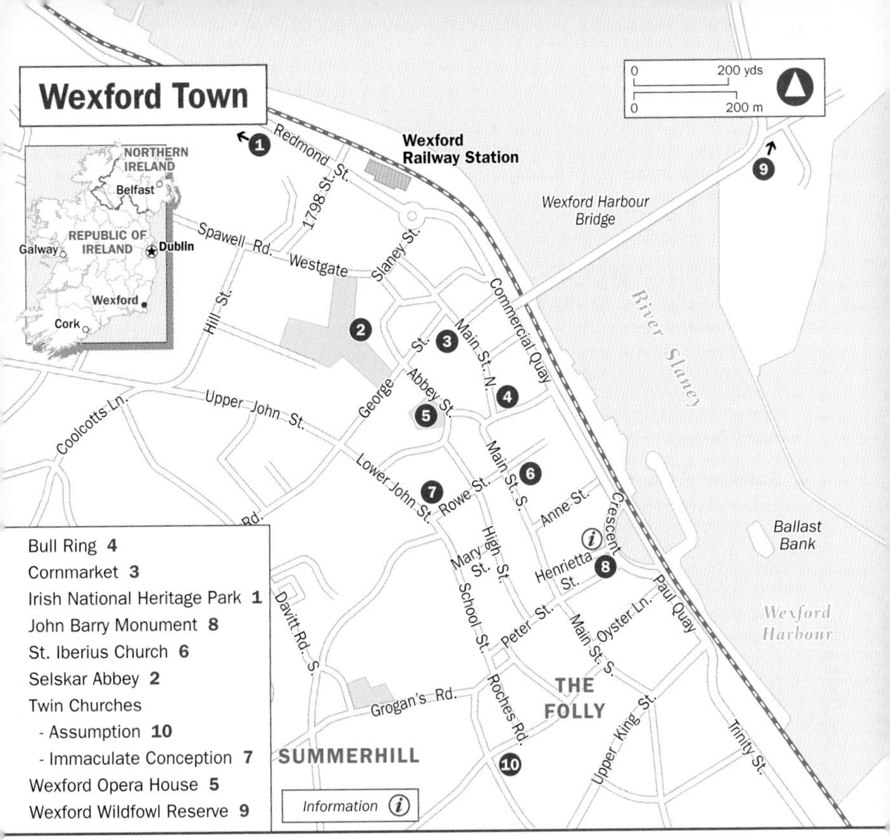

Cornmarket ★ Until a century ago, this central marketplace buzzed with the activity of cobblers, publicans, and more than 20 other businesses. Today it's just a wide street dominated by the Wexford Arts Centre, a structure dating from 1775.

Off Upper George's St., Wexford, Co. Wexford.

Irish National Heritage Park ★★ This 14-hectare (35-acre) living-history park on the banks of the River Slaney just outside of Wexford Town provides an ideal introduction for visitors of all ages to life in ancient Ireland, from the Stone Age to the Norman invasion. Each reconstructed glimpse into Irish history is well crafted and has its own natural setting and wildlife. There's also a nature trail and interpretive center, complete with gift shop and cafe. Kids can easily be amused for half a day here.

Ferrycarrig (about 4.8km/3 miles west of Wexford, signposted from N11), Co. Wexford. ✆ **053/912-0733.** www.inhp.com. Admission €9 adults; €7 seniors and students; €4.50 children 13–18; €4 children 4–12; children under 4 free; €24 families. May–Aug 9:30am–6:30pm (last admission 5pm); Sept–Apr 9:30am–5:30pm (last admission 3–3:30pm, according to daylight).

John Barry Monument ★ This bronze statue, a gift from the American people in 1956, faces out to the sea as a tribute to the titular Mr. Barry, a Wexford native who became the father of the American Navy. Born at Ballysampson,

Tacumshane, 16km (10 miles) southeast of Wexford Town, Barry immigrated to the colonies while in his teens and volunteered to fight in the American Revolution. One of the U.S. Navy's first commissioned officers, he became captain of the *Lexington*. In 1797 George Washington appointed him commander in chief of the U.S. Navy.

Crescent Quay, Wexford, Co. Wexford.

St. Iberius Church ★ Erected in 1660, St. Iberius was built on hallowed ground—the land has been used for houses of worship since Norse times. The church has a lovely Georgian facade and an interior known for its superb acoustics. Free guided tours are given according to demand.

N. Main St., Wexford, Co. Wexford. No phone. www.wexford.ferns.anglican.org/iberius.html. Free admission; donations welcome. May–Sept daily 10am–5pm; Oct–Apr Tues–Sat 10am–3pm.

Selskar Abbey and Westgate Heritage Centre ★ This picturesque abbey dates from the early 12th century, and it has often been the scene of synods and parliaments. The first Anglo-Irish treaty was signed here in 1169, and it's said that Henry II spent Lent 1172 at the abbey doing penance for having Thomas à Becket beheaded. Although the abbey is mostly in ruins, its choir is part of a Church of Ireland edifice, and a portion of the original tower is a vesting room. Connected to the abbey (and operated as a single attraction) is the **Westgate Heritage Centre.** Housed in what was once a tollgate on the western approach to the city—part of the 12th century defensive walls—the center has some diverting exhibits relating to the history of the town, plus an informative film. Opening times are somewhat variable, so it's a good idea to call ahead.

Westgate St., Wexford, Co. Wexford. ✆ **053/914-6506.** Admission €7 adults; €3 children and students. May–Aug Mon–Fri 10am–6pm, Sat–Sun noon–6pm; Sept–Apr Mon–Fri 10am–5pm.

The Twin Churches: Church of the Assumption and Church of the Immaculate Conception ★ These twin Gothic structures (1851–58) were designed by architect Robert Pierce, a pupil of Augustus Pugin. Their 69m (226-ft.) spires dominate Wexford's skyline. Mosaics on the main doors of both churches give a good bit of local history.

Bride and Rowe sts., Wexford, County Wexford. ✆ **053/912-2055.** Free admission; donations welcome. Daily 8am–6pm.

Wexford Opera House ★ This shiny, modern opera house is a somewhat awkward addition to the Wexford skyline, with its large but rather garish copper-plated tower. The biggest event in the opera houses' calendar is, unsurprisingly, the Wexford Festival Opera. Held over two weeks each October/November, this prestigious event attracts aficionados from all over Ireland and beyond. Opera lovers will be in heaven—but book early if there's something you want to see. Tickets start at around €10, rising to about €100 for the best seats.

High St., Wexford, Co. Wexford. ✆ **053/912-2144.** www.wexfordoperahouse.ie. Ticket prices vary; generally between €10–€40. Event times vary; call ahead.

Wexford Walking Tours ★★ Proud of their town's ancient streets and antique buildings, the people of Wexford began conducting guided tours for visitors more than 30 years ago. Now the tourism office runs the tours on a more formal basis, but they're still led by locals, whose knowledge of the town and its history is unrivaled. The regular historical tour runs March to October and costs €4 per person. It departs daily at 11am from the Tourist Office (see p. 206), who also handle booking. The whole tour takes about 90 minutes. They also offer ghost tours and a walk of the surviving sections of the medieval town walls.

Departs from the Wexford Tourist Office on Crescent Quay, Wexford Town, Co. Wexford. ✆ **086/352-6133.** www.wexfordwalkingtours.net. Tour €4. Mar–Oct Mon–Sat 11am.

Wexford Wildfowl Reserve ★ This national nature reserve is part of the unfortunately named North Slob, adjacent to Wexford Harbour, 5km (3 miles) east of Wexford Town. About 10,000 Greenland white-fronted geese—more than one-third of the world's population—winter here, as do brent geese, Bewick's swans, and wigeons. The reserve has a visitor center, an informational film, an exhibition hall, and an observation tower and blinds.

North Slob, Wexford, Co. Wexford. ✆ **053/912-3129.** www.wexfordwildfowlreserve.ie. Free admission. Daily 9am–5pm.

Further Afield in County Wexford

Hook Lighthouse & Heritage Centre ★★★ The Hook Head Peninsula is one of southern Ireland's loveliest drives, full of captivating vistas and hidden byways to discover. Nestled at the end of it all is this picturesque old lighthouse, the oldest part of which dates from the 13th century, making it the world's oldest lighthouse still in continuous use. Guided tours do an excellent job of telling the history of the lighthouse, and the surrounding peninsula, which has been occupied since at least the 5th century A.D. There is an active program of special events too, from art courses to ghost tours. ***Tip:*** The drive from Waterford is drastically shorter if you take the Passage East Car Ferry; see "Fast Facts" at the start of this chapter for details.

Hook Head, Co. Wexford. ✆ **051/397-055.** www.hookheritage.ie. Admission €6 adults; €4.50 seniors and students; €3.50 children 5–16; children 4 and under free; €18–€20 families. Visitor center: June–Aug daily 9:30am–6pm; May, Sept 9:30am–5:30pm; Oct–Apr 9:30am–5pm. Lighthouse tours: June–Aug half-hourly 10am–5:30pm; Sept–May hourly 11am–5pm. 30km (18⅔ miles) southeast of Waterford, 47km (29 miles) southwest of Wexford.

Irish Agricultural Museum and Famine Exhibition ★★ An extremely absorbing and at times affecting place, this excellent museum on the grounds of Johnstown Castle tells the story of agriculture and how important it was to the history of this region. Some rooms feature exhibits devoted to, among other things, dairy farming, country furniture, traditional crafts, and historic machinery. Of course no farming museum in Ireland would be complete without mention of its greatest catastrophe—the Great Famine, which killed about a million people in the mid-19th century (and was responsible for the emigration of a million more). A special section puts it all into perspective in a thought-provoking way. Johnstown Castle was built in the 1400s; today it's used as a government building, but you can still wander the beautiful grounds.

Johnstown Castle Estate, Bridgetown Road, off Wexford-Rosslare Road (N25), Wexford, Co. Wexford. ✆ **053/918-4671.** www.irishagrimuseum.ie. Gardens and museum: €8 adults; €6 seniors; €4; €24 families. Museum: Apr–Oct Mon–Fri 9am–5pm; Sat–Sun and public holidays 11am–5pm. Nov–Mar Mon–Fri 9am–4pm; Sat–Sun and public holidays 11am–4pm. Gardens: Apr–Oct daily 9am–5:30pm; Nov–Mar daily 9am–4:30pm.

A TRIP THROUGH history: EXPLORING THE RING OF HOOK

The **Hook Peninsula** in southwest County Wexford is a picturesque place of rocky headlands and secluded beaches between Bannow Bay and Waterford Harbour. These were significant inlets in medieval times for travelers from Britain to Ireland, and the abundance of archaeological remains reflects that. The end of the peninsula, with its sturdy old lighthouse, is popular with birders as a site for watching the spring and fall passerine migration. The route described below will guide you through a driving or biking tour, and hikers can see most of the places listed from the Wexford Coastal Pathway.

Start your exploration of the peninsula at the town of **Wellington Bridge.** Just west of town on R733 is a roadside stop on the left by a cemetery; from here you can look across Bannow Bay to the ruins of **Clonmines**—a Norman village established in the 13th century. It's a fine example of a walled medieval settlement, with remains of two churches, three tower houses, and an Augustinian priory. You can drive to the ruins—just follow R733 another mile west to a left turn posted for the Wicklow Coastal Pathway, and continue straight on this road where the pathway turns right. The ruins are on private land, so you should ask permission at the farmhouse at the end of the road.

Continuing west on R733, turn left on R734 at the sign for the Ring of Hook, and turn right at the sign for **Tintern Abbey** (see p. 212). The abbey was founded by the monks of Tintern in South Wales in the 13th century, but it has been much altered over the centuries. The grounds are beautiful and contain a restored stone bridge that spans a narrow sea inlet.

At **Baginbun Head,** a fine beach nestles against the cliffs, from which you can see the outline of the Norman earthwork fortifications on the head. The Norman presence in Ireland was first established here with the victory of Norman forces over the Irish at the Battle of Baginbun.

The **tip of the peninsula,** with its line of low cliffs eroded in places for blowholes, has been famous for shipwrecks since Norman times. A **lighthouse** has long been on this site; the present structure consists of a massive base, built in the early 13th century, and a narrower top dating from the 19th century.

The Ring of Hook road returns along the western side of the peninsula, passing the beaches at **Booley Bay** and **Dollar Bay.** On a promontory overlooking the town of Duncannon is a **fort** built in 1588 to protect Waterford Harbour from the Spanish Armada. Just north of Duncannon, along the coast at the village of **Ballyhack,** a ferry runs to County Waterford, and a Knights Hospitallers castle (see Ballyhack Castle, below) stands on a hill.

A visit to the Hook Peninsula wouldn't be complete without a stop at **Dunbrody Abbey,** in a field beside the road about 6.5km (4 miles) north of Duncannon. The abbey, founded in 1170, is a magnificent ruin and one of the largest Cistercian abbeys in Ireland. Despite its grand size, it bears remarkably little ornamentation. Tours are sometimes available; inquire at the visitor center across the road.

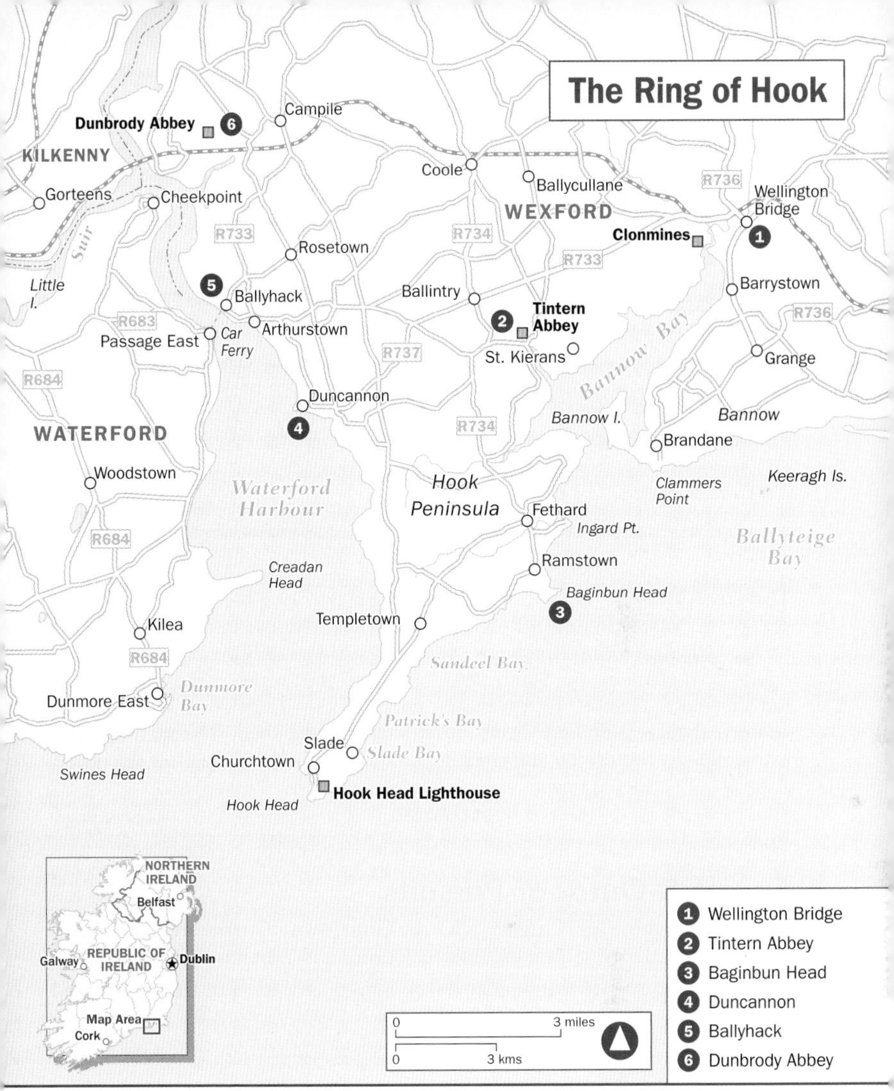

SS Dunbrody Famine Ship Experience ★★★ This huge, life-sized reconstruction of a 19th-century tall ship is exactly the kind of vessel on which a million or more people emigrated from Ireland to escape the Great Famine. An interpretive history center, the SS *Dunbrody* is an engaging way to learn about that history—particularly for youngsters, who will find it less stuffy than a conventional museum. Actors in period dress lead the tours, describing in great detail what life on board was like for the passengers. The SS *Dunbrody* is in New Ross, 36km (22⅓ miles) west of Wexford.

The Quay, New Ross, Co. Wexford. ✆ **051/425239.** www.dunbrody.com. Admission €8.50 adults; €7 seniors; €5 students and children; €20–€25 families. Apr–Sept daily 9am–6pm (first tour 9:45am, last tour 5pm); Oct–Mar daily 9am–5pm (first tour 10am, last tour 4pm).

LOCAL JFK: son OF NEW ROSS

New Ross was the birthplace of Patrick Kennedy (1823–58), great-grandfather of John F. Kennedy, the 35th President of the United States. You can visit the **Kennedy Homestead** (✆ **051/388264;** www.kennedyhomestead.ie), where Patrick and his family lived, in the tiny village of Dunganstown, 8km (5 miles) south of New Ross. It's open daily from 9:30am to 5:30pm; entry costs €7.50 adults, €6.50 seniors, €5 students, and €20 families. Another JFK site of interest is the **Kennedy Memorial Arboretum** (✆ **051/388171;** www.heritageireland.ie), a beautiful lakeside garden and wildlife haven dedicated to the late President. It's signposted from R733, about 12km (7½ miles) south of New Ross. Opening times are: May to August, daily 10am to 8pm; April and September, daily 10am to 6pm; and October to March, daily 10am to 5pm. Entry costs €3 adults, €2 seniors, €1 students and children, and €8 families.

Tintern Abbey ★ In a lovely rural setting overlooking Bannow Bay, Tintern Abbey was founded in the 12th century by William Marshall, the Earl of Pembroke, as thanks to God after he nearly died at sea. The early monks were Cistercians from Tintern in South Wales (hence the name). The parts that remain—nave, chancel, tower, chapel, and cloister—date from the early 13th century, though they have been much altered since then. The grounds are extraordinarily beautiful and include a stone bridge spanning a narrow sea inlet. A small coffee shop is on site.

Saltmills, New Ross, Co. Wexford. ✆ **051/562650.** Free admission. Mid-May–late Sept daily 10am–5pm. Signposted 19km (12 miles) south of New Ross off of R733.

Sports & Outdoor Pursuits

BEACHES County Wexford's beaches at **Courtown, Curracloe, Duncannon,** and **Rosslare** are ideal for walking, jogging, and swimming.

CYCLING You can rent mountain bikes in Wexford Town at **Hayes Cycle Shop,** 108 S. Main St. (✆ **053/912-2462;** www.hayescycles.com). From Wexford, the road north up the coast through Curracloe to Blackwater is a scenic day trip.

BIRD-WATCHING A good starting place for bird-watching in the region is the **Wexford Wildfowl Reserve** (see p. 209). The on-site warden can direct you to other places of interest.

The **Great Saltee Island** is excellent for watching seabirds, especially during May, June, and July, when it's mobbed with nesting parents and their young. Like something out of a Hitchcock feature, the cliffs on the island's southernmost point are packed to overflowing with raucous avian residents. You can get up close and personal with puffins, which nest in underground burrows, or graceful guillemots. Other species include cormorants, kittiwakes, gannets, and Manx shearwaters. The island is privately owned, but visitors are welcome on the condition that they do nothing to disturb the bird habitat and the island's natural beauty. You can usually charter a boat to the

Saltees from the Kilmore Quay; alternatively, contact **Kilmore Quay Angling Charters** (✆ **053/912-9637** or 087/292-6469), or **Sailing Island** (✆ **086/171-3800**). Landings generally take place only in summer, and not in rough weather.

Hook Head is a good spot for watching the spring and autumn passerine migration—the lack of sizable cliffs means that it isn't popular with summer nesting seabirds. In addition to swallows, swifts, and warblers, look out for the less common cuckoos, turtledoves, redstarts, and blackcaps.

While driving south from Gorey toward Ballycanew on R741, keep an eye out for a reddish **cliff** on the left, about 2km (1¼ miles) out of Gorey; this is a well-known peregrine aerie, with birds nesting until the early summer. The land is private, but you can watch the birds from the road.

DIVING The Kilmore Quay area, south of Wexford Town, offers some of the most spectacular diving in Ireland, especially around the Saltee Islands and Con-ningbeg rocks. For all your diving needs, consult the **Pier House Diving Centre,** Kilmore Quay (✆ **053/29703;** email scubabreaks@eircom.net).

GOLF In recent years, Wexford has blossomed as a golfing venue. One of the newest developments is an 18-hole championship seaside par-72 course at **St. Helens Bay Golf Club,** Kilrane (✆ **053/913-3234;** www.sthelensbay.com). Greens fees are €18 to €30. The **Enniscorthy Golf Club,** Knockmarshall, Enniscorthy (✆ **054/923-3191;** www.enniscorthygc.ie), is an inland par-70 course with greens fees of €20 on weekdays, €55 on weekends.

SAILING/FISHING The town of **Kilmore Quay,** south of Wexford Town on R739, is a center for sea angling in Wexford. The most popular rivers for fishing are the Barrow and the Slaney, where the sea trout travel upstream from mid-June to the end of August. **Blackwater Anglers** (✆ **053/912-7318**) offer fishing on a lake stocked with rainbow and brown trout from spring until late in the year.

WALKING Along the entire coastline you'll see brown signs with a picture of a hiker on them. The signs mark the **Wexford Coastal Path,** which meanders along the coast via pristine beaches and country lanes. Unfortunately, the roads are often too busy for it to be a good idea to walk the whole route—especially on the bypass around Wexford Town. The markers are handy, however, for shorter walks between Wexford's beaches. In the northern part of the county, the section of beach from Clogga Head (County Wicklow) to Tara Hill, 14km (8 miles) south, is especially lovely, as is the walk to the top of Tara Hill, which offers views across sloping pastures to the sea. Farther south, the path veers off the roads and sticks to the beach from Cahore Point south to Raven Point and from Rosslare Harbour to Kilmore Quay.

Another good coastal walk is near the town of Wexford in the **Raven Nature Reserve,** an area of forested dunes and uncrowded beaches. To get there, take R741 north out of Wexford, turn right on R742 to Curracloe just out of town, and in the village of Curracloe, turn right and continue for just over a mile to the beach parking lot. The nature reserve is to your right. You can get there by car, driving a half-mile south, or walk the distance along the beach. The beach extends another 5km (3 miles) to Raven Point, where at low tide you can see the remains of a shipwreck, half-buried in the sand.

On the border between counties Wexford and Carlow, the long, rounded ridge of peaks are the **Blackstairs Mountains,** which allow for plenty of walks in an area unspoiled by tourism. Get a guidebook and maps from any sizable Wexford tourist office.

Where to Stay in County Wexford

In Wexford, choice within the town is limited; you'll do much better opting for a place in the countryside, where a satisfying mixture of bucolic farmhouses and luxurious getaways are well worth splurging for.

Riverbank House Hotel ★★ This cozy midsize hotel just outside the town center in Wexford has lovely views of the River Slaney. Rooms overlooking the river have suitably huge picture windows. Beds are comfortable and very large; some are four-poster. Family rooms cost just €30 more than doubles (though they are not that much bigger, with one double and one single bed.) The bar and restaurant are pleasant spaces, filled with polished wood and natural light. The casual pub-style food is good too—think unfussy, international dishes of the something-for-everyone variety—and in good weather you can dine on the terrace overlooking the river. The genuinely cheerful staff helps things run smoothly. All in all, this is a thoroughly decent, near-budget option about a 10-minute walk from central Wexford.

The Bridge, Wexford, Co. Wexford. ✆ **053/912-3611.** www.riverbankhousehotel.com. 23 units. €79–€130 double. Parking (free). Rates include breakfast. **Amenities:** Wi-Fi (free); restaurant; bar; room service.

Monart Spa ★★★ A luxurious, grown-up retreat, Monart is consistently named among the top spas in Ireland—and for good reason. It's a sumptuous, impeccably designed place, nestled beside a lake and a verdant forest. Guestrooms are surrounded by woodland, and some have little balconies overlooking the grounds. The restaurant is excellent, though expensive (€40 for three courses, and many dishes have an extra cost). The heavenly spa has a thermal suite (free to use for guests) equipped with two pools, a salt grotto, indoor and outdoor saunas, and an aroma steam room. Packages and short breaks are a good value—for example, a 3-night stay, including breakfast, dinner, and a spa treatment, for €315. To maintain the air of serenity, no children are allowed at Monart. This is a strictly adults-only zone.

On L6124, The Still, Enniscorthy, Co. Wexford. ✆ **053/923-8999.** www.monart.ie. 70 units. €95–€175 double; €895–€995 suite. Parking (free). Rates include breakfast. Dinner, bed and breakfast, and spa treatment packages available. **Amenities:** 2 restaurants; bar; room service; afternoon tea; cafe; spa; pool. About 5.2km (3⅓ miles) west of Enniscorthy.

Where to Dine in County Wexford

Forde's Restaurant ★★ BISTRO The dining room here has a beautiful view of Wexford Harbour, and the bistro-style menu is an excellent value. Seafood is a specialty, and like all the best seaside restaurants, the exact line up of the menu depends on what's fresh each day. Expect lemon sole in basil sauce or salmon encased in seaweed. Carnivores may prefer pork stuffed with cashew nuts and apples or perhaps a succulent rib-eye steak. Unusual for a place that takes such pride in its bistro-style cooking, Forde's has almost as many vegetarian and vegan choices on the menu as meat dishes.

Crescent Quay, Wexford, Co. Wexford. ✆ **053/912-3832.** www.fordesrestaurant.com. Main courses €15–€19. Mon–Sat 6–10pm; Sun 5–10pm.

EXPLORING COUNTY KILKENNY

Like so many Irish towns, Kilkenny City stands on the site of an old monastery from which it takes its name. A priory was founded here in the 6th century by St. Canice; in Gaelic, *Cill Choinnigh* means "Canice's Church." In medieval times it was a prosperous walled city. Much of its medieval architecture has been skillfully preserved, including long sections of the medieval wall. Further afield from the county seat, the gentle countryside is full of captivating old ruins, from the majestic Kells Priory to the haunting remains of Jerpoint Abbey.

Visitor Information

The **Kilkenny Tourist Office** is at Shee Alms House, Rose Inn Street, Kilkenny (✆ **056/775-1500;** www.kilkennytourism.ie). It's open May to September, Monday to Saturday 9am to 6pm, Sunday 10:30am to 4pm; October to April, Monday to Saturday 9:15am to 5pm.

Exploring Kilkenny City

Black Abbey ★ Nobody is sure why this Dominican church, founded in 1225, is named Black Abbey. It may be because the Dominicans wore black capes over their white habits, or perhaps because the Black Plague claimed the

Colorful shop fronts in affluent Kilkenny City.

lives of eight priests in 1348. The Black Abbey's darkest days came in 1650, when Oliver Cromwell used it as a courthouse before destroying it; by the time he left, all that remained was the walls. The abbey was rebuilt, and opened in 1816 as a church, a new nave was completed in 1866, and the entire building was fully restored in 1979. Among the elements remaining from the original abbey are an alabaster sculpture of the Holy Trinity that dates from 1400, and a pre-Reformation statue of St. Dominic carved in Irish oak, which is believed to be the oldest such piece in the world. The huge Rosary Window, a stained-glass work of nearly 45 sq. m (484 sq. ft.) representing the 15 mysteries of the rosary, was created in 1892 by Mayers of Munich.

Kilkenny Castle and the River Nore

Abbey St. (off Parliament St.), Kilkenny, County Kilkenny. ✆ **056/772-1279.** www.blackabbey.ie. Free admission; donations welcome. Apr–Sept Mon–Sat 7:30am–7pm, Sun 9am–7pm. Oct–Mar Mon–Sat 7:30am–5:30pm. No visits during worship.

Kilkenny Castle ★★★ Standing majestically beside the River Nore on the south side of Kilkenny City, this landmark medieval castle was built in the 12th century and remodeled in Victorian times. From its sturdy corner towers to its battlements, Kilkenny Castle retains the imposing lines of an authentic fortress and sets the tone for the city. The exquisitely restored interior includes a library, drawing room, and bedrooms, all decorated in 1830s style. The former servants' quarters are now an art gallery. The 20-hectare (49-acre) grounds include a riverside walk, extensive gardens, and a well-equipped children's playground. Access to the main body of the castle is by guided tour only, prefaced by an informative video on the rise, demise, and restoration of the structure. This is a very busy site, so arrive early (or quite late) to avoid waiting.

The Parade, Kilkenny, Co. Kilkenny. ✆ **056/770-4100.** www.kilkennycastle.ie. Admission €6 adults; €4 seniors; €2.50 students and children 6 and over; €14 families. Apr–May, Sept 9:30am–5:30pm; June–Aug 9am–5:30pm; Oct–Feb 9:30am–4:30pm; Mar 9:30am–5pm.

Kilkenny Walking Tours ★★ Local historian Pat Tynan leads you through the streets and lanes of medieval Kilkenny on this lively walking tour, providing historical facts and anecdotes along the way. Tours depart daily from the tourist office, Rose Inn Street.

C/o Kilkenny Tourist Office, Rose Inn St., Kilkenny, Co. Kilkenny. ✆ **087/265-1745.** tynantours@eircom.net. Tickets €7 adults; €6.50 seniors and students. Mid-Mar–Apr, June–Oct Mon–Sat 10:30am, 12:15, 3pm; May Mon–Sat 10:30am, 12:15, 3pm, Sun 11:15am, 12:30pm.

Kyteler's Inn ★ This atmospheric old inn with a fascinating tale to tell has been in business for over six centuries. They serve decent pub food, but it's the

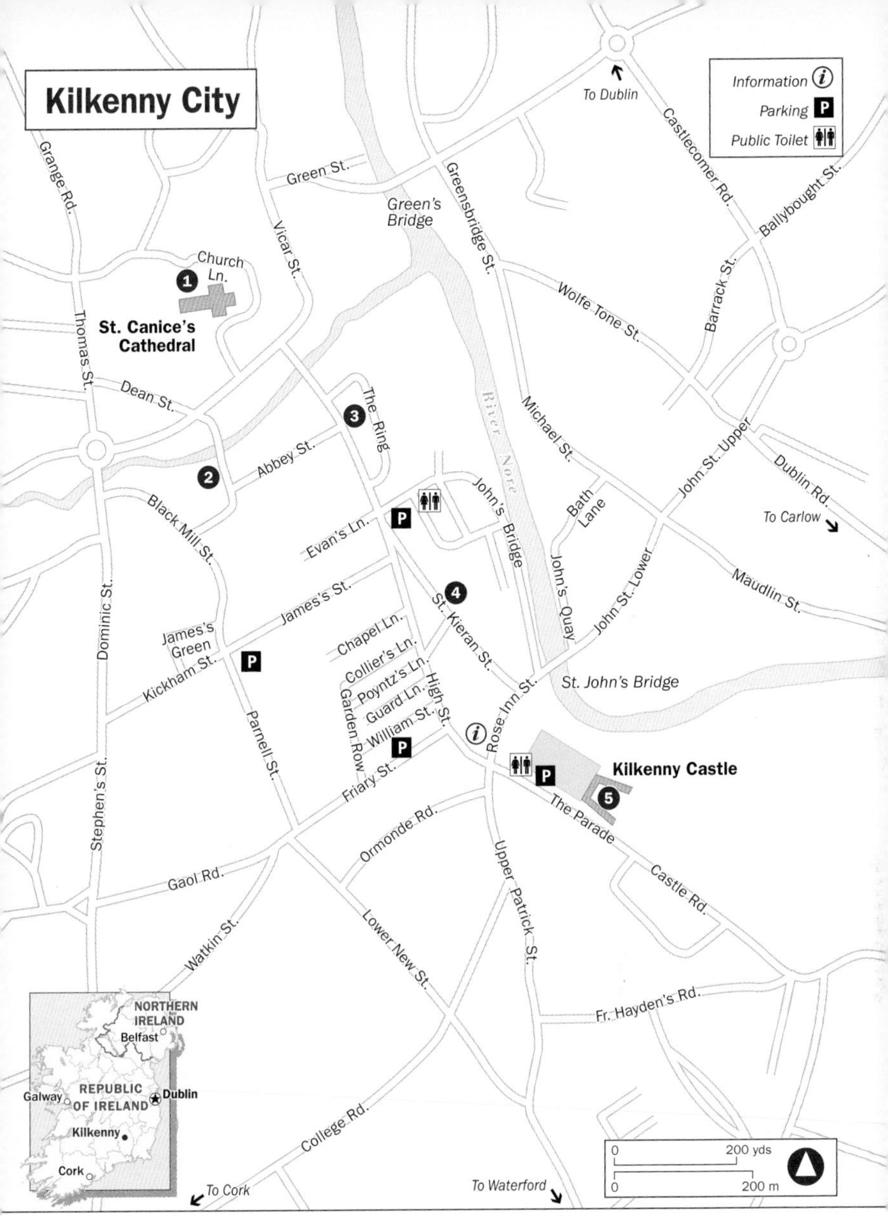

Black Abbey **2**

Kilkenny Castle **5**

Kyteler's Inn **4**

St. Canice's Cathedral **1**

St. Francis Abbey Brewery **3**

vibe you really come for—all exposed flagstones and cozy nooks, it's hard to think of a more satisfying Irish-looking pub. The place is named after former resident Alice Kyteler, who died in 1324. She poisoned at least three of her husbands, ran the Inn as a den of debauchery, and was sentenced to be burned as a witch. She escaped, but nobody saw nor heard from her again. Unless, that is, you believe some of the more colorful tales about this place after dark . . .

Kieran St., Kilkenny, Co. Kilkenny. ✆ **056/772-1064.** www.kytelersinn.com. Daily noon–around midnight.

St. Canice's Cathedral ★★ The church that gave Kilkenny its name is at the northern end of the city. It was built in the 12th century, but was restored after the English invasion led by Oliver Cromwell in the mid-17th century. It is noteworthy for the rich interior timber and stone carvings, its colorful glasswork, and the structure itself. On the grounds, amid the tombstones in the churchyard, is a massive round tower, believed to be a relic of the ancient church (although its original conical top has been replaced by a slightly domed roof). If you want to climb to the tip of the tower, it will cost you a couple of euro and more calories than you can count. The steps up to the cathedral were constructed in 1614, and the carvings on the wall at the top of the stairs date from medieval times.

The Close, Coach Rd., Kilkenny, Co. Kilkenny. ✆ **056/776-4971.** www.stcanicescathedral.com. Cathedral: €4 adults; €3 seniors, students and children; €12 families. Round Tower: €3 adults; €2.50 seniors, students and children; €12 families. Combined ticket: €6 adults; €5.50 seniors, students and children; €15 families. May–Sept Mon–Sat 9:30am–5pm, Sun 9:30am–4:30pm. Apr–May, Sept Mon–Sat 10am–1pm, 2–5pm; Sun 2–5pm. June–Aug Mon–Sat 9am–6pm; Sun 1–6pm. Oct–Mar Cathedral: Mon–Sat 10am–1pm, 2–4pm; Sun 2–4pm. Round Tower: Mon–Sat noon–4pm; Sun 3–4pm. No children under 12 allowed to climb the round tower.

St. Francis Abbey Brewery ★ Established in 1710 by John Smithwick, the brewery occupies a site that once belonged to the 12th-century Abbey of St. Francis. A popular local beer called Smithwick's is produced here, as are Budweiser and Land Kilkenny Irish beer. Tours of the brewery have an unusual selling point—you get to see the rather sorry remains of the original, 12th century St. Francis Abbey, located on the brewery grounds. Though certainly not unimpressive in themselves, the ruins are hardly done justice by being sandwiched between some industrial warehouses and a large parking lot.

Parliament St., Kilkenny, Co. Kilkenny. ✆ **056/779-6498.** www.smithwicks.ie. Admission €10. No children. No high heels or open-toe sandals. Tours Tues–Sat 12:30, 1, 3, 4:30pm.

Further Afield in County Kilkenny

Duiske Abbey ★ Duiske Abbey (1204) is a fine example of an early Cistercian abbey. It was suppressed in 1536, but its monks continued to occupy the site for many years. In 1774 the tower of the abbey church collapsed. In 1813 the roof was replaced and religious services returned to the church, but the abbey didn't approach its former glory until the 1970s, when a group of locals mounted a reconstruction effort. Now, with its fine lancet windows and a large effigy of a Norman knight, the abbey is the pride of Graiguenamanagh. The adjacent visitor center has an exhibit of Christian art and artifacts.

Graiguenamanagh, Co. Kilkenny. ✆ **059/972-4238.** Free admission; donations welcome. Daily 10am–5pm.

Dunmore Cave ★ This gloomy series of chambers, formed over millions of years, contains some fine calcite formations. The caves have been known to humans for at least a millennium; they are first recorded in written records from the 9th and 10th centuries. These records, known as the *Triads of Ireland*, indicate that a bloody Viking massacre took place here in the year A.D. 928. No conclusive proof has ever been found, but evidence unearthed by archaeologists in more recent years at least confirms that Vikings used the caves. Exhibits at the visitor center tell the story. Access to the cave is by guided tour only. Dunmore is about 11km (7 miles) from Kilkenny City.

Off Castlecomer Rd. (N78), Ballyfoyle, Co. Kilkenny. ✆ **056/776-7726.** Admission €3 adults; €2 seniors; €1 students and children; €8 families. Mid-Mar–mid-June, mid-Sept–Oct daily 9:30am–5pm (last tour 4pm); mid-June–mid-Sept daily 9:30am–6:30pm (last tour 5pm); Nov–mid-Mar Wed–Sun and holidays 9:30am–5pm (last tour 3pm).

Jerpoint Abbey ★★ About 18km (11 miles) southeast of Kilkenny, this outstanding Cistercian monastery dates from the 12th century. Preserved in a peaceful country setting, the abbey's highlights include a sculptured cloister arcade, unique stone carvings on medieval tombs, and Romanesque architecture in the north nave. The staff is as friendly and knowledgeable about the local area as they come. Ask for details of where to find the mysterious ruins of the **Church of the Long Man,** about 16km (10 miles) away. If you're lucky, they'll be able to direct you—it's impossible to find otherwise, and a local secret you may find yourself

Jerpoint Abbey

sworn to keep. ***Tip:*** If you're here in spring or autumn, plan your visit toward the end of the day. Wandering around these ancient places as the setting sun blushes the walls in peach and gold is an unforgettable experience.

On N8, 2.5km (1½ miles) southwest of Thomastown. ✆ **056/772-4623.** www.heritageireland.ie. Admission €3 adults; €2 seniors; €1 students and children; €8 families. Early Mar–Sept 9am–5:30pm; Oct daily 9am–5pm; Nov–early Dec daily 9:30–4pm. Closed Dec–early Mar.

The thick fortifications of Kells Priory have survived since the 13th century.

Jerpoint Glass Studio ★ Here you can witness the creation of Jerpoint glass, which you've probably been admiring in shops all across Ireland. The lines of the glasses, goblets, and pitchers are simple and fluid, highlighted with swirls of color. You can watch the glass being blown and then blow your budget next door at the shop.

Stoneyford, Co. Kilkenny. ✆ **056/772-4350.** www.jerpointglass.com. Shop and gallery: Mar–Oct Mon–Sat 10am–6pm; Sun and public holidays noon–5pm. Nov–Feb Mon–Sat 10am–5pm; Sun and public holidays noon–5pm. Glassblowing demonstrations: Mon–Thurs 10am–4pm; Fri 10am–1pm.

Kells Priory ★★ With its encompassing fortification walls and towers, as well as complex monastic ruins enfolded into the sloping south bank of the King's River, Kells is a glorious ruin. In 1193 Baron Geoffrey FitzRobert founded the priory and established a Norman-style town beside it. The current ruins date from the 13th to 15th centuries. The priory's wall has been carefully restored, and it connects seven towers, the remains of an abbey, and foundations of chapels and houses. You can tell by the thick walls that this monastery was well fortified, and those walls were built for a reason—it was frequently attacked. In the 13th century, it was the subject of two major battles and burned to the ground. The priory is less than a half-mile from the village of Kells, so if you have some time to spare, cross the footbridge behind it, which takes you on a beautiful stroll across the river and intersects a riverside walk leading to a picturesque old mill.

Kells, Co. Kilkenny. ✆ **056/775-1500.** Free admission. Take N76 south from Kilkenny, follow signs for R699/Callan and stay on R699 until you see signs for Kells.

Sports & Outdoor Pursuits

FISHING The **River Nore,** southeast of Kilkenny, is known for salmon and trout. For advice, permits, and supplies, visit the **Sports Shop,** 82 High St., Kilkenny (✆ **056/772-1517**).

GOLF **Mount Juliet Golf and Country Club,** Thomastown (✆ **056/777-3071;** www.mountjuliet.ie), is an excellent course 16km (10 miles) south of

Kilkenny City. The 18-hole, par-72 championship course, designed by Jack Nicklaus, charges greens fees of €60 to €120. Alternatively, try the 18-hole championship course at the **Kilkenny Golf Club,** Glendine, County Kilkenny (✆ **056/776-5400;** www.kilkennygolfclub.com), an inland par-71 layout, just 1.6km (1 mile) from the city. Greens fees are €30 to €50.

Where to Stay in County Kilkenny

Lawcus Farm Guesthouse ★★★ Make no mistake that you're staying on a real farm at this wonderful guesthouse ("helping us on the farm at feeding time is greatly appreciated" says the website). The early-19th-century building has been beautifully renovated. Guestrooms are cozy and decent-sized, with plenty of natural light; some have original fireplaces; one has exposed gray stone walls and an antique-style brass bed. Hosts Mark and Anne-Marie take real pride in welcoming guests—and how could they not, in such a beautiful setting? You're right next to a river, where you can go wild water swimming, or even try your hand at fishing for trout. Home-cooked breakfasts are delicious, but you have to fend for yourself at dinner. Luckily Mark and Anne-Marie can recommend a string of nearby places. The only snag in this rural idyll? Lawcus Farm doesn't accept credit cards or checks, so make sure you're able to pay in cash.

Stoneyford, Co. Kilkenny. ✆ **086/603-1667.** www.lawcusfarmguesthouse.com. 5 units. €100 double. Parking (free). Rates include breakfast. Discounts for stays of 2 or more nights. Children under 5 free (1 per party). **Amenities:** Wi-Fi (free). Driving from Dublin: After passing Stoneyford sign, take turning to the right of the small bridge and follow signs to B&B. From Waterford: As Dublin, but approach to Stoneyford is from opposite direction. From Cork: At Colnmel take N76 (towards Kilkenny), then turn off through Callan and Kells. When entering Kells, look out for sign pointing to Lawcus Farm beside pub on right. Keep following signs past priory on left.

Pembroke Hotel ★★ Just a few streets away from Kilkenny Castle (you can see the turrets poking up invitingly over rooftops from the upper floors), this is a comfortable, cosmopolitan hotel in the center of Kilkenny City. Bedrooms are modern and comfortable, with plenty of room, although not a great deal of character. The in-house **Statham's Restaurant** serves good, modern Irish cuisine, and certain nights in the summer feature barbecue. The sophisticated bar is a lively spot for a cocktail or glass of wine. Guests get free use of a local gym and pool, a 10-minute walk away.

Patrick St., Kilkenny, Co. Kilkenny. ✆ **056/778-3500.** www.kilkennypembrokehotel.com. 74 units. €65–€188 double. Parking (free). Rates include breakfast. **Amenities:** Wi-Fi (free); restaurant; bar; room service; gym and pool (10-min. walk).

Rosquil House ★★ Comfortable and friendly, this modest little B&B is an outstanding value for money. Your hosts, Rhoda and Phil, greet guests with genuine warmth and enthusiasm, making you feel immediately at home. The house was purposely built as a B&B, so the bedrooms are spacious and well proportioned. One room is fully accessible for those with mobility problems. Public areas, including a large guest lounge, are tastefully decorated in color schemes of chocolate and cream, with polished wood floors. The breakfasts cooked by Phil are delicious. The only downside is that you're a little far from the action, but central Kilkenny is only about a 15-minute walk away.

Castlecomer Rd., Kilkenny, Co. Kilkenny. ✆ **056/772-1419.** www.rosquilhouse.com. 7 units. €80–€85 double. Parking at nearby lots (no discount) 3.50€–5€ overnight; 5€–16€ 24 hr. Rates include breakfast. **Amenities:** Wi-Fi (free).

Where to Dine in County Kilkenny

Café Mocha ★ CAFE A good choice for a quick light lunch—or, even better, a slice of cake—this popular little cafe on Kilkenny's main street has a delightfully shabby chic vibe. Lavender walls and battered old furniture cluttered with ornaments give it the air of a broken dollhouse. Lunches are tasty and healthy with a variety of sandwiches, quiches, and salads. To indulge, choose from one of the homemade cakes, tarts, or desserts—each delectable. The upper floor location makes it a great spot to sink into a comfy sofa, cup of tea in hand, and watch the world go by.

84 High St., Kilkenny, County Kilkenny. ✆ **056/777-0074.** Main courses €5–€12. Mon–Thurs 9am–6pm; Fri–Sat 9am–10pm; Sun 10am–6pm.

Campagne ★★★ BISTRO The chef at this outstanding French-Irish restaurant, about a 10-minute walk from Kilkenny Castle, used to run the kitchen at the superlative Chapter One in Dublin (see p. 143). The dining room is sleek and atmospherically lit, with colorful modern art on the walls. The menu is short but subtly inventive: duck with cabbage, turnips and blackberries, or perhaps turbot served with a rich crab bisque. For dessert, try the lime parfait served with deliciously tart lemon curd ice cream. The only downside is that this place is quite pricey, but plenty of locals will tell you it's their go-to for a special dinner. The extensive wine list is well chosen, with particularly strong French options.

5 The Arches, Gashouse Lane, Kilkenny, Co. Kilkenny. ✆ **056/777-2858.** www.campagne.ie. Main courses €27–€29. Tues–Thurs 6–10pm; Fri 12:30–2:30pm, 6–10pm; Sat 12:30–2:30pm, 5:30–10pm; Sun 12:30–3pm. Closed Sun for dinner except on public holiday weekends. Closed Tues nights following Monday public holiday.

Gourmet Store ★ DELI/CAFE Very good for a quick lunch on the go, this little cafe in the center of Kilkenny is popular with local office workers who come for tasty sandwiches and bagels. There's also a great stock of deli goods, so you can put together your own picnic hamper, or the folks behind the counter can even do it for you—perfect for when you need to snatch a quick bite on the road. A lot of the off-the-shelf products are local and small-brand, including jams, chutneys, and other upscale nibbles, so stock up on gifts and edible souvenirs to take home.

56 High St., Kilkenny, Co. Kilkenny. ✆ **056/777-1727.** www.thegourmetstorekilkenny.com. All items €4–€10. Mon–Sat 8am–6pm.

Rinuccini ★★★ ITALIAN This extremely popular restaurant, opposite Kilkenny Castle (see p. 216), packs in diners for its delicious Italian food with an Irish accent. The basement-level dining room can get packed, but the food more than makes up for it. Fresh spaghettini may be served with Kilmore Quay prawns, basil, and chili or perhaps a simple fettuccine with the house Bolognese sauce and fresh cream. Desserts are equally good—try the homemade chocolate mousse, or if your belt buckle will go out that far, the tasty cheese plate, filled with specialty selections imported from Italy and sprinkled with black truffle. It's a bit of a splurge, but worth it. Due to Rinuccini's popularity with locals, you should book reservations if you're coming on a weekend.

1 The Parade, Kilkenny, Co. Kilkenny. ✆ **056/776-1575.** www.rinuccini.com. Main courses €17–€30. Mon–Fri noon–3pm, 5–10pm; Sat noon–3:30pm, 5–10pm; Sun noon–3:30pm, 5–9:30pm.

COUNTY CORK

8

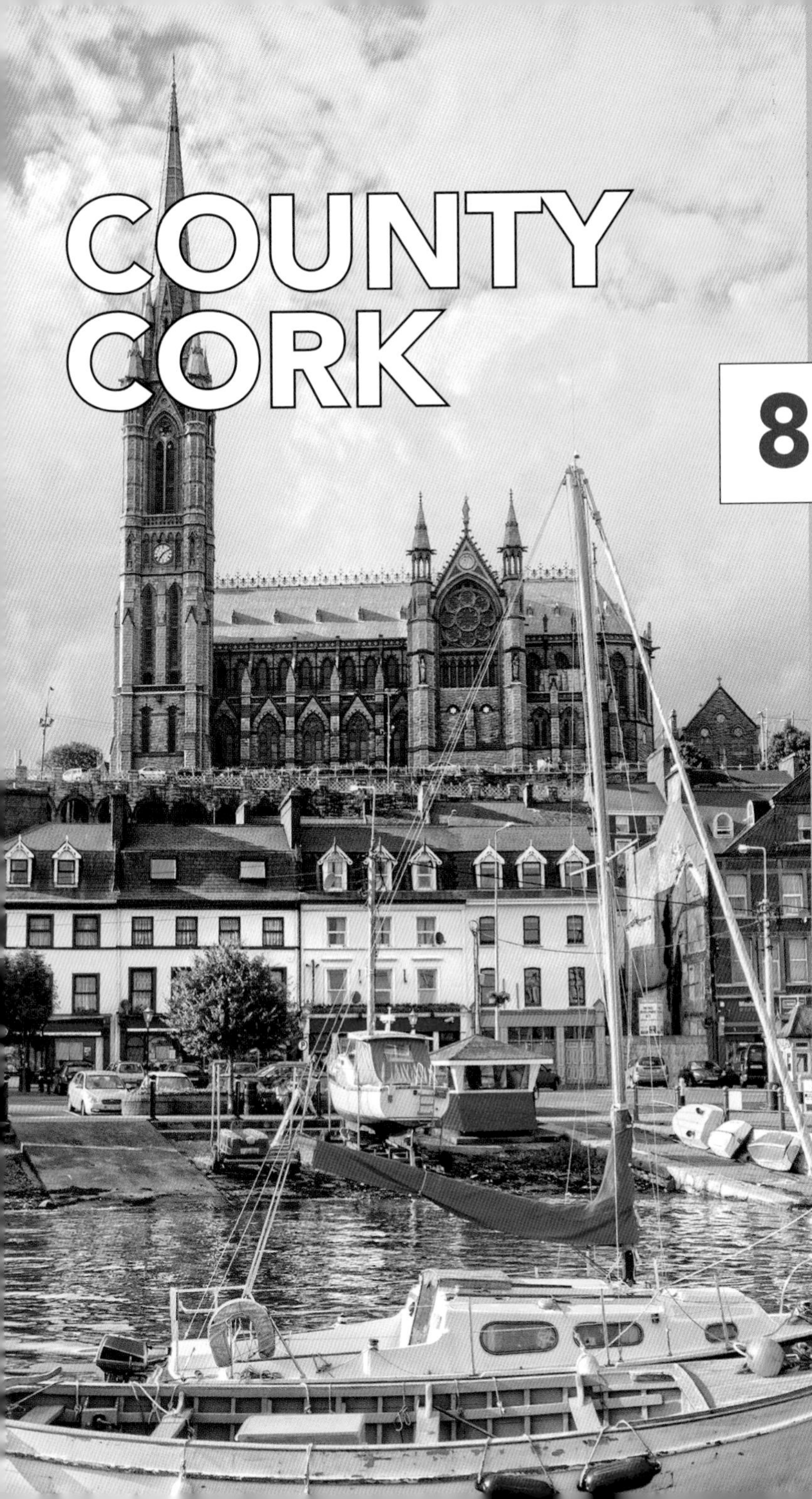

Cork is the largest of Ireland's counties, and one of its most diverse. It encompasses a lively capital city, quiet country villages, rocky hills, picturesque beaches, and long stretches of flat, green farmland. Here, modern tourism (this is where you find the Blarney Castle, after all) meets workaday Irish life, and somehow they manage to coexist side by side in peace. St. Finbarre founded Cork in the 6th century, when he built a monastery on a swampy estuary of the River Lee. He gave the place the rather generic Gaelic name of Corcaigh—which, unromantically, means "marsh." Cork City is worth a day or so to explore, but it can feel congested and gritty. Far more captivating is Kinsale, a pretty harbor town with a reputation as something of a gourmet's paradise, due to its plethora of outstanding restaurants. Farther afield, a clutch of historic sites, the storied seaport of Cobh, and the barren beauty of Cape Clear Island provide more to explore.

ESSENTIALS

Arriving

BY BUS From Dublin Airport, **AirCoach** (**✆ 01/844-7118;** www.aircoach.ie) runs a regular, non-stop service to the center of Cork City. One-way tickets are €20 adults, €8 children. The journey time is 3¾ hours. In Cork City, **Bus Éireann** (**✆ 021/450-8188;** www.buseireann.ie) runs from the **Parnell Place Bus Station** (**✆ 021/450-8188;** www.buseireann.ie) to all parts of the Republic. Bus 249 connects Cork with Kinsale. Buses also arrive on Pier Road, across from the tourist office.

BY TRAIN **Iarnród Éireann/Irish Rail** (**✆ 185/036-6222;** www.irishrail.ie) travels to Cork from Dublin and other parts of Ireland. Trains arrive at Kent Station, Lower Glanmire Road, in eastern Cork City (**✆ 021/455-7277**). Kinsale does not have a train station.

BY FERRY Ferry routes into Cork from Britain include service from Swansea on Fastnet Line (**✆ 021/487-8892;** www.fastnetline.com); and from Roscoff, France on Brittany Ferries (**✆ 021/427-7801;** www.brittany-ferries.com). Boats dock at Cork's Ringaskiddy Ferryport.

BY CAR Cork is reachable on the N8 from Dublin, N25 from Waterford, and N22 from Killarney. To hire a car in Cork try **Enterprise Rent-A-Car,** Kinsale Road (**✆ 021/497-5133**) or **Hertz** at Cork Airport (**021/496-5849**).

BY PLANE **Cork Airport,** Kinsale Road (**✆ 021/413131;** www.cork-airport.com), is served by **Aer Lingus** and **Ryanair.**

PREVIOUS PAGE: **St. Colman's Cathedral in Cobh.**

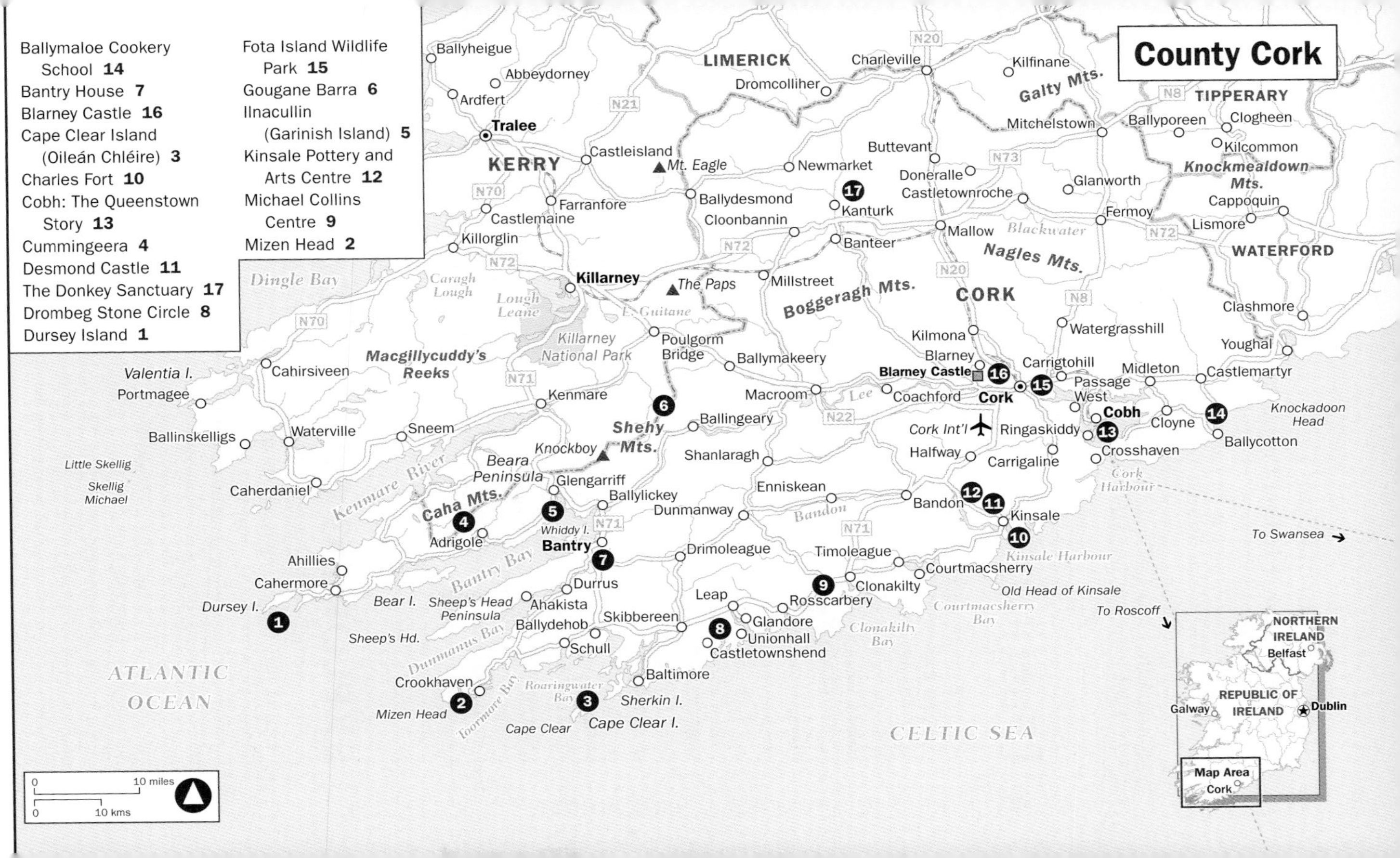
County Cork
Ballymaloe Cookery School 14
Bantry House 7
Blarney Castle 16
Cape Clear Island (Oileán Chléire) 3
Charles Fort 10
Cobh: The Queenstown Story 13
Cummingeera 4
Desmond Castle 11
The Donkey Sanctuary 17
Drombeg Stone Circle 8
Dursey Island 1
Fota Island Wildlife Park 15
Gougane Barra 6
Ilnacullin (Garinish Island) 5
Kinsale Pottery and Arts Centre 12
Michael Collins Centre 9
Mizen Head 2
LIMERICK
TIPPERARY
KERRY
CORK
WATERFORD
Galty Mts.
Knockmealdown Mts.
Nagles Mts.
Boggeragh Mts.
Macgillycuddy's Reeks
Shehy Mts.
Caha Mts.
Beara Peninsula
Sheep's Head Peninsula
Killarney National Park
Mt. Eagle
The Paps
Knockboy
Ballyheigue
Abbeydorney
Ardfert
Tralee
Castleisland
Farranfore
Castlemaine
Killorglin
Killarney
Charleville
Dromcolliher
Kilfinane
Mitchelstown
Ballyporeen
Clogheen
Kilcommon
Buttevant
Newmarket
Doneralle
Castletownroche
Glanworth
Cappoquin
Lismore
Fermoy
Mallow
Kanturk
Ballydesmond
Cloonbannin
Banteer
Millstreet
Clashmore
Youghal
Watergrasshill
Kilmona
Blarney
Blarney Castle
Carrigtohill
Passage West
Midleton
Castlemartyr
Cork
Cobh
Cloyne
Ballycotton
Knockadoon Head
Cork Int'l
Ringaskiddy
Crosshaven
Halfway
Carrigaline
Cork Harbour
Coachford
Macroom
Ballymakeery
Poulgorm Bridge
Ballingeary
Shanlaragh
Enniskean
Bandon
Kinsale
Kinsale Harbour
Old Head of Kinsale
Courtmacsherry
Courtmacsherry Bay
Timoleague
Clonakilty
Clonakilty Bay
Rosscarbery
Dunmanway
Drimoleague
Leap
Glandore
Unionhall
Castletownshend
Skibbereen
Baltimore
Sherkin I.
Cape Clear I.
Cape Clear
Roaringwater Bay
Schull
Ballydehob
Durrus
Ahakista
Bantry
Bantry Bay
Whiddy I.
Ballylickey
Glengarriff
Adrigole
Kenmare
Kenmare River
Sneem
Waterville
Caherdaniel
Cahirsiveen
Valentia I.
Portmagee
Ballinskelligs
Little Skellig
Skellig Michael
Ahillies
Cahermore
Dursey I.
Bear I.
Sheep's Hd.
Dunmanus Bay
Crookhaven
Mizen Head
Toormore Bay
Dingle Bay
Caragh Lough
Lough Leane
Lee
Blackwater
Bandon
ATLANTIC OCEAN
CELTIC SEA
To Swansea
To Roscoff
N20
N21
N70
N71
N72
N73
N8
N22
NORTHERN IRELAND
Belfast
REPUBLIC OF IRELAND
Galway
Dublin
Map Area
Cork
0
10 miles
0
10 kms

Visitor Information

The **Cork Discover Ireland Centre** is at the appropriately named Tourist House at 42 Grand Parade, Cork (✆ **021/425-5100;** www.corkcity.ie). The **Kinsale Tourist Office** is on Pier Road, Kinsale (✆ **021/477-2234;** www.kinsale.ie). The **Cobh Tourist Office** is in the Sirius Arts Centre, the Old Yacht Club Building, Lower Road., Cobh (✆ **024/481-3790**). **Seasonal tourist offices** operate at the Jameson Centre, Midleton (✆ **021/461-3702**), and Market Square, Youghal (✆ **024/20170**).

[FastFACTS] COUNTY CORK

ATMs/Banks In Cork City try **Ulster Bank** (88 Patrick St.; ✆ **021/427-0618**). In Kinsale try **Bank of Ireland,** Emmett Place (✆ **021/477-2521**).

Dentists For dental emergencies, your hotel will usually contact a dentist for you; otherwise, in Cork try **Smiles Town Dental,** 112 Oliver Plunkett St., Cork (✆ **021/427-4706**); in Kinsale, **Catherine McCarthy,** Market Sq. (✆ **021/477-4133**).

Doctors For medical emergencies dial ✆ **999.** For non-emergencies, your hotel should call you a doctor. Otherwise in Cork you could try the **Patrick Street Medical Centre,** 9 Patrick St., Cork (✆ **021/427-8699**); and in Kinsale, **The Medical Centre,** Emmet Place (✆ **021/477-2253**).

Emergencies For police, fire, or other emergencies, dial ✆ **999.**

Internet Access **Cork City Library** at 57 Grand Parade (✆ **021/492-4900**) has internet terminals that non-members can use for €1 per half-hour.

Pharmacies In Cork try **Murphy's Pharmacy,** 48 North Main St. (✆ **021/427-4121**) or **Marian Pharmacy** on Friar's Walk (✆ **021/496-3821**). In Kinsale try **John Collins**, Market Place (✆ **021/477-2077**).

Post Office In Cork the main post office is on Oliver Plunkett St. (✆ **021/485-1032**). In Kinsale it's at 10 Pearse St. (✆ **021/477-2246**).

Taxis The main taxi ranks are along St. Patrick's Street, along the South Mall, and outside major hotels. To call, try **ABC Cabs** (✆ **021/496-1961**), or **Cork Taxi Co-Op** (✆ **021/427-2222**). In Kinsale, try **Kinsale Cabs** (✆ **021/477-2642**), or **Cab 3000** (✆ **021/477-3000**). In Cobh, try **Island Taxis** (✆ **021/481-1111**).

EXPLORING COUNTY CORK

A busy, artsy hub where urban conveniences are seasoned by an appreciation for rural life, Cork City is also home to a major university which keeps the population young, the creative class dynamic, the pubs interesting, and the number of affordable restaurants plentiful. Not far from the city, Blarney Castle is an impressive sight—although it would take a starry-eyed Medievalist indeed to claim that the experience wasn't somewhat marred by the rather cynical, touristy atmosphere. Meanwhile, 25km (15½ miles) to the south of the city, the adorable harbor town of Kinsale is both an attractive hideaway and a major restaurant destination. The only disadvantage is that it's hardly undiscovered, but that somehow fails to dent its charm. To the east of Cork City the two great attractions are Fota Island, a brilliantly designed wildlife

St. Patrick's Quay on the north channel of River Lee in Cork City.

park, and Cobh, which was the last port of call in Ireland for millions of emigrants in the 19th and early 20th centuries.

Cork City

Cork City might as well be called Dublin South. It's far smaller than the capital, with 125,000 residents, but it's a busy, attractive, cultured place. However, Cork also has severe traffic congestion and can feel gritty and crowded. For its fans, these flaws merely make Cork a more interesting place, underscoring the sense that it's a real, working city. For visitors, the offerings within the county's eponymous first city are wonderfully varied. You can fight the crowds at **Blarney Castle** to find out if kissing a rock can make you loquacious, explore extraordinary collection of works by Irish artists at the **Crawford Art Gallery,** and climb to the top of the 300-year-old tower at **St. Anne's Church** to take in the sweeping views and ring the **Shandon Bells.** Because of the limited parking, Cork is best seen on foot, but don't try to do it all in a day. The South Bank and the central part, or flat, of the city can easily take a day to explore; save the Cork Hills and the North Bank for another day. You might want to follow the signposted Tourist Trail to guide you to the major sights. There's also a good local bus service.

CITY LAYOUT

Cork's center is on an island between two branches of the River Lee. The city is divided into three sections:

EXPLORING CORK CITY: THE GIFT OF gab (OR IS IT JUST BLARNEY?)

The much-beloved myth that being held upside down and backward from the top of a tall castle to kiss a rock brings you the ability to talk up a storm is actually quite new, although the Blarney association with the gift of gab goes back a long way. It is believed to have been Queen Elizabeth I who created it in the 16th century, in a fit of exasperation at the ability of then–Lord Blarney to prattle on at great length without actually ever agreeing to what she wanted. The custom of kissing the stone, though, is less than a century old. Nobody knows quite why it started, but around here they've got a thousand possible tales, some involving witches and others the crusaders, but don't believe them. It's all a bunch of . . .

FLAT OF THE CITY The city's downtown core is bounded by channels of the River Lee, and its main thoroughfare is **St. Patrick Street,** a graceful avenue lined with shops. A favorite meeting place here is by the statue of 19th-century priest Father Theobald Matthew, a crusader against drink who is fondly called the "Apostle of Temperance." The statue stands at the point where St. Patrick Street reaches St. Patrick's Bridge.

Nearby, the **South Mall** is a wide tree-lined street with attractive Georgian architecture and a row of banks, insurance companies, and legal offices, while the **Grand Parade** is a spacious thoroughfare that blends 18th-century bow-fronted houses with the remains of the old city walls. It has lots of offices and shops as well as the **Bishop Lucey Park.**

NORTH BANK St. Patrick's Bridge leads over the river to the north side of the city, a hilly, terraced area where St. Patrick Street becomes **St. Patrick's Hill.** And is it ever a hill, with an incline so steep that it's virtually San Franciscan. If you climb the stepped sidewalks of St. Patrick's Hill, you will be rewarded with a sweeping view of the Cork skyline.

East of St. Patrick's Hill, **MacCurtain Street** is a commercial thoroughfare that runs east, leading to Summerhill Road and up into the Cork hills to the residential districts of St. Luke's and Montenotte. West of St. Patrick's Hill is one of the city's oldest neighborhoods, **St. Ann's Shandon Church,** and the city's original Butter Market building.

SOUTH BANK The South Bank of the River Lee encompasses the grounds of **St. Fin Barre's Cathedral,** the site of St. Finbarre's 6th-century monastery, and also includes 17th-century city walls, the remains of Elizabeth Fort, and the City Hall (built in 1936).

EXPLORING CORK CITY

Blarney Castle ★ Though a runaway favorite for the title of "cheesiest tourist attraction in Ireland," Blarney Castle is still an impressive building. Constructed in the late 15th century, it was once much bigger, but the massive square tower is all that remains today. The famous "Blarney Stone" is wedged far enough underneath the battlements to make it uncomfortable to reach, but not far enough that countless tourists don't bend over backward, hang upside

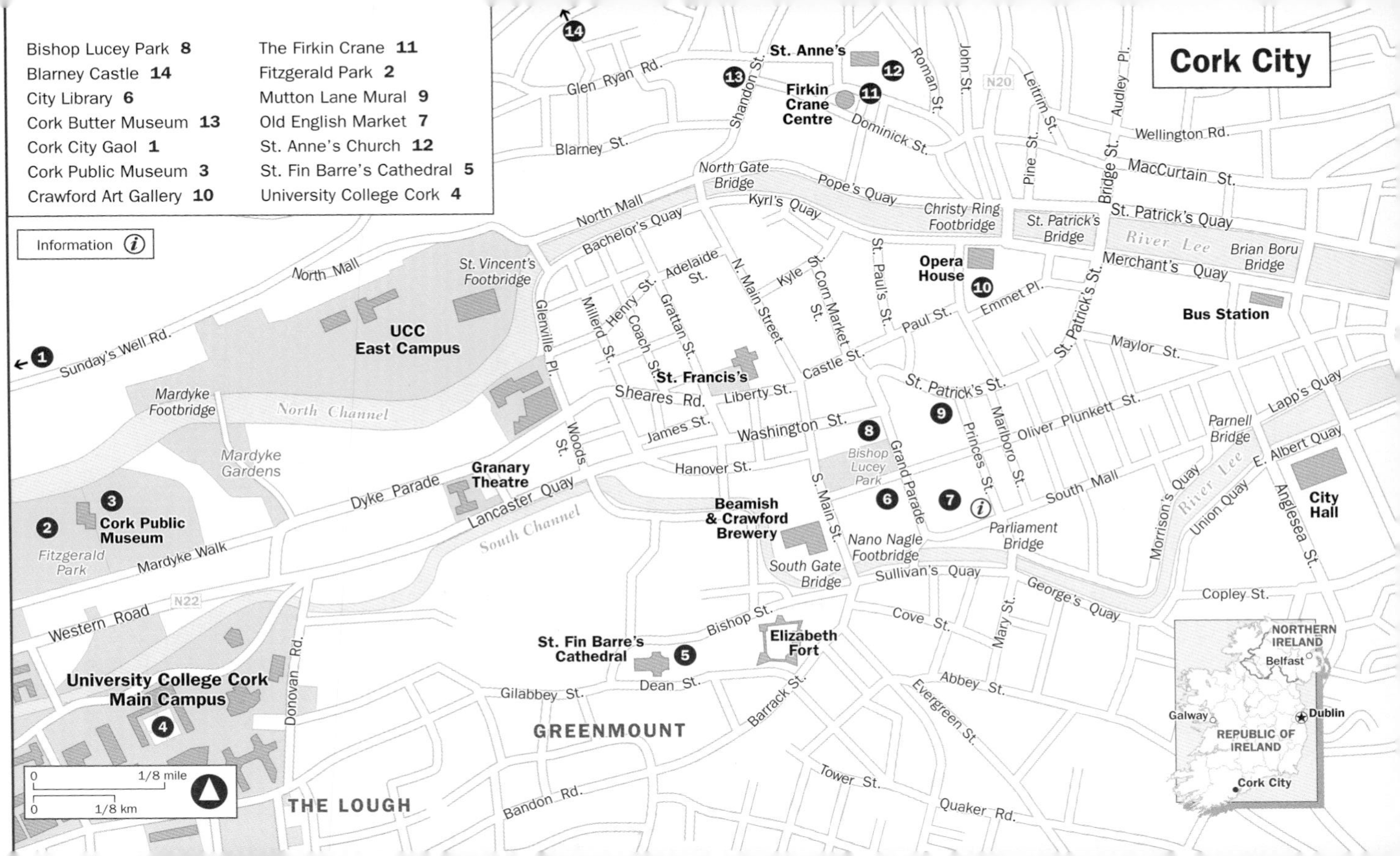

Cork City
Bishop Lucey Park 8
Blarney Castle 14
City Library 6
Cork Butter Museum 13
Cork City Gaol 1
Cork Public Museum 3
Crawford Art Gallery 10
The Firkin Crane 11
Fitzgerald Park 2
Mutton Lane Mural 9
Old English Market 7
St. Anne's Church 12
St. Fin Barre's Cathedral 5
University College Cork 4
Information
St. Anne's
Firkin Crane Centre
Opera House
Bus Station
St. Francis's
UCC East Campus
Granary Theatre
Cork Public Museum
Fitzgerald Park
Beamish & Crawford Brewery
Elizabeth Fort
St. Fin Barre's Cathedral
City Hall
University College Cork Main Campus
GREENMOUNT
THE LOUGH
Mardyke Gardens
Bishop Lucey Park
River Lee
North Channel
South Channel
Glen Ryan Rd.
Blarney St.
Shandon St.
Roman St.
John St.
N20
Leitrim St.
Audley Pl.
Wellington Rd.
Dominick St.
Pine St.
Bridge St.
MacCurtain St.
North Gate Bridge
Pope's Quay
Christy Ring Footbridge
St. Patrick's Bridge
St. Patrick's Quay
Brian Boru Bridge
Merchant's Quay
North Mall
Bachelor's Quay
Kyrl's Quay
St. Vincent's Footbridge
Adelaide St.
Henry St.
Coach St.
Grattan St.
Millerd St.
Glenville Pl.
N. Main Street
Kyle St.
Corn Market St.
St. Paul's St.
Paul St.
Emmet Pl.
St. Patrick's St.
Maylor St.
Sunday's Well Rd.
Mardyke Footbridge
Castle St.
Sheares Rd.
Liberty St.
James St.
Washington St.
Woods St.
Hanover St.
Princes St.
Marlboro St.
Oliver Plunkett St.
Lapp's Quay
Parnell Bridge
E. Albert Quay
Grand Parade
South Mall
Morrison's Quay
Union Quay
Anglesea St.
Dyke Parade
Lancaster Quay
S. Main St.
Nano Nagle Footbridge
Parliament Bridge
Mardyke Walk
South Gate Bridge
Sullivan's Quay
George's Quay
Copley St.
N22
Western Road
Bishop St.
Cove St.
Mary St.
Donovan Rd.
Gilabbey St.
Dean St.
Barrack St.
Abbey St.
Evergreen St.
Tower St.
Bandon Rd.
Quaker Rd.
0 1/8 mile
0 1/8 km
NORTHERN IRELAND
Belfast
Galway
Dublin
REPUBLIC OF IRELAND
Cork City

down in a parapet, and kiss it in hopes of achieving lifelong loquaciousness. It's customary to tip the attendant who holds your legs (you might want to do it *before* he hangs you over the edge). If you need a break from the masses, the gardens are pretty and much less crowded. Also check out the dungeons penetrating the rock at the base of the castle. Blarney Castle is 8km (5 miles) outside the city. You can easily get here by bus, and the number 215 stops about twice an hour (once per hour on Sundays). Ask the driver to let you off at the stop nearest the castle.

Blarney, Co. Cork. ✆ **021/438-5252.** www.blarneycastle.ie. Admission €12 adults; €10 seniors and students; €5 children 8–14; €30 families. May, Sept Mon–Sat 9am–6:30pm; Sun 9am–5:30pm. June–Aug Mon–Sat 9am–7pm; Sun 9am–5:30pm. Oct–Apr Mon–Sat 9am–5:30pm (or dusk if earlier); Sun 9am–dusk. 8km (5 miles) from Cork City on R617.

Cork Butter Museum ★ Going by the name alone this could make it onto any list entitled "world's oddest museums," but the quirky little Cork Butter Museum isn't merely a celebration of tasty Irish dairy produce. From 1770 until the 1920s, Cork was actually the largest exporter of butter in the world, peaking at half a million casks annually by the turn of the 20th century. The museum chronicles that industrial past, using butter as a springboard to explore wider stories about Irish farming, society, and industry, from the middle ages onwards. It's an oddity, for sure, but a charming one.

John Redmond St., Cork, Co. Cork. ✆ **021/430-0600.** www.corkbutter.museum. Admission €4 adults; €3 seniors and students; €1.50 children 17 and under; free for children 11 and under. Mar–June, Sept–Oct daily 10am–5pm; July–Aug daily 10am–6pm; Nov–Feb Sat–Sun 10am–3:30pm.

Cork City Gaol ★ Like something straight out of a Victorian novel, this early 19th-century jail is an austere, impressive, and highly atmospheric building. It opened in 1824 as a women's prison. Its famous inmates included the extraordinary Constance Markievicz, the first woman elected to the British parliament. She was sentenced to execution after the 1916 Easter Rising, in which she took part—though her sentence was commuted. Earlier in its history, this was the last place in Ireland many convicts were held before being shipped off to Australia. This colorful history is well presented, with the (perhaps inevitable) aid of costumed mannequins in key positions. Somewhat incongruously, in 1927, after the building ceased to be used as a prison, it became the site of Ireland's first radio station. A small museum tells this story, complete with a restored studio from the period.

Milking It: An Unlikely Debut

A neat story about the birth of radio broadcasting in Ireland is told at the Radio Museum, in Cork City Gaol (see above). Meticulous planning went into the launch of Station 2RN, in 1926, right down to a permanent armed guard to make sure nothing went wrong. However, the first Irish radio star turned out to be an unlikely participant. In order to test the signal, very early one morning, a technician pointed a microphone out of the window—just as a local horse and cart happened to be passing by. Thus, the first sound broadcast in Ireland was those of an unwitting milkman, quietly making his rounds.

Convent Avenue, Sunday's Well, Cork, Co. Cork. ✆ **021/430-5022.** www.corkcitygaol.com. Admission €8 adults; €7 seniors and students; €4.50 children; €24 families. Radio Museum €2. Mar–Oct daily 9:30am–5pm; Nov–Feb daily 10am–4pm.

Cork City Tours These open-top buses let you hop on and off to explore the sights of Ireland's second city. They run all day in a loop from March through October (as frequently as every half-hour in July and August), so when you see something you want to explore, just get off and rejoin the tour later. Or you can stay on the bus and use the tour to get oriented. Tour highlights include the Cork City Gaol, St. Ann's Church, and U.C.C. (University College, Cork). You can buy your ticket on the bus if you get on at any of these stops, or buy a ticket and board the bus at the tourist office. You can also drop in at the tourist office for a leaflet containing a list of pick-up points, or check them out online at **www.corkcitytour.com/timetables**.

Various stops around Cork, Co. Cork. ✆ **021/430-9090.** www.corkcitytour.com. Tickets €14 adults; €12 seniors and students; €5 children 5–17; children 4 and under free; €34 families (up to 4 children). Mar–Oct daily, with hours and number of tours reflecting seasonal demand (usually 9:30am–4:30pm).

Cork Public Museum ★ This simple rather endearing civic museum is a good place to get an overview of the city's history. Displays include a few objects from Cork's ancient past, but it's strongest when it comes to the traditional crafts made in the city during the 19th and 20th centuries—including silverware and intricate lace from the Victorian period. There are also very good collections relating to the lives of local revolutionaries, including Michael Collins. The museum is located on the west side of Cork, in the middle of Fitzgerald Park—parallel to the Western Road, where many of the city's B&Bs are located (see "Where to Stay" on p. 242).

Fitzgerald Park, Cork, Co. Cork. ✆ **021/427-0679.** www.corkcity.ie. Free admission. Apr–Sept Mon–Fri 11am–1pm, 2:15–5pm; Sat 11am–1pm, 2:15–4pm; Sun 3–5pm. Oct–Mar Mon–Fri 11am–1pm, 2:15–5pm, Sat 11am–1pm, 2:15–4pm.

Crawford Art Gallery ★★★ One of the best art galleries in Ireland, the Crawford has impressive collections of sculpture and painting. The Irish School is particularly well represented with works from John Butts (1728–65), including his beautiful 1755 panorama of Cork City, and Harry Clarke (1889–1931), a Dubliner who was not only one of the most celebrated illustrators of the early 20th century but also produced some extraordinary, early Deco-influenced stained glass. There's also a strong collection of works by female Irish artists from the mid-19th century onwards; check out the extraordinary abstract work of Mainie Jellet (1897–1944) and the Cubist painter Norah McGuinness (1901–80). The gallery also has a program of temporary exhibitions, and the excellent Crawford Gallery Café (see p. 245) is a good spot for a light lunch.

Emmet Place, Cork, Co. Cork. ✆ **021/480-5042.** www.crawfordartgallery.ie. Free admission. Mon–Wed, Fri–Sat 10am–5pm; Wed 10am–5pm. 2nd floor closes 4:45. Closed public holidays.

The Firkin Crane Cultural Centre ★★ Once part of Cork's Butter Museum (see p. 230), the Firkin Crane is one of Ireland's major centers for contemporary dance. It hosts touring companies in addition to showcasing new talent. Many performances are free. The only downside is that performances are

THE GUINNESS CORK jazz festival

Held every year since 1978, this is Ireland's biggest and most prestigious jazz festival. Big names such as Ella Fitzgerald, Oscar Peterson, and Stephane Grappelli have played here over the years, and more than 1,000 performers from all over the world take part annually. It's held at various citywide venues in late October. Visit www.corkjazzfestival.com for details. Tickets go on sale in early September; prices vary and some events are free.

infrequent—the most headline-grabbing tend to be during the Guinness Jazz Festival (see below). And the name? It comes from two Danish words for measurements of butter.

John Redmond St., Shandon, Cork, Co. Cork. ✆ **021/450-7487.** www.firkincrane.ie. Ticket prices and performance times vary by event.

Mutton Lane Mural ★ This giant mural along the walls of Mutton Lane depicts musicians performing the traditional Pana Shuffle, and is a vivid and colorful evocation of peace and community spirit. Intended to represent the essence of Cork, many of the characters depicted are based on real local people. The mural, which runs the length of the Mutton Lane alleyway, was painted by local artist Anthony Ruby in 2004. Its provenance can, in part, be dated by the message painted into the colorful scene, which was intended as a commentary on world events at the time: "dedicated to everyone except George Bush."

Mutton Lane, off St. Patrick St., Cork, Co. Cork.

Old English Market ★★ The name of this bustling food market harks back to the days of English rule. Quite a long way back, in fact: It was first granted a charter in 1610 during the reign of King James I. The current market building dates from 1788, although it was redesigned after being gutted by fire in the 1980s. Inside is a cornucopia of fresh produce, including super-traditional Cork delicacies—some of them tempting, others less palatable to outsiders. Tripe, anyone? How about pig's trotters? Happily, more modern style refreshments and takeaway snacks are readily available.

Grand Parade; enter from Patrick St., Grand Parade, Oliver Plunkett St., or Princes St., Cork, Co. Cork. ✆ **085/763-2259.** www.englishmarket.ie. Free admission; individual food stall prices vary. Mon–Sat 8am–6pm.

St. Anne's Church ★ Cork's most recognizable landmark, also known as Shandon Church, is famous for its giant pepper pot steeple and eight melodious bells. No matter where you stand in the downtown area, you can see the stone tower crowned with a gilt ball and a unique fish weather vane. Until a few years ago, due to a quirk of clockworks, it was known as "the four-faced liar" because each of its four clock faces showed a different time—except on the hour when they all managed to synchronize. Somewhat sadly, that charming quirk has now been repaired. Climb the 1722 belfry for the chance to ring the famous Shandon Bells. If you continue on the somewhat precarious climb past the bells, you'll be rewarded with spectacular views over the surrounding countryside.

The red sandstone and limestone clock tower of St. Anne's distinguishes Cork's skyline.

Church St., Shandon, Cork, Co. Cork. ✆ **021/450-5906.** www.shandonbells.ie. Admission €5 adults; €4 seniors and students; €2.50 children; €12 families. June–Aug Mon–Sat 10am–5pm; Sun 11:30am–4:30pm. Mar–May, Oct Mon–Sat 10am–4pm; Sun 11:30am–4pm. Nov–Feb Mon–Sat 11am–3pm; Sun 11:30am–3pm.

St. Fin Barre's Cathedral ★ This Church of Ireland cathedral sits on the spot St. Finbarre chose in A.D. 600 for his church and school. A much smaller medieval tower was demolished to make way for the current building, which dates from the early 1860s—there's nothing left of the original, although a few pieces of decorative stonework salvaged during the demolition can be viewed inside. The architect, William Burges (1827–81), was the winner of a competition that was staged to create a new Anglican Cathedral in the city; his winning design embraced the French Gothic style that was popular at the time, including its most prominent feature—three soaring spires, which still dominate the skyline. The interior is highly ornamented with unique mosaic work. The bells were inherited from the 1735 church that previously stood on this site. The Cathedral also hosts occasional exhibitions; check the website for listings of what's on.

Bishop St., Cork, Co. Cork. ✆ **021/496-3387.** www.cathedral.cork.anglican.org. Admission €5 adults; €3 students and children. Apr–Nov Mon–Sat 9:30am–5:30pm, Sun 12:30–5pm. Dec–Mar Mon–Sat 9:30am–5:30pm. Closed certain bank holidays; call to check.

St. Fin Barre's Cathedral in Cork.

University College Cork ★★ Part of Ireland's national university, with about 7,000 students, this center of learning is housed in a pretty quadrangle of Gothic Revival–style buildings. Colorful gardens and wooded grounds grace the campus. An audio tour of the grounds takes in the Crawford Observatory, the Harry Clarke stained glass windows in the Honan Chapel, a landscaped garden, and the Stone Corridor, a collection of stones inscribed with the ancient Irish *ogham* written language. Also on the campus is the **Lewis Glucksman Gallery** (✆ **021/490-1844;** www.glucksman.org), an innovative art center that has an excellent program of exhibitions. Expect to see innovative photography, painting, sculpture, and a few items from the university's ever-expanding permanent collection. A good cafe and shop are also on site. Admission to the Glucksman is free, though a donation of €5 per person is requested.

Visitor Centre: North Wing, Main Quad, Western Rd., Cork, Co. Cork. ✆ **021/490-1876.** visitorscentre.ucc.ie. Self-guided tours €10. Visitor Centre: Mon–Fri 9am–5pm, Sat noon–5pm. Glucksman Gallery: Tues–Sat 10am–5pm; Sun 2–5pm.

SPORTS & OUTDOOR PURSUITS

Spectator Sports

GAELIC GAMES Hurling and Gaelic football are both played on summer Sunday afternoons at Cork's **Pairc Ui Chaoimh Stadium,** Marina Walk (✆ **021/496-3311**). Check the local newspapers for details or log on to the Gaelic Athletics Association's site at www.gaa.ie.

GREYHOUND RACING Go to the dogs, as they say in Cork, only now in distinctly 21st-century style, at the **Cork Greyhound Stadium,** Curraheen Park, Cork (✆ **0189/026-9969**), on Thursday, Friday, and Saturday. Gates open 6:45pm, first race starts 7:50pm. Tickets are €10 adults, €5 seniors and students, €4 children age 13 to 17, €1 children age 12 and under, €20 families (up to three children). No Thursday races in winter.

HORSE RACING The nearest racetrack is **Cork Racecourse,** Killarney Road, Mallow (✆ **022/50207;** www.corkracecourse.ie), approximately 32km (20 miles) north of Cork. Races are scheduled year-round, but particularly in mid-May, July, August, early October, and November. Admission is around €15 adults, €10 seniors and students, and free for children 13 and under (must be with an adult).

Outdoor Pursuits

CYCLING Although walking is probably the ideal way to get around Cork, you can rent a bike at **Cyclescene,** 396 Blarney St. (✆ **021/430-1183;** www.cyclescene.ie). It costs €15 to €20 per day or €80 per week, plus a refundable deposit of €100. Open Monday to Friday 9am to 5:30pm and Saturday 9am to 5pm.

FISHING The **River Lee,** which runs through Cork, the nearby **Blackwater River,** and the many area lakes present fine opportunities. Salmon licenses, lake fishing permits, tackle, and equipment can be obtained from **T. W. Murray,** 87 St. Patrick St. (✆ **021/427-1089**).

GOLF Local clubs that welcome visitors are the **Cork Golf Club,** Little Island (✆ **021/435-3451;** www.corkgolfclub.ie), 8km (5 miles) east of Cork, with greens fees of about €50 to €80, and a special seniors rate of €20; and **Douglas Golf Club,** Maryboro Hill, Douglas (✆ **021/489-5297;** www.douglasgolfclub.ie), 4.8km (3 miles) south of Cork, with greens fees of abound €50 to €60.

WALKING The **Old Railway Line** is a dismantled train route running from Cork to the old maritime town of Passage West. It is from here in 1837 that Captain Roberts set out and crossed the Atlantic in the first passenger steamship, the *SS Sirius.* Following along the rails, a scenic walk affords the visitor excellent views of the inner harbor.

SHOPPING

St. Patrick Street is the main shopping thoroughfare, and many stores are scattered throughout the city on side streets and in lanes. In general, shops are open Monday to Saturday 9:30am to 6pm, unless indicated otherwise. In the summer many shops remain open until 9:30pm on Thursday and Friday, and some are open on Sunday.

Winthrop Arcade, off Winthrop Street, is the best of a small handful of covered shopping arcades in Cork City. Meanwhile, the main full-size shopping mall is **Merchant's Quay Shopping Centre,** Merchant's Quay and St. Patrick Street (✆ **021/427-5466;** www.merchantsquaycork.com).

Cork's best department store is **Brown Thomas,** 18 St. Patrick St. (✆ **021/480-5555**). It has three floors filled with the same kind of upscale items found in its famous sister shop in Dublin (p. 150).

Books

Vibes and Scribes ★ This cheery secondhand bookstore on Lavitt's Quay has titles in a huge array of genres. They also sell little gifts and crafty knick-knacks. They have a second branch, selling stationary, art and craft supplies, at 3 Bridge Street (✆ **021/450-5370**). 21 Lavitt's Quay, Cork, Co. Cork. ✆ **021/427-9535.** www.vibesandscribes.ie.

Crafts, Design & Housewares

Meadows & Byrne ★★ The Cork branch of this very popular Irish lifestyle chain sells housewares, furniture and various other pieces of attractive crafts, from crystal and kitchenware, to bed and bath products. Academy St., Cork, Co. Cork. ✆ **021/427-2324.** www.meadowsandbyrne.com.

Shandon Craft Centre ★ In the same building as the Cork Butter Museum (see p. 230), this center is where various local craftspeople come to sell their wares. Part of the attraction is never knowing quite what you're going to find. Occasionally in summer you'll come across free concerts here. At the Cork Butter Museum, John Redmond St., Cork, Co. Cork. ✆ **021/450-3936.**

Fashion & Clothing

Blarney Woollen Mills ★ On the grounds of Blarney Castle (see p. 228), this is the flagship outlet of an Irish chain that specializes in traditional Irish gear—Aran sweaters, cashmere and other knitwear, tweeds, country clothing, capes, and accessories. They also stock a large range of Irish crafts, such as Waterford crystal and Celtic-style jewelry. It's open until 6pm daily. On the grounds of Blarney Castle, Blarney, Co. Cork. ✆ **021/451-6111.** www.blarney.ie.

Brocade and Lime ★★★ This wonderful vintage-style clothing store sells retro fashions from the 1940s, 50s, and 60s. It's all the work of a talented coterie of Irish designers, including Orla Kiely, who specializes in swinging 60s prints; Alicia Estrada, whose brilliantly named Stop Staring label specializes in clothes inspired 1940s film noir; and What Katie Did, a super-cool brand of 1950s-influenced lingerie, favored by celebrities including Kate Moss, Lana Del Ray, and Christina Hendricks. 4 Cornmarket St., Cork, Co. Cork. ✆ **021/427-8882.** www.brocadeandlime.ie.

Monreal ★★ Designer handbags, belts, and other designer accessories are on sale at this boutique in the Winthrop Arcade. They also have a gorgeous stock of shoes, including some rather cool lace-up wellington boots—a handy way of staying stylish, whatever the Irish weather throws at you. Winthrop Arcade, off Winthrop St., Cork, Co. Cork. ✆ **021/480-6746.** www.monreal.ie.

CORK: THE rebel CITY

Cork has had a long and rebellious history, which has been for centuries tied intrinsically to Ireland's struggle for independence.

For 600 years after its foundation by St. Finbarre, *Corcaigh* (the Gaelic name for Cork) steadily grew as a center of power. It ultimately became the seat of the kingdom of *Deas-Mhumhain*—meaning South Munster, often Anglicized as "Desmond"—the name by which this part of Ireland was known when it was a sovereign entity in the middle ages.

As England's influence over Ireland grew, however, Cork would change hands many times as the English and the Irish struggled for control. It resisted Cromwell's forces, only to lose to William of Orange.

Once firmly under English control, Cork thrived until the 18th century, when it was battered by the potato famine, which drained the region of its wealth and, ultimately, of its population.

The county earned its nickname, "Rebel Cork," because it was a center of the 19th-century Fenian movement, and also played an active part in Ireland's 20th-century battle for independence. Most of Cork City, including the library, the City Hall, and most of the buildings on St. Patrick Street, were burned to the ground during the British occupation and the subsequent brutal civil war of the 1920s.

British troops in Cork—nicknamed the "Black and Tans" for the color of their uniforms—were among the most repressive in Ireland. This helped ensure that the fighting here was long and ugly. Thomas MacCurtain, a mayor of Cork City, was killed by British forces in 1920. His successor, Terence MacSwiney, died in a London prison after a hunger strike lasting 75 days.

During the negotiations that ended the War of Independence and created the Irish Free State, Cork became a center of fierce opposition to the deal. The treaty was bitterly controversial, because while it conferred *de facto* independence on Ireland, it retained the British monarch as ceremonial head of state, while also splitting off six counties in the north that would remain part of the United Kingdom. Michael Collins, a Cork native, led negotiations on the Irish side. He was assassinated on a return visit to his home county in 1922. (For more on Michael Collins, see p. 254)

Independence finally brought peace to Cork, but it was not until much later in the 20th century that the region found its new personality as a vibrant, cultured, and affluent region. The county's eponymous capital, Cork, is a university town, which keeps the population young and the arts scene ever evolving, and this also ensures that it has affordable restaurants and buzzing pubs and bars.

CORK CITY AFTER DARK

Pubs

An Spailpin Fánac ★★ One of Cork's oldest pubs (it opened in 1779), this is a wonderful spot to hang out with a pint and while away an hour or two. It's also one of the best pubs in the city for live music (see p. 237). 28–29 S. Main St., Cork, Co. Cork. ✆ **021/427-7949.**

The Idle Hour ★ This is the sort of place you go if you want some good, lively craic, loud music, and a young crowd. It's an extremely popular pub, especially

a tuneful pint: **CORK'S MOST MUSICAL PUBS**

Cork has a deserved reputation as home to some of Ireland's best pubs for live, traditional music. It's virtually a rite of passage to catch a session while enjoying a pint or two (and it's stout in these parts, by the way—Murphy's or Beamish, not Guinness—if you really want to fit in). You can just follow your ears to find the best places, but here are a few of the most respected to get you started. **An Bodhran** (the name refers to a type of drum made from goatskin) at 42 Oliver Plunkett St. (✆ **021/427-4544**) has live sessions nightly, as does the cozy **An Spailpín Fánach** (which means "The Wandering Migrant Worker") at 27 South Main St. (✆ **021/427-7949**). **Sin é** (literally, "That's It"), 8 Coburg St. (✆ **021/450-2266**) has been one of Cork's top live music pubs for decades, long before it became a popular tourist activity. They have sessions most nights, but those on Tuesdays, Fridays, and Sundays tend to be particularly good. There's trad every Thursday night at the atmospheric **Long Valley** (✆ **021/427-2144**)—but if you've had your fill of the penny-whistle by this point, come on Monday nights to catch their lively program of spoken word events; see www.obheal.ie for more details.

during sports matches, which are shown here on huge TVs. Albert Quay, Cork, Co. Cork. ✆ **021/496-5704.**

John Henchy & Sons ★★ This fantastic pub looks like it has hardly changed since it first opened in 1884. It's full of appealing Victorian features, including a private area ("snug") that was originally built to allow ladies to visit the pub without fear of impropriety. 40 St. Luke's, Cork, Co. Cork. ✆ **021/450-7833.**

The Long Valley ★★ A cheerful, gregarious air pervades at this colorful bar, which is another long-standing favorite of the Cork pub scene. The crowd is a good mix of stalwart locals and hip young things. They also have a good program of live music and spoken word. 10 Winthrop St., Cork, Co. Cork ✆ **021/427-2144.**

Clubs: Comedy, Dance & Music

Bowery ★★ This is one of the coolest nightspots in Cork. Two sophisticated bars are downstairs—the Bowery and the Berwick Room, which cultivates a decadent vibe with just a hint of the bordello. Go upstairs, however, and you have DJs spinning the latest cuts and eclectic sets in the Stage Room, and the Rooftop Bar, overlooking the nearby park. It's open Friday and Sunday from 10:30pm until 2am, and Sunday from 9pm until 1am. 21 Tuckey St., Cork, Co. Cork. ✆ **021/425-1438.** www.bowery.ie. Cover €10 and up.

Havana Browns ★ This busy nightclub attracts the kind of young party crowd who are drawn to a bit of glamour like moths to a flame. After negotiating your way past the notoriously surly bouncers, relax in one of the three bars or just get straight on the dance floor, with its high tech LED illuminations. The club is open every night 11pm until 2am. Hanover St., Cork, Co. Cork. ✆ **021/465-8100.** www.havanabrowns.ie. Cover €10 and up.

The Performing Arts

Cork Opera House ★ Near the river on Emmet Place, the Cork Opera House is the region's preeminent venue when it comes to opera and other live concerts (classical, trad, folk, rock, country, and more), plus dance, standup, and more. Emmet Place, Cork, Co. Cork. ✆ **021/427-0022.** www.corkoperahouse.ie. Tickets €18–€50.

The Firkin Crane Cultural Centre ★★ Although actual performances here are frustratingly infrequent, this is one of Ireland's premier locations for contemporary dance. For full review see p. 231. John Redmond St., Cork, Co. Cork. ✆ **021/450-7487.** www.firkincrane.ie. Tickets €10–€25.

Kinsale

Only 29km (18 miles) south of Cork City, **Kinsale** is a charming fishing village sitting on a picturesque harbor, surrounded by green hills. Considered the gateway to the western Cork seacoast, this artsy town of 3,000 residents enchants with its narrow, winding streets, well-kept 18th-century houses, imaginatively painted shop fronts, window boxes overflowing with colorful flowers, and harbor full of sailboats. Kinsale has a more eventful history than you might think, however. In 1601 it was the scene of a major sea battle, between Protestant England and Catholic Spain—one in which Irish rebels played a covert part. You can learn all about this fascinating conflict on one of local man Don Herlihy's absorbing "Historic Strolls".

The harbor of Kinsale

James Fort built by the English shortly after the Battle of Kinsale.

EXPLORING KINSALE

Charles Fort ★ Southeast of Kinsale, at the head of the harbor, this coastal landmark dates from the late 17th century. A classic star-shaped fort, it was constructed after the Battle of Kinsale to prevent foreign invaders from entering the port. The building was strengthened throughout the 18th and 19th centuries, and the fort remained in use as a military garrison right up until the British left in 1921. Charles Fort was named after Charles II, who was king of England and Ireland at the time it was built. Across the river is the smaller James Fort that dates back to the reign of King James I (1603–25). Local lore has it that until the 19th century, access to this stretch of water was controlled by a massive chain floating on timber kegs between the two shores that could be drawn tight at a moment's notice.

Summercove, Kinsale, Co. Cork. ✆ **021/477-2263.** www.heritageireland.ie. Admission €4 adults; €3 seniors; €2 students and children; €10 families. Mid-Mar–Oct 10am–6pm; Nov–mid-Mar 10am–5pm.

Desmond Castle ★ This small, squat stone fortress doesn't really look like a castle, in part because it incongruously sits half way up a residential street. It was built around 1500 as the customs house for Kinsale Harbour. In the late 17th century it was turned into a prison, at which time its history took several dark detours, including a fire that gutted the building in 1747, roasting alive the 54 French soldiers who were imprisoned within. Later, during the potato famine, it was used as a workhouse. An unusual but interesting little museum is inside,

THE scilly WALK

This signposted pedestrian path runs along the sea from Scilly, the community across the harbor from Kinsale, to Charles Fort. You can pick up maps of the full route at the Kinsale tourism office.

Technically a separate village, Scilly is effectively a miniscule suburb of Kinsale but retains a strong sense of its own identity. Pronounced "silly," its unusual name is thought to hark back to fishermen from the Scilly Isles (off the coast of Cornwall, England) who settled here during the 17th century.

Take the right-hand road around the village, skirting along the coast, and join the marked pedestrian trail by the waterside. Along here are lovely views across to Kinsale, and across the harbor you'll see the stout remains of **James Fort.** Named for King James I, it was built by the English shortly after the Battle of Kinsale to guard the entrance to the port and ensure against further insurrection. It was captured by the forces of the (Protestant) King William I during his war with the deposed (Catholic) James II in 1690—part of the same conflict that is still commemorated today by the Protestant "Orange marches" in Northern Ireland.

Another tiny hamlet on the outskirts of Kinsale, **Summer Cove** is as sweet a place as its halcyon name suggests. Black and white toy town houses, with splashes of green and red, face the harbor as gulls circle overhead and the waves froth and bubble along the harbor walls.

A short walk uphill from Summer Cove lies **Charles Fort** (see p. 239). This impressive military structure was the site of Ringcurran Castle in medieval times, an important defensive position used by the Spanish during the Battle of Kinsale in 1601. After a lengthy fight, the English army defeated the allied Irish and Spanish troops, and reduced the castle to rubble. In 1678, a permanent fortress was built here to reinforce the defenses of James Fort. Charles Fort remained in use as a barracks until the end of British rule in the early 20th century. It suffered extensive damage during the civil war, and has only recently been restored.

The Scilly Walk ends here. If you continue to walk south along the sea, you'll find another path that follows the headland to the tip of **Frower Point,** which affords great views across the harbor to the Old Head of Kinsale.

detailing the story of the Irish exiles who helped transform the global wine trade from the 17th century onwards.

Cork St., Kinsale, Co. Cork. ✆ **021/477-4855.** www.heritageireland.ie. Admission €3 adults; €2 seniors; €1 students and children; €8 families. Apr–mid-Sept daily 10am–6pm.

Kinsale Historic Stroll ★★★ One of the most pleasant ways to spend an hour in these parts is to take local resident Don Herlihy's excellent walking tour—or Historic Stroll, as he prefers to call it—of Kinsale town. Don and his fellow guide, Barry Moloney, have been leading visitors around the main sights since the mid-1990s, and their local knowledge is second to none. Highlights include the 12th-century St. Multose Church; a walk past Desmond Castle (see p. 239); and the harbor, where the 17th-century Battle of Kinsale is recounted with an enthusiasm only found in people who really love their subject. The tour starts outside the tourist office at 11:15am every day. On weekdays from May to September is an earlier tour at 9:15am. You pay at the end or, in their words, "drop out for free if you're not delighted." That probably doesn't happen very often. If you pre-book, you're given a free historic chart designed by Don.

Departs from Kinsale Tourist Office, Pier Road, Kinsale, Co. Cork. ✆ **021/477-2873** or 087/250-0731. www.historicstrollkinsale.com. Admission €6 adults; €1 children. May–Sept Mon–Sat 9:15, 11:15am; Sun 11:15am. Oct–Apr daily 11:15am.

Kinsale Pottery and Arts Centre ★ This excellent ceramics workshop outside of Kinsale sells beautiful, original items of pottery from delicate tea sets and tableware to ornamental masks. The shop is full of surprises, and prices aren't too steep for the quality of what's on offer. A two-floor gallery always has some interesting pieces on display. If you're looking for an alternative way to spend a day or more, the workshop also runs pottery courses where you can learn the basics of the craft and go home with your own creations at the end. Prices start at €75 for a 6½-hour courses, including all materials.

Ballinacurra, Kinsale, Co. Cork. ✆ **021/477-2771.** www.kinsaleceramics.com. Free admission. Daily 10am–6pm. From Kinsale: from Pearse St., turn left at the junction with the Blue Haven hotel on your right, then follow signs to Bandon and Innishannon. Take this road up the big hill, past Woodlands B&B and the Kinsale GAA sports ground, then look out for signs to Kinsale Pottery after about ⅓km (⅕ miles) on the left.

SPORTS & OUTDOOR PURSUITS

CYCLING Kinsale Harbour is perfectly designed for biking. To rent a bike, drop by **Mylie Murphy's Shop,** 8 Pearse St. (✆ **021/477-2703**). Rates are around €25 per day.

FISHING Kinsale is one of the southern Irish coast's sea angling centers. There are numerous shipwrecks in the area for wreck fishing (not the least of them the *Lusitania,* near the Old Head of Kinsale). Try **Kinsale Angling** (1 Rampart Lane, The Ramparts, ✆**021/477-4946;** www.kinsale-angling.com) for charter boats. They also run whale- and dolphin-watching trips. Also the similarly named **Angling Kinsale,** Crohane (✆ **021/477-8054** or 086/103-6905; www.angling kinsale.com), arranges sea fishing from Kinsale Harbor, as well as dolphin- and whale-watching expeditions. Prices vary widely, so call or e-mail for more information.

GOLF Embraced by the sea on three sides, the nothing-short-of-spectacular **Old Head Golf Links** (✆ **021/477-8444;** www.oldhead.com) is Tiger Woods's favorite Irish course. Named one of *Golf Magazine*'s "Top 100 Courses in the World" in the 2000s, it is hauntingly beautiful, rain or shine. The course retains a resident environmentalist to ensure that crucial wildlife habitats are not disturbed. But golfing here costs big money: Greens fees in summer are a whopping €220 for one 18-hole round, and €325 for 36 holes. If you really want to experience it but can't quite swing the price, come after 3pm, when rates go down to €115 for 18 holes (€95 in the off season). Caddy fees run €25 for a junior caddy or €40 for a senior caddy, and golf carts can be rented for €60.

If that's still too rich for your blood, there's a fine par-72 championship course at the **Fota Island Golf Club,** Carrigtwohill (✆ **021/488-3700;** www.fotaisland.ie), with greens fees of €50 to €95. Even less expensive is the

Kinsale Golf Club, Kinsale (✆ **021/477-4722;** www.kinsalegolf.ie), which has two courses, about 5km (3 miles) north of town. The 18-hole, par-71 course has greens fees of €20 to €40.

SAILING Excellent sailing is to be had out from Kinsale Head. **Sovereign Sailing** (✆ **021/477-4145;** www.sovereignsailing.com) offers a full range of yacht-sailing options for all ages and levels of experience. Between March and November, full-day or half-day sails from Kinsale leave every day. Rates vary widely based on the kind of sailing you try. They also offer yacht racing packages, but these don't come cheap.

WALKING The **Scilly Walk** is a signposted pedestrian path along the sea that runs from Scilly, the community across the harbor from Kinsale, all the way to Charles Fort. (See p. 239 for a detailed description of the route.) If you continue to walk south along the sea from Charles Fort, you'll find another path that follows the headland to the tip of **Frower Point,** which offers great views across the harbor to the Old Head of Kinsale. The complete walk from Kinsale to Frower Point is 8km (5 miles) each way, and every part of it is quite rewarding. Drop in at the tourism office to pick up their leaflet about the walk, which includes a short but comprehensive guide and map.

One of the most pleasant ways to spend an hour in these parts is to take local resident Don Herily's excellent walking tour—or **Historic Stroll ★★★**, as he prefers to call it—of Kinsale town. See listing on p. 240.

WATERSPORTS The **Oysterhaven Activity Centre** (✆ **021/477-0738;** www.oysterhaven.com), 8km (5 miles) from Kinsale, rents windsurf gear, dinghies, and kayaks. The cost ranges from €20 to €40 for windsurfing kit, €12 to €20 for kayaks' and €30 to €45 for dinghys. They also run windsurfing lessons costing €50 for a 2½ hour taster session, to €95 for a full day. They get pretty busy during summer, so try to book ahead as much as possible.

WHALE WATCHING Whale watching is a popular activity in summer, and one of the best companies is **Whale of a Time** (✆ **086/328-3250;** www.whaleofatime.ie), which uses rigid inflatable boats to cause less disruption to the creatures of the deep. Prices are €35 for a 90-minute "family trip," or €70 for a 4-hour "enthusiasts trip." **Kinsale Angling** (see "Fishing," above) also offers dolphin, whale, and seal watching trips, as does its near-namesake, **Angling Kinsale** (✆ **021/477-8054;** www.anglingkinsale.com).

Where to Stay in Cork City

Cork City is filled with B&Bs and small hotels, particularly along Western Road. They vary in quality, but among them are some interesting, decently priced options. Away from the city, the pretty harbor town of Kinsale contains several elegant, high-quality B&Bs and boutique-style accommodations.

Avondale ★★ The exterior of this excellent little B&B next door to Cork's University College is so innocuous that you could almost miss it. The welcome you get from the wonderful Dolores will quickly dispel any thoughts that you were in the wrong place, as she's a charming host, with a talent for making you feel welcome and at home. Guestrooms are modern and uncluttered with bright, spring-like color schemes of oatmeal and buttermilk. The hearty breakfasts are served in a tiny room overlooking the garden, which feels more akin to a family lounge than a formal dining area. But by that point, you may feel so much like a houseguest that you don't even notice.

1 St. Mary's Villas, Western Rd., Cork, Co. Cork. ✆ **021/490-5874.** www.avondalebb.com. 4 units. €70–€80 double. Free parking. Rates include breakfast. **Amenities:** Wi-Fi (free).

Garnish House ★★ One of several B&Bs and hotels in this neighborhood, Garnish House is a sweet and friendly place to stay. You're hardly through the door before being offered an afternoon tea, complete with delicious home-made scones. Guestrooms are pleasant with well-sized beds, and some rooms even have Jacuzzi baths. Breakfasts are outstanding; in addition to the usual hearty "full Irish" options, you could have French toast, pancakes, lentil ragout, stuffed tomatoes, salmon and dill tarts, scrambled eggs with avocado—more choices than plenty of restaurants around here would offer at dinner. There are self-catering options available for those who want a little extra free-dom, including a one-bedroom apartment and a full townhouse directly across the street.

1 St. Mary's Villas, Western Rd., Cork, Co. Cork. www.garnish.ie. ✆ **021/427-5111.** 14 units. €79–€148 double. Free parking. Rates include breakfast. **Amenities:** Wi-Fi (free).

Lancaster Lodge ★ Another small hotel on Western Road, Lancaster Lodge is modern, well run, and a good value for your money. The purple color scheme in some of the public areas might be a bit garish for some, but guestrooms are big with contemporary furnishings. Suites, which aren't a great deal more than the standard doubles, come with Jacuzzi baths. Breakfast is better than you might expect from a budget hotel, and while they don't serve dinner, central Cork is only a short walk away.

Lancaster Quay, Western Road, Cork, Co. Cork. ✆ **021/425-1125.** www.lancasterlodge.com. 48 units. €71–€106 double. Free parking. Breakfast not included in lower rates. **Amenities:** Wi-Fi (free); room service.

Where to Stay in Kinsale

Actons Hotel ★ This pleasant, well-run property looks out over Kinsale Harbour. Built in the mid-19th century, it's been a hotel since the 1940s, though a recent renovation has smoothed out a few old wrinkles. Guestrooms aren't huge, but they're nicely designed, with very large beds and lovely harbor views. In a town where it's easy to find accommodations with character but not modern conveniences, you'll welcome the few extras such as an elevator (you'd be surprised how rare that is around here) and a swimming pool. The hotel's two restaurants are good, but Kinsale is full of wonderful restaurants within a short walk.

Pier Rd., Kinsale, Co. Cork. ✆ **021/477-9900.** www.actonshotelkinsale.com. 74 units. €130–€170 double. Free parking. Rates include breakfast. Dinner, bed and breakfast packages available. **Amenities:** Wi-Fi (free); 2 restaurants; bar; room service; gym; pool; accessible rooms.

Blue Haven Hotel ★★ There's something wonderfully old-school about this chic townhouse hotel in the middle of Kinsale. The rooms are traditionally deco-rated with antique-style furniture and heritage print wallpaper. The friendly staff run things very professionally, and the in-house restaurant, the **Fishmarket** (see p. 246), is excellent. Frequent special offers can bring the hotel price down considerably. For example, midweek dinner, bed-and-breakfast deals for well under €100 are common, and enticing package deals for golfers, including access to one of the best courses in Ireland, can be had. The only snag is that you can get street noise here, so ask for an upper floor window if you're a light sleeper.

3-4 Pearse St., Kinsale, Co. Cork. ✆ **021/477-2209.** www.bluehavenkinsale.com. 17 units. €120–€140 double. Parking at nearby lots (no discount) around €1.30 per hour. Rates include breakfast. Dinner, bed and breakfast packages and 2-night midweek and weekend deals available. **Amenities:** Wi-Fi (free); 2 restaurants; bar; room service.

Desmond House ★★ This lovely, historic old B&B is one of the best places to stay in Kinsale. Desmond House was built in the mid-18th century, and, according to host Michael McLaughlin, is one of the oldest and best-preserved Georgian buildings in town. Michael is a genuine and charming man; his policy of charging American visitors according to whichever exchange rate works out best with the euro—on the day you booked or the day you check out—is a particularly considerate gesture. Guestrooms are generous with big, comfortable beds, and the modern bathrooms are furnished with whirlpool tubs. Many of the ingredients for the delicious breakfasts come straight from the **Old English Market** in Cork (see p. 232).

42 Cork St., Kinsale, Co. Cork. ✆ **021/477-3575.** www.desmondhousekinsale.com. 4 units. €140 double. Parking at nearby lots (no discount) around €1.30 per hour. Rates include breakfast. **Amenities:** Wi-Fi (free).

Pier House ★★ There's something wonderfully bright and cheerful about this sweet place in Kinsale. Hosts Pat and Anne have done a beautiful job in converting the 19th-century townhouse into a B&B. The chic color schemes and subtle splashes of modern art lift the mood beautifully. A few of the bedrooms have little balconies, and guests are welcome to bring wine back with them if they want to spend a leisurely hour admiring the views of the harbor or garden. Breakfasts are delicious and plentiful. You'll have to fend for yourself at dinner, but this is hardly a chore in foodie-friendly Kinsale.

Pier Road, Kinsale, Co. Cork. ✆ **021/477-4169.** www.pierhousekinsale.com. 10 units. €100–€140 double. Parking for bikes and motorbikes only; car parking at nearby lots around €1.30 per hour. Rates include breakfast. **Amenities:** Wi-Fi (free).

Where to Dine in Cork City

Cork's reputation as a kind of cultural "Dublin south" is burnished by its restaurant scene smattered with trendy eateries. However, it's Kinsale where the county really goes to let its collective belt out. Over the last 20 years, the town has transformed itself from a sleepy fishing village into one of Ireland's premier food destinations.

Cafe Paradiso ★★ VEGETARIAN An inventive, classy vegetarian restaurant, Cafe Paradiso does such magnificent things without meat that even passionate carnivores will find plenty to love. Start with roast eggplant with honey and cardamom, or cauliflower soup with braised shiitake mushrooms, before moving on to deep fried squash blossoms with smoked pepperonata and green onion polenta. Desserts are heavenly, so try the rich chocolate mousse (made with olive oil—trust us, it works) and spicy almond brittle. The excellent wine list is reasonably priced. If you can't quite run to dinner here, come before 7pm for the early bird menu. Or for those who prefer to roll straight from table to bed, they also have guestrooms for €100 per night (dinner included).

16 Lancaster Quay, Cork, Co. Cork. ✆ **021/427-7939.** www.cafeparadiso.ie. Fixed-price menus: 2 courses €33, 3 courses €36–€40. Mon–Fri 5:30–10pm; Sat noon–2:30pm, 5:30–10pm. No children after 7pm.

Crawford Gallery Café ★★ CAFE A big step up from the average cafe tacked onto an art gallery, the Crawford is as much a great little bistro as it is a convenient spot for a coffee or light nibble. It's open for breakfast, which certainly provides some excellent options if you can't face another hotel morning meal. You'll find spiced scones, American-style pancakes, and delicious eggs Florentine with organic spinach on the menu. Lunchtime is when this place gets busiest though, and the line-up changes regularly with plenty of daily specials like chorizo bean cassoulet or smoked salmon salad with horseradish dressing. On Thursdays the cafe stays open until 8pm for early-evening suppers.

Brewing Up Loyalty

Ireland is known for its love of Guinness, but in Cork you're more likely to find locals drinking Murphy's or Beamish—the two locally brewed stouts. There is a definite sense of civic loyalty when it comes to drinking stout in this town. In fact, walk into any pub and order a "home and away" and you'll be presented with a pint of Murphy's and one of Guinness.

At the Crawford Gallery, Emmet Place, Cork, Co. Cork. ✆ **021/427-4415.** www.crawfordgallerycafe.com. Breakfast: €3–€11; lunch: €11–€15. Mon–Wed, Fri–Sat 8:30–11:30am, noon–4pm; Thurs 8:30am–8pm.

Electric ★★ SEAFOOD/MODERN IRISH With a dining room overlooking the river and the city skyline beyond, it's easy to get swept up in the romantic atmosphere of this trendy but unpretentious restaurant. The menu isn't large, but it's honest and beautifully done with steaks, dill battered fish and chips, and a juicy house burger topped with Wicklow blue cheese. In addition to the main restaurant is the **Fish Bar** (Wed–Sat only), where you can eat super-fresh seafood while perched on bar stools overlooking the river. Despite its popularity, you can usually get a table at Electric if you arrive early—a full fifth are held back every night—and the Fish Bar doesn't take reservations at all.

41 South Mall, Cork, Co. Cork. ✆ **021/422-2990.** www.electriccork.com/restaurant. Main courses €15–€24. Thurs–Sat noon–10pm; Sun–Mon noon–9pm. No children in the Fish Bar.

Market Lane ★★ IRISH This friendly, informal restaurant serves Irish-inflected bistro food. It's a let-your-hair-down kind of place, and the menu strikes a good line between traditional, unpretentious cooking with just a few more adventurous touches. Typical mains include gin-marinated pork with black pudding and hake with summer greens and roasted garlic. Lunches are just as good, and if you're not in the mood to linger over a full meal, pick something from the small but well-judged menu of sandwiches and salads. The early bird menu is outstanding value at just €20 for three courses (daily until 7pm, except Fri and Sat).

5–6 Oliver Plunkett St., Cork, Co. Cork. ✆ **021/427-4710.** www.marketlane.ie. Main courses €14–€26. Mon–Thurs noon–10pm; Fri–Sat noon–10:30pm; Sun 1–9pm (10pm on public holidays).

Orso ★★★ IRISH/MEDITERRANEAN This place is like a ray of warm Mediterranean sunshine. Traditional flavors of southern Europe are mixed with Irish influences, and the result is nothing short of delightful. It's open all day so you can pop in for a breakfast of flatbread with banana and cinnamon or granola with Greek yogurt and berry compote. The lunch menu is long and varied, but it's really at dinnertime when the excellent cooking comes into its own. Plates include schiacciata (a type of gossamer-thin pizza made with olive oil and sea salt) alongside sesame seed-encrusted schiacciata. Nearly everything on the wine list is available by the glass, and the small cocktail menu is intriguing—try the zingy mint and lime spritzer.

8 Pembroke St., Cork, Co. Cork. ✆ **021/243-8000.** www.orso.ie. Main courses €8–€19. Mon–Tues 8am–6pm; Wed–Sat 8am–11pm.

Where to Dine in Kinsale

Crackpots ★★★ SEAFOOD/MODERN IRISH A happy marriage of designer pottery shop and outstandingly good restaurant, Crackpots specializes in fresh, delicious seafood. The ingredients are all locally sourced, so exactly what appears on the menu depends on what's freshest. In recent past, grilled langoustine with spinach and lime pesto or baked salmon flavored with lemongrass and served with potato rosti were a few of our favorites. It's not all seafood; the menu is also filled with items like roast duck, lamb, or a simple steak served in a sauce of brandy and peppercorn, plus a vegetarian option or two. The dining room is decorated with some interesting art (most of which is for sale), or you can sit in a heated garden terrace out back if the weather's fine.

3 Cork St., Kinsale, Co. Cork. ✆ **021/477-2847.** www.crackpots.ie. Main courses €16–€28. Mon–Sat 6–9pm; Sun 1–3pm.

Finn's Table ★★★ MODERN IRISH The menu here is ambitious without being overly complicated and with plenty of space to let the ingredients breathe. As you'd expect from Kinsale, the seafood on the menu comes directly from the harbor, so you never know exactly what will end up in the kitchen. However, on a typical night plates can include some tender squid fried with salt and pepper, monkfish and scallops served with parmesan cream, or lemon sole with glazed asparagus and a carrot and lime buerre blanc. Though the standout dishes tend to be seafood, there's plenty more to choose from, and the meats are all sourced from the owner's parents, who run a butcher shop in nearby Mitchelstown.

6 Main St., Kinsale, Co. Cork. ✆ **021/470-9636.** www.finnstable.com. Main courses €20–€35. Wed–Mon 5:30–10pm.

The Fishmarket ★★ SEAFOOD/INTERNATIONAL Another excellent seafood restaurant packed with the grand choices Kinsale is known for, the Fishmarket is the in-house restaurant at the **Blue Haven Hotel** (see p. 243). The short menu has a nice balance of traditional seafood dishes—classic fish and chips or hake filet with lemon and chive butter—together with some meatier options such as Thai red curry or steak in peppercorn sauce. Vegetarian choices and Celiac-friendly dishes are on the menu, too. The tempting dessert menu features such diet-busting delights as Guinness and Belgian chocolate pecan brownie served with ice cream and chocolate sauce.

3-4 Pearse St., Kinsale, Co. Cork. ✆ **021/477-2209.** www.bluehavenkinsale.com. Main courses €13–€24. Daily 6–10pm.

THE GREAT GOURMET GATHERING: kinsale food festival

Food lovers from all over Ireland—and even farther afield—descend on Kinsale for a weekend each October when the **Kinsale Gourmet Festival** takes over town. The event's calendar changes every year, but always includes plenty of cooking demonstrations and other lively activities. Restaurants join in the fun by hosting parties, special tastings, "meet the chef" events, and other culinary happenings. Many of them are free, although some of the bigger events and banquets charge about €20 to €100 per ticket. It's magnificent, Bacchanalian fun. Learn more and book tickets at www.kinsalerestaurants.com.

Fishy Fishy Café ★★★ SEAFOOD Widely respected, hugely popular, and yet brilliantly simple, the Fishy Fishy is one of the best restaurants in Kinsale. The owners also have a gourmet store and fish and chip shop on Guardwell Street, but this is their flagship. The beautifully prepared, fresh seafood comes from a small number of trusted suppliers. And we do mean local. Shane catches the cod and turbot, Maurice provides the crab, Christy, David, and Jimmy catch the prawns—you get the idea. Exactly what's cooking that day depends on the catch, but you can expect to find the signature Fishy Fishy pie of salmon and shellfish in a creamy sauce with a breadcrumb topping. Reservations are only taken for dinner, so this place gets packed during lunchtime.

Crowleys Quay, Kinsale, Co. Cork. ✆ **021/470-0415.** www.fishyfishy.ie. Main courses €16–€25. Mar–Oct daily noon–9pm; Nov–Feb Sun–Wed noon–4pm, Thurs–Sat noon–9pm.

Janey Mac ★★ CAFE There's a nice little story behind the name to this artisan bakery and cafe. "Janey Mac" isn't a person, rather it was a phrase invented by the residents of Kinsale in the 1950s as an alternative expletive to the blasphemous (and therefore, in those days, verboten) "Jesus Christ." Since then, this building has housed several businesses of wildly disparate kinds, but most of them have kept the same name. The homemade cakes, scones, brownies, and other baked treats here are delicious, and they serve great sandwiches at lunchtime too. The little dining room is decorated in a shabby chic style, scattered with cushions and other appealing touches. Look out for the wry "thought for the day," scrawled on a blackboard at the back.

38 Main St., Kinsale, Co. Cork. ✆ **086/811-1848.** www.janeymackinsale.com. Main courses €3–€9. Mon–Sat 9am–5pm.

Max's ★★★ MODERN IRISH A husband-and-wife team has run Max's since the '90s, and they're still effortlessly adept at making diners feel welcome. The menu changes seasonally, but the main flavors are French, with dishes like black sole with herb butter or lobster broth prepared with Chardonnay and tarragon. Irish influences include regionally sourced meats and wild game, some prepared with local cider. The specials board invariably features a selection of fresh, local seafood. The early bird menu (a thoroughly reasonable €30 for three courses) is served until 7:30pm and 7pm on Saturdays.

48 Main St., Kinsale, Co. Cork. ✆ **021/477-2443.** www.maxs.ie. Main courses €21–€30. Apr–mid-Dec daily 6–10pm.

The Spaniard ★★ BISTRO The portrait on the sign of this atmospheric old inn shows Don Juan de Aguila, the Spanish commander who led a force of 4,000 men, assisted by local Irish revolutionaries, against the English at the Battle of Kinsale in 1601. The English won but Don Juan became a hero in local folklore. The present inn dates from around 50 years after the battle, and it's still a satisfying place with an old-world look. They serve excellent, homey pub food in the restaurant, but the bar menu is just as good, and cheaper too. An eclectic program of live music features everything from straight-up Irish folk to Russian Gypsy bands.

Junction of Scilly and Lower Road, Kinsale, Co. Cork. ✆ **021/477-2436.** www.thespaniard.ie. Main courses €18–€25. Mon–Fri 12:30–3pm, 6–9pm; Sat 12:30–3pm, 6–10pm; Sun 12:30–3pm, 6:30–10pm.

East Cork

Lying 24km (15 miles) east of Cork City, the harbor town of **Cobh** (pronounced *cove,* meaning "haven" in Irish), was once Ireland's chief port of emigration, with three or four transatlantic liners calling each week. For thousands of Irish emigrants, particularly during the famine years and in the early part of the 20th century, Cobh was the last bit of Ireland they ever saw. The county's major coastal town is **Youghal** (pronounced *Yawl*), near the Waterford border. A leading beach resort and fishing port, Youghal is loosely associated with Sir Walter Raleigh, who was once the mayor and is said to have planted Ireland's first potatoes here. From a tourist's-eye view, present-day Youghal is a moderately attractive, congested town with a grand stretch of beach just beyond the center.

ARRIVING

If you're driving from Cork City, take the main Waterford road (N25) east. Exit at R624 for Fota and Cobh, or R632 for Shanagarry and Ballycotton. Midleton and Youghal have their own signposted exits. If you're coming from West Cork and want to bypass Cork City (a good idea during rush hour), take the car ferry operated by **Cross River Ferries Ltd.,** Atlantic Quay, Cobh (✆ **021/420-2900;** www.scottcobh.ie). It links Carrigaloe, near Cobh, with Glenbrook, south of Cork City. Cars cost a few euro each way and the journey lasts under 5 minutes.

Irish Rail (✆ **021/455-7277;** www.irishrail.ie) operates daily train service between Cork City and Cobh via Fota Island. The journey takes about half an hour. **Bus Éireann** (✆ **021/450-8188;** www.buseireann.ie) also provides daily service from Cork City to Cobh and other points in East Cork.

EXPLORING EAST CORK

Ballymaloe Cookery School ★★★ Professional and amateur cooks flock here from all over the world to sit near the whisk of Darina Allen. It all started with Darina's mother-in-law, Myrtle, whose evangelization of Ireland's bounty of fresh produce at Ballymaloe House restaurant (see p. 250) elevated Irish "country house" cooking to gourmet status. The Allen family's success led to the founding of this cooking school, the most famous in Ireland, which offers dozens of courses ranging in length from a half-day to 12 weeks. Half-day courses include "canapés, finger food and tasty bites," "afternoon tea and cakes," "irresistible breakfasts." Prices start at about €75. The beautiful, extensive **gardens** on the grounds are open to visitors all year. Admission to the gardens is €6. The

Students cooking up a storm at Ballymaloe Cookery School, run by Ireland's most famous chef, Darina Allen.

Ballymaloe Shop, open 10am to 5pm daily, sells kitchen produce (including Ballymaloe's own delicious brand of relish) and crafty knick-knacks. And the aptly-named **Café at the End of the Shop** sells light lunches, afternoon tea, and lip-smackingly good cakes.

Shanagarry, Co. Cork. ✆ **021/464-6785.** www.cookingisfun.ie. Half-day courses from €75–€125. Open year-round; schedule varies.

Fota Island & Wildlife Park ★★ If only all zoos were like the Fota Wildlife Park. Most of the animals at this thoughtfully designed park are free to roam without any apparent barriers mingling with each other and human visitors. Kangaroos, macaws, and lemurs have the run of 16 hectares (40 acres) of grassland; only the cheetahs are behind conventional fencing. If close contact with a menagerie of exotic creatures doesn't delight the kids (unlikely though it sounds), try the small amusement park, tour train, picnic area, or gift shop on site. The Park's Savannah Café has a view of the meerkat exhibition, so you may find yourself being watched by curious eyes while eating your lunch.

Fota Island, Carrigtwohill, Co. Cork. ✆ **021/481-2678.** www.fotawildlife.ie. Admission €14.30 adults; €9.20 seniors, disabled, and children; €44–€56 families. Mon–Sat 10am–6pm; Sun 10:30am–6pm. Last entry 1 hr. before closing.

Where to Stay in East Cork

Bayview Hotel ★★ This hotel must have one of the best views of any in Ireland: miles of coastline, dotted with islands, and boats bobbing gently in the harbor. Guestrooms are basic but pleasant, with modern furnishings. Each has a view of the sea. The restaurant serves good modern Irish cuisine, using plenty of

point of departure: **A DAY IN COBH**

If you're a foreigner with an Irish surname, this bustling, lively seaside town could be more important to you than you realize. Cobh (pronounced *cove*, meaning "haven") used to be called Queenstown, and it was once Ireland's chief port of emigration. During the early 20th century, several transatlantic liners departed from here every week. It was also the last port of call for the RMS *Titanic* before it sank in April 1912. That story is expertly told at **Cobh: the Queenstown Story** (Deepwater Quay; ✆ **021/481-3591;** www.cobhheritage.com). Part of the Cobh Heritage Centre, the exhibition is open Monday to Saturday from 9:30am to 6pm and Sunday and bank holidays from 11am to 6pm.

Defining the Cobh skyline, **St. Colman's Cathedral** (✆ **021/481-3222;** www.cobhcathedral.ie) is an excellent example of neo-Gothic church architecture. Started in 1868, the cathedral was the country's most expensive religious building of its time. The largest of its 47 bells weighs 3.5 tons, and the organ has nearly 2,500 pipes. The interior is vast and ornate, including a beautiful nave and precipitously high chancel arch. It is also a popular venue for concerts and recitals.

A short walk from St. Colman's Cathedral, the ***Lusitania* Memorial** (Casement Sq.) commemorates the British passenger liner sunk by a German U-boat on May 7, 1915, killing 1,198 passengers, including several victims buried in Cobh cemetery.

And if you want to discover more about Cobh's role in the *Titanic* story, an hour-long **walking tour** takes in a variety of related sites, putting it all into the context of the town's maritime history. In truth this is more of a general historical tour of the town with just a couple of actual *Titanic* connections, but it's informative nonetheless. The tour departs from the Commodore Hotel, 4 Westbourne Place, at 11am and 2pm daily. (The tour doesn't run from October to March if there are no pre-bookings). It costs €9.50 adults, €4.75 children. For bookings call ✆ **021/481-5211,** or visit www.titanic.ie.

local produce, including fish direct from the pier and meat from local and regional farms. However, prices are high (€20–€28 for a main course), and you're not exactly spoiled for alternatives around here. Guests have free use of a swanky new spa and health club at the sister Garryvoe Hotel, about a 5-minute drive down the coast. Check the website for good deals and special offers, including dinner, bed and breakfast packages and seniors discounts. The Bayview is closed from November to early April.

Ballycotton, Cork, Co. Cork. ✆ **021/464-6746.** www.thebayviewhotel.com. 35 units. €95–€145 double; €155–€205 suite. Rates include full breakfast. Dinner, bed and breakfast packages available. Closed Nov–early Apr. **Amenities:** Wi-Fi (free); restaurant; bar; room service; use of nearby health club.

Ballymaloe House ★★★ Most famous for being Ireland's best-known cookery school—you can take wonderful day and half-day courses here (see p. 248)—Ballymaloe is also an inviting countryside hotel. Comfortable guestrooms are decorated in traditional country house style, with floral print wallpaper, antique-style furniture, and original art on the walls. The house itself is an attractive fusion of Georgian farmhouse and medieval castle, surrounded by beautiful grounds. If you want a bit more privacy you can choose from several self-catering options, including cottages, a faux castle tower (complete with balcony on the battlements), and several cabin-style chalets. Unsurprisingly, the kitchen is the real draw here—the restaurant produces fantastic gourmet dinners nightly. These are lavish, five-course affairs, with seasonal menus (€70 per person); Sunday features a slightly simpler buffet spread—just as well if you've already had the €45 Sunday lunch. The wine list is extensive, and unusually high tech—ask to be given the iPad version to try out video information pages alongside the largely French selection.

Shanagarry, Midleton, Co. Cork. ✆ **800/323-5463** in the U.S., or 021/465-2531. www.ballymaloe.ie. 33 units. €110–€140 double. Rates include full breakfast. **Amenities:** Restaurant; room service.

Where to Dine in East Cork

See also "Where to Stay in East Cork" above.

The Coach House ★★ BISTRO This is a great option for lunch on the road—a fine range of delicious salads (tempura prawns with chipotle, or perhaps spinach with candied walnuts), and tasty sandwiches, burgers, and paninis. The full menu presents a heartier selection of Irish bistro-style favorites, from steaks and seafood to gourmet fish and chips.

16 Casement Sq. Cobh, Co. Cork. ✆ **021/481-3754.** Snacks and light meals €5–€13; main courses €10–€23. Daily 11:30am–10pm.

Trade Winds ★ INTERNATIONAL This popular spot overlooks the harbor in Cobh, just a 5-minute walk from **Cobh: The Queenstown Story** (see p. 250). You might start with some smoked salmon or a delicious fishcake, before moving on to a main of fresh seafood, traditional bangers and mash, or perhaps one of the extremely generous steaks. They also do lighter lunches, such as sandwiches, ciabattas, and soups. Some evenings include live music.

16 Casement Sq. Cobh, Co. Cork. ✆ **021/481-3754.** Main courses €8–€18. Daily noon–9pm.

West Cork

Some say West Cork is like County Kerry without the crowds. It shares with Kerry a photo-friendly craggy topography and jagged coastline. It's impossible to make good time on the roads here, as they tend to be narrow and sinuous, twisting along rivers, through valleys, around mountains, and passing through lovely small towns. Those willing to slow down and go with the flow are amply rewarded. You'll probably come across at least one puzzling rural intersection that's completely lacking in signage, and have to slow down for a herd of sheep slowly making its way down a country lane. In places, the public route that hugs the coast narrows to just one lane and delivers heart-stopping views. Over time, you may even come to think of the roads here as one of West Cork's great pleasures. Some of the most beautiful coastal scenery (and severe weather) is on the islands.

Cape Clear ★, home to a bird-watching observatory, is also a well-known Gaeltacht: Both schoolchildren and adults come here to work on their Gaelic skills each summer. **Dursey Island,** off the tip of the Beara Peninsula, is accessible by cable car. **Garinish Island** in Glengarriff is the site of Ilnacullin, an elaborate Italianate garden.

THE sheep's head LOOP

For a magnificent drive, take the **Sheep's Head Loop** that begins outside Bantry along the tiny road to Kilcrohane. It takes you through Ahakista, and on to Durrus. The north side is all sheer cliffs and stark beauty (the sunsets are unbelievable) while the more lush south-side road runs right alongside the wondrous Dunmanus Bay.

ARRIVING

N71 is the main road into West Cork from north and south; from Cork and points east, N22 also leads to West Cork. **Bus Éireann** (✆ **021/450-8188;** www.buseireann.ie) provides daily bus service to and from the principal towns in West Cork.

EXPLORING WEST CORK

Bantry House ★★ This Georgian house was built around 1750 for the earls of Bantry. It holds furniture and objects d'art from all over Europe, including Aubusson and Gobelin tapestries said to have been made for Marie Antoinette. The gardens, with original statuary, are beautifully kept—climb the steps behind the building for a panoramic view of the house, gardens, and Bantry Bay. There is also an informative exhibition on the ill-fated Spanish Armada, which, led by the Irish rebel Wolfe Tone, attempted to invade the country near Bantry House in 1769. If you really love it, you can spend the night (rooms €170–€200).

Bantry, Co. Cork. ✆ **027/50047.** www.bantryhouse.com. Admission €11 adults; €3 children 6–16; children 5 and under free; €26 families. Tues–Sun 10am–5pm.

Cape Clear Island (Oileán Chléire) ★★ The southernmost inhabited point in Ireland, 13km (8 miles) off the mainland, Cape Clear Island has a permanent population of just a hundred residents. It is a bleak place with a craggy coastline and no trees to break the rush of sea wind, but it's also starkly beautiful—rough, irregular, and graceful. In early summer, wildflowers brighten the landscape, and in October, passerine migrants, some on their way from North America and Siberia, fill the air. Seabirds are abundant during the nesting season, especially from July to September. You can get to the island by ferry (see below) and explore it all at your own pace; alternatively, **Fastnet Tours** (✆ **028/39159;** www.fastnettour.com) run a twice-weekly tour. After visiting the island's tiny heritage center, you're taken out for a boat ride around **Fastnet Rock,** a craggy outcrop in the Atlantic. Home to nothing but a weather-beaten lighthouse, Fastnet was traditionally known as "Teardrop Island," not for its shape, but because it was the last piece of Ireland that emigrants saw on their way to America. The tours, which only go ahead in good weather, leave from the pier in Baltimore on Wednesdays and Saturdays at 11, but frustratingly, you can only book online. They cost €32 per person.

Cape Clear Island, Co. Cork. ✆ **Ferry: 028/39159** or 41923. www.oilean-chleire.ie. Return ferry: €16 adults; €8 children; €40 families. Generally 4 times daily in summer, twice daily in winter. Schedule may change according to weather.

Cummingeera ★ Stark and eerie, Cummingeera is an abandoned village near Lauragh at the base of a cliff in a wild, remote valley. The walk to the village gives you a taste for the rough beauty of this mountainous area, and a sense of the extent to which people in pre-Famine Ireland would go to find a patch of arable land. To get to the start of the walk, take R571 heading east from the village of Derreen. From this road, take the turning for Glanmore Lake, signposted on the left after approximately 1km (⅔ mile). Then turn right at the road posted for "stone circle." Continue 2km (1¼ miles) to the point at which the road becomes dirt, and park on the roadside. From here, there is no trail—just walk up the valley to its terminus, about 2km (1¼ miles) away, where the ruins of a village hug the cliff's base. Where the valley is blocked by a headland, take the route around to the left, which is less steep. Return the way you came; the whole walk—4km (2½ miles)—is of moderate difficulty.

Near Lauragh, Co. Cork.

The Donkey Sanctuary ★ A real heartbreaker, this one: a charity that rescues abandoned and abused donkeys and nurses them back to health. A few of the beasts of burden here have been voluntarily relinquished by owners who are no longer able to care for them, but the majority have sadder histories. The donkeys live out their days at this quiet and bucolic place, where they receive medical aid and plenty of TLC. Visitors can meet the gentle patients and learn their stories. The emphasis is on happy endings. Seeing these animals given a new lease on life can be a touching and even quite profound experience for kids.

Liscarroll, near Mallow, Co. Cork. ✆ **022/48398.** www.thedonkeysanctuary.ie. Free admission. Mon–Fri 9am–4:30pm; Sat, Sun, and Bank Holidays 10am–5pm.

Drombeg Stone Circle ★★ This ring of 13 standing stones is the finest example of a megalithic stone circle in County Cork. The circle dates from 153 B.C., and little is known about its ritual purpose. However, the remains of two huts and a cooking place, just to the west of the circle, give some clue; it is thought that heated stones were placed in a water trough (which can be seen adjacent to the huts), and the hot water was used for cooking. This section has been dated to sometime between A.D. 368 and 608. While you're out this way, consider stopping at the charming little village of **Ballydehob (Béal Átha Dá Chab)**. An artsy place with an ancient stone bridge and some brightly painted houses, it's one big photo opportunity. Ballydehob is also signposted from R597 between Rosscarbery and Glandore.

Off R597 between Rosscarbery and Glandore, Co. Cork. No phone. Free admission (open site). The turning for Drombeg Stone Circle is signposted just after the sign for Drombeg (if approaching from the direction of Rosscarbery); if approaching from Glandore it's about 0.5km (⅓ miles) after the whitewashed church in Drombeg village.

Dursey Island ★★ This is a real adventure—a barren promontory extending into the sea at the tip of the Beara Peninsula. It offers no amenities for tourists, but the adventurous will find beautiful seaside walks, a 200 year-old signal tower, and a memorable passage from the mainland via cable car. To get there, take R571 past Cahermore to its terminus. As you sway wildly in the wooden cable car, you'll wonder whether or not to be reassured that someone saw fit to leave the text of Psalm 91 inside ("If you say 'the Lord is my refuge,' and you make the most high your dwelling, no harm will overtake you"). You

local hero: **MICHAEL COLLINS**

Much of County Cork, and particularly the little town of Clonakilty, seems obsessed with Michael Collins, and when you learn a bit about him, you can understand why. Collins, also known as "the Big Fella," was one of the heroes of the Irish struggle for independence—the commander in chief of the army of the Irish Free State, which under his command won the Republic's independence from Britain in 1921.

Collins was born in 1890 and, along with his seven brothers and sisters, was raised on a farm in Sam's Cross, just outside Clonakilty. He emigrated to England at 15 and, like many other young Irish men, found work in London. In his 20s, he joined the Irish revolutionary group, the Irish Republican Brotherhood (I.R.B.). He first came to fame in 1916, as one of the planners and leaders of the Easter Rising, fighting alongside Patrick Pearse at the General Post Office in Dublin. It may have roused passions among the population, but the Rising was a military disaster, and Collins—young but clever—railed against its amateurism. He was furious about the seizure of prominent buildings—such as the GPO—that were impossible to defend, impossible to escape from, and difficult to get supplies into.

After the battle, Collins was arrested and sent to an internment camp in Britain, along with hundreds of other rebels. There his stature within the I.R.B. grew, and by the time he was released, he had become one of the leaders of the Republican movement. In 1918, he was elected a member of the British Parliament, but like many other Irish members, refused to go to London, instead announcing that he would sit only in an Irish parliament in Dublin. Most of the rebel Irish MPs (including Eamon de Valera) were arrested by British troops for their actions, but Collins avoided arrest, and later helped de Valera escape from prison. Over the subsequent years, de Valera and Collins worked together to create an Irish state.

After lengthy negotiations and much bloodshed (Collins orchestrated an assassination that essentially wiped out the British secret service in Ireland), Collins was sent by de Valera in 1921 to negotiate a treaty with the British government. In the meeting, British Prime Minister David Lloyd George agreed to allow Ireland to become a free republic, as long as that republic did not include

may even be sharing your car with sheep or cows, as it's also used to transport livestock to and from the island. At this point you might wonder whether a ferry would have been a wiser option. It wouldn't. Apparently the channel between the island and mainland is just too treacherous to permit regular crossing by boat. Cables run all year, Monday to Saturday, from 9 to 10:30am, 2:30 to 4:30pm and 7 to 7:30pm, and Sunday from 9 to 10am, 1 to 2pm and 7 to 7:30pm. Summertime has extended hours; from June to September they sometimes run continuously all day. However, since the island has no shops, pubs, restaurants or lodging of any kind, it's very important to check return times with the operator before you go. You should also bring food and water. For up-to-date information on any changes to the schedule, call the Skibbereen Tourist Office on ✆ **028/21766.**

Dursey Island, about 21km (14 miles) west of Castletown-Bearhaven, Co. Cork (follow R572). No phone. www.durseyisland.ie. Cable car round-trip €8 adults; €4 children.

the counties of Ulster (a move designed to appease the Unionists in Northern Ireland). Those largely Protestant counties would stay part of the United Kingdom. Knowing he could not get more at the time and hoping to renegotiate later, Collins reluctantly agreed to sign the treaty, deciding that it was time to stop the bloodshed. (Along with Lloyd George, Winston Churchill, then a government minister, also signed the treaty.) After signing the document Collins said, "I have just signed my death warrant."

As he'd expected, the plan tore the new Republic apart, dividing the group now known as the IRA into two factions—those who wanted to continue fighting for all of Ireland, and those who favored the treaty. Fighting soon broke out in Dublin, and the civil war was underway.

Collins had learned many lessons from the Easter debacle, and now his strategy was completely different. His soldiers operated as "flying columns," waging a guerrilla war against the enemy—suddenly attacking, and then just as suddenly withdrawing, thus minimizing their losses, and leaving the opposition never knowing what to expect next. The battle stretched on for 10 months.

In August 1922, Collins was weary of the war, and was on a peace mission in his home county. After visiting various factions, and stopping at a pub near his mother's birthplace, he and his escort were on the road near Béal na Bláth when Collins was shot and killed. Precisely who killed him—whether it was his own men or the opposition—is not known. He had made, on his rapid rise to the top, too many enemies. He was 31 years old.

The **Michael Collins Centre** (✆ **023/884-6107;** www.michaelcollinscentre.com), located on the farm where he grew up, is a good place to learn more about the man. In addition to an hour-long tour, featuring a film and a visit to actual ambush site, the center runs in-depth guided trips around the local area. These are probably for Collins devotees only, though, due to the 3½-hour running time. The center is signposted off N71, 5.6km (3½ miles) west of Clonakilty. It's open mid-June to mid-September, Mondays to Fridays from 10:30am to 5pm, and Saturdays from 11am-2pm. Admission is free.

Gougane Barra ★★ One of Ireland's most beautiful spots, Gougane Barra (which means "St. Fin Barre's Cleft") is the name of both a tiny old settlement and a forest park a little northeast of the Pass of Keimaneigh, 24km (15 miles) northeast of Bantry, and well signposted off R584, about halfway between Macroom and Glengarriff. Its most beautiful feature is a still, dark, romantic lake, which is the source of the River Lee. This is where St. Finbarre founded a monastery, supposedly on the small island connected by a causeway to the mainland. Though nothing remains of the saint's 6th-century community, the setting is idyllic, with rhododendrons spilling into the still waters where swans glide by. The island now holds an elfin chapel and eight small circular cells dating from the early 1700s, as well as a modern chapel. Signposted walks and drives lead through the wooded hills, although you have to pay a small admission charge per car to enter the park.

7km (4½ miles) west of Ballingeary, Co. Cork (signposted off R584).

Ilnacullin (Garinish Island) ★★ Officially known as Ilnacullin, but usually referred to as Garinish (or "Garnish"), this little island is a beautiful and tranquil place. It used to be little more than a barren outcrop, whose only distinguishing feature was a Martello tower left over from the Napoleonic Wars. Then, in 1919, the English landscaper Harold Peto was commissioned to create an elaborately planned Italianate garden, with classical pavilions and myriad unusual plants and flowers. The island's unusually mild microclimate allows a number of subtropical plant species to thrive here; indeed, George Bernard Shaw is said to have written *St. Joan* under the shade of its palm trees. The island can be reached for a round-trip fee of €10 per person (€5 children age 6–15) on a covered ferry operated by **Blue Pool Ferry,** the Blue Pool, Glengarriff (✆ **027/63333;** www.bluepoolferry.com), or **Harbour Queen Ferries,** the Harbour, Glengarriff (✆ **027/63116;** www.harbourqueenferry.com). Boats run back and forth about every 20 minutes. ***Note:*** The Harbour Queen doesn't take credit cards. The nearest ATMs are in Bantry and Kenmare, Co. Kerry (see p. 268).

Glengarriff, Co. Cork. ✆ **027/63040.** www.garnishisland.com. Admission (gardens) €4 adults; €3 seniors; €2 students and children; €10 families. Mid-Mar–Apr Mon–Sat 10am–5:30pm; Sun 1–6pm. May, Sept Mon–Sat 10am–6pm; Sun noon–6pm. June Mon–Sat 10am–6pm; Sun 11am–6pm. July–Aug Mon–Sat 9:30am–6pm; Sun 11am–6pm. Oct Mon–Sat 10am–4pm; Sun 1–5pm. Last landing 1 hr. before closing.

Mizen Head ★★★ At Mizen Head, the very extreme southwest tip of Ireland, the land falls precipitously into the Atlantic breakers in a procession of spectacular 210m (689-ft.) sea cliffs. You can cross a suspension bridge to an old signal station, now a visitor center, and stand on a rock promontory at the southernmost point of the mainland. The sea view is spectacular, and it's worth a trip regardless of the weather. On wild days, tremendous Atlantic waves assault the cliffs, while on a clear day, dolphins leap from the waves and seals bask on the rocks. A huge renovation a couple of years ago added new bridges, viewing platforms, and a ship's bridge simulator. On the way out to Mizen Head, you'll pass Barleycove Beach, a gorgeous stretch of sand and rock.

From Cork: take N71 to Ballydehob, then R592 and R591 to Golleen and follow signs to Mizen Head. ✆ **028/35115** or 35225. www.mizenhead.ie. Admission €6 adults; €4.50 seniors and students; €3.50 children 6–11; children under 5 free; €18 families. Mid-Mar–May, Sept–Oct daily 10:30am–5pm. June–Aug daily 10am–6pm. Nov–mid-Mar 11am–4pm.

SPORTS & OUTDOOR PURSUITS

BEACHES **Barleycove Beach** is a vast expanse of pristine sand with a fine view out toward the Mizen Head cliffs; despite the trailer park and holiday homes on the far side of the dunes, large parts of the beach never seem to get crowded. Take R591 to Goleen, and follow signs for Mizen Head. A public parking lot is at the Barleycove Hotel.

Inchydoney Beach, on Clonakilty Bay, is famous for both its gorgeous beach and the salubrious **Inchydoney Lodge & Spa** (see p. 258).

BIRD-WATCHING **Cape Clear Island** is the prime birding spot in West Cork, and one of the best places in Europe to watch seabirds (see p. 252). The best time for seabirds is July to September, and October is the busiest month for migratory passerines (and for bird-watchers, who flock to the island). A bird observatory is at the **North Harbour,** with a warden in residence from March to November. **Ciarán and Mary O'Driscoll** (✆ **028/39153** or 087/268-0760;

www.capeclearisland.eu), who operate a B&B on the island, also run boat trips for bird-watchers and have a keen eye for vagrants and rarities.

CYCLING The **Mizen Head, Sheep's Head,** and **Beara peninsulas** offer fine roads for cycling, with great scenery and few cars. The Beara Peninsula is the most spectacular; the other two are less likely to be crowded with tourists during peak season. The loop around Mizen Head, starting in Skibbereen, is a good 2- to 3-day trip, and a loop around the Beara Peninsula from Bantry, Glengarriff, or Kenmare takes at least 3 days at a casual pace.

In Skibbereen, 18- and 21-speed bicycles can be rented from **Roycroft Cycles,** Heron Court, Town Car Park (✆ **028/21235;** www.westcorkcycles.ie); expect to pay around €70 per week, depending on the season.

DIVING The **Baltimore Diving Centre,** Baltimore, County Cork (✆ **028/20300;** www.baltimorediving.com), provides equipment and boats to certified divers for exploring the many shipwrecks, reefs, and caves in this region. The cost starts at around €30 per dive if you bring your own gear, or €50 with hired equipment (plus around €25 for a guide). Various 2-hour to 15-day certified PADI courses are available for all levels of experience.

FISHING The West Cork coast is known for its many shipwrecks, making this one of the best places in Ireland for wreck fishing. **Courtmacsherry Sea Angling Centre,** Woodpoint House, Courtmacsherry (✆ **023/46427;** www.courtmacsherryangling.ie), offer packages that include bed and breakfast in their idyllic 18th century stone farmhouse and a day's sea angling aboard one of their two Aquastar fishing boats. A day's fishing costs around €60 per person (€70 if you want to go out to a wreck). They also run dolphin and whale watching excursions for €35 per person, or €100 per hour for groups of up to 12.

KAYAKING With hundreds of islands, numerous inviting inlets, and a plethora of sea caves, the coast of West Cork is a sea kayaker's paradise. **Lough Ine** offers warm, still waters for beginners, a tidal rapid for the intrepid, and access to a nearby headland riddled with caves that demand exploration. In Skibbereen, **Atlantic Sea Kayaking** (✆ **028/21058;** www.atlanticseakayaking.com) specializes in guided trips around Galley Head in Clonakilty and Mizen Head.

SAILING **Sail Cork** (East Hill, Cobh, ✆**021/4811237;** www.sailcork.com) runs courses on just about every aspect of sailing, yachting, and power boating, for all levels and ages.

WALKING One of the most beautiful coastal walks in West Cork begins along the banks of **Lough Ine,** one of the largest saltwater lakes in Europe. Connected to the sea by a narrow isthmus, the lake is in a lush valley of exceptional beauty. To get there, follow signs for Lough Ine along R595 between Skibbereen and Baltimore; a parking lot is at the northwest corner of the lake. The wide trail proceeds gradually upward from the parking lot through the woods on the west slope of the valley, with several viewpoints toward the lake and the sea beyond. Once you reach the hilltop, you'll see a sweeping view of the coast from Mizen Head to Galley Head. Walking time to the top and back is about 1½ hours.

Near Lauragh on the Beara Peninsula is the abandoned town of **Cummingeera,** at the base of a cliff in a wild, remote valley. For details see p. 253.

An easy seaside walk on the **Beara Peninsula** begins at Dunboy Castle, just over a mile west of Castletownbere on R572. This stretch of trail is part of the O'Sullivan Beara trail. You can park your car along the road, by the castellated gatehouse, or drive up to the castle. The castle is a ruined 19th-century manor house overlooking the bay, with some graceful marble arches spanning the grand central hall. Just down the road are the sparse ruins of a medieval fortress. Beyond, the trail continues to the tip of Fair Head through rhododendrons, with fine views across to Bere Island. A walk from the gatehouse parking lot to the tip of Fair Head and back takes about 2 hours.

The **Sheep's Head Way,** voted "Best Walk in Ireland" by *Country Walking* magazine a few years ago, makes an 89km (55-mile) loop and incorporates numerous smaller day loops. The *Guide to the Sheep's Head Way,* available in local stores and tourist offices, combines history, poetry, and topography in a fantastic introduction to the region. It is a rough place, and you won't find many tourists in its more remote reaches. The treasures to be found include several ancient ring forts and burial mounds, but you will have to work a little harder to locate them here than in regions long since "discovered."

One of Ireland's most beautiful spots, **Gougane Barra** is a lake 24km (15 miles) northeast of Bantry. For details, see p. 255.

WINDSURFING Weeklong courses and equipment rental are available at the **Oysterhaven Activity Centre** (see p. 242) near Kinsale. Beginners can get started at a sheltered beach in Courtmacsherry and another nearby beach is good for wave jumping.

Where to Stay in West Cork

Glebe Country House ★★ A short drive west of Kinsale, this place was built as a rectory in the late 17th century. Bedrooms are comfortable and traditionally furnished, with views of the idyllic gardens. The owners are real foodies: The breakfast menu is longer and more imaginative than most places this size (try the cheesy French toast), and beautifully prepared five-course dinners, made with plenty of local produce, are delicious. They're thoroughly reasonable at €35 per head too, although you must book by noon. If you're after a bit more seclusion, two self-catering cottages are on the grounds.

Balinadee (off Balinadee center), Bandon, Co. Cork. ✆ **021/477-8294.** www.glebecountryhouse.ie. 9 units. €70 double. Free parking. Rates include breakfast. €325–€570 per week self-catering apts. **Amenities:** Wi-Fi (free); restaurant.

Inchydoney ★★★ So close to the beach, you could almost dive into the Atlantic from the balcony, this famously luxurious spa is one of the best in the region. They specialize in Thalasso treatments, using seawater, although the full list of what's on offer is enough to make you feel more relaxed just by reading it. Guestrooms are sophisticated and modern, with huge windows that open out onto amazing views of the sea (of course). The Gulfstream Restaurant serves French and Mediterranean-influenced cooking, with fresh seafood being a particular specialty. There's also a pub and bistro if you're after something a little simpler. Unlike some high-end spas, Inchydoney is a great option for families, with its dedicated Children's Lounge daycare; the hotel can also arrange family-friendly activities such as kayaking, whale watching and cycle hire.

Clonakilty, Co. Cork. ✆ **023/883-3143.** www.inchydoneyisland.com. 67 units. €160–€280 double; €380 suite. Free parking. Rates include breakfast. **Amenities:** Wi-Fi (free); 2 restaurants; bar; room service; spa; pool.

Longueville House Hotel ★★ This grand but delightfully relaxed country house was built in 1720. The bright pink frontage gives some indication that this isn't a place to stand on ceremony, and your hosts the O'Callaghan family are adept at making you feel right at home. William O'Callaghan trained with the renowned French chef Raymond Blanc, and he puts the skills he learned from such a master to wonderful use in the kitchens here (see p. 260). They also do a proper afternoon tea and Sunday lunch. Spacious bedrooms reflect the heritage of the building, with appealingly traditional style and antique furniture. The hotel and restaurant are closed on Monday and Tuesday, April to October, and from Monday to Thursday, November to March.

Mallow, Co. Cork. ✆ **022/47156.** www.longuevillehouse.ie. 22 units. €75–€190 double; €225 suite. Free parking. Rates include breakfast. **Amenities:** Restaurant; room service.

Where to Dine in West Cork

Blair's Cove ★★ IRISH This has to have one of the most picturesque dining rooms in Ireland—a former barn, which may or may not have originated as an 18th century watchtower. The menu isn't cutting edge, but that's kind of the point. Instead what you get (after a charmingly retro buffet of starters) are traditional Irish flavors such as grilled lamb with jus, haddock soufflé with chive butter, or perhaps a plate of fresh scallops from Dunmore Bay. Desserts are rich and moreish. If you really want to make a night of it, they also do B&B for €95 to €130 per night.

Barley Cove Rd., Durrus, Co. Cork. ✆ **027/61127.** www.blairscove.ie. Fixed-price menus: 2 courses €46; 3 courses €58. Mid-Mar–Oct Tues–Sun 6:30–10pm. Closed Nov–mid-Mar.

Good Things Café ★★ MODERN EUROPEAN It's not hard to see why this restaurant gets things so right: a simple menu, using plenty of local produce, done beautifully. Though the main flavors are Irish, there's more than a hint of pan-European influence here, especially French—so you might find a rich coq au vin or an Andalusian monkfish prepared with honey and saffron, alongside more traditional flavors such as pork baked in bay leaves and brandy. They also run their own cookery school; 1-day courses start at about €140.

Ahakista Rd., Cork, Co. Cork. ✆ **027/61426.** www.thegoodthingscafe.com. Main courses €16–€26. Thurs–Mon noon–2pm, 6:30–9pm. Hours can vary in winter; call to check times.

The Heron's Cove ★★ SEAFOOD It's all about the bounty of the sea at this laid back restaurant about 15km (9 miles) from Mizen Head (see p. 256). All the seafood is caught on the West Cork coastline; expect Bantry Bay salmon, tempura monkfish, or perhaps just a fresh catch of the day. Carnivores are also taken care of, courtesy of such specials as the "collops 'n scallops"—a variation on surf 'n turf, featuring Goleen lamb chops and Dunmanus Bay scallops. You can sit outside on a terrace overlooking the harbor if the weather's good. They also do B&B in pleasant guestrooms with views of the harbor for €70 per night.

16 Lancaster Quay, Cork, Co. Cork. ✆ **021/427-7939.** www.heronscove.com. Main courses €17–€27. Mar–Oct daily 7–10pm. Closed Oct–Apr.

Mary Anne's ★ SEAFOOD/PUB FOOD The handsome exterior of this friendly pub in Castletownshend, near Skibbereen, is a photo op waiting to happen, with its ochre paint and neat, black windows. Inside it all feels as satisfying pub-like as you'd expect—and the food is excellent too. This being the West Cork coast, Mary Anne's specializes in super-fresh local seafood—you might start with some baked crab before moving on to a main of fish pie, or perhaps some simple (but delicious) fish and chips. They also have steaks and other meaty options. You can eat in a little courtyard terrace if you're blessed with sunshine.

Castletownshend, Skibbereen, Co. Cork. ✆ **028/36146.** Main courses €15–€26. Daily 12:30–2pm, 6–9pm. Closed holidays. Hours can vary in winter; call to check times.

The President's Restaurant ★★★ FRENCH/IRISH The restaurant of the excellent **Longueville House Hotel** (see p. 258) is one of the finest in the region. Chef William O'Callaghan—who, along with his wife, Aisling, also runs the hotel—trained under French chef Raymond Blanc at Le Manoir aux Quat' Saisons, one of the most famous restaurants in England. Local ingredients (many from their own farm and kitchen garden) feature heavily in the Irish-French menus, including Blackwater River salmon, Lounguevile lamb, and even honey from their own hive. They also serve lunch on Sundays. Just make sure you book ahead, at least 24 hours in advance for all sittings. The restaurant is closed Monday and Tuesday, April to October, and from Monday to Thursday, November to March.

Mallow, Co. Cork. ✆ **022/47156.** www.longuevillehouse.ie. Set menu €55; tasting menu €70. Reservations essential. Wed–Thurs 6:30–8:30pm; Fri–Sat 6:30–9pm; Sun 12:30–2:15pm, 6:30–8:30pm.

COUNTY KERRY

9

With its softly rolling green fields, sweeping seascapes, and vibrant little towns, it's easy to see why so many visitors make a beeline for County Kerry. Charming villages like colorful Kenmare and bustling historic towns like Killarney seem as familiar as the Irish folk songs written about them. Craggy mountain ranges punctuated by peaceful green valley's are just what you hope for when you come to Ireland. Unfortunately this idyllic beauty cuts both ways: This is extremely well trodden territory and up to a couple of million tourists flock here every year. With that in mind, the height of summer can be the worst time to visit—ideally you want to hit these hills in the late spring or autumn. The antidote for even the busiest times? Should you find that the crowded roads on the **Ring of Kerry** are getting to you, simply turn off onto a small country lane, and within seconds, you'll find yourself virtually alone in the peaceful Irish countryside.

ESSENTIALS

Arriving

BY BUS **Bus Éireann** (✆ **064/663-0011;** www.buseireann.ie) operates regularly scheduled service into Killarney and Dingle from all parts of Ireland.

BY TRAIN Trains from Dublin, Cork, and Galway arrive daily at the Killarney Railway Station (✆ **064/663-1067;** www.irishrail.ie), Railway Road, off East Avenue Road. Kenmare or Dingle do not have train stations.

BY CAR Unless you join an organized tour (see p. 264), a car is the only feasible way to get around the Ring of Kerry. Getting to Killarney from Cork is easy—just head northeast out of the city on N22; the distance is about 85km (53 miles). To get to Killarney from Dublin, take M7 southwest to Limerick and then N21; the journey is about 310km (193 miles). Kenmare and Killarney are connected by the main N71 Ring of Kerry Road; they're only 33km (20½ miles) apart, but allow plenty of time due to the winding nature of the road (and, in summer, tour bus traffic). To hire a car in Killarney try **Budget** on Kenmare Place (✆ **064/663-4341;** www.budget.ie) or **Enterprise** on Upper Park Road (✆ **066/711-9304;** www.enterprise.ie).

BY PLANE **Aer Lingus** (✆ **081/836-5000;** www.aerlingus.com) has two flights per day from Dublin into the miniscule Kerry County Airport, Farandole, Co. Kerry (✆ **066/976-4644;** www.kerryairport.ie), about 16km (10 miles) north of Killarney. Flights from London's Lupton Airport are operated by **Ryanair** (✆ **0871/246-0000** in the U.K. or 1520/444-004; www.ryanair.com).

PREVIOUS PAGE: **Rock climbing in Dingle.**

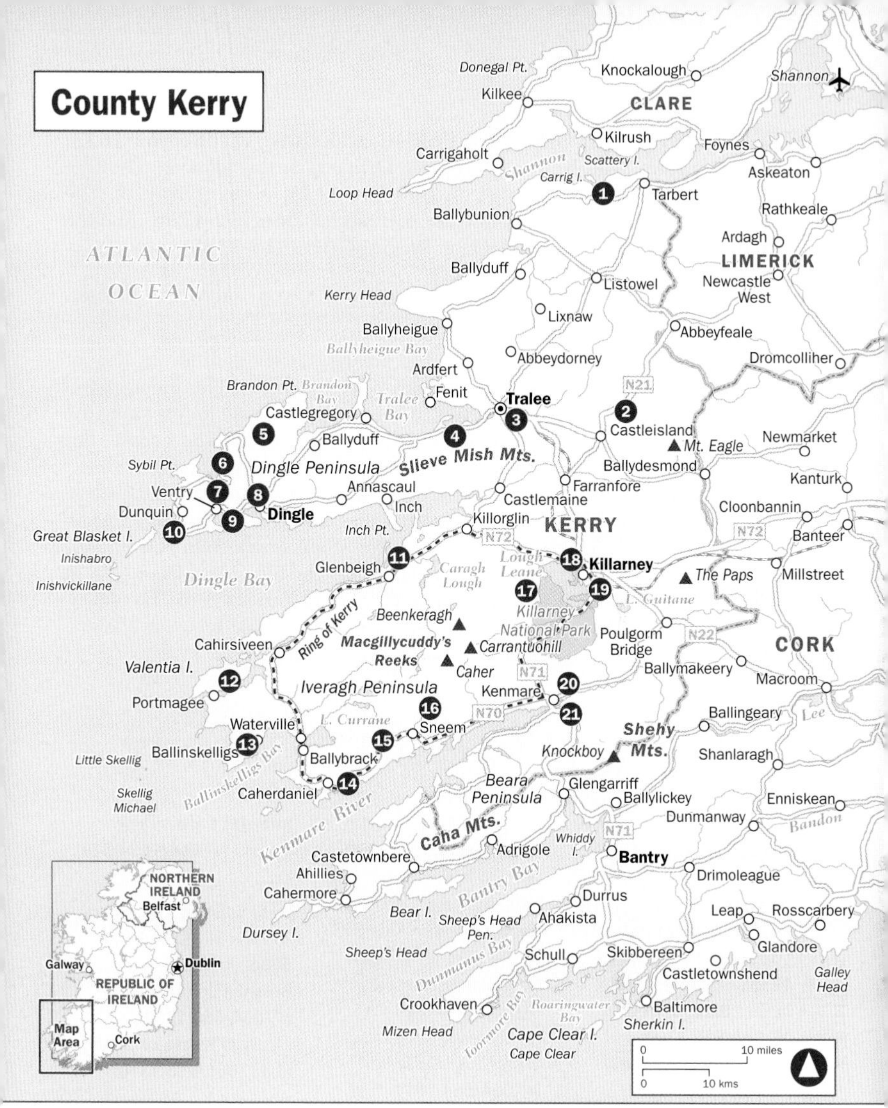

Ballinskelligs **13**
Blueberry Hill Farm **16**
Blennerville Windmill **4**
Carrigafoyle Castle **1**
Crag Cave **2**
Derrynane House National Historical Park **14**
Dingle Oceanworld Aquarium **8**
Eask Tower **9**
Fungie the Dingle Dolphin Cruise **8**
Gallarus Oratory **6**
Gap of Dunloe **17**
Ionad An Bhlascaoid Mhoir/The Blasket Centre **10**
Irish Famine Cottage **7**
Kenmare Druid Circle **21**
Kenmare Farmer's Market **21**
Kerry Bog Village Museum **11**
Kerry County Museum **3**
Knockreer Estate **18**
Muckross House, Gardens, and Farms **19**
Seafari Eco-nature Cruises **20**
The Seanchaí: Kerry Literary & Cultural Centre **5**
The Skellig Experience **12**
Staigue Fort **15**

Visitor Information

The **Killarney Tourist Office** is on Beech Road, Killarney (✆ **064/663-1633;** www.killarney.ie). The **Kenmare Tourist Office** is at the Kenmare Heritage Centre, Market Square, Kenmare (✆ **064/664-1233;** www.kenmare.ie). The **Tralee Tourist Office** is on Denny Street, Tralee (✆ **066/712-1288**).And the **Dingle Tourist Office** is on the Quay, Dingle (✆ **066/915-1188;** www.dingle-peninsula.ie). All stay open year-round.

Organized Tours

If you're not confident in hiring a car and driving yourself around the Ring of Kerry, a plethora of companies will take you to see the major sights on organized bus tours. Most depart from **Killarney,** the most popular base for exploring the Ring (see p. 273). Prices vary enormously according to what you choose, but expect to pay somewhere in the region of €20 to €40 per person.

Two recommended operators are **Corcoran's Chauffeur Tours,** 8 College St. (✆ **064/663-6666;** www.corcorantours.com); and **Doro's Tours,** 22 Main St. (✆ **064/663-1251** or 663-1567; www.derostours.com). Both run full-day tours of the Ring of Kerry, and tours to Dingle and the Slea Head Peninsula, in addition to a variety of tours centered around Killarney National Park. The downside, of course, is that you won't possibly have enough time to see everything properly.

[FastFACTS] COUNTY KERRY

ATMs/Banks In Killarney a branch of Allied Irish Banks (**AIB**) is at 25 Main St. (✆ **064/663-1047**). In Kenmare try **Bank of Ireland** in The Square (✆ **064/664-1255**). On Main St. in Dingle is a **Bank of Ireland** (✆ **066/915-1100**) and an **AIB** (✆ **066/915-1400**).

Dentists For dental emergencies, your hotel should contact a dentist for you; otherwise, in Killarney try the **Torch View Dental Surgery,** Park Rd., Killarney (✆ **066/662-6999**); in Kenmare, try **Con O'Leary,** The Square (✆ **064/664-2621**); in Dingle, try **Bryan Long,** Main St. Upper (✆ **066/915-1527**).

Doctors For medical emergencies dial ✆ **999.** For non-emergencies, your hotel should call you a doctor. Otherwise in Killarney try the Killarney Medical Centre at 47 New St. (✆ **064/662-0628**); in Kenmare, try The Medical Centre on Railway Rd. (✆ **064/664-1514**); and in Dingle, try the Dingle Medical Centre (✆ **066/915-2225**).

Emergencies For police, fire, or other emergencies, dial ✆ **999.**

Internet Access **O'Sheas** on Main St., Kenmare (✆ **064/664-0808**) has a small Internet cafe; in Dingle try **The Old Forge Internet Café** on Holyground (✆ **066/915-0523**).

Pharmacies In Killarney try **O'Sullivan's Pharmacy,** 81 New St. (✆ **064/663-5886**); in Kenmare try **Brosnan** on Henry St. (✆ **064/664-1318**); in Dingle try **O'Keefe** on Strand St. (✆ **066/915-1310**).

Post Office In Killarney the main post office is on New St. (✆ **064/663-1461**); in Kenmare it's on Henry St. (✆ **064/664-1490**); and in Dingle it's on Main St. (✆ **066/915-1661**).

Taxis In Killarney, taxis line up at the rank on **College Square** (✆ **064/663-1331**). You can also phone **Killarney Cabs**

(✆ **064/663-7444**), or **Kerry Autocabs** (✆ **087/296-3636**). In Kenmare, try the **Kenmare Taxi Service** (✆ **087/614-7222**). In Dingle, try **Dial-a-Cab** (✆ **087/222-2248**). In Tralee try **Tralee Radio Taxis** (✆ **066/712-5451**; www.traleeradiotaxis.com).

THE IVERAGH PENINSULA

Millions of tourists who come to County Kerry each year are dependent upon the turn of a bus driver's wheel for their tour of the Iveragh Peninsula—which means they see nothing save for the famed two-lane road known as the Ring of Kerry. There's certainly plenty to see there, but it's worth mentioning that the 178km (110-mile) road traces only the edges. In total, the peninsula is nearly 1,813 sq. km (700 sq. miles) of wild splendor, which you'll only see if you're able to get off the tourist strip. Admittedly, almost everyone who gets this far feels compelled to "do" the Ring of Kerry, so once it's done, why not take an unplanned turn, get a little lost, and let serendipity lead you to the county's unspoiled heart?

The **Ring of Kerry** is the name for the small highway that skirts the edges of the Iveragh Peninsula. It is both the actual name of the road—or, if you want to be pedantic, a section of the N70, N71, and N72 highways—and the collective name given to the many attractions in the area. Nearly all of County Kerry's most popular sights are either on or within a short distance of the Ring.

TAKING A (moon) SHINE TO POTCHEEN

"Keep your eyes well peeled today, the excise men are on their way, searching for the mountain tay, in the hills of Connemara . . ."

Potcheen is a potent form of Irish moonshine, traditionally brewed from grain or potatoes. It was banned by the English crown in 1661, an act that effectively criminalized thousands of distillers overnight. Unsurprisingly, that didn't stop people from making the stuff, and after 336 years on the wrong side of the law, potcheen was finally made legal again in 1997.

One 17th-century writer said of potcheen that "it enlighteneth ye heart, casts off melancholy, keeps back old age and breaketh ye wind." Its usefulness didn't stop there, evidently, as history records the drink being used as everything from a bath tonic to a substitute for dynamite.

Potcheen has long been used in fiction as a symbol of Irish nationalism, its contraband status rich with rebellious overtones. The traditional folk song "The Hills of Connemara" describes potcheen being secretly distributed under the noses of excise men.

In 2008, the European Union awarded the drink "Geographical Indicative" protection. This means that only the genuine Irish product is allowed to carry the name (the same status enjoyed by champagne and Parma ham).

You'll find potcheen for sale in a few souvenir stores. Like most liquors it can be drunk straight, on the rocks, or with a mixer, but at anything from 80 to a massive 180 proof, potcheen packs a mean punch, so enjoy . . . cautiously.

At the western end of the county, the less visited **Dingle Peninsula** also has much to offer. To call it "undiscovered" would be too generous—in the summer, Dingle Town is packed with travelers—but it's not as ruthlessly jammed as the Ring of Kerry. And from time to time, even in the high season, you can find yourself blissfully alone amid its natural beauty.

The Ring of Kerry

Undoubtedly Ireland's most popular scenic route, the Ring of Kerry winds its way along a panorama of rugged coastline, tall mountains, pristine lakes, and beautiful small towns and villages. What you won't find, at least in the summertime, is much in the way of peace. Bicyclists avoid the route because of the scores of tour buses thundering down it from early morning until late in the day. Most people traveling the route start and finish at its largest hub, **Killarney,** but the town of **Kenmare** makes for a more charming (and certainly more quiet) base. You can drive either way along the Ring of Kerry, but a counterclockwise route gives you the most spectacular views. Very large vehicles are always meant to travel this way to avoid accidents and nasty traffic jams around the Ring's perilously narrow bends.

Originally called Neidin (pronounced Nay-*deen,* meaning "little nest" in Irish), **Kenmare** is indeed a little nest of verdant foliage and colorful buildings nestled between the River Roughty and Kenmare Bay. It's an enchanting little place with flower boxes at every window, sparkling clean sidewalks, and lots of restaurants and plenty of places to stay.

From Kenmare to busy **Killarney,** the Ring road takes you through a scenic mountain stretch known as **Moll's Gap.** Killarney is best known for its glorious surroundings, in particular the spectacular landscapes of **Killarney National Park,** which includes the **Killarney Lakes** and the scenic **Gap of Dunloe.** The town itself, though, while colorful and bustling, is a victim of its own success. Tourism is more in-your-face here than perhaps anywhere else in Kerry, with generic leprechaun-laden souvenir shops and overpriced restaurants on every corner. So, to avoid becoming jaded, head out of town and get back on the road as quickly as possible. Along the way, you'll pass the lovely seaside town of **Portmagee,** which is connected by a bridge to leafy **Valentia Island.**

Departing Killarney, follow the signs for **Killorglin,** a smallish town that lights up in mid-August when it has a traditional horse, sheep, and cattle fair. It's officially called the **Puck Fair,** because local residents capture a wild goat (symbolizing the *puka* or *puki,* a mischievous sprite in Celtic legend) from the mountains and enthrone it in the center of town as a sign of unrestricted merrymaking. A whimsical statue of a goat is by the river in honor of this town's love of the *puka.*

Continue on the N70, and glimpses of Dingle Bay will soon appear on your right. **Carrantuohill,** Ireland's tallest mountain at 1,041m (3,414 ft.), is to your left, and bleak views of open bog land constantly come into view.

The Ring winds around cliffs and the edges of mountains, with nothing but the sea below—another reason you will probably average only 50kmph (31 mph), at best. As you go along, you'll notice the remnants of many stone cottages dotting the fields along the way. Most date from the mid-19th-century Great Famine, when millions of people starved to death or were forced to emigrate. This area was hard hit, and the peninsula alone lost three-quarters of its population.

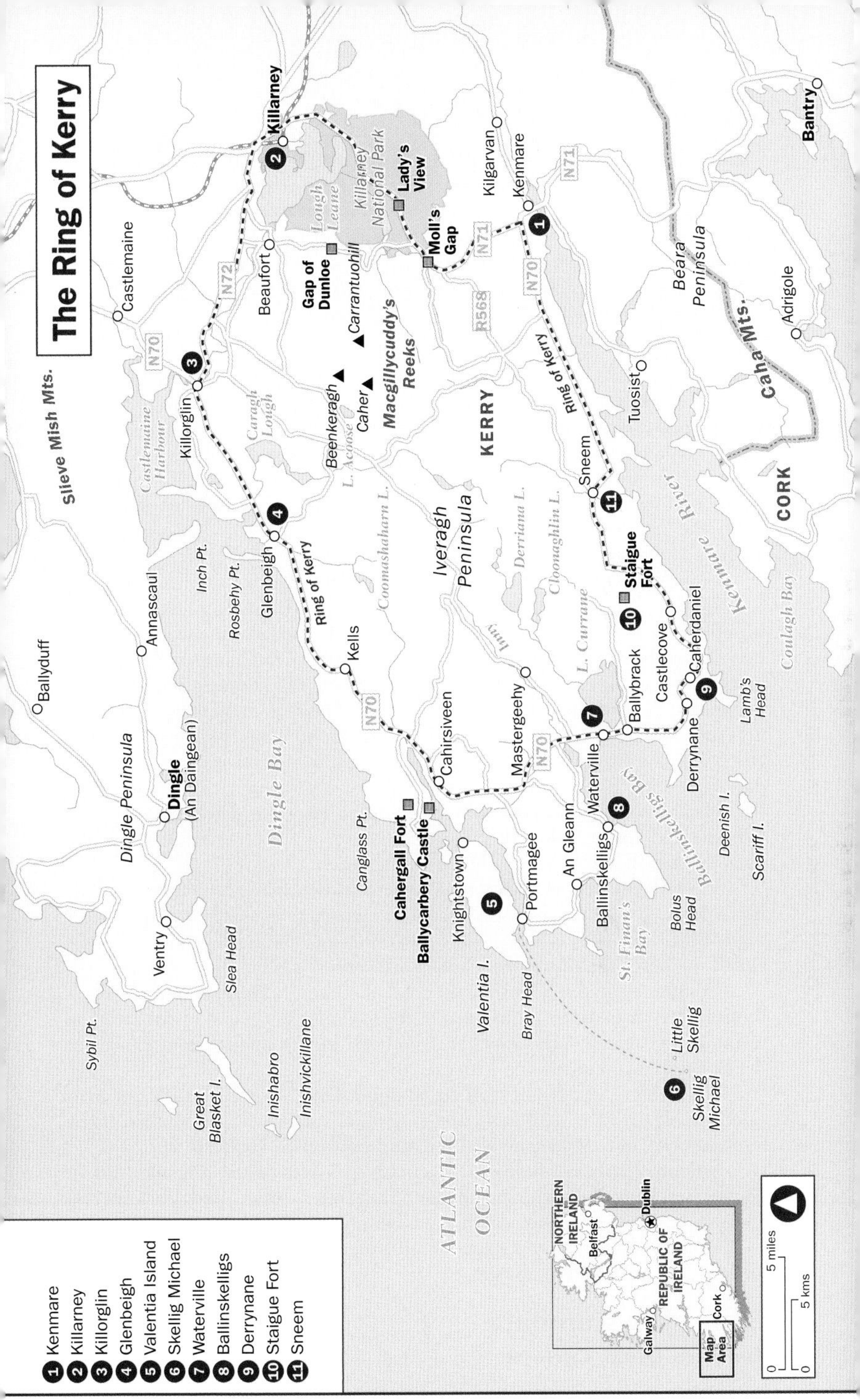

The Ring of Kerry
1 Kenmare
2 Killarney
3 Killorglin
4 Glenbeigh
5 Valentia Island
6 Skellig Michael
7 Waterville
8 Ballinskelligs
9 Derrynane
10 Staigue Fort
11 Sneem
Slieve Mish Mts.
Castlemaine
Castlemaine Harbour
Killorglin
Killarney
Lough Leane
Killarney National Park
Lady's View
Moll's Gap
Kilgarvan
Kenmare
Bantry
Beaufort
Gap of Dunloe
Carrantuohill
Macgillycuddy's Reeks
Beenkeragh
Caher
Caragh Lough
L. Acoose
KERRY
Ring of Kerry
N70
N71
N72
R568
Beara Peninsula
Caha Mts.
Adrigole
Tuosist
Sneem
CORK
Kenmare River
Coulagh Bay
Glenbeigh
Inch Pt.
Rosbehy Pt.
Coomasaharn L.
Iveragh Peninsula
Derriana L.
Cloonaghlin L.
Staigue Fort
L. Currane
Inny
Annascaul
Ballyduff
Dingle Peninsula
Dingle (An Daingean)
Dingle Bay
Kells
Cahirsiveen
Mastergeehy
Waterville
Ballybrack
Castlecove
Caherdaniel
Lamb's Head
Derrynane
Deenish I.
Scariff I.
Ballinskelligs Bay
Canglass Pt.
Cahergall Fort
Ballycarbery Castle
Knightstown
Portmagee
An Gleann
Ballinskelligs
St. Finan's Bay
Bolus Head
Ventry
Slea Head
Valentia I.
Bray Head
Little Skellig
Skellig Michael
Sybil Pt.
Great Blasket I.
Inishabro
Inishvickillane
ATLANTIC OCEAN
NORTHERN IRELAND
Belfast
Dublin
REPUBLIC OF IRELAND
Galway
Cork
Map Area
0 5 miles
0 5 kms

What's the Frequency Kerry?

In 1866, Valentia Island became the first place in Europe to have a permanent telegraph link with North America, via an undersea cable. A true feat of 19th-century engineering, the cable was used for precisely 100 years. You can still see the old receiving station (although it's just a shell) at the aptly named Telegraph Field, on the cliffs above Foilhomurrum Bay. A short distance away, a simple, black marble monument stands in muted commemoration of Ireland's role in bringing the world closer together.

Glenbeigh is next on the Ring, and it's a sweet little seafront town with streets lined with palm trees and a sandy beach. It makes a good spot for a break, or you could continue along the sea's edge to **Cahersiveen,** where you can zip across to the little island of **Valentia.** In the 18th century, the Valentia harbor was notorious as a refuge for smugglers and privateers; it's said that John Paul Jones, the Scottish-born American naval officer in the War of Independence, also anchored here quite often.

From Valentia you can hop a ferry to arguably the most magical site of the Ring of Kerry, an island just off its shore: **Skellig Michael,** a rocky pinnacle towering over the sea, where medieval monks built a monastery in exquisite isolation. Today, the ruins of their church, reached by way of rambling stone staircases up the sides of cliffs at the edge of the cobalt sea, still convey a sense of deep spirituality. Seabirds nest here in abundance, and more than 20,000 pairs of gannets inhabit neighboring **Little Skellig** during the summer nesting season. The crossing to the island can be rough, so you'll want to visit on as clear and calm a day as possible.

Head next for **Waterville,** an idyllic beach resort located between Lough Currane and Ballinskelligs Bay. For years it was a favorite retreat of Charlie Chaplin, and there's a statue of him near the beach.

If you follow the sea road north of town to the Irish-speaking village of **Ballinskelligs,** you'll see where the medieval monastery is slowly rotting away. A sandy Blue Flag beach is just past the post office by Ballinskelligs Bay, and at the end of the beach are the remnants of a 16th-century castle.

Continuing on the N70, the next point of interest is **Derrynane,** at **Caherdaniel.** Derrynane is the former seat of the O'Connell clan and erstwhile home to Daniel O'Connell ("the Liberator" who freed Irish Catholics from the last of the English Penal Laws in the 19th century).

From there, watch for signs to **Staigue Fort** (see p. 290), about 3km (2 miles) off the main road in a farmer's field. Historians are still unsure of the fort's purpose, but we do know that it dates from around 1000 B.C.

Sneem, the next village on the circuit, is a colorful little hamlet, where houses are painted in vibrant shades. The colors—blue, pink, yellow, and orange—burst out on a rainy day, like a little touch of the Mediterranean.

From here, you're no distance at all from your starting point, and you've made your way around the Ring.

Exploring Kenmare

Kenmare Druid Circle ★ On a small hill near the market square (see below), this large Bronze Age druid stone circle is magnificently intact, featuring

ALL'S fair IN KENMARE ON AUGUST 15TH

One day of the year Kenmare is no less overrun with visitors than Killarney: August 15, **Fair Day.** This is a working agricultural market, and the streets are taken over by farmers selling all manner of livestock, while a small army of onlookers descends on the town to witness the picturesque congregation. Stalls and other amusements provide fresh food, souvenirs, and even fortune telling.

15 standing stones arranged around a central boulder that still bears signs (circular holes, a shallow dent at the center) of having been used in ceremonies. To find it, walk down to the market square and follow signs on the left side of the road. There's no visitor center, and no admission fee; it's just sitting in a small paddock, passed by the traffic of everyday life.

Off the Square, Kenmare, Co. Kerry.

Kenmare Farmer's Market ★ If you're visiting midweek, be sure to check out this small but lively open air market held every Wednesday in Kenmare's main square. The emphasis is on food produce from small, artisan producers from across the region and beyond. You'll also find rustic crafts. Traders can come here from quite far afield to sell their wares, although the bulk of what's on offer is locally sourced. It's a fun and lively market to browse your way through.

The Square. Kenmare, Co. Kerry. Wed 10am–5pm. Some stalls may close in bad weather.

Seafari ★★ This is a good option for families who want to interest their kids in Kenmare Bay—aboard a 15m (49-ft.) covered boat. The 2-hour cruise covers 16km (10 miles) and features guides well versed in local history and wildlife such as dolphins, sea otters, and gray seals frolicking nearby. Boats depart from the pier next to the Kenmare suspension bridge. The family ticket includes coffee, tea, cookies, a lollipop for the kids, and a drink of rum for the grown-ups. They'll also lend you a pair of binoculars if you need one. Live entertainment sometimes follows you on board, from kid-friendly puppet shows to traditional Irish music. Reservations are recommended.

3 The Pier, Kenmare, Co. Kerry. ✆ **064/664-2059.** www.seafariireland.com. Tour €20 adults; €17.50 students; €15 teenagers; €12.50 children 11 and under then €7.50 per extra child; €60 families. Apr–Oct, 2 sailings daily; call or check website for departure times.

Sports & Outdoor Pursuits

ADVENTURE SPORTS Eclipse Ireland, Blackwater Bridge, Kenmare (✆ **064/668-2965;** www.eclipseireland.com), offers a host of high-thrills activities and outdoor fun, including kayaking, archery, raft building, mud surfing, and trekking. Their list of activities doesn't stop at the high-energy kind, however; to exercise your soul as well as your body, you can opt for a session of laughter yoga. See the website for the full list.

CYCLING Bicycles can be hired from **Finnegan's Corner** at 37 Henry St., Kenmare (✆ **064/664-1083;** www.finneganscornerkenmare.com) or from the **Eclipse Ireland,** Blackwater Bridge, Kenmare (✆ **064/668-2965;** www.eclipseireland.com). Rates are around €20 per day.

SOS: GPS

You can drive either way along the Ring of Kerry, but we recommend a **counter-clockwise** route for the most spectacular views. Drivers of very large vehicles also stick to this direction in order to avoid bottlenecks on the perilously narrow bends. This all worked fine for years—until modern technology intervened with the spread of GPS technology. Now some drivers unfamiliar with the route are sent in a clockwise direction, thus causing all sorts of chaos, including some of the worst traffic jams ever seen on the Ring. These problems don't happen every day, but nonetheless, proceed with caution, and perhaps plan on taking a different route if you absolutely have to get somewhere on time.

GOLF The **Kenmare Golf Club,** Kenmare (✆ **064/664-1291;** www.kenmaregolfclub.com), is a parkland par-71 course where greens fees run €30 weekdays, €35 weekends.

HORSEBACK RIDING In addition to the activities listed above, **Eclipse Ireland** (✆ **064/668-2965;** www.eclipseireland.com) also offers various horseriding options. As a guide to prices, an hour's trekking costs €30; 2 hours €55.

WALKING The low, long-distance path, the **Kerry Way,** traverses the extraordinary scenery of the Ring of Kerry. The first stage, from Killarney National Park to Glenbeigh, travels inland over rolling hills and past pastoral scenes. The second stage circles the Iveragh Peninsula via the towns of Cahersiveen, Waterville, Caherdaniel, Sneem, and Kenmare with a farther inland walk along the old Kenmare Road back to Killarney, for a total of 202km (125 miles). For more information see **www.kerryway.net**.

Where to Stay in Kenmare

Though Killarney is the obvious hub of the area, if you have the freedom of a car, consider nearby Kenmare as an alternative base. It's quieter and just as convenient for exploring the Ring of Kerry.

Sallyport House ★★ This peaceful 1930s mansion-turned-B&B in Kenmare is an extremely good value for the money. It's filled to the brim with interesting antiques, lending a touch of old school luxury to its already traditional charms. (Thanks to a wealthy industrialist ancestor, there's a story behind the presence of most of them.) Guestrooms are comfortable and spacious. A few rooms have intricately carved antique four-poster beds. The house is surrounded by beautiful countryside, and some rooms look out over an idyllic lake. Breakfasts are delicious, and the service is warm and accommodating without ever being intrusive.

Shelbourne St., Kenmare (just south of junction with Pier Rd.), Co. Kerry. ✆ **064/664-2066.** www.sallyporthouse.com. 5 units. €110–€130 double. Free parking. Breakfast included. **Amenities:** Wi-Fi (free).

Sea Shore Farm ★★ A modern house overlooking Kenmare Bay and the mountains beyond, this is a special place to stay. Big, floor-to-ceiling windows take full advantage of the magnificent surroundings. The guestrooms are large (very large in some cases) and tastefully furnished. The guest lounge has a library of travel books, though you may find yourself too distracted by the views to concentrate. Kenmare is a short drive away or just a captivating, 15-minute walk through the countryside—the better to work off those indulgent breakfasts. Hosts Mary and Owen make everything run smoothly and are always full of helpful suggestions for things to do. They have an encyclopedic knowledge of the local area.

Sea Shore, Tubrid, Kenmare, Co. Kerry. ✆ **064/664-1270.** www.seashorekenmare.com. 5 units. €110–€150 double. Free parking. Breakfast included. **Amenities:** Wi-Fi (free).

Shelburne Lodge ★★ This cozy 18th-century house has quite a storied history. It was originally the country home of William Petty, the Lord Shelburne (1737–1805), a Dublin-born landowner who was responsible for building much of the modern town of Kenmare. He later became Prime Minister of Great Britain and Ireland, and he signed the Treaty of Paris that formally ended the American War of Independence in 1783 and brought peace between Britain and the U.S. His home is in good hands nowadays, thanks to the wonderful hosts Tom and Maura Foley. Rooms have an old-fashioned air with color schemes of yellow and peach, antique furniture, and huge beds. Public areas have a similar feel, like the guest sitting room, so packed with handsome furniture that it's like walking through an antique shop. A lovely, manicured lawn is out back, and the center of Kenmare is only a short walk away.

Cork Rd., Kenmare, Co. Kerry. ✆ **064/664-1013.** www.shelburnelodge.com. 9 units. €100–€160 double. Free parking. Breakfast included. **Amenities:** Wi-Fi (free).

Where to Dine in Kenmare

Though relatively light on standout, first-class restaurants, Kerry has a wide variety of options—including great pubs and family-friendly eateries. Kenmare and Killarney take the lion's share of the best places, but the countryside has some enticing surprises.

The Boathouse ★ BISTRO/SEAFOOD This pleasant seafood bistro at Dromquinna Manor has an outside seating area overlooking Kenmare Bay. The menu serves dishes like creamy seafood chowder or local crab claws served with ginger, lime, and coriander butter. Or you could just have a cheeseburger served with sea-salted French fries and take in the wonderful view. This is a good stop for lunch on a sunny day, especially when the weather's fine and you can sit outside.

On N70, 5km (3 miles) west of Kenmare, Co. Kerry. ✆ **064/664-2888.** www.dromquinnamanor.com. Main courses €11–€25. May, June, Sept Tues–Sun 12:30–9pm; July–Aug daily 12:30–9pm; Oct Thurs–Sun 12:30–9pm.

The Lime Tree ★★★ MODERN IRISH This outstanding restaurant housed in a historic building has been one of the area's go-to fine dining establishments since 1985. The modern Irish menu is sophisticated without being overly complicated. You'll find plenty of locally sourced ingredients and plates such as rack of Kerry lamb served with a mini shepherd's pie (a traditional dish made with minced lamb and mashed potatoes) and garlic confit. The free range duck breast is accompanied by a zingy rhubarb and ginger chutney. Desserts are like upscale comfort food: a rich terrine of white and dark chocolate with black currant sorbet or a classic crème brulee. The wine list is unsurprisingly excellent, but surprisingly filled with plenty of very affordable choices. Shelbourne St., Kenmare, Co. Kerry. ✆ **064/664-1225.** www.limetreerestaurant.com. Main courses €19–€27. Daily 6:30–9:30pm.

Ocean Blue Seafood Bar ★★ FISH & CHIPS Not all the best food comes in gourmet style. This fish and chip shop in Kenmare is one of the best fast food restaurants in the region. There's nothing fancy, but that's the point; it's all about perfectly made, crispy fish and chips. Choose from fresh wild cod, plaice, hake, or whiting, all battered and served with chunky chips (thick fries). A couple of more unusual options include tempura battered crab claws and a small menu of Chinese dishes, but it's the classics that keep the locals coming back.

Main St., Kenmare, Co. Kerry. ✆ **085/139-6121.** Main courses €7–€18. Daily noon–around 11pm.

Packie's ★★ IRISH One of the best and most durable restaurants in Kenmare, Packie's has been a favorite in this town for years. The candlelit dining room is atmospheric, and the crowd is as much local as visitors. And it's easy to understand why—the food is unpretentious but delicious using a bounty of local ingredients. You might choose to sample steak, lamb, or perhaps super-fresh seafood, all simply prepared but melt-in-your-mouth tasty. Desserts are worth adding an extra notch to your belt for. The reasonably priced wine list does the job and offers plenty of choices available by the glass.

Henry St., Kenmare, Co. Kerry. ✆ **064/664-1508.** www.kenmarerestaurants.com/packies. Main courses €16–€30. Tues–Sat 6–10pm. Closed Feb.

Purple Heather ★ IRISH This sweet little place in Kenmare is simple and cozy. Its popularity with locals speaks to its authenticity. You can sit with a leisurely pint at the bar in front, but at lunchtime, venture toward the back to sample the menu of tasty snacks. Think salads, hearty sandwiches, fluffy omelets, homemade soups, and bowls of chowder. It's nothing complicated, but it's all well done, with a cordial, unpretentious atmosphere to boot.

Henry St., Kenmare, Co. Kerry. ✆ **064/664-1016.** www.thepurpleheatherkenmare.com. Main courses €7–€18. Mon–Sat 11am–5:30pm. Closed bank holidays.

Shopping

The Ring of Kerry has many good craft and souvenir shops, but those in and around Kenmare offer some of the best choices in terms of quality. Kenmare shops are open year-round, usually Monday to Saturday 9am to 6pm. From May to September, many shops remain open until 9 or 10pm, and some open on Sunday from noon to 5 or 6pm.

Avoca at Moll's Gap ★★★ Creative, colorful, and with what must be one of the world's best appointed parking lots, this branch of Avoca is on a mountain pass just off the main Ring of Kerry Road, north of Kenmare. Though quite small, it sells a good selection of the crafts, knitwear, and upscale knick-knacks for which the Wicklow-based company is famous. The café upstairs is also a great pitstop for a light lunch or restorative cup of tea and slice of cake. Molls Gap (on R568, signposted from main N71 (Ring of Kerry Rd.), Kenmare, Co. Kerry. ✆ **064/663-4720.** www.avoca.ie. Mon–Fri 9:30am–6pm; Sat–Sun 10am–6pm. Café closes 5pm.

De Barra Jewellery ★★★ Young jewelry designer Shane de Barra runs this exquisite little boutique in the center of Kenmare. His creations in gold and other precious materials have a unique, subtle beauty. He has an especially deft touch with freshwater pearls that he forms into lovely necklaces strung together with tiny threads of gold. Prices aren't too high, considering the quality. A true original. Main St., Kenmare, Co. Kerry. ✆ **064/664-1867.**

Quills Woollen Market ★ This long-standing business is housed in a delightfully multicolored row of shops in the center of Kenmare. They specialize in traditional Irish knitwear—particularly heavy knit Aran sweaters, coats, and cardigans. They also sell Irish tweeds, shawls, linens, and various pieces of home goods like plush sheepskin rugs. It's a great place to stock up on authentic souvenirs. Other branches of Quills are in Killarney, Glengarriff, Ballingeary, and Sneem. Main St., Kenmare, Co. Kerry. ✆ **064/664-1078.** www.irishgiftsandsweaters.com.

Killarney

Perhaps the busiest tourist hub in rural Ireland, Killarney's sidewalks are spacious enough in the winter, but in the summertime, they're absolutely packed, as the streets become one giant tour bus traffic jam and horse-and-buggy drivers risk life and limb to push their way through. The locals are well practiced at dispensing a professional brand of Irish charm, even as they hike up the hotel and restaurant prices to capitalize on the hordes descending from the buses. It all feels a bit cynical, with a few too many cheesy leprechaun-themed gift shops for its own good. It's a bit much for some people, and hardly the bucolic, gentle Ireland that many are looking for. Luckily, it's easy enough to resist Killarney's gravitational pull and spend your time exploring the quieter countryside around it. You can always sneak into town from time to time for dinner or a night out in the pub with lots of people from your homeland.

Ironically, Killarney's popularity has little to do with the town itself; the attraction is the valley in which it nestles—a verdant landscape of lakes and mountains so spectacular that author and playwright Brendan Behan once said, "Even an ad man would be ashamed to eulogize it." Exploring its glories is certainly easy—just walk (or drive) from the town parking lot toward the cathedral and turn left. In a matter of minutes, you'll forget all that Killarney stress amid the quiet rural splendor of the 65-sq.-km (25-sq.-mile) **Killarney National Park.**

TOWN LAYOUT

Killarney is small, with a full-time population of about 7,000. The town is built around one central thoroughfare, Main Street, which, mercurially, changes its name to High Street at midpoint. The principal offshoots of Main Street are Plunkett Street, which becomes College Street, and New Street. The Deenagh River edges the western side of town and East Avenue Road edges the eastern side.

The busiest section of town is at the southern tip of Main Street, where it meets East Avenue Road. Here the road curves and heads southward out to the Muckross road and the entrance to Killarney National Park.

Killarney town is so small and compact that there is no local bus service; the best way to get around is on foot. For a quick and easy tour, follow the signposted

Tourist Trail for the highlights of the main streets. It takes less than 2 hours to complete. Pick up a booklet outlining the sights along the trail at the tourist office.

EXPLORING KILLARNEY

Gap of Dunloe ★★ A narrow pass between the Purple Mountains and the MacGillycuddy's Reeks, the winding Gap of Dunloe rises through mountains and wetlands on the western side of Killarney National Park. The route through the gap passes craggy hills, meandering streams, and deep gullies, and it ends in the park at the Upper Lake. Some of the roads can be difficult around here, so many people choose to explore by bicycle (try **Killarney Rent-a-Bike,** Lower New Street, Killarney (✆ **064/663-1282;** www.killarneyrentabike.com) or by "jarvey" (see p. 276). These can be booked at the National Park Visitor Centre at Muckross House (see p. 276) or from **Killarney Jaunting Cars,** Muckross Close (✆ **064/663-3358;** www.killarneyjauntingcars.ie).

Signposted from N72 (Ring of Kerry Rd.), Killarney, Co. Kerry.

Innisfallen ★★ Shrouded in forest, this small island appears to float peacefully on the Lower Lake. Behind the trees is what's left of a 7th-century monastery that flourished for 1,000 years. It's thought that Brian Boru, the great Irish chieftain, and St. Brendan the Navigator received their education here. From 950 to 1320, the "Annals of Innisfallen," a chronicle of early Irish history,

Gap of Dunloe reflected in Auger Lake, Killarney.

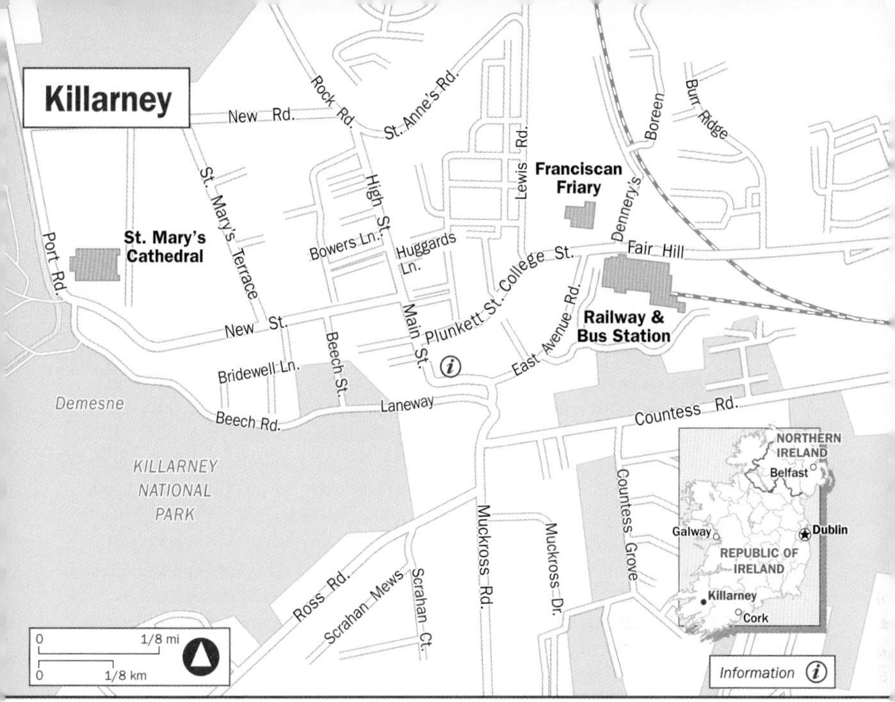

was written at the monastery. You can reach Innisfallen by rowboat, available for rental at Ross Castle (see p. 278).

Lower Lake, opposite Ross Castle, Ross Rd., (signposted from N71, Ring of Kerry Rd.), Killarney, Co. Kerry.

Killarney Lakes Cruise ★ From the harbor at Ross Castle (see p. 278), the **MV Pride of the Lake** takes you on an hour-long waterborne tour. The covered boat ride is a little on the touristy side—and very popular, so you might want to make reservations—but the views of the park from the lake are gorgeous. You can also take a tour that combines a lake cruise with a "jaunting car" ride around the park. ***Note:*** You can get to the pier by Ross Castle on a free shuttle bus from Killarney town center. It leaves Scotts Street (by the junction with East Avenue Road) a quarter of an hour before each sailing.

The Pier, Ross Castle, Ross Rd., off N71 (Ring of Kerry Rd.), Killarney, Co. Kerry. ✆ **064/662-7737.** www.killarneylaketours.ie. Tickets €13 adults; €7 children 11 and under. Apr–Oct sailings 11am, 12:30, 2:30, 4, 5:15pm. Times may change according to weather.

What's in a Name: MacGillycuddy's Reeks

This marvelously named range of mountains just west of Killarney is beautiful to look at—they were formed by red sandstone that was gradually shaved down by glaciers until they reached the gentle shape they hold today. The name, though, is a bit baffling. It turns out the mountains were named after an ancient clan that once predominated in this area—the Mac Gilla Machudas. The word "reek" is an old Irish term for a peaked hill. So these are the mountains of the Mac Gilla Machudas, just in case you were wondering.

killarney NATIONAL PARK

A bucolic refuge with breathtaking scenery just steps from the fracas of Killarney, this national park is the most essential stop along the Ring. If peace and quiet is what you seek, you could skip the Ring altogether and spend the whole day here. Cars are banned from most of the ferny trails, so take a hike or hire a **"jarvey,"** or "jaunting car"—an old-fashioned horse-and-buggy available at not-too-steep prices. The drivers congregate behind the visitor center at Muckross House (see below).

Within the park's limits are two estates, **Muckross** and **Knockreer** (see below), along with the romantic remains of medieval abbeys and castles. At almost every turn, you'll see Killarney's own botanical wonder, the arbutus, or "strawberry tree," plus eucalyptus, redwoods, and native oak.

For many, the main attractions are the park's three lakes. The largest of these, the **Lower Lake,** is sometimes called Lough Leane or Lough Lein, translated as "the lake of learning". It's more than 6km (3¾ miles) long and is dotted with 30 small islands. The most celebrated of Killarney's islands, **Innisfallen** (see p. 274), seems to float peacefully in the Lower Lake. Nearby are the Middle Lake or Muckross Lake, and the smallest of the three, the Upper Lake.

The main visitor center for the park is at **Muckross House** (✆ **064/663-1440**) and is clearly signposted from the main Ring of Kerry Road (N71), a couple of miles south of Killarney. Drop by here to pick up maps and other information about the park to explore the many walking trails (see p. 278). The visitor center is open daily from 9am to 5:30pm; hours may vary in winter.

For more information on the park visit **www.killarneynationalpark.ie**.

Knockreer Estate ★ The grand old house that once stood here burned down in the early 20th century. A modern building of the same name on the same site serves as the park's education center, but the estate's lovely old gardens still exist. Here 200-year-old trees mix with sweet wildflowers and azaleas to fragrant effect. A signposted walk takes you past beautiful views of the Lower Lake and the valley; a pathway leads down to the River Deenagh. Main access to Knockreer is through Deenagh Lodge Gate, opposite the cathedral.

Main entrance near St. Mary's Cathedral on Cathedral Place, off New St., Killarney, Co. Kerry. Free admission.

Muckross House & Gardens ★★ This elegant, Neo-Gothic Victorian house at the entrance to Killarney National Park was built in 1843. The rooms are presented much as they would have been in the mid-19th century, from the grand, *Downton Abbey*–like formal dining room to the stark contrast of the Victorian kitchens and servants' quarters below the stairs. The landscaped gardens are beautiful and a riot of color in high summer. The pleasant cafe, overlooking some manicured flowerbeds, is a lovely spot to linger. A traditional weavers' and craft shop is also on the grounds along with the ruin of the 15th-century **Muckross Abbey,** founded about 1448 and burned by Cromwell's troops in 1652, near the house. The abbey's central feature is a vaulted cloister around a courtyard that contains a huge yew tree, thought to be as old as the abbey itself. William Makepeace Thackeray once called it "the prettiest little bijou of a ruined abbey ever seen."

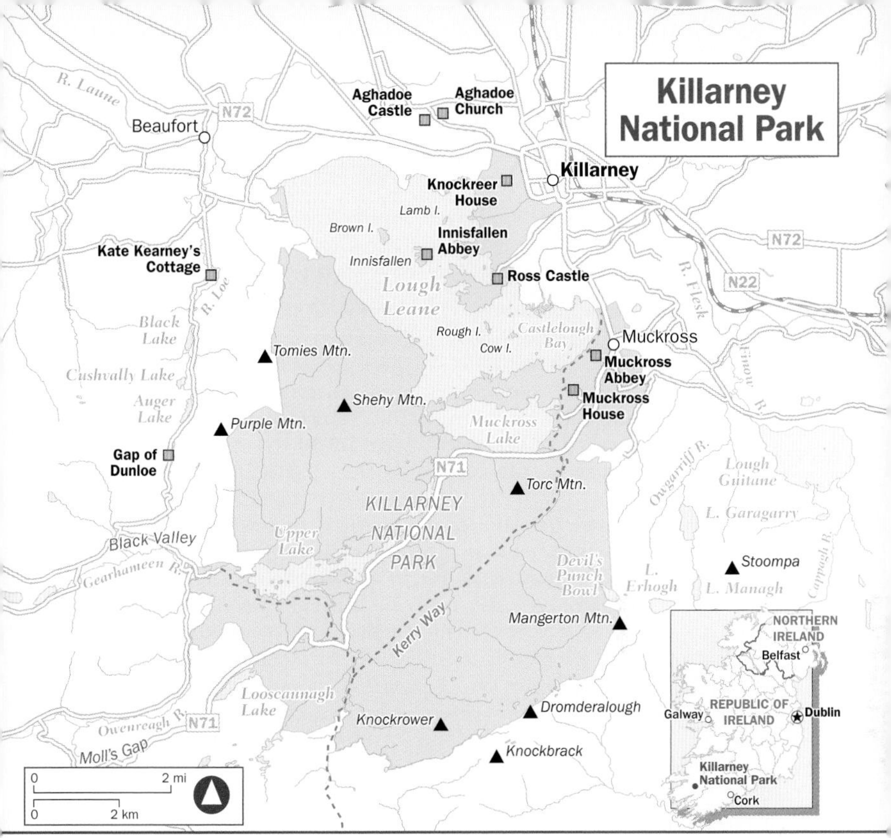

On N71 (Ring of Kerry Rd.), 6km (3¾ miles) south of Killarney, Co. Kerry. ✆ **064/667-0144.** www.muckross-house.ie. Admission €7.50 adults; €6 seniors; €4 students and children; €22 families. Joint ticket with Muckross Traditional Farms: €12.50 adults; €10.50 seniors; €7 students and children; €35 families. Sept–June daily 9am–5:30pm; July–Aug daily 9am–7pm.

Muckross Traditional Farms ★★ Not far from the Muckross House estate, these farms are designed to demonstrate a real feel for traditional life as it was in previous centuries in County Kerry. It's cleverly done—the farmhouses and barns are so authentically detailed that you feel as if you've dropped in on the real deal. Work really does go on here: Farmhands work the fields, while the blacksmith, carpenter, and wheelwright ply their trades. Women draw water from the wells and cook meals in historically accurate kitchens. There's also a petting zoo, where kids can get to handle some of the animals. A coach constantly circles the grounds, ferrying those with mobility problems between the different areas of the farm. ***Note:*** A combination ticket allows you to visit Muckross House and Gardens for a small extra fee.

Kenmare Rd. (N71), Killarney, Co. Kerry. ✆ **064/663-0804.** www.muckross-house.ie. Admission €7.50 adults; €6 seniors; €4 students and children; €22 families. Join ticket with Muckross House and Gardens: €12.50 adults; €10.50 seniors; €7 students and children; €35 families. Mar–Apr, Oct weekends and bank holidays 1–6pm; May, Sept daily 1–6pm; June–Aug daily 10am–6pm. Closed Nov–Apr.

walk this way: THE TRAILS OF KILLARNEY NATIONAL PARK

Cars are banned on most of Killarney National Park's walking trails, where the ground is a soft carpet of moss and the air is fragrant with wildflowers. Here are some of the best walking trails. Trail maps are available at the Muckross House visitor center.

Blue Pool Nature Trail: Starting behind the Muckross Park Hotel, this trail winds for a relaxing 2.3km (1½ miles) through coniferous woodland beside a small lake. The trail is named for the lake's unusually deep blue-green color, a result of copper deposits in the soil.

Cloghereen Nature Trail: Incorporated into a small section of the Blue Pool trail (see above), this walk is fully accessible to blind visitors. A guide rope leads you along the route, lined by plants identifiable by scent and touch. An audio guide is available from the Muckross House visitor center for a small deposit.

Mossy Woods Nature Trail: One of the park's gentler trails, this route starts from Muckross Lake and runs just under 2km (1¼ miles). The moss-covered trees and rocks it passes are a major habitat for bird life. You'll also see several strawberry trees *(Arbutus)*, something of a botanical mystery, along the route. They're commonplace around these parts but found almost nowhere else in Northern Europe. The route offers some incredible views of the Torc Mountains and the MacGillycuddy's Reeks.

Serious hikers might be interested in the **Kerry Way,** a long-distance trail that roughly follows the Ring of Kerry. Ireland's longest marked hiking trail, the 202km (126-mile) route follows several "green roads" (old, unused roads built as famine relief projects and now converted into walking paths). Maps outlining the route are available from the Killarney and Kenmare tourist offices. For more information see **www.kerryway.com**.

Ross Castle ★ Just outside Killarney Town, this 15th-century fortress still guards the edge of the Lower Lake. Built by the O'Donoghue chieftains, the castle was the last stronghold in Munster to surrender to Cromwell's forces in 1652. But it could not withstand time as well as the English army, and all that remains today is a tower house surrounded by a fortified *bawn* (walled garden) with rounded turrets. The tower has been furnished in the style of the late 16th and early 17th centuries. While you can wander the grounds at will, you can only see inside the castle on a guided tour. The tours tend to be a bit tedious, as the guides seem to scrounge around a bit for facts interesting enough to justify the ticket price. In good weather, the best way to reach it is via a lakeside walk (it's 3km/2 miles from Killarney to the castle). From the castle, you can take boat tours of the lake (see p. 275).

Ross Rd., signposted from N71 (Ring of Kerry Rd.), Killarney, Co. Kerry. ✆ **064/663-5851.** www.heritageireland.ie. Admission €4 adults; €3 seniors; €2 students and children; €10 families. Mid-Mar–Oct daily 9:30am–5:45pm. Last admission 45 min. before closing. No photography.

St. Mary's Cathedral ★ If you think this limestone cathedral looks more Castle Dracula than parish church, it may be because New Street was once the home of Bram Stoker. He spent summers in Killarney while he was a student at Trinity College. Officially known as the Catholic Church of St. Mary of the Assumption, it's designed in the Gothic Revival style and laid out in the shape of a cross. Construction began in 1842, was interrupted by the famine, and finally concluded in 1855 (although the towering spire wasn't added until 1912).

Cathedral Place, off New St., Killarney, Co. Kerry. ✆ **064/663-1014.** Free admission. Daily 10:30am–6pm.

Torc Mountain Walk ★★ Rising steeply from the south shore of Muckross Lake, Torc Mountain provides spectacular views of the Killarney Lakes and nearby, moody MacGillycuddy's Reeks mountain range. Start at the Torc Waterfall parking lot, about 6km (3¾ miles) south of Killarney, and follow the trail to the top of the falls. At a T-intersection, turn left toward the top parking lot, then almost immediately turn right onto Old Kenmare Road following a small stream along the south slopes of Torc Mountain. After leaving the woods, you will see Torc Mountain on your right. Look for a crescent-shaped gouge in the side of the road, about 9m (30 ft.) across, with a small cairn at its far edge. This is the beginning of the path to the ridge top, marked somewhat erratically by cairns along the way. Return the way you came; the whole moderately difficult trip is just under 10km (6 miles) and takes about 4 hours.

In Killarney National Park, Killarney, Co. Kerry. Start at Torc Waterfall parking lot, about 6km (3¾ miles) south of Killarney on N71 (Ring of Kerry Rd.). Also accessible on 4.5km (3 mile) looped walking trail from Muckross House.

SPORTS & OUTDOOR PURSUITS

Spectator Sports

GAELIC GAMES The people of Killarney are passionately devoted to the national sports of hurling and Gaelic football, and games are played almost every Sunday afternoon during the summer at **Fitzgerald Stadium,** Lewis Road (✆ **064/663-1700;** www.gaa.ie). For complete details, consult the local *Kerryman* newspaper or the Killarney Tourist Office.

HORSE RACING Killarney has two annual horse racing meets, in early May and mid-July. Each event lasts for 3 or 4 days and draws large crowds. For more information, contact the **Killarney Racecourse,** Fossa (✆ **064/663-1125;** www.killarneyraces.ie), or the tourist office.

Outdoor Pursuits

CYCLING **Killarney National Park,** with its lakeside and forest pathways, trails, and roads, is a paradise for bikers. If you haven't brought your own wheels, you can rent whatever you need here, from 21-speed touring bikes to mountain bikes to tandems. Rental charges average around €15 to €20 per day, €80 per week. Bicycles can be rented from **David O'Sullivan's Cycles,** Beech Road, Killarney (✆ **064/663-1282;** www.killarneyrentabike.com). Another Killarney-based rental store is **Lyne's Rent-a-Bike,** Muckross Road (✆**087/122-1277;** www.rentabikekillarney.com).

One great ride beginning in Killarney takes you through the Gap of Dunloe along a dirt forest road, where you'll see some of the best mountain scenery in the area. It can be made into a 56km (35-mile) loop if you return on N71. Ask at the bike rental store or the tourism office for more information.

FISHING Fishing for salmon and brown trout in Killarney's unpolluted lakes and rivers is a popular pastime around here. Brown trout fishing is free on the lakes, but a permit is necessary for the rivers Flesk and Laune. Salmon fishing anywhere requires a permit.

Permits, tackle, bait, rod rental, and other fishing gear can be obtained from **O'Neill's,** 6 Plunkett St. (✆ **064/663-1970**). The shop also arranges the hire of boats and *ghillies* (fishing guides) for around €50 to €100 per day on the Killarney Lakes, leaving from Ross Castle.

GOLF Visitors are always welcome at the twin 18-hole championship courses of the **Killarney Golf & Fishing Club,** Killorglin Road, Fossa (✆ **064/663-1034;** www.killarney-golf.com), 5km (3 miles) west of the town center. Widely praised as one of the most scenic golf settings in the world, these courses, known as Killeen and Mahony's Point, have gorgeous lake and mountain settings. Greens fees are €40 to €100, depending on the course and the time of day.

HORSEBACK RIDING Many trails in the Killarney area are suitable for horseback riding. Hiring a horse costs about €35 per hour at **Killarney Riding Stables,** N72, Ballydowney (✆ **064/663-1686;** www.killarney-trail-riding.com), and **Rocklands Stables,** Rockfield, Tralee Road (✆ **064/663-2592**). Lessons and weeklong trail rides can also be arranged.

WALKING Several signposted nature trails are in the **Killarney National Park.** The **Mossy Woods Nature Trail** starts near Muckross House, by Muckross Lake, and rambles 2.4km (1½ miles) through yew woods along low cliffs. The **Blue Pool Nature Trail** (2.4km/1½ miles) travels from Muckross village through woodlands and past a small peaceful lake known as the Blue Pool. Maps of the four trails are available at the park's visitor center. In addition, the **Cloghereen Nature Trail** is a small section of the Blue Pool trail that's designed to be fully accessible to blind visitors. For more on these trails, see "Walk This Way" on p. 278.

Other trails within the park include the **Old Boat House Nature Trail,** which begins at the 19th-century boathouse below Muckross Gardens and leads .8km (½ mile) around a small peninsula by Muckross Lake. And **Arthur Young's Walk** (4.8km/3 miles) starts on the road to Dinis, traverses natural yew woods, then follows a 200-year-old road on the Muckross Peninsula. Audio guides for all the trails can be obtained from Muckross House for a small deposit.

The **Torc Mountain Walk** is a moderately difficult, 10km (6 mile) walk that allows beautiful views of the Killarney Lakes and **MacGillycuddy's Reeks.** It starts at the **Torc Waterfall** parking lot, approximately 6km (3¾ miles) south of Killarney.

If you prefer a little guidance, you could choose a guided walking tour of some length (from 1 day to a weekend to a full week). A number of walks and walking holidays of varying lengths are offered by **SouthWestWalks Ireland** (✆ **066/718-6181;** www.southwestwalksireland.com). Or you can arrange in advance to meet up with **the Wayfarers,** an international organization of passionate pedestrians, who schedule 5-week-long footloose circuits of the Ring of Kerry each spring, summer, and fall. To receive a schedule, contact **the Wayfarers,** 174 Bellevue Ave., Newport, RI 02840 (✆ **800/249-4620;** www.thewayfarers.com).

For long-distance walkers, the 202km (125-mile) **Kerry Way** is a signposted walking route that extends from Killarney around the Ring of Kerry (see "Walk This Way" on p. 278).

WHERE TO STAY IN KILLARNEY

As the main tourist hub of County Kerry, it should come as no surprise that it's in and around Killarney where you'll find by far the greatest choice of accommodations.

Aghadoe Heights ★★★ This seductive retreat just north of Killarney is worth the splurge; luxurious and welcoming, it's one of the best spas in Ireland. The large guestrooms are decorated in soothing tones of white, gray, and oatmeal. Beds are extremely comfortable and bathrooms impeccably modern. It's worth spending a little extra to get a room at the front to appreciate the stunning views of the Lower Lake in Killarney National Park. There is a huge list of treatments in the opulent, futuristic spa (they even have a "precious stone chamber" for some of the more exotic-sounding options), and the thermal suite is full of high tech touches such as showers infused with refreshing essential oils. On site are two excellent restaurants and a bar overlooking the lake.

Aghadoe, Killarney, Co. Kerry. ✆ **064/663-1766.** www.aghadoeheights.com. 74 units. €150–€210 double; €249–€419 suite. Free parking. Rates include breakfast. Spa and dinner, bed and breakfast packages available. **Amenities:** Wi-Fi; 2 restaurants; bar; pool; spa; room service. Head north out of Killarney on N22; Aghadoe Heights is signposted about 2.7km (1 mile) after the second of the two roundabouts on the north side of the town center (just after the turning for Birch Hill).

Cahernane House ★★★ A neo-Gothic mansion on the outskirts of Killarney National Park, Cahernane has been exquisitely transformed into a luxury retreat. The decor is authentically grandiose. The public areas have the feel of an old gentlemen's club filled with antique furniture, stag heads on the wall, and roaring fires in the open grates. Guestrooms are more modern, though no less elegant, and some bathrooms come with deep claw-foot tubs. Many of the rooms have private patios. The house has two restaurants—the excellent, formal **Herbert Room,** and the more relaxed **Cellar Bar,** where you can take lighter meals among the beautifully lit arches of the old wine cellar. Fields and farmland surround the hotel, and the misty mountains of the park linger in the distance. Dinner, bed and breakfast packages start at around €115 per person.

Muckross Rd., Killarney, Co. Kerry. ✆ **064/663-1895.** www.cahernane.com. 38 units. €130–€240 double; €300 suite. Free parking. Rates include breakfast. **Amenities:** Restaurant; bar; room service.

Earls Court House ★★ Just outside the center of Killarney, on a quiet street with views of the mountains, Earls Court House is a pleasingly old-fashioned kind of B&B. Guestrooms are simple but elegant, featuring polished wood furniture and buttermilk-colored walls. A few have canopy or four-poster beds. Flatscreen TVs mounted to the walls add a touch of modern convenience. You can take afternoon tea in one of the two guest lounges (included in the price of your room), and light suppers are served until early evening. The excellent, varied breakfasts include fresh, home-baked bread and pastries. Check the website for special offers; one or two deals is on offer per season.

Woodlawn Rd., Killarney, Co. Kerry. ✆ **064/663-4009.** www.killarney-earlscourt.ie. 24 units. €100–€120 double. Free parking. Rates include breakfast. 2-night minimum on some summer weekends. **Amenities:** Wi-Fi (free); library.

ENJOYING spa life, IRISH STYLE

Times may be harder than they have been in recent years, economically speaking, but Ireland still has more than its share of top-rated spas—and some of the top spas cluster around Kenmare and Killarney. In this region, the best spas use the exquisite natural settings to spectacular effect, and borrow their treatments from the Irish countryside. Everything from Irish spring water to Irish peat mud and Irish river stones can be used to coax forth beauty from tired, work-dulled skin and hair. None of these spas are cheap, but they're a wonderful way to treat yourself on the road.

All guests at the **Aghadoe Heights Hotel & Spa** (see above) outside Killarney are welcome to spend an hour in its exquisite thermal suite for the fairly small fee of €25. With the wide array of steam rooms, saunas, tropical showers, cooling rooms, and hot tubs, it is a luxuriant 60 minutes. Once you're fully relaxed, you might sample one of the spa's numerous massages or facials, using Aveda products. Treatments range from about €65 to €145.

The **Easanna Spa** at the **Sheen Falls Lodge,** off N71, Kenmare (✆ **064/664-1600;** www.sheenfallslodge.ie) features a pool shaped like a flower—each petal forming a kind of private relaxation space. You can have a hot stone massage or facial and then float off in total relaxation. Room rates here start at around €180, although the typical price is more like €220 for a standard double. Treatments range from about €60 to €155.

The spa at the **Killarney Park Hotel,** off East Avenue in the center of Killarney (✆ **064/663-5555;** www.killarneyparkhotel.ie), is a modern, peaceful oasis, with a soothing pool and such exotic treatments as the 3-hour Absolute Spa Ritual for €270 in which you are rubbed with coconut before being wrapped in a milk-and-lavender essence and then massaged. It's purported to cure jet lag. Rooms here start at around €250 (not including breakfast). Treatments range from about €65 to an eye-watering €380.

The **Sámas spa** in the super-pricey **Park Hotel Kenmare,** Shelbourne Street, Kenmare (✆ **064/664-1200;** www.parkkenmare.com) has won awards for its unique design. You can soak in the warm spa pool while gazing out over the

Friars Glen ★★★ Nestled in the cleft of a lush and verdant glen inside Killarney National Park, this delightful B&B could hardly be friendlier or better run. Hosts John and Mary (and their two dogs) welcome guests like old friends; they really enjoy what they do and take pride in helping visitors plan their explorations of the park and the Ring of Kerry. They will even organize tours on your behalf and can provide babysitting in the evenings with a bit of notice. The building itself looks like an old farmhouse, but it is actually contemporary and very well designed, with plenty of authentic materials and exposed stone. Guestrooms are cozy and simple, complete with wood furniture and decent-sized bathrooms. Ask for a room with a view; the vistas across the surrounding glen are inspiring. Breakfast is served until a very civilized 10am. Dinner isn't offered, but the place is only a short drive from Killarney, and Molly Darcy's pub (see p. 285) is within walking distance.

Mangerton Rd., Muckross, Killarney, Co. Kerry. ✆ **064/663-7500.** www.friarsglen.ie. 10 units. €90–€110 double. Free parking. Rates include breakfast. **Amenities:** Wi-Fi (free). Head south

Old-world gentility and a 21st-century spa offer the best of both worlds to guests at the Park Hotel Kenmare.

mountains nearby. Spend an hour relaxing in the thermal suite (rock sauna, ice fountain, tropical mist shower), before moving on to your facial, wrap, or massage. Unlike those above, the spa is strictly for residents only, although they sometimes make exceptions when it's not too busy. Rooms here *start* at about €300 during the summer months, though, so you'll have to have deep pockets to dip your toes in their waters. Treatments range from €145 up to around €280.

from Killarney on N71 for about 4km (2½ miles) then turn left immediately after Molly Darcy's Pub. The turning for Friar's Glen is on the right immediately after the Muckross Garden Centre. (From Kenmare, take N71 towards Killarney and then take a right immediately before Molly Darcy's pub.)

Larkinley Lodge ★★ A great option just a few blocks from the center of Killarney, Larkinley Lodge is a stylish, modern B&B in a beautifully converted townhouse. Guestrooms are spotlessly clean with muted, neutral color schemes and wood furniture. Toni and Danny Sheehan are gregarious owners whose warm personalities shine through. Breakfasts are traditional and excellent. The location is only about a 10-minute walk into central Killarney, not far from great pubs and restaurants. However, it's in a quiet neighborhood, so you can easily escape the evening street noise that can sometimes be a problem in this lively town.

Lewis Rd., Killarney, Co. Kerry. ✆ **064/663-5142.** www.larkinley.com. 6 units. €80–€90 double. Free parking. Rates include breakfast. **Amenities:** Wi-Fi (free).

COUNTY KERRY: A poet's EYE VIEW

Irish writer **John Millington Synge** (1871–1909), best known today as the author of *Playboy of the Western World*, was a great lover of County Kerry. His last work, published posthumously in 1912, was a book of essays entitled *In Wicklow and West Kerry*, in which he wrote lovingly about this part of the country. The following extract sums up its unique appeal more perfectly than a whole guidebook's worth of description could hope to achieve:

"I walked up this morning along the slope from the east to the top of Sybil Head, where one comes out suddenly on the brow of a cliff with a straight fall of many hundreds of feet into the sea. It is a place of indescribable grandeur, where one can see Carrantuohill and the Skelligs and Loop Head and the full sweep of the Atlantic, and over all, the wonderfully tender and searching light that is seen only in Kerry. One wonders in these places why there is anyone left in Dublin, or London, or Paris, when it would be better, one would think, to live in a tent or hut with this magnificent sea and sky, and to breathe this wonderful air, which is like wine in one's teeth."

WHERE TO DINE IN KILLARNEY

Bricin ★★ IRISH Rather incongruously located above a craft shop, this is a long-standing favorite of the Killarney dining scene. *Bricin* means "little trout" in Gaelic, and seafood is often the strong point of the traditional Irish menu. Plates feature locally reared meat, often served with interesting sauces—rack of roast lamb with Madeira and rosemary sauce, for example, or steak with brandy, bourbon, and pepper. However, it's the house specialty for which this place is renowned: boxty, a classic pancake stuffed with several different types of filling. The dining room is an old-fashioned type of place, complete with stained glass windows and an open fireplace. Bricin serves two early bird menus (€19 for two courses, €29 for three) until 6:30pm.

26 High St., Killarney, Co. Kerry. ✆ **064/663-4902.** www.bricin.com. Main courses €19–€26. Tues–Sat 6–9pm. Closed early Jan–early Mar.

Cellar One ★★ MODERN EUROPEAN The basement dining room here is either a wry, colorful design statement or just garishly camp. However, the food is an extremely successful mix of modern European dishes, Irish flavors, and the odd hint of something more exotic. You might opt for some spicy chickpea cakes to start, followed by tiger prawns prepared in chili, garlic, and tequila, or maybe some crab-encrusted cod with wilted spinach in a coconut and ginger sauce. Desserts go down a more traditional route with choices like chocolate pudding or the wonderfully named knickerbocker glory—a super-retro style ice cream sundae served with fruit, chocolate brownies, and meringue. Service is excellent, and the atmosphere deliciously good fun.

At the Ross Hotel, Church Lane, Killarney, Co. Kerry. ✆ **064/663-1855.** www.theross.ie. Main courses €19–€28. Daily noon–9:30pm.

Kate Kearney's Cottage ★ INTERNATIONAL Unofficially considered the gateway to the Gap of Dunloe, this cheerful pub is hugely popular. It's a little touristy (a dead giveaway is the in-house souvenir shop), but the atmosphere is upbeat and traditional, and the stick-to-your-ribs pub food is pretty tasty. Think steaks, ribs, burgers, and bistro-style classics, all washed down with a restorative pint. In summer a full "Traditional Irish Night" is every Wednesday, Friday, and Sunday. Dinner is accompanied by a show of live music and Irish dancing. The pub is named after a feisty local woman who carved out a reputation as a maker of illegal potcheen (moonshine) that she called Mountain Dew.

Gap of Dunloe, Gap of Dunloe, signposted from N72 (Ring of Kerry Rd.), Beaufort, Killarney, Co. Kerry. ✆ **064/664-4146.** www.katekearneyscottage.com. Main courses €12–€17. Daily noon–11pm (food 6:30–9:30pm).

The Laurels ★ INTERNATIONAL The menu at this busy pub in the center of Killarney is a mix of bistro dishes and more populist fare. Starters include deep fried brie with red currant sauce and chicken wings, while mains range from a generous steak served with peppercorn sauce and rosti to a tureen of white wine poached mussels with citrus cream sauce. They also serve stone-baked pizzas, made fresh to order—none of this menu business, you just choose the toppings you want. The lunch menu is much simpler serving "doorstep" (very thick cut) sandwiches, burgers, salads, and the like. In summer features lively music sessions several times a week.

Main St., Killarney, Co. Kerry. ✆ **064/663-1149.** www.thelaurelspub.com. Main courses €15–€30. Mon–Thurs 10:30am–11:30pm; Fri–Sat 10:30am–12:30am; Sun 12:30–11pm. (Food served until about 9:30pm).

Molly Darcy's ★ IRISH This popular pub on the outskirts of Killarney National Park is a festive spot. It's quite touristy, so don't come here looking for much in the way of authenticity, but the interior has oodles of rustic charm. The menu sticks to traditional pub food—fish and chips, catch of the day, homemade pies, lamb stew—though the house burger served with mozzarella, arugula, and basil shakes things up a bit. Vegetarians are catered to with almost as many options as the meat and fish dishes. July to September features a show of live music and Irish dancing every night except Sunday and Monday; during October, the show is on Tuesdays and Thursdays.

At the Muckross Park Hotel, Muckross Rd., Killarney, Co. Kerry. ✆ **064/662-3400.** Main courses €14–€22. Daily noon–11pm (food 6:30 to about 9:30pm).

Pay as You Please ★★ INTERNATIONAL Well this is interesting: a restaurant with no prices. Literally. Instead, you pay whatever you think the food is worth. The owners describe the concept as a "postmodern" restaurant; the hippie ethos is one reason it has attracted a lot of attention since opening in 2011. But the genuine popularity of this place proves it to be more than a novelty, and that comes down to one key fact: The food is top-notch. The menu is kept very short, but there are specials daily like delicious soup or crispy, thin-crust pizzas with creative toppings such as salami, goat's cheese, and roasted garlic. Dessert comes in the form of home-baked cakes. The dining room is tiny, but the funky vibe and friendly atmosphere add up to a unique dining experience. Opening times can be unpredictable, so call ahead.

New Market Lane, Killarney, Co. Kerry. ✆ **087/190-2567.** www.payasyouplease.ie. No set charge. Thurs and Sun 12:30–4pm; Fri–Sat 7–10pm. On busy nights, times may be altered to two sittings at 7 and 9pm.

SHOPPING

Shopping hours in Killarney are usually Monday to Saturday 9am to 6pm, but from May through September or October, many stores are open every day until 9 or 10pm. Although Killarney has more souvenir and craft shops than you can shake a shillelagh at, here are a few of the best.

The Candle Shop ★★ The clue's in the name here—this place sells candles of all shapes and sizes, plus handmade soaps and skincare products. A good choice if you're looking for authentic souvenirs. 22 Plunkett St., Killarney, Co. Kerry. ✆ **064/662-1636.**

Christy's Irish Stores ★ This enormous gift emporium on the corner of Plunett Street has a huge array of Irish souvenir items, from fripperies and touristy tat to really quite nice knitwear, crystal, and other craft items. 10 Main St., Killarney, Co. Kerry. ✆ **064/642-3311.** www.christysirishstores.com.

Frank Lewis Gallery ★★ Regularly changing exhibitions of contemporary visual arts are on display at this excellent little gallery. The emphasis is on emerging talent and the standard is high. 6 Bridewell Lane, Killarney, Co. Kerry. ✆ **064/663-1108.** www.franklewisgallery.com.

Killarney Art Gallery ★★ This gallery in Aghadoe, north of central Killarney, showcases work from respected Irish artists as well as new and local talent. Aghadoe, Killarney, Co. Kerry. ✆ **064/663-4628.** www.killarneyartgallery.com.

Killarney Bookshop ★ his sweet little independent bookstore has a great section on local history and folklore. They also sell maps and other titles of Irish interest. 32 Main St., Killarney, Co. Kerry. ✆ **064/663-4108.** www.killarneybookshop.ie.

Mucros Craft Centre ★★ Part of the Walled Garden, a small shopping complex on the grounds of Muckross House (see p. 276), this place has a good stock of Irish crafts, pottery, clothing, cards, and quality gifts—and many items are made locally. Muckross House, Muckross Rd., Killarney, Co. Kerry. ✆ **064/667-014.** www.muckross-house.ie.

Serendipity ★★ Another good place to buy local crafts, this delightful shop in central Killarney also sells artisan jewelry. 15 College St., Killarney, Co. Kerry. ✆ **064/663-1056.**

KILLARNEY AFTER DARK

The mainstay of nightlife in Killarney is the lively pub scene. The town has more than its fair share of good places to enjoy a pint and some live traditional music. Unsurprisingly for such a popular tourist town, all of these places can get pretty packed on a busy summer's night—so come early to stand a chance of getting a seat.

Killarney Grand ★★ This hugely popular pub—officially known as Sheehan's Bar, although the signs out front say both—is one of the best places in the region to hear traditional Irish music. Nightly lively sessions nightly start at 9pm; after 11pm it turns into a nightclub. The atmosphere gets pretty raucous, and the crowds can really pack in here (definitely standing room only), but the music is always good. Some of the biggest names in Irish music have played here over the years, and you never know when you might catch the next big thing. A "neat" dress code is enforced on the door. In other words, you don't have to wear your best duds, but don't be too scruffy either. Main St., Killarney, Co. Kerry. ✆ **064/663-1159.** www.killarneygrand.com.

The Laurels ★ Another very popular pub for live music, here the traditional music sessions are on several times a week, usually starting at around 9pm. They also serve good food, including a range of stone-baked pizzas (see p. 285). Main St., Killarney, Co. Kerry. ✆ **064/663-1149.** www.thelaurelspub.com.

O'Connors ★★ This is a proper, traditional-feeling pub. The program of live music is extensive, and it doesn't stop there—you might catch a play, some standup comedy, or even a spoken word event. 7 High St., Killarney, Co. Kerry. ✆ **064/663-1115.**

Tatler Jack ★ For Gaelic sports fans, this is the place to go in Killarney. Football and hurling matches are shown on big screen TVs and traditional music is on many nights in summer. The atmosphere is invariably raucous. Plunkett St., Killarney, Co. Kerry. ✆ **064/663-2361.** www.tatlerjack.com.

The Rest of the Ring of Kerry

Often the greatest pleasures along the Ring of Kerry can be found during a scenic drive along the road or on a quiet byway just begging to be explored. Give in to those temptations—real treasure is waiting in these hills. The following points of interest are listed alphabetically, though all are on, or within easy reach of, the route described above.

The beehive huts atop Skellig Michael, where 6th-century Christian monks lived, worked, and prayed in severe isolation from the mainland.

Ballinskelligs and the Skellig Ring ★★ West of Waterville, across a small bay, the coastal village of **Ballinskelligs** contains the absurdly picturesque ruins of St. Michael Ballinskelligs, a medieval priory overlooking the sea. A sandy beach also features the remnants of a 16th-century castle. Ballinskelligs is a starting point for the so-called **Skellig Ring,** a stunning coastal drive that takes in some of the best viewpoints of the mysterious Skellig Islands (see below). It also passes through some of the most spectacular scenery in the county, and with the merest fraction of the traffic that can clog the Ring of Kerry. However, be warned: Its very remoteness means this route can be tough going, and the roads are very mountainous in places. This is also the edge of Gaeltacht territory, where Irish is the primary language on road signs. To find the Ring, head south through Ballinskelligs. About 0.5km (⅓ mile) after the pink An Post building, you'll come to a crossroads. The Skellig Ring (*Morchuaird na Sceilge* in Gaelic) is signposted to the right. The signs continue throughout the route.

Visitor Information Point: Barbara's Beach Café, Ballinskelligs Beach, Ballinskelligs, Co. Kerry. Tourist Office: Cahersiveen Community Centre, Church St., Cahersiveen, Co. Kerry. ✆ **066/947-2589** (Cahersiveen, summer only). www.visitballinskelligs.ie.

Blueberry Hill Farm ★★ A good way to amuse younger children for half a day, this working farm still does as much as possible according to traditional methods. As part of the half-day tours, you can help milk cows, make butter, and take part in a treasure hunt. Children get to interact with the animals and even help out at feeding time. There's also a cafe selling tasty homemade scones and other treats. The whole experience is very friendly, authentic, and can be quite delightful for the little ones. Full-day courses in such skills as basket weaving, blacksmithing, food preserving, and beekeeping are available for adults.

Signposted from R568 (Sneem-Killarney Rd.), Sneem, Co. Kerry. ✆ **086/356-1150** or 086/316-0224. www.blueberryhillfarm.ie. Admission €15 adults and children; €60 families. Tours at 10am, 3pm.

Crag Cave ★★ Although they are believed to be more than a million years old, these limestone caves were not discovered until 1983. Today, they're open for the wandering (via guided tour only, of course). The guides accompany you 3,753m (12,310 ft.) into the well-lit cave passage on a 40-minute tour revealing massive stalactites and fascinating caverns. If need be, you can get your souvenir fix at the crafts shop. There is also a children's play area (endearingly called **Crazy Cave**), although it costs extra. The Garden Restaurant is a useful stop for lunch if you need a quick bite. It's very touristy but interesting nonetheless. On the same site is the **Kingdom Falconry** center, where you can watch birds of prey fly and be guided by handlers.

College Rd., Castleisland, Co. Kerry. ✆ **066/714-1244.** www.cragcave.com. Caves: €12 adults; €9 seniors and students; €5 children; €30–€25 families. Kingdom Falconry: €8 adults, seniors, and students; €5 children. Crazy Cave: €8 children (accompanying adults free). Combination tickets: €20 adults; €17 seniors and students; €18 children (includes Crazy Cave). Apr–Dec daily 10am–6pm; Dec–Mar Sat–Sun 10am–6pm. Tour times: May–Aug, every ½ hr.; Jan–Apr, Sept–Dec 10:45am, noon, 2:30, 4, 5:30pm.

GREAT, mysterious WONDER: A TRIP TO THE SKELLIG ISLANDS

"Whoever has not stood in the graveyard on the summit of that cliff, among the beehive dwellings and beehive oratory, does not know Ireland through and through . . ."

–George Bernard Shaw

The craggy, inhospitable Skellig Islands rise precipitously from the sea. Here gray skies meet stormy horizons about 14km (8 miles) off the coast of the Iveragh Peninsula. From the mainland, Skellig Michael and Little Skellig appear impossibly sharp-angled and daunting even today, even though the mere act of getting there isn't perilous, as it was in the 6th and 7th centuries. Back then a group of monks built a community on the steepest, most wind-battered peaks. Over time, they carved 600 steps into the cliffs and built monastic buildings hundreds of feet above the ocean. The complex is now a UNESCO World Heritage Site.

Landing is only possible on **Skellig Michael,** the largest of the islands. There is something tragic and beautiful about the remains of the ancient oratories and beehive cells there. Historians know very little about these monks and how they lived, although they obviously sought intense isolation. Records relating to the Skelligs indicate that even here, all but completely hidden, the Vikings found the monastery and punished it as they did all the Irish monastic settlements. Monks were kidnapped and killed in attacks in the 8th century, but the settlement always recovered. To this day, nobody knows why the monks finally abandoned the rock in the 12th century.

Start your exploration at the **Skellig Experience** (✆ **066/947-6306;** www.skelligexperience.com) on Valentia Island, which is reached via road bridge in Portmagee. The well-designed visitor center tells you all about the extraordinary history of these ancient edifices and also offers boat trips out to see the islands. It's open daily, May, June, and September from 10am to 6pm, and until 7pm in July and August; in March, April, October, and November it's open on weekdays only from 10am to 5pm. Last entry is 45 minutes before closing. Admission costs €5 adults, €4 seniors and students, €3 children, and €14 families.

If you add a cruise to see the Skelligs, the cost is €27.50 adults, €24.50 seniors and students, €14.50 children, and €71.50 families—but note that, at present, the visitor center's own boat trips only cruise *around* the Skelligs, and **do not make landfall.** If you want to see the ruins on Skellig Michael up close, you have to go with one of the many independent boat operators who work the route. A list of endorsed skippers is on the Skellig Experience website; if you use **Des Lavelle** (✆ **086/947-6124** or 087/237-1017) or **Eoin Walsh** (✆ **066/947-6327** or 087/283-3522) the fee includes entry to the visitor center. They both charge €50 per person.

There are also "unofficial" ways of reaching the islands, although they're very much at your own risk. For a negotiated fee, you can almost always find a fisherman who's willing to take you over, wait, and then bring you back. The crossing will be rougher but certainly more adventurous.

Derrynane House National Historic Park ★★ Daniel O'Connell (1775–1847) was an Irish political leader and Member of Parliament, who became known as "the Great Liberator" for his successful campaign to repeal the laws that barred Catholics from holding office. He became particularly famous in his lifetime for his so-called "monster meetings," vast public rallies held across the country (one, on the Hill of Tara, was reckoned to have been attended by nearly a million supporters). His house, at Caherdaniel, is open to the public. It contains a museum devoted to his life featuring various artifacts and items from his personal archives. Not everything will be of interest to those who aren't already familiar with his story, but a few pieces—such as the gilded carriage from which he triumphantly greeted crowds after a brief spell as a political prisoner—are definitely worth seeing. The vast grounds are a scenic spot to wander through.

Signposted from N70 (Ring of Kerry Rd.), approx. 2.5km (1½ miles) from Caherdaniel, Co. Kerry. ✆ **066/947-5113.** www.heritageireland.ie. Admission €3 adults; €2 seniors; €1 students and children; €8 families. Late March–Apr, Oct–mid-Nov Wed–Sun and bank holidays 10:30am–5pm; May–mid-Sept daily 10:30am–6pm.

Kerry Bog Village Museum ★ This interesting little museum recreates life in a Kerry bog village in the early 1800s. The site has laborer's cottages, tradesmen houses, and a blacksmith's. It's all quite basic but an informative diversion nonetheless. A little bar and restaurant are on site.

Ring of Kerry Rd. (N71), Ballycleave, Glenbeigh, Co. Kerry. ✆ **066/976-9184.** www.kerrybogvillage.ie. Admission €6.50 adults; €5.50 seniors and students; €4.50 children. Daily 8:30am–6pm.

Staigue Fort ★★ This well-preserved, surprisingly large, prehistoric fort is built of rough stones without mortar of any kind. The walls are 4m (13 ft.) thick at the base. Historians are not certain what purpose it served—it may have been

KILLORGLIN: THE puck STOPS HERE

The first major stop on the Ring of Kerry northward from Killarney, **Killorglin** is a sleepy little town—until August 10, at least, when the annual **Puck Fair** (www.puckfair.ie) incites a 3-day explosion of merrymaking and pageantry.

One of Ireland's last remaining traditional fairs, it's technically an agricultural show; the apex of the event involves capturing a mountain goat (which symbolizes the *puka* or *puki*, a mischievous Celtic sprite) that is then declared *King Puck* and paraded around town on a throne, wearing a crown. It's bonkers but quite a lot fun.

Nobody knows how it began, but one story dates to Cromwell's invasion of Ireland in the mid-17th century. English soldiers were foraging for food in the hills above the town and tried to capture a herd of goats. One escaped to Killorglin and alerted the villagers to mount a defence. Others say the fair is pre-Christian, connected with the Pagan feast of Lughnasa on August 1.

For the rest of the year, Killorglin is a pretty, quiet town, well worth a wander. The River Laune runs straight through the town center. As you cross the old stone bridge, look out for the whimsical statue of the goat on the eastern side—and know that it stands in honor of this town's love for the *puka*.

a fortress or just a kind of prehistoric community center—but experts think it probably dates from around 1000 B.C. It's an open site with no visitor center; just this ancient structure, alone and open to the elements in the middle of a farmer's field.

4 km (2½ miles) off N70 just outside Castlecove, Co. Kerry, on a small farm road (follow signs).

Tralee

Sandwiched between the Ring of Kerry and the Dingle Peninsula, Tralee doesn't quite live up to its singsong pretty name. With a population of 22,000, the town is three times the size of Killarney, and it feels like it. This is more a workaday town than a tourist center, and there's not much here for visitors to do. In fact, it can feel a bit rough at times—especially on weekend nights, when the town's many bars are packed, and walking the streets can feel a bit of a health hazard. However, it has some attractive Georgian architecture and a few sights worth seeing. Mostly it's a place you go *through*, rather than to, with maybe a stop along the way to hit the high points and stock up. The countryside nearby has a couple more offerings.

EXPLORING IN & AROUND TRALEE

Blennerville Windmill ★★ Reaching 20m (66 ft.) into the sky, this must surely be the most photographed object in Tralee. This picturesque windmill at the edge of a river still works, and that makes it quite rare in this part of the world. Built in 1800, it flourished until 1850, when it was largely abandoned. After decades of neglect, it was restored, and is now fully operational. You can climb to the top of the windmill, and see some of its complex inner workings in detail. The visitor complex has an exhibition on the famine years (when Blennerville was a major point of emigration), plus an audiovisual theater, craft workshops, and a cafe. The windmill is 5km (3 miles) west of Tralee.

Windmill St., Blennerville, Co. Kerry. ✆ **066/712-1064.** Admission €5 adults; €3 seniors, students, and children 6 and over; free for children 5 and under; €15 families. Apr–May, Sept–Oct daily 9:30am–5:30pm; June–Aug daily 9am–6pm. Closed Nov–Mar.

Carrigafoyle Castle ★ This rugged medieval castle, surrounded entirely by water, dates from the 15th century. Its name comes from the Gaelic *Carragain Phoill* (or "Rock of the Hole"), and probably describes its location in the channel between the land and Carrig Island. It was once the seat of the O'Connor clan, who ruled most of the Kerry clan for a century or so—it was besieged by English forces in the late 16th century and taken again by Cromwell less than a century later. Although it's a ruin, the tower is almost as tall as that of Blarney Castle (see p. 228). One wall is new, however—modern safety regulations wouldn't allow access to the upper part of the tower without it. Still, it blends in well, and it does mean that you can climb all 104 steps to the top to see the magnificent views.

2km (1¼ miles) west of Ballylongford, Co. Kerry. ✆ **068/43304**. Free admission. May–Sept daily 9am–6pm.

Kerry County Museum ★ This museum spans the history of County Kerry from several thousand in the past, up to the present day. Several galleries cover (among other subjects) Kerry's ancient past; the coming of the Normans and the medieval period; the famine years; and the struggle for independence. The high tech audiovisual presentation includes a tour of the county using archive footage

COULD YOU BE THE rose OF TRALEE?

Beauty pageants may have gone out of fashion in much of the world, but at the annual **Rose of Tralee,** these cheesy, retro institutions are still going strong.

A 19th-century song about a pretty local girl named Mary O'Connor is at the root of this world-famous beauty contest. William Mulchinock's tear-jerker of a song about the girl he was stopped by fate from marrying so caught the public's imagination that more than 100 years later, it is still performed in Irish pubs worldwide. Thus, in 1959 was the idea born for a contest to find the prettiest girl in Tralee and crown her.

Every August, the town fills with pretty young women, those who make them beautiful, and those who want to look at them. The contest rules are fairly generous in terms of just who is Irish, not to mention Traleean—the rules require contestants to be of Irish birth *or ancestry,* so past winners have been from places as far flung as the U.S. and Australia. The festival lasts 5 days, during which time the entire town becomes somewhat obsessed with it—restaurants, pubs, and theaters all get involved in hosting events related to the Rose of Tralee. In recent years they've also added a men's section, the "Escort of the Year."

If you want to join in the fun, or if you know a pretty girl with an Irish last name, contact the **Rose of Tralee Festival Office** (✆ **066/712-1322;** www.roseoftralee.ie).

to show how it looked half a century ago. In the Knight's Hall and Medieval Experience, you can wander around a recreated medieval town, with requisite sound effects, dressed-up mannequins and the like. The museum is in the same building as the Tralee tourism office.

Ashe Memorial Hall, Denny St., Tralee, Co. Kerry. ✆ **066/712-7777.** www.kerrymuseum.ie. Admission €5 adults; accompanied children free; €10 families. June–Aug daily 9:30am–5:30pm; Sep–May Tues–Sat 9:30am–5pm.

The Seanchaí: Kerry Literary and Cultural Centre ★ This imaginative museum is devoted to the literary heritage of County Kerry. Rooms are divided into innovative display that often feel more like art installations devoted to the life and work of various Kerry writers from the past and present. Some of those mentioned here will be familiar, but part of the pleasure is discovering new names and hitherto unfamiliar works. A busy schedule of events fills the summer months; check the website for details. Listowel is 26km (16 miles) northeast of Tralee on N69.

24 The Square, Listowel, Co. Kerry. ✆ **068/22212.** www.kerrywritersmuseum.com. Free admission. Guided tours €4 adults; €3 seniors, students, and children. June–Aug daily 9:30am–5:30pm; Sept–Nov, Mar–May Mon–Fri 10am–4pm. Last tour 1 hr. before closing.

SPORTS & OUTDOOR PURSUITS

Spectator Sports

DOG RACING Greyhounds race year-round on Tuesday and Friday starting at 8pm at the **Kingdom Greyhound Racing Track,** Oakview, Brewery Road (✆ **066/712-4033**). Admission is €10 per person;, €5 seniors and students, €15 families.

HORSE RACING Horse racing takes place twice a year (in early June and late August) at **Tralee Racecourse,** Ballybeggan Park (✆ **066/712-6490**). Post time is usually 2:30pm. Tickets to races start at around €14 for adults, €7 for seniors and students.

Outdoor Pursuits

GOLF The **Tralee Golf Club,** Fenit/Churchill Road, West Barrow, Ardfert (✆ **066/713-6379;** www.traleegolfclub.com), overlooking the Atlantic 13km (8 miles) northwest of town, is an Arnold Palmer–designed course. It's one of the most spectacularly-situated courses in Ireland. Greens fees are a pricey €175, although this also allows you to play a second round within a week of the first.

About 40km (25 miles) north of Tralee in the northwest corner of County Kerry is Bill Clinton's favorite Irish course, the **Ballybunion Golf Club,** Ballybunion (✆ **068/27146;** www.ballybuniongolfclub.ie). This facility offers the chance to play on two challenging 18-hole seaside links, both on cliffs overlooking the Shannon River estuary and the Atlantic. Tom Watson has rated the Old Course one of the finest in the world, while the Cashen Course was designed by Robert Trent Jones, Sr. Greens fees are €55 to €180 or €110 to €200 for golf on both courses within a week, depending on the time of year.

Where to Stay in the Rest of the Ring of Kerry

Ballygarry House ★★ On the outer edge of the otherwise unlovely Tralee, this pleasant country inn is ensconced in gardens. Built as a manor house in the 18th century, plenty of the original features have been retained, even though the facilities are thoroughly modern. Elegant guestrooms maintain the country mansion air; superior rooms are surprisingly spacious, with king size beds. Family rooms are an excellent value at usually the same price as doubles. The fantastic in-house spa is a relaxing, revitalizing hideaway, while the outdoor hot tub, overlooking fields and distant mountains, is a calming oasis. Special inclusive spa offers change monthly—massage, facial, and access to the spa facilities for around €100 is the kind of deal you can expect. The Brooks restaurant serves excellent, modern Irish food.

Signposted off N21, Leebrook, approx. 3.3km (2 miles) west of central Tralee, Co. Kerry. ✆ **066/712-3322.** www.ballygarryhouse.com. 46 units. €86–€172 double. Free parking. Rates include breakfast. **Amenities:** Wi-Fi (free); restaurant; bar; spa.

Coffey River's Edge ★★ A bright, cheery building overlooking the River Laune in the center of Killorglin, one of the main stops on the Ring of Kerry, Coffey's is an exceptional value for the money. Owners Finbarr and Anne are charming and congenial hosts, and nothing seems like too much trouble to make their guests feel at ease. Rooms are decently sized with large beds and contemporary wood furniture. Breakfasts are served in the dining room overlooking the river and picturesque stone bridge, and a large guest balcony and deck outside. No evening meal is on offer, but the rest of pretty Killorglin is just a short, leisurely stroll away. Finbarr and Anne are both keen golfers and will happily arrange for you to have a game at a local course.

The Bridge, Killorglin, Co. Kerry. ✆ **066/976-1750.** www.coffeysriversedge.com. 11 units. €60–€65 double. Free parking. Breakfast included. **Amenities:** Wi-Fi (free).

Derrynane Hotel ★ The view from this place is striking—perched on a promontory overlooking Kenmare Bay, guests look out across a dramatic coastal inlet streaked with tiny green islands and a smattering of pleasure boats cruising around the coast. Accommodations have few frills; some are nicely designed, if rather spartan, and others could do with an upgrade. Package deals include "Golden Breaks," with special discounts for seniors. This place is really geared toward families, with standard rooms that actually sleep up to three for the same cost. Plus, some handy extras include an indoor playroom and child-friendly menus at dinner. Other relaxing amenities include a small outdoor pool, sauna, and a seaweed bath treatment room. A small herb garden on the grounds provides ingredients for the in-house restaurant.

Caherdaniel (signposted from N70 Ring of Kerry Rd.) Co. Kerry. ✆ **066/947-5136.** www.derrynane.com. 70 units. €59–€111 double. Free parking. Breakfast not included in lower rates. **Amenities:** Restaurant; bar; room service; pool; gym; treatment room.

Iskeroon ★★★ In a spectacularly beautiful setting on the Ring of Kerry, looking out across the Derrynane coast and out to the Skellig Islands, this extraordinary bed and breakfast is a serene and special place to stay. Built in the 1930s, the house isn't large, but this merely adds to the feeling of special care and attention you experience from the moment you walk through the door. The two suites, with stone floors, king-sized beds, handmade furniture, and beautiful pieces of art, have been beautifully renovated. Fresh ingredients are provided for breakfast, but you prepare it yourself in the little kitchenette that comes with your suite as there's no better location to enjoy a leisurely breakfast than your balcony overlooking the sea. The only downside is the 3-night minimum stay, but it hardly feels like a negative once you're here. The former coach house on the grounds is rented out as a full self-catering accommodation for €450–€500 per week (depending on the time of year).

Bunavalla (halfway between Waterville and Caherdaniel), Co. Kerry. ✆ **066/947-5119.** www.iskeroon.com. 2 units. €100 double. Free parking. Breakfast included. 3-night minimum stay. **Amenities:** Wi-Fi; DVD player and library; kitchenette. At the Scariff Inn, follow signs for Bunavalla Pier, then follow signs to Iskeroon near the bottom of the hill.

QC's ★★ More of a restaurant-with-rooms than a small hotel, QC's is nonetheless a stylish and unique place to stay on the Ring of Kerry. Accommodations are open plan, contemporary spaces with a minimalist vibe; polished wood floors, huge skylights, and claw-foot tubs next to the bed. A few high tech extras include Bose stereos. The guest lounge looks like it's tumbled from the pages of a magazine featuring deep velvet sofas and a cozy wood-burning stove. The superb downstairs restaurant specializes in fresh seafood. They take pride in local flavors cooked to perfection such as roast hake with samphire and lemon risotto or local meats served with seasonal vegetables and delicious sauces.

Main St., Cahersiveen, Co. Kerry. ✆ **066/947-2244.** www.qcbar.com. 5 units. €85–€95 double. Free parking. Breakfast included. **Amenities:** Wi-Fi.

Where to Dine in the Rest of the Ring of Kerry

The Blind Piper ★ IRISH This friendly and lively pub is one of the top places to eat in Caherdaniel. The high-quality bar menu strikes a nice line between straightforward traditional pub grub and something a little more sophisticated. Think Guinness stew with fresh soda bread, fish and chips, excellent hamburgers, and Thai fishcakes. The charming staff makes you feel right at home, and in summer the bar is often enlivened by live traditional music sessions. The Blind Piper is a bit hard to find, partly because it doesn't have a proper street address. Take the main N70 road through Caherdaniel, and then take the turn next to the big red building in the center of the village. (There's usually a handmade sign here pointing you in the right direction.) The pub is painted bright yellow.

Off main Ring of Kerry Rd. (N70), Caherdaniel, Co. Kerry. ✆ **066/947-5126.** Main courses €10–€20. Mon–Thurs 11am–11:30pm; Fri–Sat 11am–midnight; Sun noon–11pm (food until about 9pm).

The Blue Bull ★ IRISH This great little pub in tiny, picturesque Sneem serves traditional fare in a couple of cozy dining spaces. The menu doesn't deviate too far from Irish pub classics, but it does it all very well—fish and chips, mussels in garlic sauce, steaks, sandwiches, and salads. The crowd, a good mix of hungry tourists and easy-going locals settling down at the bar, makes for a congenial atmosphere. This is a straight-up traditional pub with a bar area in the front separate from the dining rooms. It's a great spot for standing at the bar, eavesdropping on a few conversations, and possibly being asked your opinion about the topic of the day.

South Square, Sneem, Co. Kerry. ✆ **066/947-5126.** Main courses €6–€20. Mon–Sat 11am–around midnight; Sun noon–11pm (food until about 9pm).

Denny Lane ★ BISTRO A good option for a quick and tasty lunch in Tralee, Denny Lane serves tasty soups, salads, sandwiches, and light lunch specials. It's nothing fancy, but the food is good and the atmosphere congenial. They also do breakfast until a very civilized noon (or brunch till 2pm). Dinner on weekends includes a selection of steaks, seafood, burgers and other crowd-pleasing favorites all mixed up with a popular tapas menu.

11 Denny St., Tralee, Co. Kerry. ✆ **066/719-4319.** www.dennylane.ie. Lunch main courses €5–€11. Dinner main courses €16–€26. Mon–Thurs 10am–4pm; Fri–Sat 10am–11pm (last orders 9pm).

Jack's Coastguard Restaurant ★★★ SEAFOOD/MODERN IRISH This cheery restaurant lists "Water's Edge" as its address. That's not so much a name as a description; it's right on the harbor in Cromane, a tiny village near Killorglin. The dining room is a bright, modern space boasting beautiful views of the bay, while a pianist plays away in the corner. The menu strikes elegant notes with choices like hake filet with an almond and herb crust and turbot with a side of potatoes, prepared with raisins and orange. Meat dishes are kept simple, and you'll find lamb with potatoes boiled in sea salt topped with rosemary jus. The restaurant is attached to a popular local pub, and live music plays every Monday night in summer.

Water's Edge, Cromane Lower, Killorglin, Co. Kerry. ✆ **066/976-9102.** www.jackscromane.com. Main courses €17–€35. May–Sept Wed–Mon noon–9pm; Oct Wed–Sun noon–9pm; Nov–Dec Thurs–Sun noon-9pm; Feb–Apr Thurs–Sun noon–9pm. Closed Jan.

Nick's Restaurant and Piano Bar ★★ SEAFOOD/IRISH The rather Rat Pack feel to this restaurant's name says everything about its old school credentials. Nick's is quite famous in Ireland—it's been here since 1978—and while you won't find cutting edge modern cuisine here, it's still deserving of its reputation as one of the better places to eat along the Ring of Kerry. Choose from two dining areas: a formal restaurant and a bar, where a simpler (and less expensive) selection is served in more relaxed surroundings. On the main menu are several catches of the day (naturally), grilled sole, shellfish mornay, or a classic seafood platter. It's not all about the fruits of the sea, as you can also order steaks, lamb, and a chicken supreme with whiskey cream sauce. The bar menu is more of the fish and chips or steak sandwich variety, but it's still good. Everything is served to the gentle melodies of a live piano accompaniment. Just the same as it ever was.

Lower Bridge St., Killorglin, Co. Kerry. ✆ **066/976-1219.** www.nicks.ie. Main courses €20–€34. Wed–Sun 5:30–10pm.

Smuggler's Inn ★ SEAFOOD/IRISH Overlooking the beach in Waterville, this is a great option for lunch. The menu is mostly seafood caught fresh from Ballinskelligs Bay—think oysters, black sole, and seafood chowder. Meat options run the gamut from tender steaks and pot roasts, to roast chicken or duck. Most of the ingredients have been sourced locally, so the menu is heavy on seasonal choices. The conservatory dining room has lovely views of the bay, or you can sit outside and take in the full glory of it all. The Smuggler's Inn also does bed and breakfast accommodations for around €70 to €110 per night.

Cliff Rd., Waterville, Co. Kerry. ✆ **066/947-4330.** www.the-smugglers-inn.com. Main courses €15–€30. Daily noon–3pm, 6–9pm. No children after 8pm. Closed Nov–Easter.

THE DINGLE PENINSULA

A quieter, shorter alternative to the Ring of Kerry, the Dingle Peninsula loop is an exhilarating, sometimes vertigo inducing drive full of heart-stopping dips and breathtaking panoramas (acrophobes should avoid the R561 coast road between Milltown and Annascaul).

Dingle ***(An Daingean)*** is a charming, brightly colored little town at the foot of steep hills and on the edge of a gorgeous stretch of coast. You won't find much to do here, but it has plenty of hotels and restaurants and makes a good base for exploring the region. The town's most famous resident is a dolphin that adopted the place years ago and has been bringing in dolphin-loving tourists ever since. Its busiest time is in August, when the Dingle Races bring in crowds from throughout the area to watch the horses run every other weekend. (The racetrack is just outside of town on the N86.) In the last week of August, the Dingle Regatta fills the harbor with traditional Irish currach boats in a vivid display of color and history.

When leaving Dingle, heading west takes you on the **Slea Head Drive,** a gorgeous stretch of road known for its collection of ancient sites (see "The Slea Head Drive" on p. 299).

Not far from Dingle, **Gallarus Oratory** is a beautifully preserved, early Christian church building. A few miles away, the village of **Ballyferriter** ***(Baile an Fheirtearaigh)*** is a sleepy place with some quite spectacularly grim nomenclature (see "A Gruesome Tale in Ballyferriter" on p. 303).

The village of **Dunquin** ***(Dún Chaion),*** stunningly situated between Slea Head and Clogher Head, is where you catch ferries (✆ **066/335-3805;** www.blasketislands.ie) to the **Blasket Islands** ***(Na Blascaodaí).*** Until they were evacuated in 1953, the islands were famous for having an entirely Gaelic-speaking population. These days it's inhabited only by seals and seabirds. If you're up to it, you can take a 13km (8-mile) walk to the west end of Great Blasket and back.

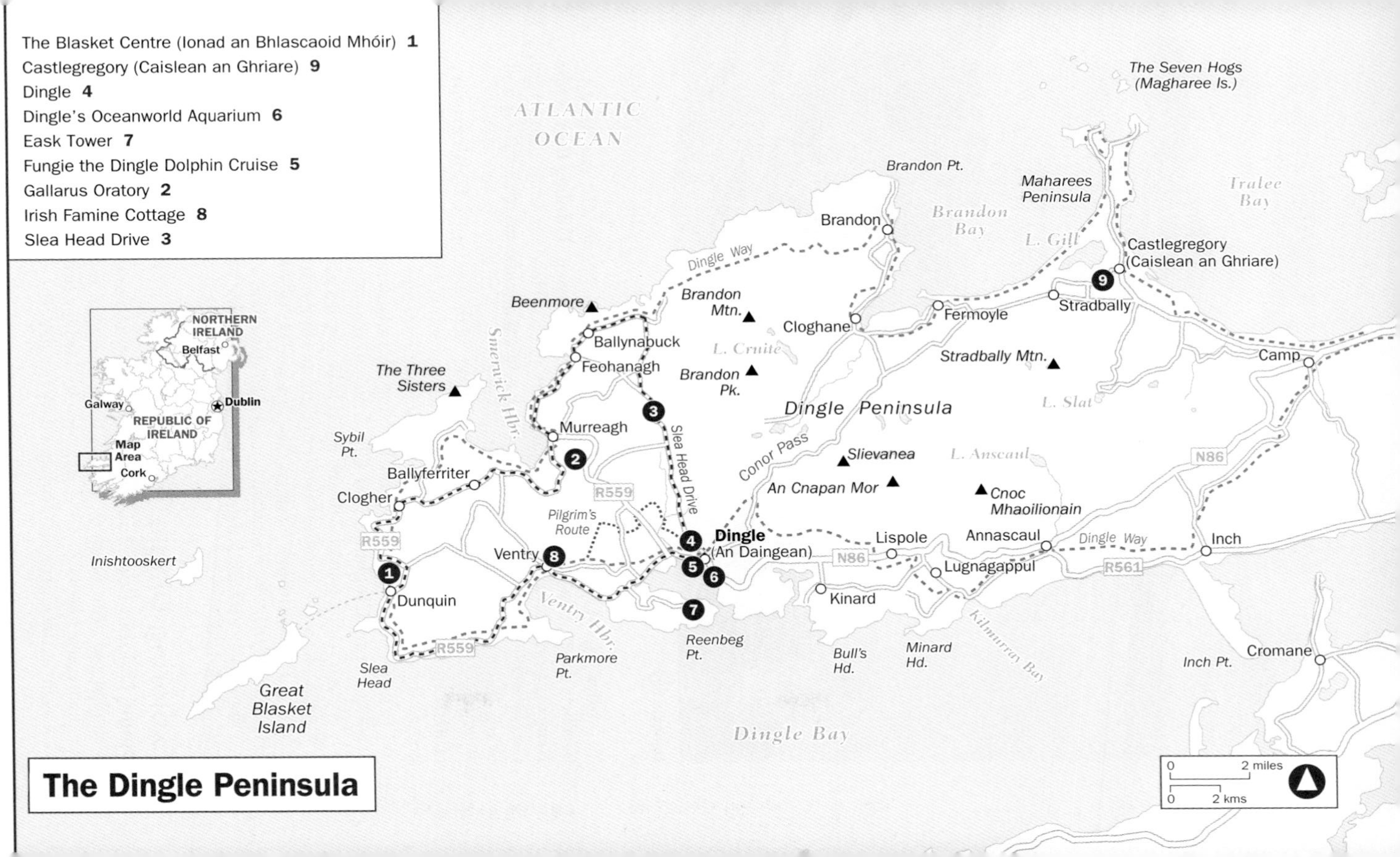
The Blasket Centre (Ionad an Bhlascaoid Mhóir) 1
Castlegregory (Caislean an Ghriare) 9
Dingle 4
Dingle's Oceanworld Aquarium 6
Eask Tower 7
Fungie the Dingle Dolphin Cruise 5
Gallarus Oratory 2
Irish Famine Cottage 8
Slea Head Drive 3
The Dingle Peninsula
ATLANTIC OCEAN
NORTHERN IRELAND
Belfast
Galway
Dublin
REPUBLIC OF IRELAND
Map Area
Cork
The Seven Hogs (Magharee Is.)
Tralee Bay
Brandon Pt.
Maharees Peninsula
Brandon Bay
L. Gill
Brandon
Castlegregory (Caislean an Ghriare)
Dingle Way
Beenmore
Brandon Mtn.
Cloghane
Fermoyle
Stradbally
Ballynabuck
Feohanagh
L. Cruite
Stradbally Mtn.
Camp
The Three Sisters
Smerwick Hbr.
Brandon Pk.
Dingle Peninsula
L. Slat
Murreagh
Slea Head Drive
Sybil Pt.
Conor Pass
Slievanea
L. Anscaul
N86
Ballyferriter
R559
An Cnapan Mor
Cnoc Mhaoilionain
Clogher
Pilgrim's Route
Dingle (An Daingean)
Lispole
Annascaul
Inch
R559
Inishtooskert
Ventry
N86
Lugnagappul
R561
Dunquin
Kinard
Ventry Hbr.
Reenbeg Pt.
Kilmurray Bay
R559
Slea Head
Parkmore Pt.
Bull's Hd.
Minard Hd.
Inch Pt.
Cromane
Great Blasket Island
Dingle Bay
0 2 miles
0 2 kms

Dunquin Bay

Slea Head, at the southwestern edge of the peninsula, has pristine beaches, great walks, and extensive archaeological remains. **Dunbeg Fort *(Dún Beag)*** sits on a rocky promontory just south of Slea Head, its walls rising from the cliff edge. Although much of the fort has fallen into the sea, the place is well worth a visit at the bargain-basement rate of €3.

Back on the mainland and on the north side of the peninsula, **Castlegregory *(Caislean an Ghriare)*** is a seaside village with two wide, sandy beaches. It's known for its good diving waters, and scuba divers and watersports fans flock to the place in summer. It's a bit bustling for isolationists, who are better off heading to tiny **Cloghane *(An Clochán)*** on the southern edge of Brandon Bay. With a population of 270 and a lovely beach, it's got much to offer. It also is a good place for climbers interested in tackling nearby **Mount Brandon *(Cnoc Bhréannain)*,** which is Ireland's second-highest mountain (951m/3,120 ft.). The mountain is a good all-day climb and has gorgeous views, but don't try it without a map and compass and some experience scaling considerable heights.

Exploring Dingle Town

Dingle Dolphin Boat Tours ★★ The story of Fungie the Dingle Dolphin is strange and heartwarming. The bottlenose dolphin was first spotted by Dingle's lighthouse keeper in 1983, as it escorted fishing boats out to sea and then back again at the end of their voyages day after day. The sailors named him, and he became a harbor fixture. Fishermen took their children out to swim with him, and he seemed to love human contact. Now people come from miles around to have a few minutes' time with Fungie, and the fishermen ferry them out to meet him. Trips last about 60 minutes and depart roughly every 2 hours in low season and as often as every half-hour in high season. Fungie swims right up to the boats that stay out long enough to afford views of the picturesque bay. You pay at the end, and no charge if he doesn't show. However, while the little fella is still packing the crowds in at the time of writing, nobody quite knows how old Fungie is. So before you get the little ones too excited you might want to call ahead . . . discreetly.

The Pier, Dingle, Co. Kerry. ✆ **066/915-2626.** www.dingledolphin.com. Tour starts at €16 adults, €8 children 11 and under. Daily 11:30am–4pm, weather permitting.

Dingle Oceanworld Aquarium ★ This is a nicely designed aquarium, although it's quite small, given the ticket price. As is the norm at such places, there are lots of sea critters in creatively designed tanks. You can walk through an aquarium tunnel with fish swimming above and around you, and members of the young staff carry around live lobsters, crabs, starfish, and other "inner space" creatures and introduce them up close to kids. They also have some super-cute Antarctic Gentoo penguins. This is a compact, hands-on, interactive place that is a good way of rewarding your kids for being so patient while you took pictures of a pile of rocks back up the road. You get a 10% discount if you buy tickets online.

Dingle Harbour, Dingle, Co. Kerry. ✆ **066/915-2111.** www.dingle-oceanworld.ie. Admission €13 adults; €9 seniors and students; €7.50 children; €30–€36 families. July–Aug daily 10am–6pm; Sept–June daily 10am–5pm.

Eask Tower ★ Built in 1847 as a famine relief project, this is a remarkable edifice, a 12m (39-ft.) tower built of solid stone nearly 5m (16 ft.) thick with a wooden arrow pointing to the mouth of the harbor. It is certainly interesting to look at, but the main reason for making the 1.6km (1-mile) climb to the summit of Carhoo Hill is not to see the tower, but the incredible views of Dingle Harbour, Connor Pass, and, on the far side of the bay, the peaks of the Iveragh Peninsula. This is a great place to get your bearings, but save a trip here for a clear day.

Carhoo Hill, Dingle, Co. Kerry. From Dingle, follow Slea Head Rd. 3.2km (2 miles), turn left at road signposted for Colâiste Ide, and continue another 3.2km (2 miles).

THE slea head DRIVE

When leaving Dingle by car, head west along R559 and you'll encounter the **Slea Head Drive,** a spectacular stretch of road known for its collection of ancient sites—including the **Gallarus Oratory** (see p. 302), one of the best-preserved pieces of early Christian architecture in Ireland. At any tourist information center, you can get a guide to the various ruined abbeys and old forts along the way. ***Note:*** This is serious Gaeltacht territory, so by law, all signs—even road hazard signs—are in Gaelic only.

Sciuird Archaeological Adventures ★ For serious history buffs, these are a great opportunity to get deeper insight into ancient local history. Led by a local historian, the tours last about a half-day and involve a short bus journey and some easy walking. Four or five monuments, from the Stone Age to medieval times, are on the route. All tours, limited to 8 to 10 people, start from the top of the pier, although pickups from your hotel are possible if you're staying locally. Reservations are required, at least a day or so in advance if possible.

Holy Ground, Dingle, Co. Kerry. ✆ **066/915-1606.** Tour €20 per person. Apr–Sept daily 10:30am and 2pm; rest of year by appointment.

Where to Stay in Dingle

Castlewood House ★★★ Overlooking the glassy expanse of Dingle Bay, this lovely, whitewashed house is filled with art and antique knick-knacks. The location is just breathtaking; views of the shimmering water, framed by distant mountains, are fully exploited by the huge bay windows, flooding the bright guestrooms with natural light. Beds are chic and comfortable, and accommodations are heavy on designer furniture and well-chosen art. Bathrooms have Jacuzzi tubs. Breakfasts are outstanding—porridge with a dash of whiskey, homemade breads, oranges in caramel, kippers with scrambled egg, or even a light and fluffy omelet with smoked salmon. Husband-and-wife team Brian and Helen Woods-Heaton are expert and charming hosts. Despite the beautifully rural feel to the location, Dingle Marina is, in fact, only about a 10-minute walk away.

The Wood, Dingle, Co. Kerry. ✆ **066/915-2788.** www.castlewooddingle.com. 14 units. €130–€160 double. Free parking. Rates include breakfast. **Amenities:** Wi-Fi (free).

Greenmount House ★★★ A welcoming B&B overlooking Dingle Bay, Greenmount House is one of the best places to stay in the area. The view from the front is like a cliché of what you might imagine all of Ireland to be like: rolling green slopes falling gently into the sea at Dingle Bay with the streets of quaint Dingle city curving around the coastline below. The public areas are arranged at the front as much as possible, so that you can admire the view from the guest lounge or breakfast room. The garden has an enclosed hot tub where you can savor a glass of wine. Guestrooms are bright and spacious; some have polished wood floors and others have skylights, letting the daylight pour in. Breakfasts are delicious and plentiful—try the tasty smoked salmon and scrambled eggs. Hosts Mary and John are incredibly friendly and will even arrange personal tours of the area for you, escorted by a member of their own family.

Upper John St., Dingle, Co. Kerry. ✆ **066/915-1414.** www.greenmounthouse.ie. 14 units. €100–€150 double. Free parking. Rates include breakfast. **Amenities:** Wi-Fi (free).

Where to Dine in Dingle

Dingle is one of the best places in Ireland for gourmet seafood, not to mention its more low-rent (but delicious) cousin, fish and chips.

The Chart House ★★ IRISH This friendly restaurant on the outskirts of Dingle is one of the most popular places to indulge in the local bounty. The menu is short but impeccably judged, filled with regional flavor and a hint of global influences. Dishes include mussels served with lemongrass and coconut broth, beef filet with colcannon (a traditional Irish dish made with potato and cabbage), and duck with juniper gravy. Almost everything on the menu is sourced from providers within the Dingle Peninsula. The early bird deal has almost as much choice as the evening service and costs just €27 for three courses.

The Mall, Dingle, Co. Kerry. ✆ **066/915-2255.** www.thecharthousedingle.com. Main courses €18–€27. Daily 6–10pm. Times may vary in winter. Closed Jan–mid-Feb.

Doyle's Seafood Bar ★★★ SEAFOOD This is one of the best places in Dingle to go for top-notch seafood. It's not cheap, but the food is beautifully prepared. As you'd expect from a place like this, what you find on the menu will depend on the catch of the day; however, specialties include fish stew made with white wine and saffron, turbot with red pepper and chive sauce, or black sole with a lemon and parsley butter. Carnivores are taken care of with a simple steak or lamb dish—perfectly cooked, but hardly the reason why people flock here. The wine list is extensive, and the early bird menu is served until 7:30pm (€28 for three courses).

4 John St., Dingle, Co. Kerry. ✆ **066/915-2674.** www.doylesofdingle.ie. Main courses €24–€35. Mon–Sat 5–9:30pm.

Reel Dingle Fish ★★ FISH & CHIPS Dingle is not short of an authentic "chipper" or two, and this is one of the best in town. Everything's cooked the traditional way—fish in batter, with piping hot chips, and no messing around—but there's a greater than average choice of fresh fish to choose from including hake, monkfish, pollock, and locally smoked haddock, in addition to the more usual cod and plaice. They also sell homemade burgers crafted from local beef.

Bridge St., Dingle, Co. Kerry. ✆ **066/915-1713.** Fish and chips €5–€12. Daily noon–around 11pm.

Shopping

Dingle has several interesting little craft stores and galleries dotted around the town center and in its environs. Here are a few of the best.

Brian de Staic Jewellery Workshop ★★ Brian is a highly respected jewelry designer who has built up quite a following since he first appeared on the scene over 30 years ago. He specializes in modern interpretations of ancient Celtic motifs, and you'll find everything from pendants and brooches to earrings, bracelets, and crosses. Some of his work is based on instantly recognizable designs; others are more subtle and abstract. It's all exquisite quality. Green St., Dingle, Co. Kerry. ✆ **066/915-1298.** www.briandestaic.com.

Greenlane Gallery ★★ A great selection of new, contemporary art is on sale at this interesting gallery. Styles vary from abstract watercolors and oils to challenging sculpture. Prices vary, inevitably, but several pieces are really quite affordable. Green St., Dingle, Co. Kerry. ✆ **066/915-2018.** www.greenlanegallery.com.

The Weavers' Shop ★★ Lisbeth Mulcahy is a talented weaver and fashion designer. She creates lovely, colorful items of knitwear, hats, throws, and wall hangings. You can also take a peek at the latest creations being made in the studio out back. The shop is closed on Sundays from October to May. Green St., Dingle, Co. Kerry. ✆ **066/915-1688.** www.lisbethmulcahy.com.

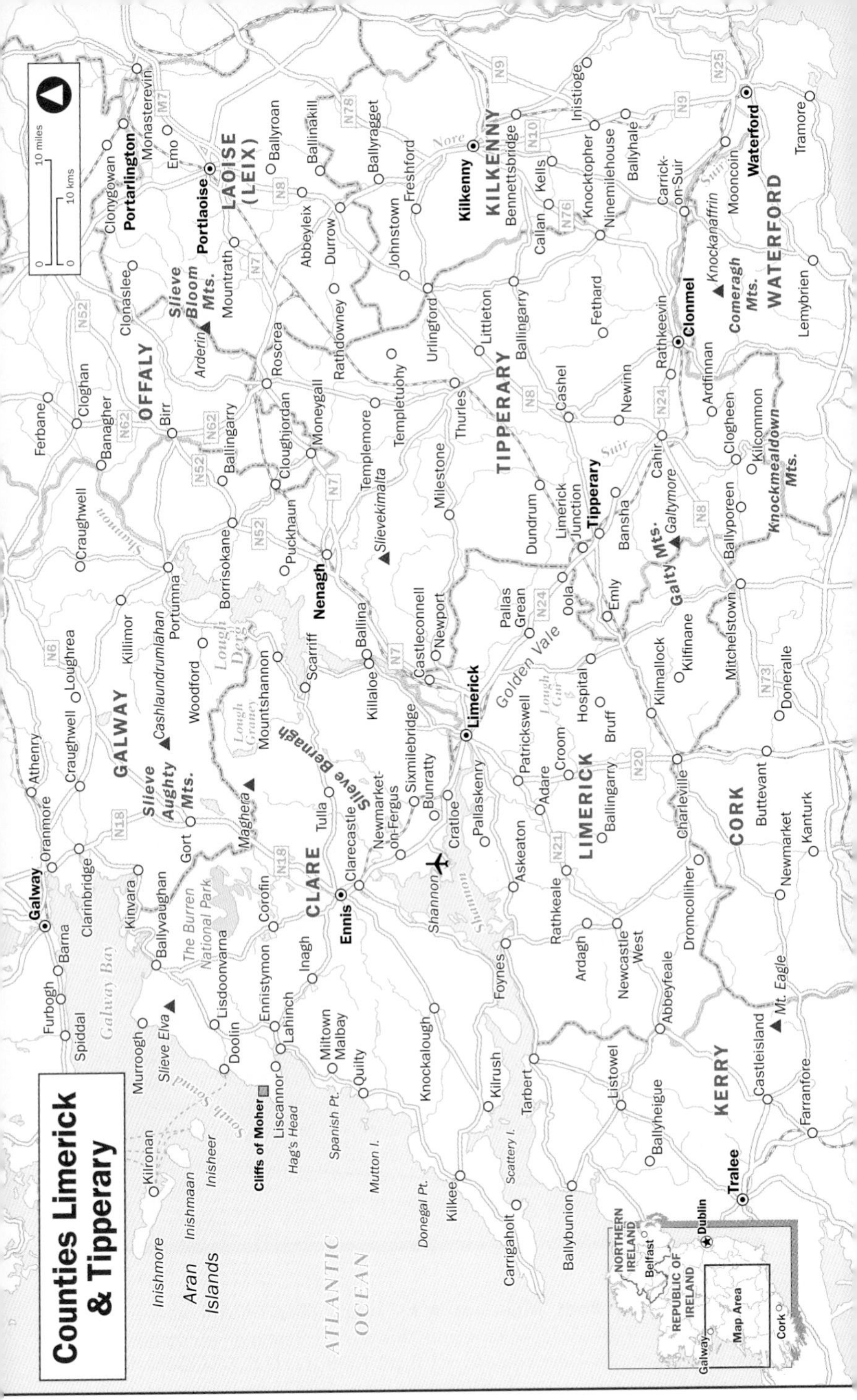

Counties Limerick & Tipperary
0 10 miles
0 10 kms
N
ATLANTIC OCEAN
Aran Islands
Inishmore
Inishmaan
Inisheer
Kilronan
South Sound
Galway Bay
Cliffs of Moher
Hag's Head
Spanish Pt.
Mutton I.
Donegal Pt.
Scattery I.
GALWAY
CLARE
LIMERICK
TIPPERARY
KERRY
CORK
WATERFORD
KILKENNY
OFFALY
LAOISE (LEIX)
Galway
Barna
Furbogh
Spiddal
Oranmore
Athenry
Clarinbridge
Craughwell
Loughrea
Kilimor
Kinvara
Ballyvaughan
Murroogh
Slieve Elva
The Burren National Park
Lisdoonvarna
Doolin
Ennistymon
Lahinch
Liscannor
Corofin
Inagh
Miltown Malbay
Quilty
Ennis
Clarecastle
Newmarket-on-Fergus
Sixmilebridge
Bunratty
Cratloe
Shannon
Knockalough
Kilrush
Kilkee
Carrigaholt
Tarbert
Foynes
Ballybunion
Listowel
Ballyheigue
Tralee
Farranfore
Castleisland
Mt. Eagle
Abbeyfeale
Newcastle West
Ardagh
Rathkeale
Askeaton
Pallaskenry
Adare
Croom
Patrickswell
Ballingarry
Dromcolliher
Newmarket
Kanturk
Charleville
Buttevant
Doneraile
Kilmallock
Bruff
Hospital
Lough Gur
Golden Vale
Limerick
Castleconnell
Newport
Pallas Grean
Oola
Emly
Kilfinane
Galty Mts.
Galtymore
Mitchelstown
Ballyporeen
Knockmealdown Mts.
Clogheen
Kilcommon
Cahir
Bansha
Tipperary
Limerick Junction
Dundrum
Cashel
Newinn
Ardfinnan
Clonmel
Rathkeevin
Fethard
Comeragh Mts.
Knockanaffrin
Lemybrien
Carrick-on-Suir
Mooncoin
Waterford
Tramore
Kilmacthomas
Ballingarry
Littleton
Thurles
Templetuohy
Templemore
Milestone
Slievekimalta
Nenagh
Puckhaun
Ballina
Killaloe
Scarriff
Mountshannon
Lough Derg
Lough Graney
Slieve Bernagh
Tulla
Woodford
Portumna
Borrisokane
Cashlaundrumlahan
Slieve Aughty Mts.
Gort
Maghera
Birr
Banagher
Cloghan
Ferbane
Ballingarry
Cloughjordan
Moneygall
Roscrea
Arderin
Slieve Bloom Mts.
Mountrath
Clonaslee
Portlaoise
Portarlington
Clonygowan
Monasterevin
Emo
Ballyroan
Abbeyleix
Ballinakill
Durrow
Ballyragget
Rathdowney
Johnstown
Freshford
Urlingford
Kilkenny
Bennettsbridge
Kells
Callan
Knocktopher
Ninemilehouse
Ballyhale
Inistioge
Nore
Suir
Shannon
N6
N7
N8
N9
N10
N18
N20
N21
N24
N25
N52
N62
N73
N76
N77
N78
NORTHERN IRELAND
REPUBLIC OF IRELAND
Belfast
Dublin
Galway
Cork
Map Area

Louis Mulchay Workshop ★★ The Mulcahys are a talented bunch—Lisbeth's husband, Louis, is a big name in designer Irish pottery. He designs everything on sale and personally crafts a great deal of the pieces—chances are you'll be able to come away with a true original. It's all beautifully made, from Deco-influenced vases to kitchenware, tea sets, and ornaments. Considering what a name he is, Louis's prices are pretty reasonable too. The workshop also has a handy cafe. Clogher is 16.5km (10⅓ miles) northwest of Dingle on R559. On R559, Clogher, Ballyferriter, near Dingle, Co. Kerry. ✆ **066/915-6229.** www.louismulcahy.com. Workshop: May–Sept Mon–9am–7pm, Sat–Sun 10am–7pm; Oct–Feb, Mon–Fri 9am–5:30pm, Sat–Sun 10am–5:30pm; Mar, Apr Mon–Fri 9am–6pm, Sat–Sun 10am–6pm. Cafe opens 10am Mon–Fri and closes 2 hr. before workshop, year-round.

The Rest of the Dingle Peninsula

The Blasket Islands ★★ Overshadowed by the more famous Skelligs (see above), the Blaskets are another group of mysterious, abandoned islands off the Kerry coast, but with a more recent story to tell. For hundreds of years these were home to an isolated community with a rich tradition of storytelling and folklore that was well documented in the late 1800s. In the 1950s, however, the Irish government ordered a mandatory evacuation when the islands were considered too dangerous for habitation. You can visit the largest of the islands, **Great Blasket,** where a few crumbling buildings and skeletal edifices remain. The main attraction is the eerie, ghost town–like atmosphere in an outstandingly beautiful setting. It's all capped off by a stunning 13km (8-mile) walking route that stretches to the west end of the island, passing sea cliffs and beaches of ivory sand. You can pick up maps and other information from the **Blasket Centre** on the mainland in Dunquin. **Blasket Island Ferries** (✆ **086/335-3805;** www.blasketislands.ie) in Dunquin runs return trips to Great Blasket for €20.

The Blasket Centre (Ionad an Bhlascaoid): Dunquin (Dún Chaoin) , Co. Kerry. ✆ **066/915-6444.** www.blasketislands.ie. Admission €4 adults; €3 seniors; €2 children; €10 families. Mid-Mar–Oct daily 10am–6pm. Last admission 45 min. before closing.

Gallarus Oratory ★ This small, beehive-shaped church is one of the best-preserved pieces of early Christian architecture in Ireland. Built between the 7th and the 9th centuries A.D., its walls and roof are made entirely from dry stones without mortar—yet the interior stays remarkably dry. (Not quite dry enough, sadly, to avoid minor damage sustained during the heavy floods that hit Ireland in early 2014). The small visitor center features displays on the history of the Oratory, plus the obligatory information film. Nearby is the single surviving tower of **Gallarus Castle** that was built in the 15th century.

4.8km (3 miles) east of Ballyferriter, Co. Kerry. ✆ **064/663-2402.** www.heritageireland.ie. Free admission. May–Aug daily 10am–6pm. Signposted down small farm road off R559, just east of Gallarus. Approx. 6.3km (4 miles) northeast of Dingle, turn off R559 at signs for Boile an Fheirteoraigh, Wine Strand and Louis Mulcahy Pottery; then after about 0.1km (100 yds.) take the right hand fork in the road. Gallarus Oratory is signposted on the right a short distance down this road, up a small track.

Irish Famine Cottage ★ This cottage isn't a replica; it's a real dwelling, maintained as it would have been at the time it was abandoned (including eerie, scattered pieces of furniture) during the famine years of the mid-19th

A gruesome TALE IN BALLYFERRITER

The unassuming village of **Ballyferriter *(Baile an Fheirtearaigh)***, part of the Slea Head Drive, is named after a local rebel named Piaras Ferriter. He was a poet and soldier who fought in the 1641 rebellion and ultimately became the last area commander to surrender to Oliver Cromwell's English troops.

Just north of the village, you can follow signs to the moody ruins of the **Dún an Oir Fort,** a defensive citadel dating from the Iron Age. A small memorial here is dedicated to 600 Spanish and Irish troops who were massacred here by the English in 1580. Most were beheaded—a fact commemorated by the highly gruesome local names for two adjacent fields nearby. The first, where the executions were carried out, is called "the Field of the Cutting." The second, where their partial remains were buried, is "the Field of the Heads."

century. The humble stone building is a stark and haunting sight, perched on a windswept cliff, overlooking the coast, while sheep and horses graze nearby. You can't go inside, but looking in through the windows gives a powerful enough impression of what life was really like for the rural poor. The ticket price includes a bag of feed you can take up with you for the curious farm animals who watch your approach. ***Note:*** The cottage is a 2-minute walk up hill from the parking lot, so it may not be suitable for those with mobility problems.

Signposted from R559 (Slea Head Drive), Ventry, Co. Kerry. ✆ **066/915-6241.** Admission €4 adults; €3 children. Apr–Oct daily 10am–6pm. If approaching from the west, sign is just after the turning for Dunbeg Fort.

SPORTS & OUTDOOR PURSUITS

BEACHES The Dingle Peninsula has some of the most dramatic beaches in Ireland. The most famous is **Inch Strand**—a 5km-long (3-mile) creamy stretch of sand dunes in the town of Inch *(Inse)*—but one of the most striking is **Kilmurray Bay at Minard ★★** where, in the shadow of Minard Castle, giant sandstone boulders form a beach unlike anything you've ever seen. It's definitely not safe for swimming, but ideal for a picnic.

Like Minard, **Trabeg Beach** confronts the southwest storms of the Atlantic head on. Here, during ebb tide, you will find exquisite wave-sculptured, maroon sandstone shapes below sheer rock cliffs, and small sea caves lined with veins of crystalline quartz. The beauty of the rock sculptures combined with the roar of the surf is magical.

Some of the calmest beaches in this area for swimming are east of Castlegregory, on the more protected west side of Tralee Bay. The beach at **Maherabeg** has a coveted European Blue Flag (meaning it is exceptionally unpolluted and environmentally safe), and the beaches of **Brandon Bay** are particularly scenic—great for walking and swimming.

BIRD-WATCHING In summer, the small, uninhabited islands surrounding Great Blasket attract flocks of nesting seabirds, including vast numbers of storm petrels. From Clogher Head north of Dunquin at the western extremity of the Dingle Peninsula, rare autumn migrants can sometimes be seen. Inch Peninsula, extending into Castlemaine Harbour south of Inch town, is a wintering ground for brent geese, which arrive in late August and move on in April; there is also a large wigeon population in the fall.

CYCLING Mountain bikes can be rented at **Foxy John Moriarty,** Main Street, Dingle (✆ **066/915-1316**). Alternatively, the staff at the **Mountain Man Outdoor Shop,** Strand Street, Dingle (✆ **066/915-2400;** www.themountainmanshop.com), can handle the arrangements for you. The cost is normally around €15 to €20 per day, or €55 to €80 per week. Employees at both shops know the area well, and can suggest a number of day trips or overnight touring options. Foxy John's has the added advantage of also being a pub, although you might want to save your pints until after your bike ride.

One possible day trip is to take the road out to the tip of the peninsula past Slea Head and Clogher Head. The scenery is outrageously beautiful and the journey is hilly, but not ridiculously so.

DIVING On the North Dingle Peninsula, **Waterworld,** Harbour House, Scraggane Pier, Castlegregory, County Kerry (✆ **066/713-9292;** www.waterworld.ie), is a diving center that offers packages including diving, room, and board at good rates. Classes for beginners are available. The house is a short boat ride from most of the diving sites.

GOLF Sixteen kilometers (10 miles) west of Dingle Town, on the western edge of the Dingle Peninsula, overlooking the Atlantic, the **Dingle Golf Club (Ceann Sibéal),** Ballyferriter (✆ **066/915-6255;** www.dinglelinks.com), welcomes visitors to play its 18-hole, par-72 course. Greens fees for 18 holes are €30 to €60, and for 32 holes, €75 to €85, depending on the season.

HORSEBACK RIDING At **Dingle Horse Riding,** Ballinaboula House, Dingle (✆ **086/821-1225;** www.dinglehorseriding.com), rides are available along nearby beaches or through the mountains. A 1-hour mountain ride starts at €35. Half-day, full-day, and 3- to 5-day packages, including accommodations, meals, and riding, can be arranged.

SAILING The **Dingle Sailing Club,** The Marina, Dingle (✆ **087/390-4816;** www.dinglesailingclub.com), offers an array of courses taught by experienced, certified instructors. Summer courses cost from about €130 to €200.

SEA ANGLING For packages and day trips, contact Nick or Maureen O'Connor at **Angler's Rest,** Ventry (✆ **066/915-9947;** www.iol.ie/~avalon).

WALKING The **Dingle Way** begins in Tralee and circles the peninsula, covering 153km (95 miles) of gorgeous mountain and coastal landscape. The most rugged section is along Brandon Head, where the trail passes between Mount Brandon and the ocean. The views are tremendous, but the walk is long (about 24km/15 miles, averaging 9 hr.) and strenuous, and should be attempted only by experienced walkers and in good weather. The section between Dunquin and Ballyferriter (also 24km/15 miles) follows an especially lovely stretch of coast. For more information, pick up maps from local tourist offices.

Another good walk is the ascent up **Mount Brandon.** The approach from the west is a more gradual climb, but the walk from the eastern, Cloghane side is far more interesting and passes the pastoral beauty of the Paternoster Lakes. The road to the trail head is signposted just past Cloghane on the road to Brandon town; drive about 5km (3 miles) on this road to a small parking lot

Horseback riding in Dingle.

and the Lopsided Tea House. Be sure to bring plenty of water and food, gear for wind and rain, and a good map. The trail climbs through fields, past an elaborate grotto, and along the slope of an open hillside where red-and-white poles clearly mark the way. As you round the corner of the high open hillside, the Paternoster Lakes and Brandon come into view. The walk through this glacial valley toward the base of the mountain is the most beautiful part—if the weather's bad, you won't have wasted your time if you turn around before reaching the summit.

The only seriously strenuous leg is the climb out of this valley to the ridge, a short but intense scramble over boulders and around ledges. Once you reach the ridge top, turn left and follow the trail another .4km (¼ mile) or so to the summit. You can return the way you came or continue south along the ridge, returning to Cloghane on the Pilgrim's Route, an old track that circumnavigates the Dingle Peninsula. Although this is a day hike (about 4 hr. to the summit and back), and very well marked, it shouldn't be taken lightly and certainly isn't for amateurs—bring all necessary supplies and let someone know when you expect to return. Information on routes and weather conditions is available at the Cloghane visitor center.

Hidden Ireland Tours, Dingle (✆ **251/478-7519** in the U.S., or 087/258-1966; www.hiddenirelandtours.com), offers a week of easy to moderate guided hiking through some of Ireland's most beautiful scenery. It takes in parts of the Kerry Way, Killarney National Park, Beara Peninsula in County Cork, Skellig Michael, and the Dingle Peninsula. The cost, including luggage transfers and accommodations, runs around €2,300 per person. Hikes are available April to September.

WINDSURFING The beaches around Castlegregory offer a variety of conditions for windsurfing. Those on the eastern side of the peninsula are generally calmer than those to the west. Equipment can be hired from **Jamie Knox Watersports,** Brandon Bay, Castlegregory, County Kerry (✆ **066/713-9411;** www.jamieknox.com), on the road between Castlegregory and Fahamore. The cost runs from €15 for 1 hour to €70 for the whole day. They also offer lessons for surfers of all skill levels; a 2-hour beginner's taster costs €40 adults, €30 kids 15 and under.

10

THE BURREN & BEYOND: LIMERICK, TIPPERARY & CLARE

North of Kerry and Cork lies County Limerick, a name with poetic associations (of a sort). But despite the 50,000 bad jokes and dirty songs for which it can arguably be blamed, Limerick is actually rather a quiet, rural county, distinguished by the swirls and eddies of the Shannon River and its valley—although you may want to give its eponymous capital city a miss.

To the east, Tipperary is filled with pleasant, emerald green farmland (yes the clichés are true). In truth the county doesn't contain much else that's worth going out of the way for, with one major exception: the Rock of Cashel. As one of Ireland's most spectacular medieval ruins, it's worth a trip across the county all on its own.

County Clare, however, could hardly be a starker contrast. The region's biggest draw is the unique, wild region known as the Burren. Dotted with mysterious ancient stone dolmens and graced with stark, breathtaking vistas, its lunar landscape is quite unlike anywhere else in the country. As if that wasn't enough to impress, Clare also has the famous Cliffs of Moher, a place of high drama and majestic beauty.

And those who don't mind a bit of cheesy entertainment will also find rich pickings here; this region is medieval banquet central, with at least two of its biggest castles packing in the crowds for a nightly dose of ye olde funne.

ARRIVING

BY PLANE Several major airlines operate regular, scheduled flights into **Shannon Airport,** off the Limerick-Ennis road (N18), County Clare (✆ **061/712000;** www.shannonairport.com), 24km (15 miles) west of Limerick. Aer Lingus and Ryanair operate flights to London, Birmingham, and Bristol in England. A taxi from the airport to the city center costs about €35; you can catch one at the airport or pre-book with **Shannon Airport Cabs** (✆ **061/333-366;** www.shannonairportcabs.com).

BY BUS **Bus Éireann** (✆ **061/313333;** www.buseireann.ie) provides the regular Shannonlink bus service from Shannon Airport to **Colbert Station,** Limerick's railway station, on Parnell Street. Bus services from all parts of Ireland come to this station. They also operate services from Limerick, Wexford, and Rosslare, into Clonmel Train Station, Thomas Street, Clonmel, County Tipperary (✆ **052/612-1982;** www.buseireann.ie). In County Clare, most of the small towns and countryside attractions listed in this chapter—including Bunratty, Kilfenora, Doolin, and the Cliffs of Moher—are all accessible on Bus Éireann, although frequency of services can be low in the most rural areas.

PREVIOUS PAGE: **Poulnabrone, an ancient dolmen in the limestone karst landscape of the Burren, County Clare.**

BY TRAIN **Irish Rail** operates direct trains from Dublin, Cork, and Killarney, with connections from other parts of Ireland. They arrive at Limerick's **Colbert Station,** Parnell Street (✆ **061/315555;** www.irishrail.ie). **Irish Rail** runs several trains a day into Clonmel, County Tipperary from Limerick and Waterford. It serves Clonmel Station, Thomas Street, Clonmel, Tipperary (✆ **052/612-1982;** www.irishrail.ie). The station is a 10-minute walk from the town center.

BY CAR Although several of the major sights in this region can be reached on public transportation, you really need a car for the more remote and hard to get to places. Shannon Airport has offices of: **Avis** (✆ **061/715600;** www.avis.ie), **Budget** (✆ **061/471361;** www.budget.ie), and **Hertz** (✆ **061/471369;** www.hertz.ie). Several local firms also maintain desks at the airport; among the most reliable is **Dan Dooley Rent-A-Car** (✆ **061/471098;** www.dan-dooley.ie).

[FastFACTS] LIMERICK, TIPPERARY & CLARE

ATMs/Banks In Clonmel, a branch of **AIB** (✆ **056/612-2500**) is on O'Connell Street. A handy ATM is at Bunratty Castle and Folk Park. Otherwise ATMs are frustratingly rare in the countryside, so make sure you get cash when you can.

Doctors For medical emergencies dial ✆ **999.** For non-emergencies, your hotel should call you a doctor. Otherwise in Clonmel try the **Western House Medical Centre,** Western Rd. (✆ **052/612-5312**). In Limerick City, try the **Abbeygrove Surgery** in Sir Harry's Mall, off Island Road (✆ **061/419121**). In Ballyvaughan, try the **Ballyvaughan Medical Centre** (✆ **065/707-7035**). In Doolin, try **Dr. Catherine O'Loughlin** on Fisher Street (✆ **065/707-4990**).

Emergencies For police, fire, or other emergencies, dial ✆ **999.**

Pharmacies In Clonmel, try **McCormack's Pharmacy,** Mary St. (✆ **052/619-9329**). In Limerick City, try **Boots the Chemist** on Childers Rd. (✆ **061/422017**). In the rural areas of County Clare covered in this chapter, drugstores are fairly scarce, though in Ballyvaughan you could try the **Burren Pharmacy** on Ennis Road (✆ **065/707-7029**).

Taxis In Clonmel try **Dessie's Cabs** (✆ **052/6124425**). In Limerick City, try **Munster Cabs** (✆ **061/639474**). Taxis further out into the countryside, in small towns and villages are rare; the best bet is to ask your hotel, B&B or restaurant to call you one.

COUNTY LIMERICK

The majority of County Limerick is peaceful, pleasant farmland. The picture-postcard village of Adare is definitely worth a visit (although you'll see everything from the end of a row of tourist buses), as are Lough Gurr, and Rathkeale. Sadly the same cannot be said of Limerick City (see p. 312); despite the best efforts of the Tourist Board to shake up its image, the city is a rather gritty, unpleasant place. Things have improved a little since the late 2000s, most notably with the recent redevelopment of the visitor center at **King John's Castle,** but unless you're *really* trying to see everything this island has to offer, it's hard to see why Limerick would demand much of your time.

Visitor Information

The **Limerick Tourist Information Centre** is on Arthur's Quay, Limerick (✆ **061/317522**). It is open Monday to Friday 9am to 5pm; in summer it's usually open weekends too, but call ahead to check.

Another office is located in the **Adare Heritage Centre,** Main Street, Adare (✆ **061/396225;** www.adareheritagecentre.ie). It is open daily, year-round, from 9am to 6pm.

Exploring County Limerick

Adare ★★ *"O sweet Adare"* wrote the poet Gerald Griffin (1803–40), *"O soft retreat of sylvan splendor/ Nor summer sun nor morning gale/ E'er hailed a scene more softly tender."* Like a town plucked from a book of fairy tales, Adare has thatched cottages, black-and-white timbered houses, lichen-covered churches, and romantic ruins, strewn along the banks of the River Maigue. Drop in at the **Adare Heritage Centre** while you're there—part-visitor center, part museum on the history of the town, part craft store. The center is on the main street through Adare village center. Yes, this place has been seriously discovered by the tour-bus crowds (even by May, which is still officially off season, the roads can get clogged at times), but it's still absolutely worth a stop.

Adare, Co. Limerick. Heritage Centre. ✆ **061/396666.** www.adareheritagecentre.ie. Historical Exhibition €4.50 adults; €3.50 seniors, students, and children. Daily 9am–6pm (sometimes closed for lunch).

THERE ONCE WAS A poet FROM LIMERICK . . .

To find out how a genre of bawdy pub poetry came to be associated with this unassuming Irish town requires looking back nearly 300 years. Nobody really knows who wrote the first sharply worded, five-line poem, but the style gained popularity in the 18th century and is credited to a group of poets who lived in the town of Croom in County Limerick. Known as the *Fili na Maighe*, or the "Gaelic poets of the Maigue," the poets wrote sardonic, quick-witted poems in Irish that soon became all the rage. Their style was adopted across the region, and within a century, everybody was doing it. Most anthologies on the subject list 42 poets and Irish scholars in the county in the 19th century, who were known for composing limericks, most with themes of romance, drinking, personal squabbles, and politics.

But it's possible that the true rise of the limerick came as a result of an 18th-century battle of wills between a poet and pub owner, Sean O'Tuama, and his friend Andrias MacCraith. Boyhood friends O'Tuama and MacCraith grew up in County Limerick and were well educated. The two fell out quite spectacularly (nobody remembers over what) and then wrote a series of castigating verses about each other. These became enormously popular, and the modern limerick was born. In retrospect, they're kind of cute, although the meter was sometimes a little stretched. As MacCraith once wrote:

O'Tuama! You boast yourself handy,
At selling good ale and bright brandy
But the fact is your liquor
Makes everyone sicker,
I tell you this, I, your good friend, Andy.

LIMERICK CITY: worth A VISIT?

It is synonymous the world over with a particular brand of cheerful verse, but spend much time in Limerick's eponymous capital and you might find yourself making up a few off-color rhymes of your own. In such a small country, its population of 60,000 is enough to make it the Republic's fourth largest city (only Dublin, Cork, and Galway are bigger), yet it has the kind of gritty, urban feel usually associated with much larger places. It also has a crime problem, including gang-related crime. In 2008 it even suffered the ignominy of being named the murder capital of Europe, while the same report declared Ireland to be Europe's safest country overall. During the economic crash that started in that fateful year, what had been a sharply growing business sector in the city collapsed, leading to a population drain of around 5%.

Simply put, Limerick just isn't very nice.

That said, there are genuine efforts to make things better. The tourist board is doing its part to clean the place up, with a certain amount of success. A prime example is **King John's Castle ★** (Nicholas Street, ✆ **061/411201;** www.shannonheritage.com). The stern riverside fortress, dating from 1210, is the centerpiece of Limerick's historic area. But rarely has an historic building been so poorly treated in the modern age; during the 1950s, in an astonishing act of government vandalism, it even had a public housing project built within its central courtyard. Thankfully that's long gone, but the big, modern visitor center building that's gone up in its place still rather spoils the effect. That said, a recent renovation has greatly modernized and improved the visitor facilities, including high-tech interactive displays. Admission costs €8 adults, €7 seniors, €4.50 children 5 to 16, €21 to €24 families (free for children 4 and under). It's open April to September from 9:30am to 5:30pm, and October to March from 9:30am to 4:30pm (last admission an hour before closing).

The **Limerick City Gallery of Art ★** (People's Park, at the corner of Perry Square and Mallow St., ✆ **061/310633;** www.gallery.limerick.ie) has a good, regularly changing program of contemporary art exhibitions. Its permanent collection includes work by Irish painters Jack B. Yeats and Sir John Lavery. Its opening times are Monday, Wednesday, and Friday 10am to 5:30pm; Tuesday 11am to 5:30pm; Thursday 10am to 8:30pm; Saturday 10am to 5pm; and Sunday noon to 5pm (closed on public holidays). Admission is free.

Perhaps the greatest attraction in Limerick is the **Hunt Museum ★★,** Rutland Street (✆ **061/312833;** www.huntmuseum.com). Located in the old customs building, the museum's 18th century Palladian front is modeled on the Petit Trianon at the Palace of Versailles in France. It has exhibits on ancient Greece and Rome, and paintings by Picasso and Renoir. Admission costs €5 adults, €3.50 seniors and students, €2.50 children and €12 families. It's open Monday to Saturday from 10am to 5pm, and Sunday from 2 to 5pm.

Foynes Flying Boat Museum ★★ When Shannon Airport was just a remote patch of undeveloped farmland, this was the center of international aviation in Europe. The first commercial flight from the U.S. to Europe touched down at Foynes Airport, one hot July morning in 1937; 5 years later this became

IF THE story FITZ . . .

Between Adare and Limerick, the small town of Patrickswell is home to the bijou **Honey Fitz Theatre** (✆ **061/385386;** www.loughgur.com). This is the main venue for the **Lough Gur Storytelling Festival,** a 5-day event in late October that celebrates the art of the good yarn, through a program of music, drama, and poetry. Honey Fitz was the nickname of John Fitzgerald (1863–1950), grandfather to President John F. Kennedy. According to the biographer Robert Dallek, Fitz had a reputation for being "the only politician who could sing *Sweet Adeline* sober and get away with it." The theater was opened in 1994 by Fitzgerald's granddaughter, Jean Kennedy Smith (who was then U.S. Ambassador). *Sweet Adeline* was sung during the ceremony.

one end of the first ever regular service between the two continents. (It's absolutely no coincidence that, in the same year, Foynes was also the birthplace of the Irish coffee. The story goes that a flight to New York had to turn back after a particularly violent storm. The bartender was asked to hurriedly prepare something to both warm up and steady the nerves of the unfortunate passengers. Not knowing what else to do, he served hot coffee and threw shots of whiskey in for good measure.) At this engaging museum you can see a replica of the original Pan Am "flying boat," which may make you swear never to complain about a modern flight again. You can also tour the actual terminal building, kept as it was when the airport closed in 1945, and experience a replica 1940s cinema.

Foynes, Co. Limerick. ✆ **069/65416.** www.flyingboatmuseum.com. Admission €11 adults; €9 seniors and students; €6 children 5–13; children 4 and under free; €28 families. Mar–May daily 9:30am–5pm; June–Sept 9am–6pm; last admission 1 hr. before closing.

Lough Gur ★★ An unusual preponderance of ancient sites surrounds this lovely lake. Most of the sights are well signposted on the R512, the drive that skirts around the lake's edge. Lough Gur was occupied continuously from the Neolithic period to late medieval times. Archaeologists have uncovered foundations of a small farmstead built around the year 900, a lake island dwelling built between 500 and 1000, a wedge-shaped tomb that was a communal grave around 2,500 B.C., and the extraordinary Grange Stone Circle, which is a 4,000-year-old site with 113 upright stones forming the largest prehistoric stone circle in Ireland. An interesting Heritage Centre helps put it all into context. To find the center, head south through the village of Ballyneety; about 6½km (4 miles) on you'll come to Reardons Pub in Holycross. Take the first left afterwards, keep to the left, and this road will take you straight there. The lake itself is a great place to explore and have a picnic.

11km (6¾ miles) SE of Limerick City on R512, Lough Gur, Co. Limerick. ✆ **061/385386.** www.loughgur.com. Free access to Lough; Heritage Centre €5 adults; €4 seniors and students; €3 children; €15 families. Heritage Center Mar–Oct.

Sports & Outdoor Pursuits

FISHING Get information, licenses, permits, and equipment at the **Fishing, Shooting and Archery Store,** The Milk Market, Carr Street, Limerick

(✆ **061/413484**). **Celtic Angling,** in nearby Ballingarry, Adare (✆ **069/68202;** www.celticangling.com), sells all the supplies you need. They also offer daylong salmon-fishing excursions on the Shannon, including pickup from Limerick City, equipment, and licenses. A day's fishing will cost on average €170 to €300 for one person, plus €50 to €200 for each additional person in a group; equipment rental is included in the price. (Owner Paddy Dunworth also offers guided sightseeing trips and hillwalking excursions; check the website for details.)

GOLF The par-70 inland course at the **Limerick Golf Club,** Ballyclough (✆ **061/415146;** www.limerickgolfclub.ie), 4.8km (3 miles) south of Limerick, has greens fees of €50 weekdays, €70 weekends, year-round. The par-71 inland course at **Castletroy Golf Club,** Castletroy, County Limerick (✆ **061/335753;** www.castletroygolfclub.ie), 4.8km (3 miles) east of Limerick, charges greens fees of €40 Monday to Thursday, €50 Friday to Sunday, year-round.

HORSEBACK RIDING The county's fields provide good turf for horseback riding. Rates run about €25 to €30 per hour. The **Clonshire Equestrian Centre,** Adare, County Limerick (✆ **061/396770;** www.clonshire.com), offers riding holidays for adults and children. They're also one of the only riding schools in Ireland to offer riding for disabled visitors.

Where to Stay in County Limerick

Limerick City's economic growth spurt in the 1990s and 2000s led to the construction of several large, impersonal chain hotels there. But why would you bother? The real finds are to be had in the rural parts of County Limerick, where you can hide away in a lovely old cottage on a tranquil farm, or splurge on a night in a grand country house retreat.

Adare Manor ★★ Surrounded by a whopping 340 hectares (840 acres) of landscaped grounds, on the very edge of lovely Adare village, this luxurious resort looks impressively Victorian gothic from the outside. Indoors you'll find a beautifully restored and converted manor house; mostly 19th century, although check out the elaborately-carved 15th century doors on the ground floor. Guestrooms are spacious and individually decorated in traditional (some might say fussy) style. Hidden away on the grounds are 15 modern 3-bedroom self-catering villas, plus 18 townhouses. There's also a swimming pool and a pampering spa. Adare Manor is renowned as something of a golfer's paradise, with a highly rated 18-hole championship course. Archery, clay pigeon shooting, and horseback riding can all be easily arranged. The Oak Room restaurant is one of the best in the area (see p. 316).

Adare, Co. Limerick. ✆ **061/605200.** www.adaremanor.com. 62 units. €440–€700 double; €300–€720 villas. Free parking. Breakfast included. **Amenities:** 2 restaurants; bar; room service; spa; pool; gym; golf course.

Courtyard Cottage ★ A former cowshed may not sound like the height of glamour, but this is a beautifully converted, elegant space. You really feel away from the herd (no pun intended), with 202 hectares (500 acres) of farmland between you and civilization. But what could be more civilized than going up to the manor house, where the charming owner and family resides, for dinner—or even having it brought to your door if you prefer? (€25; or you can fend for yourself in the cottage's own kitchen.) You can rent this place as a fully self-catering option, or as a B&B, with tasty Irish breakfasts cooked every morning up at the house.

Askeaton, Co. Limerick. ✆ **061/392112.** 2 units. €100–€150 B&B; €540–€660 per week self-catering. Free parking. Breakfast included in B&B rate. **Amenities:** Dinner on request (notice required); kitchen; tennis court.

Echo Lodge ★★ This place was once a convent, before being converted into a chic and stylish hotel. Bedrooms are reasonably small, but decorated in such a way that they could be described as "traditional" without the acres of chintz that usually implies—instead they use vintage print wallpapers, tasteful color schemes, and pleasantly eccentric, *objects d'art* touches here and there, such as mini-Ionic columns for bedside tables. There's usually a good handful deals and special offers listed on the website.

Ballingarry, Co. Limerick (13km/8 miles south of Adare). ✆ **069/68508.** 76 units. €130–€320 double. Free parking. Breakfast included. **Amenities:** Wi-Fi (free, public areas only); restaurant (The Mustard Seed, see below); bar; room service.

Fitzgerald's Woodlands House Hotel ★★ The bedrooms at this pleasant, modern hotel aren't particularly fancy, but they're enormous—rare for a place that will give you change when you hand over a €100 bill to pay for the night. The hotel makes a big deal out of how good its beds are, thanks to a full 10cm (4 in.) down mattress topper on each of the beds. The in-house Revas Spa offers relaxation treatments and a thermal suite to while away the last hint of travel fatigue; you can book couples' packages that include massages and afternoon tea for two for around €270.

Adare, Co. Limerick. ✆ **061/605120.** www.woodlands-hotel.ie. 94 units. €80–€140 double. Free parking. Breakfast included. **Amenities:** Wi-Fi (free); restaurant; bar; room service; spa.

Where to Dine in County Limerick

Dutifully demolishing the rule of thumb that the best restaurants are usually found in cities, the rural byways of Counties Limerick and Claire contain several places to eat that would be serious contenders on any "best of" lists for Ireland.

Foley's ★ PUB FOOD/GRILL Nearly 16km (9 miles) southwest of Adare, just off the main N21 road, is this friendly little bar and grill. The menu focuses on hearty, unpretentious comfort food, such as steaks, stews, or maybe a sizzling platter of spicy chicken. They sometimes have live music here in the evening, though it's more of the local rock band variety than flutes and fiddles. Heading from the direction of Adare, take the R523 turnoff signposted for Athea. Foley's is located on the right, just after the road straightens out.

On R523, about 4km (2½ miles) southwest of Rathkeale, Co. Limerick. ✆ **062/62688.** www.ryansdaughter.ie. Main courses €3–€10. Daily 9am–4pm.

Mortell's ★★ SEAFOOD/DELI This great deli restaurant is an excellent lunch option if you're in Limerick City. The seafood (much of it local) is beautifully prepared, and cooked right in front of your eyes, although you can also opt for a burger or simply a cup of coffee and a sandwich. The lively, chatty staff keep everything running smoothly.

40 Roaches St., Limerick, Co. Limerick. ✆ **061/415457.** Lunch main courses €5–€14. Mon–Sat 8am–5pm.

The Mustard Seed ★★★ MODERN EUROPEAN The in-house restaurant of the excellent Echo Lodge hotel (see above) is one of the best-loved, and most widely known, in the region. The restaurant has its own kitchen garden that supplies many of the ingredients. The four-course menus are imaginative and scintillating; after a starter of warm strawberry salad, made with beet meringues and elderflower syrup, you could go for spring lamb with chargrilled zucchini cream, or guinea fowl with Parmesan custard and a vegetable fricassee. Dinner and bed and breakfast deals are usually on offer on the website.

At the Echo Lodge hotel, Ballingarry, Co. Limerick (13km/8 miles south of Adare). ✆ **069/68508.** www.mustardseed.ie. Fixed-price 4-course dinner €60. Daily 6:45–9:15pm.

The Oak Room ★★★ MODERN IRISH Another superb hotel restaurant, the Oak Room is part of Adare Manor (see p. 314). The high stone windows and silver candelabra of the dining room here should leave you in no doubt that this is a place where you're expected to sit up straight—gentlemen, a tie if you please. The food certainly lives up to the promise of being something special. Herb and citron marinated salmon makes a deliciously piquant starter before a main of beef filet with cracked pepper jus, or rack of lamb with a wild garlic crust. And if you're liking the place too much to leave at the end of the meal . . . well you probably should anyway, the cheapest rooms here cost about €400.

Adare, Co. Limerick. ✆ **061/605200.** www.adaremanor.com. Main courses €25–€35. Daily 6:30–10pm.

The Wild Geese ★★★ MODERN IRISH What is it about Adare that breeds superlative restaurants? The Wild Geese, in the center of the village, mixes fresh, local ingredients with hints of the global village. A main of roast chicken could be stuffed with soft Bluebell Falls goat's cheese, a specialty from County Clare; or some monkfish may arrive accompanied by a potato and spinach pancake, finished off with some lemongrass sauce. Sunday lunch, which often features dishes seen on the evening menu, is significantly cheaper than dinner service, at just €20 for two courses.

Adare, Co. Limerick. ✆ **061/605200.** www.adaremanor.com. Main courses €25–€32. May–Sept Tues–Sat 6:30–10pm, Sun noon–3pm, 5:30–10pm; Oct–Apr Tues–Sat 6:30–10pm, Sun noon–3pm. Closed most of Jan.

COUNTY TIPPERARY

In many ways County Tipperary is a bit mysterious. Everybody's heard of it, but few have actually been. It's a bit out of the way—too far from most major tourist hot spots for an easy day trip—and its attractions are few. This works to its advantage, though, since far from the tour buses and the bleeping of digital camera shutters, you may just find the Ireland everyone is looking for: welcoming, unspoiled, green, and peaceful.

Visitor Information

The **Clonmel Tourist Office** is at 6 Sarsfield St., Clonmel (✆ **052/612-2960**). It's open year-round, Monday to Friday, from 9:30am to 1pm and 2pm to 4:30pm. The small **Cashel Tourist Office** is at the Heritage Centre, Main Street, Cashel (✆ **062/62511**), open March to October daily 9:30am to 5:30pm and November to February 9:30am to 5:30pm Monday to Friday. A **seasonal office** is at Castle Street, Cahir (✆ **052/714-1453**), open April to October, Monday to Saturday, from 9:30am to 6pm.

Exploring County Tipperary

Clonmel, the capital of Tipperary, is the unassuming gateway to the region. A working town, largely unspoiled by tourism, Clonmel (whose name in Gaelic, *Cluaín Meala,* means "Meadows of Honey") makes a strategic, pleasant base in the Southeast. Looking at the sleepy rural town, poised on the banks of the Suir, it's hard to believe that it once withstood a Cromwellian siege for 3 brutal months.

North of Clonmel and deep in the Tipperary countryside, **Cashel,** with its monastic buildings and dramatic setting, is not to be missed. Because it's on the main N8 road, most people pass through en route from Dublin to Cork.

Meanwhile, at Cahir, head north through the scenic **Galtee Mountains** to the Glen of Aherlow for a gorgeous drive. The pristine 11km (7-mile) Glen of Aherlow is a secluded and scenic pass between the plains of counties Tipperary and Limerick.

Ahenny High Crosses ★ You're likely to have this little-known and rarely visited site to yourself, except for the cows whose pasture you will cross to reach it. The setting is idyllic and gorgeous on a bright day. The well-preserved Ahenny high crosses date from the 8th or 9th century. Tradition associates them with seven saintly bishops, all brothers who were said to have been waylaid and murdered. Their unusual stone "caps," thought by some to be bishops' miters, more likely suggest the transition from wood crosses, which would have had small roofs to shelter them from the rain. Also note their intricate spiral and cable ornamentation in remarkably high relief, which may have been inspired by earlier Celtic metalwork.

Kil Crispeen Churchyard, Ahenny, Co. Tipperary. 8km (5 miles) north of Carrick-on-Suir, signposted off R697. Free admission (box for donations).

Athassel Priory ★ Although it is in ruins, many delightful details from the original medieval priory that once stood here still remain. This was an Augustinian priory, founded in the late 12th century, and it was once elaborately decorated. The main approach is over a low stone bridge and through a gatehouse. The church entrance is a beautifully carved doorway at its west end, while to the south of the church is the cloister, its graceful arches eroded by time. Look for a carved face protruding from the southwest corner of the chapel tower, about 9m (30 ft.) above ground level.

3km (2 miles) south of Golden, Co. Tipperary. Take signposted road from Golden, on the N74; the priory is in a field just east of the road.

The Bolton Library ★ Not far from the Rock of Cashel (see p. 319), this curious and unexpected library has a great collection of valuable antiquarian manuscripts, including some early medieval books. The collection on display features works by, among others, Jonathan Swift, Dante, Machiavelli, and Sir Isaac Newton. It also contains what is supposedly the smallest book in the world.

On the grounds of St. John the Baptist Church, John St., Cashel, Co. Tipperary. ✆ **062/61944.** Admission €2 adults; children free. Mon–Wed 10am–3pm, Thurs 10am–2:30pm.

Cahir Castle ★★ On a rock in the middle of the River Suir, this remarkably complete medieval fortress can trace its history from the 3rd century, when a fort was first built on the rock—hence the town's Gaelic name, "City of the Fishing Fort". The present structure, which belonged to the Butler

PETTICOAT loose & OTHER SCENIC DIVERSIONS

If you're driving this way from County Waterford, you might want to travel via the **Vee Gap.** This 18km-long (11-mile) road winds through the Knockmealdown Mountains from Lismore and Cappoquin in County Waterford, to Clogheen in County Tipperary. It's a dramatic drive, which peaks at the Tipperary-Waterford border, where the two slopes of the pass converge to frame the patchwork fields of the Galtee Valley far below. At this point, numerous walking trails lead to the nearby peaks and down to the mountain lake of **Petticoat Loose**—named after a, shall we say, lady of flexible morals. A more edifying local character was Samuel Grubb, of Castle Grace, who so loved these slopes that he left instructions to be buried upright overlooking them. And so he was. The rounded stone cairn you might notice off the road between Clogheen and the Vee Gap is where he stands in place, entombed, facing the Golden Vale of Tipperary.

The Vee Gap also has some terrific walking paths. About 2km (1¼ miles) north of R669 and R668, you reach the highest point in the gap; a parking lot is here, as well as a dirt road continuing down to a lake nestled into the slope below. This is Bay Lough, and the dirt road used to be the main thoroughfare over the gap. It now offers a fine walk to the shores of the lake, with outstanding views of the valley to the north. For a panoramic perspective of the region, start walking due east from the gap parking lot to the summit of Sugarloaf Hill; the hike is extremely steep, but well worth the effort—the views from the ridge are superb.

family for 600 years, 1375 to 1961, is Norman. It has a massive keep, high walls, spacious courtyards, original gateways with portcullis still intact, and a fully restored great hall. The interpretive center has an engaging 20-minute video introduction to the region's major historic sites, and you can take a guided tour of the castle grounds. But do take the time to walk through the castle buildings, which are not included in the tour.

Cahir, Co. Tipperary. ✆ **052/744-1011.** Admission €3 adults; €2 seniors; €1 students and children; €8 families. Mar–mid-June daily 9:30am–5:30pm; mid-June–Aug daily 9am–6:30pm; Sept–mid-Oct daily 9:30am–5:30pm; mid-Oct–Feb daily 9:30am–4:30pm.

Ormond Castle ★ This mid-15th-century castle built by Sir Edward MacRichard Butler on a strategic bend of the River Suir has lain in ruins for centuries. What still stands, attached to the ancient battlements, is the last surviving Tudor manor house in Ireland. Trusting that "if he built it, she would come," Thomas Butler constructed an extensive manor in honor of his most successful relation, Queen Elizabeth I. He was to be disappointed. Elizabeth never dropped by, but many others have, especially since the Heritage Service partially restored this impressive piece of Irish history. The manor's plasterwork, carvings, period furniture, and collection of original 17th- and 18th-century royal charters will make you glad you bothered to visit and wonder why Good Queen Bess never did.

Signposted from the center of Carrick-on-Suir, Carrick-on-Suir, Co. Tipperary. ✆ **051/640787.** Free admission. Apr–late Sept daily 10am–1:30pm, 2–6pm. Closed late Sept–Feb. Last admission 45 min. before closing.

The Rock of Cashel ★★★ Worth the long drive it takes to get here from almost anywhere useful, this is one of Ireland's most iconic—and most impressive—medieval ruins. The extraordinary, dramatic outline of this craggy abbey, atop a hill in the center of Cashel, dominates views for miles around. An outcrop of limestone reaching some 60m (197 ft.) into the sky, the so-called "Rock" tells the tales of 16 centuries. It was the seat of the kings of Munster at least as far back as 360, and it remained a royal fortress until 1101, when King Murtagh O'Brien granted it to the church. Among Cashel's many great moments was the legendary baptism of King Aengus by St. Patrick in 448. Remaining on the rock are the ruins of a two-towered chapel, a cruciform cathedral, a 28m (92-ft.) round tower, and a cluster of other medieval monuments. Inside the cathedral, extraordinary and detailed ancient carvings survive in excellent condition. The views of and from the Rock are spectacular.

Cashel, Co. Tipperary. Admission €6 adults; €4 seniors; €2 children and students; €14 families. Mid-Mar–early June daily 9am–5:30pm; early June–mid-Sept daily 9am–7pm; mid-Sept–mid-Oct 9am–5:30pm; mid-Oct–mid-Mar daily 9am–4:30pm; last admission 45 min. before closing.

Swiss Cottage ★ The earls of Glengall used the Swiss Cottage as a hunting and fishing lodge as far back as 1812. It's a superb example of *cottage orné:* a rustic house embodying the ideal of simplicity that so appealed to the Romantics of the early 19th century. The thatched-roof cottage has extensive timberwork, usually not seen in Ireland, and is believed to have been designed by John Nash, a

Lough Derg

THE lough derg DRIVE

At the meeting point of Counties Clare, Limerick, and Tipperary, Lough Derg creates a stunning waterscape. Often called an inland sea, Lough Derg is the Shannon River's largest lake and widest point: 40km (25 miles) long and almost 16km (10 miles) wide.

The road that circles the lake for 153km (95 miles), the **Lough Derg Drive,** is another of Ireland's great scenic drives. It's one continuous photo opportunity, where panoramas of hilly farmlands, gentle mountains, and glistening waters are unspoiled by commercialization.

The drive is also a collage of colorful shoreline towns, starting with **Killaloe,** County Clare, and **Ballina,** County Tipperary. They're so close that they are essentially one community—only a splendid 13-arch bridge over the Shannon separates them. In the summer, its pubs and bars fill with weekend sailors.

Kincora, on the highest ground at Killaloe, was the royal settlement of Brian Boru and the other O'Brien kings, although no trace of any buildings survives. **Killaloe** is a picturesque town with lakeside views at almost every turn and restaurants and pubs perched on the shore.

Eight kilometers (5 miles) inland from Lough Derg's lower southeast shores is **Nenagh,** the chief town of north Tipperary. It lies in a fertile valley between the Silvermine and Arra mountains.

On the north shore of the lake in County Galway, **Portumna** is worth a visit for its forest park and castle.

Memorable little towns and harborside villages like **Mountshannon** and **Dromineer** dot the rest of the Lough Derg Drive. Some towns, like **Terryglass** and **Woodford,** are known for atmospheric old pubs where spontaneous sessions of traditional Irish music are likely to break out. Others, like **Puckane** and **Ballinderry,** offer unique crafts.

The best way to get to Lough Derg is by car or boat. Since the area has limited public transportation, you will need a car to get around the lake. Major roads that lead to Lough Derg are the main Limerick-Dublin road (N7) from points east and south, N6 and N65 from Galway and the west, and N52 from the north. The Lough Derg Drive, which is well signposted, is a combination of R352 on the west bank of the lake and R493, R494, and R495 on the east bank.

royal architect. The interior has some of the first wallpaper commercially produced in Paris. A guided tour (the only way to see the building) lasts approximately 40 minutes.

Off Dublin-Cork Rd. (N8), Kilcommon, Cahir, Co. Tipperary. ✆ **052/41144.** Guided tour €3 adults; €2 seniors; €1 students and children; €8 families. Apr–late Oct daily 10am–6pm; last tour 45 min. before closing.

Sports & Outdoor Pursuits

BIRD-WATCHING As many as 15 species of Irish water birds—including mute swans, coots, gadwalls, and gray herons—can be seen at the **Marlfield Lake Wildfowl Refuge,** several miles west of Clonmel in Marlfield. On your way, you will pass signposts for **St. Patrick's Well,** less than 1.6km (1 mile) away, a tranquil spot with an effervescent pool of reputedly healing crystalline water. In the middle of the pool rises an ancient Celtic cross. The legend that St. Patrick himself visited here seems more solidly rooted than most such claims.

CYCLING Centered around the town of Nenagh, the **North Tipperary Cycle Network** is the collective name given to three scenic cycling routes around the north Tipperary countryside. The signposted routes pass Lough Derg, small riverside villages, and farmland, before looping back to Nenagh. They vary in length from 30km (18½ miles) to 67km (41½ miles). Maps and other information about the loops can be found at **www.everytrail.com**. To hire a bike locally, contact **Moynana**, 4 Cecil Walk, Nenagh (✆ **067/31293;** www.moynans.com).

FISHING The **River Suir,** from Carrick-on-Suir to Thurles, was once one of the finest salmon rivers in Europe, but recent excessive trawling at its mouth has threatened its stock. It's still a decent salmon river, especially in the February run and from June to September. Trout (brown and rainbow) are in abundance here in the summer. Here you'll find some of the least expensive game fishing in Ireland; single weekday permits cost around €45. Trout permits are issued by local fishing clubs, and prices vary. The fishing season lasts from St. Patrick's Day to the end of September. Get in touch with the local tourist offices for more details. The **River Nore** and the nearby **River Barrow** are also known for good salmon and trout fishing.

WALKING In the Clonmel area are excellent river and hill walks, some more challenging than others. The most spectacular is the ascent of famed **Slievenamon,** a mountain rich in myth. Inexpensive, detailed trail maps for at least a half-dozen walks are available at the Clonmel Tourist Office on Sarsfield Street, Clonmel. Also available is a free leaflet guide to the birds, butterflies, and flora of nearby **Wilderness Gorge.**

The **Galtee Mountains,** northwest of the Knockmealdowns, offer some great long and short walks. One beautiful route on a well-defined trail is the circuit of **Lake Muskry,** on the north side of the range. To get there, take R663 west out of Bansha, and follow signs for the town of Rossadrehid. To get to the trail, ask for directions in Rossadrehid; there are several turns, and the landmarks change frequently because of logging. The trail leads you up a glaciated valley to the base of a ring of cliffs where the crystalline waters of Lake Muskry lie; from here you can walk around the lake, take in the tremendous views of the valley, and return the way you came. Walking time to the lake and back is 3 hours.

Another option on this walk is to continue up past the lake to the top of the ridge, and from there along the ridge top to Galtymore, a prominent dome-shaped peak about 5km (3 miles) west of Lake Muskry. It is a beautiful but extremely demanding walk, about 6 hours to Galtymore and back. This is only one of many extraordinary walks in the Glen of Aherlow. Trail maps and all the information and assistance you need are available at the **Glen of Aherlow Fáilte Society,** just behind the Coach Road pub, Coach Road, Newtown (✆ **062/56331;** www.aherlow.com). It's open daily June to October from 9am to 6pm, with variable hours at other times of year.

Some great walks begin at the **Vee Gap,** a dramatic notch in the Knockmealdown Mountains. For more on this area, see "Petticoat Loose & Other Scenic Diversions" on p. 318.

Where to Stay in County Tipperary

Ashley Park House ★★ The enchanting quality of this 18th century manor house hotel overlooking Lough Ourna is helped by the fact that you can row out to an island on the lake and explore an overgrown ruined castle from here. The house is decorated with heavy references to its historic origins, with

Regency style color schemes and quality antique furniture. Fishing can be arranged on the Lough, as can horseback riding; or you could just stroll around the beautiful gardens, with their vast swathes of peaceful woodland. Four-course dinners, served in the elegant red dining room, can be arranged for around €45 per head.

Adare, Co. Limerick. ✆ **067/38223.** www.cashel-palace.ie. 5 units. €100–€140 double. Free parking. Breakfast included. **Amenities:** Wi-Fi (free); dinners on request (notice required).

Bansha House ★ This Georgian manor house in tiny Bansha, in the shadow of the Galtee Mountains, is 18km (11 miles) southwest of Cashel. Guestrooms are simple and a bit old fashioned—not all have private bathrooms, for instance, so make sure you ask for one if that's important—but it's cheerful, cozy, and well run. Guests are free to wander the enormous grounds, and the owners also run a horse-breeding stable next door—ask and they'll take you to meet the occupants. A self-catering cottage on the grounds, overlooking where the horses run, sleeps up to five.

Bansha, Co. Tipperary. ✆ **062/54194.** 7 units. €95 double. Free parking. Breakfast included.

Cashel Palace Hotel ★★ The word "palace" might be just a touch grand to describe this 1730s mansion—the name used to be given to Church of Ireland bishops' residences, not just royalty—but nonetheless this is certainly a very elegant and handsome hotel. You're actually right in the middle of Cashel, although it's easy to forget, being surrounded by the gardens here. Bedrooms are good sized and traditionally decorated—check out the delightfully old-fashioned wooden washbasins in the bathrooms. Some rooms overlook the Rock of Cashel (see p. 319), which means you get to see it at its most grand and imposing, floodlit at night. (Rooms with a view of the rock do cost a bit extra, though). Also overlooking the Rock is the **Bishop's Buttery** restaurant, serving good modern Irish cuisine. Be sure to make a dining reservation on weekends.

Main St., Cashel, Co. Tipperary. ✆ **062/62707.** www.cashel-palace.ie. 23 units. €134–€170 double; €224 suites. Free parking. Breakfast included. **Amenities:** Restaurant; bar; room service.

Dundrum House Hotel ★★ Another fine Georgian house hotel—this one's about 10km (10 miles) northwest of the town—Dundrum House is surrounded by verdant green hills and pretty gardens. Large guestrooms have countryside views; some have iron-framed four-poster beds. Family rooms are exceptionally good value here, sleeping up to four for around €100 per night. Very good deals can also be had on dinner and bed and breakfast packages by booking online. Two- and 3-bedroom self-catering cottages and apartments are decently priced too, at between €520 and €655 per week. **Lady Clementine's Restaurant** serves upmarket bistro fare made with plenty of local produce. Make sure you stay for a drink in the bar—it's set in the house's original chapel.

Dundrum, Co. Tipperary. ✆ **062/71116.** www.dundrumhousehotel.com. 86 units. €65–€81 double; €224 suite. Free parking. Breakfast included. **Amenities:** Wi-Fi (free); restaurant; bar; pool; golf course.

Where to Dine in County Tipperary

The pickings are a little thin in Tipperary—it's more of a lunch-on-the-go kind of place—but it's not without interesting and unique dining options of its own.

Befani's ★★ MEDITERRANEAN/TAPAS This cheerful little restaurant in Clonmel is a pleasant surprise in a land where Irish cooking is king. The tapas menu is short but satisfying, with a couple of nods to exotic flavors (Thai prawns with lemongrass and chili tempura, for instance). Entrees combine Irish and Mediterranean flavors, so hake filet comes with pasta *al Nero di Seppia* (a sauce made with squid ink); seared scallops come with black pudding and fig jam.

6 Sarsfield St., Clonmel, Co. Tipperary. ✆ **061/617-7893.** www.befani.com. Tapas €6–€8; main courses €16–€26. Mon–Sat 9–11am, 12:30–2:30pm, 5:30–9:30pm; Sun 9–11am, 12:30–4pm, 5:30–9:30pm. Tapas served Mon–Sat 12:30pm–2:30pm.

Chez Hans ★★ EUROPEAN Located in a converted church building—which, rather wonderfully, was bought with 1,000-year lease on terms of one shilling per year in the 1860s—Chez Hans is one of the most reliable restaurants in Cashel. Menus change several times a week, based on what's freshest and best. Seafood features heavily (Kilmore Quay scallops with salad Nicoise perhaps, or organic salmon served with seasonal vegetables), or you could opt for a local T-bone steak, served with pink pepper sauce. The dining room is a beautiful space, redolent of the building's past life. Reservations are recommended. The restaurant is a 2-minute walk from the Rock of Cashel.

Rockside, Cashel, Co. Tipperary. ✆ **062/61177.** www.chezhans.net. Main courses €24–€38. Tues–Sat 6–10pm.

Mr. Bumbles ★ INTERNATIONAL A casual and friendly restaurant (how could it *not* be both of those things with a name like "Mr. Bumbles"?), this is a great option for lunch or an unfussy dinner. The menu is a mix of international favorites (enchiladas, Cajun chicken salad, tandoori chicken wings) and traditional Irish staples, such as the all-day "mixed grill"—essentially the same full Irish breakfast you've seen in every hotel, with the addition of steak, thus injecting that extra half pound of meat you've thought it needed. Fish and chips cost just €5 every Friday. In the evening things get a little more refined, so you could start with some duck, bacon, and pistachio pate before having a main of spinach and ricotta tortellini, or perhaps a fresh catch of the day.

Richmond House, Kickham St., Clonmel, Co. Tipperary. ✆ **052/612-9188.** www.mrbumbles.ie. Lunch €8–€17. Dinner €19–€27. Daily 9:30am–9:30pm.

The Lazy Bean Café ★ CAFE This is a place that takes coffee and tea seriously. In addition to an exceptionally fine coffee, you can order tea that comes in a suki teapot (a traditional Japanese teapot). They serve very good wraps, bagels, and focaccia sandwiches at lunchtime, or you can choose from the varied all-day breakfast menu. They also have free Wi-Fi.

The Square, Cahir, Co. Tipperary. ✆ **052/744-2038.** www.thelazybeancafe.com. Lunch €7. Daily 9am–6pm.

Ryan's Daughter ★ IRISH/CAFE Good for a satisfyingly traditional lunch, this cute little cafe is not far from the Rock of Cashel (see p. 319). Mains are hearty and old-school. Choose from homemade pies, stews, roast chicken, pork, or beef, piled high with steaming hot vegetables. Portions are so generous you probably won't be hungry for dinner. The flat-rate of €10 per main course is a great value; alternatively, you could reward yourself for making the climb up and down from the Rock with a restorative coffee and a tasty slice of cake for just a couple of euro.

Ladyswell St., Cashel, Co. Tipperary. ✆ **062/62688.** www.ryansdaughter.ie. Main courses €10. Daily 9am–4pm.

COUNTY CLARE

With its miles of pasture and green, softly rolling fields, Clare seems, at first, a pleasantly pastoral place. But head to the coast and a dramatic landscape awaits you, with plunging cliffs and crashing waves. Turn north, and you'll find visual drama of a different kind, courtesy of the lunar landscapes of the Burren.

Visitor Information

The **Burren Centre** in Kilfenora (✆ **065/708-8030**) is the place to go for information on the Burren region. In addition, visitor information points are on Main Street in **Ballyvaughan** (✆ **065/707-7464**) and at the **Cliffs of Moher** (✆ **065/708-1171**).

Exploring the Burren

The **Burren National Park** is by far and away the county's greatest attraction. You could spend several days exploring its profound wilderness, although a day is plenty to hit the high points.

Lisdoonvarna, on the western edge, is a charmingly old-fashioned spa town that has long been known for its natural mineral springs (see "Loved Up in Lisdoonvarna" on p. 333). Each summer, it draws thousands of people to bathe in its sulfuric streams, iron creeks, and iodine lakes.

One of the best ways to explore the Burren is to take the R480. Through a series of corkscrew turns, the road curves from **Corofin** through gorgeous scenery to **Ballyvaughan,** a delightful little village overlooking the blue waters of Galway Bay.

Wildflower spotting in the Burren.

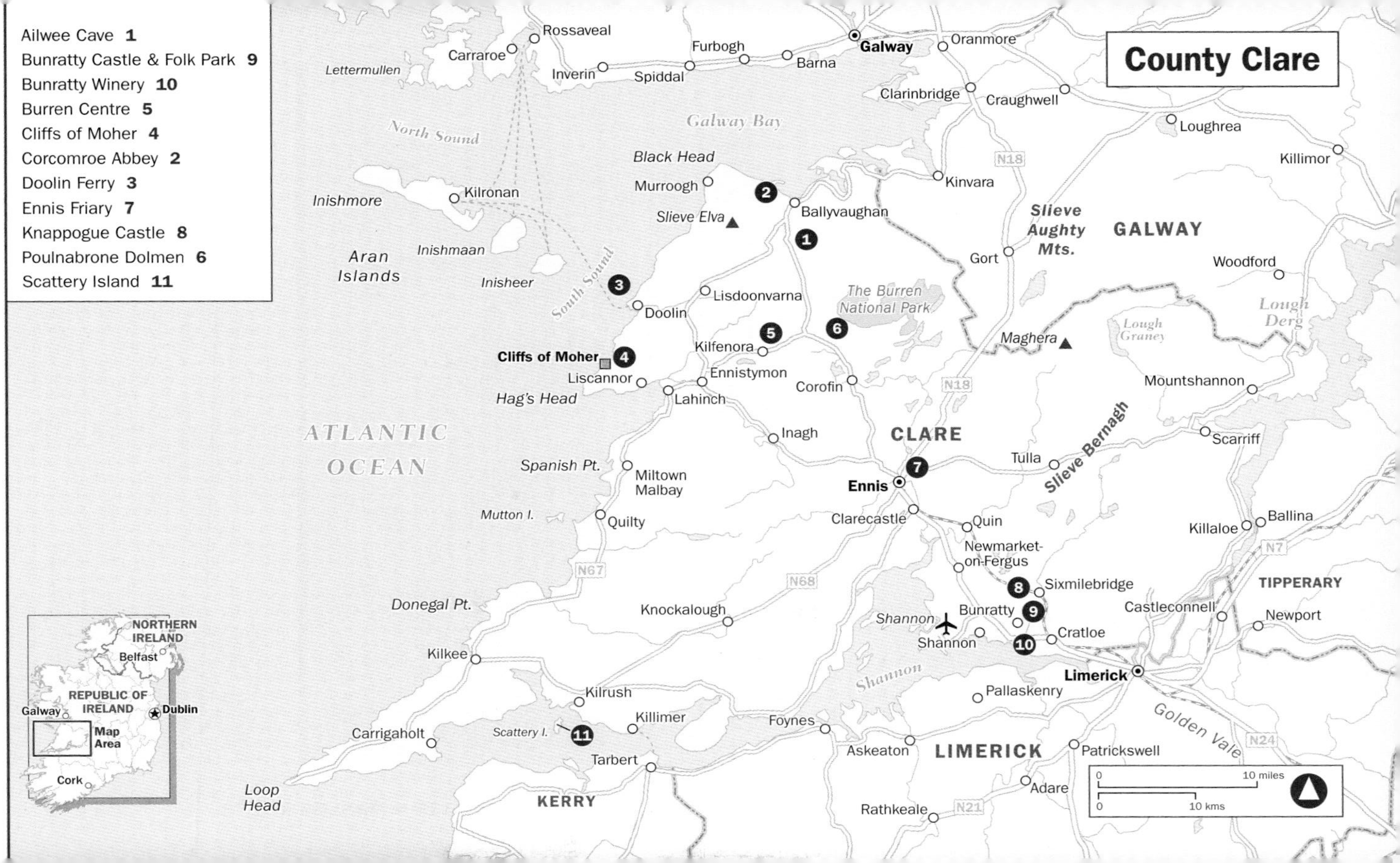
County Clare
Ailwee Cave 1
Bunratty Castle & Folk Park 9
Bunratty Winery 10
Burren Centre 5
Cliffs of Moher 4
Corcomroe Abbey 2
Doolin Ferry 3
Ennis Friary 7
Knappogue Castle 8
Poulnabrone Dolmen 6
Scattery Island 11
Rossaveal
Carraroe
Lettermullen
Inverin
Spiddal
Furbogh
Barna
Galway
Oranmore
Clarinbridge
Craughwell
Loughrea
Killimor
Galway Bay
North Sound
Black Head
Murroogh
Kinvara
Kilronan
Inishmore
Ballyvaughan
Slieve Elva
Slieve Aughty Mts.
GALWAY
Gort
Aran Islands
Inishmaan
Inisheer
South Sound
Doolin
Lisdoonvarna
The Burren National Park
Woodford
Lough Derg
Lough Graney
Maghera
Kilfenora
Cliffs of Moher
Ennistymon
Liscannor
Corofin
Hag's Head
Lahinch
Mountshannon
ATLANTIC OCEAN
Inagh
CLARE
Slieve Bernagh
Scarriff
Tulla
Spanish Pt.
Miltown Malbay
Ennis
Mutton I.
Quilty
Clarecastle
Quin
Killaloe
Ballina
Newmarket-on-Fergus
N18
N67
N68
N7
N24
N21
Sixmilebridge
TIPPERARY
Donegal Pt.
Knockalough
Shannon
Bunratty
Castleconnell
Newport
Cratloe
Kilkee
Limerick
Kilrush
Pallaskenry
Golden Vale
Killimer
Foynes
Carrigaholt
Scattery I.
Askeaton
LIMERICK
Patrickswell
Tarbert
Loop Head
KERRY
Adare
Rathkeale
0
10 miles
10 kms
NORTHERN IRELAND
Belfast
REPUBLIC OF IRELAND
Galway
Dublin
Map Area
Cork

THE burren NATIONAL PARK

The stark, otherworldly landscape of **the Burren National Park** spreads across 1,653 hectares (4,083 acres) and continually acquires more land as it becomes available. Carved by nature from bare carboniferous limestone, the Burren manages to be both desolate and beautiful. Sheets of rock jut and undulate in a kind of moonscape as far as you can see. Amid the rocks, delicate wildflowers somehow find enough dirt to thrive, and ferns curl gently around boulders, moss softens hard edges, orchids flower exotically, and violets brighten the landscape. With the flowers come butterflies that thrive on the rare flora. Even the Burren's animals are unusual: The pine marten (small weasels), stoat (ermine), and badger, all rare in the rest of Ireland, are common here.

The Burren began to get its strange and unforgettable appearance 300 million years ago when layers of shells and sediment were deposited under a tropical sea. Many millions of years later, those layers were exposed by erosion and poor prehistoric farming methods, and since then, it's all been battered by the Irish rain and winds, producing all that you see today.

About 7,000 years ago, when this landscape was already very old indeed, humans first began to leave their mark here. The park is particularly rich in archaeological remains from the Neolithic through the medieval periods—dolmens and wedge tombs (approximately 120 of them), ring forts (500 of those), round towers, ancient churches, high crosses, monasteries, and holy wells.

The park is centered at Mullaghmore Mountain, but there are no official entrance points—and like all National Parks in Ireland, it's completely free to enter. **The Burren Centre,** on R476 to Kilfenora, is a fine place to get acquainted with all facets of the area. Using films, landscape models, and interpretive displays, it gives an informative overview of the Burren's unique landscape and history. A craft shop and tearoom are also on site. Local guide **Tony Kirby** leads 2½-hour guided walks from outside the center at 12:30pm, on Saturdays, Sundays, Tuesdays, and Thursdays in summertime. The cost is €20, including entry to the exhibition. Contact the visitor center for more details.

The visitor center is on the main road through Kilfenora, County Clare (✆ **065/708-8030;** www.theburren.ie). Admission to the center costs €6 adults, €5 seniors and students, €4 children age 6 to 16, and €20 families (free for children 5 and under). It's open from mid-March to May, September and October daily from 10am to 5pm; and from June to August daily from 9:30am to 5:30pm.

Aillwee Cave ★★ This deep cave was undiscovered for thousands of years until a local farmer followed a dog into it 50 years ago. Inside he found a huge cavern with 1,000m (3,280 ft.) of passages running straight into the heart of a mountain. He kept it to himself for decades before eventually spreading the word. Professional cave explorers later uncovered its magnificent bridged chasms, deep caverns, a frozen waterfall, and hollows created by hibernating brown bears. (Brown bears have been extinct in Ireland for 10,000 years.) Guided tours are excellent here—generally led by geology students from area universities. Enjoy the scary moment when they turn out the lights for a minute so you can experience the depth of the darkness inside. Tours last approximately 30 minutes, and are conducted continuously. A couple of other attractions are on the same site. The **Burren Birds of Prey Centre** is a working aviary designed to mimic the natural habitat of the buzzards, falcons, eagles, and owls that live there. And at the **Wolf's Den** you can take part in 2-hour courses, where you'll learn traditional countryside crafts such as bow making and wood carving.

Ballyvaughan, Co. Clare. ✆ **065/707-7036.** www.aillweecave.ie. Admission to caves: €12 adults; €5.50 children; €29–€35 families. Birds of Prey Centre: €8 adults; €6 children. Combined ticket: €17 adults; €10 children; €49 families. May–June daily 10am–5:30pm; July–Aug daily 10am–6:30pm; Sept–Oct, Mar–Apr daily 10am–5:30pm; Jan–Feb, Nov–Dec daily 10am–5pm. (Times are first and last tour). Wolf's Den sessions daily at noon and 3pm.

Ailwee Cave was unknown in modern times until a farmer stumbled into it in the mid-20th century.

Corcomroe Abbey ★★ Set jewel-like in a languid, green valley bounded by rolling hills, the jagged ruins of this Cistercian abbey are breathtaking. Donal Mór O'Brien founded the abbey in 1194, and his grandson, a former king of Thomond, is entombed in the structure's northern wall. Some interesting medieval and Romanesque carvings are in the stone, including one of a bishop with a crosier. Corcomroe is a lonely spot,

WALK THIS WAY: hiking IN THE BURREN

With its unique terrain and meandering walking paths, the Burren lends itself beautifully to walking. One of the best ways to amble through the limestone pavements and terraces, shale uplands, and lakes is to follow the **Burren Way.**

The 42km (26-mile) signposted route stretches from Ballyvaughan to Liscannor. It includes old "green roads": former highways that crisscross the Burren landscape in inaccessible areas. Most of these unpaved roads were created during the Great Famine as work projects for starving locals, although some are more ancient roads, of indeterminate origin. These unused routes are also famous for harboring rare and beautiful wildflowers, such as orchids and deep blue gentians.

If you're not up for the whole thing, it's easy to pick up the Burren Way in sections, walk a stretch of it, and then head back to your car. An information sheet outlining the route is available from any tourist office. And for more information, including a downloadable map, visit **www.shannonregiontrails.ie**.

except for Easter morning, when people come from miles around to celebrate Mass. It's meant to be quite a sight. Look out for a mound, surrounded by trees, beside the road on the way out—it's the remains of an ancient ring fort.

Signposted from L1014, near Oughtmama, Co. Clare. No phone. Free admission (open site).

Poulnabrone Dolmen ★ This portal tomb is an exquisitely preserved, prehistoric site made all the more peculiar and arresting by the alien Burren landscape in which it sits. Its dolmen (or stone table) is huge, and surrounded by a natural pavement of rocks. The tomb has been dated back 5,000 years. When it was excavated in the 1980s, the remains of 16 people were found. And yet, the greatest mystery remains how the gigantic boulders were moved and lifted—the capstone alone weighs 4½ tonnes (5 tons). In the summer, you probably won't have much trouble finding this sight—just look for all the tour buses. At times they literally block the road.

On R480, 8km (5 miles) south of Aillwee Cave (see p. 326). Free admission (open site).

Exploring the Rest of County Clare

One of Ireland's most photographed places, the **Cliffs of Moher** draw thousands of visitors to Clare's remote reaches every day of the year—rain or shine. Rising to vertiginous heights 210m (689 ft.) above the Atlantic and stretching along about 8km (5 miles) of coastline, the cliffs are undeniably impressive. In bad weather, access to the cliffs is (understandably) limited, as the wind can blow very hard here and it's a long way down. When the weather is fine, the guardrail offers you a small sense of security as you peek over the edge, though some foolhardy visitors treat it with startling disdain, climbing over it for a better view of the sheer drop (although a fierce new anti-climb policy is intended to put a stop to that). It's all well worth a visit, but be aware that in the high season, the crowds can rather spoil the effect.

Farther along the Clare Coast, **Lahinch** is an old-fashioned Victorian seaside resort, with a wide beach and long promenade curving along the horseshoe bay. Golfers will already know all they need to know about this town, as it's renowned for its outstandingly good golf course (see p. 332).

Traditional Irish music is always on heavy rotation in Clare, which is well known for a vibrant music scene. The secluded fishing village of **Doolin,** near Lahinch, is the unofficial capital of Irish traditional music. The village is also a departure point for the short boat trip to the beautiful and isolated **Aran Islands** (see p. 343).

The Clare Coast is dotted with **seaside resorts** with varying degrees of crowds and beauty, and the best include places such as **Kilrush, Kilkee, Miltown Malbay,** and **Ennistymon.** This part of the county is a marvelous place to take amusing pictures of signs denoting the presence of tiny villages and beauty spots with quirky names like Puffing Hole, Intrinsic Bay, Chimney Hill, Elephant's Teeth, Mutton Island, and Lover's Leap.

Bunratty Castle & Folk Park ★★ An impressive, early-15th-century castle, Bunratty is the home for two major tourist attractions: a "living history" recreation of a 19th-century village, and a riotous nighttime medieval banquet. You can tour the interior of the castle, which is surprisingly complete, and the beautiful, restored walled garden. However, the folk park is the big attraction here. Actors in period costume wander around as you walk through the impressive-looking village center, complete with everything from a post office and schoolroom to a doctor's office. You can go inside each one and chat to the occupants. Meanwhile, professional craftspeople work their trades, using authentically traditional methods. There's even a Victorian-style pub. It's all excellent fun, and a brilliant way to imbue kids with a sense of history. In the evenings, the medieval banquet takes over the castle's Great Hall. After a full, sit-down meal, there's a lively a show of music, dancing, and folk stories—all performed by actors and musicians in medieval garb. There are two sittings nightly, at 5:30 and 8:45pm. Booking is essential.

Signposted from N18 (Shannon-Limerick Rd.), Bunratty, Co. Clare. ✆ **061/361-511.** www.shannonheritage.com. Admission €15 adults; €10 seniors and students; €9 children; €34–€38 families. Medieval banquet: €49 adults; €37 children 10–12; €25 children 6–9; children 0–5 free. Daily 9am–5:30pm. Last admission 45 min. before closing.

Bunratty Winery ★ In a coach house dating from 1816, this winery produces traditional medieval wines including mead—a drink made from honey, fermented grape juice, water, matured spirits, and herbs, a historical favorite of the upper classes. The winery is also one of only a couple of distilleries officially licensed to brew Irish potcheen, a heady potato whiskey that was so popular and pernicious, it was banned in 1661—and was only made legal again in 1997. (For more on potcheen, see p. 265). Most of the products are made for Bunratty Castle's medieval-style banquets, but visitors are welcome at the working winery to watch the production in progress and taste the brew.

Next to Bunratty Castle, Bunrarry, Co. Clare. ✆ **061/362-222.** www.bunrattymead.net. Free admission. Weekdays 9:30am–5:30pm.

Cliffs of Moher ★★ The cries of nesting seabirds are faintly audible amid the roar of the Atlantic crashing against the base of these breathtaking cliffs that undulate for 8km (5 miles) along the coast, towering as high as 214m (702 ft.) over the sea. On a clear day, you can see the Aran Islands in Galway Bay as misty shapes in the distance. Look the other way, and you'll see a constant throng of tour buses, cars, and tacky souvenir stalls set up along the footpath. The enormous visitor center houses gift shops, a high-tech "Cliffs of Moher Experience," and various other exhibits. Furthermore, the visitor center has the only (legal) car park, which you can't use without buying entry tickets to the whole center—effectively turning it into a steep *per person* parking charge. If this doesn't put you off the whole place, head up the path beside the visitor center to **O'Brien's Tower** for the best view of the cliffs. The 19th century tower is a knockout spot for photos—though you have to pay an extra couple of euro to climb the stairs.

Nr. Liscannor, Co. Clare. ✆ **065/708-6141.** www.cliffsofmoher.ie. Admission €6 adults; €4 seniors and students; children 15 and under free. Price includes parking and visitor center admission. Mar, Oct Mon–Fri 9am–6pm, Sat–Sun 9am–6:30pm; Apr Mon–Fri 9am–6pm, Sat–Sun 9am–6:30pm; May, Sept Mon–Fri 9am–7pm, Sat–Sun 9am–7:30pm; June Mon–Fri 9am–7:30pm, Sat–Sun 9am–8pm; July–Aug daily 9am–9pm; Nov–Feb daily 9am–5pm.

Doolin ★★ Doolin's old pubs and restaurants ring with the sound of fiddle and accordion all year long, earning this secluded fishing village a reputation as the unofficial capital of Irish traditional music. Most famous among them is **Gus O'Connor's Pub** (Fisher St.; **065/707-4168;** www.gusoconnorsdoolin.com), set among a row of thatched fisherman's cottages, about a 10-minute walk from the seafront. Great though the craic is here, the pub's fame inevitably draws crowds, and it can get packed to the rafters on a busy night. If you're

DOOLIN: SPELUNKER'S gold

The area around Doolin is well known among cavers for its many intriguing potholes and caves. The area is riddled with them—the ground underneath your feet may look solid, but it's really like Swiss cheese. If you're interested in joining the spelunkers, you can stop by the tourist office and pick up brochures from local caving guides, as well as maps.

The most extraordinary single cave is **Poll na gColm,** just northeast of Lisdoonvarna. This is one of Ireland's longest caves, and its caverns wander for miles through underground passageways, vaults, and natural wonders.

For divers, there's a cluster of underwater caves just north of Doolin's harbor called the **Green Holes of Doolin** that are said to be simply extraordinary. You can get a peek at what divers will see at an area known as "Hell," where the roof of a cave has worn away, and the water rushes through an open cavern into a series of undersea pathways.

Novices should definitely not go caving on their own without training or guides. To get one or both of those, check out the homepage of the Speleological Union of Ireland, **www.caving.ie**.

looking for something a little more authentic, head up the road to **McGann's** (Main St.; **065/707-4133;** www.mcgannspubdoolin.com); it's less well known and not so unrelentingly jammed as Gus O'Connor's. In fact, on many nights, there are no locals in Gus's at all—they're all here, downing pints of Guinness and listening to the fiddles. Feel free to join them. Doolin is on R479, about 7.8km (4¾ miles) west of Lisdoonvarna.

Tourist Information Point: at the Hotel Doolin, Fitz's Cross, Doolin, Co. Clare. ✆ **065/707-4111** or 086/856-9725.

Ennis Friary ★ When you walk around Ennis Friary, it can be hard to get a sense of scale, but if it helps you to understand it, consider that records show that in 1375 it was the home and workplace for 350 friars and 600 students. Founded in 1241, this Franciscan abbey, a famous seat of learning in medieval times, made Ennis a focal point of Western Europe for many years. It was finally forced to close in 1692, and thereafter fell into ruin, but it's been partly restored, and contains many beautifully sculpted medieval tombs, decorative fragments, and carvings, including the famous McMahon tomb, with its striking representations of the Passion. The nave and chancel are the oldest parts of the friary, but other structures, such as the 15th-century tower, transept, and sacristy, are also rich in architectural detail. ***Note:*** At this writing the friary was undergoing extensive renovation work. It should be completed by 2014, but it's worth calling ahead to check opening times and prices.

Abbey St., Ennis, Co. Clare. ✆ **065/682-9100.** www.heritageireland.ie. Admission €4 adults; €3 seniors; €2 children and students; €9 families. Easter–Sept daily 10am–6pm; Oct daily 10am–5pm. Last admission 45 min. before closing.

Knappogue Castle & Walled Gardens ★★ Midway between Bunratty and Ennis, this regal castle was built in 1467 as the home of the MacNamara clan—who, along with the O'Briens, dominated the area for more than 1,000 years. Oliver Cromwell used the castle as a base in the mid-17th century while pillaging the countryside and thus, unlike many castles, it was largely left intact. The original Norman structure also has elaborate late-Georgian and Regency wings, added in the early and mid-19th century. Later, in the 20th century, it fell into disrepair, but was rescued by Texan Mark Edwin Andrews, a former U.S. Assistant Secretary of the Navy. He and his wife, Lavone, an architect, worked closely with area historical societies and returned the castle to its former glory, even furnishing it with 15th-century furniture. The Andrews family then turned Knappogue over to the Irish people. The peaceful walled gardens have been meticulously restored to their Victorian condition—look out for the wonderful statue of Bacchus. The gardens supply herbs for the **medieval banquets,** held nightly at 6:30pm, from April to October. Call or see the castle's website for details. ***Note:*** There is no cafe or restaurant on site during the day.

Quin, Co. Clare. ✆ **061/360-788.** Admission €6 adults; €3.50 seniors; €3 children 5–16; children 5 and under free; €15–€17.50 families. Apr–Oct daily 9:30am–5:15pm. Last admission 45 min. before closing.

Scattery Island ★ This unspoiled island in the Shannon Estuary near Kilrush has atmospheric monastic ruins dating from the 6th century. A high, round tower and several churches are all that remain of an extensive settlement that was founded by St. Senan. To visit the island, speak to one of the boat operators who arrange the 20-minute ferry rides from the Marina in Kilrush. Frequency depends on demand, and even in summer there may be only one trip per day. Or you can ask at the Kilrush information center, just past the pier. Kilrush is on N68, 43km (28 miles) southwest of Ennis.

Information center: Merchants Quay, Kilrush, Co. Clare. ✆ **065/905-1577.** Free admission. Ferry prices vary; usually around €15–€20 round trip.

Sports & Outdoor Pursuits

BIRD-WATCHING The **Bridges of Ross,** on the north side of **Loop Head,** is one of the prime autumn bird-watching sites in Ireland, especially during northwest gales, when several rare species have been seen with some consistency. The **lighthouse** at the tip of the head is also a popular spot for watching seabirds.

DOLPHIN-WATCHING The Shannon Estuary is home to about 70 bottlenose dolphins, one of four such resident groups of dolphins in Europe. Two- and four-hour cruises run by **Dolphinwatch** (✆ **065/905-8156;** www.dolphinwatch.ie). Fees start at €26 for adults, €14 for children ages 6 to 16, and €5 for children 5 and under. Advance bookins is essential.

GOLF **Doonbeg Golf Club,** Doonbeg (✆ **065/905-5600;** www.doonbeggolfclub.com), has links designed by golf pro Greg Norman in a breathtaking setting. The magnificent 15th hole ends in a funnel-shaped green surrounded by

The Mass Hole

To say golf is a religious experience in Ireland wouldn't just be hyperbole. Only in Ireland can you experience the unique hazard of the "Mass hole". When the celebration of Mass was outlawed during penal times, secret Masses were often held in hidden dales, culverts, and gorges, out of sight of the British. Some golf links incorporate such places into their courses.

Atlantic winds and stunning views are a constant distraction at the seaside Lahinch Golf Course.

sky-high dunes. With a helipad and a complex that includes a country club, hotel, and cottages, Doonbeg has quickly become a haunt for the moneyed set, so it should come as no surprise that greens fees hefty; expect to pay around €150 to €200 per person.

Also famous, and just as pricey, is **Lahinch Golf Club,** Lahinch (✆ **065/708-1003;** www.lahinchgolf.com). It has two attractive 18-hole links courses, and the "Old Course"—the longer championship links course—is the one that has given Lahinch its far-reaching reputation. This course's elevations, especially at the 9th and 13th holes, make for great views, but it also makes wind an integral part of play. Watch the goats, Lahinch's legendary weather forecasters: If they huddle by the clubhouse, it means a storm is approaching. Visitors are welcome to play, especially on weekdays; greens fees are €50 to €150 for the Old Course, €20 to €35 for a 9-hole game, depending on the time of year. On the newer Castle Course, however, the rate is a much more affordable €55. Meanwhile the **East Clare Golf Club,** Scariff/Killaloe Road, Bodyke, County Clare (✆ **061/921322;** www.eastclare.com), is an 18-hole championship course. Greens fees are about €30 to €50.

SURFING & OTHER WATERSPORTS If you enjoy boating, tubing, water-skiing, windsurfing, canoeing, or other water activities, this is the place for you. If you've always wanted to try surfing, here's your chance: **Lahinch Surf School** (✆ **065/708-2061** or 087/960-9667; www.lahinchsurfschool.com) is set up in a hut on Lahinch promenade, and they specialize in getting people suited up and out on the waves—whether you surf every weekend or have never hit a board in your life. They're friendly and know their stuff; besides, surfing is good for you, apparently. Wet suits, surfboards, and lessons included. Private lessons cost around €100 to €140, depending on the time of year; group lessons cost around €40.

Students look forward to their next break at the Lahinch Surf School.

LOVED UP IN lisdoonvarna

If you've been looking for love in all the wrong places, clearly you've never been to Lisdoonvarna. This County Clare town lives for *l'amour*. There's a Matchmaker Pub on the main street (inside the Imperial Hotel); two local residents call themselves professional matchmakers (Willie Daly, a horse dealer, and James White, an hotelier); and every autumn, the town hosts the month-long **Lisdoonvarna Matchmaking Festival** (www.matchmakerireland.com). Thousands of lovelorn singletons come in search of The One, and locals cheer them on. Up and down each street, every atmospheric corner is used for mixers and minglers. Residents stir the pot by hosting romantic breakfasts, dinners, games, and dances. So good are their intentions and so charming is their belief in true love—in the idea that there really is somebody out there for everybody, and that they should all come together in a far-flung corner of western Ireland to find one another—that you may just fall for it. Lisdoonvarna can be found on the main N67 road, between Ballyvaughan and Ennistimon.

Meanwhile, another watersport that's big business in this part of the country is **river cruising.** If you're experienced, you can rent a barge or cruiser and make your own way, or you can rent a cruiser or barge complete with crew, or take a cabin on a shared cruiser. It all depends on your level of expertise, and the depth of your pockets. Several companies rent cabin cruisers along this stretch of the river including **Emerald Star Line,** The Marina, Carrick-on-Shannon, County Leitrim (✆ **084/4273-1901;** www.emeraldstar.ie).

SWIMMING Lough Derg in the southern part of the county is known for clear, unpolluted water that's ideal for swimming, particularly at **Castle Lough, Dromineer,** and **Portumna Bay.** Portumna Bay has changing rooms and showers.

WALKING **Portumna Forest Park,** at the northern tip of Lough Derg, has some excellent walks, as does the shoreline. For a touch of scenic wilderness, walk a portion of the **Slieve Bloom Way,** a circular 34km (21-mile) signposted trail that begins and ends in Glenbarrow, County Laois; see **www.slievebloom.ie** for details.

Where to Stay in County Clare

County Clare that contains the most unique and special places to stay in the region. That said, it's perhaps a little surprising that there aren't more of them.

Aran View House Hotel ★★ The clue's in the name at this small but friendly hotel in Doolin: The house looks across an expanse of lawn and sea, out to the Aran Islands in the distance. It was built in the mid-17th century and has good-sized guestrooms that maintain a traditional feel, with heavy wood furniture and color schemes of peach or buttermilk. The bar wisely takes full advantage of the amazing view out front, making this a lovely spot for an early evening pint as the sun goes down. The helpful staff runs things very efficiently, and breakfasts are good too. Doolin is about a 10-minute drive up the coast from the Cliffs of Moher.

Coast Rd., Doolin, Co. Clare. ✆ **065/707-4420.** 13 units. €100–€110 double. Free parking. Breakfast included. **Amenities:** Restaurant; bar.

Fergus View ★★ More breathtaking views are to be had at this sweet B&B near Corofin, one of the gateways to the Burren. You could sit for ages marveling at the long vista of rolling fields and rambling hills, joined by the wonderful owner, Mary, as she brings you a fortifying tray of tea to sip by the open fire. Mary is also an expert on the Burren and all this area has to offer visitors, and will happily share her encyclopedic knowledge. Guestrooms are small and simple, but the beds are comfortable. On the grounds is a self-catering lodge that sleeps five. Fergus View is closed from November to Easter.

Kilnaboy, 3.2km (2 miles) north of Corofin on road to Kilfenora, Co. Clare. ✆ **065/683-7606.** www.fergusview.com. 6 units. €76 double. Free parking. Breakfast included.

Gregan's Castle Hotel ★★★ An elegant 18th-century house in an extraordinary setting, Gregan's is one of the most unique and peaceful hotels in this part of Ireland. Manager Simon Haden is the second generation of hoteliers in his family to run this place, although it's been a hotel for much longer—famous guests of the 20th century included J. R. R. Tolkien, who was apparently so inspired by the lunar-like views of the surrounding Burren that he drew on them to describe Mordor in *The Lord of the Rings*. Guestrooms are design-magazine chic, with modern furnishings and bay windows. Televisions are banned in the hotel, to enable guests to get maximum benefit from the peace and tranquility of the surroundings. Even if you can't stretch to the cost of a night here, consider booking a table in the superb **restaurant** (see p. 336). Chef David Hurley's modern Irish cooking is utterly superlative. Check the website for some attractive dinner, bed and breakfast packages, and midweek deals.

Ballyvaughan, Co. Clare. ✆ **065/707-7005.** www.gregans.ie. 22 units. €195–€325 double; €238–€460 suite. Free parking. Breakfast included. **Amenities:** Wi-Fi (free); restaurant; bar.

Durty Nelly's pub in Bunratty, County Clare, lies right in the shadow of Bunratty Castle.

Moy House ★★ An extraordinary squat tower house built in the 19th century, overlooking the crashing waves of the Atlantic Ocean, Moy House is a unique place. You can climb the four-story central tower for the best view out to sea, although the view from some of the guestrooms is almost as good. (The cheaper ones have views of the grounds, not the sea). Rooms are designed in muted, modern tones, with large beds and modern bathrooms. In what has to be a unique feature, one bathroom even has an original, glass-covered well. You can walk down to the beach for a stroll along the dramatic shoreline, or relax in the drawing room—the house is packed with bookshelves, filled with interesting tomes. The restaurant is excellent, with a very strong emphasis on seasonal produce, but it's certainly not cheap at €75 per person for a five-course, fixed-price menu. Check the website for good package deals that can really lower the price, including 2- night getaways for around €230.

On N67, 1.6km (1 mile) south of Lahinch, Co. Clare. ✆ **065/708-2800.** www.moyhouse.com. 9 units. €185–€234 double; €239–€310 suite. Free parking. Breakfast included. **Amenities:** Restaurant.

Where to Dine in County Clare

Barrtra Seafood Restaurant ★★ SEAFOOD A friendly, family-run place with a good line up of simple, tasty seafood, this restaurant looks out over Liscannor Bay. Just look at a map and you'll quickly see why that makes this such a lovely spot in the late evening—the sun sets over the sea on a virtually direct line to the dining room. The menu is simple and fresh, focusing on locally caught seafood served with tasty sauces or unadorned, and a few well-chosen vegetables on the side. It's not all fishy—you could go for a hearty steak and horseradish crème fraiche instead, or perhaps mix the two up with the popular surf 'n' turf (steak served with scallops and garlic butter). It's advisable to call ahead to check opening times outside the summer season.

Miltown Malbay Rd., Lahinch, Co. Clare. ✆ **065/708-1280.** www.barrtra.com. 3 course fixed-price menu €35. Daily noon–2:30pm, 6–10pm. Closed Jan–Feb.

Bay Fish & Chips ★ FISH & CHIPS A 10-minute drive from the Cliffs of Moher, the Bay serves extremely fresh fish and chips. There's nothing fancy here—battered seafood and chunky, steaming chips—but it's the simplicity of this dish that makes it such a universally loved staple in this part of the world. Specials always include a fresh catch of the day. Portions are formidable, and the staff will happily chat to you while you wait for the batter to turn that irresistible shade of golden brown. To get here from the Cliffs, just head south on R478 for a little over 5.5km (3½ miles). It's on the main street as you drive through Liscannor—look out for the small white building with a blue wave painted on one end.

Main St., Liscannor, Co. Clare. ✆ **083/112-3351.** Fish and chips €5–€10. Daily noon–around 11pm.

The Cherry Tree ★★★ MODERN IRISH Overlooking a lake in the sweet village of Killaloe, the Cherry Tree has raked in awards over the years, and with good reason. The menu, which uses plenty of local ingredients, is simple yet sophisticated, wisely giving space for those local flavors to come to the fore. A starter of crab cakes with chili jam could lead on to seabass filet served with braised leaks and lemon butter sauce, or maybe some pan-roasted Tipperary steak with horseradish mash. The early bird menu, served until 9pm on Thursday and 7:30pm on Friday and Saturday, is a great value at €26 for three courses. Booking is advisable.

Lakeside, Ballina, Killaloe, Co. Clare. ✆ **061/375688.** www.cherrytreerestaurant.ie. Main courses €16–€27. Thurs–Sat 6–10pm; Sun 12:30–3pm.

Durty Nelly's ★ IRISH/PUB FOOD You don't walk into a pub called Durty Nelly's expecting haute cuisine. Nonetheless, a few welcome surprises are to be found here. Think genuine, appetizing pub food—fish and chips, steak sandwiches, burgers, or salads. Those who don't mind a bit of cheesy tourist novelty can have their picture taken while pouring their own pint of Guinness. The proximity to Bunratty Castle (see p. 328) will mean that most travelers will probably see it as more of a lunch spot than a dinner destination, but there are actually three dining rooms here—the more refined Oyster and Loft restaurants offer an upmarket version of the same food (good steaks, Thai curries, fresh seafood, and so on). And if you're wondering about the name, "Durty Nelly" was a somewhat ribald heroine of Irish folklore, said to have invented the magical cure-all (and highly alcoholic) moonshine, potcheen (see p. 265).

Next to Bunratty Castle, Bunratty, Co. Clare. ✆ **061/364-861.** www.durtynellys.ie. Main courses €11–€25. Mon–Thurs, Sun 10:30am–12:30am; Fri–Sat 10:30am–2am (food served noon–10pm). Oyster Restaurant: daily noon–5:30pm, 5:30–10pm. Loft Restaurant: daily 5:30–10pm.

Gregan's Castle ★★★ MODERN IRISH The hugely talented David Hurley is the head chef at the exceptional in-house restaurant of the Gregan's Castle

Hotel in Ballyvaughan. His menus are exquisite; easily the equal of the kind of top-level restaurants one may mistakenly think are confined to major cities. The seven-course tasting menu forms the entirety of the dinner service, although a slightly cheaper, three-course dinner menu is available until 7:30pm. A typical meal could start with a few expertly prepared impeccable canapés, before moving on to chicken and sweetbread terrine, wild Wicklow venison, or perhaps some perfectly prepared local seafood. Desserts are sumptuous; compressed pineapple with coconut and lime, for instance. If you love Gregan's so much that you don't want to leave (and that would be perfectly understandable), rooms start at just under €200 per night during high season. For more on the hotel, see p. 334.

Ballyvaughan, Co. Clare. ✆ **065/707-7005.** www.gregans.ie. Fixed-price menu €69; 7-course tasting menu €75, or €115 with wines. Daily 6–9pm.

11

COUNTY GALWAY & CONNEMARA

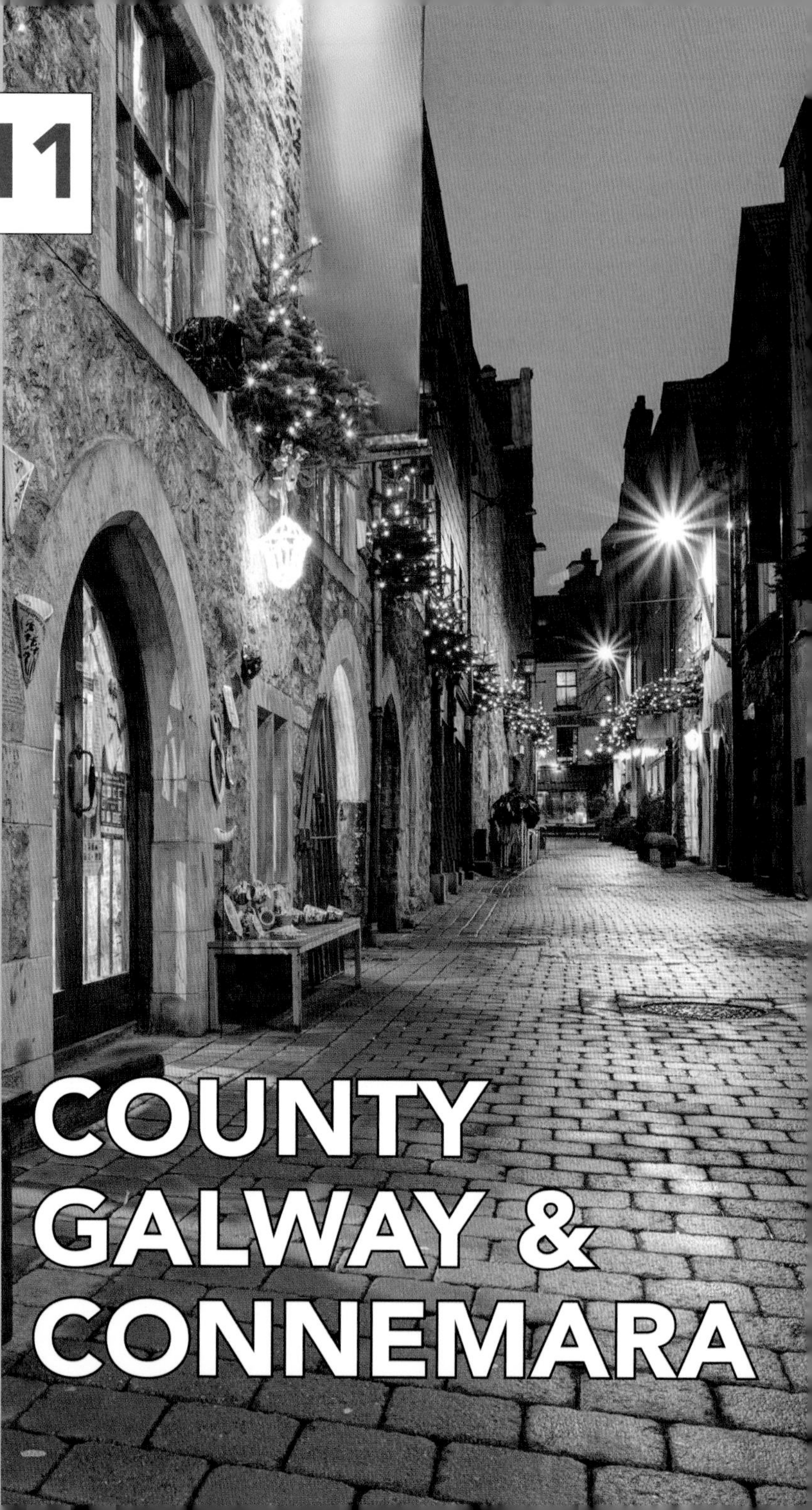

Galway is far enough west to escape the tourist crowds of Kerry or Cork, which is part of its attraction. Here you can climb hills, catch fish, explore history, and get away from it all in the Irish countryside. With its misty, mountain-fringed lakes, rugged coastline, and extensive wilderness, County Galway is a wild and wooly area. And yet, nestled just outside its most dramatic and unkempt part—the windswept, boggy expanse of Connemara—is one of Ireland's artsiest and sophisticated cities. The diminutive city of Galway has long been a center for the arts, and the winding, medieval streets of its oldest quarter retain a seductively bohemian air. Though small, the city is a natural hub for exploring the region. For many travelers to Ireland, Galway is the farthest edge of their journey. Part of the reason they draw the line here is because the county looks so otherworldly—with its bleak bogs, heather-clad moors, and extraordinary light—they think that it must be the end of all that's worth seeing in Ireland (if not the end of the world). It isn't, of course, but Galway is just far enough from the touristy bustle to feel far away.

ARRIVING

BY BUS Buses from all parts of Ireland arrive daily at **Bus Éireann Travel Centre**, Ceannt Station, off Eyre Square, Galway, County Galway (✆ **091/562000;** www.buseireann.ie). They also provide daily service to Clifden.

BY TRAIN Trains from Dublin and other points arrive daily at Ceannt Station in Galway City, off Eyre Square.

BY CAR Galway is on the main N18, N17, N63, N67, and M6 roads. Journey time from Dublin is about 2 hours; from Killarney it's about 3 hours; and from Cork it's about 2½ hours. Outside of Galway City, which is easily accessible by public transportation, your options in this region get pretty limited if you don't have a car. Buses to rural areas sometimes run only a handful of times per day, and remote sites may be completely inaccessible without a car. To hire one in Galway, try **Budget,** 12 Eyre Square (✆ **091/564-570;** www.budget.ie) or **Irish Car Rentals** at Motorpark, Headford Road (✆ **061/206-086;** www.irishcarrentals.com).

BY PLANE Galway has an airport, but at this writing it has not been used for regular, commercial flights since 2011. As of 2014 this situation is unchanged, but there's a possibility they will resume in future. It may be worth checking www.galwayairport.com for updates.

PREVIOUS PAGE: **Kirwan's Lane in Galway.**

[FastFACTS] GALWAY & CLARE

ATMs/Banks In Galway, a **Bank of Ireland** (✆ **091/567-321**) and an **AIB** (✆ **091/561-151**) are on Eyre Square. There's also an AIB on Courthouse Square in Clifden (✆ **095/21129**). ATMs are frustratingly rare the further you get into the countryside, so make sure you get cash when you can.

Dentists For dental emergencies, your hotel should contact a dentist for you; otherwise, in Galway City try **Eyre Square Dental Clinic** on Prospect Hill, Eyre Square (✆ **091/562-932**).

Doctors For medical emergencies dial ✆ **999.** For non-emergencies, your hotel should call you a doctor. Otherwise in Galway City try the **Crescent Medical Centre,** 1 The Crescent (✆ **091/587-213**). In Clifden, try **Dr. Ciaran MacLoughlin** on Main St. (✆ **095/21141**).

Emergencies For police, fire, or other emergencies, dial ✆ **999.**

Internet Access In Galway City, **Chat 'R Net,** 2 Eyre Square (✆ **091/539-912**), offers Internet access and low-cost international calls. You'll be lucky to find any place in the countryside, although the majority of even the small rural B&Bs listed in this chapter have Wi-Fi.

Pharmacies In Galway City, try **Eyre Square Pharmacy,** 2 Eyre Square (✆ **091/567-740**). If you need a drugstore after hours, the **University Late Night Pharmacy,** opposite the University College Hospital on Newcastle Road (✆ **091/520-115**) is open until 9pm weekdays, though it doesn't stay open late on weekends.

Taxis In Galway City try **Abby Taxis** (✆ **091/533-333**) or **Galway Taxis** (✆ **091/561-111**).Taxis in small towns and villages are rare; the best bet is to ask at your hotel or B&B.

COUNTY GALWAY

The majority of top attractions in County Galway are split between two regions: the area around busy Galway City and the wild, untamed landscapes to the west, known as Connemara. Here you'll find windswept, boggy countryside peppered with breathtaking views, dramatic old buildings, and sweet little towns.

Visitor Information

The **Galway Tourist Office** is on Forster Street, Galway (✆ **091/537-700;** www.galway.ie). The city also has a smaller tourist information point on Eyre Square. The **Aran Islands Tourist Office** is in Kilronan, Inishmore (✆ **099/61263**). The **Clifden Tourist Office** is on Galway Road, Clifden (✆ **095/21163**). The Clifden office is closed in winter.

Galway City

A small but thriving and cultured city, Galway still has its winding medieval lanes, but it also has a cosmopolitan core. The city's hub is busy **Eyre Square** (pronounced Air Square), which is a few minutes' walk from everywhere. The charming, artsy medieval district is a tiny, tangled area, so getting lost is half the fun of going there.

CITY LAYOUT

The downtown Galway core lies between Eyre Square on the east and the River Corrib on the west. The main thoroughfare begins west of Eyre Square.

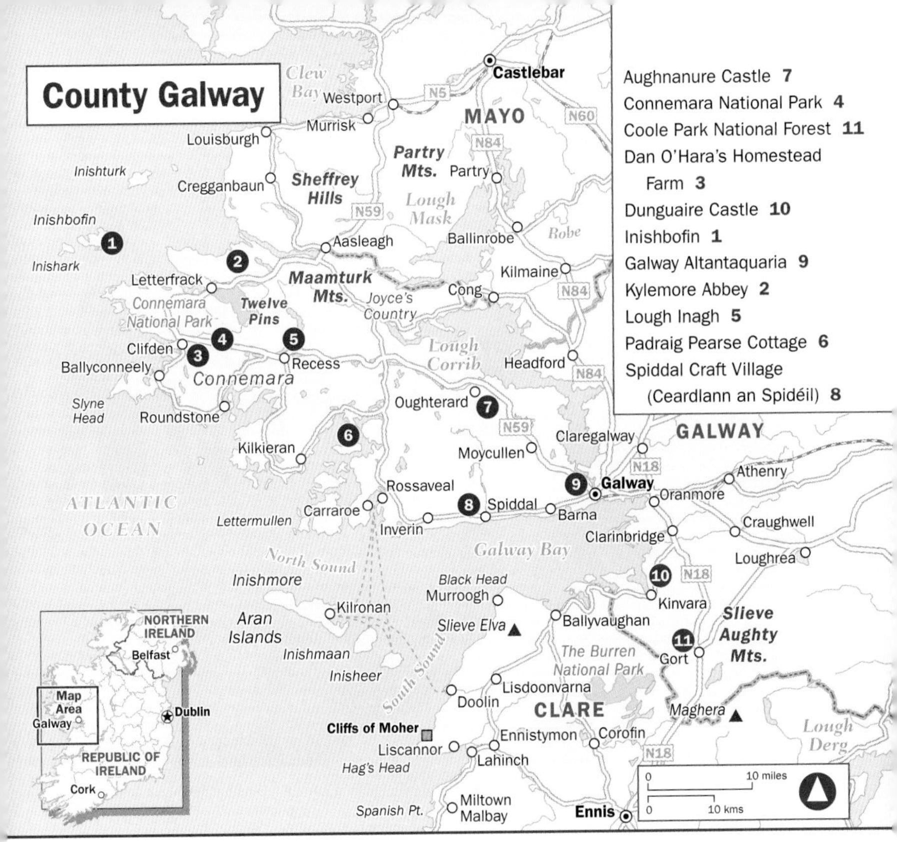

Its name changes—from William to Shop, Main Guard, and Bridge—before it crosses the River Corrib and changes again. If that sounds confusing, well, it is a bit. But the streets are all short and well marked, and it's fairly simple to find your way around the city center. The medieval town center, with its medieval arches, narrow alleyways, and cobblestone lanes, is best explored on foot (wear comfortable shoes). Once you check in at your hotel or guesthouse, park your car and tour by walking. (To see the highlights, follow the signposts on the Tourist Trail of Old Galway. A handy booklet, available at the tourist office and at most bookshops, provides historical and architectural details.) If you must bring your car into the center of town, park it and then walk.

Many of Galway's top attractions are outdoors and free of charge. In the center of town, for example, on Shop Street, is **Lynch's Castle** (see p. 346), dating from 1490 and renovated in the 19th century. It's now a branch of the Allied Irish Bank, and you can walk in and look around. The stern exterior is watched over by a handful of amusing gargoyles.

Close to the city docks, you can still see the area where Spanish merchants unloaded cargo from their galleons. The **Spanish Arch** was one of four arches built in 1594, and the **Spanish Parade** is a small open square, which, like Eyre Square, is great for people-watching.

The bustling streets in Galway, known since the 15th century as the City of Tribes.

The Tribes of Galway

By the 15th century, 14 wealthy merchant families ruled Galway Town, giving it a nickname it still bears today—"City of Tribes." These families, mostly of Welsh and Norman origin, ruled as an oligarchy, and you still see storefronts and businesses bearing these names today: Athy, Blake, Bodkin, Browne, Darcy, Deane, Font, French, Joyce, Kirwan, Lynch, Martin, Morris, and Skerret.

EXPLORING GALWAY CITY

Corrib Princess Cruise ★ Sit back and take in the view from this 157-passenger, two-deck boat, as it cruises along the River Corrib out of Galway City. The journey along the river takes in castles, historical sites, and assorted wildlife. An enthusiastic hostess shows passengers how to fix the perfect Irish coffee and will often try to liven things up with a bit of traditional dancing. It's not for those averse to the tourist experience, but the 90-minute trip is very picturesque. You can buy tickets at the dock or at the *Corrib Princess* desk in the tourist office. It's advisable to call ahead or check the website for up-to-date sailing times.

Departs from Woodquay, Galway, Co. Galway. ✆ **091/592-447.** www.corribprincess.ie. €15 adults; €13 seniors and students; €7 children 4–16; €35 families. Sailings May–June, Sept daily 2:30, 4:30pm; July–Aug daily 12:30, 2:30, 4:30pm.

Druid Theatre ★★ Highly respected across Ireland and beyond for its original, cutting-edge productions, the Druid has been one of the region's foremost arts institutions since the 1970s. They're particularly known for premiering new work from up-and-coming writers, so expect to find challenging, intelligent material being staged here. They also produce new versions of classic plays by Irish,

THE aran islands

"I have heard that, at that time, the ruling proprietor and magistrate of the north island used to give any man who had done wrong a letter to a jailer in Galway, and send him off by himself to serve a term of imprisonment."

—J. M. Synge

When you see the ghostly shapes of the Aran Islands floating 48km (30 miles) out at sea like misty Brigadoon, you instantly understand why the sea-battered and wind-whipped Aran Islands have been the subject of fable, song, and film for thousands of years.

The islands—**Inis Mor** (Inishmore), **Inis Meain** (Inishmaan), and **Inis Oirr** (Inisheer)—are outposts of Gaelic culture and language. All the islands are rather strange looking, with a ring of rocks around their outer edges and, inside, small farms surrounded by soft green grass and wildflowers. Life on the islands is deeply isolated. To this day, many of the 1,500 inhabitants maintain a somewhat traditional life, fishing from currachs (small crafts made of tarred canvas stretched over timber frames), living in stone cottages, relying on pony-drawn wagons to get around, and speaking Gaelic. They still wear the classic, creamy, handmade *bainin* sweaters that originated here, as there's nothing better for keeping out the chill.

Of the islands, **Inishmore** is the largest and easiest to reach from Galway. Its easy transport means you can escape the crowds if you wish. Most visitors disembark from the ferries at **Kilronan,** Inishmore's main town (though it's only the size of a village). It's an easy enough place in which to arrange or rent transportation. The mode is up to you: horse-drawn buggies can be hailed like taxis as you step off the boat, minivans stand at the ready, and bicycle-rental shops are within sight. Drop in at **Oifig Fáilte** (Aran Island Tourist Information), in Kilronan, to pick up walking maps, ask questions, and generally get yourself going here.

The islands have some excellent geological sights, including the magnificent **Dún Aengus,** a vast, 2,000-year-old stone fortress on Inishmore, on the edge of a cliff that drops 90m (295 ft.) to the sea. Its original purpose is unknown—some think it was a military structure, others say it was a vast ceremonial theater. From the top are spectacular views of Galway Bay, the Burren, and Connemara.

Aran Island Ferries (✆ **091/568-903;** www.aranislandferries.com) runs daily service to Inishmore and Inishmaan. Boats leave from Rossaveal (Ros a' Mhíl) (37km/23 miles) west of Galway City. The crossing takes 40 minutes. Call for sailing times. The booking office is at 4 Forster Street in Galway. A shuttle bus goes from nearby Queen's Street to the ferry port, but you must check in at the booking office least 90 minutes before the sailing time if you want to take it. The return crossing costs €25 adults, €20 seniors and students, €13 children. The shuttle bus costs €7 adults, €6 seniors and students, €4 children.

British, and European dramatists. Shows can sell out some time in advance, however, and are often out on the road (the Druid is a touring company), so it's advisable to check out what's on and make bookings as far in advance as possible. Ticket prices range from around €15 to €45.

Flood St., Galway, Co. Galway. ✆ **091/568-660.** www.druid.ie. Ticket prices and performance times vary by show.

Galway Arts Centre ★★ Once the home of W. B. Yeats's patron, Lady Gregory, this attractive town house for many years housed local governmental offices. Today it offers an excellent program of concerts, readings, and exhibitions by Irish and international artists, returning, in a way, to a form Lady Gregory would have appreciated. Usually two or three exhibitions run at any one time. The Arts Centre also manages a second building at 23 Nuns Island. The permanent home of the Galway Youth Theatre, it's used by them and other groups for performances, concerts, and films. For details, call the main arts center number.

47 Dominick St., Galway, Co. Galway. ✆ **091/565-886.** www.galwayartscentre.ie. Free admission. Mon–Fri 10am–5:30pm; Sat 10am–2pm.

Galway Cathedral ★ It's easy to understand why this church's nickname is so short and simple, given that its official name is "Cathedral of Our Lady Assumed into Heaven and St. Nicholas". Although the impressive, domed exterior looks much more classical in style, it was actually built in the 1960s. The striking interior has rows of symmetrical stone archways and dramatic lighting. Contemporary Irish artisans designed the statues, colorful mosaics, and stained glass windows. The limestone for the walls was cut from local quarries, while the polished floor is made from Connemara marble.

University and Gaol rds. beside the Salmon Weir Bridge on the river's west bank. ✆ **091/563-577** (select option 4). www.galwaycathedral.ie. Free admission, donations welcome. Daily 8:30am–6:30pm.

Galway City Museum ★ A rather endearing little museum overlooking the Spanish Arch, this is a good place to spend half an hour acquainting yourself with the city's history. The permanent galleries downstairs relate to Galway's prehistoric and medieval periods, while the upper levels deal with the city's more recent past, including its relationship with the arts. Highlights include a large collection of intricate embroidered textiles, made by a local order of nuns between the 17th and 20th centuries, and some engaging exhibits relating to the history of cinema going in the city. A lively program of special events includes talks, touring exhibitions, and hands-on arts workshops.

Spanish Parade, Galway, Co. Galway. ✆ **091/532-460.** www.galwaycitymuseum.ie. Free admission. Tues–Sat 10am–5pm. Closed Sun and Mon.

Galway Irish Crystal Heritage Centre ★★ Not as well-known as its feted Waterford rival, Galway Crystal is just as unique and beautiful. At this modern visitor center you can observe the master craftspeople at their work, from blowing the molten glass to cutting the finished product (weekdays only, although the center is open daily). Needless to say, the shop is extremely well stocked.

East of the city on the main Dublin Rd. (N6), Merlin Park, Galway, Co. Galway. ✆ **091/757311.** www.galwaycrystal.ie. Free admission. Mon–Fri 9am–5:30pm; Sat 10am–5:30pm; Sun 11am–5pm.

Corrib Princess **1**
Druid Theatre **10**
Eyre Square
Shopping Centre **8**
Ferry to Aran Islands **13**
Galway Arts Centre **9**
Galway Cathedral **2**
Galway City Museum **11**
Galway Irish Crystal
Heritage Centre **4**
Lynch's Castle **7**
Lynch Memorial Window **6**
Nora Barnacle House **3**
St. Nicholas'
Collegiate Church **5**
Spanish Arch **12**

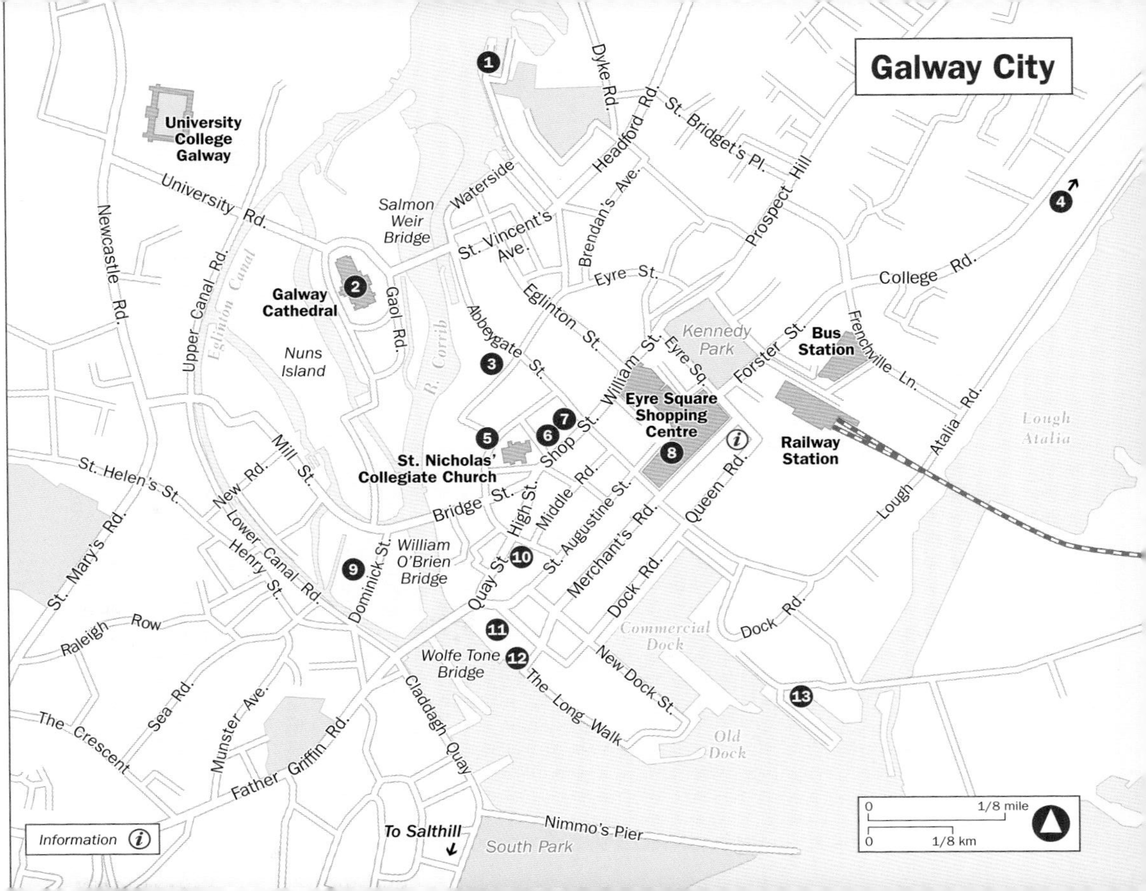

The Tragic Tale of Lynch's Window

One block away from Eyre Square on Market Street, the **Lynch Memorial Window** sits in a wall above a built-up Gothic doorway. It commemorates the tragic story of the 16th-century Galway mayor James Lynch FitzStephen, who condemned his own son to death for the murder of a Spanish merchant. After finding no one to carry out the deed, he executed the boy himself. The act destroyed him and he retreated into a life of seclusion.

Lynch's Castle ★ Dating from 1490 and renovated in the 19th century, this impressive structure was once home to the Lynch family, who ruled the city for many years. It's one of the oldest medieval town houses in Ireland and is now a branch of the Allied Irish Bank. Gargoyles preside over the exterior, while inside is a small display telling the building's history.

Abbeygate St. and Shop St. Free admission. Mon–Wed, Fri 10am–4pm; Thurs 10am–5pm.

Nora Barnacle House ★ This tiny museum (which claims to be the smallest in Ireland) was the childhood home of Nora Barnacle—lover, muse, and eventually wife to James Joyce. The small terraced house was built in the 19th century, and has been lovingly restored to how it would have looked in the early 1900s, around the time Joyce would have first come here. It contains various exhibits relating to the life of Nora and James, including photos and a correspondence between the two. It's probably of limited interest to non-Joyce fans, but looking around is worth the scant entry fee.

Bowling Green, off Shop St., Galway, Co. Galway. ✆ **091/564-743.** Admission €2.50 adults; €2 seniors, students, and children. Late May–mid-Sept Tues–Sat 10am–1pm, 2–5pm.

St. Nicholas' Collegiate Church ★★ This is Galway's oldest church—it's said that Christopher Columbus prayed here in 1477 before sailing away on one of his attempts to reach the New World. Established about 1320, it has changed from Roman Catholic to Church of Ireland and back again at least four times. Currently, it's under the aegis of the latter denomination. Inside are a 12th-century crusader's tomb with a Norman inscription, a carved font from the 16th or 17th century, and a stone lectern with barley-sugar twist columns from the 15th century. You can arrange guided tours conducted by a knowledgeable and enthusiastic church representative. Call or ask at the church for details.

Jcn. of Mainguard St. and Lombard St., Galway, Co. Galway. ✆ **086/389-8777.** www.stnicholas.ie. Free admission (donations requested). Daily 9am–6pm; opening times may vary in winter. No tours Sunday morning.

SPORTS & OUTDOOR PURSUITS

Spectator Sports

GREYHOUND RACING The hounds race year-round Thursday to Saturday at the modern **Galway Greyhound Track,** College Road, off Eyre Square (✆ **091/562273**). Doors open 7pm and admission is around €10 adults, €5 seniors and students, and €.50 children.

HORSE RACING Galway has one of the most famous racetracks in Europe—the subject of fable and song. Horses pound the track at the **Galway Racecourse,**

A DAY AT THE races

Almost as big a social event as it is a sporting one, the **Galway Races** are a big deal in the Irish horse-racing calendar. People dress up in posh frocks and big hats, and the crowds cheer enthusiastically as the competing racehorses pound the turf. Horse lovers and high rollers still pour in from around the country for the race weeks in July, August, and September. The animals are the best around, and the atmosphere is electric. Ticket prices vary depending on the event and day of the week, but expect to pay from around €20 to upwards of €40 for a ticket. Multi-day and season tickets are also available. The racetrack is in Ballybrit, on the north side of the city. See www.galwayraces or call the track directly on ✆ **091/735-870** to find out more.

Ballybrit (✆ **091/753870;** www.galwayraces.com), less than 3km (2 miles) east of town. See "A Day at the Races" below for more details.

Outdoor Pursuits

CYCLING To rent a bike, contact **Richard Walsh Cycles,** Headford Road, Woodquay (✆ **091/565710**).

FISHING Set beside the River Corrib, Galway City and nearby Connemara are popular fishing centers for salmon and sea trout. For gear and equipment, try **Duffy's Fishing & Shooting,** 5 Main Guard St. (✆ **091/562367**), or **Great Outdoors Sports Centre,** Eglinton Street (✆ **091/562869**).

GOLF Less than 3km (2 miles) west of the city is the 18-hole, par-69 seaside course at **Galway Golf Club,** Blackrock, Galway (✆ **091/522033;** www.galwaygolf.com). Greens fees are €40.

HORSEBACK RIDING Riding enthusiasts head to **Aille Cross Equestrian Centre,** Aille Cross, Loughrea, County Galway (✆ **091/843968;** www.connemara-trails.com), about 32km (20 miles) east of Galway. Run by personable Willy Leahy (who has appeared often on American television), this facility is one of the largest in Ireland, with 50 horses and 20 Connemara ponies. For about €25 to €50 an hour, you can ride through nearby farmlands, woodlands, forest trails, and along beaches.

SHOPPING

Given its status as both a tourist hub and a vibrant arts community, it's unsurprising that Galway has fairly good shopping. Some of the best is in tiny clusters of shops in historic buildings, such as the **Cornstore** on Middle Street or the **Grainstore** on Lower Abbeygate Street. **Eyre Square Centre,** the downtown area's largest shopping mall, with around 50 shops, incorporates a section of Galway's medieval town wall into its complex.

Most shops are open Monday to Saturday 9 or 10am to 5:30 or 6pm. In July and August, many stay open late, usually until 9pm on weekdays, and some also open on Sunday from noon to 5pm.

Antiques & Vintage Curios

The Gaiety Antique & Vintage Store ★ The owners of this friendly store are third-generation antiques dealers and furniture restorers. They specialize in

Artsy shops and pubs line the cobblestone streets of thriving, prosperous Galway.

antique furniture, ornaments and other curios, from Ireland and further afield. 3 St. Frances St., Galway, Co. Galway. ✆ **091/564966.** www.charliebyrne.com.

Books

Charlie Byrne's Bookshop ★★ This wonderfully chaotic bookshop is packed floor to ceiling with books—secondhand, antiquarian, and new. They have a huge stock covering just about anything. The Irish Times named this the best bookshop in Ireland in 2013. Cornstore Mall, Middle St., Galway, Co. Galway. ✆ **091/561766.** www.charliebyrne.com.

Kenny's Book Shop and Galleries Ltd ★ Another long-standing favorite of Galway bibliophiles, Kenny's has a great selection of new books on all topics, plus and secondhand and hard-to-find antiquarian titles. They also have an interesting little art gallery in the same store. Lisobun Retail Park, Tuam Rd., Galway, Co. Galway. ✆ **091/709350.** www.bookshop.kennys.ie.

Crystal, China & Souvenirs

Galway Irish Crystal ★★ This local brand of fine crystal may not be as famous as Waterford Crystal, but it's really just as shiny. At the factory on the edge of town you can watch the craftspeople at work and purchase armfuls of the stuff yourself. See p. 201 for more details. Dublin Rd., Merlin Park. ✆ **091/757311.** www.galwaycrystal.ie.

Treasure Chest ★ This large craft store and gift emporium in the town center sells china (including Belleek and Royal Doulton), plus Aran sweaters, Irish linens, handicrafts, and a host of other souvenirs. 31–33 William St. and Castle St. ✆ **091/563862.** www.treasurechest.ie.

ESSENTIAL SOUVENIR: THE claddagh RING

The delicate **Claddagh** (pronounced *Clod*-uh) ring has become synonymous with Ireland and its diaspora. It originated here, or more precisely, just over the Father Griffin Bridge, on the west bank of the River Corrib, in the town of Claddagh. It's now a residential satellite to Galway, but in ancient times it was a kingdom with its own laws, fleet, and customs. The earliest known Claddagh ring was made in the 17th century for a wedding.

The ring features two hands holding a heart topped by a crown. The hands are said to represent friendship, the crown loyalty, and the heart love—the three ingredients of a perfect marriage. Originally, the ring was a wedding band worn facing out for engagement and facing in for marriage. Though no longer widely worn as a symbol of marriage, it is still frequently worn as a friendship ring and makes a lovely memento.

Thomas Dillon's jewelry store on Quay Street claims to be the original creator of the Claddagh ring—it's been selling them since 1750.

Jewelry

Cobwebs ★★ Located opposite the Spanish Arch, this great little store sells antique and modern jewelry, plus curios, antiques and objects d'art. There are always treasures to be discovered here. 7 Quay Lane, Galway, Co. Galway. ✆ **091/564388.** www.cobwebs.ie.

Fallers of Galway ★ Fallers make and sell the Claddagh ring, a traditional Galway souvenir that symbolizes love and friendship (see "Essential Souvenir" above). They also have a large stock of other jewelry with Celtic motifs. Williamsgate St., Galway, Co. Galway. ✆ **091/561226.** www.fallers.com.

Hartmann & Son Ltd. ★ Another maker of Claddagh rings, Hartmann's also specialize in watches and diamonds. This is one of Galway's real high-end jewelry stores. 29 William St. ✆ **091/562063.** www.hartmanns.ie.

Thomas Dillon's Claddagh Gold ★ This chirpily colored little store makes two bold claims: to be the original maker of Claddagh rings, and the oldest jewelry store in Ireland as a whole. If the date they were established is anything to go by—1750—it's probably true. The shop has a tiny little museum displaying some early Claddagh rings from the 1700s. 1 Quay St., Galway, Co. Galway ✆ **091/566365.** www.claddaghring.ie.

The Winding Stair ★ Another long-standing Galway antiques store, this place specializes in beautiful antique jewelry and silver. They also stock a good range of art prints. 4 Mainguard St., Galway, Co. Galway. ✆ **091/561682.**

Music & Musical Instruments

P. Powell and Sons ★ Usually just called Powell's, this is an excellent stockiest of instruments—including whistles, bodhráns and the like—as well as a good range of traditional music CDs. The Four Corners, Williams St., Galway, Co. Galway. ✆ **091/562295.**

Tweeds, Woolens & Clothing

Faller's Sweater Shop ★ One of several stores in Galway that specializes in traditional Irish knitwear, this one also sells various gifts and souvenirs. The store is located on the ground floor of the Corbett Court Shopping Centre on Williamsgate Street. Williamsgate St., Galway, Co. Galway. ✆ **091/565249.**

Mac Eocagain/Galway Woollen Market ★ This colorful store is one of the best for traditional, hand-loomed Aran knits, plus lace and other traditional textiles. Visitors who live outside the European Union don't have to pay sales tax on items bought from here. 21 High St., Galway, Co. Galway. ✆ **091/562491.**

O'Máille (O'Malley) ★ Another excellent place to buy Aran knitwear and other Irish knits, this store also has a claim to fame of its own—when *The Quiet Man* was filmed near here in 1951, they provided the costumes for all the actors, including John Wayne. 16 High St., Galway, Co. Galway. ✆ **091/562696.** www.omaille.com.

GALWAY CITY AFTER DARK

Pubs & Bars

Crane Bar ★★ Considered one of the best pubs in the city for traditional music, the Crane Bar has live bands every night from 9:30, and on some weekend afternoons too. Admission is usually free, but some sessions in the upstairs bar cost anything from a couple of euro to around €20. 2 Sea Rd., Galway, Co. Galway. ✆ **091/587419.** www.thecranebar.com.

Front Door ★ This cheerful pub, which sprawls over two floors, is a wonderfully social place where you can saunter in at lunchtime for a tasty sandwich and a pint, and find yourself staying for hours. They sometimes show Irish sports on big TV screens. High St., Galway Co. Galway. ✆ **091/563757.** www.frontdoorpub.com.

Halo ★★ Playful decadence is the vibe at this popular nightclub, which pitches itself at a young-but-not-too-young demographic (under 23s are not admitted). They have five bars and a good, slightly retro cocktail menu (though it's quite pricey). 36 Upper Abbeygate St., Galway, Co. Galway. ✆ **091/565976.** www.halonightclub.com.

Murty Rabbitt's ★★ This charming and unspoiled late 19th-century pub has a delightfully old-fashioned feel. (It's still run by the same family who owned it all the way back then, too. How's that for tradition?) Rabbitt's sometimes has live music in the evening. 23–25 Forster St., Galway, Co. Galway. ✆ **091/566490.**

The Quays ★★ Another good place to hear live music, the Quays has the highly unusual distinction of having interior decor that was reclaimed from a French church dating back to the Middle Ages. The what's on list is a real mixed bag—you could find anything from trad to 80s rock, hip hop to indie. Expect the fun to kick off around 9pm. Quay St. and Chapel Lane, Galway, Co. Galway. ✆ **091/568347.**

Roisin Dubh ★★ This place is as much a concert venue as it is a bar, but one that gets great acts—expect to see a few famous names crop up among the packed program of live music and standup comedy. Dominic St., Galway, Co. Galway. ✆ **091/586540.** www.roisindubh.net.

WHERE TO STAY IN GALWAY CITY

Galway City has a handful of good, reasonably priced accommodations, although as with many Irish cities, you'll get more for your money by staying in the 'burbs—in this case, pretty Salthill, a mile or two to the west of the center.

The G ★★★ When the G opened in the mid-2000s it was considered a true symbol of Galway's uber-hip status as a sophisticated and monied enclave. This is a modern and luxurious hotel, full of chic designer flourishes and contemporary art. The hotel overlooks the glassy waters of Lough Atalia and Galway Bay, and many bedrooms have floor-to-ceiling windows to take full advantage of those views, flooding the place with natural light. Service is outstanding, with charming and attentive staff. Treatments in the beautifully designed spa aren't cheap, but excellent package deals are on offer, including a massage, use of the thermal suite (usually €20), dinner in the hotel restaurant, and tickets to the movie of your choice at a nearby cinema for just €120 per person. **Gigi's** restaurant serves good modern Irish food, with plenty of local meats and seafood. The menu also carries a nice innovation—you can choose from one of three set menus, which are ordered by price ("Treat" will set you back €25 for three courses, while "Indulge" is a much steeper €55 for four courses).

Wellpark, Galway, Co. Galway. ✆ **091/865-200.** www.marlesshouse.com. 101 units. €125–€215 double; €256–€480 suite. Free parking. Breakfast included. **Amenities:** Wi-Fi (free); restaurant; bar; room service; spa; gym.

The House Hotel ★ This upbeat, funky hotel in the heart of Galway City has a modern vibe. The public areas are filled with playful design statements, from polka dot chairs to hot pink sofas. Guestrooms, however, are far more muted and restful, with oatmeal, white, or green color schemes, with the

The Latin Quarter of Galway

slightest hint of a retro theme. The restaurant is good, and surprisingly reasonable for a hotel of this size in the center of the city. The in-house cocktail bar is a lively nightspot. That said, you're spoiled for choice when it comes to nightlife in this neighborhood— Galway's buzzing Latin Quarter is literally on your doorstep. The House Hotel runs frequent deals, such as a 2-night dinner, bed and breakfast package for an impressive €160 per person.

Spanish Parade, Galway, Co. Galway. ✆ **091/755-111.** www.flanneryshotelgalway.com. 134 units. €129–€169 double. Discounted parking at nearby lot (€8 for 24 hr.). Breakfast not included in lower rates. **Amenities:** Wi-Fi (free); restaurant; bar; room service.

Marless House ★ This pleasant, friendly B&B in Salthill, a small seaside commuter town immediately to the west of Galway, is an exceptionally good value for the money. Guestrooms are spacious and spotlessly clean, though some have slightly overwhelming floral color schemes. Mary and Tom are thoughtful hosts; they have arrangements with several local tour groups, so if you want to book an organized trip to one of the major sights in the region—including the Aran Islands and the Cliffs of Moher—the coach will come and pick you up directly from here, and drop you back at the end of the day. Mary is also a fount of sightseeing information for the local area, and will cheerfully help you draw up an itinerary. Breakfasts are delicious and filling.

8 Threadneedle Rd., Salthill, Galway, Co. Galway. ✆ **091/523-931.** www.marlesshouse.com. 6 units. €70–€80 double. Free parking. Breakfast included. **Amenities:** Wi-Fi (free).

Sea Breeze Lodge ★★ Another good option in Salthill, just outside Galway City, this stylish little B&B overlooks Galway Bay. The modern, gray exterior gives way to stylish, contemporary spaces inside. Guestrooms are spacious and contemporary, with polished wood floors and big windows, looking out over the bay or garden. Beds are enormous—the larger ones are super king-size (the European equivalent of an American king-size), and all have luxurious memory foam mattresses. Breakfasts are served in a pleasant little conservatory overlooking the garden. The hotel can arrange tours of the major sights in the area, including an all-day trip to the Aran Islands for €25 per person. There's no restaurant, but the center of Galway is only about 5km (3 miles) by car or taxi.

9 Cashelmara, Salthill, Galway, Co. Galway. ✆ **091/529-581.** www.seabreezelodge.org. 6 units. €90–€120 double. Free parking. Rates include breakfast. **Amenities:** Wi-Fi (free).

WHERE TO DINE IN GALWAY CITY

Unsurprisingly, Galway City is the focus of the region's culinary scene. That's not to say that the range of options is particularly varied, but there are some excellent places—particularly if you're after some good, fresh, local seafood.

Aniar ★★★ MODERN IRISH This achingly fashionable, Michelin-starred restaurant in the center of Galway City is one of the best places to eat in the region. Head chef Ultan Cooke has won as many fans for his passionately slow-food ethos as for his delicious food. Well, almost as many. It's mainly the food. The menu is tiny, but impeccably judged, and always designed firmly according to what's best and in season. The central ingredients are given subtly innovative twists—duck served with dandelion, for example, or filet of John Dory with mussels and monk's beard (the leaves of the soda plant). The only downside is the cost. This is not a cheap night out, although the five-course tasting menu for €60 (€90 with a different glass of wine per course) is less expensive than you might expect from a place as on trend as this. Needless to say, reservations are essential.

53 Lower Dominick St., Galway, Co. Galway. ✆ **091/535-947.** www.aniarrestaurant.ie. Main courses €30–€35. Tues–Sat 6–10pm.

Ard Bia at Nimmo's ★★ SEAFOOD/BISTRO/CAFE The pleasantly rustic dining room at this fashionable restaurant in Galway City doubles as a popular cafe during the day. At any time, the emphasis is the same: delicious, homey flavors, with local and seasonal produce. Stop in for some tasty, creative sandwiches at lunch, or maybe some fresh hummus with roast vegetables. In the evening, expect local fish with wilted greens and saffron aioli or perhaps some lamb marinated in harissa. The wine list is excellent, and reasonably priced—you can pop in just for a glass or two without eating, if you don't mind perching on a barstool. They also do a popular brunch on weekends.

Spanish Arch, Long Walk, Galway, Co. Galway. ✆ **091/561-114.** www.ardbia.com. Lunch main courses: €5–€10. Dinner main courses: €19–€24. Mon–Fri 10am–3:30pm (lunch served from noon), 6–10pm; Sat–Sun 10am–3:30pm (brunch only), 6–10pm.

G.B.C. (Galway Bakery Company) ★★ BAKERY/BISTRO A cheerful bakery and cafe downstairs during the evening, and a busy restaurant upstairs. Both are hugely popular with locals. The cafe serves breakfast, fresh bakery goods, and light meals all day. It's a buzzing spot for a cup of coffee and a mid-afternoon treat. Meanwhile, upstairs is proper sit-down bistro, albeit a pleasantly informal one, serving steak, roast chicken, fajitas, pasta, and fresh salmon. The evening set menu offers much the same hearty kind of fare, but the early bird menu tends to have a couple of different options—such as burgers, open sandwiches, and even an extremely late-in-the-day full Irish breakfast.

Williamsgate St., Galway, Co. Galway. ✆ **091/563-087.** www.gbcgalway.com. Main courses €4–€17. Cafe: daily 8am–9pm. Restaurant: Sun–Thurs noon–8pm; Fri–Sat noon–9pm.

Gourmet Tart Company ★★ BAKERY/INTERNATIONAL A French-style bakery and patisserie with a restaurant attached, the Gourmet Tart Company is very popular with locals for snacks, light meals, and sweet treats. The home-baked cakes, tarts, and pastries make for a tempting mid-afternoon snack or a breakfast on the go. (They also do a very good sit-down breakfast if you want to linger.) At lunch they sell sandwiches and assorted deli items to take out. At night, however, a full menu of delicious, international fare at very reasonable prices suddenly appears. Think filet of sole with new potatoes, Thai

THE GALWAY oyster FESTIVAL

On the main road south (N18) of Galway are two small fishing villages, **Clarenbridge** and **Kilcolgan.** Each year at the end of September, these villages play host to the annual **Galway Oyster Festival** (www.galwayoysterfest.com). Now in its 61st year, the 5-day festival is packed with traditional music, song, dancing, sports, art exhibits, and, above all, oyster-tasting events and oyster shucking competitions.

curry with coconut rice, or perhaps a salad of Parma ham, pears, and Cashel blue cheese. Brunch is popular on Sundays. The Gourmet Tart Company also has smaller (deli/bakery only) branches on Abbeygate Street and Headford Road in Galway City.

Jameson Court, Salthill, Galway, Co. Galway. ✆ **091/861-667.** www.gourmettartco.com. Breakfast: €2–€9. Lunch main courses: €8–€11. Dinner main courses: €8–€17. Wed–Sat 7:30am–11pm (last orders 9pm); Sun–Tues 7:30am–7pm (last orders 6pm).

Kirwan's Lane ★★ MODERN IRISH/SEAFOOD The exposed stone walls of the elegant downstairs dining room at this popular restaurant speak to the building's medieval origins. Open the menu, however, and everything suddenly seems bang up to date—this is one of the most popular and reliable restaurants in Galway City for modern Irish cuisine. Seafood is a specialty, all expertly prepared and presented. Think prawn and clam linguine with chili, garlic, and lemon, or perhaps some Connemara mussels prepared with lemongrass and coconut cream. Carnivores are not overlooked, with a good selection of meat dishes too (try the duckling with orange and mango puree).

Kirwan's Lane, Galway, Co. Galway. ✆ **091/568-266.** www.kirwanslane.com. Main courses €11–€27. Mon–Sat 12:30–2:30pm, 6–10pm; Sun 6–10pm.

Martine's Quay Street ★★ BISTRO A friendly, cozy restaurant in the center of Galway City, Martine's serves excellent, Irish-influenced bistro style cooking, with just a hint of an international accent. The menu is short but well judged: dishes like tempura of hake or goat's cheese salad, followed by a juicy steak or catch of the day. They take their meat seriously here: The specials board includes a "cut of the day," according to what's best. The early bird menu is an excellent value at €20 for two courses (or €25 for three). It's also not really early bird at all—it's available all night, every night. This is also a good choice for a simple but delicious lunch of salads, sandwiches, and a few sit-down lunch dishes, all for around €10 or less.

21 Quay St., Galway, Co. Galway. ✆ **091/565-662.** www.winebar.ie. Main courses €13–€23. Wed, Thurs, and Sun noon–3pm, 4–10:30pm; Fri–Sat noon–10:30pm; Sun–Tues noon–3pm, 4–10:30pm.

Oscars Seafood Bistro ★★★ SEAFOOD Another of the standout places to go for seafood in Galway City, Oscar's is a cheerful, relaxed kind of place. The dining room is filled with modern art and fabric drapes across the ceiling providing a slightly bohemian touch. You could start with some prawns, cooked simply in garlic and butter, before moving on to some Clare Island salmon with seasonal vegetables, or perhaps some seared scallops with lime drizzle. The ingredients are sourced from local producers and farmers' markets. The fixed-price menu is exceptional value, at just €15 for two courses (served Mon–Thurs and Fri until 7pm).

Dominick St., Galway, Co. Galway. ✆ **091/852-180.** www.oscarsbistro.ie. Main courses €15–€25. Daily noon–9pm.

The Pie Maker ★★ PIES Just try and beat *this* for an authentic Irish food experience. With its old style red-and-gold frontage and dimly lit, quirkily decorated dining room, it could virtually have tumbled fully formed out of the Victorian age. The menu consists of pies, pies, and more pies, in light, fresh pastry crusts. There are a couple of sweet options, but most are savory with hot, fresh fillings of meat and vegetables, such as roast beef, curried chicken, chicken and mushroom, or sausage and mozzarella. Super-traditional sides come in the form of creamy mashed potatoes and garden peas. And if by some miracle you have room for dessert, try the amazing Banoffee pie, a heavenly combination of whipped cream, banana, and toffee, with a crumbly base. Pies can also be ordered to go. The Pie Maker is open until an astonishingly late 4am on Fridays and Saturdays, should you feel yourself in need of a late—or should that be early?—snack. ***Note:*** The Pie Maker doesn't take cards; it's cash only around here.

10 Cross St. Upper, Galway, Co. Galway. ✆ **085/758-1581.** Main courses €5–€10. Mon–Thurs 11am–9pm; Fri–Sat 11am–4am; Sun noon–9pm.

Sheridan's Cheesemongers ★ DELI/WINE BAR Well this is an unusual idea—an artisan cheese shop and deli, doubling up as a bar where you can order a glass of wine and some nibbles. Food comes in the form of delicious cheeseboards and charcuterie, much of it locally produced. So simple, so delicious, and hugely popular too—you might struggle to get one of the few tables during busy times. This is a really good alternative to heavy restaurant food when all you really want is a chat and a sophisticated snack. Oh, and the selection of cheeses is sensational. The shop is open Monday to Friday from 10am to 7pm, Saturday from 9am to 6pm, and Sunday from noon to 5pm. See below for food service times.

Church Yard St., Galway, Co. Galway. ✆ **091/564-829.** www.sheridanscheesemongers.com. Main courses €5–€10. Tues–Thurs 1pm–10pm; Fri 1pm–midnight; Sat noon–midnight.

Side Trips from Galway City

Heading west out of Galway City, the winding R336 coast road snakes along the edge of Galway Bay. The first major stop on the headland is the busy, unromantic modern beach resort, **Salthill *(Bóthar na Trá),*** a summer favorite of Irish families, which is somewhat reminiscent of the Jersey shore in the U.S., or Blackpool in England. It has a boardwalk and a fine beach, plus lots of bars, fast food, amusement rides, and game arcades, which can be good if you've got children looking for an alternative to historic sights (so long as you don't mind the crowds). Farther along the scenic road are charming little historic towns including Gaelic-speaking **Spiddal *(An Spidéal),*** which is also an ideal spot to shop for locally made Aran knit sweaters and other handicrafts.

The road continues as far as **Inverin *(Indreabhán),*** then turns northward, with signposts for **Rossaveal *(Ros an Mhíl).*** From Rossaveal, you can make the shortest sea crossing from the Galway mainland to the Aran Islands (see p. 343), and on a sunny day, you might want to combine this coastal drive with a trip to the islands.

If you continue on R336, you'll leave the Galway Bay coast and travel past the rocky and remote scenery approaching the center of Connemara. Along the way you'll pass **Ros Muc,** site of the **Padraig Pearse Cottage.** This simple, rather bleak thatched-roof structure served as a retreat for Dublin-based Pearse (1879–1916), who was one of the leaders of Ireland's 1916 Easter Rising. He used his time here to improve his knowledge of the Irish language. Now a national monument, the cottage contains documents, photographs, and other memorabilia. Admission costs just a couple of euro. It's open from mid-June to mid-September daily 9:30am to 5:30pm.

Salthill is a popular beach town for Irish families.

On the main road inland from Galway City, heading south and east, are a string of attractions related to one of Ireland's greatest poets, W.B. Yeats (1965–1939). You can visit his summerhouse, **Thoor Ballylee,** and wander the sylvan grounds of **Coole Park,** which was the childhood home of his patron, the dramatist and poet **Lady Gregory** (1852–1932).

Other worthwhile attractions within a short drive of Galway City include **Athenry,** a well-preserved medieval town with a small castle and the picturesque ruins of a Dominican Priory.

Galway Atlantaquaria ★★★ Also known as the National Aquarium of Ireland (the largest in the country), this is a fantastic way to reward kids for trudging around all those historic ruins. One's imagination is captured right from the first exhibit—a dramatic "splash room," where a large, one tonne (just under a ton) capacity tank goes off every minute or so with a giant splash, which is designed to imitate the natural movement of waves on the Galway coast. Highlights of the thoughtful exhibits include the enormous ocean tank, set over two floors and housing a couple of hundred sea creatures, including small sharks; a wreck tank home to dangerous conger eels; and touch pools in which kids can handle tame sea creatures such as starfish and hermit crabs, under supervision from the aquarium staff. There's also the opportunity to tickle some inquisitive rays, though make sure your hands are wet first or your touch can burn their skin.

The Promenade, Salthill, Galway, Co. Galway. ✆ **091/585-100.** www.nationalaquarium.ie. Admission €11 adults; €7.50 seniors and students; €7 children 3–16; €4 extra children; €21–€30 families. Daily 10am–6pm.

Medieval Banquet at Dunguaire Castle ★ One of the better *ye olde worlde* style entertainments in this part of Ireland, the medieval banquet at Dungaire Castle is actually pretty good fun. It's best not to worry about the accuracy

ATHENRY: FADED medieval SPLENDOR

About a 25-minute drive east from Galway, the pretty little town of **Athenry** is notable for its medieval town walls, which are some of the best-preserved in Ireland. The walls were constructed in the 1300s, and well over half of the original 2km (1⅓ mile) circuit still survives—up to 5m (16½ ft.) tall in places.

Start with a visit to the **Athenry Heritage Centre** on The Square, in the town center (✆ **091/844661;** www.athenryheritagecentre.com). As well as providing all the usual orientation—including maps for walking routes and the best sections of wall—it has a lively **Medieval Experience.** Aimed mostly at kids, it has plenty of interactive exhibits, dressing up, and recreations of a torture dungeon and medieval street. You can also play Robin Hood by having a go at archery. It costs €7.50 adults, €5 children, €26 families. Opening times are Monday to Friday, 11am to 6pm.

Just a 10-minute walk away, on Court Lane, is the medieval **Athenry Castle.** The modest tower keep is the only substantial part that survives, although you can go inside. Look out for some interesting carvings on the main doorway and on the interior side of the window arches. Admission costs €3 adults, €2 seniors, €1 students and children, and €8 families. It's open 10am to 6pm daily from Easter to October.

Also worth checking out are the ruins of a **Dominican Priory,** just around the corner from the castle on Bridge Street. Built in the mid-13th century, it was comprehensively destroyed by Cromwell's forces 400 years later. Today it's just a picturesque ruin, incongruously surrounded by modern houses; to medievalists, however, it's of particular interest because of its elaborately carved gravestones.

To reach Athenry from Galway, take the main M5 motorway east of the city for about 25km (15½ miles). The turnoff is well signposted at junction 17, for Athenry and Craughwell. Athenry also has a little train station; trains go about every once an hour and take between 15 and 30 minutes. The return fare is around €6.

of its supposed medievalness, but that's hardly the point. After being welcomed with a goblet of mead, you're seated in a satisfyingly atmospheric, candle-lit hall, with long communal tables. A (mostly) traditional Irish-style dinner is served—smoked salmon, leek and potato soup, that kind of thing—with jugs of wine left on the table to lubricate the proceedings. A live show follows, featuring song and poetry from some of the great Irish writers. (None of them medieval, but remember what we told you about not worrying?) There are two sittings nightly, and reservations are essential as far in advance as possible, as the midsummer dates can get booked up. Dunguaire Castle itself is worth a look around; a tower house-style late medieval castle built in 1520, it overlooks Galway Bay. Outside of the banquet, it's open 10am to 5pm.

On N67 (Ballyvaughan Rd.), Dunguaire, Co. Galway. ✆ **061/360-788.** www.shannonheritage.com/EveningEntertainments/DunguaireCastleBanquet. Banquet €40 adults; €30 children 9–12; €20 children 6–9. Reservations essential. May–Sept daily 5:30, 8:45pm. Dunguaire is near Kinvara, approx. 26km (16 miles) southeast of Galway.

Spiddal Craft Village (Ceardlann an Spidéil) ★★ On the main road as you enter Spiddal from Galway, this is a fantastic collection of cottage-style crafts stores and workshops. The artists in residence here change, but selection is always diverse. At this writing, they include a basket maker; a store selling Irish language books and creative, artsy gifts; a wonderful contemporary ceramicist; a jeweler specializing in pieces made from pre-euro Irish coins; a traditional weaver; a stained glass artist; and a couple of very talented painters. Plenty for sale is affordable enough, in addition to some more exclusive work. Even if you're not buying, however, it's an inspiring place to browse. The on-site **Builín**

FOLLOWING IN THE footsteps OF POETS

About 36km (22⅓ miles) southeast of Galway City, near the northern border of the Burren (see chapter 10), you'll see signs to the beautiful **Coole Park National Forest** (✆ **091/631804;** www.coolepark.ie). This was once a country home of the dramatist and arts patron Lady Gregory, who, along with W. B. Yeats and Edward Martyn, founded the Abbey Theatre in Dublin (see p. 161). Sadly, her house no longer stands, but her influence is memorialized in a tree on the grounds on which the following people carved their initials while visiting with her: George Bernard Shaw, Sean O'Casey, John Masefield, Oliver St. John Gogarty, W. B. Yeats, and Douglas Hyde, the first president of Ireland. Clearly, this is an exceptional place. The visitor center shows a number of films on Lady Gregory and Coole Park, and has a tearoom, picnic tables, and some lovely nature trails for wandering. The visitor center is open daily 10am to 5pm in late March to June and September, with extended hours from 10am to 6pm in July to August. Admission is free.

Not too far away from the home of his friend, W. B. Yeats had his own summer home in Gort at **Thoor Ballylee** (✆ **091/631436**). The restored 16th-century Norman tower house served as the inspiration for his poems "The Winding Stair" and "The Tower". In the interpretive center, an audiovisual presentation examines the poet's life. Also on the grounds are the original Ballylee Mill, partially restored, and a bookshop specializing in Anglo-Irish literature. The tower suffered severe flood damage in early 2014, but is expected to reopen by the 2015 season. The site is on the N18 at Gort. Admission is €6 for adults, €5.50 for seniors and students, €2.50 for children 12 and over, €1.50 for children 11 and under, and €12 for families. It's open from May to September daily 10am to 6pm.

Not too far away from Yeats's and Lady Gregory's summer homes, west off the main road, between Gort and Kilcolgan, **Dunguaire Castle,** Kinvara (✆ **061/360788;** www.shannonheritage.com), sits on the south shore of Galway Bay. Once the royal seat of the 7th-century King Guaire of Connaught, the castle was taken over later by the legendary Oliver St. John Gogarty (1878–1957), Irish surgeon, author, poet, and wit. Yeats and Lady Gregory were great friends and frequent guests. Together the three must have had a kind of Bloomsbury Society West in the summertime, when all of Dublin's greatest literary minds decamped to their manor homes. Today Dunguaire's greatest appeal is the exquisite view from its battlements of the nearby Burren and Galway Bay. Stay for a **medieval banquet** here on a summer evenings (see p. 356). Dunguaire is on the N67 just east of Kinvara.

Blasta Café sells delicious bakery goods, snacks, and light meals, in addition to takeaway deli items. You can contact the individual artists via the main website.

About 15km (9 miles) west of Galway on R336, Spiddal, Co. Galway. ✆ **086/806-7352.** www.ceardlann.com. Mon–Sat 9:30am–6pm; Sun noon–5pm.

SPORTS & OUTDOOR PURSUITS

FISHING As you might surmise, this area is prime territory for sea fishing, especially for mackerel, pollock, cod and turbot—though you'll need to obtain a license. Ask at whichever store you rent your fishing gear from for details. For a couple of good places in Galway City, see p. 340.

Those who prefer trout fishing might want to check out the **Crumlin Lodge Fisheries,** Inverin, County Galway (✆ **091/593105**). This fishery has a lake stocked with sea-reared rainbow trout and allows two fish per person to be taken per day. Prices range from around €20 to €50, depending on whether you fish from a bank or a boat. Fishing starts at 9am daily; reservations must be made at least a day in advance.

SWIMMING The Silver Strand at Barna and the beach at Spiddal are clean, sandy, and ideal for swimming.

WHERE TO STAY ON THE ARAN ISLANDS

Kilmurvey House ★★ Overlooking Dún Aengus Fort (see p. 343), this is probably the best place to stay on the Aran Islands. At first view, the gray stone manor looks somewhat austere; inside, however, it's all cheerful, bright rooms and polished wood floors. Owner Teresa Joyce is extremely welcoming, and her home-cooked breakfasts are delicious (try her porridge made with whiskey). She occasionally cooks dinner too, although generally not for small groups—check in advance if you want to try and arrange this. She'll happily serve you a glass of wine and a plate of crackers and cheese, however, if you just want a snack. Guestrooms are enormous; you could probably fit an average European city B&B bedroom into one of these bright, light-filled spaces several times over.

Kilmurvey, Inis Mor, Aran Islands, Co. Galway. ✆ **099/61218.** www.kilmurveyhouse.com. 12 units. €90–€110 double. Free parking. Breakfast included.

WHERE TO DINE ON THE ARAN ISLANDS

Teach Nan Phaidi ★★ CAFE/IRISH The Aran Islands aren't exactly awash with fine restaurants, and so as a captive audience you might be forgiven for lowering your expectations. But this little cafe-restaurant near the Dún Aengus Fort is nothing short of delightful. The Irish country cottage interior is cheery and atmospheric, with exposed wood beams and jauntily painted furniture. The menu is straightforward and unfussy but quite delicious. Cakes, stews, sandwiches and soups—comfort food, in other words, and incredibly welcome after a blustery day on the island. Most of the ingredients are locally sourced, and there's a special children's menu too. The homemade desserts, particularly the cakes, are absolutely delicious. Service is upbeat and cheerful.

Kilmurvey, Inis Mor, Aran Islands, Co. Galway. ✆ **099/20975.** Main courses €4–€13. Daily 11am–5pm.

CONNEMARA

If you look for Connemara on road signs, you may be looking forever, because it's not a city or county, but rather an area or region. Like the Burren in County Clare, the boundaries are a bit hazy, but most agree that Connemara is west of Galway City, starting at Oughterard and continuing toward the Atlantic. You know it when you see it, as it's an area of heartbreaking barrenness and unique beauty, with dark bogs and tall jagged mountains punctuated by curving glassy lakes dotted with green islands. The desolate landscape is caused, in part, by an absence of trees that were felled and dragged off long ago for building ships, houses, and furniture. Connemara is part of the **Gaeltacht,** or Irish-speaking area, so many signs are in Gaelic only.

It's a varied place—in fact, you could say that there are two Connemaras. South of the Galway-Clifden road is a vast bog-mantled moorland dotted with lakes, and with a low, indented, rocky coastline. North of the Galway-Clifden road, tall quartzite domes and cones form the Maumturks and the **Twelve Bens** (also called the Twelve Pins), rising toward the breathtaking Killary fiord—the only fiord in the 6,000 or so islands that make up the British Isles—near where Mayo takes over from Galway. Oscar Wilde wrote, "Connemara is a savage beauty." Now you can see that for yourself.

Exploring Connemara

The seaside town of **Clifden** ***(An Clochán)*** has an enviable location at the edge of the blue waters of Clifden Bay, where miles of curving, sandy beaches skirt the rugged coastline. It's a small, attractive Victorian town with colorful shop fronts and church steeples thrusting skyward through a veil of trees. With its plentiful restaurants, shops, hotels, and pubs, it makes a handy base for exploring the area, so it's quite touristy. If you prefer a quieter location, you might want to look at one of the many smaller towns and villages in the area, such as the small fishing port of **Roundstone** ***(Cloch na Rón)*** ★ about 24km (15 miles) away, which, while still relatively peaceful, is also equipped with all of the essentials: pristine beaches, comfortable guesthouses, good restaurants, shops to explore, and more than its share of natural charm.

From Roundstone, you can head on to the little community of **Letterfrack** ***(Leitir Fraic)*** at the edge of Connemara National Park, close to the extraordinary Gothic Kylemore Abbey. The tiny village, founded by Quakers, has a handful of pubs and B&Bs in a glorious natural setting. It's near the bright white sands of **Glassillaun Beach** and **Lettergesh,** where horses raced across the sand in the film *The Quiet Man.*

Aughnanure Castle ★ Standing on an outcrop of rock surrounded by forest and pasture, this sturdy fortress is a well-preserved Irish tower castle with an unusual double *bawn* (a fortified enclosure) and a still-complete watchtower that you can climb. It was built around A.D. 1500 as a stronghold of the "Ferocious" O'Flaherty clan, who dominated the region and terrified their neighbors in their day. The castle's fireplaces are so big that you could fit a double bed in them. The ruined banqueting hall contains the remains of a dry harbor.

Oughterard, Co. Galway. ✆ **091/552-214.** www.heritageireland.ie. Admission €3 adults; €2 seniors; €1 children; €8 families. Late Mar–mid-Oct daily 9:30am–6pm.

Clifden (An Clochán) ★ In many ways Clifden is a typical seaside resort, in that it can feel crowded and touristy in summer, but slightly faded when empty.

DARE YOU TAKE . . . THE spooky SHORTCUT?

If you're planning a drive across the Connemara National Park to Clifden, you may want to make a shortcut across the rough but beautiful "bog road" more prosaically known as R341. Unless you're traveling at night, that is. A hotel manager in these parts once told us that many locals consider the road to be haunted, and won't take it after dark. Spooks or not, it's certainly dark and scary at night, and should be avoided in bad weather.

That said, it has sandy beaches, a dramatic coastline, and plenty of attractive Victorian buildings. Although you certainly could base yourself here, most visitors will probably experience it as a welcome stop on a tour of the Connemara countryside; somewhere to happily wander for an hour or two. If you prefer somewhere even more off the beaten path, take a detour to **Roundstone (*Cloch na Rón*)** on your way out of town. About 24km (15 miles) south on R341, it's a smaller, sleepier fishing port, with pristine beaches.

Clifden, Co. Galway.

Connemara National Park ★★★ This gorgeous national park encompasses over 2,000 hectares (4,940 acres) of mountains, bogs, grasslands, and hiking trails. Some of the best lead through the peaceful ***Gleann Mór* (Big Glen),** with its River Polladirk, or up to the **Twelve Bens** (also called the Twelve Pins), a small, quartzite mountain range north of the Galway-Clifden road. Nearby are the lesser-known, equally lovely **Maumturk** range and the breathtaking **Killary Fiord**—the only fiord in Ireland. None of the Twelve Bens rises above 730m (2,392 ft.), which makes their summits quite accessible to those who don't mind walking at a steep incline. Frequent rainfall produces dozens of tiny streams and waterfalls, and the views are spectacular. The excellent visitor center south of the crossroads in **Letterfrack** dispenses general information on the park and sustenance in the form of tea, sandwiches, and fresh-baked goods.

Visitor Centre: signposted from N59, Letterfrack, Co. Galway. ✆ **076/100-2528.** www.connemaranationalpark.ie. Free admission. Visitor Centre: Mar–Oct 9am–5:30pm. Park: daily, year-round.

Connemara Walking Centre ★★ This company's expert local guides lead walking tours of Connemara with an emphasis on history, archaeology, and wildlife. The walks cover different sections—from the Renvyle Peninsula and Roundstone Bog to the Kylemore Valley, the Maumturk Mountains, and Sky Road. Weeklong trips are based at Dun Gibbons, a center dedicated to exploring Connemara's countryside. Walks gather at Island House on Market Street in Clifden and include bus transportation to the walking site.

Market St., Clifden. ✆ **095/21379.** Tours around €20, depending on tour. Mar–Oct.

Dan O'Hara's Homestead Farm ★★ This excellent heritage center and open-air museum tells the story of Connemara, its people, and how they worked this rocky and inhospitable land. Dan O'Hara was a real person who

CONNEMARA pony TREKKING

The sturdy yet elegant Connemara pony is the only horse breed native to Ireland, though it has received an infusion of Spanish blood over the centuries. Often raised in tiny fields with limestone pastures, the ponies are known for their stamina and gentleness, which make them ideal for amateur riders and young people. They are also born and bred to traverse the region's rugged terrain, so they are adept at scaling short, steep hills and delicately picking their way along rocky shores.

Because much of the countryside is well off the beaten track, pony trekking is actually a fantastic way to cover ground. It gets you off the busy roads and out into the countryside and onto the white-sand beaches near Roundstone and elsewhere along the coast. The **Aille Cross Equestrian Centre** near Loughrea (✆ **091/841-216;** www.aillecross.com) can set you up with guided treks for all levels of ability.

farmed 3 hectares (8 acres) of land for himself and his family, until the potato famine destroyed their livelihood and they were evicted. His tragic tale—recounted at the museum—ends with Dan's children being taken into care and him dying broke in New York, where he eked out a living as a match seller. The reconstructed farmstead is set up exactly how it would have been in the years before the famine, complete with farm dwellings. The heritage center has exhibits and an informative historical film. Also on the grounds of the museum is a dolmen and prehistoric tomb. The farm also does B&B and self-catering if this kind of isolation is your idea of a rural idyll.

About 6.5km (4 miles) east of Clifden off N59, Lettershea, Clifden, Co. Galway. ✆ **095/21246.** www.connemaraheritage.com Admission €8 adults; €7 seniors and students; €4 children; €20 families. Apr–Oct daily 10am–6pm; last admission 1 hr. before closing.

Inishbofin ★★ This small emerald-green gem lies 11km (6¾ miles) off the northwest coast of Connemara and offers seclusion and spectacular beauty, provided the skies are clear enough to deliver the unforgettable views of and from its shores. Once the domain of monks, then the lair of pirate queen Grace O'Malley (see p. 392), later Cromwell's infamous priest prison—you can still see his original, star-shaped barracks—Inishbofin is currently home to just 180 year-round human residents, a seal colony, and a sea bird sanctuary. Numerous ferries to the island operate from the port of Cleggan (13km/8 miles northwest of Clifden off N59) daily April through October. **Inishbofin Island Discovery,** Cloonamore, Inishbofin Island, County Galway (✆ **095/45819** or 095/45894; www.inishbofinislanddiscovery.com), sails between the island and Cleggan on the mainland, twice a day. Tickets cost €20, €15 seniors and students, €10 children 12 and older, €5 children 5 to 11, and €5 children age 3 to 5. ***Note:*** Reservations are essential, and evening sail times are liable to be brought forward in bad weather—so make sure you keep an eye on the hour.

Inishbofin, Co. Galway.

Kylemore Abbey ★★ As you round yet another bend on the particularly barren stretch of country road around Kylemore, this extraordinary neo-Gothic abbey looms into view, at the base of a wooded hill across the mirror-like Kylemore Lake. The facade of the main building—a vast, crenelated 19th-century house—is a splendid example of neo-Gothic architecture. In 1920, its owners donated it to the Benedictine nuns, and the sisters have run a convent boarding school here ever since. You can see a little of the interior, but it's disappointingly plain; the exterior and the grounds are the attraction here and are impressive enough to justify a visit. The highlight is the restored Gothic chapel, an exquisite cathedral in miniature with a plain, somber cemetery to one side; a lavish Victorian walled garden; and the breathtaking views of it all from across the lake. The complex includes a decent restaurant that serves produce grown on the nuns' farm, as well as tea and good scones, a shop with a working pottery studio, and a visitor center. The abbey is most atmospheric when the bells are rung for midday office or for vespers at 6pm.

Kylemore, Co. Galway (follow signs from N59). ✆ **095/52011.** www.kylemoreabbey.com. Admission €12.50 adults; €10 seniors; €9 students and children 11–17; €25–€34 families. Children 10 and under free. Mar, Oct 9am–5:30pm; Apr–June, Sept 9am–6pm; July–Aug 9am–7pm; Nov, Feb 9:30am–5pm; Dec 9:30am–4:30pm; Jan 10am–4:30pm.

Sports & Outdoor Pursuits

CYCLING Bicycles can be rented year-round from **Mannion Cycles,** Bridge Street, Clifden, County Galway (✆ **095/21160**). The rate for a regular touring bike in high season starts at €15 per day, €90 per week. Touring bikes can also be hired from May through October at the **Little Killary Adventure Company,** Leenane, County Galway (✆ **095/43411;** www.killary.com). They go for €18 per day.

DIVING You can rent equipment and receive instruction at **Scubadive West,** Renvyle, County Galway (✆ **095/43922;** www.scubadivewest.com).

FISHING Lough Corrib is renowned for brown-trout and salmon fishing. Brown-trout fishing is usually good from the middle of February, and salmon is best from the end of May. The mayfly fishing begins around the middle of May and continues for up to 3 weeks.

For salmon and sea trout, the **Ballynahinch Castle Hotel** at Ballynahinch, Recess, County Galway (✆ **095/31006;** www.ballynahinch-castle.com), is an angler's paradise. State fishing licenses, tackle hire and sales, maps, and advice are available at the hotel.

At **Portarra Lodge,** Tullykyne, Moycullen, County Galway (✆ **091/555-051;** www.portarralodge.com), packages are available, including B&B accommodations in a modern guesthouse on the shores of Lough Corrib, dinners, and boats and tackle. Michael Canney is an avid angler and a great guide to this part of Galway. Weekly packages that include half-board, boat, and *ghillie* (guide) are available.

GOLF Visitors are welcome at the 18-hole, par-72 championship seaside course of the **Connemara Golf Club,** Ballyconneely, Clifden, County Galway (✆ **095/23502;** www.connemaragolflinks.com), nestled in the heart of Connemara and overlooking the Atlantic. Greens fees are €50 to €75.

The **Oughterard Golf Club,** Oughterard, County Galway (✆ **091/552131;** www.oughterardgolfclub.com), is an 18-hole, par-70 inland course. Greens fees are €25.

HORSEBACK RIDING See the beaches of Connemara from horseback on a trek with the **Cleggan Beach Riding Centre,** Clegan, County Galway

LOUGH INAGH & THE walk TO MAUM EAN ORATORY

Lough Inagh, nestled between the Maumturk and the Twelve Bens mountains in the heart of Connemara, is in a spectacularly beautiful valley, where mountain slopes rise precipitously from the valley floor and small streams cascade into the lake in a series of sparkling waterfalls. The R344 cuts through the valley, linking Recess to the south and Kylemore Lake to the north.

The **Western Way,** a walking route that traverses the high country of Galway and Mayo, follows a quiet country road above the R344 through the Lough Inagh Valley. To reach the beginning of the walk, drive north on the R344, turning right on a side road—the sign for Maum Ean—about 200m (656 ft.) before the Lough Inagh Lodge Hotel. Continue on this side of the road for about 6km (3¾ miles) to a large gravel parking lot on the left. Park here, and follow the well-worn trail 2km (1¼ miles) to the top of the pass, through glorious mountain scenery.

This short (4km/2½-mile) walk follows the Western Way to the top of a mountain pass that has long been associated with St. Patrick and is now the site of a small oratory, a hollow in the rock known as **Patrick's Bed,** a life-size statue of the saint, and a series of cairns marking the Stations of the Cross. Together, these monuments make a striking ensemble, strangely eerie when the mists descend and conceal the far slopes in their shifting haze. A clear day offers great views, with the Atlantic Ocean and Bertraghboy Bay to the southwest and more mountains to the northeast. The round-trip walking time is about 1 hour.

(✆ **095/44746;** www.clegganridingcentre.com). The center offers beach and mountain treks, and the most popular is a 3-hour ride to Omey Island at low tide. Or explore with **Connemara and Coast Trails,** Loughrea, County Galway (✆ **091/843968;** www.connemara-trails.com). Rides are for experienced and beginning riders alike. Expect to pay from around €20 to €50 per person per hour.

WALKING The town of **Leenane** is the start of any number of exhilarating walks. One of the best takes you to the picturesque Aasleagh Waterfall (Eas Liath) east of the Killary Harbor. Another walk around that harbor, Ireland's only fiord, follows the Green Road. It was once the primary route from the Rinvyle Peninsula to Leenane, and is now largely a sheep track. The path passes a ghost town (an abandoned pre-famine village) on the far side of the harbor, where the fields rise at a devilishly steep slope from the ruined cottages clustered at the water's edge. Excellent walking trails are also in **Connemara National Park** (see p. 361), some of which lead up the sides of the Twelve Bens. You can get maps at the park's visitor center.

WATERSPORTS Hobie Cat sailing and sailboarding can be arranged at the **Little Killary Adventure Company,** Leenane, County Galway (✆ **095/43411;** www.killary.com). Rates start at around €60 per day (two sessions), which entitles you to use the watersports equipment and participate in all the center's supervised sporting activities, including kayaking, water-skiing, hill and coastal walking, rock climbing, archery, and more.

Where to Stay in Connemara

The Anglers Return ★ This lovely, artsy retreat is surrounded by beautiful gardens. The house was built as a hunting lodge in the 19th century; today it's run with great charm by Lynn Hill, a talented artist who also hosts painting and photography classes here. Bedrooms are simple and modestly sized, furnished with antiques. The views over the grounds and nearby river are gorgeous. The only downside is that none of the rooms have private bathrooms—you have to use one of two bathrooms located down the corridor, although robes are thoughtfully provided. Guests are free to wander the gardens, which are practically an attraction all of their own. Those wanting more seclusion, and a touch of adventure, may want to rent a yurt on the grounds. The Anglers Return doesn't accept credit cards; it's cash or check only around here.

Toombeola, Rounstone, Co. Galway. ✆ **095/21204.** www.anglersreturn.com. 3 units. €110 double Free parking. Breakfast included. Closed Dec–Jan.

Dolphin Beach House ★★★ This is an incredibly special place to stay. A beautifully restored early-20th-century homestead, Dolphin Beach House has awe-inspiring views of the bay at Clifden. The guestrooms are huge and light-filled, with handmade wood beds and high ceilings. The dining room looks out across acres of green fields, giving way to the azure sea beyond. Delicious evening meals are served here, such as local lamb or a catch of the day. The vegetables for the table are grown in the house's own organic garden. Breakfasts are good too. Fearghus Foyle is an easy, charming host and also a passionate environmentalist; the house is almost entirely powered by renewable energy sources, and there's rainwater collection and recycling system. Check the website for good midweek discount deals. ***Note:*** Dinner must be booked in advance, before you arrive.

Lower Sky Rd., Clifden, Co. Galway. ✆ **095/21204.** www.dolphinbeachhouse.com. 4 units. €130–€180. Free parking. Breakfast included. 3 course dinner €40. **Amenities:** Wi-Fi (free); restaurant. No children under 12.

GONE TO THE bogs

Connemara's **bog lands** began forming 2,500 years ago. During the Iron Age, the Celts preserved butter in the bog. Today, with one-third of Connemara classified as bog, the turf (or peat) that's cut from the bog remains an important source of fuel. Cutting and drying turf is an integral part of the rhythm of the seasons in Connemara. Cutting requires a special tool, a spade called a *slane,* which slices the turf into bricks about 46cm (18 in.) long. The bricks are first spread out flat to dry, and then stacked in pyramids for further drying. If you spend enough time in Ireland, you'll get used to the strong, smoky smell of burning turf. You can always tell when turf is burning in a home's fireplace—the smoke coming out of the chimney is blue and sweet scented. It's an evocative scent, quintessentially Irish, and so liable to provoke feelings of intense nostalgia among those who grow to love it.

Where to Dine in Connemara

Though Galway City may be the big culinary attraction, the rest of counties Galway and Clare are not without a few top-notch places either, plus a liberal smattering of cheap and cheerful lunch spots.

O'Dowd's ★★ SEAFOOD There's not much room in this tiny pub in tiny Roundstone, which means you'll be fighting for space with dozens of hungry locals. But trust them, for they know exactly what they're here for: extremely good, fresh seafood, simple and beautifully prepared. There's nothing complicated about the menu, and that's part of the appeal—Connemara salmon or seafood au gratin, served with boiled potatoes or fries, or perhaps a simple lamb stew to keep carnivores happy. Try the delicious chowder if it's on offer. Needless to say, booking is advisable.

Roundstone, Co. Galway. ✆ **095/35809.** Main courses €13–€22. Mon–Sat 10am–5:30pm.

The Steam Café ★ CAFE This cute and simple little cafe is one of the best places in Clifden for lunch. The menu isn't fancy, but it's all good—wraps, sandwiches, light meals, and daily specials, all made with quality ingredients. The salads come from the cafe's own organic vegetable garden. The soups are particularly tasty, with ever-changing daily specials, but you may find minestrone, tomato and herb, or even carrot and orange. They also do tasty cakes and desserts—great to wash down the excellent coffee. The Steam Café is in the Station House Hotel, which is on the main N59 road, in Clifden town center.

Station House Hotel Courtyard, off N59 (Galway Rd.), Clifden, Co. Galway. ✆ **095/30600.** Main courses €4–€12. Mon–Sat 10am–5:30pm.

12

THE MIDLANDS

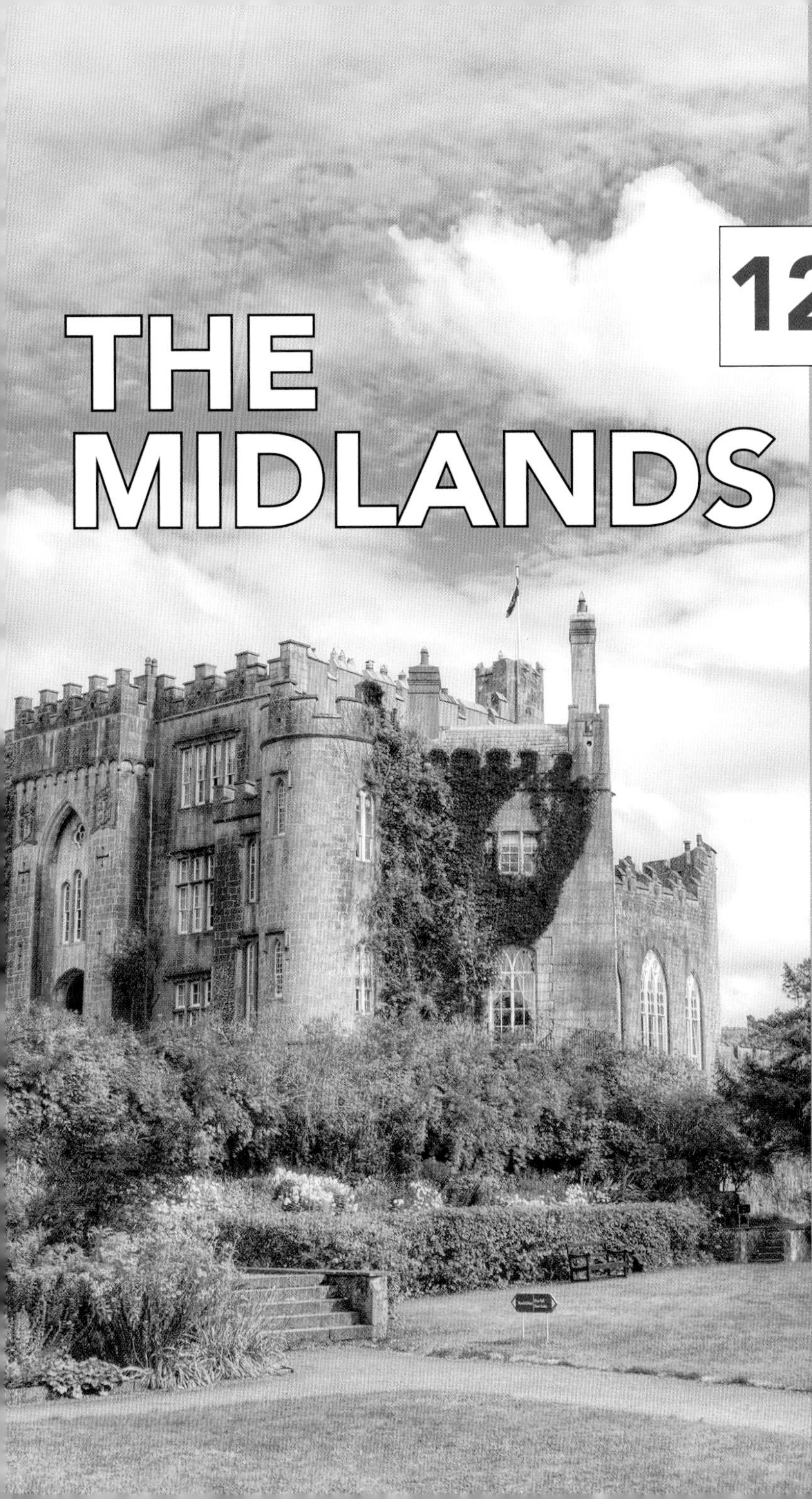

Not all that many tourists make it to the middle part of Ireland, which is odd since so many must go *through* it on their way between the far more visited east and west coasts. And while on some level that's a shame, it would take an optimistic act of PR by the region's tourist board to suggest that the region is teeming with attractions to draw people in. Plainly speaking, compared to places like Cork, Kerry or Galway, there's just not a great deal to do here.

That said, if you know where to look, you'll find real gems here. Seek out the romantic medieval castles that simply drip with history and atmosphere, such as **Charleville** and **Birr;** and the extraordinary ancient sites, such as the ancient monastic site at **Clonmacnoise** and the surprisingly little-known (and really old) **Corlea Trackway.**

This region was also where, in the late 17th century, the final battle for supremacy took place between two English kings: the Protestant William III and the Catholic King James II. William won, thus cementing the hold of a Protestant establishment in Ireland for centuries to come. The lavishly high-tech museum at Athlone Castle is the best of several in the region that tell this important story.

ESSENTIALS

Arriving

BY CAR By far the best way to get to and around the Midlands is by car. Although Athlone is easy to reach by public transportation from Galway or Dublin, you're still best off with a car in order to see the smaller towns and remote sites. Major roads that lead to this area are the main Galway-Dublin road (N6) from points east and west, N62 from the south, and N55 and N61 from the north. You can also boat through the region along the Shannon River, which cuts a swath through the region.

BY BUS **Bus Éireann** (✆ **061/313333;** www.buseireann.ie) runs hourly buses from the main bus station in Galway City to Athlone (about 90 min.) and several buses a day to Birr (around 4 hr.). From the main bus station in Dublin, buses also go to Athlone every hour (2 hr. journey time), and a handful of times a day to Birr (3–4 hr.).

BY TRAIN **Irish Rail** operates direct trains from Galway to Athlone Station, Southern Station Road (✆ **090/647-3300**) every 1 to 2 hours; the journey takes 90 minutes. From Dublin trains go to Athlone about every hour; the journey also takes 90 minutes.

PREVIOUS PAGE: **Birr Castle and Gardens in County Offaly.**

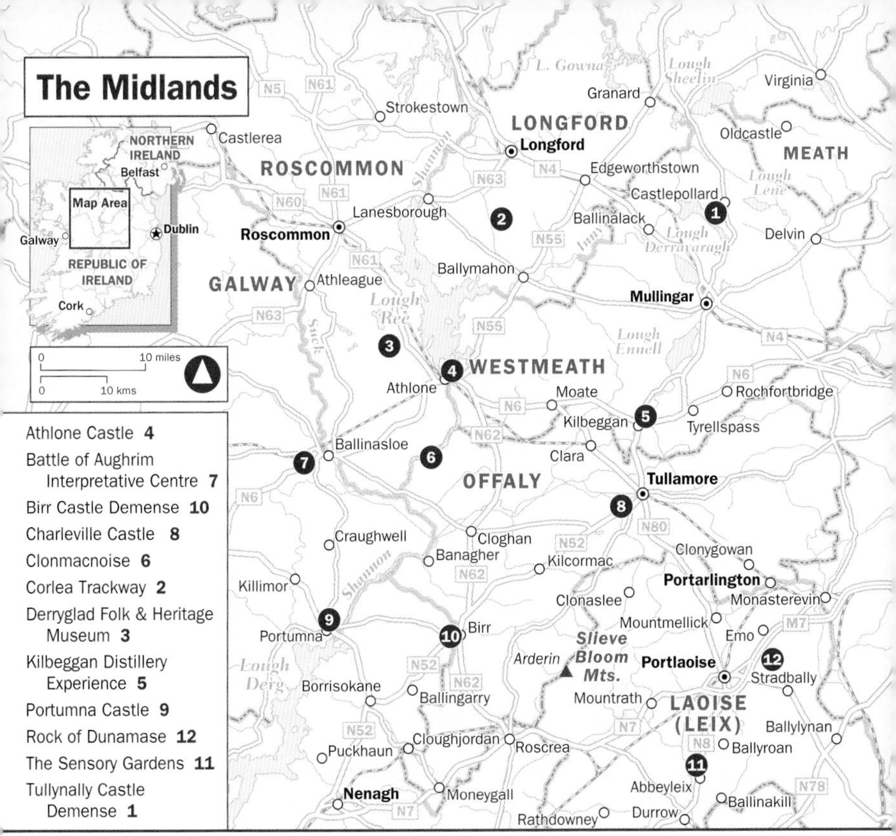

A Note on Listings

Officially the Midlands region covers the counties of Laois, Longford, Offaly, and Westmeath; however, we've included a couple of sights in the far eastern part of County Galway in this chapter, due to their close proximity. Given how spread out the top attractions in this region are, we've also decided to present them together, rather than split them up further by county. This is yet another reason why hiring a car is the only real way you'll be able to see what the Midlands can offer.

[Fast FACTS] THE MIDLANDS

ATMs/Banks In Athlone, a **Bank of Ireland** is at 31 Church St. (✆ **090/647-5111.** In Birr you can use the **Ulster Bank** ATM inside the **Londis** convenience store on Townsend St. (✆ **057/9121250**). In Abbeyleix try the **Bank of Ireland** on Main St. (✆ **057/873-1212**). And in Tullamore, a branch of **AIB** is at 5 William St. (✆ **057/932-1514**).

Dentists In the first instance you should ask your hotel or B&B to contact a dentist for you.

Alternatively, in Athlone, you could try **Ballantyne Dental Practise** on Garden Vale (✆ **090/647-5387**); in Birr, try **Catherine Barry**, the Green (✆ **057/291-0488**).

Doctors For medical emergencies dial ✆ **999.** For non-emergencies, your hotel should call you a doctor. Otherwise in Athlone try **Dr. Patrick O'Meara** on Garden Vale (✆ **090/647-2172**); in Birr, try **Dr. PJ McAuliffe** on Elm Park (✆ **057/912-1356**); in Tullamore, try **Dr Breda Scanlon** on Church St. (✆ **057/932-1170**); and in Abbeyleix, try **Dr. John Madden** on Main St. (✆ **057/873-1772**).

Emergencies For police, fire, or other emergencies, dial ✆ **999.**

Internet Access Even out in the boondocks, most—though not all—hotels now have internet access of one kind of another. Alternatively, if you need to get online in Athlone, you could try the **Netcafé** at 1 Paynes Lane, Irishtown (✆ **090/647-8888**), on the south side of the town.

Pharmacies In Athlone, try **Naylor's Pharmacy** at 23 Pearse St. (✆ **090/649-2259**); in Birr, try **Fox's Pharmacy** on O'Connell St. (✆ **057/912-0166**); in Tullamore, try **Fahey's** on Patrick St. (✆ **057/932-1540**) and in Abbeyleix, try **Frank O'Donnell** at the Medical Hall on Main St. (✆ **057/873-1294**)

Taxis In the countryside, the best way to get a cab is nearly always to ask your B&B or restaurant to call you one. Alternatively, in Athlone you could try **Dial-a-Cab** (✆ **090/649-3030**) or **Athlone Cabs** (✆ **090/647-4400**); in Birr, try **PL Dolan** (✆ **057/912-0006**; in Tullamore), try **Tullamore Taxis** (✆ **087/996-2264**); and in Abbeyleix try **Coffs Cabs** (✆ **087/224-9587**).

EXPLORING THE MIDLANDS

Eastern Galway segues smoothly into Offaly and Westmeath, and the rugged countryside becomes a bit softer and greener as you head inland. This is farming country, and pastures stretch as far as the eye can see, punctuated by historic sites and small farming communities. The early Christian settlement of **Clonmacnoise** ***(Cluain Mhic Nóis)*** occupies a beautiful stretch of land by the river, with its stone chapels and mysterious round towers. Farther along, you might want to stop by the town of **Birr** ***(Biorra),*** known for its magnificent and historic gardens, and **Banagher** ***(Beannchar na Sionna),*** a sleepy, working town with a picturesque harbor—although in recent years, sadly, it's got a little rougher and more rundown than it used to be. Later, the river winds and curls its way to **Athlone** ***(Baile Átha Luain),*** a vibrant, colorful place where the buildings are all brightly painted, and house plenty of interesting craft stores and boutiques. It is certainly the region's most appealing town of any size—although with a population of just over 15,500, it's hardly a teeming metropolis.

Athlone Castle ★★ Athlone Castle has protected the town for centuries. Built in 1210 for King John of England, this mighty stone fortress sits on the edge of the Shannon atop the ruins of an earlier fort built in 1129 as the seat of the chiefs of Connaught. It was besieged for almost 6 months in 1641, and again in 1690, but it fell in 1691 after an intense bombardment by forces sent by William of Orange. The Dutch military commander who took the town, Godard van Glinkel, was rewarded for his efforts with the earldom of Athlone. The castle underwent a multimillion-euro renovation in 2012; it now houses eight separate galleries on the history of Athlone, with plenty of high-tech

Athlone and the Shannon River in County Westmeath.

wizardry. Several tell the story of the Siege of Athlone (1690–91), a key event in the war that would cement the Protestant establishment in Ireland and ensure British rule, all the way up to the War of Independence in the 1920s. The castle's original medieval walls have been preserved, as have two large cannons dating from the reign of George II and a pair of 25cm (10-in.) mortars cast in 1856.

Athlone, Co. Westmeath. ✆ **090/644-2130.** Admission €8 adults; €6 seniors and students; €4 children 14 and under; €20 families. Tues–Sat 11am–5pm; Sun noon–5pm. On the riverbank, signposted from all directions.

Battle of Aughrim Interpretative Centre ★ About midway between Galway City and Athlone, just off the M5 motorway, lies this interesting little museum and interpretive center. The Battle of Aughrim wasn't the most famous, nor arguably the most important of the war between Protestant King William and Catholic King James—but it was the decisive one, with the final defeat of the so-called Jacobite forces of James II, thus ending the prospect of a Catholic Ireland for almost two and a half centuries. The center does a competent job of telling the story through displays and exhibits, plus the obligatory visitor center film.

Galway-Dublin Rd. (N6), Aughrim, near Ballinasloe, Co. Galway. ✆ **090/967-3939.** Admission €5 adults; €4 seniors and students; €3 children 11 and under; €12 families. May–early Sept Tues–Sat 10:30am–4pm, Sun 2–5pm. Closed early Sept–Apr.

Birr Castle Demesne ★★ The 17th-century castle is not open to the public, but people come here anyway, just to see the extraordinary gardens. The demesne (estate) of the Parsons family, now the earls of Rosse, wraps around a peaceful lake and along the banks of the two rivers. The box hedges have been featured in the *Guinness Book of Records* as the tallest in the world, and the hornbeam cloisters are lovely. The grounds contain an engaging exhibition on science in the 19th century, when Birr Castle was a hub of research into astronomy, photography, and botany. Antique scientific instruments are on display—including the jewel in their crown, **the Great Telescope.** The enormous astronomical machine, which resembles a medieval siege engine, was built in the 1840s; at the time it was the biggest telescope in the world. It was here that the Third Earl discovered that certain galaxies were shaped like spirals. This remained the only place in the world where the phenomenon could be observed until 1914. The telescope was recently restored to full working order, and demonstrations are held regularly in summer—call to check times.

Birr, Co. Offaly. ✆ **057/912-0336.** www.birrcastle.com. Admission €9 adults; €7.50 seniors and youth age 13–17; €5 children 5–12; free for children 4 and under; €25 families. Mid-Mar–late Oct daily 9am–6pm; late Oct–mid-Mar daily 10am–4pm. Take N52 37km (23 miles) southwest of Tullamore.

Charleville Castle ★★ Now, *this* is a castle. Designed in 1798 by Francis Johnston, this spooky, Gothic, crenellated masterpiece took 12 years to build. Today it's considered one of the best of Ireland's early-19th-century castles, and those who believe in such things say it is haunted. (It featured on the TV show Ghost Hunters in 2008.) It has fine limestone walls and plenty of towers, turrets, and battlements. Inside is spectacular plasterwork and hand-carved stairways, as well as secret passageways and dungeons. Charleville is run by volunteers, so opening times can be a little unpredictable. Tours run every day in the summer, and there are occasional night tours—but call ahead, particularly if you're planning to visit in the off season. Prices are a little on the high side, but the money is very obviously needed for ongoing restoration work. The fact that the staff, so dedicated and enthusiastic, are all unpaid, makes paying that little bit extra a lot easier to justify.

Off Birr Rd. (N52), Tullamore, Co. Offaly. ✆ **087/766-4110** or 057/932-3040. www.charlevillecastle.ie. Guided tour €16 adults; €8 students age 17–18; €4 children 6–16; free for children 5 and under. Apr–Aug tours daily 1–5:30pm. Tours by appointment at other times of year by.

castlepalooza MUSIC & ARTS FESTIVAL

Haunted it may or may not be, but Charleville Castle (see above) certainly comes to life in early August, when the delightfully laidback and bohemian **Castlepalooza** takes over the grounds. The 3-day festival—which won the award for "best small festival in Europe" in 2009, 10, and 11—attracts indie and alternative bands from Ireland and beyond. There are also arts workshops, film screenings, spoken word performances, and the like. Camping is available on site during the festival. For more information, and to book tickets, visit **www.castlepalooza.com**.

Clonmacnoise, an early Christian settlement north of Shannonbridge in County Offaly.

Clonmacnoise ★★★ Resting somberly on the east bank of the Shannon, this is one of Ireland's most profound ancient sites. St. Ciaran founded the monastic community of Clonmacnoise in 548 at the crucial intersection of the Shannon and the Dublin-Galway land route, and it soon became one of Europe's great centers of learning and culture. For nearly 1,000 years, Clonmacnoise flourished under the patronage of Irish chiefs. The last high king, Rory O'Connor, was buried here in 1198. Clonmacnoise was raided repeatedly by native chiefs, Danes, and Anglo-Normans, until it was finally destroyed by English troops in 1552. Previously the monks always had something to rebuild, but this time the English carried away everything—the roofs from the buildings, the doors, even the panes from the windows. By the time they'd finished, according to a report written by a monk from that time, "There was not left a bell, small or large, an image or an altar, or a book, or a gem, or even glass in a window, from the wall of the church out, which was not carried off." Today you can see what was left of the cathedral, a castle, eight churches, two round towers, three sculpted high crosses, and more than 200 monumental slabs, including some stones on which the old carvings can still be seen with thoughtful messages in ancient Celtic writing saying things like, "A prayer for Daniel."

On R357, 6.5km (4 miles) north of Shannonbridge, Co. Offaly. ✆ **090/967-4195.** Admission €6 adults; €4 seniors; €2 students and children; €14 families. Mid-Mar–May, Sept–Oct daily 10am–6pm; June–Aug daily 9am–6:30pm; Nov–mid-Mar daily 10am–5:30pm.

Corlea Trackway ★★ This is one of those places that, despite being very low key, makes you stand back and marvel at just how *old* Ireland is. A modern interpretive center, situated in a bog, contains what at first glance looks like an elevated wooden platform, made of planks nailed into place along rails, of the kind that you would see in a marsh or swamp today. It is, in fact, an excavated wooden trackway that has been carbon dated to the year 148 B.C. Roughly 18m (59 ft.) of original track has been uncovered so far and can be seen on a (free) guided tour. The center also contains an exhibition and a film to put the whole thing into context. A replica version of the track crosses a starkly beautiful section of bog, roughly where the rest of the track is believed to be buried. The weird thing is that the modern version really doesn't look all that different. One interesting tidbit: there is some disagreement among archaeologists over whether the track was built merely as a bridge over the bog, or whether it had some religious significance, enabling people to reach a part of the bog considered sacred for some reason.

Kenagh, Co. Longford. ✆ **043/332-2386.** www.heritageireland.ie. Free admission. Easter–Sept daily 10am–6pm. Last tour 1 hr. before closing; last admission 45 min. before closing.

Derryglad Folk & Heritage Museum ★ This rather sweet little museum just outside Athlone is a highly concentrated dose of mid-20th century nostalgia. You walk through a series of recreated businesses, each little building jam packed with memorabilia and antiques—a "medical hall" (drugstore), grocery store, hardware store—and a few farmer's crofts. Also intriguing is the **McCormack Photography Room,** which preserves the collection of a real photography studio that operated in Athlone from 1948 until 2002. As well as antique cameras and developing equipment, it displays photographs from the decades the shop was in operation. Museum guides could hardly be more helpful and keen to impart their encyclopedic knowledge.

Curraghboy, Co. Roscommon (13.8km/8½ miles northwest of Athlone on R362). ✆ **090/648-8192.** www.derrygladfolkmuseum.com. Admission €5 adults; €4.50 seniors and students; €3.50 children. May–Sept Mon–Sat 10am–6pm. Closed Oct–Apr.

The Kilbeggan Distillery Museum ★ The oldest *licensed* distillery in Ireland, Kilbeggan has been producing whiskey here since 1757. Well, almost—it closed in 1957, and was virtually derelict for 25 years, until the local people revived it as a smalltime distillery and museum. Full production resumed here in the late 2000s, using partly traditional methods, including a two-century-old copper still—thought to be the oldest still in day-to-day use anywhere in the world—and oak mash tuns. (They also have a working waterwheel and a steam-powered engine, although these are mostly for show.) Unlike most distilleries, you can wander around yourself, or choose one of the guided tours. The silver medal tour (€13; 10am and 3pm daily) includes a tasting of three whiskeys (or, if you prefer, samples to take home); while the gold medal (€25; 1pm daily) allows you to meet the distillers themselves, and take part in a four-whiskey masterclass tasting.

On N6, east of Athlone, Kilbeggan, Co. Westmeath. ✆ **057/933-2134.** www.lockesdistillerymuseum.ie. Self-guided tour €8; guided tours €13–€25. No children on tours. Apr–Oct daily 9am–6pm; Nov–Mar daily 10am–4pm.

Portumna Castle and Forest Park ★★ Built in 1609 by Earl Richard Burke, this massive, noble structure on the northern shores of Lough Derg is a particularly fine manor house. Had it not been gutted by fire in 1826, who knows what billionaire might own it now? The fire spared much of the impressive exterior, including its Dutch-style decorative gables and rows of stone mullioned windows; the ground floor is open to the public, and contains exhibits on the history of the castle, and the so-called "Flight of the Wild Geese," when the Jacobite forces of James II fled Ireland in defeat. The grounds contain a restored walled

A somber SORT OF GRANDEUR: STROKESTOWN PARK

Strokestown Park House (✆ **071/963-3013;** www.strokestownpark.ie) was the seat of the Pakenham-Mahon family from 1600 to 1979. King Charles II granted the vast estate, which stretches for miles in every direction, to Nicholas Mahon after the Restoration in appreciation of his support of the House of Stewart during the bloody English Civil War. It was quite a reward. The original house, completed in 1697, was considered to be too small and unimposing by Nicholas's grandson, Thomas. So he hired Richard Cassels (also known as Richard Castle) to build him something bigger and more impressive. The result is this 45-room Palladian mansion.

The north wing houses Ireland's last existing galleried kitchen (where the lady of the house could observe the culinary activity without being part of it). The south wing is an elaborate vaulted stable so magnificent that it has been described as an "equine cathedral."

These days Strokestown is also the permanent home of the **Irish National Famine Museum,** one of the country's very best museums devoted to that deadly period in Irish history. It sets out the terrible mixture of natural disaster and shocking cruelty of the British establishment that led to the deaths of around a million people and the emigration of a million more. Exhibits include letters penned by some of the tenants of Strokestown during the Famine years.

The reasoning behind this somber but incongruous pairing of historic attractions becomes clearer when you understand a little more of the history behind the grand Strokestown estate—particularly the behavior of one man, Major Denis Mahon, who was the landlord at Strokestown during the 1840s. When the potato blight struck, and famine started to spread, Mahon and his land agents could have done many things to help the hundreds of starving peasants who lived and worked on the property, but instead they evicted them as soon as it became clear they would not be able to pay their rent. He even went so far as to charter ships to send them away from Ireland. In 1847 Major Mahon was shot to death near Strokestown, and two men were hastily (and dubiously) convicted of the crime. But it seems clear that many hungry people had motives.

Strokestown Park is on the main Dublin-Castlebar Road (N5), in Strokestown, County Roscommon. It's about 77km (41 miles) south of Sligo Town. Admission costs €13.50 adults, €5.50 children, and €27.50 families. It's open from mid-March to October daily from 10:30am to 5:30pm, and November to mid-March daily from 10:30am to 4pm. The house can only be seen on a guided tour, at noon, 2:30 and 4:30pm (2:30pm only during the winter season).

kitchen garden and a willow maze. The castle is within the beautiful, 560-hectare (1,383-acre) expanse of **Portumna Forest Park.** It offers trails and signposted walks, plus viewing points, picnic areas, and the remains of a 13th century Cistercian abbey. Admission to the Forest Park is free.

Off N65, Portumna, Co. Galway. ✆ **090/974-1658.** Castle €3 adults; €2 seniors; €1 children and students; €8 families. Free admission to gardens. Apr–late Sept daily 9:30am–6pm; late Sept–late Oct Sat–Sun 9:30am–5pm. Last admission 45 min. before closing.

Portumna Castle, built in 1609 by Earl Richard Burke on the shores of Lough Derg in County Galway.

The Rock of Dunamase ★ There isn't much left of the castle that once stood atop this rocky outcrop overlooking a valley near the town of Portlaoise; however, what remains is an artful and quite striking sight. The ruins were once **Dunamase Castle** (though nobody really calls it that), built sometime during the 12th century. It clearly didn't last long, however; records indicate that it was a total ruin by as early as 1350. A much earlier fort is believed to have stood on the same sight. A few arched gateways survive intact, and the scattered remains of walls and turrets give a good idea of how impressive a sight it must once have been. The stunning view from among the ruins, over rolling green fields towards the Slieve Mountains in the distance, is worth the visit alone. Unfortunately the Rock isn't signposted from the main road; to get there, follow these directions. Leave Portlaoise on N80, heading in the direction of Carlow. Shortly after crossing over the main M7 motorway, just outside the town limits, you'll pass some large green industrial sheds. Approximately 1.8km (just over 1 mile) after this you will come to some scattered houses, with a turning on the left, next to a triangular patch of lawn and a telegraph pole. Take this turning; you will start to see the Rock on the hill to your left in about 0.5km (550 yds.).

Signposted on N80 (Portlaoise-Carlow Rd.), about 9km/5½ miles east of Portlaoise, Co. Laois. Free admission. Daily dawn–dusk.

leprechauns: **YOU'RE DOING IT ALL WRONG**

The word "leprechaun" comes from the Irish *leath bhrógan*, meaning "shoemaker". In folklore, leprechauns were often depicted as shoemakers by trade. They were mischievous creatures, not evil exactly, but certainly not averse to some very malicious practical jokes.

Different regions of Ireland all had their own versions of the Leprechaun folklore. There was disagreement over how they looked, too, although there were a few elements of common ground—including, most interestingly, a fondness for *red* coats, not green ones. The green came to be added later, presumably by foreigners, out of an association with Ireland in general.

Today the word also has less whimsical connotations. It's used to describe the more crass side of the tourism industry (with good reason—after all, the Ring of Kerry really does have "Leprechaun Crossing" signs). And on an even less pleasant note, it's used by some Northern Irish Unionists as a term of abuse for the Gaelic language.

The Sensory Gardens ★ These imaginative gardens are on the grounds of a convent in the town of Abbeyleix, not far from the border between counties Laois and Kilkenny. Designed entirely by people with learning difficulties, the gardens are intended to be accessible and stimulating to disabled visitors. Plants are chosen for their particularly strong effect on the senses, whether it be for their vibrant colors, powerful scent, or tactile appeal. Touches like wind chimes here and there, and even an innovative "humming stone," make this an ingenious and pleasant place to wander.

At Dove House, Main St., Abbeyleix, Co. Laois. ✆ **057/873-1325.** Free admission. June–Sept Mon–Fri 9am–4pm, Sat–Sun 2–6pm; Oct–May Mon–Fri 9am–4pm (Bank Holidays 2–6pm).

Tullynally Castle Demense ★ A turreted and towered Gothic Revival manor, this creamy white castle home is dazzling. It has been the home of the Pakenham family, the earls of Longford, since 1655. Frustratingly, given its inviting, fairytale-like exterior, the building itself is only open to pre-booked groups of 20 or more. However, the 12-hectare (30-acre) grounds are an attraction in themselves. Highlights include a large kitchen garden, where the grass is kept short by grazing llamas; forest trails and a riverside walk; and an idyllic path leading to a Victorian grotto. Tullynally is near Lough Derravaragh, a tranquil spot featured in the legendary Irish tale *The Children of Lir.*

About 32km (20 miles) east of Longford and 21km (13 miles) north of Mullingar, off the main Dublin-Sligo Rd. (N4), Castlepollard, Co. Westmeath. ✆ **044/966-1159.** www.tullynallycastle.com. Gardens €6 adults; €3 children; €16 families. Castle only open for pre-booked group tours—call in advance for information. Garden May–Aug Thurs–Sun and holidays 1–6pm.

THE slieve bloom MOUNTAINS

Linking Counties Laois and Offaly, this lush and gentle mountain range is great hill-walking territory— its tallest peak is just 527m (1,729 ft.), which clocks in at about the same as the 44th tallest in the Wicklow Mountains (see chapter 6). They also have the great advantage of being decidedly under-visited, so you're likely to find peace and solitude a lot easier to come by.

The park has several looped hiking trails, including several around **Lough Boora;** one of them has its own sculpture trail. Another takes you through the tiny but charming village of **Clonaslee,** and up to the **Rickets Rock waterfall.** Several trained guides live locally and will offer their services if you'd prefer to be taken around by an expert; a full list with contact details is available at **www.slievebloom.ie/index.php?page=walking-guides**.

The terrain also lends itself particularly well to horseback riding; the **Birr Equestrian Centre,** Kingsborough House, Birr, County Offaly (✆ **087/244-5545;** www.birrequestrian.ie) organizes regular treks and special trips.

Several castles are to be found within the boundaries of the Slieves, including **Charleville** (see p. 372) and **Portumna** (see p. 374).

For more information visit **www.slievebloom.ie**.

Sports & Outdoor Pursuits

BOATING The following companies rent cabin cruisers, usually for a minimum of 1 week, along this section of the Shannon: **Athlone Cruisers,** Jolly Mariner Marina, Athlone, County Westmeath (✆ **090/647-2892**); and **Silverline Cruisers,** The Marina, Banagher, County Offaly (✆ **057/915-1112;** www.silverlinecruisers.com). Crafts range from four to six berths; range from €700 to €3,600 per week in high season.

CYCLING Bikes can be rented from **D.B. Cycles & Babyland,** Unit 3, Magazine Road, Athlone, County Westmeath (✆ **090/649-2280**), for €15 per day or €50 per week.

GOLF **Birr Golf Club,** The Glens, Birr, County Offaly (✆ **057/912-0082;** www.birrgolfclub.com), is an 18-hole course on 45 hectares (111 acres) of parkland countryside; the greens fees are €25 to €35.

In the Athlone area is the 18-hole **Athlone Golf Club,** Hodson Bay, Athlone, County Westmeath (✆ **090/649-2073;** www.athlonegolfclub.ie), with greens fees of €30 to €35; and the 18-hole championship **Mount Temple Golf Club,** Moate, County Westmeath (✆ **090/648-1841;** www.mounttemplegolfclub.com), 8km (5 miles) east of Athlone, with greens fees of €20 to €25. The **Glasson Golf Hotel & Country Club,** Glasson, County Westmeath (✆ **090/648-5120;** www.glassongolfhotel.ie), is on the shores of Lough Ree, 10km (6¼ miles) north of Athlone. Greens fees are €40 to €50.

Lovely parkland and woodland golfing in the Lough Derg area is offered at 18-hole clubs such as **Portumna Golf Club,** Ennis Road, Portumna, County Galway (✆ **090/974-1059;** www.portumnagolfclub.ie), with greens fees of €20 to €25, with a special midweek rate for seniors of €15.

HORSE RACING The horse racing runs from July to September at the **Kilbeggan Racecourse,** Loughnagore, Kilbeggan, County Westmeath (✆ **057/933-2176;** www.kilbegganraces.com), off the main Mullingar road (N52), 1.6km (1 mile) from town. Tickets cost €12 adults, €10 seniors and students, €20 families (2 adults with children aged 15 or under), free for children 15 and under.

WALKING The **Slieve Bloom Mountains** (see p. 378) contain several excellent several looped walking paths and trails.

WHERE TO STAY IN THE MIDLANDS

Athlone, on the southern tip of Lough Rea and almost half way between Galway and Dublin, makes a natural base from which to explore the Midlands region. It has a couple of modern chain hotels, although it seems a shame to come all this way and stay in one when you could be waking up to a home cooked breakfast in a sweet little Irish farmhouse instead. Otherwise, the Midlands are by no means the richest region in the country for interesting hotels and B&Bs, but some real standouts are to be found scattered around the countryside.

Bastion ★★ This delightful B&B is run by the lovely Anthony and Vinny McCay, who have converted an old Athlone townhouse into a chic, rather bohemian getaway. The decor helps fill the place with light and cheer, from the whitewashed walls and polished wood floors in the bedrooms, to the sophisticated furniture and slightly Moroccan-style accent pieces strewn around the public areas. Breakfasts are plentiful and healthy; a buffet laid out with home baked bread, fruit and other welcome alternatives to the ubiquitous full Irish. Two minor downsides: two of the bedrooms have shared bathrooms, and those with mobility problems should be sure to ask for a room on the lower floors—there are quite a few stairs to climb.

2 Bastion St., Athlone, Co. Westmeath. ✆ **090/649-4954.** www.thebastion.net. 7 units. €55–€75 double. No parking (street parking nearby). Breakfast not included in lower rates. **Amenities:** Wi-Fi (free).

Emmett House ★ A corner terrace house with a cozy, authentic interior, Emmett House is a satisfyingly traditional B&B. Bedrooms are a bit of a mixture; some nicely reference the 18th century origins of the house, with antique-style furniture (including a beautiful four poster in one room), but others are rather more plain and modern. They're a decent enough size, though (given their age) and everything is spotlessly clean. Breakfasts are tasty and filling, and the welcome from host Maureen is genuine and warm.

Emmett Square, Co. Offaly. ✆ **057/916-9885.** www.emmethouse.com. 4 units. €80–€100 double. No parking (street parking nearby). Breakfast included. **Amenities:** Wi-Fi (free).

Viewmount House ★★ A warm welcome, good food, and tranquil, elegant gardens await at this lovely country house B&B just outside Longford. Bedrooms are done in a pleasingly old-fashioned style, with heavy, antique wood furniture and plenty of space. Some have little sitting areas and roll top tubs in the bathrooms. However, Viewmount also has a deserved reputation for being one of the best places to eat in the area; the **VM Restaurant** serves superb modern Irish cuisine, and worth the splurge at €53 for four courses. Check the website for special offers, including good midweek dinner, bed and breakfast discounts.

Dublin Rd., Longford, Co. Longford. ✆ **043-3341919.** www.viewmounthouse.com. 12 units. €120 double; €150 suite. Free parking. Breakfast included. **Amenities:** Wi-Fi (free); restaurant.

St. Ruth's Farmhouse ★ Your welcome could hardly be warmer at this charming farmhouse B&B, courtesy of hostess Helen and the delicious homemade cakes and pies she lays on for every new arrival. From the outside, St Ruth's is precisely how you'd imagine an Irish farmhouse to look—all stone walls, lush green lawns and flowerpots around the cute yellow front door—and inside she's done a wonderful job of keeping the decor traditional without tipping over into twee. Breakfasts are delicious, with several ingredients coming straight from the farm.

Milltown, Athlone, Co. Westmeath. ✆ **090/648-8090.** www.struths.com. 5 units. €70 double. Free parking. Breakfast included. **Amenities:** Wi-Fi (free).

Wineport Lodge ★★★ This romantic, modern hotel overlooking Lough Rea is a truly relaxing getaway. The contemporary bedrooms have plenty of space, and little balconies with views of the Lough—great for watching the glassy waters turn orange as the sun goes down. The hotel spa is surprisingly good value for a place like this; you could choose from a simple aromatherapy bath for €35, or a deeply relaxing full body hot stone massage for €95. It should come as no surprise that the restaurant is equally excellent. Good value dinner, bed and breakfast packages are available.

Glasson, Athlone, Co. Westmeath. www.wineport.ie. ✆ **090/643-9010.** 30 units. €100–€198 double; €166–€240 suite. Free parking. **Amenities:** Wi-Fi (free); restaurant; bar; room service; spa.

WHERE TO DINE IN THE MIDLANDS

Most small towns in this area have little in the way of restaurant life. In some villages, the only place in town making food at all is the pub. But **Athlone** has a reasonably vibrant restaurant scene, with some sophisticated restaurants and coffee shops to choose from. Along with the choices below, see the hotels listed above, as most have excellent restaurants.

Beans & Leaves ★ CAFE This cheerful cafe-deli is a great place to know when you're after a quick, tasty, and healthy lunch in Athlone. In addition to excellent sandwiches, they also do tasty light meals—fishcakes, seafood chowder, or perhaps a steaming hot plate of chicken curry. They also make some exceedingly moreish desserts.

Lloyds Lane, Athlone, Co. Westmeath. ✆ **090/643-3534.** Lunch main courses €5–€12. Mon–Sat 9:30am–5:30pm; Sun 11am–5pm.

The Blue Apron ★★ IRISH This great little bistro is in Tullamore, about 3.4km (2 miles) northeast of Charleville Castle (see p. 372). The menu isn't long, but it's well judged and expertly done. Go for some pear and Cashel blue cheese salad or scallops to start, before maybe choosing from such mains as honey and thyme glazed duck breast or rainbow trout served with roast fennel and saffron cream. The fixed-price Sunday lunch menu (€27 for three courses) is a great choice for a proper, full lunch, although don't expect to get much done afterwards.

Harbour St., Tullamore, Co. Offaly. ✆ **057/936-0106.** www.theblueapronrestaurant.ie. Main courses €15–€24. Wed–Thurs 5:30–9:30pm; Fri–Sat 5:30–10:30pm; Sun 12:30–9pm. Set menus only Wed–Fri, Sun lunch.

The Coffee Club ★ Café This busy, friendly cafe in Tullamore is an extremely popular spot for lunch. They serve a huge range of sandwiches from their deli counter, plus delicious, healthy stir-frys (you choose the ingredients), salads, and other snacks. The upstairs dining room, which is lined with shelves full of secondhand books, is a quieter, more relaxed space. Appropriately enough, given the name, they also serve an extremely fine cup of coffee. They have live music—of a jazz-or-salsa variety—on Sundays from 2 until 4pm.

Harbour St., Tullamore, Co. Offaly. No phone. www.thecoffee-club.com. Main courses €5–€12. Mon–Sat 8am–6pm; Sun 10am–5pm.

The Fatted Calf ★★ MODERN IRISH/INTERNATIONAL A funky ambience pervades at this gastropub just outside Athlone. They take their local, seasonal produce seriously here—as well they might, as the owner has been a national commissioner for a European-wide chef's organization since the 90s. The menu takes Irish flavors and gives them an infusion of global influences, meaning you might start with some Dublin Bay prawn wontons, before moving on to some spiced Irish chicken fried in buttermilk and served with pico de gallo, or some sweet potato pancakes served with chickpea cassoulet and tomato chili jam. They also serve a menu of imaginative salads and lighter meals at lunchtime. Glasson is about 8km (5 miles) northeast of Athlone on N55.

Glasson, Co. Westmeath. ✆ **090/648-5208.** www.thefattedcalf.ie. Main courses €18–€28. Wed–Sat 12:30–3:45pm, 5:15–9:30pm; Sun 12:30–3:45pm , 5:15–7:45pm.

THE OLDEST pub IN IRELAND

The question of who gets to claim the title of Ireland's oldest pub is a vexed one, with several contenders battling it out to have their claim taken most seriously. The Brazen Head in Dublin (see p. 158) has been serving customers since 1198, making it an oft-cited candidate for the honor—although detractors would point to the fact that most of the building was replaced in the 17th century as cause at least for reasonable doubt.

The other big contender is **Sean's Bar** on Main Street in Athlone (✆ **096/649-2358;** www.seansbar.lightholderproductions.com). Records show that there has been a drinking establishment of some kind or another on this site since the quite astonishingly faraway date of 900 A.D. The owners can even point to the fact that a small section of its walls are thought to be original as further strength for their claim—but again, the extent to which it can be considered the *same* pub is open to debate.

The dispute was finally settled in the mid-2000s, when the *Guinness Book of Records* ruled in favor of Sean's, which presumably means it's now acceptable to call it officially Ireland's oldest pub. Today it's a pleasant enough spot, although somewhat disappointingly lacking in *olde worlde* features; you'd never guess to look at the place that it's been serving customers since half a millennia before Columbus sailed to America.

The Old Fort ★★ IRISH/INTERNATIONAL Well this is certainly a unique place for a restaurant: a converted artillery fortification, constructed to guard against a potential French invasion in the early 19th century. The building has been interestingly restored, with slightly wry touches like lighting sconces in the dining room shaped like old-fashioned rifles (the effect is subtler than it sounds). The menu keeps things simple, with plenty of traditional flavors; a starter of crab claws or calamari, perhaps, followed by roast duck with honey and clove sauce, or maybe a simple but delicious steak with pepper cream sauce. A simpler, more international set menu goes right along with the à la carte options.

Shannonbridge, Co. Roscommon. ✆ **090/967-4973.** Main courses €21–€29. Wed–Sat 5–9pm; Sun 12:30–4pm. Call to check opening in winter, particularly Wed and Thurs.

Preston House ★★ IRISH Classic Irish food, elegantly prepared and presented is the mainstay of this popular fine dining restaurant in the center of Abbeyleix. This is very much a special occasion kind of restaurant locally, with all the seasonal ingredients and technical skill that you'd expect. A starter of goats cheese soufflé is presented in thoroughly modern style with delicate squares of saffron gel; for main course you could have some wild seabass with pappardelle and cep voulete, or perhaps some woodland pigeon, served in its own jus with puy lentils. It's not all formality and fuss, however; come to the cafe (in the same building) before 5pm for the simple but very good lunch menu on offer for around €10 per main course (less if you opt for a sandwich). Preston House is also a very good B&B, with prices starting at €120 for a double.

Main St., Abbeyleix, Co. Laois. ✆ **057/873-1432.** www.prestonhouse.ie. Main courses €18–€32; 7-course tasting menu €60 without wine, €80 with wines. Restaurant: Tues–Sat noon–2pm, 6–10pm; Sun noon–3pm. Closed Sun Nov–Feb. Cafe: Tues–Sat 10am–5pm.

Thyme ★★★ MODERN IRISH Offering fine dining without being overly fussy or formal, this excellent bistro is one of the best places to eat in Athlone. Local ingredients feature heavily on the imaginative bistro-style menu; you may be offered Fivemiletown goats cheese panna cotta or smoked mackerel and leek croquettes to start, then maybe a local sirloin served with red chard and polenta, or some beautifully presented duck breast with organic turnip puree and blackberry jus. The "value menu," served until 6pm on Friday and Saturday but all night in the rest of the week, offers similar dishes at a very reasonable €23 for two courses, or €28 with dessert. You should try and make reservations, especially on weekends.

Costume Place, Athlone, Co. Westmeath. ✆ **090/647-8850.** www.thymerestaurant.ie. Main courses €15–€26. Mon–Sat 5–10pm; Sun noon–8pm.

13

MAYO, SLIGO & THE NORTH SHANNON VALLEY

The strikingly beautiful landscape of Galway continues to the strikingly beautiful landscape of southern Mayo without fanfare. Like Galway, Mayo is marked by dramatic scenery tumbling over rocky cliffs plunging down into the opaque blue waters of the icy sea. If you head farther north, you'll reach the smooth pastures of County Sligo. The main appeal here is not its towns, which tend to be functional farm communities, but the countryside. This is the landscape that inspired the poet William Butler Yeats. Its unspoiled marvels are still a healing tonic—though the region is rich with fairy-tale castles and mysterious prehistoric sites, its biggest gift to the visitor is tranquility. Heading inland from Sligo, you'll reach the upper Shannon River valley, with its sprawling lakes, promising fresh trout and salmon, and nearly limitless watersports in the summer.

ARRIVING

BY BUS **Bus Éireann** runs daily bus service to Sligo Town from Dublin, Galway, and other points including Derry in Northern Ireland. It provides daily service to major towns in Mayo. The bus station in Sligo is on Lord Edward Street.

BY TRAIN Trains from Dublin and other major points arrive daily at Westport in Mayo, and Sligo Town in Sligo. The train station in Westport is on Altamont Street; about a 10-minute walk from the town center; in Sligo it's on Lord Edward Street, next to the bus station.

BY CAR Four major roads lead to Sligo: N4 from Dublin and the east, N17 from Galway and the south, N15 from Donegal to the north, and N16 from Northern Ireland.

BY PLANE **Ireland West Airport Knock** in Charlestown, County Mayo (✆ **094/936-8100;** www.knockairport.com) is becoming quite a popular hub for budget airlines from the U.K. **Aer Lingus** (✆ **081/836-5000;** www.aerlingus.com) or **Ryanair** (✆ **0871/246-0000** in the U.K. or 152/044-4004; www.ryanair.com) run daily scheduled flights from London, Liverpool, Edinburgh, and Bristol. **Flybe** (✆ **087/1700-2000** in the U.K. or 0044/1392-683-152) also has three flights per week from Manchester and Edinburgh. There are no flights to the airport from other points within Ireland.

PREVIOUS PAGE: **View from Croagh Patrick, County Mayo.**

[Fast FACTS] THE NORTHWEST

ATMs/Banks In Westport, a branch of **AIB** is on Shop Street (✆ **098/25466**). In Ballina, a **Bank of Ireland** is on Pearse Street (✆ **096/21144**). In Sligo Town, try the **AIB** on Stephen Street (✆ **071/914-2157**).

Dentists For dental emergencies, your hotel should contact a dentist for you; otherwise, in Westport try **Dr. Richard Lee Kin** on Upper James Street (✆ **098/26611**). In Sligo Town, try **Dr. Brendan Flanagan** on Wine Street (✆ **091/916-0953**).

Doctors For medical emergencies dial ✆ **999.** For non-emergencies, your hotel should call you a doctor. Otherwise in Westport try the **Westport Medical Clinic,** Market Lane (✆ **098/27500**); in Ballina, try the **Moyview Family Practise** on Dillon Terrace (✆ **095/22933**). In Sligo Town the **Medicentre** is on Barrack Street (✆ **071/914-2550**).

Emergencies For police, fire, or other emergencies, dial ✆ **999.**

Internet Access In Westport, you can get online at the **Mayo County Library** on the Crescent (✆ **098/25747**). In Sligo Town try **Café Online** at Cairy Court (✆ **071/914-4892**).

Pharmacies In Westport, try **Treacy's** on James Street (✆ **098/25474**). In Ballina, **Quinn's Chemist** is on Pearse Street (✆ **096/21365**). Sligo Town has a branch of **Boots** on O'Connell Street (✆ **071/914-9445**).

Post Offices In Westport, the main post office is on North Mall (✆ **098/27210**). In Ballina, Bury Street (✆ **096/21798**). In Sligo Town, Castle Street (✆ **071/914-3078**).

Taxis If you need a cab home from a restaurant, the management should be able to call a recommended one for you—particularly in rural areas, where taxi firms can be few and far between. Otherwise, in Ballina you could try the **Ballina Taxi Company** (✆ **087/295-8787**). In Westport, try **AA Taxis** (✆ **087/237-7070**); in Sligo Town, try **Ace Cabs** (✆ **071/914-4444**).

COUNTY MAYO

Serenely beautiful, County Mayo sits in the shadow of its more famous neighbor, Galway, and doesn't seem to mind. For experienced Ireland travelers, Mayo is a kind of Galway Lite—its rugged coastal scenery is similar to that of Galway, but it has less of the traffic or tourist overload from which Galway suffers in the summer. This is peaceful, pleasant Ireland, with striking seascapes and inland scenery that ranges from lush and green to stark, desert-like, and mountainous. It's an unpredictable place, where the terrain changes at the turn of a steering wheel. This region was hit so hard by the potato famine that, in some ways, it's only now recovering. Starvation and emigration emptied it then, and that emptiness is still noticeable. It feels as you leave Galway as if it all goes quiet.

For some, the county's most familiar history is cinematic. The village of **Cong** was the setting for the 1951 John Ford film *The Quiet Man,* starring John Wayne and Maureen O'Hara. Among Mayo's other attractions are the mysterious 5,000-year-old settlement at **Céide Fields,** the religious shrine at **Knock,** and some of Europe's best fishing waters at **Lough Conn, Lough Mask,** and the **River Moy. Ballina** ***(Béal an Átha),*** Mayo's largest town, calls itself the home of the Irish salmon. And **Westport** is a little resort town guaranteed to steal your heart.

Visitor Information

The main tourist information center for County Mayo is the **Westport Tourist Office,** James Street, Westport (✆ **098/25711;** www.mayo.ie). Other offices are on Pearse Street, **Ballina** (✆ **096/72800**) and in the Old Courthouse in the center of **Cong** (✆ **094/954-6542**). **Ireland Centre** is on the Quay, Donegal Town (✆ **074/972-1148**).

Exploring County Mayo

Because it's a rural county with no major cities or many large towns, County Mayo feels a bit like a place without a center. Towns like Castlebar, Claremorris, Westport, and Ballinrobe in the southern part of the county, and Ballina in the northern reaches, make good places to stop, refill the tank, and have lunch, but they offer little to make you linger. The county's attractions lie in the countryside, and in smaller communities like Foxford, Ballycastle, Louisburgh, and Newport.

County Mayo's loveliest town, **Westport *(Cathair na Mairt)*** ★, nestles on the shores of Clew Bay. Once a major port, it was designed by Richard Castle with a tree-lined mall, rows of Georgian buildings, and an octagonal central mall where a vibrant market adds zest to the town on Thursdays.

Southeast of Westport, **Croagh Patrick,** a 750m (2,460-ft.) mountain, dominates the views of western Mayo for miles. St. Patrick is said to have spent the 40 days of Lent praying here in the year 441. To commemorate that, on the last Sunday of July, thousands of Irish people make a pilgrimage to the site, which has become known as St. Patrick's Holy Mountain.

Heading west, the bleak and starkly beautiful coast provides a magnificent backdrop as you head towards **Achill Island *(An Caol)***, a wild and beautiful outpost (see p. 394). **Clare Island,** once the home of Mayo's legendary "Pirate Queen," Grace O'Malley, is another scenic isle, south of Achill in Clew Bay.

Like the drive to Achill Island, the road from Ballina along the edge of the northern coast to Downpatrick Head is breathtaking. It passes through **Killala** (***Cill Alaidh*** or ***Cill Ála***), a small, secluded harbor village that came close to changing the course of Ireland's history. In 1798, the French General Amable Humbert landed here with 1,100 troops in an attempt to help the Irish defeat the British forces. After several surprisingly successful fights with troops under British command, particularly a thorough routing at Castlebar, Humbert had attracted thousands of Irish volunteers who fought by his side. At that point, the British sent General Cornwallis (the same general who surrendered to Washington at Yorktown in 1781) to take him on in Longford, with thousands of well-armed troops. The battle lasted only half an hour before Humbert surrendered. The French soldiers were treated honorably, but the Irish volunteers who had fought with Humbert, and anybody suspected of sympathizing with him, were slaughtered.

Outside Killala on the road R314 to **Ballina *(Béal an Átha)*** are several ruined friaries worth a stop for those who love the blurred beauty of ancient abbeys. **Moyne Abbey** was established in the mid-1400s and destroyed by Richard Bingham, the English governor of Connaught, in the 16th century. It's a peaceful place, and you can see why the monks chose it. The same is true, even

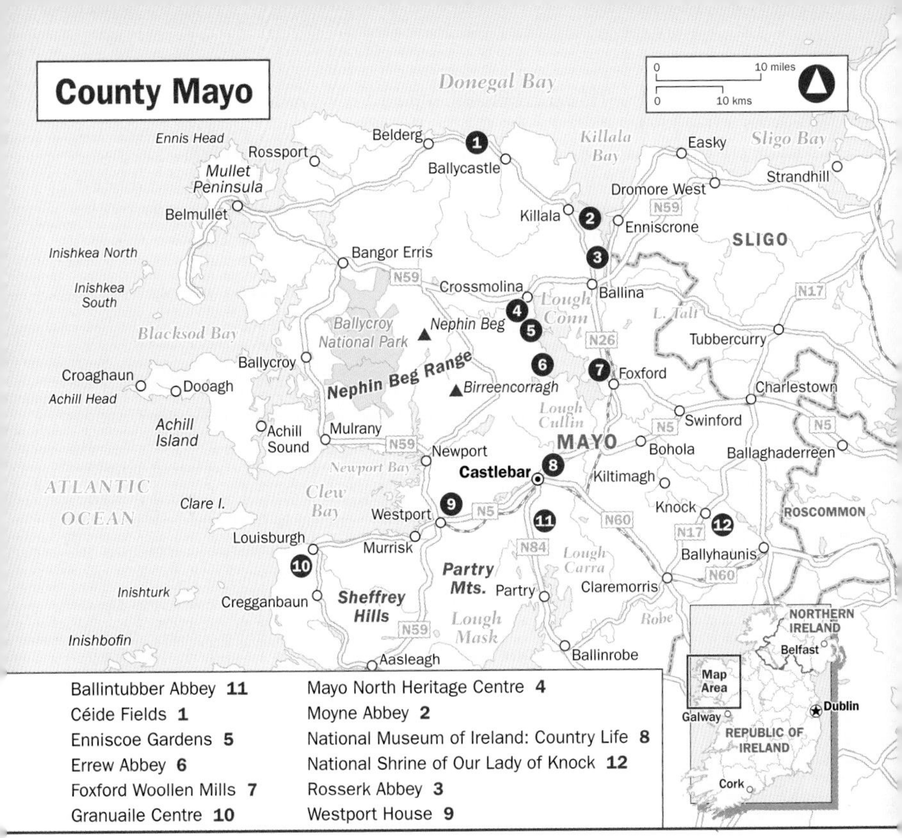

more so, of **Rosserk Abbey** about 3km (2 miles) away. Sitting at the edge of the River Rosserk, the abbey is in much better shape than the Moyne: Its chapel windows are well preserved. You can climb a winding stone stair to look out across the bay. The piscina of the church (once used for washing altar vessels) is still here, carved with angels, and on its lower-left-hand column is a delightful detail: a tiny, elegant carving of a round tower that recalls its 23m-tall (75-ft.) counterpart in nearby Killala. The Rosserk Abbey was built at the same time as the Moyne and also destroyed by Bingham's troops.

Around Ballina

Enniscoe Gardens ★ Part of the huge Enniscoe estate—which also includes the Mayo North Heritage Centre (see p. 388) and where you can stay in the charming manor house (see p. 397)—these beautiful gardens comprise woods, parkland and part of Lough Conn. One of the highlights is an 18th century walled garden that has been restored to the layout it would have had in the estate's Victorian heyday.

On Lough Conn, about 3.2km (2 miles) south of Crossmolina, off R315, Enniscoe, Castlehill, Ballina, Co. Mayo. ✆ **096/31809.** www.northmayogenealogy.com. Gardens: €6 adults; €5 seniors and students; €2 children; €12 families. Combined ticket with museum: €8 adults; €5 seniors; €3 students and children; €15 families. Apr–Oct Mon–Fri 10am–6pm; Sat–Sun 2–6pm.

Errew Abbey ★ This atmospheric, ruined 13th-century Augustinian church sits on a tiny peninsula in Lough Conn. The cloister is well preserved, as is the chancel with altar and piscina, a stone basin used for disposing of the water used during Mass. The oratory of massive stone walls in fields adjacent to the abbey is on the site of a church founded in the 6th century. It's known locally by the marvellous, tongue-twistery name *Templenagalliaghdoo,* which means "Church of the Black Nun."

Signposted about 3.2km (2 miles) south of Crossmolina on the Castlebar Rd., then 5km (3 miles) down a side road, County Mayo. No phone. Free admission (open site). Crossmolina is about 11.7km (7⅓ miles) west of Ballina.

Foxford Woollen Mills Visitor Centre ★ This popular Irish brand of knitwear and tweed has a noble origin story. It was founded by Mother Agnes Morragh Bernard, a nun, in the late 19th century. Mother Agnes's idea was to build a new local industry to try and ameliorate the effects of the Great Famine by providing employment to locals. Ever since then the mill has thrived producing rugs, clothing, and the like. Not only did her scheme help to stave off poverty for the local workforce, but the brand became hugely successful in Ireland and beyond. You can tour the mills, and visit the on-site museum that tells the story in detail. The guided tour (free of charge) leaves every 20 minutes and takes 45 minutes or so; alternatively you can borrow a self-guided multimedia version that takes around an hour to complete. Also on site are two art galleries, a jewelry workshop, a restaurant, and of course a gift shop, where you can stock up on the stylish products themselves.

St. Joseph's Place, Foxford, Co. Mayo. ✆ **094/925-6104.** www.foxfordwoollenmills.com/working-mills.php. Free admission. May–Oct Mon–Sat 10am–6pm; Sun noon–6pm. Nov–Apr Mon–Sat 10am–6pm; Sun 2–6pm. Last guided tour 5:30pm. Tours after noon on Sun do not include working mills. Foxford is 16km (10 miles) south of Ballina on N26.

Mayo North Heritage Centre ★ This is the ideal place to start if you're in the region checking out your roots. The extensive records available to view here include church registers (Catholic, Presbyterian, Methodist, and others); registers of births, marriages, and deaths; estate and probate records; property leases and rent rolls; school registers; emigrant rolls; and census records. Research fees, with their expert genealogists, range from €30 for a basic search (best suited to those who are just starting out with their research, or don't already know much about their family tree), to more extensive searches, including full reports, which cost anything from €95 to €150 and take several weeks to finish. The on-site museum displays a somewhat random collection of historic farm equipment and household items from the early to mid-20th century. The **Enniscoe Gardens** (see p. 387) are directly next door and combined tickets are available.

On Lough Conn, about 3.2km (2 miles) south of Crossmolina, off R315, Enniscoe, Castlehill, Ballina, Co. Mayo. ✆ **096/31809.** www.northmayogenealogy.com. Museum: €6 adults; €3 seniors; €2 students and children; €8 families. Combined ticket with gardens: €8 adults; €5 seniors; €3 students and children; €15 families. Mon–Fri 9:30am–4:00pm.

Moyne Abbey ★ Established in the mid-1400s and destroyed by Richard Bingham, the English governor of Connaught in the 16th century, Moyne Abbey is an atmospheric ruin between Killala and Ballina. Parts of the exterior are relatively complete (minus the roof, which is completely gone). The closer you get the more of a ruin you realize it is, although the tower is pretty well preserved—until you look to the upper level, that is, where the whole structure looks like it's been snapped off by a giant hand. Moyne Abbey is a peaceful place, and looking through its moldering old windows, or over a misty carpet of green fields, you can fully understand why the monks chose this spot.

On R314 between Killala and Ballina. No phone. Free admission (open site).

In & Around Westport

Ballintubber Abbey ★★ This abbey is a real survivor—one of only a few Irish churches in continuous use for almost 800 years. Founded in 1216 by Cathal O'Connor, king of Connaught, it has endured fires, numerous attacks, illnesses, and anti-Catholic pogroms. Although Oliver Cromwell's forces so thoroughly dismantled the abbey that they even carried off its roof in 1653 in an effort to finally suppress it, clerics continued discreetly conducting religious rites. Today it's an impressive church, with 13th-century windows on the right side of the nave and a doorway dating to the 15th century. It was completely restored in 1966. A helpful visitor center illuminates its troubled and fascinating history. Guided tours are available weekdays from 10am to 5pm; there's no charge but donations of €4 per person are requested.

Off the main Galway-Castlebar Rd. (N84), about 21.5km (13½ miles) east of Westport, Ballintubber, Co. Mayo. ✆ **094/903-0934.** www.ballintubberabbey.ie. Free admission; donations requested. Daily 9am–midnight.

Granuaile Centre ★ This small but rather charming museum is devoted to a particularly cool local hero: Grace O'Malley, also known as "the Pirate Queen"—or, in Gaelic, *Granuaile*, (pronounced *Grawn-yawayl*). To call Grace's

THE quiet MAN: WHEN THE GOLDEN AGE OF HOLLYWOOD CAME TO COUNTY MAYO

The sweet little town of **Cong,** County Mayo, was the setting for the classic 1951 John Ford film *The Quiet Man,* starring John Wayne and Maureen O'Hara. Ever since then, the town has been a popular tourist destination, and you can still see the scant remains of the stone cottage used in the film, which has been gradually torn apart over the years by people who want to bring home one of its stones. (We strongly request that you do not take anything except photographs—as do the locals.)

Guided tours of the locations used in the film are available from **Inisfree Experience.** Tours are individually tailored, so can work out to be quite expensive unless you're in a group. Call Paddy on ✆ **087/243-9760** or visit www.inisfreeexperience.com for more information.

Aside from the Quiet Man, Cong is most famous as the location of **Ashford Castle.** Built in the 13th century, it is one of Ireland's biggest and most complete medieval castles. Unfortunately (unless palatial luxury is within your price range), it is now a super-exclusive hotel and resort, and there are no public tours. However, there's nothing to stop you driving up and having a wander of the grounds. And if you want to spend a little more time here on a slightly more realistic budget, consider the more modest splurge of dinner at **Wilde's** (see p. 399), an outstanding restaurant in the former estate keeper's lodge.

Cong is roughly half way between Galway and Westport, on R344, R345 and R346.

life story colorful would be an understatement, but today she is considered a defender of the rights of the people of Mayo as much as she was a ruthless pirate. But the pirate stuff is inevitably more fun. The center is in a former church building and has some engaging exhibits that tell the story of her life, plus a few more exhibits on the history of the area in general. It's engaging if you're interested in the subject, but the slightly out-of-the-way location means that the opening times can be unpredictable, so it's best to call ahead before making the journey. For more on this extraordinary woman, see p. 392.

Church St., Louisburgh, Co. Mayo. ✆ **098/66341.** Admission €4 adults; €2 seniors and students; children free. Mon–Fri 10am–4pm. Louisburgh is 21km (13 miles) west of Westport on R334; Church St. is near the center of the village.

The National Museum of Ireland: Country Life ★★ The countryside outpost of Ireland's multi-site national museum (the others are all in Dublin, see chapter 5), this one specializes in Irish life, trade, culture, and tradition since the mid-19th century. Permanent exhibitions deal with folklore; the natural environment and how local communities have relied on it for survival; political and social upheaval, particularly in the years preceding the Great Famine; traditional trades and crafts; and the changing life of the Irish people at home and at work. They also have a thoughtful program of changing exhibitions. Like all the National Museum sites, entry is completely free.

Signposted from N5, Turlough Park, about 8km (5 miles) east of Castlebar, Co. Mayo. ✆ **094/903-1755.** www.museum.ie. Free admission. Tues–Sat 10am–5pm; Sun 2–5pm.

Westport House and Pirate Adventure Park ★★ At the edge of the town of Westport, this late-18th-century residence is the home of Lord Altamont, the Marquess of Sligo and a descendant, it is said, of Pirate Queen Grace

THE ROOLABOOLA CHILDREN'S arts FESTIVAL

RoolaBoola is a festival of children's theater, film, and arts workshops at the Linenhall Arts Centre in Castlebar. The festival has been growing in prominence over the last decade and now attracts professional theater companies from all over the world. What particularly appeals about this festival is that, although the plays are aimed very firmly at children, they are intelligent, well-produced pieces of theater that don't talk down to their audience. Recent productions have included a funny and touching play about two hobos who live in a world of discarded objects, and a fantasy play about a magical creature who collects forgotten memories. The festival also includes film screenings and workshops on everything from Cubist art for 5 to 7 year-olds to circus skills. Not everything has to be pre-booked and some events are free; otherwise, tickets cost anything between €1 and about €8, with family discounts available. For more information and details on how to book, call the box office at ✆ **094/902-3733,** or visit the festival website, www.thelinenhall.com/children/roolaboola-festival.php. The festival program runs for a week in late October, and the program is usually announced in early September.

Westport House in County Mayo.

O'Malley (witness the bronze statue of her on the grounds). The work of Richard Cassels and James Wyatt, the house has a graceful staircase of ornate white Sicilian marble, unusual Art Nouveau glass and carvings, family heirlooms, and silver. The grandeur of the residence is undeniable, but purists might be put off by the fact that the sprawling gardens are a commercial enterprise these days, home to the **Pirate Adventure Park.** Kids, however, will be far more interested in the log ride, the swinging pirate ship, swan-shaped pedal boats on the lake, giant bouncy castle, and a child-size train tooting its way through the gardens. Probably because of that, prices are quite high (and a few attractions, such as the Pirate's Den play area for young children, cost extra).

The Westport Demense, Westport, Co. Mayo. ✆ **098/27766.** www.westporthouse.ie. House and Gardens: €12 adults; €9.50 seniors and students; €6.50 children. House, Gardens and Pirate Park: €20 adults; €18 seniors and students; €16.50 students; €59–€75 families. Pirate's Den play area: €6.50 children 4 and over; €3.50 children 3 and under. Pitch and Putt Golf: €6. June Wed–Fri 10am–3pm; Sat–Sun noon–6pm. July–Aug daily 11am–6pm. Also over 2 week Easter school holidays daily 11am–6pm; first weekend in May (May Bank Holiday) Fri–Mon 11am–6pm and 1 week October school holidays daily 1–5pm. Closed Nov–Mar (until Easter school holidays).

Exploring the Rest of County Mayo

Clare Island ★★ Floating about 5km (3 miles) off the Mayo coast, just beyond Clew Bay, Clare Island is a place of unspoiled splendor. Inhabited for 5,000 years and once quite populous—1,700 people lived there in the early 19th century—Clare is now home to 150 year-round islanders, plus perhaps as many sheep. But the island is best known as the haunt of Grace O'Malley, the "Pirate Queen," who controlled the coastal waters 400 years ago (see p. 392). O'Malley's modest castle and the partially restored Cistercian abbey where she is buried are among the island's few attractions. The rest of the draw is its remote natural beauty. Two ferry services operate out of Roonagh Harbour, 29km (18 miles) south of Westport: **O'Malley's Ferry Service** (✆ **098/25045;** www.omalleyferries.com); and **Clare Island Ferries** (✆ **098/26307;** www.clareislandferry.com). The round-trip fare for the 15-minute journey is around €15.

Co. Mayo. www.clareisland.info.

local hero: GRACE O'MALLEY, THE PIRATE QUEEN

Grace O'Malley, the "Pirate Queen," was born in 1530 on **Clare Island** (see p. 391). She was, by all accounts, ahead of her time. A heroine, adventurer, pirate, gambler, mercenary, traitor, chieftain, and noblewoman, she is remembered now with affection, although at the time she was feared and despised. Even as a child, she was fiercely independent. When her mother refused to let her sail with her father, she cut off her hair and dressed in boys' clothing. Her father called her *"Grainne Mhaol,"* or "Bald Grace," later shortened to Granuaile (pronounced *Graw-nya-wayl*), a nickname she'd carry all her life.

At 16, Grace married Donal O'Flaherty, second in line to the O'Flaherty clan chieftain, who ruled all of Connacht. A few years later, her career as a pirate began when the city of Galway, one of the largest trade centers in the British Isles, refused to trade with the O'Flahertys. Grace used her fleet of fast galleys to waylay slower vessels on their way into Galway Harbour. She then offered safe passage for a fee in lieu of pillaging the ships.

She is most fondly remembered for refusing to trade her lands in return for an English title, a common practice of the day.

When the English captured her sons in 1593, she went to London to try to secure their release. In an extraordinary turn of events, she actually secured a meeting with Queen Elizabeth. History records that, just as remarkably, the two women got on quite well (although legend has it that Grace initially tried to smuggle a knife in with her, in case things went differently). A deal was struck; Elizabeth agreed to release her sons and to return some captured lands, if Grace would agree to renounce piracy. This she did and returned to Ireland triumphantly.

Grace O'Malley, the "Pirate Queen" of Galway, known as a hero and defender of the Gaelic way of life.

The truce did not last, however. She got her sons back, but not her property. She took up piracy again and continued it until her death from natural causes in 1600.

At Céide Fields, a seaside bog preserved the remains of a Stone Age farm settlement for more than 5,000 years.

Céide Fields ★★ In a breathtaking setting above huge chalk cliffs that plunge hundreds of feet down into a deep blue sea, an ancient people once lived, worked, and buried their dead here. However, nobody knew this until the 1930s, when a local farmer noticed stones piled in strange patterns in his fields. More than 40 years later, his archaeologist son explored the discovery further. Under the turf, he found Stone Age fields, megalithic tombs, and the foundations of a village. Standing amid it now, you can see a pattern of farm fields as they were laid out 5,000 years ago (predating the Egyptian pyramids). Preserved for millennia beneath the bog, the site is both fascinating and inscrutable. To a casual observer, it's little more than piles of stones, but the visitor center makes it meaningful in a series of displays, films, and tours. The pyramid-shaped center itself is designed to fit in with the dramatic surroundings—you can see the building from miles away. It also contains a cafeteria, which comes as a relief since this site is 20 hilly, rocky kilometers (12 miles) of winding roads from anywhere.

On R314, 8km (5 miles) west of Ballycastle, Co. Mayo. ✆ **096/43325.** Admission €4 adults; €3.50 seniors; €2 students and children; €10 families. Apr–May, Oct daily 10am–5pm; June–Sept daily 10am–6pm; last tour 1 hr. before closing. Céide Fields is about 34km (21 miles) northwest of Ballina.

National Shrine of Our Lady of Knock and the Church of the Apparition ★ This is Ireland's version of Lourdes, and Catholic pilgrims (mostly Irish Catholic) come here in droves. It all dates from a day in August 1879 when two young local girls said they saw Joseph, Mary, and St. John standing in bright light in front of the southern tower of the parish church. Soon, 13 other witnesses claimed to have seen the same thing, and the Church declared it a miracle. Before long, miracles were occurring fast and furious, as sick and lame visitors

A TRIP TO achill island

The rugged, bog-filled, sparsely populated coast of counties Mayo and Sligo makes for scenic drives to secluded outposts. Leading the list is **Achill Island,** a heather-filled slip of land with sandy beaches and spectacular views of waves crashing against rocky cliffs. The drive from the mainland and then across the island to the little town of **Keel** requires patience and skill but rewards you with a camera full of photos. The unrelenting wind off the Atlantic Ocean means that Achill Island is ideal for windsurfing, hang gliding, or any activity that involves a breeze.

About 5.7km (3½ miles) west of Keel is the secluded Blue Flag beach of **Keem Bay.** It was once a major fishing ground—basking shark were caught here commercially up until the 1950s—but no more. You can reach the bay along a small cliff-top road, which passes by cliff faces containing, so we're told, rich seams of glittering amethyst. Apparently it's not uncommon to find chunks of the stuff lying loose after heavy rainfall.

Speaking of remarkable finds: Hidden on the slopes of **Mount Slievemore,** Achill's tallest mountain, are the remains of an **abandoned village.** The hundred or so crumbling stone cottages of the nameless ghost town date back to sometime around the 12th century. It was deserted during the Great Famine, although some cottages are known to have been in occasional use until the very early years of the 20th century, as the traditional practice of "booleying"—seasonal occupation by farming communities—continued here long after it had died out in the rest of Ireland. Mount Slievemore is between Keel and Doogort, in the central northeastern part of Achill Island.

At Kildavnet, between Derreen and Coughmore, in the southeastern corner of the island, you'll find **Granuaile's Tower.** This impressive 15th-century tower house was owned by Grace O'Malley, the "Pirate Queen," who caused all manner of havoc for the English around these parts in the 16th century (see p. 392). There's not a great deal to see, but it's a stunning spot to

claimed to be healed after visits to the church. Knock came to the world's attention in 1979, when Pope John Paul II visited the shrine. There's not much to the town of Knock on the whole—it sits unspectacularly at the intersection of the N17 and R323 roads (it's not even on some maps of Ireland, it's so small)—but it's filled with increasingly large, modern religious structures, including a huge circular basilica that seats 7,000 and contains artifacts or furnishings from every county in Ireland. The grounds also hold a folk museum (with a few letters relating to the original testimonies) and a religious bookshop.

On the N17 Galway Rd. Knock, Co. Mayo. ✆ **094/938-8100.** www.knock-shrine.ie. Free admission to shrine. Museum €4 adults; €3 seniors and children age 5 and over; €3.50 students; children 4 and under free. Shrine and grounds: daily 8am–6pm or later. Museum: daily 10am–6pm. Knock is about 44km (27⅓ miles) southeast of Ballina, 30km (18½ miles) east of Castlebar.

Sports & Outdoor Pursuits

FISHING The waters of the River Moy and loughs Carrowmore and Conn are known for good fishing, particularly for salmon and trout. To arrange a day's fishing, contact **Cloonamoyne Fishery ★**, Castlehill, near Crossmolina, Ballina

Walking on Achill Island.

admire. Nearby **Kildavnet Church** is thought by some archaeologists to date from the 8th century.

To get to the Achill Island crossing, take N59 heading northwest out of Westport, then join R319, signposted to Achill. The drive from Westport to the crossing is about 42km (26 miles) and should take around 40 minutes. Once you're on Achill Island, Keel is about another 14km (8⅔ miles) down the same road.

(✆ **096/51156** or 087/314-8449; www.cloonamoynefishery.com). This professional angling service will advise and equip you to fish the local waters: for brown trout on loughs Conn and Cullin; for salmon on loughs Beltra, Furnace, and Feeagh; and for salmon and sea trout on the rivers Moy and Deel. The fishery rents fully equipped boats and tackle, teaches fly-casting, and provides transport to and from all fishing. Daily rates are €30 for a rowboat, €60 for a boat with engine, and €120 for a boat with engine and *ghillie* (guide).

County Mayo is also home to the **Pontoon Bridge Hotel Fly Fishing School,** Pontoon, County Mayo (✆ **094/925-6120;** www.pontoonbridge.com), where you don't need to be a hotel guest to enjoy the fly fishing school, run by local expert Jack Mellette. The courses last from 10am to 5pm, including an hour's stop on Glass Island in the middle of the Lough Conn, and cost €95. They also offer dinner, bed and breakfast packages for €200.

Obtain a permit and state fishing license at the **Mayo Angling Advice Centre,** at the Tiernan Bros. fishing tackle shop, Upper Main Street, Foxford, County Mayo (✆ **094/945-6731;** www.tiernanbrothers.8k.com). It also offers a range of services, including boat hire and *ghillies.*

For fishing tackle, try **Kingfisher Bates,** Pier Road, Enniscrone, County Mayo (✆ **096/36733**), or **Ridge Pool Tackle Shop,** Cathedral Road, Ballina, County Mayo (✆ **096/72656**). On Achill Island, get sea-angling gear at **O'Malley's Island Sports** on the main road (next to the post office) in Keel (✆ **098/43125**). O'Malley's can also arrange boat hire and bike hire.

GOLF County Mayo's 18-hole golf courses include a par-71 inland course at **Castlebar Golf Club,** Rocklands, Castlebar, County Mayo (✆ **094/902-1649;** www.castlebargolfclub.ie), with greens fees of around €25 weekdays and €35 weekends. They sometimes run special deals that include a meal at the clubhouse for very little extra, especially out of season. The par-73 championship course at **Westport Golf Club,** County Mayo (✆ **098/28262;** www.golfwestport.com), charges greens fees of around €30 weekdays, €50 weekends. On the shores of Clew Bay, the challenging and scenic course winds around the slopes of Croagh Patrick Mountain.

KAYAKING Courses for adults and children are at the **Atlantic Adventure Centre,** in Lecanvey, just outside of Westport, County Mayo (✆ **098/64806;** www.atlanticadventurecentre.com). Most of the kayaking is done at the Blue Flag beaches at Old Head, Bertra, and Carramore. Very reasonable accommodations rates are available for campers. The adventure center has all you need for a wide range of activities, from canoeing to rock climbing. Call for details.

WALKING The region to the east of the Mullet peninsula has a spectacular array of sheer sea cliffs and craggy islands. The small, secluded beach at **Portacloy,** 14km (8⅔ miles) north of Glenamoy on the R314, is a good starting point for a dramatic walk. On a sunny day, its aquamarine waters and fine-grained white sand recall the Mediterranean more than the North Atlantic. At its western edge is a concrete quay. From here, head north up the steep green slopes of the nearest hill. ***Safety note: Don't be too distracted by the fantastic view or adorable little sheep—the boggy slopes on which you are walking end precipitously at an unmarked cliff edge. The walk is therefore not recommended for children, or in bad weather.*** Exercise caution and resist the urge to try to get a better view of the mysterious sea caves or to reach the outermost extent of the coast's promontories. Instead, use a farmer's fence as a guide and head west toward the striking profile of **Benwee Head,** about 2.4km (1½ miles) away. Return the same way to have a swim in the chilly, tranquil waters of Portacloy.

WINDSURFING & OTHER WATERSPORTS The constant wind off the Atlantic Ocean means that Achill Island is ideal for windsurfing, hang gliding, or any activities that involve a breeze. If you want to try it out, talk with Richie O'Hara at **McDowell's Hotel & Activity Centre** (Slievemore Road, near Dugort; ✆ **098/43148**). He also gives surfing instructions and advice on rock climbing, and rents out canoes and surfboards. For other options, contact the useful Atlantic Adventure Centre (see above).

Where to Stay in County Mayo

This region of Ireland has few rich pickings when it comes to the quantity of top places to stay. Even the major towns have only a smattering of decent B&Bs and small hotels. However, some gems are to be found in the deepest reaches of the countryside. It takes effort to get to these places, but the journey will be worth it.

Ashford Castle ★★★ This extraordinary, fairytale-like castle has entertained plenty of famous guests over the years; Grace Kelly, Ronald Regan, Brad Pitt, Pierce Brosnan, and Tony Blair are just a few of the luminaries to have been cosseted within its luxurious walls. It was also named the best resort hotel in Europe by *Condé Nast Traveler* in 2010, and if you've got a spare couple of hundred euros burning a hole in your wallet, you too can join the ranks of its illustrious fans. Ashford Castle was built in the 13th century and still looks every inch the palatial abode, thanks to the suits of armor and priceless antiques lining the walls and the huge four-poster beds filling the sumptuous guestrooms. The grounds are stunning—the castle overlooks Lough Corrib, and you have acres of forest and landscaped gardens in which to get lost. A range of spa treatments is available. The restaurant is as excellent as you'd expect (don't even think about dressing down) although a less formal eatery is on the grounds too. Hotel experiences in Ireland don't come much more splurge-y than this, but that's the cost of living like royalty—even for a night. Check the website for special deals, especially in the off season.

On R346, on the eastern approach to Cong, Co. Mayo. ✆ **094/954-6003.** www.ashford.ie. 83 units. €354–€1046 double; €628–€1380 suite. Free parking. Breakfast included. **Amenities:** Wi-Fi (free); 2 restaurants; bar; gym; massage treatments; estate sports including golf, fishing and clay pigeon shooting.

The Bervie ★★★ Overlooking the Atlantic Ocean on Achill Island, reached by bridge across Achill Sound, the Bervie is an inspiring place to stay. Husband-and-wife hosts, John and Elizabeth Barrett, spent years lovingly restoring the place. Elizabeth actually grew up here; it's been a B&B since the 1930s, although today it's a far more sophisticated place than she remembers from her childhood. Guestrooms are large and spacious, with well-chosen furniture (most of it made locally) and tasteful art. Some rooms directly overlook the sea—and what a view! You can see some of the other islands dotted around the bay from some rooms, while others have a dramatic view of cliffs. Light pours in from huge windows, and the whispering of the waves soothes you off to a restful sleep. Elizabeth's home-cooked breakfasts are to die for, and after years of being advance notice-only, the outstanding dinners are a permanent fixture. Think roast lamb served with Madeira jus or rib-eye steak with onion marmalade and blue cheese mushrooms—all with excellent use of local ingredients. There's a reasonably priced wine list too.

The Strand, Keel, Achill, Co. Mayo. ✆ **098/43114.** www.bervie-guesthouse-achill.com. 14 units. €110–€130 double. Free parking. Breakfast included. Dinner €45. **Amenities:** Wi-Fi (free); restaurant. Take N59 to Achill Island, then follow R319 to Keel. The Bervie is signposted from the edge of the village.

Enniscoe House ★★ Flanked by Mount Nephin on one side and the shimmering waters of Lough Conn on the other, Enniscoe is a stunningly restored mid-18th-century mansion. Very little has been significantly altered from the original structure, so the place is overflowing with wonderful period details (one room even has its original silk wallpaper). Bedrooms are spacious with big windows and antique, half-tester beds. Bathrooms are modern and elegantly designed. Susan Kellett and her son, DJ, run the place with a natural flair for hospitality. Susan is a great cook too; make sure you book one of her excellent dinners. The grounds are big, and with enough to do that you could spend a day here without leaving, should you wish. They're open to the public, with a cafe and even a **Heritage Centre,** complete with a local history museum, a genealogical service, and a small antiques shop. The Enniscoe estate also has a couple of self-catering cottages available if you want even more privacy.

Castlehill, Ballina, Co. Mayo. ✆ **096/31112.** www.enniscoe.com. 6 units. €160–€180 double. Dinner €50. Free parking. Breakfast included. **Amenities:** Guest lounge.

Windmill Cottages ★★ Your host, Pierre Blezat, fell so in love with the area when he first came here that he left his native France to run Windmill Cottage as a B&B. He restored the small complex of farm buildings personally, and each displays a personal touch. The effect is like a series of cozy, modern country cabins with exposed pine walls decked, modern art, and contemporary furniture. The cottages are a stone's throw (literally) from the sea, with views of the water and distant mountains. The breakfast room takes full advantage of the view and sometimes doubles as a dining room in the evenings, where Pierre serves delicious French-Irish meals that must be booked in advance. Pierre can also arrange a chauffeur service to Westport train station for €15; transfers from further afield are possible too.

Carraholly, about 2 km (1¼ miles) west of Westport Golf Club, Co. Mayo. ✆ **098/56006.** www.windmill-cottage.com. 6 units. €100–€150 double. Dinner €30. Free parking. Breakfast included. **Amenities:** Wi-Fi (free); bike hire. Closed Oct–Mar.

Where to Dine in County Mayo

Standout restaurants in this part of the country are few and far between. However, they often can be found in hotels and the better B&Bs. You will find some good, reliable choices in Westport.

An Port Mor ★★ SEAFOOD/MODERN IRISH This multi-award winning restaurant in Westport specializes in seafood. Local catches dominate the menu, so you could easily find Clew bay crab cakes and scallops, or blue trout (yes, *blue*) from Curran served with tarragon and canola. The seafood is excellent, but it's not all that's on offer—expect to find a juicy sirloin served with red onion marmalade, or perhaps some local lamb. Everything is impeccably presented, and the atmosphere in the cheerful dining room is relaxed. Service is excellent too.

Bridge St., Westport, Co. Mayo. ✆ **098/26730.** www.anportmor.com. Main courses €15–€23. Tues–Sun 6pm–midnight.

Bayside Bistro ★ BISTRO There aren't many restaurants in Keel, the main town on little Achill Island, but this place is a cheerful and reasonably inexpensive option. You might start with stir-fried squid with sweet chili, before moving on to duck in cranberry and red wine, or a simple steak with peppercorn sauce and fries. There's always a wide selection of daily seafood specials, too. Lunches are simpler—salads, ciabatta sandwiches, crostini (grilled bread with assorted toppings), or even fish tacos.

On R319, Keel, Achill Island, Co. Mayo (next to the general store and post office in the center of the village). ✆ **098/43798.** www.baysidebistro.ie. Main courses €15–€20. Daily noon–10pm.

The Helm ★ SEAFOOD/BISTRO This laid back bar-restaurant specializes in local seafood. Portions are generous—tackle the delicious fisherman's platter only if very hungry—but it's all tasty and cheerfully served. Main dishes include steaks, rack of lamb, and pork chops, in addition to the fishy options. Creamy seafood chowder is a particular specialty. Lunch service is heartier and more traditional, with Irish stew and mash alongside lasagna and chips. Desserts are all comfort food like pies, crumbles, and even jelly and ice cream. The Helm is also a B&B with a few self-catering apartments available too.

The Harbour, Westport, Co. Mayo. ✆ **098/26398.** www.thehelm.ie. Main courses €19–€23. Daily 8am–about midnight. Food served until about 9:30pm.

The Hungry Monk ★ CAFE The Hungry Monk is just the kind of place you want to break up a long day's sightseeing: simple cooking, light lunches and snacks, served in a cozy, cottage atmosphere. The lunch menu consists mostly of tasty sandwiches and salads, creatively prepared with local ingredients. Or you could just linger over a cup of coffee and a something to nibble on such as the delicious cheesecake. The Hungry Monk doesn't serve dinner, but snacks and light meals are served until late afternoon.

Abbey St., Cong, Co. Mayo. ✆ **094/954-5842.** Main courses €4–€12. Mon–Sat 10am–6pm; Sun 11am–5pm.

Wilde's at Lisloughrey Lodge ★★★ CONTEMPORARY IRISH If you can't quite swing a night at Ashford Castle (see p. 397), then, like the other 99 percent of us, you might find this a viable alternative. Lisloughrey was once home to the estate managers of Ashford, but now it's run as a boutique hotel with a fantastic restaurant. Wilde's is overseen by Jonathan Keane, an up-and-coming star of the Irish culinary world. His modern Irish cooking is deliciously inventive, and just a glance at the menu is enough to give you an idea of his celebratory, joyous approach to food. A starter of goat cheese, profiteroles, and mango is "birds nest on the roof," while the "Atlantic sea spray lamb" is prepared with pistachio, seaweed, samphire, mint . . . and Coca-Cola. The dining room has a fantastic view of Lough Corrib. If you want to spend the night, doubles start at around €120.

On the grounds of Ashford Castle, Cong, Co. Mayo. ✆ **094/954-5400.** www.lisloughreylodge.com. Fixed-price menus (3 courses) €42. Mon–Sat 6–10pm; Sun 1–3:30pm, 6–10pm.

COUNTY SLIGO

County Sligo is known for its extraordinary concentration of ancient burial grounds and pagan sites, most of which are in easy reach of the county capital. Chief among these are the Stone Age cemeteries at **Carrowmore** and **Carrowkeel,** but just driving down the country lanes, you can't help spotting a **dolmen** (ancient stone table) in some pasture or other, with sheep or ponies grazing casually around it. **Sligo Town** isn't busy, historic, or pretty enough to require much of your time, but it is a handy place to base yourself if you want to explore the bucolic farmland that has become, thanks to the impressive energy of the County Sligo tourism offices, "Yeats Country." Although he was born in Dublin, the poet W. B. Yeats spent so much time in County Sligo that it became a part of him, and he a part of it—literally, as he is buried here. As you'll quickly discover, every hill, cottage, vale, and lake seems to bear a plaque indicating its relation to the poet or his works. When you plan your itinerary, allow plenty of time to explore the countryside that so inspired him.

Visitor Information

The **Sligo Tourist Office** is on the ground floor of the Bank Building, O'Connell Street, Sligo Town (© **071/916-1201;** www.sligotourism.ie).

Exploring County Sligo

Sligo Town (pop. 20,000) is a small farm town on the south side of the River Garavogue, surrounded on three sides by mountains, the most famous of which are Ben Bulben to the north and Knocknarea to the south. A gray and somber place, with a mix of historic and less interesting modern architecture, Sligo has undergone something of a renaissance in recent years—albeit one that, like the rest of the country, hit difficult times in the post-2008 recession. From a visitor's perspective, the focus of this has been Sligo's new "Left Bank," where cafes and restaurants spill onto the waterfront promenade whenever weather permits.

SLIGO TOWN LAYOUT

Edged by Sligo Bay to the west, Sligo Town is bisected by the Garavogue River, with most of its commercial district on the river's south bank. **O'Connell Street** is the main north-south artery (and the location of the tourist office). The main east-west thoroughfare is **Stephen Street,** which becomes Wine Street and then Lord Edward Street. Three bridges span the river; the **Douglas Hyde Bridge,** named for Ireland's first president, is the main link between the two sides.

EXPLORING SLIGO TOWN

The Model ★★ One of Ireland's most renowned contemporary art museums, the Model houses an impressive collection of paintings and other visual art. It includes probably the best collection of works by Jack B. Yeats (1871–1957) outside the National Gallery in Dublin (see p. 105). Brother of William, Jack was one of the foremost Irish painters of the 20th century. Other luminaries of the Irish art world represented here include Louis le Brocquy (1916–2012), an extraordinary figurative painter; and the portraitist Estella Solomons (1882–1968). Their program of temporary and special exhibitions is varied and imaginative. The Model is also a venue for live music and film screenings. Check the website for up-to-date listings.

The Mall, Sligo, Co. Sligo. © **071/914-1405.** www.themodel.ie. Free admission to exhibitions; tickets to other events free to around €25. Tues–Sat 10am–5:30pm; Sun noon–5pm.

Sligo Abbey ★ Founded as a Dominican house in 1252 by Maurice Fitzgerald, Earl of Kildare, Sligo Abbey was the center of early Sligo Town. It thrived for centuries and flourished in medieval times when it was the burial place of the chiefs and earls of Sligo. But, as with other affluent religious settlements, the abbey was under constant attack, and it was finally destroyed in 1641. Much restoration work has been done in recent years, and the cloisters contain outstanding examples of stone carving; the 15th-century altar is one of few intact medieval altars in Ireland.

Abbey St., Sligo, Co. Sligo. © **071/914-6406.** www.heritageireland.ie. Admission €3 adults; €2 seniors; €1 students and children; €8 families. Apr–mid-Oct daily 10am–6pm; last admission 45 min. before closing.

County Sligo
Carrowkeel Passage Tomb Cemetery 8
Carrowmore Megalithic Cemetery 4
Drumcliffe & Yeats's Grave 2
Eagles Flying 7
Inishmurray 1
Knocknarea 3
Lough Gill Drive 5
Parke's Castle 6
NORTHERN IRELAND
Belfast
Map Area
Galway
Dublin
REPUBLIC OF IRELAND
Cork
Donegal Bay
Inver Bay
Killybegs
Ballintra
DONEGAL
Ballyshannon
Tullaghan
Bundoran
Lower Lough Erne
Lough Melvin
Inishmurray
Cliffoney
Benbulben
Dartry Mts.
Glencar L.
Drumcliffe
Rosses Point
Sligo Bay
Strandhill
Sligo
Manorhamilton
L. Macnean
Enniskillen
Belcoo
NORTHERN IRELAND
Upper Lough Erne
Ballycastle
Easky
Killala Bay
Dromore West
Lough Gill
Dromahair
Killala
Enniscrone
Knockalongy
Ballysadare
Collooney
Slieve Gamph (Ox Mts.)
Glengavlen
Drumkeeran
Riverstown
SLIGO
LEITRIM
CAVAN
Crossmolina
Ballina
L. Talt
Ballymote
Castlebaldwin
Lough Arrow
Lough Allen
Iron Mts.
Ballyconnell
MAYO
Tubbercurry
Ballyfarnon
Drumshanbo
Ballinamore
Lough Conn
Lough Key
Lough Oughter
Ballinafad
Curlew Mts.
Foxford
Birreencorragh
Lough Cullin
Charlestown
Lough Gara
Boyle
Carrick-on-Shannon
Swinford
Drumsna
Mohill
Arva
Bohola
Ballaghaderreen
ROSCOMMON
Lough Boderg
Brosna
LONGFORD
N15
N16
N4
N59
N17
N26
N5
N61
N87
A47
A46
A4
A32
A509
0
10 miles
10 kms

Sligo County Museum ★ This museum in the center of Sligo Town does a good job of giving you an overview of the county's history, from ancient times to the present day. The most interesting sections cover the region's extraordinary prehistoric heritage, including a couple of ancient artifacts. (Sligo is, after all, where you'll find the world's oldest building by some measures—see the listing for Carrowmore Megalithic Cemetery on p. 405). The other standout sections are devoted to two of Sligo's most famous residents: W. B. Yeats, one of the 20th century's foremost poets, whose mother was from Sligo and whose affinity with the county drastically influenced his work, and Constance Markievicz (1868–1927), an aristocrat who grew up in Sligo, and went on to become both the first woman elected to the British Parliament and a prominent Irish revolutionary.

Stephen St., Sligo, Co. Sligo. ✆ **071/914-2212.** Free admission. Tues–Sat 10am–noon, 2–4:30pm. Closed Oct–May.

In Sligo Town, the Yeats Memorial Building houses a library devoted to William Butler's life and work.

Yeats Memorial Building ★ Located in a distinctive red-and-white townhouse building on the Douglas Hyde Bridge, this engaging little museum, art gallery, and heritage center acts as a kind of focal point for the Yeats-related attractions in County Sligo. Exhibitions focus on the life and work of the great poet, and the 19th and 20th century literary canon of which he was a part. The center also has an art gallery, featuring work by contemporary artists, many of them Sligo-based; courses, workshops, and lectures during the summer months; and **Lily's & Lolly's Café** (see p. 410).

Douglas Hyde Bridge, Sligo, Co. Sligo. ✆ **071/914-2693.** www.yeats-sligo.com. Free admission. Mon–Fri 10am–5pm.

SHOPPING

Sligo has some great little boutiques and independent local businesses that are worth dropping in to explore. Most Sligo shops are open Monday to Saturday 9am to 6pm, and some may have extended hours during July and August.

The Cat & the Moon ★★ This is a great place to shop for Irish crafts and jewelry. They design their own silver rings and pendants with Celtic motifs. In addition they stock an interesting range of art, ceramics, candles, and other handcrafts, which always seem to offer something in the way of unique finds and souvenirs. 4 Castle St., Sligo, County Sligo. ✆ **071/914-3686.** www.thecatandthemoon.com.

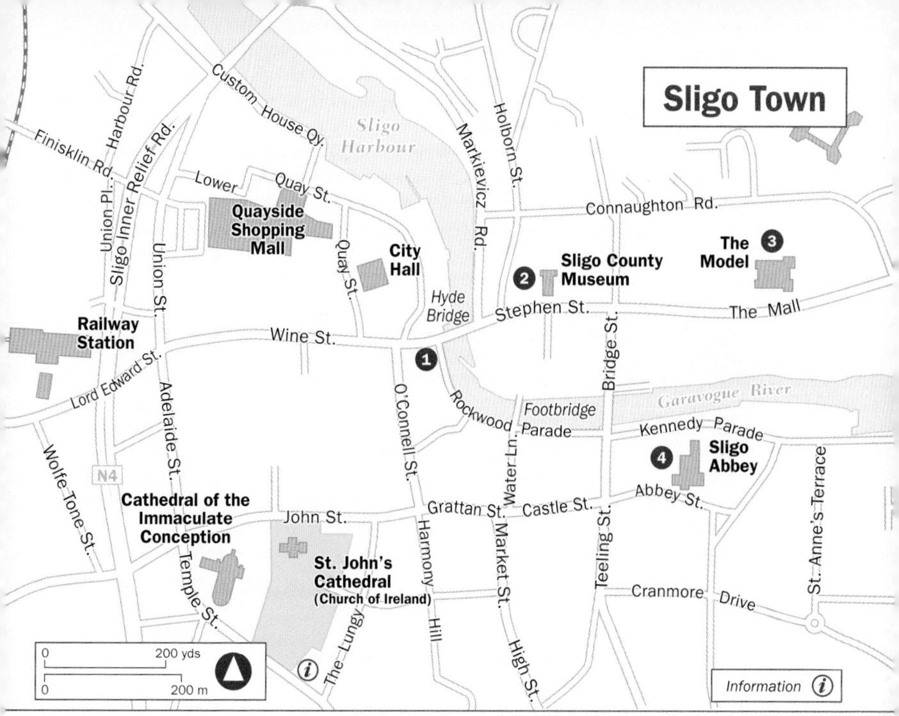

The Model **3**
Sligo Abbey **4**
Sligo County Museum **2**
Yeats Memorial Building **1**

The Gingham Duck ★ Knitters won't want to miss this friendly little store on Harmony Hill, a 5-minute walk from Sligo Abbey (see p. 400). They stock a huge selection of wool, including traditional Aran yarn. They also sell cute little teddy bears and rag dolls. 4 Castle St., Sligo, County Sligo. ✆ **071/914-3686.** www.thecatandthemoon.com.

Michael Quirke ★★ Michael Quirke is a real Sligo character. He used to be a butcher, but got bored of it and decided to follow his real passion instead—woodcarving. Out went the meat and in came the artisan tools, as his shop was turned into a studio. Now he spends his time carving and selling exquisite statues, ornaments, and *objects d'art* out of Irish wood, with a particular focus on

THE cat & THE MOON

The cat went here and there
And the moon spun round like a top,
And the nearest kin of the moon,
The creeping cat, looked up.
Black Minnaloushe stared at the moon,
For, wander and wail as he would,
The pure cold light in the sky
Troubled his animal blood.
Minnaloushe runs in the grass
Lifting his delicate feet.
Do you dance, Minnaloushe, do you dance?
When two close kindred meet,
What better than call a dance?
Maybe the moon may learn,
Tired of that courtly fashion,
A new dance turn.
Minnaloushe creeps through the grass
From moonlit place to place,
The sacred moon overhead
Has taken a new phase.
Does Minnaloushe know that his pupils
Will pass from change to change,
And that from round to crescent,
From crescent to round they range?
Minnaloushe creeps through the grass
Alone, important and wise,
And lifts to the changing moon
His changing eyes.

—W.B Yeats (1919)

figures from Irish mythology. His carvings are quite affordable for the quality. Wine St., Sligo, County Sligo. ✆ **071/914-2624.**

Wehrly Bros. Ltd ★★ This place is the granddaddy of Sligo jewelry stores, having been trading from behind its elegant black and gold storefront since 1875. They specialize in diamond rings, watches, and pearls, although there's a wide range of designer jewelry here. They also sell Waterford crystal. 3 O'Connell St., Sligo, County Sligo. ✆ **071/914-2252.** www.wehrlybros.ie.

Out from Sligo Town

The area around Sligo Town is known for its ancient burial grounds and pagan sites, some dating from the Stone Age. As you drive down country lanes, you'll often spy a **dolmen** (ancient stone table) in pastures with sheep or ponies grazing casually around it. The presence of so many burial sites and of the stacked stones of mysterious ancient religions makes this a particularly fascinating section of the country. Some are open to the public, but most are not, and the Irish are passionate about property rights, so don't go clambering over a fence for a better photo without getting permission first.

To plunge in at the deep end of ancient sites, stop by the vast and strangely beautiful **Carrowmore** (see listing below). It's a huge Neolithic cemetery that once contained as many as 200 passage tombs, some predating Newgrange by 500 years. From Carrowmore, you can see the hilltop cairn grave of **Knocknarea** as a lump atop the large hill in the distance. Local legend has it that this is the grave of the "fairy queen" Queen Maeve (Queen Mab in Shakespeare plays). If you have the energy to make the relatively gentle 30-minute climb to the top, the views are extraordinary. (Knocknarea is on the same road as Carrowmore—follow signs for mescan meadhbha chambered cairn.) From Carrowmore and Knocknarea, it's about an hour's drive to the Neolithic mountaintop cemetery of **Carrowkeel,** which offers an unforgettable experience. After a breathtaking ascent on foot, you'll find yourself alone with the past. The tombs face Carrowmore below and are aligned with the summer solstice.

At the foot of Knocknarea is **Strandhill,** 8km (5 miles) from Sligo Town. This delightful resort area stretches into Sligo Bay, with a sand dune beach and a patch of land nearby called Coney Island, which is usually credited with lending its name to the New York beach amusement area. Across the bay is another resort, Rosses Point.

Carrowkeel Passage Tomb Cemetery ★★ Atop a hill overlooking Lough Arrow, this ancient passage tomb cemetery is impressive, isolated, and frequently empty. Its 14 cairns, dolmens, and stone circles date from the Stone Age (ca. 5000 B.C.), and it's easy to feel that history, standing among the cold, ageless rocks. The walk uphill from the parking lot takes about 20 minutes, so be ready to get a little exercise. It's worth the effort. This is a simple site—no visitor center, no tea shop, no admission fee—nothing but ancient mystery.

Signposted on N4 between Sligo Town and Boyle, Co. Sligo. No phone. www.heritageireland.ie. Free admission (open site).

Carrowmore Megalithic Cemetery ★★★ This is one of the great sacred landscapes of the ancient world. At the center of the Coolera Peninsula sits a massive passage grave that once had a Stonehenge-like stone circle of its own. Encircling that were as many as 200 additional stone circles and passage graves arranged in an intricate and mysterious design. Over the years, some of the stones have been moved, but more than 60 circles and passage graves still exist, although the site spreads out so far that many of them are in adjacent farmland. Look out for your first dolmen in a paddock next to the road about a mile before you reach the site. The dolmens were the actual graves, once covered in stones and earth. Some of these sites are open to visitors, and you can get a map to them from the visitor center. On the main site, Tomb 52A (which was only excavated in 1998) is estimated to be 7,400 years old, making it the earliest known piece of free-standing stone architecture in the entire world. From Carrowmore, you can see the hilltop cairn grave of **Knocknarea** in the distance (see p. 406). The visitor center has good exhibits and guided tours.

Carrowmore, Co. Sligo. (Follow signs from Woodville Rd. heading west out of Sligo Town, or from R292 at Ransboro). ✆ **071/916-1534.** www.heritageireland.ie. Admission €3 adults; €2 seniors; €1 students and children; €8 families. Apr–Sept daily 10am–6pm. Closed Oct–Mar.

Drumcliffe Church ★ This small stone church is the final resting place of W. B. Yeats (1865–1939) and as no surprise, has become something of a pilgrimage site for his legions of fans. As you walk in, Yeats's grave is marked with a dark, modest stone just to the left of the church. He's buried alongside his young wife, Georgie Hyde-Lee (when they married in 1917, he was 52 and she was 23). The moving epitaph, "Cast a cold eye on life, on death . . ." comes from his poem "Under Ben Bulben". The church sits atop the 6th-century foundations of the monastery St. Columba, and the round tower on the main road dates from that earlier building. The high cross in the churchyard is from the 11th century, and its faded eastern side shows Christ, Daniel in the lions' den, Adam and Eve, and Cain murdering Abel. The little visitor center has a few gifts and doodads and an excellent teashop with marvelous cakes, hearty sandwiches, and fresh hot soup.

Drumcliffe Churchyard, Drumcliffe (on N15), Co. Sligo. No phone. Free admission.

Eagles Flying ★★ You can see some of the biggest birds of prey in the world at this aviary and educational center near Ballymote. Eagles, vultures, owls, and

local hero: WILLIAM BUTLER YEATS

The landscape of County Sligo deeply influenced the work of Ireland's first of four Nobel laureates, **William Butler Yeats** (1865–1939). The poet, playwright, and two-term Irish senator grew up amid Sligo's verdant hills and dales, now known as "Yeats Country"—a moniker the tourism board won't let you forget, through signposts and plaques mounted throughout the region and a plethora of Yeats-related activities. You can cruise Lough Gill while listening to a live recital of Yeats's poetry; take Yeats trails and buy a hundred items of Yeats memorabilia; and visit dozens of his purported haunts—some reputedly still spooked by his ghost, and some of which have only tenuous connections with the man.

Yeats died in Menton, on the French Riviera, in 1939. Knowing he was ill, he stated, "If I die here, bury me up there on the mountain, and then after a year or so, dig me up and bring me privately to Sligo." True to his wishes, in 1948 his body was moved to Sligo, and reinterred at Drumcliffe Church (see p. 405), where his great-grandfather had been a rector.

falcons take part in an hour-long flying show daily at 11am and 3pm—outside or in a purpose-built arena. Most of the awesome birds who live at the center can be handled by visitors (under close supervision, of course). For young children who prefer their animals just a little less intimidating, there's also petting zoo, home to horses, hedgehogs, rabbits, chinchillas, and even raccoons (which are not native to Ireland but have slowly been spreading here as an invasive species since about 2011).

Ballymote, Co. Sligo. ✆ **071/918-9310.** www.eaglesflying.com. Admission €10 adults; €9 students; €6 children 3–16; free for children 2 and under; €30 families (up to 4; additional children €5). No credit cards. Apr–early Nov daily 10:30am–12:30pm, 2:30–4:30pm.

Inishmurray ★★ Northwest of Sligo Bay, 6km (3¾ miles), lies this tiny, uninhabited island. It encompasses the haunting ruins of St. Molaise, a very early monastic settlement founded in the 6th century and destroyed by the Vikings in 807. Within its circular walls are the remains of several churches, beehive cells, altars, and an assemblage of "cursing stones" once used to bring ruin on those who presumably deserved it. In the 19th and early 20th centuries, Inishmurray harbored a thriving, illicit trade in the distilling of moonshine whiskey. The last permanent residents left the island in 1948; their ruined houses can still be seen, battered by the elements. **Inishmurray Island Trips** (✆ **087/254-0190;** www.inishmurrayislandtrips.com) and **Ewing's Sea Angling and Boat Charters** (✆ **086/891-3618;** www.sligoboatcharters.com) both run boat trips to the island. Expect to pay around €40 adults, €35 children, and you may need a minimum group size of four. Call or visit the website for details of sailing times.

Northwest of Sligo Bay, 6km (3¾ miles) offshore. Ferries leave from Mullaghmore or Rosses Point.

Knocknarea ★ From the low vantage point of Carrowmore (see p. 405), if you study the distant mountain ranges that ring the surrounding valley, you'll notice a stone cairn in the center of each one. (They're easy to spot—as any local schoolchild will tell you—due to their uncannily breast-like shape). One of these is the unexcavated **Knocknarea.** Local legend has it that this is the grave of the "fairy queen" Queen Maeve—better known to most people these days as Queen Mab, the subject of one of the most famous speeches written by William Shakespeare in *Romeo and Juliet*. If you have the energy to make the relatively gentle 30-minute climb to the top, the views are extraordinary. Knocknarea is on the same road as Carrowmore; follow signs for **Mescan Meadhbha Chambered Cairn.**

Knocknarea, about 6.4km (4 miles) west of Sligo, Co. Sligo. No phone. Free admission (open site). Signposted from small farm road between Cullenduff and Knocknarea, and from R292 heading south from Strandhill.

Parke's Castle ★ On the north side of the Lough Gill Drive (see below), just over the County Leitrim side of the border, Parke's Castle stands out as a lone outpost amid the natural tableau of lake view and woodland scenery. Named after an English family that gained possession of it during the 1620 plantation of Leitrim (when land was confiscated from the Irish and given to favored English families), this castle was originally the stronghold of the O'Rourke clan, rulers of the Kingdom of Breffni. Beautifully restored using Irish oak and traditional craftsmanship, it exemplifies the 17th-century fortified manor house. In the visitor center, informative exhibits and a splendid audio-visual show illustrate the history of the castle and introduce visitors to the rich, diverse sites of interest in the surrounding area.

On R286, 11.2km (7 miles) east of Sligo Town, Co. Leitrim. ✆ **071/916-4149.** www.heritageireland.ie. Admission €3 adults; €2 seniors; €1 students and children; €8 families. Apr–mid-Sept daily 10am–6pm; last admission 45 min. before closing.

THE lough gill DRIVE

This beautiful lake figured prominently in the writings of W.B. Yeats, and this 42km (26-mile) drive-yourself tour around the perimeter is well signposted.

To start, head 1.6km (1 mile) south of town and follow the signs for Lough Gill. Within 3.2km (2 miles) you'll be on the lower edge of the shoreline. Among the sites are **Parke's Castle** (see above); **Dooney Rock,** with its own nature trail and lakeside walk (inspiration for the poem "Fiddler of Dooney"); the **Lake Isle of Innisfree,** made famous in Yeats's poetry and in song; and the **Hazelwood Sculpture Trail,** a unique forest walk along the shores of Lough Gill, with 13 wood sculptures. The storied Innisfree is one of 22 islands in Lough Gill.

You can drive the lakeside circuit in less than an hour, or you can stop at the east end and visit **Dromahair,** a delightful village on the River Bonet. The road along Lough Gill's upper shore brings you back to the northern end of Sligo Town. Continue north on the main road (N15), and you'll see the graceful profile of **Ben Bulben** (519m/1,702 ft.), one of the Dartry Mountains, rising off to your right.

If you prefer to see all this beautiful scenery from the water itself, **Lough Gill Cruises** take you around Lough Gill and the Garavogue River aboard the 72-passenger *Wild Rose* waterbus as you listen to the poetry of Yeats. The boat departs from Parke's Castle; call ✆ **071/916-4266** or visit www.roseofinnisfree.com for departure times and booking. Trips to Innisfree, sunset cruises, and dinner cruises are also scheduled. Tickets start at around €15 adults, €8 children.

Sports & Outdoor Pursuits

BEACHES Safe sandy beaches for walking, jogging, or swimming, and complete with promenades are at **Strandhill, Rosses Point,** and **Enniscrone** on the Sligo Bay coast.

CYCLING With its lakes and woodlands, Yeats Country is particularly good biking territory. To rent a bike, contact **Flanagans Cycles,** Market Square, Sligo (✆ **071/914-4477;** www.flanagancycles.com).

FISHING For fishing gear and tackle, see **Barton Smith,** Hyde Bridge, Sligo (✆ **071/914-2356;** www.bartonsmith.ie). For boat rental, see **Kingfisher Bates,** Pier Road, Enniscrone (✆ **096/36733**).

GOLF With its seascapes, mountain valleys, and lakesides, County Sligo is known for challenging golf courses. Leading the list is **County Sligo Golf Club** ★, Rosses Point Road, Rosses Point (✆ **071/917-7134;** www.countysligogolfclub.ie), overlooking Sligo Bay under the shadow of Ben Bulben mountain. It's an 18-hole, par-71 championship seaside links famed for its wild, natural terrain and constant winds. Greens fees range from around €25 to €95 weekends, depending on the number of holes and day of the week.

In the southwestern corner of the county, about 40km (25 miles) from Sligo Town and overlooking Sligo Bay, the **Enniscrone Golf Club,** Enniscrone (✆ **096/36297;** www.enniscronegolf.com), is a seaside par-72 course. Greens fees are €30 to €70.

HORSEBACK RIDING An hour's or a day's riding on the beach, in the countryside, or over mountain trails can be arranged at **Sligo Riding Centre,** Carrowmore (✆ **087/230-4828;** www.sligoridingcentre.com), or at **Woodlands Equestrian Centre,** Loughill, Lavagh, Tubbercurry, County Sligo (✆ **071/918-4207**). Rates average around €20 to €40 per hour.

Where to Stay in County Sligo

As with County Mayo, the best places to stay in County Sligo are hidden in the countryside.

The Glasshouse ★ Another solid, modern option in Sligo Town, The Glasshouse resembles a gleaming, modern ship from the outside and overlooks the River Garavogue. The public areas inside either look bold and funky or like an explosion in a kitsch factory, depending on your point of view: multicolored circles on the carpet, misshapen blue sofas, and a bright orange signature color in the towering atrium. Bedrooms are a little more refined, with muted tones and modern art on the walls. There is an in-house restaurant, although you could certainly eat more cheaply in town. The appropriately named View Bar looks out over Sligo Town and has live music, although that can be a drawback due to noise, so ask for a room away from the bar when you book. Just a short few years ago places like this were all but unheard of in Sligo, and the Glasshouse offers a good alternative for those who want a decently priced, convenient, and contemporary place to stay.

Swan Point, Sligo, Co. Sligo. ✆ **071/919-4300.** www.theglasshouse.ie. 116 units. €70–€160 double. Free parking. Breakfast not included in lower rates. **Amenities:** Internet (broadband/via TV), restaurant; 2 bars; room service.

Ross Farmhouse ★★ Not far from Carrowkeel (see p. 405), Ross Farmhouse is a restored 19th-century cottage, surrounded by acres and acres of rolling farmland. The cheerful owners, Nicholas and Oriel Hill-Wilkinson, see this place as their pride and joy, and it shows in the gregarious welcome they give guests. Bedrooms are reasonably sized, with simple, unfussy furnishings. One is a family room, and another is fully accessible to wheelchairs. Downstairs are two lovely guest lounges, filled with antiques. An open peat fire warms the hearth in winter. Breakfasts are good, and they'll cook for you in the evenings if you book in advance (very reasonable at €35 per person; there's a good wine list too, or you can bring your own). In addition to all the countryside walks, ancient ruins, and sweet little towns you could wish for, the area also has some of the best horse riding in Ireland—ask if you'd like recommendations for local riding centers. ***Note:*** Not all bedrooms have a private bathroom, so specify when you book if you want one.

Riverstown, Co. Sligo. (Follow signs from Drumfin on N4 or Coola on R284). ✆ **071/916-5140.** www.rossfarmhousesligo.com. 6 units. €90 double. Free parking. Breakfast included. **Amenities:** Wi-Fi (free).

Sligo Park Hotel ★ A pleasant little park surrounds this convenient, cheap-ish hotel in Sligo Town; one of just a handful of modern accommodations in the county's capital. Guestrooms are simply furnished in a contemporary style, with muted color schemes of gray and brown, and good-sized bathrooms. One or two rooms could do with some TLC around the edges, though the public areas are sleek and well designed. Family rooms are a good value for money. This hotel won't win any awards for inspiring, heart-of-Ireland countryside experiences, but as a clean, modern base, it's a good option in a region that's short on choice. One word of caution: the hotel is also a popular venue for weddings and other events, so noise can sometimes be a problem on weekends. You might want to ask for a room as far away from the bar as possible.

Pearse Rd., Sligo, Co. Sligo. ✆ **071/919-0400.** www.sligoparkhotel.com. 136 units. €75–€100 double. Free parking. Breakfast not included in lower rates. **Amenities:** Wi-Fi (free); restaurant; bar; room service; pool.

Temple House ★★★ This is quite simply *the* place you need to try and stay in the northwest if you're after a truly unique and historic B&B experience. Temple House is not full of five star extras—but you'll find it hard to beat for historical authenticity, beautiful surroundings, and sheer charm. The 1665 manor house has been restored, bit by painstaking bit, by the charming young custodians of the estate, Roderick and Helena Perceval. The place is dripping with history; once a thriving country estate, it fell slowly into near-ruin during the turbulent years of the 20th century. The huge guest rooms are packed with interesting antiques, yet have completely modern bathrooms. Nightly dinners are more akin to parties, with all guests seated around an enormous old table enjoying the outstanding food. Breakfasts hit the spot too, with plenty of homemade treats. The beautiful grounds are full of secrets, including a boating lake, a walled garden, and even a ruined Knights Templar castle. Supposedly a couple of resident ghosts are roaming around, although they must be of a very Bacchanalian kind, with such a welcoming and convivial atmosphere as this. There is also a self-catering cottage on the grounds.

Ballymote, Ballinacarrow, Co. Sligo. ✆ **071/918-3329.** www.templehouse.ie. 6 units. €150–€180 double. Dinner €45. Free parking. Breakfast included. **Amenities:** Wi-Fi (free). Closed Dec–Mar. No dinner Sun.

Where to Dine in & Around Sligo Town

Happily, the dining scene in Sligo Town has improved dramatically over the last couple of years.

Coach Lane at Donaghy's Bar ★★ IRISH/INTERNATIONAL A very popular spot with locals, Coach Lane has two dining rooms: a bar, serving easy crowd pleasers, such as burgers, fish and chips, and shepherd's pie; and a more upmarket, gastropub-style restaurant. The menu is divided into salad, pasta, meat, or seafood options, so after an appetizer of buffalo wings or smoked salmon, you could move on to a Caesar salad or rib-eye steak. There's always a great selection of seafood too, including black sole in a white wine sauce, buttered shrimp with garlic and lemon, and salmon served with teriyaki and ginger.

1–2 Lord Edward St., Sligo, Co. Sligo. ✆ **071/916-2417.** www.coachlane.ie. Main courses €18–€25. Bar food: daily 3–10pm. Restaurant: daily 5:30–10pm.

Eala Bhan ★ INTERNATIONAL This popular restaurant in Sligo Town specializes in steaks and seafood. Enormous T-bones or tender sirloins come with satisfyingly traditional steakhouse sides—onion rings, French fries, or maybe a creamy potato gratin. The seafood is good: local (of course) hake or a catch of the day. The lunch menu is almost as extensive as dinner, with a few lighter options such as roast chicken salad or seafood chowder. The early bird menu (served until 6:30 daily) is great value at just €20 for three courses.

Rockwood Parade, Sligo, Co. Sligo. ✆ **071/914-5823.** www.ealabhan.ie. Main courses €15–€25. Daily 12–3:30pm, 5–9:30pm.

Kate's Kitchen ★★ DELI This great delicatessen in central Sligo has a large stock of gourmet foods, Irish cheese, fresh bread, scones, salads, chutneys, and other tasty items that just beg to be put together to make an elegant picnic or lunch on the go. They also sell bath products and a particularly nice range of handmade chocolates—perfect for gifts, if you can keep yourself from raiding them before the journey home.

3 Castle St., Sligo, County Sligo. ✆ **071/914-3022.** www.kateskitchen.ie. Most items €4–€8. Mon–Sat 8:45am–6:15pm.

Lily's & Loly's Café ★ CAFE Handy for a quick and tasty lunch, this cheery cafe is at the Yeats Memorial Building (see p. 402). They serve reasonably priced wraps, panini, and light meals, in addition to homemade cakes and pies. The cafe is next to the Garavogue River, and you can sit outside on a sunny little terrace when the weather's fine.

At the Yeats Memorial Building, Douglas Hyde Bridge, Sligo, Co. Sligo. ✆ **087/166-2266.** www.yeatssociety.com/lilys-and-lollys-cafe.html. Sandwiches €4–€8. Mon–Sat 9am–5pm.

Osta Café and Wine Bar ★ CAFE The owners of this sweet cafe overlooking the river in Sligo are big believers in the slow food and organic movements. This is reflected in their delicious, healthful food that makes superb use of ingredients from small, local producers. Daily specials could include boxty, a traditional Irish potato pancake, made with leeks and cheese; a delicious spinach quiche; or just a plate of fresh sandwiches. (The bread comes from a local bakery.) They also serve wonderful homemade soups.

Garavogue Weir, off Stephen St., Sligo Town, Co. Sligo. ✆ **071/914-4639.** www.osta.ie. Main courses €4–€12. Mon–Wed 8am–7pm; Thurs–Fri 8am–9pm; Sat 8am–8pm; Sun 9am–6pm.

Trá Bán ★★ INTERNATIONAL Another fine place for steaks and seafood, Trá Bán is above a popular bar in Strandhill, a little seaside town about 8km (5 miles) west of Sligo Town. Typical starters include crab claws in garlic butter or salmon sushi. For your main course try the "reef on beef" (sirloin, filet, or beef medallions with a lobster tail on top), or red snapper served with stir-fried vegetables and red pepper coulis. They also offer a special children's menu (three courses for €14). The atmosphere is relaxed and easygoing, with a cheery and efficient staff. Reservations are recommended, especially on weekends.

Above the Strand Bar, Strandhill, Co. Sligo. ✆ **071/912-8402.** www.trabansligo.ie. Main courses €17–€24. Tues–Sun 5–9:30pm. Closed early Jan–early Feb.

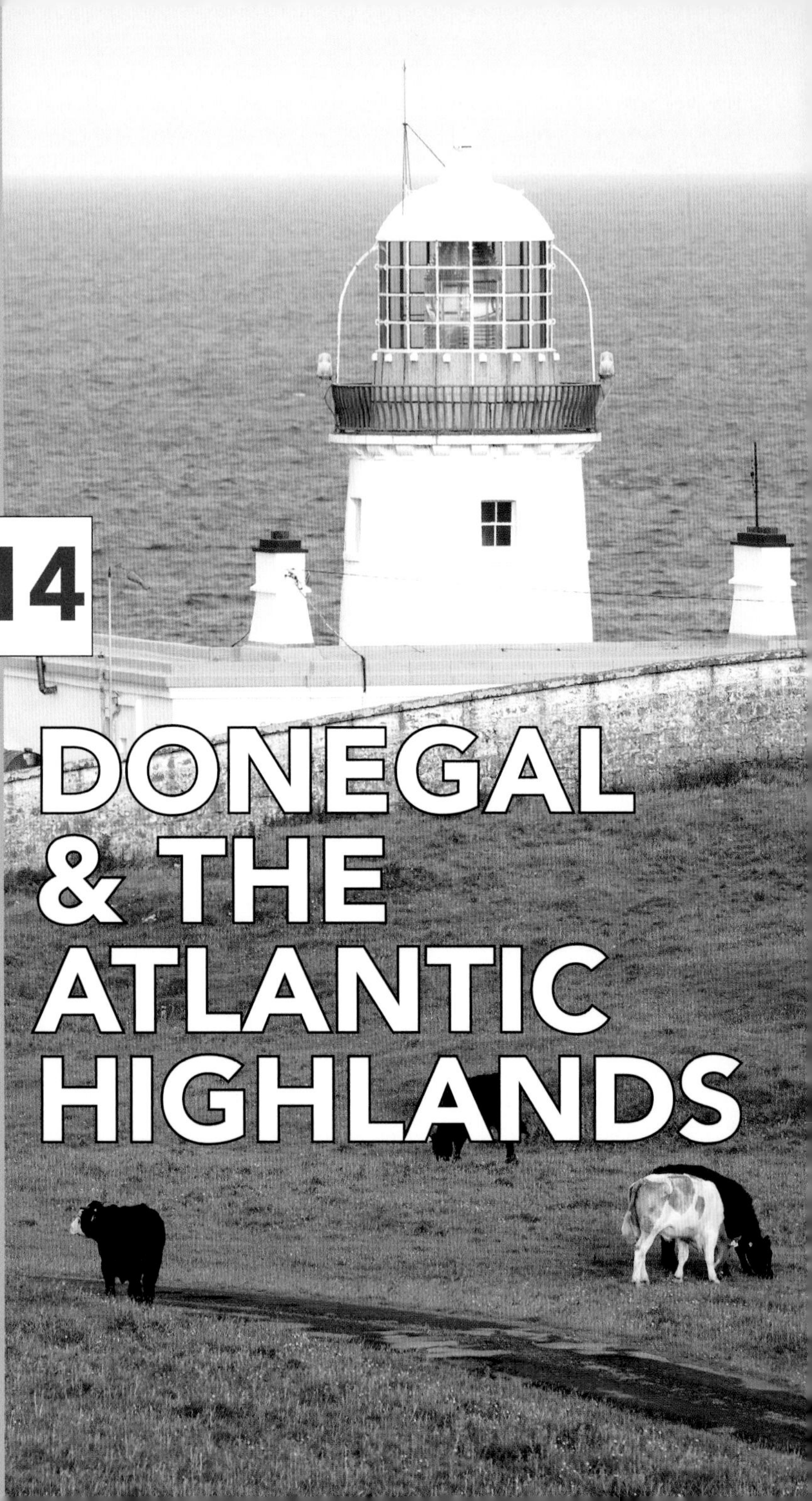

14

DONEGAL & THE ATLANTIC HIGHLANDS

Beyond Sligo, the topography changes and the roads twist and turn through tortuous corkscrews. When the signs change into Gaelic, the landscape opens up into great sweeping views of rocky hills and barren shores, and a freezing mist blows off the sea, you know you've reached Donegal. The austere beauty of this county can be almost too bleak, but it is also unforgettable. On a sunny day, you can stand at the edge of the sea at Malin Head and, despite the sun, the sea spray will blow a chill right through you—it feels as if you're standing at the edge of the world. County Donegal's natural wonders include the magnificent Slieve League cliffs and the remote beaches tucked into the bays and inlets of its sharply indented coast.

The towns of Donegal are perhaps the least developed for tourism in Ireland. Donegal has some truly fantastic places to stay, though you have to really search for them. As with counties Mayo and Sligo to the south, the standout accommodations are to be found hidden away deep within the breathtaking, mountainous roads and tiny, bucolic seaside towns. Few tourists make it this far. Buildings are made of cold stone and villages perch on the slopes of precipitous hillsides. When you stop to take a wander, you can't help but worry whether the car's brakes will hold. But take the chance. The people in Donegal are as nice as can be, and meeting them is worth the trip in itself. Of course, fewer tourists mean fewer amenities, so it's harder to find good restaurants and modern guesthouses. In addition, you'll have to contend with road signs that vary from cryptic to nonexistent. You will spend half your time lost. But Ireland is a small place; wherever you're headed, you'll get there eventually and not without a few adventures along the way.

ARRIVING

BY BUS **Bus Éireann** (✆ **074/912-1309;** www.buseireann.ie) operates daily bus service to Donegal Town from Dublin, Derry, Sligo, Galway, and other points.

BY TRAIN Trains in this part of the country are extremely scarce. Donegal Town no longer even has a train station.

BY CAR The only remotely practical way to get around the remote attractions of County Donegal is by car. If you're driving from the south, Donegal is reached on N15 from Sligo or A46 or A47 from Northern Ireland; from the east and north, it's N15 and N56; from the west, N56 leads to Donegal Town.

BY PLANE **Donegal Airport,** Carrickfin, near Letterkenny, Co. Donegal (✆ **074/954-8284;** www.donegalairport.ie), also known as Carrickfinn Airport, is very slowly growing as a budget airline hub. Currently a couple of scheduled flights connect per day with Dublin; **Flybe** (✆ **087/1700-2000** in the U.K. or 0044/1392-683-152) also operates regular flights from Glasgow, Scotland.

PREVIOUS PAGE: **Lighthouse on St. John's Point in County Donegal.**

[FastFACTS] COUNTY DONEGAL

ATMs/Banks Donegal Town's central shopping area—known as "The Diamond"—has branches of **Permanent TSB** and **AIB.** ATMs get seriously few and far between in the Donegal countryside, so get cash before you strike out into the boondocks.

Dentists For dental emergencies, your hotel should contact a dentist for you. Otherwise, in Donegal Town, try **Dr. Brian McCaughey** on Upper Main Street (✆ **074/972-3066**).

Doctors For medical emergencies dial ✆ **999.** For non-emergencies, your hotel should call you a doctor. Otherwise, in Donegal Town, try **Dr. Marie Drumgoole** on Waterloo Place (✆ **074/972-1364**).

Emergencies For police, fire, or other emergencies, dial ✆ **999.**

Pharmacies In Donegal Town try **Eske Pharmacy** (✆ **071/972-2033**) or **McElwee Pharmacy** (✆ **074/952-1032**), both on Main Street.

Post Offices The main post office in Donegal Town is on Tirconaill Street (✆ **071/972-1030**).

Taxis If you need a cab home from a restaurant or hotel, the management should call one for you—in rural areas, this is often the only reliable way of getting anywhere if you don't want to drive. Otherwise, in Donegal Town, try **Quinn's Taxis** (✆ **087/262-0670**) or **McNulty Taxis** (✆ **087/256-1319**).

DONEGAL TOWN & DONEGAL BAY

Although far from Ireland's prettiest or most interesting town, the greatest attraction of **Donegal Town** is the town's layout itself: a happy mix of medieval and modern. Overseen by a low, gloomy castle at the edge of the picturesque estuary of the River Eske on Donegal Bay, this is a tiny burg, with just 2,500 residents. As recently as the 1940s, the town's central mall (called "the Diamond") was used as a market for trading livestock and goods. Today the marketing is done in the form of tweeds and tourist goods, as the Diamond is surrounded by little crafts shops and small hotels of variable quality.

Donegal Town has a couple of good, reasonably priced options; however, its size doesn't make it a wholly convenient base for touring the countryside.

DONEGAL TOWN summer FESTIVAL

If you're heading this way in early July, you may want to check out **www.donegaltown.ie** for details of the town's annual **Summer Festival.** The program is an enthusiastic mixture of free concerts (from local bands that, in all probability, you've never heard of) and family-friendly fun and games. The festival lasts 4 days, with the biggest events scheduled over a weekend.

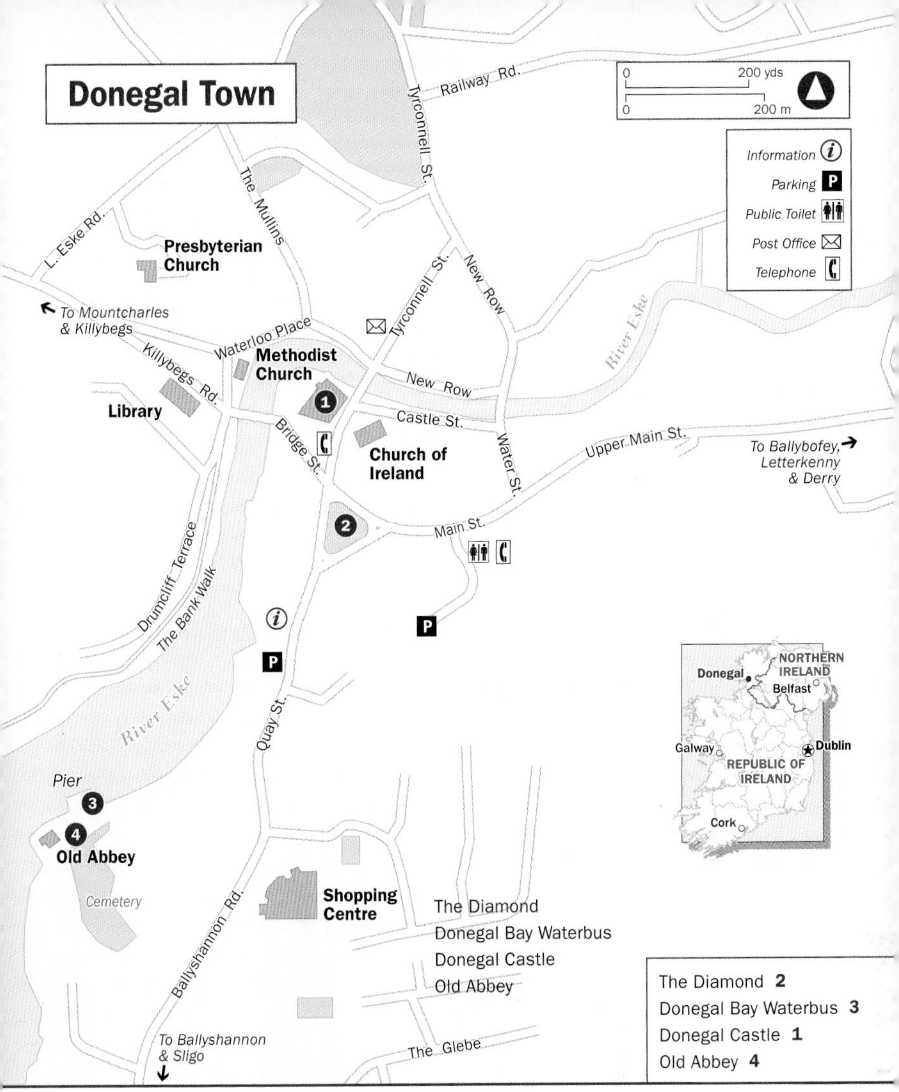

Visitor Information

The **Donegal Discover Ireland Centre** is on the Quay, Donegal Town (**✆ 074/972-1148**). The seasonal **Ardara Heritage Centre** is on the main road through Ardara; it's closed from November to Easter.

Town Layout

The town is laid out around the triangular central mall called **the Diamond,** where the roads from Killybegs, Ballyshannon, and Ballybofey converge. The Diamond is dominated by an obelisk erected in memory of four early-7th-century Irish clerics from the local abbey who wrote *The Annals of Ireland,* the first recorded history of Gaelic Ireland.

Exploring in & Around Donegal Town

Donegal Bay Waterbus ★ This modern, two-deck boat makes daily tours of Donegal Bay. The guided tour lasts 90 minutes. Points of interest along the way include the **Old Abbey** (see p. 417); **Seal Island,** home to a colony of about 200 noisy seals; and **The Hassans,** a port from which many emigrants from the northern part of the country left for the New World. The guides are enthusiastic and knowledgeable; the only downside is that the commentary is non-stop, and they will even play the keyboard to fill in moments of silence. However, the views are wonderful. Sailing times are usually morning and afternoon or evening, but are dependent upon weather and the tides, so make sure you call ahead. Tickets can be obtained from the ticket office on Quay Street—it's the white and blue building next to Dom's Pier 1 Bar.

The Pier, Donegal, Co. Donegal. ✆ **074/972-3666.** www.donegalbaywaterbus.com. Tour €15 adults; €5 children 5–17; children 4 and under free. No credit cards. Closed Oct–Apr.

Donegal Castle ★ Built in the 15th century on the banks of the River Eske, this solid, gray-stone castle was once the chief stronghold for the O'Donnells, a powerful Donegal clan. In the 17th century, during the Plantation period, it was taken over by Sir Basil Brook, who added an extension with 10 gables, a large bay window, and smaller mullioned windows in Jacobean style. Much of the building has survived the centuries, and both the interior and exterior of the castle were beautifully restored in the 1990s. Guided tours are available every hour, included in the admission price.

Castle St., Donegal, Co. Donegal. ✆ **074/972-2405.** www.heritageireland.ie. Admission €4 adults; €3 seniors; €2 students and children; €10 families. Easter–mid-Sept daily 10am–6pm; mid-Sept–Easter Thurs–Mon 9:30am–4:30pm; last admission 45 min. before closing.

Lough Derg ★★ This beautiful lake, filled with islands, lies about 16km (10 miles) east of Donegal Town. Legend has it that St. Patrick spent 40 days and 40 nights fasting in a cavern at this secluded spot, and since then it has been revered as a place of penance and pilgrimage. From June 1st to August 15th, thousands of Irish Catholics take turns coming to Lough Derg to do penance for 3 days at a time, remaining awake and eating nothing but tea and toast. It's considered one of the most rigorous pilgrimages in all of Christendom. To reach Lough Derg, take R232 to Pettigo, then R233 for 8km (5 miles).

Co. Donegal.

Donegal Town

IRISH only!

Along with counties Mayo and Kerry, Donegal is in the **Gaeltacht,** or Irish-language, section of the country. Increasingly, road signs in these regions are being changed into Irish only. We're including the Irish names as well as the English names for the places where you're likely to encounter this.

Old Abbey ★ Sitting in a peaceful spot on the quay in Donegal Town, where the River Eske meets Donegal Bay, this ruined Franciscan monastery was founded in 1474 by the first Red Hugh O'Donnell and his wife, Nuala O'Brien of Munster. It was generously endowed by the O'Donnell family and became an important center of religion and learning. Great gatherings of clergy and lay leaders assembled here in 1539. It was from this friary that some of the scholars undertook to salvage old Gaelic manuscripts and compile *The Annals of the Four Masters* (1632–36). Enough remains of its glory—ruins of a church and a cloister—to give you an idea of how magnificent it once was.

The Quay, Donegal, Co. Donegal. Free admission (open site).

Exploring the Donegal Bay Coast

The rugged coastline around Donegal Bay is wild and beautiful. The rocky land careens toward the dark blue Atlantic, where the roads end just short of the icy water. Roads corkscrew so tightly that it will almost make you dizzy, and the main speed limit is the one you impose on yourself, as speeds much above 55kmph (35 mph) are dangerous. That's just as well, since the spectacular views will cause you to stop again and again to take in the rolling hills, jagged mountains, bright green fields, and crashing seas.

The richest pickings on Donegal Bay are all to be found to the north of Donegal Town; to the south, the attractions are certainly fewer. However, a couple of villages are worth stopping by, plus a sandy beach or two. Sporty types, however, are much better served—some of the best surfing in Ireland can be found in the southern part of the bay, as can some of the best golf courses in Ireland.

Bundoran *(Bun Dobhráin)* is a tacky seaside town with little to offer to anyone except the surfers who make the most of its famously rough surf, while historic **Ballyshannon *(Béal Átha Seanaidh)*** makes for a much more interesting stop. Likewise, **Rossnowlagh *(Ross Neamblach)*** has a fine beach.

Ballyshannon *(Béal Átha Seanaidh)* ★★ The first proper town you'll come to on a drive south of Donegal is this busy, pretty little town, built on a hill, with a 15th century town center. In fact, some claim (rather dubiously) that Ballyshannon is the oldest town in Ireland, in part because traces of permanent settlements dating as far back as 4000 B.C. have been found here. Ballyshannon is also the location of **Abbey Mills** (✆ **071/985-1260**), a heritage center and craft store. Part of a ruined Cistercian abbey, the mill still has a working waterwheel. The store is a great place to stop for individual, designer crafts. It's usually open in the summer months only; hours vary but generally Monday to Saturday, 10am to 5pm. Entry is free. While you're here, check out **Catsby Cave,** about

50m (164 ft.) along the riverbank. During the years of British occupation, when Catholicism was outlawed (from the 16th until the mid-19th century), priests would give Mass here in secret. You can still see the remains of an altar, chiseled from the rock. The cave, which is so tiny you might not even recognize it as such, is a free, open site. Ballyshannon is known for its lively pubs, many of which have reliably good traditional music—never more so than during a weekend in late July or early August, when the streets come alive for the **Ballyshannon Folk Festival** (www.ballyshannonfolkfestival.com).

Tourism Office: The Bridge, Ballyshannon, Co. Donegal. © **071/982-2856.** www.ballyshannon.ie. Ballyshannon is about 22km (13½ miles) south of Donegal Town on N15.

SPORTS & OUTDOOR PURSUITS

BEACHES Donegal Bay's beaches are wide, sandy, clean, and flat—ideal for walking. **Ballyshannon** has a good beach, but it gets crowded; **Rossnowlagh** and **Bundoran** are both better options.

GOLF The Donegal Bay coast is home to two outstanding 18-hole championship seaside golf courses. **Donegal Golf Club,** Murvagh, Ballintra, County Donegal (© **074/973-4054;** www.donegalgolfclub.ie), is 5km (3 miles) north of Rossnowlagh and 11km (6¾ miles) south of Donegal Town. It's a par-73 course with greens fees of €70 weekdays, €80 weekends.

The **Bundoran Golf Club,** off the Sligo-Ballyshannon road (N15), Bundoran, County Donegal (© **071/984-1302;** www.bundorangolfclub.com), is a par-69 course designed by Harry Vardon. The greens fees are around €50 weekdays, €60 weekends.

SURFING **Bundoran** is popular with surfers for its steady waves, and has hosted the European Surfing Championships. Rossnowlagh also has excellent surf, and attracts lots of surfers. When the surf is up, you can rent boards and wet suits locally from around €5 per hour per item.

Exploring North Donegal Bay

To the north of Donegal Town, the coastal scenery is breathtaking. Follow the main road (N56) to the west out of Donegal for a slow, spectacularly scenic drive along the bay where the road winds past sheer cliffs, craggy rocks, bog land, panoramic mountain and sea views, and green pastures. You'll often see the distinctive thatched-roof cottages typical of this area—with rounded roofs held down by ropes (called *sugans*) fastened beneath the eaves to help the thatch resist the strong sea winds. It's only 48km (30 miles) from Donegal Town to the wonderful Glencolumbkille, the traditional end of the west coast drive, but these are some of the most winding roads you'll ever drive, so it can take an hour or more.

Your first stop could be at **Killybegs** ***(Ceala Beaga)***—where, if you arrive around sundown, you can watch the fishing boats unloading the day's catch—or at Studio Donegal in **Kilcar** ***(Cill Chártha)*** if you're interested in picking up Donegal tweed at a bargain. This area is where the scenery starts to get particularly breathtaking, so make sure you have plenty of space in your camera's memory card.

The first truly spectacular photo ops await at **Slieve League** ***(Sliabh Liag),*** with its perilously high sea cliffs crashing down into the waters below. (Take the turnoff for the Bunglass viewing point at Carrick.) Once at the cliffs, you must decide whether you want to merely gaze at their 300m (984-ft.)

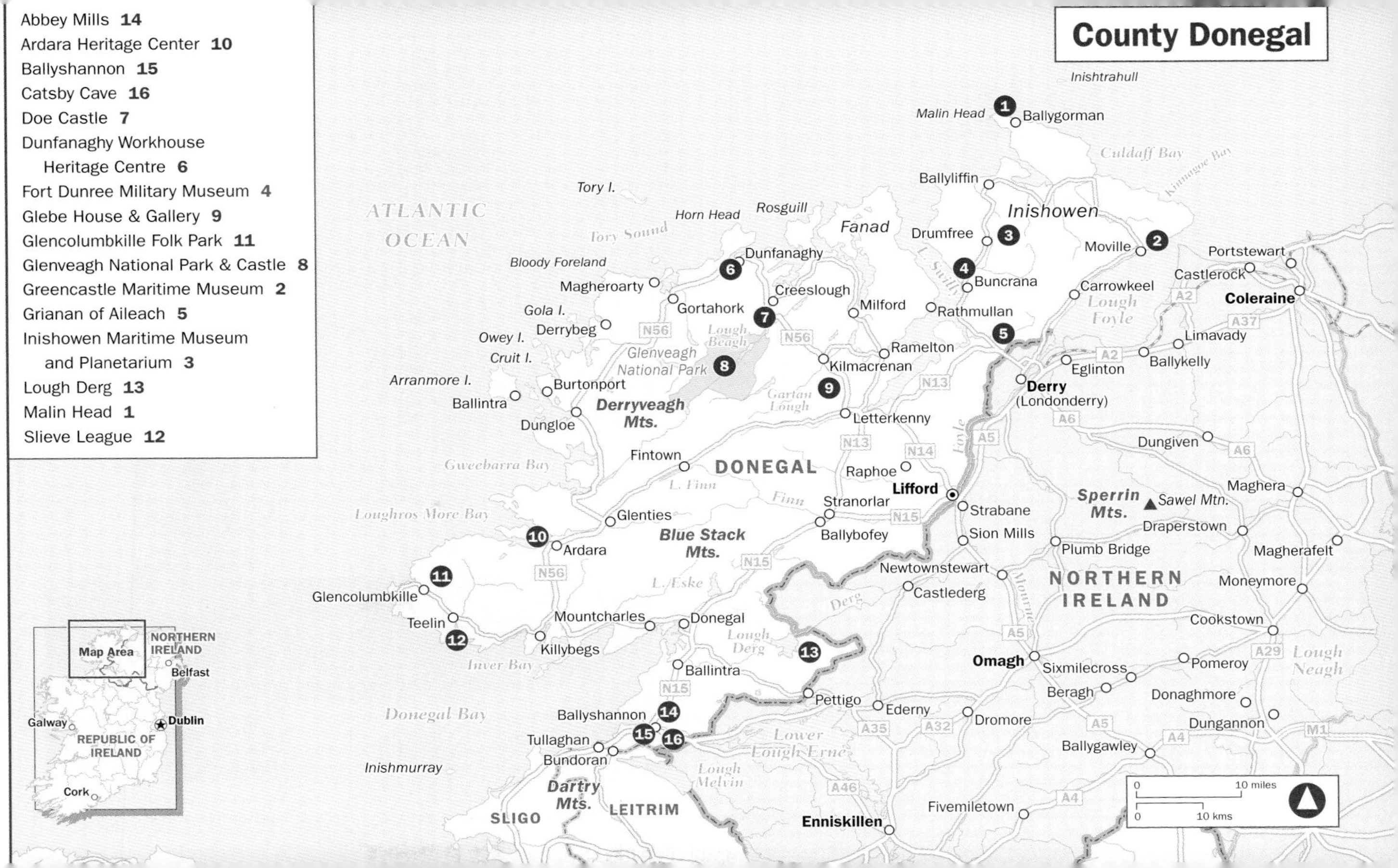
County Donegal
Abbey Mills 14
Ardara Heritage Center 10
Ballyshannon 15
Catsby Cave 16
Doe Castle 7
Dunfanaghy Workhouse Heritage Centre 6
Fort Dunree Military Museum 4
Glebe House & Gallery 9
Glencolumbkille Folk Park 11
Glenveagh National Park & Castle 8
Greencastle Maritime Museum 2
Grianan of Aileach 5
Inishowen Maritime Museum and Planetarium 3
Lough Derg 13
Malin Head 1
Slieve League 12
Inishtrahull
Malin Head
Ballygorman
Culdaff Bay
Kinnagoe Bay
Ballyliffin
Inishowen
Drumfree
Moville
Portstewart
Castlerock
Coleraine
Carrowkeel
Lough Foyle
Buncrana
Rathmullan
Limavady
Ballykelly
Eglinton
Derry (Londonderry)
Tory I.
Tory Sound
ATLANTIC OCEAN
Horn Head
Rosguill
Fanad
Bloody Foreland
Dunfanaghy
Magheroarty
Gortahork
Creeslough
Milford
Ramelton
Kilmacrenan
Gola I.
Derrybeg
Owey I.
Cruit I.
Lough Beagh
Glenveagh National Park
Gartan Lough
Arranmore I.
Ballintra
Burtonport
Dungloe
Derryveagh Mts.
Letterkenny
Dungiven
Fintown
DONEGAL
Raphoe
Lifford
Strabane
Stranorlar
Ballybofey
Sperrin Mts.
Sawel Mtn.
Maghera
Draperstown
Magherafelt
Gweebarra Bay
L. Finn
Finn
Foyle
Loughros More Bay
Glenties
Blue Stack Mts.
Sion Mills
Plumb Bridge
Ardara
Newtownstewart
Castlederg
Mourne
NORTHERN IRELAND
Moneymore
Glencolumbkille
L. Eske
Derg
Teelin
Mountcharles
Donegal
Lough Derg
Cookstown
Killybegs
Inver Bay
Ballintra
Omagh
Sixmilecross
Pomeroy
Lough Neagh
Beragh
Donaghmore
Pettigo
Ederny
Dromore
Dungannon
Donegal Bay
Ballyshannon
Lower Lough Erne
Tullaghan
Bundoran
Ballygawley
Inishmurray
Lough Melvin
Dartry Mts.
SLIGO
LEITRIM
Enniskillen
Fivemiletown
0 10 miles
0 10 kms
Map Area
NORTHERN IRELAND
Belfast
Galway
Dublin
REPUBLIC OF IRELAND
Cork
N56
N13
N14
N15
A2
A37
A6
A5
A29
A35
A32
A4
A46
M1

splendor or to brave a wind-buffeted walk along the treacherous ridge. Including the climb up and down, the rigorous hike is about 10km (6¼ miles) and takes 4 or 5 hours.

Just before you come to Killybegs, the N56 road swings inland and northward, and the landscape becomes desolate and wild. Continue on the coastal road west to discover the beauty of **Glencolumbkille *(Gleann Cholm Cille)*,** a 5,000-year-old Atlantic outpost. Those interested in the history of the place will want to stop by the **Glencolumbkille Folk Park** (**✆ 074/973-0017;** www.gleanncholmcille.ie). Built by the people of Glencolumbkille in the form of a tiny village, or *clachan,* this modest theme park of thatched cottages reflects life in this remote corner over centuries.

To continue touring from Glencolumbkille, follow the signs directing you to the charming, hilly town of **Ardara *(Árd an Rátha)*,** reached over a mountainous terrain. The road follows another breathtaking drive, through **Glengesh Pass,** a narrow, sinuous, scenic roadway that rises to a height of 270m (886 ft.) before plunging, in a tortuously zigzag pattern of hairpin curves, into the valley below. The road leads eventually to tiny Ardara, a stone village known for its tweed and woolen craft shops. From here, if you *really* want to get away from it all, you can tour the Atlantic Highlands (see p. 425).

Glencolumbkille (Gleann Cholm Cille) ★★ An extraordinarily beautiful outpost overlooking the Atlantic Ocean, Glencolumbkille is a small community about 52km (33⅓ miles) west of Donegal Town. Here the dark bogs disappear, replaced by a lush green valley. It is said that St. Columba established a

In the 6th century, St. Columba established a monastery at Glencolumbkille.

Hikers along the Slieve League, the country's most dramatic coastal walk.

monastery here in the 6th century and gave his name to the glen (its Gaelic name—*Gleann Cholm Cille*—means "Glen of Columba's Church"). Today it's home to the **Glencolumbkille Folk Park,** a wonderful "living history" park and craft village, set up and maintained entirely by the local people. In a series of small, traditional cottages, the park tells the story of this remote community in an engaging way. Guided tours are available, or you can take it at your own pace. Don't leave without browsing the *sheebeen*—a little store selling traditional, local products, including wines made from unusual ingredients, such as seaweed. There are miniature playhouses to entertain the children, while a tearoom serves traditional Irish stews and *brútin* (a stew of hot milk and potatoes). Hearty Guinness cake is a house specialty.

On R263, about 26km (16 miles) northeast of Killybegs, Co. Donegal. ✆ **074/973-0017.** www.gleanncholmcille.ie. Admission €4.50 adults; €4 seniors and students; €2.50 children 7–16; children 6 and under free; €12 families. Easter–Sept Mon–Sat 10am–6pm; Sun noon–6pm.

Slieve League ★★ It's surprising that these towering sea cliffs aren't better known, since they're almost three times the height of their far more feted southern cousins, the Cliffs of Moher (see p. 329), and arguably even more spectacular. Needless to say, given the remote location, they also get the tiniest fraction of the visitors. Start at the **Slieve League Cliffs Centre** (✆ **074/973-9077;** www.slieveleaguecliffs.ie) in Teelin, about 3km (1⅔ miles) southwest of Carrick. It's a great, friendly little visitor center, full of helpful information, with a very good cafe and a crafts store. Admission and parking are both free. The summits of the Slieve League, rising almost 600m (1,968 ft.) above the sea, are often capped in clouds, and you should think twice about undertaking the walk if there is danger of losing visibility along the way. In any case, this walk should only be for the fearless and fit. Including the climb up and then back down, the hike is about 10km (6¼ miles) and takes between 4 and 5 hours. Alternatively, the visitor center runs a shuttle bus up to the best viewing point.

Slieve League Centre: Teelin, Carrick, Co. Donegal (signposted from R263), Co. Donegal. ✆ **074/973-9077.** www.slieveleaguecliffs.ie. Free admission. Mar–Nov daily 10:30am–5:30pm.

SPORTS & OUTDOOR PURSUITS

BEACHES Glencolumbkille has two fine beaches: One is the flat, broad, sandy beach at the end of Glencolumbkille village, where the R263 swings left; the lesser known gem is a tiny beach surrounded by a horseshoe of cliffs, accessible from the small road signposted to Malin More (off the R263) about 1.6km (1 mile) southwest of town.

CYCLING If you're very fit, the north side of Donegal Bay has great cycling roads—tremendously scenic if very hilly. One good but arduous route from Donegal Town follows the coast roads west to Glencolumbkille (day 1), continues north to Ardara and Dawros Head via Glengesh Pass (day 2), and then returns to Donegal (day 3). It takes in some of the most spectacular coastal scenery in Ireland along the way, but takes place on small winding roads that must be shared with cars. Rental bikes are available in Donegal Town from **Ted's Bike Shop** (✆ **074/974-0774**), Killybegs Road, Donegal, for around €15 per day.

FISHING Surrounded by waters that hold shark, skate, pollock, conger, cod, and mackerel, **Killybegs** is one of the most active centers on the northwest coast for commercial and sport sea fishing. **Brian McGilloway** (✆ **087/220-0982;** www.killybegsangling.com) operates full-day fishing expeditions on the 12m (39-ft.) MV *Meridian,* from Blackrock Pier. Prices average €55 per person per day, plus €15 for rods and tackle, or around €450 to €700, depending on what you want to catch, for a party of 8 to 10 (8 is preferable for comfort). Alternatively he'll take you on evening mackerel fishing trips for €30 per person (minimum group size is five). The daily schedule and departure times vary according to demand; reservations are required.

WALKING The peninsula to the west of Killybegs offers some of the most spectacular coastal scenery in Ireland, and much of it is accessible only from the sea or on foot. The grandeur of the **Slieve League** cliffs (see p. 421) makes the hills popular with hikers, but only attempt them with a good map, hiking boots, and basic provisions. The best way to visit this natural monument is to hike from the Bunglass lookout point to Trabane Strand in Malin Beg, a few miles southwest of Glencolumbkille. This walk crosses the notorious "One Man's Pass," a vertigo-inducing narrow ridge with steep drops on both sides. The distance from Bunglass to Trabane Strand is 15km (9⅓ miles), and you will have to arrange a pickup at the end.

Another, lesser known walk that is just as spectacular is the coastal walk between Glencolumbkille and the town of **Maghera** (not so much a town as a small cluster of houses). Glen Head, topped by a Martello tower, overlooks Glencolumbkille to the north. This walk begins with a climb to the tower and continues along the cliff face for 24km (15 miles), passing only one remote outpost of human habitation along the way, the tiny town of **Port.** For isolated sea splendor, this is one of the finest walks in Ireland, but only experienced walkers with adequate provisions should undertake it, and only in fine weather.

Where to Stay in Donegal Town & Donegal Bay

Ard Na Breátha ★★ Beautifully converted into a comfortable, modern guesthouse, Ard Na Breátha sits on a working farm. Everything seems to have been judged with impeccable taste. Bedrooms are summery and spacious, with bright color schemes, polished wood floors, and antique-style iron frame beds in some rooms. Family rooms are only about €30 more than standard doubles. The pleasant guest lounge has a fireplace and a little bar too. Evening meals are sophisticated while unashamedly traditional in style, with plenty of local and seasonal ingredients (many supplied from their own farm, of course). Pre-booking for dinner is essential. See p. 424 for more on the restaurant. The B&B is located right on the edge of Donegal Town, though the farm makes it feel quite rural, enhanced by views of the mountains in the distance.

Railway Park, Middle Drumrooske, Donegal Town, Co. Donegal. ✆ **074/972-2288.** www.ardnabreatha.com. 6 units. €90–€130 double. Free parking. Breakfast included. **Amenities:** Wi-Fi (free); restaurant; bar. Closed mid-Jan–mid-Feb.

Bruckless House ★★ Another impeccably converted farmhouse, but with a slightly older pedigree, this property was built in the mid-1700s. Your hosts, Joan and Clive Evans, are cultured and well-traveled sorts, and their house is full of the kind of art and antiques that all tell a story. The gardens are beautiful and quite famous even with locals. A walk down the main path, past flowerbeds and lawns, will take you down to the sea. Bedrooms are simple, but tastefully decorated, and guests can use the pleasantly old-fashioned drawing room. The former Gate Lodge to the house is available as a self-catering unit; it sleeps up to four and is a good value at between €200 and €450 per week, depending on the season.

On N56, Bruckless, Co. Donegal. ✆ **074/973-7071.** www.bruckless.com. 4 units. €120 double. Free parking. Breakfast included. **Amenities:** Wi-Fi (free). From Donegal Town, Bruckless House is the first driveway on the left after the Bruckless village sign. Closed Oct–Mar.

Creevy Pier Hotel ★ The coastline in this part of Ireland isn't short of hotels and restaurants with magnificent views, but this one has to be up there with the best. The dining room looks straight out over Donegal Bay, framed by distant mountains. It's a magnificent spot from which to watch the sun go down. The Pier Restaurant is good, with plenty of local seafood options. Service is good and the staff welcoming. The bar has live music most weekends in summer. Bedrooms are fairly basic, but pleasant and well equipped. Very good value package deals are available, including 3-night midweek packages for seniors (including dinner on one night) for under €100. The only negative is it can sometimes get booked for weddings and pre-wedding parties, so you might want to check if any are planned over the dates you want to stay, to avoid any disruption.

Kildoney Glebe (signposted from R231 in Ballure), Co. Donegal. ✆ **071/985-8355.** www.creevy.ie. 10 units. €109–€120 double. Free parking. Breakfast included. **Amenities:** Wi-Fi (free); restaurant; bar; room service.

Where to Dine in Donegal Town & Donegal Bay

Ard Na Breátha ★★ MODERN IRISH The in-house restaurant at the lovely B&B of the same name (see p. 423) serves up excellent modern Irish cooking. The attractive, high-beamed dining room has a great view across rolling farmland to Donegal Town. The menu is seasonal, but depending on when you're visiting, you could be offered a starter of parsnip and apple soup or a warm goat-cheese tart, followed by chicken supreme (free range of course) or lamb shank with almonds and fresh ginger. The little bar outside the dining room is perfect for a pre-dinner drink or a nightcap while you take in the heady scent of the peat burning fire. Booking is essential.

Railway Park, Middle Drumrooske, Donegal, Co. Donegal. ✆ **074/972-2288.** www.ardnabreatha.com. Fixed-price menu (3 courses) €38. Daily 6–9:30pm. Closed mid-Jan–mid-Feb.

Pearl's Place ★★ MODERN IRISH From the outside, Pearl's Place looks nondescript, more closely resembling a family home than a restaurant. But what a surprise awaits! Delicious Irish cooking, modern in style without being overdone, served by friendly and professional staff. You could start with some duck confit with spicy lentils, then follow it up with some local lamb with tomato and mint chutney, or maybe some seabass with a side of garlic potatoes. They also have dedicated vegetarian and kids menus.

Killybegs Rd., Donegal Town, Co. Donegal. ✆ **071/972-1200.** www.pearlsplace.ie. Main courses €17–€26. Wed–Fri 6–9pm; Sat 5:30–9:30pm; Sun 1–4pm.

Smuggler's Creek Inn ★ SEAFOOD With a breathtakingly beautiful cliff-top view of Donegal Bay, this mid-19th-century inn is a fantastic place to come and watch the sun setting over the Atlantic Ocean. See if you can get a table outside or in the conservatory. Happily the food is good too. You can order steaks, lamb shank, and the like, but the seafood is really what's best here so go for the chowder, fresh hake in a cream sauce, oysters, salmon filet, or a seafood platter. There's always a catch of the day, and some vegetarian options too. Service can be slow, however, especially when it's busy.

Cliff Rd., Rossnowlagh, Co. Donegal. ✆ **071/985-2367.** www.smugglerscreekinn.com. Main courses €15–€23. Daily 12:30–3pm, 6–9:30pm.

The Village Tavern ★★ MODERN IRISH It's quite possible that you'll experience a sense of *déjà vu* when you approach the front door to this homely gastropub—the owners claim that it's been photographed several times for postcards, to convey a sense of "authentic Irishness". The place is cozy on the inside, and the food, which comes highly recommended by locals, is terrific. Although the menu is contemporary in style and presentation, there's a strong sense of tradition too, so wild salmon with coconut-flavored risotto and a spicy piri piri chicken share the menu with fish and chips or a simple box of cockles and mussels. The truly undaunted may attempt to tackle the "five steak" plate, made from two different cuts of meat, with two sauces plus sides.

Lower Main St., Mountcharles (5km/3 miles west of Donegal Town), Co. Donegal. ✆ **074/973-5622.** www.villagetavern.ie. Main courses €14–€24. Mon–Fri noon–9pm; Sat noon–9:30pm; Sun noon–7pm. Call ahead Oct–Apr. Food may not be served out of season, especially weekdays.

THE ATLANTIC HIGHLANDS

This is the most isolated part of Donegal, which is the most isolated county in Ireland, so it doesn't get much more rugged, exhilarating, and, well, *isolated* than this. At a certain point when you're driving through the highlands, the signs drop all pretense at bilingualism and switch to Gaelic. This is disconcerting, because most maps are in English, and the Gaelic names and the English names of places frequently are not even distant relatives. It's disorienting—one minute you know exactly where you are and the next you haven't a clue. It's as if somebody has stolen your compass. At that moment, which often occurs on a mountainside by a rushing stream amid rocky terrain where there's no space to pull the car over and stare more closely at the useless map, you're in the true Donegal. With its breathtaking coastal scenery, mountain ranges, and the lunar landscape of its rocky beaches, you could fill your camera's memory card here.

The best place to start a tour of Donegal's Atlantic Highlands is at **Ardara** ***(Árd an Rátha)***, an adorable village about 40km (25 miles) northwest of Donegal Town. From there, weave your way up the coast, turning inland when a place lures you to do so. This drive can take 4 hours or 4 days, depending on your schedule and interests. Our advice is to take your time. You may never come this way again, and you will want to remember every moment.

Exploring the Atlantic Highlands

Looking as if it were carved from stone, charming little **Ardara** is known for its exceptional tweed and wool creations. Astride a narrow river in a steep gulch, it is a pleasant place to stop, chat with the locals, and do a bit of shopping or maybe have a cup of tea in its small but useful **Heritage Centre** on the N56 main road through the village. It's open Easter to September, Monday to Saturday, from 10am to 6pm, and Sunday from 2 to 6pm.

If you happen to arrive in June, you may be lucky enough to catch the **Ardara Weavers Fair,** which has been going on since the 18th century, and features spectacular works in wool.

Heading north from Ardara, the landscape rolls across green hills and splashes into clear lakes. The two little resort towns here—**Naran (*An Fhearthainn*)** and **Portnoo**—are favorites with Irish families in the summer. They have lovely beaches, particularly Naran which has an excellent Blue Flag beach. A little farther along is the neat-as-a-pin little town of **Glenties *(Na Gleanta),*** which unsurprisingly has been the winner several times of the Irish Tidy Towns competition. It's excellent for fishing and for walks. The playwright Brian Friel set his play *Dancing at Lughnasa* here.

From here, the road curves inland to towns like **Gweedore *(Gaoth Dobhair),*** where Gaelic is the primary language and the countryside is increasingly desolate, but you're just a few miles from the gorgeous **Glenveagh National Park** and **Mount Errigal,** Donegal's highest mountain. The park is strewn with lakes and thick forest, and is home to rare golden eagles. At the edge of the park, Glenveagh Castle is a good place to meet other travelers, a bit of a relief after a long time driving empty roads.

Out along the coast, the road passes through Dungloe to an area known as the **Rosses,** extending from Gweebarra Bridge as far north as Crolly. It's a hard and rock-strewn land, but strangely beautiful, punctuated by mountains, rivers,

Dunlewey and the Errigal Mountains

and glassy lakes. Along the way, you'll pass **Burtonport** ***(Ailt an Chorrain),*** and it's said that more salmon and lobster are landed here than at any other port in the country.

The coastal area north of the Rosses, between Derrybeg and Gortahork, is known as the **Bloody Foreland,** from the fact that its rocks take on a ruddy color when lit by the setting sun. If you can arrange to be driving through such far-flung terrain at sunset on a clear day, you are in for a treat.

Next you'll approach the top rim of Donegal, dominated by a series of small peninsulas like fingers jabbing out into the sea. **Horn Head** ***(Corrán Binne)*** is the most extraordinary of these, with breathtaking cliffs towering 180m (590 ft.) above the ocean. But roads on this headland are a bit perilous in places, and definitely not for those uncomfortable with heights. At the base of the peninsula, **Dunfanaghy** ***(Dún Fionnachaidh)*** is one of the prettiest little towns you'll pass, with a great beach, much favored by Irish families. After Horn Head, the next peninsula to the east is **Rosguill** ***(Ros Goill).*** The 16km (10-mile) route around this peninsula is much less traumatic than the one around Horn Head, and is called the Atlantic Drive. This leads you to yet another peninsula, the **Fanad,** with a 73km (45-mile) circuit between Mulroy Bay and the glassy waters of Lough Swilly. The village of **Rathmelton** ***(Ráth Mealtain)*** is another one of those distinctive Irish villages that seems to have been hewn from the rocky hillside. It is tiny and eminently photographic, with its gray Georgian warehouses reflected in the mirrorlike water of the lake. It was once a bustling place, apparently, but then the rail line was rerouted to Letterkenny, and it all went quiet here. A few miles away, along a winding waterfront road, the village of **Rathmullan** ***(Ráth Maoláin)*** is an excellent stopping point, with a couple of good hotels (splurge on the amazing Rathmullan House if you can swing it—see p. 430); an evocative ruined abbey; and a beautiful stretch of flat, sandy beach on which to stroll or ride horses.

Doe Castle ★ This little tower house is so complete, it looks as if you could move in today and set up well-fortified housekeeping. A battlement wall with round towers at the corners encloses the central tower; the view from the battlements across the bay is superb. Built in the early 16th century, the castle was extensively restored in the 18th century and inhabited until 1843. It's a lovely little place, surrounded on three sides by the waters of Sheep Haven Bay, and on the fourth by a moat carved into the bedrock that forms its foundation. If the entrance is locked, you can get the key from the caretaker in the house nearest the castle.

5.6km (3½ miles) off N56; turnoff signposted just south of Creeslough, Co. Donegal. Free admission. Daily dawn–dusk.

Dunfanaghy Workhouse Heritage Centre ★ This rather unassuming looking building was the scene of great hardship and fear in the 19th century, when it was one of around 100,000 workhouses set up to feed and house the poor during the Great Famine. Their purpose was hardly altruistic, however; fearing that mere aid to stop the people starving would engender a "something-for-nothing" culture in the poor, the authorities decreed that they should perform backbreaking labor in return for their bread. It's estimated that workhouses killed around a million people in Ireland. This particular one housed about 300 inmates. The museum does a good job of describing their daily lives, as well as providing a history of the famine in this area. One exhibit focuses particularly on a local girl, "Wee Hannah" Herrity, who lived here and survived to tell the tale—which she did, in extensive conversation with a local biographer.

Just west of Dunfanaghy on N56, Co. Donegal. ✆ **074/913-6540.** www.dunfanaghyworkhouse.ie. Admission €4.50 adults; €3.50 seniors; €3 students and children; €11 families. June–Sept daily 10am–5pm; Oct–May Mon–Tues 9:30am–5:30pm, Wed–Fri 9:30am–4pm. Call for opening times Oct–May; actual opening times off-season are unpredictable.

Glebe House and Gallery ★★ What a surprise, in such a remote location, to find an art gallery as good as this. The early-19th-century house, on the shores of Lake Gartan, was once the home of the noted English painter Derek Hill (1916–2000). He donated the house, along with his personal art collection, to the Irish state in the 1980s. And it was quite a collection—highlights include paintings by Picasso, Renoir, Jack Yeats, and Oskar Kokoschka, rare Islamic and far Eastern art, and original William Morris prints. About 300 works are on display from the permanent collection, plus temporary and special exhibitions. The house itself is worth seeing too—a handsome Regency building, surrounded by pretty woods and gardens, stretching down to the Lough. The house can only be seen on a guided tour, and space is limited to 15 people at a time.

Church Hill, Co. Donegal. Signposted from R251, about 17km (10½ miles) northeast of Letterkenny. ✆ **074/913-7071.** www.heritageireland.ie. Admission €3 adults; €2 seniors; €1 students and children; €8 families. Gallery only: Easter week daily 11am–6:30pm; June and Sept Sat–Thurs 11am–6:30pm; July–Aug daily 11am–6:30pm; last tour 1 hr. before closing. Grounds open year-round.

Once the home of a brutal English landlord, Glenveagh Castle and its luxh gardens now belong to the Irish people.

Glenveagh National Park and Castle ★★★ This thickly wooded valley is a lush forest paradise, with the lavish Glenveagh Estate at its core. It's beautiful and pleasant now, but its history is dark. Nestling at its heart, **Glenveagh Castle** was originally the home of the infamously cruel landlord John George Adair, who evicted scores of struggling tenant farmers in the freezing winter of 1861, ostensibly because their presence on his estate was ruining his view. If the tale is true, it's a form of divine justice that his estate now belongs to all of the people of Ireland. Today the fairy-tale setting includes woodlands, herds of red deer, alpine gardens, a sylvan lake, and the highest mountain in Donegal, Mount Errigal. There's a visitor center with a little shop, and a charming tearoom in the castle. You can also go on ranger-led walks of the park here for €10. Cars aren't allowed in the park past the visitor center, but a shuttle bus can take you from there straight up to the castle for €3 round-trip. Admission to the park is free, but there's a charge to visit the castle (guided tours only).

Visitor Centre and Castle: Church Hill, Co. Donegal (signposted from R251, 24.4km/15 miles northeast of Letterkenny). ✆ **076/100-2536.** www.glenveaghnationalpark.ie. Castle: €5 adults; €3 seniors; €2 students and children; €10 families. Daily 10am–5pm. Park: Mar–Oct daily 9am–6pm; Oct–Mar daily 9am–5pm; last admission 1 hr. before closing.

Sports & Outdoor Pursuits

BEACHES The western coast of Donegal has lots of pristine and secluded beaches. If you like populated beaches, several of them spread around Dawros

Head, including **Traighmore Strand** in Rossbeg, and the Blue Flag beaches in Portnoo and Navan. **Magheroarty,** near Falcarragh on the northern coast, has a breathtaking beach, unspoiled by crowds or development. The same goes for **Tramore** beach on the western side of Horn Head near Dunfanaghy; you have to hike a short distance, but the rewards are seclusion and miles of creamy sand. Other peaceful sandy beaches ideal for walking and jogging include **Carrigart, Downings, Marble Hill,** and **Port na Blagh.**

BIRD-WATCHING **Horn Head,** just north of Dunfanaghy, is a nesting site for many species of seabirds, including a huge nesting population of razorbills.

FISHING The rivers and lakes in this area produce salmon, sea trout, and brown trout, and the coastal waters yield flounder, pollock, and cod. Fishing expeditions are offered by charter boats, fishing boats, and trawlers. For details, contact the **North Western Regional Fisheries Board,** Abbey Street, Ballina, County Mayo (✆ **096/22788;** www.northwestfisheries.ie or www.cfb.ie).

GOLF One of Ireland's most challenging golf courses is the **Rosapenna Golf Club,** Atlantic Drive, Downings, County Donegal (✆ **074/915-5000;** www.rosapenna.ie), an 18-hole championship seaside par-70 links course that was laid out in 1983 by Tom Morris of St. Andrews. It also has the newer Sandy Hills links, which was named the top course in the whole of Ireland and Britain by *Golf World* magazine in 2008. Greens fees are €80, but there's a €20 discount if you book your tee time online. They also offer a round on each links for €130 inclusive (€110 if you book online). Unusually for such a top club, prices do not rise on weekends.

Other 18-hole courses in this part of Donegal are **Dunfanaghy Golf Club,** Dunfanaghy, County Donegal (✆ **074/913-6335;** www.dunfanaghygolfclub.com), a seaside par-68 course with greens fees of €25 to €30; **Narin & Portnoo Golf Club,** Narin-Portnoo, County Donegal (✆ **074/954-5107;** www.narinportnoogolfclub.ie), a par-69 seaside course with greens fees of €25 to €70; and **Portsalon Golf Club,** Portsalon, County Donegal (✆ **074/915-9459;** www.portsalongolfclub.com), a seaside par-69 course with greens fees of €40 to €50.

HORSEBACK RIDING **Dunfanaghy Stables,** Arnold's Hotel, Dunfanaghy, County Donegal (✆ **074/913-6208;** www.dunfanaghystables.com), specializes in trail riding on the surrounding beaches, dunes, and mountain trails. An hour's ride averages €30 adults, €25 children. Between May and September they also offer guided trail riding holidays, including meals and accommodations.

WALKING A section of the **Ulster Way** passes through Donegal between the towns of Falcarragh to the north and Pettigo to the south, on the border with Fermanagh. This trail traverses some remote and wild terrain, passing Mount Errigal and Glenveagh Park before heading south into the Blue Stack Mountains, so should not be undertaken without a good map, proper attire, and supplies.

There are some incredible walks on **Hook Head,** signposted off N56 just west of Dunfanaghy. Follow Hook Head Drive to the concrete lookout point. From here you can walk out to a ruined castle on the headland and continue south along a line of impressive quartzite sea cliffs that glitter in the sun as though covered with glass. This is a moderately difficult walk.

The **Ards Forest Park** is on a peninsula jutting out into Sheep Haven Bay, about 5.6km (3½ miles) south of Dunfanaghy on N56. The park is mostly forested and includes an area of dunes along the water. The nature trails are signposted, and you can buy a guidebook as you enter the park.

Where to Stay in the Atlantic Highlands

Arnold's Hotel ★ This simple but pleasant hotel near the harbor in Dunfanaghy overlooks Sheephaven Bay. The slightly garish decor in the public areas won't win any design awards, but guestrooms are more restrained, with modern furniture and comfortable beds. Ask for a room with a view of the bay. The owners also run a horseback riding stables; week-long holiday packages, including accommodations and guided trail rides, are available. Check the website for details.

On N56, Dunfanaghy, Co. Donegal. ✆ **074/913-6208.** www.arnoldshotel.com. 32 units. €94–€150 double. Free parking. Breakfast not included in lower rates. **Amenities:** Wi-Fi (free); restaurant; bar.

Castle Grove Hotel ★★ Lancelot "Capability" Brown, the famous English landscaper who virtually invented landscape gardening in the 18th century, laid out the elegant grounds at this inviting white manor house. Inside the decor is avowedly traditional in style, with plenty of period detail and heritage paint colors. Rooms have antique furnishings (including a four-poster bed in one). All have views of the grounds. Breakfasts are outstanding, and the restaurant (see below) is one of the best in the region. Check the website for dinner, bed and breakfast packages.

Ballymaleel, off Ramelton Rd., Letterkenny, Co. Donegal. ✆ **074/915-1118.** www.castlegrove.com. 16 units. €90–€160 double; €150–€220 suite. Breakfast included. **Amenities:** Wi-Fi (free); restaurant; bar; room service; access to nearby golf courses; tennis courts.

Rathmullan House ★★★ Right on the edge of Lough Swilly, this delightful mid-18th-century mansion is one of the best places to stay in the northwest. The public areas are warm and hospitable, with sumptuous period decor. Bedrooms are spacious and extremely comfortable; those in the modern extension lose nothing in terms of style and charm to the rooms in the older section of the house. Some have fireplaces and deep, antique-style bathtubs. Superior rooms have even more space, and family rooms can work out at just slightly more expensive than standard doubles. The house has a swimming pool, or you can just take a short stroll down to the beach of the Loch. The Weeping Elm Restaurant is outstanding, and deserves its reputation as one of the best places to eat in Donegal—no bad thing, as there aren't many others within a reasonable drive. Many ingredients are supplied from the house's own garden (see p. 431). Check the website for discounts and special rates—particularly outside the busiest times of year, when you can often find deals that work out at around €100 per person, which is an incredible value for a place as good as this. They also offer dinner, bed and breakfast packages.

On R247 (Chapel Rd.), Rathmullan, Co. Donegal. ✆ **074/915-8188.** www.rathmullanhouse.com. 32 units. €180–€250 double. Parking. Breakfast included. **Amenities:** Restaurant; pool.

Where to Dine in the Atlantic Highlands

Castle Grove ★★★ IRISH The eponymous restaurant of the Castle Grove Hotel (see above) has won plenty of awards over the years, and it's easy to see why—the food is superb, and a top recommendation if you're staying here or nearby. The menu presents classic Irish dishes, made with plenty of local ingredients, and infuses them with a hint of the global village. For example, a gateaux of crab may be prepared with Thai seasoning and served with couscous, or salmon filet from Lough Swilly wrapped in Parma ham and served with red pepper coulis.

Ballymaleel, off Ramelton Rd., Letterkenny, Co. Donegal. ✆ **074/915-1118.** www.castlegrove.com. Main courses €18–€28. Daily 6:30–9:30pm. No children 9 and under allowed after 7pm.

Sheila's Coffee & Cream ★ CAFE This cozy cafe at the Ardara Heritage Centre (see p. 415) is a welcome find. Drop in for a fine cup of coffee and a restorative slice of cake, or you could stop for a light lunch—soups, Irish stew, salads, or maybe just a filling sandwich. The bread is home baked, and the ever-present Sheila herself is quite delightful. The cafe stays open until 9pm on Friday and Saturday in summer.

Ardara Heritage Centre, Ardara, Co. Donegal. ✆ **074/953-7905.** Main courses €5–€12. Daily 6:30–9:30pm. No children 9 and under allowed after 7pm.

The Weeping Elm ★★★ IRISH It's entirely befitting that, as one of the very best hotels in Donegal, Rathmullan House (see p. 430) would also have one of its best restaurants. Many of the ingredients have come no greater distance than the house's own gardens, and many of the rest haven't traveled all that much further. You could start with beetroot cured salmon, served with crab hand-picked from Wards beach, before moving on to Greencastle cod with braised lentils, or Donegal ham with parsley and bread sauce. Despite the quality, it's not the kind of place you have to sit up ruler-straight the whole time either; in addition to fancier choices they also do a fine burger, and kids get their own menu too (although younger ones are expected to be done by 7pm).

At Rathmullan House hotel, on R247 (Chapel Rd.), Rathmullan, Co. Donegal. ✆ **074/915-8188.** www.rathmullanhouse.com. Main courses €18–€28. Sun–Thurs 7–8:45pm; Fri–Sat 7–9:15pm.

THE INISHOWEN PENINSULA

To drive around the Inishowen is to traverse desolate seascapes, intimidating mountains, restful valleys, and impenetrable woodlands. This is a world apart, where residents treasure the legends of Ireland and still observe its ancient traditions. If you've made it this far, well done! You join the hardy, lucky few who have discovered the rugged, peaceful beauty of Inishowen.

Exploring the Inishowen Peninsula

To an extent, driving around the northernmost point of Ireland is worth doing just so you can say you did. You stood on Malin Head and felt the icy mist come in on a wind that hit you like a fist, and you balanced yourself on the rocky edge of the country and looked out at the true north. You have felt the satisfaction that comes from knowing there is no farther to go.

There is, however, more to this land than that. The **Inishowen *(Inis Eoghain)*** Peninsula reaches out from Lough Foyle to the east and Lough Swilly to the west toward Malin Head, its farthest point. Around the edges are ancient sites, beautiful beaches, and charming villages. At its center are gorgeous views, mountains, and quiet, vivid green pastures. If you are looking to get lost, this is a great place to do it.

In an unlikely twist, getting lost here actually won't be easy. Inexplicably, despite its clear need to be off the beaten path, and even with a decided dearth of traffic, the Inishowen Peninsula circuit is very well signposted, with all directions clearly printed in English and Irish, miles and kilometers.

To make a loop around the peninsula, start in the bustling little town of **Moville *(Bun an Phobail),*** which is a good place to stock up on gas and picnic provisions, and after a few miles of coastal road, you'll soon find yourself driving through **Greencastle *(An Cáisleá Nua),*** which holds the quirky Maritime Museum and Planetarium. From there, it's a short drive to the picturesque Inishowen Head. Follow signs off the main road onto a small side road, which you can take to the end, and then you walk the rest of the way to the headland. It's a bit eerily isolated, but the views are stupendous—on clear days, you can see all the way to the Antrim Coast. Back along the main road, look for a turnoff for **Culdaff *(Cúil Dabhcha),*** a sleepy waterfront village with a pretty beach. On its main street, the Clonca Church is a solid 17th-century structure with a high cross carved on one side with the biblical tale of loaves and fishes, and on the other with Celtic designs.

From Culdaff, it's about a 20-minute drive north to the pretty town of **Malin *(Málainn),*** with its stone bridge and village green. From Malin, it's another 20-minute drive to **Malin Head *(Cionn Mhélanna),*** a satisfyingly remote place at the end of the road (see p. 433).

There are not really many places to go here, so follow your instincts and the few signs, and meander past the small cluster of houses until you reach rocky **Banba's Crown *(Fíorcheann Éireann),*** the farthest point of the headland. Here, winds permitting, you can wander down to the rocky edge of the land and catch a glimpse of some old concrete huts built in World War II as lookout points. To the west of them is the dramatically named **Hell's Hole,** a natural land formation where waves crash deafeningly against the craggy shore. To the east, a path leads to a hermit's cave known as the **Wee House of Malin.**

Finding your way back to the main road without any signs is half the battle, and once you've done it, you're soon around the top of the peninsula and headed down the other side, through the **Gap of Mamore,** a mountain pass that rises 240m (787 ft.), then slowly descends on a corkscrew path to sea level, past a series of small, scenic villages to busy **Buncrana,** an excellent place to rest and have a meal. From the northern end of the seafront, you can find the old stone Castle Bridge that leads to **O'Doherty's Keep,** a simple, ruined tower house that served as the headquarters of the O'Doherty clan from the 15th century until it was destroyed 300 years later. The ruins next to it are all that's left of the castle that the English built to replace it. Appropriately, they are privately owned and inaccessible to the public; the O'Doherty grounds, on the other hand, can be explored for free.

About 16km (10 miles) south of Buncrana, the hilltop fort known as ***Grianan of Aileach*** is a beautifully preserved ring fort. It was built as a temple of the sun around 1700 B.C., and from the mid-5th century A.D. to the early 12th century A.D., it was the royal residence of the O'Neills, the chiefs of this area.

After you've toured the Inishowen, head south through **Letterkenny** (***Leitir Ceanainn;*** pop. 5,000). The largest town in the county, it's on a hillside overlooking the River Swilly. There you can pick up the N56, the main road, and drive to the twin towns of **Ballybofey** and **Stranorlar.** Change here to N15, which takes you to yet another scenic Donegal drive, the **Barnesmore Gap,** a vast open stretch through the Blue Stack Mountains, which leads you into Donegal Town and points south.

Fort Dunree Military Museum ★★ Rising precipitously from the cliffs beside Lough Swilly, this impressive-looking fort was constructed as a defensive lookout in case of a French invasion during the Napoleonic Wars. It later became part of Irish sea defenses in case of a German invasion during the First World War. Neither came, and today Dunree serves as an informative museum. Spread partly through subsurface bunkers, the exhibitions tell the history of the fort, and of the local area as a whole. It also serves as the starting point for scenic walks around Dunree Point along three recommended walking paths. The museum has a handy coffee shop overlooking the Lough.

Signposted on the coast road north of Buncrana, Co. Donegal. ✆ **074/936-1817.** www.dunree.pro.ie. Admission €6 adults; €4 seniors and children. Daily 10:30am–6pm.

Inishowen Maritime Museum and Planetarium ★ This small but engaging museum overlooks Loch Foyle. Exhibits pack all they can into the old coastguard building for the harbor town of Greencastle, taking the town's maritime history from the Armadas of the 16th century, through emigration, to the modern-day lifeboat crews and their selflessly heroic work. In something of a contrast, there's also a planetarium, complete with recently renovated digital projection. Shows run on request during the winter (minimum group size is six), but more or less all day during summer—call to confirm times.

The Harbour, Greencastle, Co. Donegal. ✆ **074/938-1363.** www.inishowenmaritime.com. Museum only: €5 adults; €3 seniors, students and children. Museum and planetarium: €10 adults; €6 seniors, students, and children. Easter–Sept Mon–Sat 9:30am–5:30pm, Sun noon–5:30pm; Oct–Easter Mon–Fri 9:15am–5:30pm. Last admission 30 min. before closing.

Malin Head (Cionn Mhélanna) ★★★ The remote Inishowen Peninsula, rarely visited but much admired, is a land of desolate seascapes, intimidating mountains, restful valleys, and impenetrable woodlands. The most far-flung of all the natural sights on the isolated Inishowen Peninsula is Malin Head, a stunning promontory where the road goes no further and the next stop west is New York. Even on a sunny day, the wind often howls and the temperature can be 10 degrees colder than it is just a few miles south. Get this far and you can say you've experienced Ireland more completely than all but a handful of visitors ever manage. To reach Malin Head, take R242 north until it turns into a small, unnamed road. Continue along this road all the way until it literally runs out and there's nowhere left to go. You'll find a place to pull over, and a little information board that tells you all about the Head. But you're unlikely to read the whole thing—you'll be too busy gazing at the incredible view.

Ballyhillin, Co. Donegal.

Sports & Outdoor Pursuits

BEACHES **Ballyliffin, Buncrana, Greencastle,** and **Moville** have safe, sandy beaches ideal for swimming or strolling.

BIRD-WATCHING **Malin Head** is a good site for watching migrating species in late autumn.

GOLF The Inishowen is a major center for golf in Ireland, and it has four 18-hole golf courses. Two are at the **Ballyliffin Golf Club,** Ballyliffin, County Donegal (✆ **074/937-6119;** www.ballyliffingolfclub.com). The "Old Links" is a par-71 course with greens fees of €50 to €80; the "Glashedy Links" course costs €50 to €90. The **North West Golf Club,** Fahan, Buncrana, County Donegal (✆ **074/936-1027;** www.northwestgolfclub.com), founded in 1890, is a par-69 seaside course with greens fees of €30 weekdays, €35 weekends. **Greencastle Golf Course,** Greencastle, County Donegal (✆ **074/938-1013**), is a par-69 parkland course with greens fees of around €25 to €40.

WATERSPORTS The Inishowen's long coastline, sandy beaches, and combination of open ocean and sheltered coves provide great opportunities for watersports. The northwest coast presents some of the most challenging surfing conditions in Europe. For advice and specific information, contact the **Irish Surfing Association,** Easkey Surf and Information Centre in Easkey, County Sligo (✆ **096/49428;** www.isasurf.ie).

Where to Stay on the Inishowen Peninsula

Ballyliffin Lodge ★★ With impressive views of Malin Head (see p. 433), this hotel is a relaxing place to stay. The in-house spa, **Rock Crystal,** provides a welcome respite at the end of a long day's travel. Prices are a lot more reasonable here than they would be in an equivalent place in a more visited part of the country too, with three treatments (totaling just over an hour) for €70. Bedrooms, which take full advantage of the gorgeous views, are nice and spacious, with muted, autumnal decor. The hotel can help organize plenty of activities, from horseback riding to surfing and golf.

Ballyliffin, Co. Donegal. ✆ **074/937-8200.** www.ballyliffinlodge.com. 40 units. €80–€195 double. Breakfast not included in lower rates. **Amenities:** Wi-Fi; restaurant; bar; room service; spa; gym; pool.

The Strand ★ Another place with views of Malin Head, this modest but friendly hotel also overlooks Pollan Strand, a 2-mile stretch of beach outside Ballyliffin. Accommodations aren't overly fancy, but they're modern and comfortable, with deep tubs in the bathrooms. Family rooms sleep up to 4; one room is fully accessible for wheelchair users. The hotel often teams up with local golf courses to offer packages that include access to some of the area's most highly-rated links.

Ballyliffin, Co. Donegal. ✆ **074/937-6107.** www.ballyliffin.com. 21 units. €75–€90 double. Free parking. Breakfast included. **Amenities:** Wi-Fi (free); restaurant; bar.

Where to Dine on the Inishowen Peninsula

The Drift Inn ★★ IRISH/PUB FOOD You never quite know where you are with punning restaurant names, but this cheerful place in Buncrana can be forgiven a groan because of its top quality pub food. There are plenty of names on the menu that you probably will have seen on signs while driving here, and that accounts for at least some of the freshness of the flavors too. You could opt for a 6-hour braised Donegal lamb shank served with mustard mashed potato, or Greencastle salmon filet with chili and coriander sauce. Buncrana is about a 15 minute drive south of Fort Dunree (see p. 433), and about 45 minutes south of Malin Head (see p. 433).

Railway Rd., Buncrana, Co. Donegal. ✆ **074/936-1999.** www.thedriftinn.ie. Main courses €13–€19. Thurs–Sat 1–9:15pm; Sun 1–8:30pm. Closed Thurs in winter.

Nancy's Barn ★ CAFE This is the kind of place that looks so pretty from the outside on a sunny day, with its red shutters and gray stone walls, that you stop to take a picture and end up going for lunch out of curiosity. Fortunately, chances of disappointment are low—Nancy's serves fine sandwiches, toasties, salads, soups, and other light meals. They also bake their own cakes and scones. Ballyliffin is due south of Malin Head, on the other side of the bay; to reach the town from there, take R242 and R238. The journey's only 27km (17 miles) but allow at least half an hour due to the winding roads.

On the main road through Ballyliffin, Co. Donegal. ✆ **087/211-4239.** Main courses €4–€13. Daily 10am–5pm.

15

NORTHERN IRELAND

The vibrant and beautiful six counties of Ireland still under British rule are all the more fascinating for their troubled history. Collectively they're known as Northern Ireland—although you'll hear terms such as "Ulster" and "the North" used interchangeably. Given the seemingly endless struggle that has gone on for the soul of this place, the fact that nobody knows quite what to call it is somehow appropriate. This is a colorful, exciting region filled with lively towns and countryside of breathtaking beauty. Tourism numbers in Northern Ireland have increased greatly over the last decade, but it's still far less visited than the Republic. That's both a shame and its biggest selling point. You're likely to find yourself very welcome here—and yet, outside of the busy summer months, it's not uncommon to find yourself alone in the most spectacular places.

WHAT'S ALL THE TROUBLE?

Belfast and **Derry,** the North's only cities of any size, are both quite manageable, with winding streets and grand historical monuments. But the main draw here is the magnificent countryside: the cool greens of the **Glens of Antrim,** the rugged **Mourne Mountains,** and the famously craggy coastline culminating in the extraordinary lunar **Giant's Causeway.**

For many years, however, visitors to Ireland avoided the North, for obvious reasons. In so many ways, things here aren't what they used to be. And that's a good thing. Many young adults today have spent their whole lives in Belfast or Derry and have almost no memory of a time when their cities were overshadowed by violence.

And yet, while peace reigns, the divisions remain deep. Heartbreakingly, in the most intransigent communities, this is just as true of the younger generation as it is for their parents. Time has taken away the weapons, but it has not healed all wounds.

Still, the Troubles are obviously the elephant in the Northern Irish living room. It would be a unique visit that ignored politics entirely, whether it's the unforgiving murals in West Belfast or the strident graffiti that startles you in even the most bucolic village. Everybody picks a side in the Sisyphean effort to claim this rocky soil for God and country. But whose God and which country? Herewith, a quick rundown of the history of it all.

The strife in Northern Ireland can be traced back 800 years. In fact, one apocryphal story tells of a phone call between two friends—an Irish politician and an English parliamentarian—at the start of the Irish civil war in the 1920s. According lore, the Englishman asked his Irish friend, "Is it true that there's an uprising in Ireland?" and the Irishman replied, "Aye, 'tis true." "When did it

PREVIOUS PAGE: **Giant's Causeway, Northern Ireland's UNESCO World Heritage Site in County Antrim.**

An Creagán Visitors' Centre **11**
Andrew Jackson Cottage & U.S. Rangers Centre **41**
Ards Peninsula **32**
Armagh Astronomy Centre **17**
Armagh County Museum **19**
Beaghmore Stone Circles **12**
Belleek Visitors Centre **5**
Benburb Valley Park & Castle **15**
Carrick-a-Rede Rope Bridge **46**
Carrickfergus Castle **40**
Carnlough **42**
Castle Coole **6**
Castle Espie Wetlands Centre **34**
Castle Ward **30**
Castlewellan Forest Park **25**
Crom Estate **7**
Cushendun **44**
Devenish Island **4**
Down Cathedral **28**
Drum Manor Forest Park **13**
Drumena Cashel **24**
Dundrum Castle **26**
Dunluce Castle **48**
Enniskellen Castle **3**
Florence Court **1**
Giant's Causeway & Visitor Centre **49**
Giant's Ring **37**
The Glens of Antrim **43**
Gortin Glen Forest Park **9**
Greencastle Fort **20**
Grey Abbey **33**
Legananny Dolmen **27**
Lough Neagh Discovery Centre **36**
Marble Arch Caves **2**
Mount Stewart House **39**
Mourne Mountains **21**
Navan Fort **16**
Nendrum Monastic Site **35**
Old Bushmills Distillery **47**
Peatlands Park **14**
Portaferry Castle **31**
Silent Valley Mountain Park **22**
Sperrin Heritage Centre **10**
St. Patrick Centre/Down County Museum **29**
St. Patrick's Church of Ireland Cathedral **18**
St. Patrick's Roman Catholic Cathedral **18**
Tollymore Forest Park **23**
Torr Head Scenic Road **45**
Rathlin Island Bird Sanctuary **50**
Ulster Folk & Transport Museum **38**
Ulster American Folk Park **8**

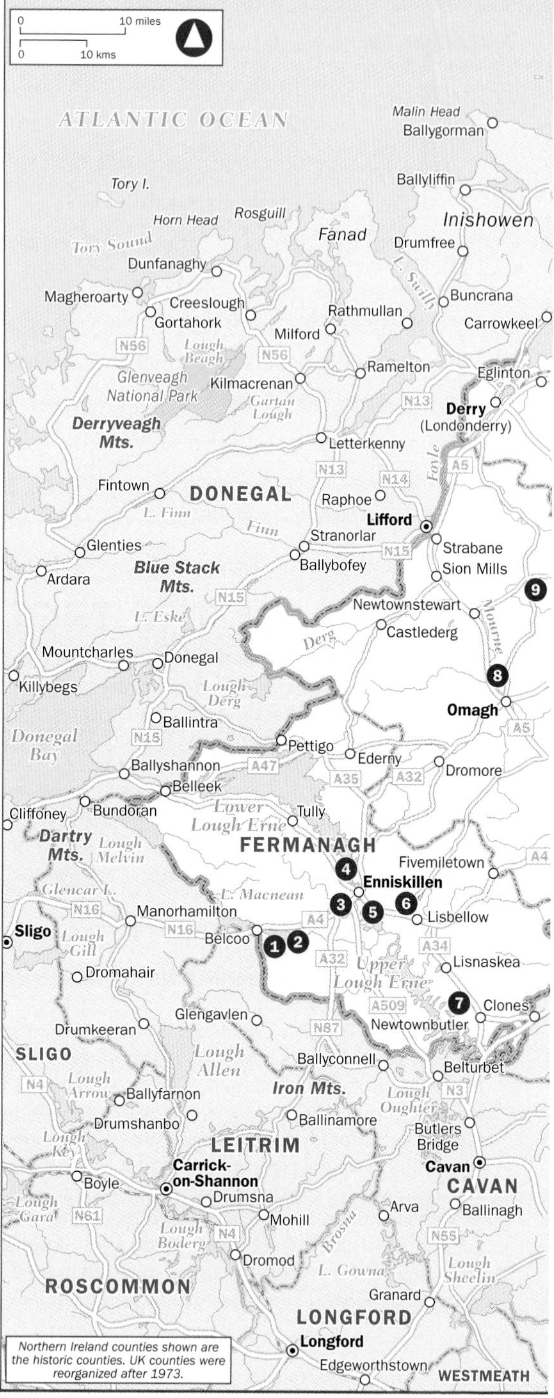

Northern Ireland
SCOTLAND
Culdaff Bay
Kinnagoe Bay
Rathlin I.
Giant's Causeway
Ballintoy
Fair Head
Mull of Kintyre
Torr Head
Portrush
Bushmills
Moville
Portstewart
Ballycastle
Castlerock
Coleraine
Armoy
Cushendun
Lough Foyle
North Channel
To Troon
Ballymoney
Red Bay
Cushendall
Limavady
Trostan
Ballykelly
To Cairnryan
Antrim Mts.
Carnlough Bay
LONDONDERRY (DERRY)
Garvagh
Bann
Carnlough
Kilrea
Glenarm
To Stranraer
ANTRIM
Dungiven
Broughshane
Sperrin Mts.
Sawel Mtn.
Maghera
Ballymena
Larne
Island Magee
Draperstown
Magherafelt
Ballyclare
Whitehead
Randalstown
Carrickfergus
Moneymore
Antrim
Greenisland
Belfast Lough
Newtownabbey
Belfast Int'l
Cookstown
Glengormley
Bangor
Donaghadee
To Douglas, Heysham, Liverpool
TYRONE
Lough Neagh
Crumlin
BELFAST
Pomeroy
Newtownards
Sixmilecross
Comber
Strangford Lough
Ards Peninsula
Coal Island
Dungannon
Lisburn
Lagan
Craigavon
Lurgan
Saintfield
Killinchy
Portavogie
Ballygawley
Augher
Portadown
Dromore
Aughnacloy
Ballynahinch
Killyleagh
Tandragee
DOWN
Portaferry
Strangford
Armagh
Banbridge
Downpatrick
Scarva
Middletown
ARMAGH
Castlewellan
Dundrum
Ardglass
Monaghan
Markethill
Rathfriland
Keady
Newcastle
Dundrum Bay
Newry
Mourne Mts.
MONAGHAN
Ballybay
Slieve Gullion
IRISH SEA
Warrenpoint
Castleblayney
Forkhill
Omeath
Annalong
Cootehill
Carlingford
Kilkeel
Greenore
Carlingford Lough
Inniskeen
Dundalk
Shercock
Fane
Carrickmacross
Louth
Bailieborough
Dundalk Bay
Dromiskin
Castlebellingham
Kingscourt
LOUTH
Dunany Point
Virginia
L. Ramor
Ardee
Dunleer
Nobber
Mullagh
Clogherhead
Collon
Oldcastle
MEATH
Tullyallen
Knowth
Drogheda
Kells (Ceanannus Mór)
Slane
Newgrange
A2
A44
A26
A37
A54
A29
A6
A42
A36
A8
A505
A5
A4
M1
A3
A1
A21
A49
A7
A50
A25
A28
N54
N2
N1
N52
10
11
12
13
14
15
16
17
18
19
20
21
22
23
24
25
26
27
28
29
30
31
32
33
34
35
36
37
38
39
40
41
42
43
44
45
46
47
48
49
50
NORTHERN IRELAND
Map Area
Belfast
Galway
Dublin
REPUBLIC OF IRELAND
Cork

start?" the Englishman asked. "When Strongbow invaded Ireland," the Irishman said. "When will it end?" asked the Englishman. "When Cromwell gets out of hell." The story alludes to the fact that when the English first invaded Ireland in the 12th century, they were led by the Earl of Pembroke, nicknamed "Strongbow". They never really left, and some Irish have never quit trying to get rid of them.

Over the centuries, the British waged a largely futile effort to make Ireland, and the Irish, British. Their tactics included outlawing the Irish language, banning Catholicism, and barring Catholics from landownership; finally, in the mid-1600s, Oliver Cromwell's New Model Army went for the more basic approach of killing them in droves. British families were brought over to take their land—essentially, physically replacing Irish Catholics with British Protestants—in a process the Irish called "planting". The descendants of those British settlers, generally speaking, form the Protestant population of Northern Ireland today.

After centuries of struggle, Ireland finally won independence of a sort from Britain in 1921. After much arguing, it was decided that the island would be divided. Twenty-six Irish counties would form an independent "Free State" (now the Republic of Ireland), while six counties in the Ulster province with predominantly Protestant populations would remain part of the United Kingdom to form Northern Ireland.

When the six counties were detached from the rest of the island, two conflicting ideological bodies emerged: **Unionists,** associated with the Protestant majority, who want to remain a part of the United Kingdom, and **Nationalists,** associated with the Catholic minority, who want the whole of Ireland united as one independent nation. Of course, being a Unionist or a Nationalist doesn't imply approval of the violence. In fact, the overwhelming majority of Northern Irish people, regardless of whether they want British rule or Irish rule, oppose the use of violence.

After the division, the British police and government in Ulster were quite brutal toward the Catholic minority. Things came to a head in the late 1960s when the Catholic population began an intense civil rights campaign. Their marches and demonstrations were crushed by the authorities, sometimes with disproportionate levels of violence, thus setting the stage for the reemergence of the Irish Republican Army (IRA), a violent paramilitary group that had first appeared early in the 20th century. After the infamous "Bloody Sunday" massacre in 1971, when the British army opened fire on a peaceful protest in Derry (see p. 487), the IRA began a campaign of bombs targeted at civilians on the British mainland.

The struggle continued—but to say it was *only* a struggle between the British/Protestant establishment and the Irish/Catholic minority would be too simplistic. There were a multitude of groups, aligned with either side, many with their very own confusing acronym and private army. The cycle of violence and retribution was almost tit-for-tat.

No wonder the unholy mess became known simply as "The Troubles."

It was a dirty fight. Throughout the 1970s and 80s, violence on all sides was a fact of everyday life. And yet the vast majority of ordinary people in Northern Ireland had nothing to do with it. By the 1990s, the population of Ulster—stunned by the sheer horror of an IRA bombing in the town of Omagh that killed 29 civilians on a busy shopping street—had had enough.

With the personal involvement of U.S. President Bill Clinton urging them to find a peaceful solution to their disagreements, on May 22, 1998, Northerners and their fellow islanders in the Republic voted to accept the so-called

CHOOSING sides: UNDERSTANDING NORTHERN IRELAND'S DIVISIONS

To understand Northern Ireland, you first must understand who is involved in the sectarian game, because the battle between **Republicans** (those who believe the North should become part of the Republic of Ireland; also called Nationalists or "the Catholics," depending on who's talking), and the **Loyalists** (those who are loyal to the British crown and think the North should stay, as it is now, part of the United Kingdom; also called Unionists or "the Protestants") defines this region to this day. The problem is that both sides have splintered over the last decade, and so it's hard to keep up with who's who.

The Republicans are now divided among devotees of the IRA (the Irish Republican Army), the "Real" IRA (a splinter faction that branched off from the IRA), and Sinn Fein (also splintered from the IRA, and now its political face). Supporters for this side often have the green, white, and orange Irish flag hanging from their homes and businesses.

The Loyalists are divided among a variety of paramilitary groups, including the UDA (Ulster Defence Association), the UDF (Ulster Defence Force), and the UVF (Ulster Volunteer Force). Much of the violence in the last decade has been the result of turf wars between those Protestant groups. Supporters of that side often have the British Union Jack flag flying from their homes and businesses.

These days, many, though not all, of these groups are more involved in organized crime than political struggle, and all of them have sometimes been lumped together by pundits under the new term "Irish mafia." Massive bank robberies (all of Northern Ireland's currency was withdrawn and reissued within 1 week in 2005 after a gang suspected to be connected with the IRA stole £22 million in a bank heist), importation and sales of illegal weaponry, and drugs are all blamed on the same factions that once battled for political power here.

Most Irish people will tell you that they're sick of the lot of them—however, don't ask unless you know the person you're talking to really well. It's an extremely sensitive subject that should not be brought up casually. If you're really curious, take one of the superb **Black Taxi tours** (see p. 448) and you can ask the brilliant and patient guides questions to your heart's content.

"Good Friday Agreement". It dismantled the claims of both Ireland and Britain to the North and acknowledged the sovereign right of the people of Northern Ireland to take charge of their political destiny, effectively separating their government from London.

Since the peace agreement was signed, it has been tested several times. In 2009, violence flared again in this region, in a series of murders and attacks on British soldiers and others involved on one side or the other of the political landscape. The situation was quickly calmed, due to the determination of all sides not to return to the bad old days. Since then there have been sporadic incidents—including a couple of car bombs, one of which, in 2011, was outside the tourism office in Derry (although nobody was hurt). And the summer of 2013 saw some pretty serious riots in Belfast; on one night alone, 56 police officers were injured and parts of the city center were vandalized. But on the whole, despite sporadic incidents, the region remains at peace.

Is Northern Ireland Safe to Visit?

In short, **yes.** But you should still be savvy. From a visitor's perspective, any violence here has always been remarkably contained. Like diplomats, foreigners have always had a kind of immunity. Belfast and Derry are safer for visitors than almost any comparable American city, and the Ulster countryside is idyllic and serene. Overall, Northern Ireland has one of the *lowest* crime rates in Europe. But nonetheless, you should follow these basic rules of thumb:

- **Do not** discuss the political situation with anyone you don't know well.
- **Never, ever** get involved in political or religious arguments relating to Northern Ireland.
- **Avoid** venturing deep into the poorer, inner city areas of Belfast or Derry without a guide.
- **Always** stay informed. Follow the news to keep abreast of current events and any likely trouble spots.

ARRIVING

BY BUS **Ulsterbus** (✆ **028/9066-6630;** www.translink.co.uk) runs buses from Dublin to Belfast and towns across Northern Ireland. From Dublin Airport, **AirCoach** (✆ **01/844-7118;** www.aircoach.ie) runs a regular, non-stop service to Belfast. One-way tickets are £17 adults, £10 children. The journey time is just under 2 hours. In Belfast, the main bus station is Europa Bus Centre on Great Victoria Street.

BY TRAIN Belfast has two train stations: Great Victoria Street Station and Belfast Central Station on East Bridge Street. Contact **Northern Ireland Railways** (✆ **028/9066-6630**) for tickets.

BY CAR Driving from Dublin to Belfast is easy; just go north up the M1 motorway. From Dublin airport the journey is about 90 minutes in good traffic. From Sligo Town take N16 and A4 west; from there it's 124 miles (200km), about 2½ hours.

BY PLANE Belfast has two airports: **Belfast International** (✆ **028/9448-4848;** www.belfastairport.com) and **Belfast City Airport** (✆ **028/9093-9093;** www.belfastcityairport.com). United Airlines (✆ **1800/864-8331;** www.united.com) runs the one regular, direct flight to Belfast from North America. Aer Lingus (✆ **01/814-1111;** www.aerlingus.com), British Airways (✆ **189/0626-747** in Ireland, or 084/4493-0787 in the U.K.), Flybe (✆ **44/139-268-3152** or 087/1700-2000 in the U.K.), and Easyjet (✆ **084/3104-1000;** www.easyjet.com) all

KEEPING up WITH THE IRISH

If you want to brush up on your knowledge of Northern Ireland, **Newshound** (www.irishcentral.com/news/thenorth) is an indispensable resource. Run by American expat John Fay, this is an extremely well-organized catalog of news articles culled from Irish newspapers, covering everything from the Troubles to dining and shopping in Belfast. A vast array of articles about the Republic (click the main "News" tab) includes culture, travel, and even dining reviews from Dublin to Donegal. The site is intelligent, user-friendly, and searchable.

operate regular scheduled flights from London to Belfast. Easyjet and Flybe fly to Belfast from Manchester, Birmingham, and Edinburgh in the U.K. You can fly direct to Belfast from several European cities.

[FastFACTS] NORTHERN IRELAND

ATMs/Banks ATMs aren't hard to come by in central Belfast; several banks are around Donegall Square, including **Ulster Bank** (✆ **028/9024-4112**) and **Bank of Ireland** (✆ **028/9043-3420**). In Enniskillen, **Santander Bank,** 4 Church St. (✆ **084/5765-4321**) has an ATM. In Omagh, try **HSBC,** 1 Dublin Rd. (✆ **084/5740-4404**). In Derry, try **Santander** on Shipquay St. (✆ **084/5765-4321**).

Currency As part of the United Kingdom, Northern Ireland uses the **pound sterling,** not the euro. The cheapest way to get local currency is to use an ATM. The pound/ euro exchange rate fluctuates as much as all major currencies, but in general it usually hovers around £0.80 to €1.

Dentists For dental emergencies, your hotel should contact a dentist for you. Otherwise, in Belfast try **Dublin Road Dental Practice,** 23 Dublin Rd., BT2 7HB (✆ **028/9032-5345**) or **Lisburn Road Dental Clinic,** 424 Lisburn Rd., BT9 6GN (✆ **028/9038-2262**); in Derry, try **Timber Quay Dental Practise,** Timber Quay, BT48 7NR (✆ **028/7122-1098**).

Doctors For medical emergencies dial ✆ **999.** For non-emergencies, your hotel should call you a doctor. Otherwise in Belfast, try **Ormeau Health Centre** (✆ **028/9032-6030**); in Enniskillen, try **Devenish Practise,** the Health Centre, Erne Rd., BT74 6NN); in Omagh try **Stule Medical Practise,** Mountjoy Rd., BT79 7BA (✆ **084/4477-3504**); and in Derry try **Park Medical,** 49 Great James St., BT48 7DH (✆ **028/7137-8500**).

Emergencies For police, fire, or other emergencies, dial ✆ **999.**

Internet Access In Belfast there's **Browsers Café,** 77 Dublin Rd., BT2 7HF (✆ **028/9032-2272**) and **Abigail's,** 140 Upper Lisburn Rd., BT10 0BG (✆ **028/9061-6825**). In Derry try **Café Connect,** 49 Strand Rd., BT48 7BN (✆ **028/7137-2101**).

Pharmacies Belfast has branches of **Boots the Chemist** at 35–47 Donegall Place, BT1 5AW (✆ **028/9024-2332**) and Great Victoria St., BT2 7GN (✆ **028/9031-0530**). In Omagh, try **Bradley's Pharmacy,** 84 Old Mountfield Rd., BT79 7ET (✆ **028/8244-1373**). In Enniskillen, try **Corry's Chemist,** 15 Darling St., BT74 7DP (✆ **028/8167-1974**). And in Derry, try the **MediCare Pharmacy,** 43 Great James St., BT48 7DF (✆ **028/7126-7004**).

Post Offices Main branches in Belfast include 16–22 Bedford St., BT2 7FD and 12–14 Bridge St., BT1 1LS.

Taxis In Belfast you can catch a taxi at train stations, ports, airports, and the taxi stand in front of City Hall. Alternatively try **Value Cabs** (✆ **028/9080-9080**), **Courtesy Cabs** (✆ **028/9002-9345**) or **Aldergrove Taxis** (✆ **028/9433-0950**). In Derry, taxi stands are at the Ulsterbus station, Foyle Street, and at the train station on Duke Street; alternatively call **City Cabs** (✆ **028/7126-4466**) or **Foyle Delta Cabs** (✆ **028/7127-9999**). In Enniskillen try **Diamond Cabs** (✆ **028/6632-8484**). In Omagh try **P&L Taxis** (✆ **028/8224-1010**). Out in the countryside taxis are rarer—the best thing to do is ask for numbers from your hotel or at a pub. Most restaurants will call one for you.

VISITING NORTHERN IRELAND: f.a.q.

What's the border crossing like?
There is no marked land border between the Republic of Ireland and Northern Ireland. The only immediate difference you are likely to notice is that the road signs change.

Will I need a passport?
You don't need a passport or a separate visa when crossing between the Republic of Ireland and Northern Ireland.

Is driving in Northern Ireland the same?
Broadly speaking, yes, but with one major difference: road signs in Northern Ireland show **miles,** not kilometers. Signs around the border usually show both. Don't forget to check that your travel insurance and any car-rental agreements are equally valid in Northern Ireland.

Does Northern Ireland use the euro?
No. The currency in Northern Ireland is the **British pound (sterling).** In practice, euros are accepted in some border areas, major tourist attractions, and hotels; however, you will almost always be given change in pounds. ATMs are the easiest and cheapest way to get currency.

What are those letters and numbers at the end of Northern Irish addresses?
They're British-style postcodes (zip codes). Postcodes are still in the process of being introduced to the Republic, but almost every address in Northern Ireland has one. This is actually a big advantage if you're driving, as it makes GPS navigation much easier. Where possible we've included postcodes for all the listings in this chapter.

Any other tips?
Your mobile phone company will treat Northern Ireland as the U.K., so inform them in advance if you think you'll be crossing the border. This might avoid higher international roaming charges.

BELFAST

Belfast is a lively, funky, and complicated town; a curious combination of faded grandeur and forward-looking optimism, complete with an artsy, edgy underbelly. Belfast boomed in the 19th century as prosperity flowed from its vast textile and shipbuilding industries. The 20th century was not so kind to the city, which spent many years in decline, but plenty of grand old Victorian buildings still reflect that time of wealth and power. Now the city's urban landscape is changing once again as the Titanic Quarter spurs new development with shiny museums and modern visitor attractions.

Visitor Information

The main tourist information center for the city is the **Belfast Welcome Centre** at 37 Donegall Place, BT1 5AD (✆ **028/9024-6609;** www.visit-belfast.com). They can help book accommodations in the city, and they also have a bureau de change and left luggage facility. Smaller visitor information points are at **Belfast International Airport** (✆ **028/9448-4677**) and **George Best Belfast City Airport** (✆ **028/9093-5372**).

City Layout

Small and easily traversed, central Belfast is best explored **walking.** The main tourist districts are as follows.

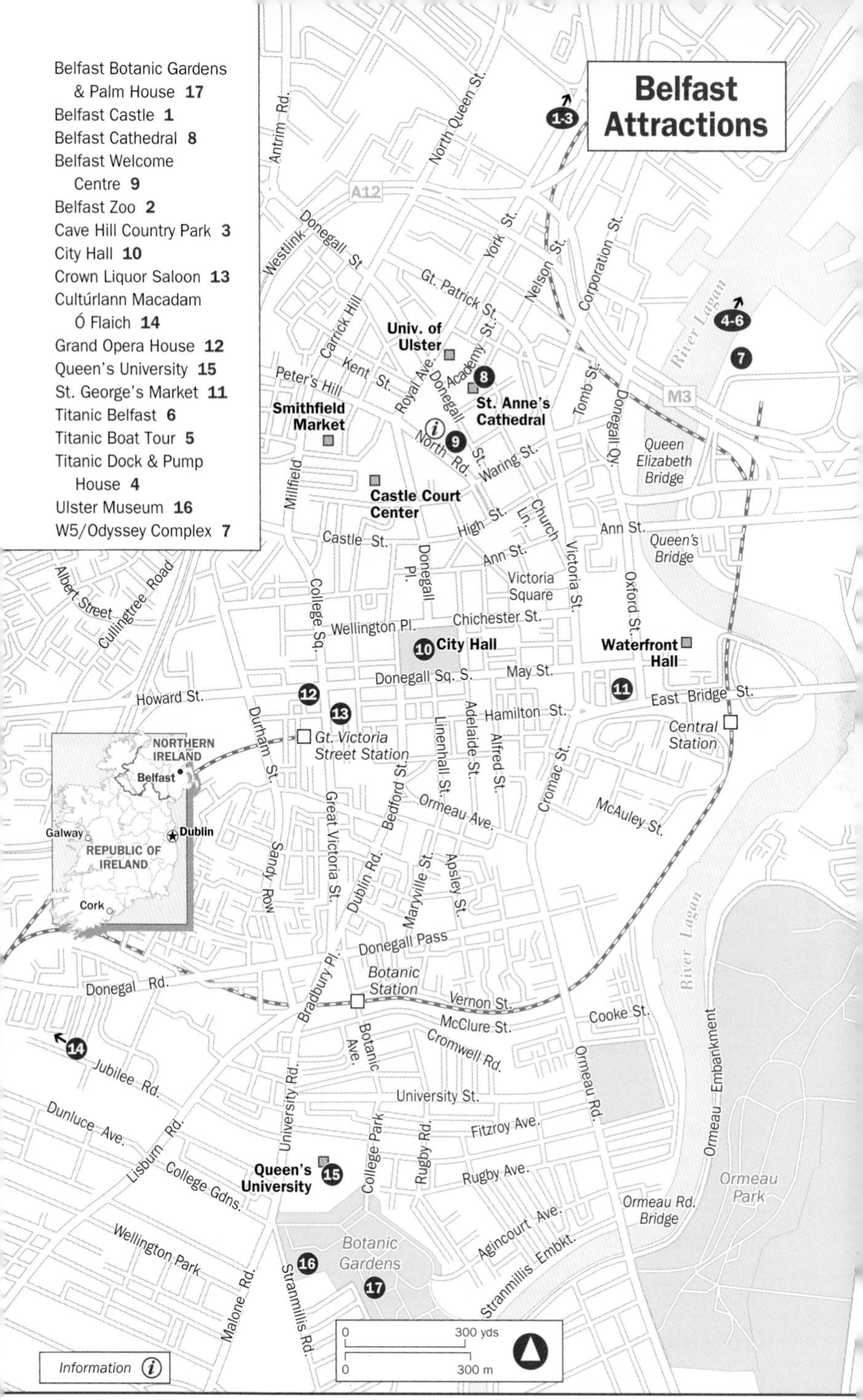
Belfast Attractions
Belfast Botanic Gardens & Palm House 17
Belfast Castle 1
Belfast Cathedral 8
Belfast Welcome Centre 9
Belfast Zoo 2
Cave Hill Country Park 3
City Hall 10
Crown Liquor Saloon 13
Cultúrlann Macadam Ó Flaich 14
Grand Opera House 12
Queen's University 15
St. George's Market 11
Titanic Belfast 6
Titanic Boat Tour 5
Titanic Dock & Pump House 4
Ulster Museum 16
W5/Odyssey Complex 7
Univ. of Ulster
St. Anne's Cathedral
Smithfield Market
Castle Court Center
City Hall
Waterfront Hall
Gt. Victoria Street Station
Central Station
Botanic Station
Queen's University
Botanic Gardens
Queen Elizabeth Bridge
Queen's Bridge
Ormeau Rd. Bridge
Ormeau Park
Victoria Square
River Lagan
A12
M3
Antrim Rd.
North Queen St.
Westlink
Donegall St.
York St.
Nelson St.
Corporation St.
Gt. Patrick St.
Carrick Hill
Academy St.
Kent St.
Peter's Hill
Royal Ave.
Donegall St.
North St.
Tomb St.
Donegall Qy.
Waring St.
Millfield
High St.
Church Ln.
Castle St.
Ann St.
Victoria St.
Donegall Pl.
Oxford St.
College Sq.
Wellington Pl.
Chichester St.
Albert Street
Cullingtree Road
Donegall Sq. S.
May St.
Howard St.
Hamilton St.
East Bridge St.
Durham St.
Linenhall St.
Adelaide St.
Alfred St.
Cromac St.
Bedford St.
Great Victoria St.
Ormeau Ave.
McAuley St.
Sandy Row
Dublin Rd.
Maryville St.
Apsley St.
Donegall Pass
Bradbury Pl.
Donegal Rd.
Vernon St.
Cooke St.
McClure St.
Cromwell Rd.
Botanic Ave.
Ormeau Rd.
Ormeau Embankment
Jubilee Rd.
University Rd.
University St.
Fitzroy Ave.
Dunluce Ave.
Lisburn Rd.
College Park
Rugby Rd.
Rugby Ave.
College Gdns.
Agincourt Ave.
Stranmillis Embkt.
Wellington Park
Malone Rd.
Stranmillis Rd.
NORTHERN IRELAND
Belfast
Galway
Dublin
REPUBLIC OF IRELAND
Cork
Information
0 300 yds
0 300 m

Belfast's City Hall on Donegall Square.

CITY CENTER Spreads out from around the impressive, domed City Hall building and bustling Donegall Square. This is the best place for shopping, particularly along **Donegall Place,** which extends north from the square, onto **Royal Avenue. Bedford Street,** which travels south from the **Donegall Square,** becomes **Dublin Road,** which, in turn, becomes:

UNIVERSITY QUARTER The leafy area around Queen's University. This is where you'll find the Botanic Gardens, art galleries, and museums, as well as a buzzing nightlife scene. Heading north from Donegall Place, it's a short distance to:

CATHEDRAL QUARTER Surrounds Donegall Street, and holds, as the name implies, the city's most important cathedrals, as well as many vast Victorian warehouses.

GOLDEN MILE The area around Great Victoria Street beyond Bradbury Place. It's considered the city's best address for restaurants and pubs, although it's a bit hyperbolically named. As one local said to us, "It's not a mile and it's not golden. But it's nice enough." Finally there's:

TITANIC QUARTER A series of big commercial developments around Belfast Harbour, to the northeast of the city center. This is where you'll find many of the city's biggest new purpose-built attractions.

Getting Around

Metro (✆ **028/9066-6630;** www.translink.co.uk) is the local bus service provider in Belfast. Buses depart from Donegall Square East, West, and North, plus

Upper Queen Street, Wellington Place, Chichester Street, and Castle Street, and from bus stops throughout the city. An information kiosk is located on Donegall Square West, and you can download timetables from the website.

If you've brought a **car** into Belfast, it's best to leave it parked and take public transportation or walk around the city. If you must drive and want to park your car downtown, look for a blue p sign that shows a parking lot or a parking area. Belfast has a number of "control zones," indicated by a pink-and-yellow sign, where no parking is permitted. In general, on-street parking is limited to an area behind City Hall (south side), Belfast (St. Anne's) Cathedral (north side), and around Queen's University and Ulster Museum.

Taxis are available at all main rail stations, ports, and airports, and in front of City Hall. Most metered taxis are London-type black cabs with a yellow disk on the window. Other taxis may not have meters, so you should ask about the fare to your destination in advance.

Exploring Belfast

Belfast's wealthy past has left the city with some handsome industrial remnants, and you could easily spend a couple of days here just exploring the more refined side of what Belfast has to offer. However, it's the more troubled, 20th century Belfast that many visitors find most intriguing, and a **Black Taxi Tour** (see p. 448) is a unique way to explore that history. Meanwhile, a whole new mini-industry of another kind has sprung up here with a tranche of new attractions related to the most famous shipwreck in history. The SS *Titanic* was built in Belfast, a fact that is a curious symbol of pride for natives of this city. The bold new **Titanic Belfast** museum and the **Titanic Dock and Pump House** are helping to draw shipwreck aficionados ("Titanoraks" as the locals rather endearingly call them) and tourists into the newly regenerated harbor district.

Belfast Castle ★ Northwest of downtown and 120m (394 ft.) above sea level stands Belfast Castle, whose 80-hectare (198-acre) estate spreads down the slopes of Cave Hill. Dating from 1870, this was the family residence of the third marquis of Donegall, and it was built in the style of Britain's Balmoral castle. The estate is a lovely place to visit, offering sweeping views of Belfast and the lough. Its cellars contain a nifty Victorian arcade, a restaurant (open 11am–5pm Wed–Mon, and 11am–9pm Tues), and a shop selling antiques and crafts. According to legend, a white cat brought the castle residents luck, so look around for carvings featuring this much-loved feline. This is also the location of the Cave Hill Country Park visitor center (see p. 450).

Signposted off Antrim Rd., 2½ miles (4km) north of the city center, Belfast, BT15 5GR. ✆ **028/9077-6925.** www.belfastcastle.co.uk. Free admission and parking. Mon–Sat 9am–10pm; Sun 9am–6pm.

Belfast Cathedral ★ The foundation stone on this monumental cathedral, also known as **St. Anne's,** was laid in 1899. It remained incomplete for more than a century; even now it still awaits a steeple. Crisscrossing architectural genres from Romanesque to Victorian to modern, the huge structure is more attractive inside than out. In the nave, the ceiling soars above the black-and-white marble walls and stone floors, and elaborate stained-glass windows fill it with color. Carvings that represent life in Belfast top the 10 pillars. The cathedral's most impressive features, though, are the delicate mosaic ceilings of the tympanum, and the baptistery constructed of thousands of pieces of glass.

Donegall St., Belfast, BT1 2HB. ✆ **028/9032-8332.** www.belfastcathedral.org. Free admission (£2 donation requested). Mon–Sat 8am–6pm; Sun 8–11am, 12:30–4pm.

Belfast Zoo ★ In a picturesque mountain park on the slopes of Cave Hill just outside of town and overlooking the city, this zoo was founded in 1920 as Bellevue Gardens and has been completely modernized in recent years. It emphasizes conservation and education, and focuses on breeding rare species, including Hawaiian geese, lowland gorillas, red lechwe (a kind of antelope), sea bears, Barbary lions, and golden lion tamarins. The Rainforest House is a tropical environment filled with birds and jungle creatures. Special tours and one-off events run all year. Most activity days are quite kid-oriented, although there are also some more grown-up events too, such as all-day photography competitions. Check the website for up-to-date listings.

Antrim Rd., Belfast, BT36 7PN. ✆ **028/9077-6277.** www.belfastzoo.co.uk. Admission £10.50 adults; £5.50 seniors, students and children; £28 families. Apr–Sept Mon–Fri 10am–6pm; Sat–Sun 10am–7pm (last admission 5pm, animal houses close 6pm). Oct–Mar daily 10am–4pm (last admission 2:30pm, animal houses close 3:30pm).

Black Taxi Tour ★★★ For many years, Belfast was best known for its most conflicted neighborhoods, where in the 1970s and '80s protest and violence occurred daily. For anyone born before 1990, the name Belfast is probably still synonymous with sectarianism, even though peace has (precariously) held on the Catholic Falls Road and its nearby parallel, the Protestant Shankill Road, for

Black Taxi Tours transport visitors safely through formerly troubled neighborhoods to see the Bogside Murals.

the art of conflict: **BELFAST'S STREET MURALS**

The huge street murals in West Belfast are painted by amateur artists, albeit immensely talented ones. Each mural tells a tale of history, strife, anger, or peace. The densest concentration is around the **Falls and Shankill roads.** During the Troubles, from the late 1960s to the mid-1990s, this area was the center of the conflict. That dark chapter officially ended with the Good Friday Agreement of 1998, but divisions between some Catholic and Protestant communities still run deep and raw.

The Falls Road is staunchly Catholic and Republican (i.e., those who want to see Ireland united as a single country). Shankill, just half a mile away, is resolutely Protestant and Loyalist (those who want Northern Ireland to remain part of the United Kingdom).

Although all are deeply political, there is a noticeable divide between the tones of the murals. Those on the Falls Road tend to be about solidarity with the downtrodden (and not just in Ireland—you'll see murals about war and oppression in other parts of the world too). On the corner of Falls Road and Sevastopol Street is the surprisingly small Sinn Fein headquarters. At one end of the building is a mural of the late hunger striker **Bobby Sands** (1954–81), arguably the most famous political mural in Ireland.

By contrast, the Shankill murals are generally darker, featuring more violent and threatening imagery, although some of the worst were removed a few years ago.

Locals in all districts are very proud of their murals and are used to people visiting to take photos. They're safe to visit, but you should still exercise the usual caution you would in any rough city neighborhood. It's also advisable to avoid these parts of town on **parade days**—ostensibly celebratory events, these tend towards unpleasant displays of nationalism, erupting into street violence. The biggest, and most controversial, is the Protestant "Orange Order" parade on July 12th. Any parades that are likely to cause trouble are well covered by the local media, though, so it's easy to know when one is coming up.

The best, safest, and certainly the most informative way to see the murals is to take a **Black Taxi Tour** (see p. 448). The tours are a real Belfast highlight, and could hardly be more convenient—the drivers will pick you up at your hotel and drop you off anywhere you like in the city.

nearly 15 years. Today there's a growing industry around exploring these infamous districts, and Black Taxi Tour is by far the best one. The tours are conducted in London-style cabs that take you through the neighborhoods, past the barbed wire, towering fences, and partisan murals, as guides explain their significance. Drivers, who are all locals, are relaxed, patient, and unbiased, with a talent for explaining this complicated history to outsiders in an easy and engaging way. Tours aren't just limited to politics; the guides will also take you to see the *Titanic* shipyard and other parts of the city if you wish. Just ask when you book. The standard tour lasts about 90 minutes, and guides will pick you up and drop you off anywhere in the city.

Belfast. ✆ **028/9064-2264.** www.belfasttours.com. £25 for up to 2 passengers, then £10 for each additional passenger, up to 6 people.

Belfast Botanic Gardens

Belfast Botanic Gardens & Palm House ★ Dating from 1828, these gardens were established by the Belfast Botanic and Horticultural Society. Ten years later, they gained a glass house, or conservatory, designed by noted Belfast architect Charles Lanyon. Now known as the Palm House, this unique structure contains an excellent variety of tropical plants, including sugar cane, coffee, cinnamon, banana, aloe, ivory nut, rubber, bamboo, guava, and spindly birds of paradise. If the weather's fine, stroll in the outdoor rose gardens that date back to 1927. They occasionally hold festivals and other special events here; check local listings for details.

College Park, Botanic Avenue, Belfast, BT7 1LP. ✆ **028/9031-4762.** Free admission. Palm House and Tropical Ravine Apr–Sept Mon–Fri daily 1–5pm; Oct–Mar daily 1–4pm. Gardens daily 7:30am–sunset.

Cave Hill Country Park ★★ This park atop a 360m (1,181-ft.) basalt cliff offers panoramic views, walking trails, and archaeological and historical sights. The park gets its name from five small caves thought to have been Neolithic iron mines; several other ancient sites are scattered about the place, often unmarked. These include stone cairns, dolmens, and **McArt's Fort**—the remains of an ancient defensive hill fort in which Wolfe Tone and his fellow United Irishmen planned the 1798 rebellion. It's mostly gone now, but you can explore the ruins, which sit atop the park's most famous viewpoint. The **Cave Hill Visitor Centre,** on the second floor of Belfast Castle (see p. 447), contains a diverting exhibition on the history of the park and the castle itself. You can also pick up maps of the park here. A great walk around the entire circuit of the park can be found on the website of Walk NI, a useful link set up to promote hiking in Northern Ireland. The route description, plus a handy map, can be downloaded from www.walkni.com/walks/79/cave-hill-country-park. It should be manageable for anyone of reasonable fitness, though it may be too challenging for children; ask for advice at the park visitor center before you set out.

Visitor Center: Belfast Castle, off Antrim Rd., 4 miles (6.5km) north of city center, Belfast, BT15 5GR. ✆ **028/9077-6925.** www.belfastcity.gov.uk/parksandopenspaces. Free admission. Visitor Center: Mon–Sat 9am–10pm; Sun 9am–5:30pm.

City Hall ★ This glorious explosion of granite, marble, and stained glass is testament to Belfast's grand industrial past. Built in classical Renaissance style in 1906, it has white Portland stone walls and a soft green copper dome. Several statues are on the grounds, including a grim-faced statue of Queen Victoria that stands out front, looking as if she wished she were anywhere else. Bronze figures around her represent the textile and shipbuilding industries that powered Belfast's success. There's also a memorial to the victims of the *Titanic* disaster. Inside the building, the elaborate entry hall is heavy with marble but lightened by stained glass and a rotunda with a painted ceiling. Somehow it all manages not to be tacky. Exhibitions are often upstairs, and to learn more about the building's history, take a free guided tour. Call or ask in the lobby for details.

Donegall Sq. North, Belfast, BT1 5GS. ✆ **028/9027-0456.** Free admission. Guided tours Mon–Fri 11am, 2, 3pm; Sat 2, 3pm; otherwise by appointment.

Crown Liquor Saloon ★★★ Easily the most impressive Victorian pub in the city, and possibly the country, the Crown Liquor Saloon piles on the atmosphere as thick as fog. The old "gin palace," as pubs of this era are known, owes its elaborate appearance to Italian workers who had come to Ireland in the late 19th century to work on churches but ended up finding work here. Some of the finer features definitely have something ecclesiastical about them, from the stained glass in the windows to the pew-like "snugs," complete with elaborately

JOINING THE national trust

Several of Ulster's best historic sites are managed by the **National Trust,** a not-for-profit organization that preserves thousands of buildings and areas of natural beauty across the U.K. (including Northern Ireland), keeping them accessible to the public. Taking out a yearly membership gives you unlimited free admission to all of them, which can work out cheaper if you plan to visit several. If you also happen to be visiting Britain on your trip, or within the same year, it could be a wise investment.

The current membership costs are £55.50 for individuals, £92 for couples, [b]26 for children, and £60.50 to £97 for families. You can sign up for membership at any National Trust property, or join in advance online at **www.nationaltrust.org.uk**.

Alternatively, American visitors can join the U.S. wing of the National Trust, the **Royal Oak Foundation.** Call ✆ **212/480-2889** or visit **www.royal-oak.org** for more information. Royal Oak members get the same benefits, plus money off lectures, tours, and other special events held in the U.S.

Queen's University in Belfast.

carved doors designed to shield the more refined class of Victorian patrons from their fellow drinkers. The floors are intricately tiled and the ceiling is made of hammered copper. This place was considered so important to the iconography of Belfast that it was actually bought for the nation by the National Trust in the 1970s. This ensures its impeccable upkeep while it continues to run as a working pub.

46 Great Victoria St., Belfast, BT2 7BA. ✆ **028/9024-3187.** www.nicholsonspubs.co.uk/thecrownliquorsaloonbelfast. Mon–Wed 11:30am–11pm; Thurs–Sat 11:30am–midnight; Sun 12:30–10pm.

Cultúrlann Macadam Ó Flaich ★ Located on the Falls Road, this cultural and arts center is a friendly, inclusive place. The former church building contains a handy cafe, a tourist information point and well stocked shop, full of Irish interest books, traditional crafts and music CDs. The **Dillon Gallery,** West Belfast's only public art gallery, showcases work by Irish artists, and those from further afield. There's also a theater, with a varied program of traditional music, plays, spoken word events and films. Check the website for listings.

216 Falls Rd., Belfast, BT12 6AH. ✆ **028/9096-4180.** www.culturlann.ie. Free admission. Mon–Thurs 9am–9pm; Fri–Sat 9am–6pm; Sun 11am–4pm.

Queen's University ★ Founded during the reign of Queen Victoria in 1845 to provide nondenominational higher education, this is Northern Ireland's most prestigious university. The main, 19th-century Tudor revival building may remind you of England's Oxford, especially because its design was based on that of the Founder's Tower at Magdalen College. But that's hardly all there is to this university, which sprawls through 250 buildings and where 17,500 students are studying at any given time. The whole neighborhood around the university is a quiet, attractive place to wander, and University Square on the north side of campus is simply beautiful. At one end of the square is the Union Theological College, dating from 1853, which housed the Northern Ireland Parliament after the partition of Ireland in 1921 until its abolition in 1972. Tours of the campus can be arranged on request; contact the university's welcome center for details. Access to parts of the campus may be restricted during exam times.

Queen's Welcome Centre, Queen's University, University Rd., Belfast, BT7 1NN. ✆ **028/9097-5252.** www.queenseventus.com/QueensWelcomeCentre. Free admission; tours £3.50 per person. Mon–Fri 9:30am–4:30pm; also Sat–Sun 11am–4pm during summer vacation.

St. George's Market ★ This eclectic street market is one of the city's oldest attractions. The current iron-and-glass structure opened in 1896, although a market has been held on this spot for much longer. Friday is the **Variety Market** that's packed with 250 stalls of fresh produce, antiques, clothing, and bric-a-brac. There's also a lively fishmarket that supplies many of the local restaurants. On Saturday the **City Food and Craft Market** specializes in artisan foods with plenty of tempting fresh snacks on offer, plus a nice assortment of local crafts. The **Sunday Market** is a happy combination of the two, although the balance tends to be in favor of crafts.

May St. at Oxford St., Belfast, BT1 3NQ. ✆ **028/9043-5704.** Free admission. Fri 6am–2pm; Sat 9am–3pm; Sun 10am–4pm.

Titanic Belfast ★★★ This ambitious new museum, which opened in 2012 to great fanfare, tells the story of the *Titanic* in revelatory detail. Located next to the very site where the doomed vessel was constructed, the enormous, angular frontage, clad in 2000 individual sheets of aluminum, juts out in four directions at the actual height of Titanic's bow. The innovative design continues across the nine well laid-out galleries covering everything from the *Titanic*'s construction to the triumphant launch, disastrous sinking, and the lasting cultural phenomenon that rose in her wake. A special ride takes you on a virtual tour of the shipyard to see how *Titanic*, and her sister ship, *Olympic*, were built. In a split-level gallery you can even "explore" the wreck yourself, via enormous high definition screens and other interactive gizmos. Finally, the **Ocean Exploration Centre** takes the story into the 21st century with high-tech exhibits on the science of sea exploration, including a live link to an undersea probe. In truth the content can sometimes feel stretched to fill the space, but it's all impressively done. Needless to say, an extremely well stocked gift shop is at the end. Crowds can swell at busy times, so it's advisable to book ahead.

1 Olympic Way, Belfast, BT3 9DP. ✆ **028/9076-6386.** www.titanicbelfast.com. Admission £13.50 adults; £10 seniors–weekdays; £11.50 seniors–weekends; £9.50 students; £7 children 5–16; children 4 and under free; £34 families. Parking £1.50 per hr. for 1st hr., then £1 per hr. afterwards. Apr–Sept daily 9am–7pm; Oct–Mar daily 10am–5pm. Last admission 1 hr. 40 min. before closing.

Titanic Boat Tour ★ Many historic shipyard buildings were demolished in the early 2000s to make way for new development, a controversial move, but one that also opened up long obscured views of the harbor from the river. This jaunty and informative boat trip takes you past many of them. Despite the name, there aren't that many *Titanic*-related sights left, but this is also a good introduction to Belfast's maritime past and a pleasant way to spend an hour. With typically dry Belfast wit, the crew t-shirts read "She was alright when she left here." In summer the tour goes as far as Musgrave Channel, home to a large breeding colony of seals. The departure point is on Donegall Quay, about 100m (330 ft.) to the left of the big fish sculpture.

The Obel, Donegall Quay, Belfast, BT3 3NG. ✆ **028/9024-0124.** www.laganboatcompany.com. Admission £10 adults; £8 seniors, students and children 6–16; children 5 and under free; £30 families. Tours daily 12:30, 2, 3:30pm (no 3:30 tour in winter). Tours daily 12:30, 2, 3:30pm. (No 3:30pm tour in winter.)

Titanic Dock and Pump House ★★ Another of Belfast's major ship-related attractions, this fascinating tour takes you around the dry docks at the old Harland and Wolff shipyard, where *Titanic* and *Olympic* were constructed from 1909–11. Designed to appeal to a general audience, not just enthusiasts, it's a great way to learn about what it was really like to work here at the turn of the last century, when Belfast was one of the world's greatest industrial cities. The enormous Edwardian pump house, that could drain a staggering 21 million gallons of water in just over an hour and a half, is worth the price of admission by itself. An audio-visual room includes some rare film footage of the Titanic in situ at the dock. Fully guided versions of the tour take place daily at 3 and 4pm; if you want to join one of these tickets cost a couple of pounds extra. The large visitor center also has plenty of interesting exhibits, a gift shop, and a cafe.

Queen's Rd., Queen's Island, Belfast, BT3 9DT. ✆ **028/9073-7813.** www.titanicsdock.com. Admission £5 adults; £4 seniors–weekdays; £4.50 seniors–weekends; £4 students; £3 children 5–16; children 4 and under free, £12 families. Mon–Thurs 10am–6pm, Fri 9:30am–6pm, Sat–Sun 10am–6pm.

Ulster Museum ★★★ This is one of Belfast's best and most comprehensive museums. The collection is impressive, from dinosaur bones and prehistoric artifacts to art and other treasures from Ireland and around the world. Highlights include a collection of 16th to 18th century Dutch and Italian paintings; a hoard of priceless 16th century Spanish jewelry, recovered off the coast near Belfast in the 1960s; clothes, textiles, and ceramics from Asia and Africa; and items relating to the Ascendancy, the period of Protestant rule in Ireland that finally came to a head with the rebellion of 1798. The collection of objects from the Classical world is particularly strong; the **Life and Death in Ancient Egypt** exhibit has about 2,000 artifacts from Pharaonic times (including a mummy), as well as items from ancient Mesopotamia, Rome, and Greece. The museum's events calendar often has special exhibitions, talks, and even the occasional concert; check the website to see what's on.

The Ulster Museum explores 9,000 years of Irish history.

Carrickfergus Castle in County Antrim.

At the Botanic Gardens, Belfast, BT9 5AB. ✆ **028/9044-0000.** www.nmni.com. Free admission. Tues–Sun 10am–5pm. Closed Mon (except Bank Holidays).

W5 ★ This great hands-on science play center for kids is part of the Odyssey Complex, a huge indoor arena on Queen's Quay that's bursting with activities. Properly known as "Whowhatwhenwherewhy"—you can see why they abbreviate it to W5—it's a high-tech, interactive learning environment. Kids can take part in over 250 individual activities, all in the spirit of science-based fun. They can do everything from create animated cartoons, try to beat a lie detector test, and even present the weather on TV. There are also plenty of special events and temporary exhibitions. The Odyssey also contains a cinema, game arcades, and a sports arena.

2 Queen's Quay, BT3 9QQ. ✆ **028/9046-7700.** www.w5online.co.uk. Admission £8 adults; £6.50 seniors and students; £6 children; £22–£38.50 families. Mon–Sat 10am–6pm, Sun noon–6pm; last admission 1 hr. before closing.

Day Trips from Belfast

Just outside Belfast off the M3 motorway, the castle town of **Carrickfergus** offers a nice break from the hustle and bustle of the city, and some fresh sea air. Locals like to say that Carrickfergus was thriving when Belfast was a sandbank, and looking around its winding medieval streets at the edge of the sea, it's easy to believe. In 1180 John de Courcy, a Norman, built a massive keep at Carrickfergus, the first real Irish castle, to guard the approach to the strategically critical **Belfast Lough.** Even today, although the town spreads for several miles in each direction along the shore, the huge, forbidding castle is still its center. The narrow streets across from the castle follow the historic winding pattern of medieval roads, and you can still find some of the old city walls.

Meanwhile, on the other side of the Lough, **Cultra** is a relatively nondescript residential suburb with one big attraction—the excellent **Ulster Folk & Transport Museum.** And a short drive south of Belfast, the charming little town of **Downpatrick** is a major destination for those with an interest in Ireland's patron saint.

Andrew Jackson Cottage and U.S. Rangers Centre ★ This recreated 18th century dwelling is built in the style of cottages once lived in by Scotch-Irish settlers—including the ancestors of Andrew Jackson (1767–1845), the 7th President of the United States. The cottage is restored to how it would have looked in the 1750s; also here is an exhibition devoted to the life of Jackson, who was the first President of Irish extraction. Though it's as faithful a reproduction as can reasonably be expected, the house isn't the actual home of the Jacksons—that was demolished in the 19th century. Next door is a small museum devoted to the U.S. Rangers, who were stationed in Carrickfergus during World War II.

2 Boneybefore, Carrickfergus, BT38 7EQ. ✆ **028/9335-8049.** Free admission. June–Sept Mon–Fri 10am–1pm; Sat–Sun 10am–1pm, 2–6pm. Oct–May Fri–Sat 11am–3pm. Hours may vary; call to check.

Carrickfergus Castle ★ This impressive Norman castle looms darkly over the entrance to Belfast Lough, where William of Orange landed on June 1690 en route to the Battle of the Boyne. The central part dates to the 12th century, the thick outer walls were completed 100 years later, and the gun ports are a relatively new addition at only 400 years old. The outside is more impressive than the inside, which has been largely dedicated to inspiring young imaginations. The use of waxwork figures (riding horses, threatening to shoot people over the walls) is a bit over-the-top, although sometimes actors in medieval costume add a touch of hammy fun. The castle has a visitor center and a small museum. In the summer, medieval banquets, a medieval fair, and a crafts market are held, all adding a touch of play and pageantry.

Marine Highway, Carrickfergus, BT38 7BG. ✆ **028/9335-1273.** Admission £5 adults £3 seniors and children. Apr–Sept daily 10am–6pm; Oct–Mar daily 10am–4pm. Carrickfergus is on A2, 12 miles northeast of Belfast.

Ulster Folk & Transport Museum ★★★ As one of Northern Ireland's best living history museums, the Ulster Folk & Transport Museum is made up of buildings rescued from demolition and reconstructed, piece by piece. The majority of the buildings are from the 19th century; they include houses, schools, a chemist, a pub, and even a working farm. The level of detail is impressive—the shops are fully decked out as they would have been in Victorian times, complete with shelves overflowing with authentic bottles, jars, and items of clothing. Costumed guides add to the sense of fun. As you wander about you may encounter a Victorian housewife engaged in some day-to-day household drudgery or watch a village blacksmith working away in a forge using authentic methods from the period. Frequent special events include craft demonstrations and classes, horse-drawn vehicle days, or wildlife hunts. The Transport Museum contains a wealth of historic vehicles, from old cars and small planes, to buses and trams.

Signposted off A2 (Bangor Rd.), Cultra, Hollywood, Co. Down, BT18 0EU. ✆ **028/9042-8428.** www.nmni.com/uftm. Folk or Transport Museum: £7.50 adults; £5 seniors and student; £4.50

children 5–17; children 4 and under free; £15.50–£21 families. Combined ticket to both museums: £9 adults; £5.50 seniors and students; £5 children 5–17, children 4 and under free; £18.50–£24 families. Mar–Sept Tues–Sun 10am–5pm; Oct–Feb Tues–Fri 10am–4pm, Sat–Sun 11am–4pm. Closed Mon (except Bank Holidays).

DOWNPATRICK: sainted TOWN

The charming town of Downpatrick is closely identified with St. Patrick. Legend has it that when Patrick came to Ireland in A.D. 432 to begin his missionary work, strong winds blew his boat here. He'd meant to sail up the coast to County Antrim, where as a young slave he had tended flocks on Slemish Mountain. Instead, he settled here and converted the local chieftain Dichu and his followers to Christianity. Over the next 30 years, Patrick roamed through Ireland carrying out his work, but this is where he died, and some believe he is buried in the graveyard of Downpatrick Cathedral, although there's no proof. Because of all of this, the town tends to be crowded, largely with Catholic pilgrims, around St. Patrick's Day, but the constant activities and religious fervor are worth witnessing.

Stop in first at the **Down County Museum,** The Mall, English St., BT30 6AH. Set in a converted jail, the museum tells the story of Down from the Stone Age to the present day. They also have an extremely flashy *son et lumiere* (sound and light) show, which is projected onto the old prison walls; and a handy tea-room. The museum opens weekdays from 10am to 5pm, and weekends from noon to 5pm.

Almost next door to the museum, at the end of the English Street cul-du-sac, is **Down Cathedral** (✆ **028/4461-4922;** www.downcathedral.org). Excavations show that Downpatrick was a *dún* (or fort), perhaps as early as the Bronze Age, and its earliest structures were built on the site where this church now sits. Ancient fortifications ultimately gave way to a series of churches, each built atop the ruins of the previous incarnation, over 1,800 years. The current cathedral is an 18th- and 19th-century reconstruction of its 13th- and 16th-century predecessors. Just south of the cathedral stands a relatively recent monolith inscribed with the name "Patric". By some accounts, it roughly marks the grave of the saint, who is said to have died at Saul, 2 miles (3km) northeast. The tradition identifying this site as Patrick's grave seems to go back no further than the 12th century, though, when John de Courcy reputedly transferred the bones of saints Columba and Brigid to lie beside those of St. Patrick. The Cathedral is open to visitors Monday to Saturday from 9:30am to 4:30pm. Entry is free.

A 5-minute walk away Is **St. Patrick Centre,** 53A Market St., BT30 6LZ (✆ **028/4461-9000;** www.saintpatrickcentre.com). Housed in a modern glass-and-steel building, the center tells the story of Ireland's patron saint, through high-tech displays and exhibits. There's also an exhibition devoted to legacy of the Irish missionaries who helped spread Christianity in Europe in the latter half of the first millennium. The center is open Monday to Saturday from 9am to 5pm; also Sunday 1 to 5pm in July and August. Entry costs £5.50 adults, £3.75 seniors and students, £3 children and £13 families.

Downpatrick is about 21 miles (34km) southeast of Belfast. To get there from the city by car take A24 then A7; the drive takes just under 40 minutes. Alternatively you can get there by bus from the main Europa Bus Station on Great Victoria St. The journey takes an hour.

Sports & Outdoor Pursuits

CYCLING Cave Hill Country Park (p. 450) has dedicated mountain bike trails. To hire a bike try **Full Cycle,** 387 Antrim Rd., Belfast, BT15 3BG (✆ **028/9074-1569** or 0845/839-3280; www.fullcyclebikeshop.com). Their service is pretty comprehensive, but they do insist that you make reservations at least 24 hours in advance, and preferably a full week.

FISHING The 5½-mile (9km) stretch of the Lagan River from the Stranmillis weir to Shaw's Bridge offers decent coarse fishing, especially on summer evenings. From May to July, Lough Neagh has good shore and boat fishing. For fishing equipment and contacts try **Get Hooked,** 4 Woodbourne Crescent, Belfast, BT11 9PH (✆ **028/9062-3431**). For info, tackle, and bait, try the **Village Tackle Shop,** 55a Newtownbreda Rd., Belfast (✆ **028/9049-1916;** www.villagetackleshopbelfast.co.uk).

GOLF The Belfast area offers four 18-hole courses within 3¾ miles (6km) of the city center. Some 3 miles (5km) southwest of the city, is the **Balmoral Golf Club,** 518 Lisburn Rd., Belfast (✆ **028/9038-1514;** www.balmoralgolf.com), with greens fees of £27 to £33. About 3¾ miles (6km) southwest of the city center the **Dunmurry Golf Club,** 91 Dunmurry Lane, Dunmurry, Belfast (✆ **028/9061-0834;** www.dunmurrygolfclub.co.uk), costs £30 to £32. About 3 miles (4.8km) south of the city center is the **Belvoir Park Golf Club,** 73 Church Rd., Newtownbreda, Belfast (✆ **028/9064-6714;** www.belvoirparkgolfclub.com), £30 to £75; and 3 miles (4.8km) north, the **Fortwilliam Golf Club,** Downview Avenue, Belfast (✆ **028/9037-0770;** www.fortwilliamgc.co.uk), £20 weekdays, £24 weekends (in truly old fashioned style, women are charged a few pounds less). Weekdays are usually better for visitors, and each club has preferred weekdays. Phone ahead.

Where to Stay in & Around Belfast

Belfast's hotel scene has grown in leaps and bounds during the last few years. A decade ago, expecting to find a top quality boutique hotel or B&B from £100 per room was a tough task; today, however, you have much more to choose from. Best of all, because Belfast is still developing as a major tourist destination, the prices are still relatively low—although depending on where you're from, that advantage can be quickly wiped out by the exchange rate, which can often be more punishing to pounds than it is to euros.

Dunnanelly Country House ★★★ This delightful country mansion is just outside Downpatrick, about 18 miles (29km) south of Belfast, but the half-hour or so it takes to drive here from the city is a very trivial price to pay for such a relaxing location. The beautiful grounds stretch on for over 32 hectares (80 acres). The decor inside mixes up a feeling of history with a playful edge; traditional, Regency-style color schemes and furnishings, offset by pieces of modern art, an interesting sculpture, or (memorably, in the entrance hall/piano room) an antique rocking horse, complete with mouth open in an oh-so-happy-to-see-you grin. The guestrooms are thoughtfully designed with large, modern bathrooms and have lovely views of the estate that's just begging to be discovered on a gentle stroll or invigorating hike. And you may need that exercise to help work off the hearty and delicious breakfasts. Guests have the use of a conservatory, a sitting room, and a separate game room. There's no

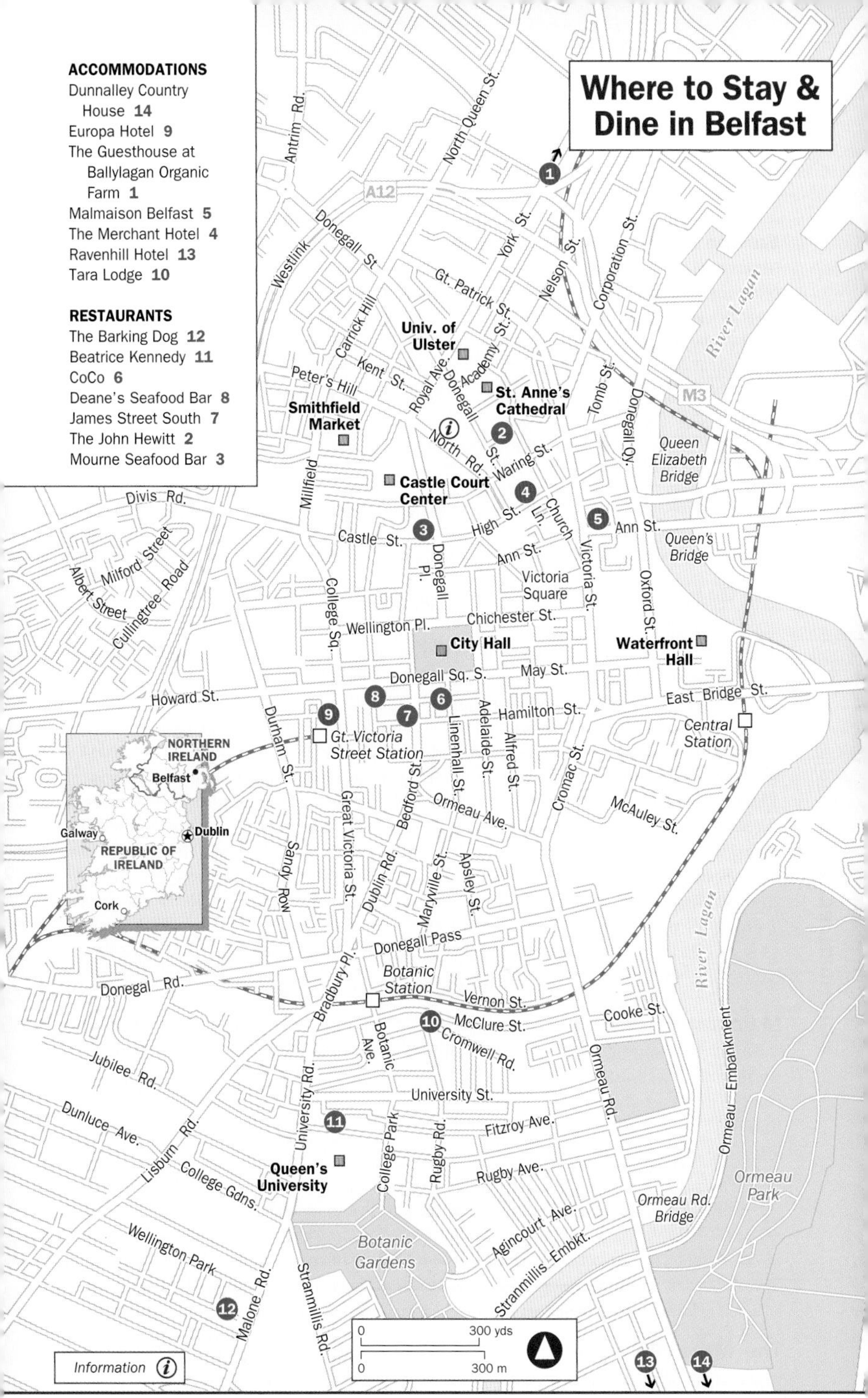
Where to Stay & Dine in Belfast
ACCOMMODATIONS
Dunnalley Country House 14
Europa Hotel 9
The Guesthouse at Ballylagan Organic Farm 1
Malmaison Belfast 5
The Merchant Hotel 4
Ravenhill Hotel 13
Tara Lodge 10
RESTAURANTS
The Barking Dog 12
Beatrice Kennedy 11
CoCo 6
Deane's Seafood Bar 8
James Street South 7
The John Hewitt 2
Mourne Seafood Bar 3
Univ. of Ulster
St. Anne's Cathedral
Smithfield Market
Castle Court Center
City Hall
Waterfront Hall
Victoria Square
Gt. Victoria Street Station
Central Station
Botanic Station
Queen's University
Botanic Gardens
Ormeau Park
Queen Elizabeth Bridge
Queen's Bridge
Ormeau Rd. Bridge
River Lagan
NORTHERN IRELAND
Belfast
Dublin
Galway
REPUBLIC OF IRELAND
Cork
0 300 yds
0 300 m
Information

dinner, but the owners can cheerfully point you in the direction of the best local pubs. This is a truly idyllic retreat.

26 Rocks Chapel Rd., Downpatrick, Co. Down, BT30 9BA. ✆ **077/1277-9085.** www.dunnanellycountryhouse.com. 3 units. £120 double. Free parking. Breakfast included. No children under 12 unless all 3 rooms booked by same group. **Amenities:** Wi-Fi (free).

Europa Hotel ★★ For some time this has been a lodging of choice for big-name politicians, diplomats, and celebrities when visiting Belfast (Hilary Clinton stayed here a couple of years ago). The large bedrooms are contemporary in style, with comfortable beds and modern furnishings. A little rubber ducky in a top hat is waiting for you as you enter the bathroom (you can take it home if you want). It's a nice touch and indicative of the attention to detail here. Downstairs is a piano bar and the laidback **Causerie** restaurant. Check the website for deals such as a theater package that includes tickets to the Grand Opera House (see p. 466) *and* return train travel from Dublin, for around £100 per couple.

Great Victoria St. Belfast, BT2 7AP. ✆ **028/9027-1066.** www.hastingshotels.com/europa-belfast. 240 units. £75–£260 double; £500–£750 suite. Free parking. Breakfast not included in lower rates. **Amenities:** Wi-Fi (free); restaurant; 2 bars; room service; gym.

The Guesthouse at Ballylagan Organic Farm ★★ Ballylagan is a working, fully certified organic farm (the first in Northern Ireland, no less) and at the center of it all is this welcoming little 1840s farmhouse. Patricia and Tom Gilbert are really passionate about what they do, and that ethos shines through everywhere, especially in the food. All the ingredients are completely organic (of course), from the fresh baked bread to the bacon and sausages at breakfast. Home-cooked dinners can be provided too, if booked in advance. (They can't serve wine, due to licensing restrictions, but you're welcome to bring your own.) The guestrooms are painted in soothing color schemes, with modern prints on the wall. They rooms are large enough to easily fit a sofa and a couple of chairs in addition to the extremely comfortable beds, so you certainly won't feel cramped here. For an extra charge of £10 per night you can have the use of a wood-burning stove in your room—and that will be smoldering away when you arrive. Ballyclare is about 13 miles (21km) north of Belfast.

12 Ballylagan Rd., Straid, Ballyclare, Belfast, BT39 9NF. ✆ **028/9332-2129.** www.ballylagan.com. 4 units. £90 double. Free parking. Rates include breakfast. **Amenities:** Wi-Fi (free).

Malmaison Belfast ★ This is the only Irish outpost of Malmaison, a British mini-chain that specializes in rescuing unusual historic buildings and turning them into hip boutique hotels. This one used to be a seed warehouse, of all things, and the chic, playful design in the public areas retains a few industrial touches. The result is deep purple carpets, gray or black walls, and steel girders left exposed here and there. Bedrooms are decorated in masculine tones of gray and brown with low lighting, huge beds, and modern bathrooms. The in-house restaurant serves decent, brasserie-style cooking (dinner, bed and breakfast packages are available) and there's a lively bar too.

34–38 Victoria St., Belfast, BT1 3GH. ✆ **084/4693-0650.** www.malmaison.com/locations/belfast. 64 units. £80–£145 double. Discounted parking at nearby lot (£10 per day). Breakfast not included in lower rates. **Amenities:** Wi-Fi (free); restaurant; bar; room service; gym.

The Merchant Hotel ★★★ One of Ireland's most luxurious hotels, a night at the Merchant is a real treat. The Victorian building used to be a bank;

it was only turned into an hotel in 2006, with a further, £17 million upgrade in 2010. The conversion is stunning, from the extraordinary dining room with its lacquered and gilded Corinthian columns, marble floors, and ceiling friezes to the elegant cocktail lounge with chandeliers and a gently curved, dark wood bar. Guest rooms are big and thoroughly modern, but ask for an Art Deco style room, as opposed to a traditional one—they're larger and better designed. There's an excellent **spa,** complete with hydrotherapy pool and treatment rooms and even a hot tub on the roof with a great view over the city. The **Great Room Restaurant** serves top-notch modern Irish cuisine. Afternoon tea is also a bit of an event here, and popular, so it's advisable to book if you want to indulge. Service is impeccable. The staff could hardly be friendlier or more helpful.

16 Skipper St., Belfast, BT1 2DZ. ✆ **028/9023-4888.** www.themerchanthotel.com. 62 units. £160–£240 double; £220–£300 suite. Valet parking. Breakfast not included in lower rates. Dinner, bed and breakfast packages available. **Amenities:** Wi-Fi (free); restaurant; bar; spa; gym.

Ravenhill Hotel ★★ A friendly welcome awaits from hosts Roger and Olive, whose handsome Victorian corner house has been converted into one of the best B&Bs in Belfast. They really know how to make guests feel at home, and nothing seems too much trouble. Bedrooms are simple but neat as a pin with print fabrics and views of the street. You're in a residential area here, but luckily not far from the action; the city center is about a 10-minute cab or bus ride. Roger cooks delicious breakfasts and guests can expect the full Ulster fry, in addition to a few lighter options such as kippers with parsley butter and scrambled eggs. They also bake their own traditional Irish wheaten bread from scratch, even down to milling their own flour. At certain times of the year you can get a discount for stays of two nights or more. You'll be hard pressed to find a better or more hospitable B&B at this price.

690 Ravenhill Rd., Belfast, BT6 0BZ. ✆ **028/9020-7444.** www.ravenhillhouse.com. 5 units. £75–£90 double. Free parking. Rates include breakfast. **Amenities:** Wi-Fi (free).

Tara Lodge ★ When Tara Lodge opened in the mid-2000s, it was part of a new wave of modern, inexpensive boutique-style small hotels in Belfast, a city where good budget accommodations were scarce. It has more competition these days, but Tara Lodge still manages to get everything just about right. Guestrooms are simple but contemporary in style, if perhaps a little small, but the beds are large and comfortable. Breakfasts are very good and offer plenty of choice. The **Botanic Gardens** (see p. 450) and **Ulster Museum** (see p. 454) are about

The Red Hand of Ulster

Around Belfast and Northern Ireland, you'll frequently come across representations of a red hand. It's carved in doorframes, painted on walls and ceilings, and even planted in red flowers in gardens. Known as the Red Hand of Ulster, it is one of the symbols of the region. According to one version of the old tale, the hand can trace its history from a battle between two men competing to be king of Ulster. They held a race (some say by boat, others say it took place on horseback) and agreed that the first man to touch Ulster soil would win. As one man fell behind, he pulled his sword and cut off his right hand, then with his left, flung the bloody hand ahead of his competitor, winning the right to rule.

10 minutes away on foot; you could walk to the city center in about 25, or it's a short cab ride. The only downside is that the hotel doesn't have a restaurant, but plenty of good options are within easy reach.

36 Cromwell Rd., Belfast, BT7 1JW. ✆ **028/9059-0900.** www.taralodge.com. 34 units. £83–£120 double. Free parking. Breakfast included. **Amenities:** Wi-Fi (free).

Where to Dine in Belfast

A prominent British journalist tells the story of ordering an Ulster fry in Belfast, sometime in the 1970s. "No sausage," he asked the waitress. When his food arrived, there were sausages on the plate. He sent it back, asking again for no sausage. But back it came, with sausages still there. "But I said no sausages," he complained. "Chef says sausage is compulsory," replied the waitress. Today the Belfast dining scene is, happily, much more cosmopolitan. The number of top restaurants in the city seems to increase year on year, from funky little gastropubs to chic fine dining.

The Barking Dog ★★ IRISH/INTERNATIONAL There's something quintessentially Belfast about this place—quirky, artsy, lively, but ultimately no nonsense. The dining room has a funky pub feel, complete with exposed brick and old candelabras balanced on battered wood tables. If you sit in the front garden, you're separated from the street by a fence with paw prints all over it. The menu is balanced and straightforward, with a juicy cheeseburger with fat French fries, for example, or a simple fish pie. The slightly more original items, such as the "nibbles and tipples" combo of tapas-style sharing plates, can be paired with house cocktails. There's a good lunch menu, and the Sunday brunch is popular.

33–35 Malone Rd., Belfast, BT9 6RU. ✆ **028/9066-1885.** www.barkingdogbelfast.com. Main courses £7–£15. Mon–Thurs noon–3pm, 5:30–10pm; Fri–Sat noon–3pm, 5:30–11pm; Sun noon–9pm. No children after 9pm.

Beatrice Kennedy ★★ IRISH This great little find in the heart of the University Quarter is great for traditional Irish cooking with a few modern flourishes. The dining room is quirky and small; maybe a little too much so, especially when it gets busy. You might start with some squid or perhaps scallops in a sweet orange sauce before moving on to some tender, pink roast duck with creamy mashed potato. Desserts are mostly sweet comfort food with some touches of invention. Try the mango and chocolate mousse if it's on offer. Early bird specials are a good value.

44 University Rd., Belfast, BT7 1NJ. ✆ **028/9020-2290.** www.beatricekennedy.co.uk. Main courses £12–£22. Tues–Fri noon–3pm, 5–9:30pm; Sat 5–10:30pm; Sun 12:30–2:30pm, 5–8:30pm.

CoCo ★★ MODERN EUROPEAN/INTERNATIONAL Coco's funky dining room is plastered in modern art along with posters and photo-collages that set the tone. The contemporary menu has an international flavor with dishes like goat cheese fritters served with essence of bell pepper, lamb with merguez sausage and couscous, and a Thai red chicken curry served with sticky rice and bok choi. The vegetarian menu is a pleasant surprise; try the "admiral pie" made with chili tofu, asparagus, sugar snap peas, and parsley cream. Prices are a little high for the evening service, but the pre-theater menu is a good value at three courses for £18. They also do a popular three-course Sunday lunch menu for £17.

7–11 Linenhall St., Belfast, BT2 8AA. ✆ **028/9031-1150.** www.cocobelfast.com. Main courses £17–£25. Mon–Fri noon–3pm, 6pm–midnight; Sat 6pm–midnight; Sun midday–4pm.

Deane's Seafood Bar ★★★ SEAFOOD Michael Deane is something of a local celebrity chef, and he's certainly come to dominate the Belfast dining scene. **Deane's,** his flagship, formal restaurant on Howard Street, still serves very good Irish-French cuisine, although the adjacent **Seafood Bar** is equally good, and (even better) less expensive. Here you'll find plates such as salt cod croquettes, tempura oysters, or crispy monkfish filet served with hot and sour peppers. At lunchtime main dishes are an astonishingly low £6.50 (plus extra for sides). Michael Deane now has four branches across Belfast, each cleverly going for a slightly different crowd, and sometimes sharing premises. There's the **Deli-Bistro** (✆ **028/902-8800**) and **Deli/Vin Café** (✆ **028/9024-8830**), a tapas bar, on Bedford Street; while in the University Quarter, next to the Ulster Museum, is the informal bistro, **Deane's at Queen's** (✆ **028/9038-2111**). The newest addition to the mini-empire is his foray into Italian cooking, **Deane and Decano** (✆ **028/9066-3108**), on Lisburn Road.

36–40 Howard St., Belfast, BT1 6PF. ✆ **028/9033-1134.** www.michaeldeane.co.uk. Main courses £13–£20. Mon–Sat noon–9:30pm.

James Street South ★★★ MODERN IRISH One of Belfast's leading restaurants, James Street South has built a great reputation on interesting, modern Irish cuisine, with an inventive twist. The food is indeed outstanding; you could start with some crispy mackerel with gooseberries, or razor clams served with a lime confit, followed by loin of lamb with glazed turnip, or turbot poached in wine with *buerre rouge* (a rich sauce made with butter, shallots, and red wine). Desserts could include a deliciously sweet lemon brulee, or you could embrace the spirit of discovery and have an assortment of Irish cheeses. Prices are surprisingly reasonable. A tasting menu is compact and interesting (£45 for four courses, or £65 with paired wines).

21 James St. South, Belfast, BT2 7GA. ✆ **028/9043-4310.** www.jamesstreetsouth.co.uk. Main courses £16–£21. Mon–Sat noon–2:45pm, 5:45–10:45pm.

The John Hewitt ★ IRISH/INTERNATIONAL This atmospheric bar near the Cathedral is a popular hangout with locals. The gastropub-style lunch menu is a real crowd pleaser, serving items like soup of the day with crusty bread, crispy squid with coriander (cilantro) rice, and a steak and onion sandwich made with Italian-style ciabatta bread and served with garlic butter. They don't serve food in the evenings or any time on Sundays, but you may still want to drop by—the John Hewitt is one of the best spots in the city for live music with bands every night from 9pm or 5:30pm on Saturday. Admission to gigs is usually free.

51 Donegall St., Belfast, BT1 2FH. ✆ **028/9023-3768.** www.thejohnhewitt.com. Main courses £4–£9. Mon–Fri 11:30am–1am; Sat noon–1am; Sun 7pm–midnight. (Food served Mon–Sat noon–3pm.)

Mourne Seafood Bar ★★★ SEAFOOD This is one of the best places in Belfast for top quality seafood. The dining room has a pleasing casual air—this is a seafood *bar* after all—but the food speaks entirely for itself. Oysters are a specialty, served traditionally, with Tabasco and lemon, or in more elaborate ways, such as with pickled ginger and soy dressing. Alternatively you could go for some crab claws with chili butter to start, before moving on to one of the fresh daily specials like seared scallops with pea risotto. The atmosphere is relaxed and convivial, and the prices are thoroughly reasonable for food this good. They don't take reservations at lunchtime, but evening booking is essential.

34–36 Bank St., Belfast, BT1 1HL. ✆ **028/9024-8544.** www.mourneseafood.com. Main courses £12–£17. Mon–Thurs noon–9:30pm; Fri, Sat noon–4pm, 5–10:30pm; Sun 1–6pm.

Shopping

Belfast is a surprisingly good place to shop. Start at Donegall Place, where the streets are lined with shops, and the Victorian arcades are filled with gift and jewelry stores. Good buys are to be had on Belleek china, linen, and crystal from County Tyrone. Shops are typically open weekdays from 9 or 9:30am to 5 or 5:30pm, and open later on weekends.

The main shopping street is **Royal Avenue,** home of several well-known chain stores, while the **Westfield Castlecourt Shopping Centre** on Royal Avenue and the glass-domed **Victoria Square** shopping center are Belfast's main downtown multistory shopping malls.

In addition to the selection below, don't forget to check out the lively and eclectic **St. George's Market** (p. 453).

ANTIQUES

Archive's Antiques Centre ★ Several dealers sell their wares at this sprawling center, with specialists in everything from silverware to pub memorabilia and militaria. 88 Donegall Pass, Belfast, BT7 1BX. ✆ **028/9023-2383.** www.archivesantique-centre.co.uk.

Oakland Antiques ★★ This enormous antiques emporium specializes in furniture, glassware, and other household items from the 18th to early 20th centuries. 135 Donegall Pass, BT7 1DS. ✆ **028/9023-0176.** www.oaklandantiques.co.uk.

BOOKS & STATIONERY

Kozo Paper ★★ A popular entry in the little black books of wedding planners all over Ireland, this great little store sells beautiful stationery from Japan and other parts of Asia. They specialize in wedding invitations, but also sell stationery for other occasions, plus notebooks and other papery delights.18 North St., Belfast, BT1 1LA. ✆ **028/9033-2321.**

No Alibis ★★ Here's a mystery to solve. You walk into this independent bookstore empty handed and come out carrying a bag filled with books and a lighter wallet. What happened in there? *J'accuse* no Alibis, with its excellent stock devoted to crime fiction from all over the world. You think your sweet little cafe out back will save you? No. You are guilty as charged. 83 Botanic Ave., Belfast, BT7 1JL. ✆ **028/9031-9601.** www.noalibis.com.

CRAFTS, DESIGN & HOMEWARE

Coppermoon ★★★ A riotously creative little boutique, Coppermoon sells interesting art and gorgeous little knick-knacks. Plenty of local designers get good representation, including makers of bags and accessories; funky, Steampunk-style jewelry; glass and ceramics; and quirky pieces of homeware, from lampshades made of bottles to wittily embroidered pillows. They also create beautiful, individually designed cards. 3 Wellington St., Belfast, BT1 6HT. ✆ **028/9023-5325.** www.coppermoon.co.uk.

Irish Linen and Gift Centre ★ This place stocks a huge range of Irish tablecloths, bed sheets and other linens, plus more traditional gift items, such as Belleek china, Aran sweaters, and a selection of Titanic merchandize. They're also an official seller of Guinness-related products, which means all the reproduction vintage posters and other branded knick-knacks you could shake a beer bottle opener at. 65 Royal Ave., Belfast, BT1 1FE. ✆ **028/9031-4272.** www.theirishlinenandgiftcentre.com.

The Wicker Man ★★ Don't be put off by how humdrum this place looks from the outside; within lies a creative and interesting selection of crafts, art and other souvenirs, from clocks and jewelry to bath products and musical instruments. This is one of the best places to shop for gifts in Belfast. 44–46 High St., Belfast, BT1 2BE. ✆ **028/9024-3550.** www.thewickerman.co.uk.

JEWELRY

The Steensons ★★★ This long-established showroom sells an outstanding collection of gold and silver jewelry. Most of what's on sale are their own designs, although they sell work by other top Irish designers too. Among their most popular lines are some elegant and tasteful limited edition pieces launched to commemorate the Titanic—the owner's grandfather was a crewmember on board. The showroom is behind Belfast City Hall. They also have a second branch on Toberwine Street in Glenarm, County Antrim (✆ **028/2884-1445**). Bedford St., Belfast, BT2 7FD. ✆ **028/9024-8269.** www.thesteensons.com.

FASHION & CLOTHING

The Bureau ★★ When this place opened in the late 1980s, it was something of a harbinger of the modern, cultured city Belfast would slowly become in the 1990s and 2000s. Today it remains one of the major men's fashion boutiques in the city, selling a fantastic range of clothes and footwear from its airy, stylish new shop on Newtownards Road, east of the Titanic Quarter. Portview, 310 Newtownards Rd., Belfast. ✆ **028/9046-0190.** www.thebureaubelfast.com.

Rojo ★★ This place is an absolute must for the well-heeled woman. Rojo specializes in women's shoes and boots, from a wide selection of top designers. They also sell beautiful purses, handbags, and other accessories. It isn't cheap, but the range is second to none in the city. 613 Lisburn Way, Belfast, BT9 7GT. ✆ **028/9066-6998.** www.rojoshoes.co.uk.

The Rusty Zip ★★ Hipster heaven! Lovers of vintage style will fall for this place instantly, with its stock of retro items from the 60s, 70s, and 80s—though a few togs can usually be found from earlier decades too. The menswear is fab, but the selection of women's clothes and boots is truly *groovy*. 28 Botanic Ave., Belfast, BT7 1JQ. ✆ **028/9024-9700.** www.therustyzip.com.

Belfast After Dark

Belfast has a plethora of historic pubs where the crowds tend to be local and friendly, but the big news here in recent years has been its fast-growing scene of hip modern bars geared toward the young and trendy. The late-night places are mostly clustered in the University Quarter, while the pubs are spread around town. If you're drawn to traditional pubs, several of the best are hidden away in the pedestrian lanes off Donegall Place. The licensing laws in Northern Ireland aren't as notoriously strict as they used to be. Pub hours are generally Monday to

Saturday from 11:30am to 11pm and Sunday from 12:30 to 2:30pm and from 7 to 10pm, although some open until 1am, especially on Friday and Saturday; bars stay open later. Nightclubs tend not to get busy until after the pubs close; admission ranges from a few pounds to about £15.

BARS & CLUBS

Apartment ★★★ This glamorous cocktail bar has a fantastic view of Belfast City Hall. It's popular with a young and sophisticated crowd, drawn by the top DJs (from about 9:30pm on weekend nights) and the excellent cocktail list. They also serve good food. 2 Donegal Sq. West, Belfast, BT1 6JA. ✆ **028/9050-9777.** www.apartmentbelfast.com.

Café Vaudeville ★★ Gilded Age glamor positively drips from the walls of this luxurious bar on Arthur Street. During the day it's a pleasant cafe; at night, come for dinner or drinks, while you listen to an old-school swing band or cabaret chanteuse—particularly on Fridays, when there's a regular Vaudeville slot. Reservations are advisable on weekends. 25–39 Arthur St., Belfast, BT1 4GA. ✆ **028/9043-9160.** www.cafevaudeville.com.

THE PERFORMING ARTS

Belfast Empire ★ This former music hall is now one of the city's busiest live venues, with live acts most Fridays and Saturdays (some big names, mostly of an indie/ alternative variety) and standup comedy every Tuesday. It's also a busy bar and nightclub, open until 1am every night except Sunday. 42 Botanic Ave., Belfast, BT1 1JQ. ✆ **028/9024-9276.** www.thebelfastempire.com.

Black Box ★ This eclectic venue has a great program of theater, spoken word, cabaret, and other live events. They also have exhibition spaces, where something interesting in the worlds of photography and visual art always seems to be going on. From Thursday to Saturday nights (and Sunday afternoons in summer), the Green Room bar opens for free, live music, beer, and pizza. The slightly bohemian crowd is a great mix of ages, and the music a similarly mixed bag of styles. 18–22 Hill St., Belfast, BT1 2LA. ✆ **028/9024-4400.** www.blackboxbelfast.com.

Grand Opera House ★★ One of the main landmarks of Belfast's "Golden Mile," the Grand Opera House opened in 1895. The interior is full of late-Victorian detail, including an extraordinarily grand auditorium, complete with an elaborately painted frieze on the high ceiling. It hasn't always been well treated. It was severely damaged twice by IRA bombs, but a full restoration in the mid-2000s returned the place to its former glory. Today it continues to be a cornerstone of the Belfast live arts scene with a tremendous variety of shows, from touring plays, ballet, and opera to big-ticket musicals, concerts, and standup comedy. Ticket prices vary greatly, but expect to pay between £15 and £30 for most shows. Check the website for a detailed listing of what's on. 2–4 Great Victoria St., Belfast, BT2 7HR. ✆ **028/9024-1919.** www.goh.co.uk.

Lyric Theatre ★★ The Lyric is a highly respected repertory theater (the only one in Northern Ireland), producing original work and hosting a varied program of touring plays all year. Ticket prices vary, but are generally between about £10 and £25. In 2011 the Lyric played a walk-on part in history, when it was the venue for a meeting between the Queen and Martin McGuinness (the former IRA commander, now Deputy First Minister of Northern Ireland). 55 Ridgeway St., Belfast, BT9 5FP. ✆ **028/9038-1081.** www.lyrictheatre.co.uk.

PUBS

Crown Liquor Saloon ★★★ There's a very real possibility that this impeccably restored Victorian "gin palace" is the most handsome pub in the world. See full review on p. 451. 46 Great Victoria St., Belfast, BT2 7BA. ✆ **028/9024-3187.** www.nicholsonspubs.co.uk/thecrownliquorsaloonbelfast.

Kelly's Cellars ★★ One of a couple of claimants to the title of Belfast's oldest pub, Kelly's Cellars certainly looks the part, with low doorways and an appealingly mismatched selection of vintage fishing nets, lanterns, and other bric-a-brac hanging from the high beamed ceiling. It's particularly well known today as one of the best pubs in Belfast for live, traditional music; sessions are usually held from Tuesday to Thursday at 8:30pm, Saturday at 4:30pm, and can last several hours. 30–32 Bank St., Belfast, BT1 1HL. ✆ **028/9024-6058.**

The Morning Star ★ Another lovely, traditional pub, the Morning Star has been in business since at least 1810. The name supposedly comes from the fact that it was once next to a stagecoach terminus; the story goes that carriages would arrive here at the crack of dawn, and customers would head straight inside for a pick-me-up. The pub is famously hard to find; Pottinger's Entry is a small, pedestrian-only alleyway off High Street, almost opposite the post office; you can spot it by the iron arch over the entrance. 17–19 Pottinger's Entry, Belfast. ✆ **028/9023-5986.** www.themorningstarbar.com.

The Crown Liquor Saloon in Belfast, a National Trust property.

White's Tavern ★★ An even older establishment than all of the above, White's Tavern has been serving liquor (as a wine shop to begin with, then a pub—hence the dispute) since 1630. It was renovated in 2014 to keep it looking… Well, decidedly *not* new, but that's exactly why people love the place. The decor is all old whiskey bottles and vintage photos, which just adds to the satisfyingly old world atmosphere. The entrance to Winecellar Entry is between High and Rosemary Streets. 2–4 Winecellar Entry, Belfast, BT1 1QN. ✆ **028/9024-3080.**

SOUTHEAST OF BELFAST & THE ARDS PENINSULA

Further afield from Belfast, the Ards Peninsula, beginning about 10 miles (16km) east of the city, curls around the western shore of **Strangford Lough.** This is a place of great natural beauty, as well as a bird sanctuary and wildlife reserve. It's also lined with historic buildings and ancient sites, from the austere **Castle Ward** and the elegant **Mount Stewart House,** to the mysterious, megalithic **Giant's Ring.**

Two roads traverse the peninsula: A20 (the Lough road) and A2 (the coast road). The Lough road is the more scenic.

At the southern tip of the Lough, car ferry service connects Portaferry with the Strangford Ferry Terminal (✆ **028/4488-1637**), in Strangford, on the mainland side. From the Portaferry side it departs at quarter past and quarter to every hour; first and last sailing times are 7:45am and 10:45pm from Monday to Friday; 8:15am and 11:15pm on Saturday; 9:45am and 10:45pm on Sunday. From the Strangford side it departs on every hour and half-hour; first and last sailing times are 7:30am and 10:30pm from Monday to Friday; 8am and 11pm on Saturday; 9:30am and 10:30pm on Sunday.

Visitor Information

The **Portaferry Tourist Information Office** is at Mountstewart House, Portaferry Rd., Newtownards, BT22 2AD (✆ **028/4278-8387**). It's open Easter to June, Monday to Saturday, 10am to 5pm, and Sunday, 1 to 5pm; and July and August, Monday to Saturday, 10am to 5:30pm, and Sunday, noon to 5pm. It's closed from September all the way through to Easter.

Exploring Southeast of Belfast & the Ards Peninsula

Castle Espie Wetland Centre ★ This marvelous wildlife center, named for a castle that has long since ceased to be, is home to a virtual UN of rare migratory geese, ducks, and swans. Some are so accustomed to visitors that they will eat grain from their hands, so children can have the disarming experience of meeting Hooper swans eye to eye. Guided trails are designed for children and families, and the center sponsors activities and events year-round. A favorite of bird-watchers in search of waterfowl, the center has thousands of pale-bellied brents in early winter. The book and gift shop is enticing, the kids' play area is excellent, and the restaurant serves good lunches and home-baked cakes.

78 Ballydrain Rd., Comber, BT23 6EA. ✆ **028/9187-4146.** www.wwt.org.uk/wetland-centres/castle-espie. Admission £7.50 adults; £5.60 seniors and students; £3.60 children 4–16; £20

families. Mar–Apr, Sept–Oct daily 10am–5pm; May–Aug Mon–Fri 10am–5pm, Sat–Sun 10am–5:30pm; Nov–Feb daily 10am–4:30pm.

Castle Ward ★★ About 1¼ miles (2km) west of Strangford village is this grand manor house dating from 1760. A hybrid of architectural styles melding Gothic with classical, it sits on a 280-hectare (692-acre) country estate of formal gardens, woodlands, lakelands, and seashore. Inside, kids can dress up in period clothes and play with period toys, while outside, they can roam its vast estate of formal gardens, woodlands, lakes, and seashore, and even ride a tractor-trailer out to see the farm animals. A theater in the stable yard that hosts operatic performances in summer. Castle Ward has achieved a degree of latter-day fame as one of the key locations for the HBO series *Game of Thrones*—albeit heavily disguised.

Park Rd., Strangford, Co. Down, BT30 7LS. ✆ **028/4488-1204.** www.nationaltrust.org.uk. Admission £7 adults; £3.50 children; £17 families. Grounds: Mar, Oct daily 10am–5pm; Apr–Sept daily 10am–8pm; Nov–Feb daily 10–4pm. House: Mar–Oct daily noon–5pm.

Giant's Ring ★★ This massive and mysterious prehistoric earthwork, 180m (590 ft.) in diameter, has at its center a megalithic chamber with a single capstone. Ancient burial rings like this were thought to be protected by fairies and were left untouched, but this one is quite an exception. In the 19th century, it was used as a racetrack, and the high embankment around it served as grandstands. Today, its dignity has been restored, and it is a place of wonder for the few tourists who make the journey.

Ballynahatty, Co. Down. 3¾ miles (6km) southwest of Belfast center, west off A24. Free admission (open site).

Grey Abbey ★ The impressive ruins of Grey Abbey sit amid a beautifully landscaped setting, perfect for a picnic. Founded in 1193 by the Cistercians, it contained one of the earliest Gothic churches in Ireland. Many Cistercian ruins

khaleesi **DOES IT**

The most popular TV show in the world is filmed in Northern Ireland, and the publicity that HBO's *Game of Thrones* has brought to the region has been a massive boon for tourism. Major filming locations have included **Castle Ward** (see above); **Cushendun** (see p. 481), and **Ballintoy** (see p. 480) on the Antrim Coast Drive; and the **Tollymore Forest Park** in County Down (see p. 474). **Brit Movie Tours** offer a bus tour of many of the most scenic places used in the show.

The tour, which will also cover a few extras like the **Giant's Causeway** (see p. 482), leaves from the City Tours office in Victoria Square, central Belfast, and returns roughly 8½ hours later. They run all year on Saturdays and Sundays, and also on Tuesdays and Thursdays from April to September. Departure time is always 10am. Tickets cost £35 adults, £20 children 11 and under, and £90 families. Private tours, for up to six people, can be booked for £400.

For details and booking call ✆ **0844/247-1007** in Northern Ireland and Britain (✆ **44/207-118-1007** in the rest of the world), or visit www.britmovietours.com.

The Leganannny Dolmen in the Mourne Mountains.

were quite elaborate, but this one is surprisingly plain. Amid the ruined choirs is a fragmented stone effigy of a knight in armor, possibly a likeness of John de Courcy, husband of the abbey's founder, Affreca of Cumbria. Grey Abbey is in the appropriately named Greyabbey, about 15 miles (24km) west of Belfast.

Greyabbey, Co. Down. No phone. Free admission. Apr–May Tues–Sun 10am–5pm; June–mid-Sept daily 10am–5pm; mid-Sept–Oct, Mar noon–4pm; Nov–Feb noon–4pm.

Legananny Dolmen ★ This renowned granite dolmen (Neolithic tomb) on the southern slope of Slieve Croob looks, in the words of archaeologist Peter Harbison, like "a coffin on stilts". This must be one of the most photographed dolmens in Ireland, and you must see it up close to fully appreciate the impressive size. The massive capstone seems weightlessly poised on its supporting uprights. The Dolmen is signposted about half way between Dromara and Castelwellan on the lower slopes of Slieve Croob Mountain, about 25 miles (40km) south of Belfast.

Signposted off Leganny Rd. Leitrim, Co. Down, BT32 3QR. No phone. Free admission (open site).

Mount Stewart House, Garden and Temple of the Winds ★★ Once the home of Lord Castlereagh, this 18th-century house sits on the eastern shore of Strangford Lough. Its lush gardens hold an impressive array of rare and unusual plants. Inside, the excellent art collection includes the *Hambletonian* by George Stubbs and family portraits by Pompeo Batoni and Anton Raphael Mengs. The Temple of the Winds, a rare 18th-century banqueting house, is also on the estate, but it's open only on public holidays. Admission to the house is by guided tour only. As of this writing a major restoration program is underway at the Mount Stewart, although access is still being allowed. It may be wise to call ahead just to check everything's open before you set out.

Portaferry Rd., Newtownards, Co. Down, BT22 2AD. ✆ **028/4278-8387.** www.nationaltrust.org.uk. House and Lakeside Garden: £6.50 adults; £3.50 children; £16 families. House: Mar–Oct daily noon–5pm. Lakeside Garden: early Nov–mid-Mar 10am–4pm; mid-Mar–early Nov 10am–6pm. Last admission 1 hr. before closing.

Nendrum Monastic Site ★ Hidden away on an isolated island, this site dates from the 5th century. This site is much older than Grey Abbey across the water, and the remains of the ancient community founded by St. Mochaoi (St. Mahee) are fascinating. Foundations show the outline of ancient churches, a round tower, and beehive cells. Other interesting details are concentric stone ramparts and a sundial, reconstructed from long-broken pieces. Its visitor center shows informative videos and has insightful exhibits. The road to Mahee Island crosses a causeway to Reagh Island and a bridge still protected by the 15th-century Mahee Castle.

Mahee Island, Ringneill Rd., Comber, Co. Down, BT23 6EP. ✆ **028/9054-3037.** Free admission. Mar and mid-Sept–Oct Tues–Sun noon–4pm; Apr–May Tues–Sun 10am–5pm; June–mid-Sept daily 10am–5pm; Nov–Feb Sun noon–4pm.

Portaferry Castle ★ This is little more than a small, 16th-century tower house, but together with another tower house in Strangford it once controlled all the ship traffic through the Narrows. It's a piece of history right beside the Portaferry visitor center, so it's worth popping your head in for a peek.

Castle St., Portaferry, County Down. Free admission. Easter–Aug daily 10am–5pm.

Sports & Outdoor Pursuits

CYCLING If you want to explore the area on two wheels, you can rent bicycles for roughly £10 to £15 a day. Cycle rental by the day or week, and delivery in the North Down/Ards area, are available from **Mike the Bike,** 53 Frances St., Newtownards (✆ **028/9181-1311;** www.kayaksatmikethebike.co.uk). He also rents kayaks.

DIVING The nearby loughs and offshore waters are a diver's dream—remarkably clear and littered with wrecks. To charter a diving expedition in Strangford Lough, contact **Des Rogers** (✆ **028/4272-8297**). One of Europe's finest training centers, **DV Diving,** 138 Mount Stewart Rd., Newtownards, County Down (✆ **028/9186-1686** or 028/9146-4671; www.dvdiving.co.uk), offers diving courses.

FISHING For info, tackle, and bait, try the **Village Tackle Shop,** 55a Newtownbreda Rd., Belfast (✆ **028/9049-1916;** www.villagetackleshopbelfast.co.uk), or **Kelly Hardware,** 54 Market St., Downpatrick, County Down (✆ **028/4461-2193;** www.kellyhardwaredownpatrick.co.uk). Sea-fishing trips from Portaferry into the waters of Strangford Lough and along the County Down coast are organized by **Norsemaid Sea Enterprises,** 152 Portaferry Rd., Newtownards, County Down (✆ **078/3113-5298;** www.salutay.co.uk). Reservations are required. To outfit yourself and fish for rainbow trout year-round, visit **Ballygrangee Trout Fishery,** Mountstewart Road, Carrowdore, County Down (✆ **028/4278-8883**).

GOLF Several well-established courses are just a short drive from Belfast in north County Down. They include the **Bangor Golf Club,** Broadway, Bangor (✆ **028/9127-0922;** www.bangorgolfclubni.co.uk), with greens fees of £22 to £35 (tell them you're a tourist and you'll get a discount); **Downpatrick Golf**

Club, 43 Saul Rd., Downpatrick (✆ **028/4461-5947;** www.downpatrickgolfclub.org.uk), with greens fees of £18 to £20; and the 71-par **Scrabo Golf Club,** 233 Scrabo Rd., Newtownards (✆ **028/9181-2355;** www.scrabogolfclub.com), with greens fees of £20 to £25, or £15 on Fridays.

THE MOURNE MOUNTAINS

South and west from Downpatrick, the rolling foothills of the Mournes make a promise that the mountains beyond fulfill. These are the highest mountains in Northern Ireland and the rocky landscape here is breathtaking—all gray granite, yellow gorse, purple heather, and white stone cottages. Remote and traversed by few roads, the mountains—complete with barren, wind-swept moors—are left to hikers and walkers. The ancestral home of the Brontës is here, in ruins. But the region is not desolate: You have forest parks, sandy beaches, lush gardens, and, of course, pubs to explore.

The region is dominated by the massive cold, barren peak of **Slieve Donard** (839m/2,752 ft.). From the top, the view takes in the full length of Strangford Lough, Lough Neagh, the Isle of Man, and, on a crystalline day, the west coasts of Wales and Scotland. (The recommended ascent of Slieve Donard is from Donard Park on the south side of Newcastle.) If that's too high for you, head to the heart of the Mournes, to the exquisite **Silent Valley Reservoir,** Silent Valley Mountain Park, Head Road, Annalong, Newcastle, County Down BT34 4HU (✆ **028/9074-6581;** car £4.50 or £1.60 adults, 60p children on foot; March–September daily 10am–6:30pm, October–April daily 10am–4pm), where easy, well-marked paths wind around the lake and a coffee shop with an information center keeps it all from feeling too far from civilization.

Besides walking and climbing and sighing at the splendor of it all, there's **Newcastle,** a lively, traditional seaside resort with a golden sand beach and one of the finest golf courses in Ireland. It makes a good base for exploring the area, but if it's too urban for you (pop. 7,500), several small coastal towns strung along the A2 road—**Kilkeel, Rostrevor,** and **Warrenpoint**—have more bucolic charms.

Wherever you stay, the mountains are the main attraction, and in Ireland you can't have cliffs and sea without soaring birds, fairytale castles, and mysterious dolmens. Finally, if your idea of nightlife has more to do with stars than bars, the Mourne Mountains provide a luminous getaway.

Visitor Information

The **Newcastle Tourist Information Centre** is at 10–14 Central Promenade, Newcastle, County Down, BT33 0AA (✆ **028/4372-2222**). It's open April to June and September, Monday to Saturday, 9:30am to 5pm, and Sunday, 2 to 6pm; July and August, Monday to Saturday, 9:30am to 7pm, and Sunday, 1 to 7pm; and October to March, Monday to Saturday, 9:30am to 5pm, and Sunday, 2 to 5pm. The **Silent Valley Visitor Centre** is on Head Road, Annalong, Newcastle, County Down, BT34 4HU (✆ **028/9035-4716**). It's open May to September, daily, 10am to 6:30pm; and October to April, daily, 10am to 4pm.

Getting There

Driving from Belfast, the A24 and A2 south from the city will take you directly down to Newcastle; the drive should take just under an hour. If you're driving up from Dublin, turn east off the Dublin-Belfast Road at Newry and take A2, following the north shore of Carlingford Lough, between the mountains and the sea. It's a drive you won't soon forget.

Exploring the Mourne Mountains

Castlewellan Forest Park ★★ Surrounding a fine trout lake and watched over by the impressive, mid-19th century Castelwellan Castle (sadly closed to the public), this forest park just begs for picnics and outdoor activities. Woodland walks, a formal walled gardens, and an interesting lakeside sculpture trail awaits. Anglers can fish for trout (brown and rainbow) in the lake. The **Peace Maze,** planted in 2000, is an enormous hedge maze, and appropriately named, given that it's meant to represent the path to peace in Northern Ireland. The real draw is the National Arboretum, opened in 1740 and now 10 times its original size. The largest of its three greenhouses features aquatic plants and a collection of free-flying tropical birds. The town of Castlewellan, elegantly laid out around two squares, is a short distance away, as is the ancient fort of Drumena Cashel (see below).

Forest Office: The Grange, Castlewellan Forest Park, Castlewellan, Co. Down, BT31 9BU. ✆ **028/4377-8664.** Admission and parking: £4.50. Daily 10am–sunset.

Drumena Cashel ★ The walls of this irregularly shaped ancient stone-ring fort—a farmstead dating from the early Christian period—were partially rebuilt in the mid-1920s and measure 2.7m (9 ft.) to 3.6m (12 ft.) thick. The *souterrain* (underground stone tunnel) is T-shaped and was likely used in ancient times for cold storage. During the age of the Viking invasions, it likely provided a degree of protection for the local population. Ireland once had thousands of such fortifications, and this is one of the better-preserved examples in this region. Castlewellan is about 30 miles (48km) south of Belfast.

Signposted from A25, 2 miles (3km) southwest of Castlewellan, Co. Down. Free (open site).

Dundrum Castle ★ The site of an early Irish fortification (of which nothing is visible now), the oldest visible portions of this castle's striking and extensive ruins date from the 12th century. The enormous keep was built in the 13th century, as was the gatehouse. It was the home of the Maginnis family until the 17th century, when it was captured by Oliver Cromwell's army, which destroyed it in 1652. The hilltop setting is lovely, and the views from the keep's parapet are panoramic. This was once one of the mightiest of the Norman castles in Northern Ireland (second only to Carrickfergus), and it still commands the imagination, if nothing else.

4 miles (6.5km) east of Newcastle, off A2, Dundrum, County Down. ✆ **028/9181-1491.** No phone. Free admission. Mid-Apr–May, Sept Tues–Sun 10am–5pm; June–Aug daily 10am–5pm.

Greencastle Fort ★ The first castle on this site, built in 1261, faced its companion, Carlingford Castle, across the lough. It was a two-story rectangular tower surrounded by a curtain wall with corner towers. Very little survives. Most of what you see is from the 14th century. It served as a royal garrison until it was destroyed by Cromwell's forces in 1652.

4 miles (6.5km) southwest of Kilkeel, Greencastle, Cranfield Point, Mouth of Carlingford Lough, Co. Down. No phone. Admission £1.40. June, Sept daily 10am–5pm; July–Aug Sat–Sun 10am–5pm. Closed Oct–May.

Silent Valley Mountain Park ★★ Between 1904 and 1922, the 22-mile (36km) dry-stone Mourne Wall and dam was built to enclose Silent Valley, creating the Silent Valley Reservoir, the major source of water for County Down. The 22-mile (36km) **Mourne Wall Trek** follows the wall that threads together 15 of the range's main peaks. The steep path is more than most hikers want to take on, and certainly shouldn't be attempted in a single day. But it is a fine, long walk for experienced ramblers and offers wonderful views. More information about the route, including maps and a photo log of every stage, can be found at www.mournewall.co.uk. A good alternative is the more modest walk from the fishing port of Kilkeel to the Silent Valley and Lough Shannagh. An even less strenuous alternative is to drive to the Silent Valley Information Centre and take the shuttle bus to the top of nearby Ben Crom. It runs on weekends during May, June, and September, and daily in July and August.

Visitor Centre: Head Rd., Annalong, Newcastle, Co. Down, BT34 4HU. ✆ **028/9035-4716.** www.niwater.com/silent-valley. Admission £4.50 per car. May–Sept daily 10am–6:30pm; Oct–Apr daily 10am–4pm.

Tollymore Forest Park ★★ All that's left of the once-glorious Tollymore House is this delightful 480-hectare (1,186-acre) wildlife and forest park. The park offers a number of walks up into the north slopes of the Mourne Mountains or along the Shimna River (which is known for its exceptionally fine salmon). The Shimna walk has several beguiling little landmarks, including caves and grottos. The park is dotted with follies, such as faux-medieval castle gatehouses and other fanciful fakes. The forest is a nature preserve inhabited by a host of local wildlife like badgers, foxes, otters, and pine martens. And don't miss the trees for the forest—some exotic species here include the magnificent Himalayan cedars and a 30-m (98-ft.) sequoia in the arboretum.

Off B180, 2 miles (3.2km) northwest of Newcastle, Tullybrannigan Rd., Newcastle, County Down. ✆ **028/4372-2428.** Free admission. Parking £4.50. Daily 10am–dusk.

Sports & Outdoor Pursuits

ADVENTURE SPORTS For canoeing, rock climbing, bushcraft, watersports, and a variety of other intrepid activities, contact **One Great Adventure,** The Grange Yard, Castlewellan Forest Park, Castlewellan, County Down, BT31 9BU (✆ **084/4770-5477;** www.onegreatadventure.com).

CYCLING The Mourne roads are narrow and often bordered by dry-stone walls up to 1.7m (5½-ft.) tall. The foothills of the Mournes around Castlewellan are ideal for cycling, with panoramic vistas and very little traffic. In these parts, the perfect year-round outfitter is **Ross Cycles,** 44 Clarkhill Rd. (✆ **028/4377-8029**), signposted from the Clough-Castlewellan Road, ½ mile (.8km) out of Castlewellan. The shop carries light-frame, highly geared mountain bikes for the whole family, with helmets and children's seats. All cycles are fully insured, as are their riders. You can park and ride, or request local delivery. Daily rates are around £10, and family and weekly rates are available.

GOLF **Royal County Down ★**, Newcastle, County Down (✆ **028/4372-3314;** www.royalcountydown.org), is nestled in huge sand dunes with the Mountains of Mourne in the background. This 18-hole, par-71 Championship course was created in 1889 and is still considered to be among the best; the Annesley links are worth a try, too. Greens fees are £170 to £185, depending on the day and time of year. (In winter prices drop to £50–£100). Not too far away, the **Kilkeel Golf Club,** Mourne Park, Ballyardle, Kilkeel (✆ **028/4176-5095;** www.kilkeelgolfclub.org), is a beautiful parkland course on the historic Kilmorey Estate. Green fees are £25 to £30; on Mondays and Wednesdays you can play a round and have a meal in the clubhouse for just £15.

HORSEBACK RIDING The **Mount Pleasant Trekking and Horse Riding Centre,** Bannonstown Road, Castlwellan, County Down, BT31 9BG (✆ **028/4377-8651;** www.mountpleasantcentre.com), offers group trekking tours into Castlewellan Forest Park (see p. 473). For riding in the Tollymore Forest Park or on local trails, contact the **Mourne Trail Riding Centre,** 96 Castlewellan Rd., Newcastle, County Down, BT33 0JP (✆ **028/4372-9107;** www.mournetrailridingcentre.co.uk). It has quality horses and offers beach rides for skilled riders. Expect to pay around £20 per hour.

Where to Stay & Dine in the Mourne Mountains

Glassdrumman Lodge Country House ★★ Overlooking the sea and the Mournes, near the Silent Valley, this is a truly warm and welcoming place to stay. The Hall family creates an atmosphere of a home away from home—albeit a rather grand and elegant one. Bedrooms are large, filled with natural light, and decorated in understated, elegant tones. A few have real fireplaces. One of the main reasons this place is so highly rated, however, is the excellent **restaurant,** where locally sourced ingredients are used to create sumptuous classic Irish meals. It comes as no surprise at all that they also run a 1-day cookery school several times per month; check the website for an up-to-date schedule.

85 Mill Rd., Annalong, Co. Down, BT34 4RH. ✆ **028/4376-8451.** www.glassdrummanlodge.com. 10 units. £90–£130 double. Free parking. Breakfast included. **Amenities:** Restaurant.

The Slieve Donard Spa and Resort ★★ The spindly, neo-Gothic turret of this 1897 hotel stands like a beacon overlooking Dundrum Bay. The surroundings are certainly dramatic, but inside this is a relaxing, luxurious place. Bedrooms are good sized and modern; many have views of the bay and Mourne Mountains. Executive bedrooms are bigger and—a bonus if you're visiting during a rare heatwave—having air conditioning. The excellent spa has a long list of enticing treatments, from Ayurvedic treatment rituals, to hot stone massages and full body salt scrubs. (Prices aren't cheap, however—expect to pay between £75 and £160 for a one to 2-hour signature treatment.) The two restaurants are the formal **Oak Room** and the more relaxed **Percy French.** Dinner, bed and breakfast packages offer good savings.

Downs Rd., Newcastle, Co. Down, BT33 0AH. ✆ **028/4372-1066.** www.hastingshotels.com. 178 units. £155–£220 double. Free parking. Breakfast included. **Amenities:** 2 restaurants; bar; room service; spa; gym; pool.

COUNTY ARMAGH

County Armagh is a green rolling stretch of gentle hills and small villages. It is also one of Northern Ireland's most rebellious Republican regions—police watchtowers are atop some hills, the occasional barracks (mostly empty these days), and until a couple of years ago, you could expect to hear the rhythmic thumping of military helicopters flying over.

Small and manageable **Armagh City** is a handsome cathedral city. Its name, from the Irish *ard Macha* (Macha's height) refers to the pagan queen Macha who is said to have built a fortress here. It's no coincidence that St. Patrick chose to base himself here when he was spreading Christianity—it was a bold challenge to the native paganism. The simple stone church that he built in the 5th century is now the giant Church of Ireland cathedral—clearly, his plan worked, at least to some extent. Armagh City actually has two St. Patrick cathedrals—one Catholic and one Protestant—and each is the seat of its primate.

The town has the kind of dignity you might expect in a seat of religion, with grand public buildings, huge churches, and big Georgian town houses along the Mall. Buildings, doorsteps, and sidewalks are made of delightful pink, yellow, and red local limestone that make the city glow even on a dull day.

Just to the east of the town center is **The Mall,** a park with an interesting history. It was used for such low activities as horse racing and cock fighting until the 18th century, when an archbishop converted it into a lush park surrounded by Georgian buildings. The courthouse at its northern end was destroyed by an IRA bomb in 1993, but then rebuilt. It dates from 1809, and was designed by a local architect, Francis Johnston, who went on to create much of Dublin's famous Georgian architecture. Opposite the courthouse, the gloomy Armagh Gaol, was built in 1780 and remained in use until 1988.

A short distance outside the city, the small town of Bessbrook has historic cottages, the forests of Slieve Gullion, and ancient Navan Fort, the most important archaeological site in Ulster.

Visitor Information

The **Armagh Tourist Information Centre,** 81 Killylead Rd., Armagh, BT60 4LD (✆ **028/3752-9644**), is the main information point for the surrounding area. It's open all year, Monday to Saturday 9am to 5pm.

Getting There

Armagh is 40 miles (64km) southwest of Belfast. To get there from the city, take M1 and A3; the journey takes around 50 minutes.

Exploring County Armagh

Armagh Astronomy Centre and Planetarium ★★ This state-of-the-art planetarium is a fantastic way to reward kids with an interest in science and astronomy. The digital projection system, which has 3D elements, is impressive. The 25-minute "Violent Universe," full of crashes and zooms and loud space facts, runs at 2pm every weekday. On Saturdays the program gets much more varied, with different shows on the hour, from 15-minute "Little Yellow Star," a rather gentle show aimed at very young children, to documentaries on constellations and astronomers. Outside the Planetarium you'll see the 200 year-old, working Armagh Observatory (not open to the public), and can wander around the Astropark, which is filled with scale models of planets. ***Note:*** All seats have to be booked in advance and you must arrived 30 minutes before start time to pick up your tickets.

College Hill, Armagh, Co. Armagh, BT61 9DB. ✆ **028/3752-3689.** www.armaghplanet.com. Admission to show and exhibition area £6 adults; £5 seniors and children; £20 families. Mon–Sat 10am–5pm. Show times Mon–Fri 2pm; Sat 11am–4pm (on the hr.).

Armagh County Museum ★ Part of the same National Museums Northern Ireland collective that includes the excellent Ulster Museum (see p. 454) and the Folk & Transport Museum (see p. 456), this one has Armagh-related artifacts going back to the Neolithic age. Highlights include a collection of 19th century Irish bog oak jewelry; Irish police uniforms from the 1820s up to the mid-20th century; and a collection of elaborate fans from around the world, from as far back as the 1700s. Rather chillingly they also have a genuine scold's bridal, an iron torture instrument and "correctional" device that was placed over a woman's head, with a spike inside her mouth to prevent her from talking.

The Mall East, Armagh, Co. Armagh, BT61 9BE. ✆ **028/3752-3070.** www.nmni.com/acm. Free admission. Mon–Fri 10am–5pm; Sat 10am–1pm, 2–5pm.

Benburb Valley Park and Castle ★★ This rather lovely, sylvan park on the River Blackwater contains the ruins of **Benburb Castle,** a squat but satisfyingly fortress-like ruin dating from the early 1600s, in an impressive cliffside spot overlooking a gorge. In 1646, an Irish army defeated an Anglo-Scottish invasion force at Benburb, thus ending the brief Scottish bid to rule Ireland. Nearby, the **Benburb Valley Heritage Centre** (✆ **028/3754-9752**), a former Linen factory, has some exhibits on the history of the area. The park also contains a working Servite priory. Benburb is 7 miles (11km) northwest of Armagh; take B128 off A29.

89 Milltown Rd., Benburb, Co. Armagh. ✆ **028/3754-8170.** Park free admission. Castle and Heritage Centre £3. Park daily until dusk. Castle and Heritage Centre Apr–Sept Mon–Sat 10am–5pm.

Navan Fort and Centre ★★ Believed to have been the royal and religious capital of Ulster from 1150 B.C. until the spread of Christianity, the Navan Fort is a mysterious place. Its central circular earthwork enclosure holds a smaller circular structure, and it all encloses an Iron Age burial mound. Even today, scientists do not really know what it was used for, although they know that it was all set on fire around 95 B.C., possibly as part of a ritual. The excellent interpretive center puts it all into context, complete with exhibition and reconstructed Iron Age houses. Admission rates are discounted slightly in the winter months. The Fort is 2 miles (3km) from Armagh on A28, signposted from Armagh center.

The Navan Centre, 81 Killylea Rd., Armagh, Co. Armagh, BT60 4LD. www.armagh.co.uk/navan-centre-fort. ✆ **028/3752-9644.** Admission £6.20 adults; £4.10 children; £5.15 seniors and students; £17 families. Apr–Sept daily 10am–6:30pm (last admission 5pm); Oct–Mar daily 10am–4pm (last admission 3pm).

Peatlands Park ★ As the name implies, Peatlands Park is a park filled with peat. It's also big—more than 240 hectares (593 acres)—and the peat bogs and small lakes are quite lovely. The whole thing is a nature reserve, so you wander through it on a well-designed system of walking paths, or, slightly more fun on rainy days, you ride through it on a narrow-gauge railway. Nature walks and events are offered through the year. Dungannon is 14 miles (23km) northeast of Benburb, just over the border with County Tyrone.

33 Derryhubbert Rd. (6¾ miles/11km southeast of Dungannon, at exit 13 off M1), Co Tyrone, BT71 6NW. ✆ **028/3885-1102.** Free admission to park. Rail ride £1 adults; £0.5 seniors and children 5–18; children 4 and under free. Vehicle access to park Oct–Mar daily 9am–4:30pm; Apr–Sept daily 9am–9pm. Railway June–Sept Sat, Sun and Bank Holidays only 1–5pm.

LOUGH neagh

Lough Neagh, at 396 sq. km (153 sq. miles), is the largest lake in Ireland. Ancient Irish lore maintains the lake was created by the mighty giant Fionn MacCumhail (Finn McCool) when he flung a chunk of earth into the sea to create the Isle of Man. But before you think about taking a dip, consider this: The lake's claim to fame is its eels. Yep, the waters are positively infested with the slimy creatures. Hundreds of tons of eels are taken from Lough Neagh and exported each year, mainly to Germany and Holland. The ages-old eel-extraction method involves "long lines," baited with up to 100 hooks. As many as 200 boats trailing these lines are on the lake each night (the best time to go fishing for eels). So, maybe take a rain check on that swim.

If you're not entirely creeped out by that, however, you can take a **boat trip** on the lovely lake. Boats depart regularly from the nearby **Kinnego Marina** (✆ **028/3832-7573**), signposted from the main road. They last about 45 minutes and cost about £10 for adults, £7 for children.

The **Lough Neagh Discovery Centre,** Oxford Island, Craigavon, Co. Armagh (✆**028/3832-2205;** www.oxfordisland.com), is open April to September daily from 10am to 6pm, and October to March, Wednesday to Sunday, from 10am to 5pom. Part of an enormous, lush nature reserve, the center has an exhibition on the Lough and its history, plus information about the best walking trails. They also host occasional guided walks trails (or "rambles") through the reserve; prices and times of any upcoming tours are advertised on the website. There's also a cafe, craft shop, and tourist information center (where, handily, you can hire a pair of binoculars). The center is open weekdays from 9am to 5pm and weekends from 10am to 5pm. During summer it closes an hour later.

St. Patrick's Church of Ireland Cathedral ★ Built on the site of St. Patrick's 5th-century church, the Anglican cathedral dates from the 13th century, although much of the structure was built in the 1830s. Inside the church are the remains of an 11th-century Celtic cross, and a strange granite carved figure known as the Tandragee Idol, which dates from the Iron Age. A stone slab on the exterior wall of the north transept marks the spot where Brian Boru, the high king of Ireland who died in the last great battle with the Vikings in 1014, is buried.

43 Abbey St, Armagh, Co. Armagh. ✆ **028/3752-3142.** Free admission; suggested donation £3 adults; £2 seniors, students and children. Apr–Oct daily 9am–5pm; Nov–Mar daily 9am–4pm. Guided tours June–Aug Mon–Sat 11:30am, 2:30pm.

St. Patrick's Roman Catholic Cathedral ★ Built at the same time as the current structure of the Anglican church—in the mid-1800s—the cathedral is a grand Gothic Revival building dominating its portion of the town. It stands on a hill that you scale by the stone stairs. Outside it's gray and hulking, but inside is another story, as vividly painted mosaics bathe it in color. Unfortunately, a renovation in the 1980s added some modern touches that stand out starkly against its otherwise perfect 19th-century authenticity.

Cathedral Rd., Armagh, Co. Armagh, BT61 7QY. ✆ **028/3752-2802.** Free admission. Daily 8am–dusk. Opening times can vary; call to check.

THE GLENS OF ANTRIM & THE ANTRIM COAST

The most extraordinary stretch of countryside in Northern Ireland, the evocatively named Glens of Antrim, are really nine green valleys stretching north and west from Belfast, and curving around toward Donegal. The names of the glens are all based on local legends, and although the meanings are largely lost to the ages, the popular translations are: Glenarm (glen of the army), Glencloy (glen of the hedges), Glenariff (ploughman's glen), Glenballyeamon (Edwardstown glen), Glenaan (glen of the rush lights), Glencorp (glen of the slaughter), Glendun (brown glen), Glenshesk (sedgy glen), and Glentaisie (Taisie's glen).

Many modern residents of this region are descendants of the ancient Irish and the Hebridean Scots, so this is one of the strongholds in Northern Ireland of the Gaelic tongue. To this day, the glen people are known to be great storytellers.

The area's attractions are formidable, and include the awe-inspiring **Giant's Causeway,** the picturesque **Carrick-a-Rede Rope Bridge,** and **Old Bushmills Distillery.** For bird-watchers, the coastal moors and cliffs and the offshore nature reserve on **Rathlin Island** are prime destinations. On the last Monday and Tuesday of August, the seaside town of **Ballycastle** plays host to the Oul' Lammas Fair, a traditional livestock and food market that has been running since the 17th century

Visitor Information

The principal tourist information centers in North Antrim are at Narrow Gauge Road, **Larne,** BT40 1XB (✆ **028/2826-0088**); Sheskburn House, 14 Bayview Rd., **Ballycastle,** BT54 6BT (✆ **028/2076-2024**); and the **Giant's Causeway Information Centre,** 44 Causeway Rd., Bushmills, BT57 8SU (✆ **028/2073-1855**).

The Larne office is open year-round, Monday to Saturday, from 9:30am to 5pm (closes 4pm Saturdays from October–May; also Sundays from 1 to 3pm from June to September).

The Ballycastle office is open year-round, Monday to Friday, from 9:30am to 5pm, Saturday 9am to 4pm (5pm in July and August), and also on Sundays in June and September from 12 to 4pm, and July and August from 1 to 5pm.

The Giant's Causeway office is open daily, April to September, from 9am to 7pm (9pm in July and August); February, March and October from 9am to 6pm; and November to January, 9am to 5pm.

Getting There

Coming from Belfast, the best starting point for the coast road is in Carrickfergus, which is 10 miles (16km) northeast of the city center on A2.

Exploring the Antrim Coast

Carnlough ★ The first major stop along the Antrim Coast Drive is this quiet village, known for its glassy harbor bobbing with sailboats. It's a lovely place to wander around the interesting little shops and restaurants. Just outside Carnlough is a peaceful, yet little known, waterfall and beautiful spot called **Cranny Falls.** You can walk there on a marked trail from the waterfront. Start by crossing the white stone bridge; from there the route goes through some idyllic countryside, following the route of an abandoned railway, past a disused quarry, until it reaches the falls after about a mile. Along the way are occasional markers, telling you more about the history of the area.

Carnlough, Co. Antrim.

THE antrim coast DRIVE

The 60-mile (96km) drive along the Antrim coast road is one of the most memorable routes in Ireland, offering sweeping views of midnight-blue seas against gray unforgiving cliffs and deep green hillsides.

A good place to start the drive is in Carrickfergus, just north of Belfast. It stretches to **Portrush,** a few miles on from the spectacular **Giant's Causeway** (see p. 482). The whole route is about 70 miles (113km), though you can skip some sections if you don't want to spend the whole day in the car. The journey is manageable in a couple of hours, but allow much longer if you can, because it's the sort of drive you want to savor. The main highlights of the drive each get their own listings in the next few pages, but here's an overview of what the route has to offer.

Once you join the coast road itself, about 16 miles (26km) or so north of Carrickfergus, the first town is **Glenarm,** decked out with castle walls and a barbican gate. In **Carnlough** (see p. 479), a quiet seaside village, you can climb the white stone bridge and walk along a path for about a mile to the Cranny Falls waterfall.

Keep going north along the coast from there and the road passes through the National Trust village of **Cushendun** (see p. 481), which is known for its teashops and whitewashed cottages. Along the way the coastal drive meanders under bridges and stone arches, passing crescent bays, sandy beaches, harbors, and huge rock formations. The ocean gleams beside you as you curve along its craggy shoreline, and the light creates intense colors. In the spring and autumn, you can often have the road all to yourself.

Later, for the most spectacular views, turn off the main coastal road at Cushendun onto the **Torr Head Scenic Road** (see p. 484). Just note that this narrow, rugged, cliffside road is vertigo inducing. It climbs in seemingly perilous fashion to the tops of hills that are bigger than you might think, and on a clear day, you can see all the way to the Mull of Kintyre in Scotland.

In the late spring and summer, you can take a ferry from the bustling beach town of **Ballycastle** to **Rathlin Island,** where seals and nesting birds make their homes at the **Kebble National Reserve.**

The heart-stopping **Carrick-a-Rede Rope Bridge** (see p. 481) allows the brave to cross on foot over to a small island just off the coast. Those not willing to wobble their way across—no matter how good the views—can press straight on to the little town of **Ballintoy,** a picture postcard waiting to happen, and filled with charming stone cottages and flowery gardens.

Ballintoy is stretched out at the edge of **Whitepark Bay,** a wide, crystalline curve of sandy beach at the foot of rocky hills surrounded by green farms. On a sunny day, you might find it hard to go farther.

The last major stop along the way is the eerily lunar **Giant's Causeway** (see p. 482), one of the world's true natural wonders. And after all that driving, don't you think you've earned yourself a tipple at the **Old Bushmills Distillery** (see p. 484)?

Carrick-a-Rede Rope Bridge ★★★ Five miles (8km) west of Ballycastle off the A2 road, this rope bridge spans a chasm 18m (59 ft.) wide and 24m (79 ft.) above the sea between the mainland and a small island. Local fishermen put up the bridge each spring to allow access to the island's salmon fishery, but visitors can use it for a thrilling walk and the chance to call out to each other, "Don't look down!" (By the way, that is *excellent* advice.) If you are acrophobic, stay clear; if you don't know whether you are, this is not the place to find out. ***Note:*** The 12-mile (19km) coastal cliff path from the Giant's Causeway to the rope bridge is always open and is worth the exhaustion.

119A Whitepark Rd., Ballintoy, Co. Antrim, BT54 6LS. ✆ **028/2076-9839.** www.nationaltrust.org.uk/carrick-a-rede. Admission £5.70 adults; £3 children; £14 families. Mar–May and Sept–Oct daily 10am–6pm; June–Aug daily 10am–7pm; Nov–Dec daily 10:30am–3:30pm.

Cushendun ★ Another 15 miles (24km) north of Carnlough, around the headland, the A2 road passes through the tiny, picturesque village of Cushendun. The place is so pretty that the National Trust bought most of it in the 1950s to preserve it from over-development. The seafront is lined with an elegant sweep of perfect white, Cornish-style cottages, and the quaint teashops do a bustling trade. The Glendun River winds its way through the village, crossed by a lovely old stone bridge, while down on the beach are some atmospheric sea caves. Just north of the village, in a field overlooking the coast, are the scant remains of **Curra Castle.** Cushendun is a good place to stop and take pictures before heading on down the main A2 road—or, if you want the most amazing views, the Torr Head Scenic Road (see p. 484), which hugs perilously to the coast.

Cushendun, Co. Antrim.

It's best not to look down as you cross the ocean on the Carrick-a-Rede Rope Bridge.

Dunluce Castle ★★ Near the Old Bushmills Distillery (see p. 484), between the Giant's Causeway and the bustling seaside town of Portrush, the coastline is dominated by the hulking skeletal outline of what must have once been a glorious castle. This was the main fort of the Irish MacDonnells, chiefs of Antrim. From the 14th to the 17th century, it was the largest and most sophisticated castle in the North, with a series of fortifications built on rocky outcrops extending into the sea. In 1639, part of the castle fell into the sea, taking some of the servants with it; soon after that, it was allowed to fall into a beautiful ruin. The 17th century courtyard survives, including a few buildings. The site incorporates two of the original Norman towers dating from 1305. One enticing footnote: a recent archaeological dig here uncovered the remains of a town that was previously thought completely destroyed during a rebellion in 1641. Only a very tiny fraction of what is now thought to exist has so far been excavated.

87 Dunluce Rd., Bushmills, Co. Antrim, BT57 8UY. ✆ **028/2073-1938.** Admission £5 adults; £3 seniors and children; £13 families. Mar, Oct–Nov daily 10am–5pm; Apr–Sept daily 10am–6pm; Dec, Jan daily 10am–4pm; last admission 30 min. before closing.

Giant's Causeway ★★★ A UNESCO World Heritage Site, this natural rock formation is extraordinary. Sitting at the foot of steep cliffs and stretching out into the sea, it is a natural formation of thousands of tightly packed basalt columns. The tops of the columns form flat steppingstones, all of which are perfectly hexagonal. They measure about 30cm (12 in.) in diameter; some are very short, others are as tall as 12m (39 ft.). Scientists believe they were formed 60 or 70 million years ago by volcanic eruptions and cooling lava. The ancients,

The lighthouse on Rathlin Island

on the other hand, believed the rock formation to be the work of giants. To reach the causeway, you walk from the parking area down a steep path for nearly 1 mile (1.6km), past amphitheaters of stone columns and formations with fanciful names like Honeycomb, Wishing Well, Giant's Granny, King and his Nobles, and Lover's Leap. If you wish, you can then climb up a wooden staircase to Benbane Head to take in the views, and then walk back along the cliff top. Regular shuttle service down from the visitor center is available for those who can't face the hike. ***Note:*** The underground visitor center has a cafe, shop, interpretive center, and hugely expensive parking. However, the Causeway is a free,

GOING TO THE birds: A TRIP TO RATHLIN ISLAND

Want to get close to nature? Plan a trip to **Rathlin Island,** 6 miles (10km) off the coast north of Ballycastle. The tiny island is 3¾ miles (6km) long, and less than 1 mile (1.5km) wide and almost completely treeless, with a rugged coast of 60m-high (197-ft.) cliffs, a small beach, and crowds of seals and seabirds in spring and summer. Once you get there you'll realize that it's not quite as isolated as it seems—it has a resident population of about 100, plus a pub, a fish and chip shop, and a couple of guesthouses, should you miss the last boat to shore.

Start with a visit to the **Boat House Museum and Visitor Centre,** near to the ferry landing at Church Bay, Rathlin Island, BT54 6RT (✆ **028/2076-2024**). The center, which was fully refurbished in 2014, contains an exhibition on the history of the islands, as well as plenty of handy visitor information. It's open from May to August

This is a favorite bird-watching spot, especially in spring and early to midsummer when the birds are nesting. Given that there's little else to do here except to take in the scenery, it's no surprise that the island's biggest draw is bird-watching at the **Kebble National Nature Reserve** on the western side of the island, and the **RSPB Rathlin Seabird Centre** (✆ **028/2076-3948**), located in an old lighthouse. There's no charge for entry but you have to be let in by the warden; call in advance to arrange a time. From here you can watch colorful puffins, guillemots, kittiwakes, fulmars, razorbills, and other birds.

Boat trips operate daily from Ballycastle pier; crossing time is 50 minutes. The round-trip fare is around £12 for adults, £6 for children, free for kids 4 and under. The number and schedule of crossings vary from season to season and from year to year, and are always subject to weather conditions, but there are usually several crossings a day. To check times and book tickets call **Rathlin Island Ferry** (✆ **028/2076-9299;** www.rathlinballycastleferry.com)

On the island, a minibus (summer only) will take you from Church Bay to the West Light Platform and the Kebble Nature Reserve for roughly £5 adults, £3 children, round-trip. Bicycles can be rented from **Soerneog View Hostel** (✆ **028/2076-3954;** closed November–April) for around £10 per day.

If you find yourself wanting to stay a little longer, **Coolnagrock B&B** (✆ **028/2076-3983**), which has distant views of the Mull of Kintyre in Scotland, costs from £70 for a double.

For more information about Rathlin visit **www.rathlin-island.co.uk**.

open site, so if you can find safe and legal parking, there's nothing to stop you from just walking straight down.

44 Causeway Rd., Bushmills, Co. Antrim, BT57 8SU. ✆ **028/2073-1855.** www.nationaltrust.org.uk/giants-causeway. Visitor center and parking: £8.50 adults; £4.50 children; £21 families. Visitor center Mar, Oct 9am–6pm; Apr–June, Sept 9am–7pm; July–Aug 9am–9pm; Nov–Jan 9am–5pm.

The Old Bushmills Distillery ★★ Licensed to distill spirits in 1608, but with historical references dating from as far back as 1276, this ancient distillery is endlessly popular. Visitors can tour the working sections and watch the whiskey-making process, starting with fresh water from the adjacent River Bush and continuing through distillation, fermentation, and bottling. At the end of the tour, you can sample the wares in the Potstill Bar, where you can learn more about the history of the distillery. Tours last about 25 minutes. The Bushmills coffee shop serves tea, coffee, homemade snacks, and lunch. ***Tip:*** Try to visit during the week for the full experience. Though tours do take place on weekends, the distillery itself is only in operation from Monday to Friday.

Main St., Bushmills, Co. Antrim, BT57 8XH. ✆ **028/2073-3272.** www.bushmills.com. Admission £7 adults; £6 seniors and students; £3.50 children 8–17; £20 families. No children under 8 on tour. Apr–Oct tours about every 20 min. throughout the day, Mar–Oct Mon–Sat 9:15am–4:45pm, Sun noon 4:45pm (last tours 4pm); Nov–Feb Mon–Sat 10am–4:45pm, Sun noon–4:45pm (last tours 3:30pm).

Torr Head Scenic Road ★★ This diversion is spectacular, but it's not for those with a fear of heights or narrow dirt roads; nor is it a good idea in bad weather. But on a sunny, dry day, the brave can follow signs from Cushendun (see p. 481), up a steep hill at the edge of town onto the **Torr Head Scenic Road.** After a precipitous climb, the road narrows further and inches its way along in rugged fashion at the edge of the cliff overlooking the sea. Along the way are places to park and take in the sweeping views. On a clear day, you can see all the way to the Mull of Kintyre in Scotland. Arguably the best views of all are to be had at Murlough Bay (follow the signs).

Torr Rd., heading north out of Cushendun, Co. Antrim.

Sports & Outdoor Pursuits

ADVENTURE SPORTS The **Ardclinis Activity Centre,** High Street, Cushendall, County Antrim (✆ **028/2177-1340;** www.ardclinis.com), offers a range of year-round outdoor programs and courses. They include everything from rock climbing and mountain biking to windsurfing and rafting, for people aged 14 and over.

GOLF North Antrim has several notable courses, including champion pro golfer Darren Clarke's home course, the **Royal Portrush Golf Club,** Dunluce Road, Portrush, County Antrim (✆ **028/7082-2311;** www.royalportrushgolfclub.com). Royal Portrush has two links courses, including the celebrated Dunluce Course, ranked number three in the United Kingdom. Greens fees here are £155 weekdays, £140 weekends, and £42.50 weekdays, £55 weekends on the smaller Valley Links course. However, rates plummet in the off-season. Just over the border in County Londonderry is the **Portstewart Golf Club,** 117 Strand Rd., Portstewart (✆ **028/7083-2015;** www.portstewartgc.co.uk). Of its three links courses, the par-72 Strand Course is the celebrated one here. Some days and times are more accessible than others for visitors, so call ahead for times and fees, which range from £10 to £80, depending on the course you choose and the day of the week.

PONY TREKKING **Watertop Farm Family Activity Centre,** 188 Cushendall Rd., Ballycastle, County Antrim (✆ **028/2076-2576;** www.watertopfarm.co.uk), offers pony trekking and other outdoor activities. In the Portrush area, contact **Maddybenny Riding Centre,** Loguestown Road, Portrush, County Antrim (✆ **028/7082-3394;** www.maddybenny.com); Maddybenny also has a B&B, which has appeared in several best-of lists for farmhouse B&Bs in Ireland over the last decade. Rooms run around £70 for a double. They also have a number of self-catering cottages. Also, in Castlerock is **Hill Farm Riding and Trekking Centre** (✆ **028/7084-8629;** www.hillfarmridingcentre.co.uk). Fees are typically around £15 to £20 per hour-long trek.

WALKING The **Ulster Way** (www.walkni.com/ulsterway), 560 miles (904km) of marked trail, follows the North Antrim Coast from Glenarm to Portstewart. The **Moyle Way** (www.walkni.com/walks/187/moyle-way) offers a spectacular detour from Ballycastle south to Glenariff. Last, but far from least, is the **Causeway Coast Path** (www.walkni.com/walks/186/causeway-coast-way). It stretches from Bushfoot Strand, near Bushmills, in the west to Ballintoy Harbour in the east. Short of sprouting wings, this is the best way to take in the full splendor of the North Antrim Coast. Comprehensive guides to each route, including downloadable maps of each stage, can be found on their respective websites.

Where to Stay on the Antrim Coast

Causeway Smithy ★★ A short hop from the Giant's Causeway (you can just see it in the distance, across rolling green fields), this warm and friendly B&B is a fantastic find. The guestrooms are simple but stylish with polished wood floors and modern print wallpaper. Big bay windows look out over the verdant countryside, flooding the rooms with light during the day. Each of the three rooms are located in a separate annex, and you have your own key, so there's more of a feeling of freedom and privacy than one might usually find from countryside B&Bs. The tasty breakfasts are served in a little guest lounge. There's no restaurant, but owner Denise is full of recommendations about where to go in the evenings.

270 Whitepark Rd., Bushmills, Co. Antrim, BT57 8SN. ✆ **075/1506-6975.** www.causewaysmithybnb.com. 2 units. £100 double. Free parking. Rates include breakfast. **Amenities:** Wi-Fi (free).

Londonderry Arms Hotel ★ A pleasant Georgian inn, the Londonderry Arms is a well-run, traditional kind of place. The building has its quirks—most of the inn is original, even with the modern extension—though the effect is more charming than inconvenient. A couple of the rooms have views of the nearby sea. Bedrooms are simple but comfortable; executive rooms have a bit more space. Spacious family rooms are a good value for your money. (Check the website for plenty of special offers, including excellent weekend packages.) The restaurant is very good, and chef Manus Jamison's delicious menus are full of regional specialties. If you want something a little simpler, a more modest bistro-style menu is available in the cozy bar. An unexpected piece of historical trivia about this place: Winston Churchill was briefly the landlord. He inherited it and sold it soon afterwards, although he is known to have stayed here at least once.

20 Harbour Rd., Carnlough, Co. Antrim, BT44 0EU. ✆ **028/2888-5255.** www.glensofantrim.com. 35 units. £85–£135 double. Limited free parking (on street). Breakfast included. **Amenities:** Restaurant; bar; room service.

Lurig View ★ The atmosphere at this sweet little B&B in Glenariff feels akin to a family home. The manager, Rose Ward, and her husband, Chris, are thoughtful hosts, friendly as can be and happy to help with planning itineraries, making dinner reservations, and so on. Bedrooms are simple but decorated with paintings of flowers chosen to match the accent colors of the room, which makes for an inventive touch. Breakfast is served outside if the weather's good. If you really must, the guests lounge has a TV, but a better choice is to get out and explore. Glenariff is a pretty little town and one of the most popular destinations along the Antrim coast. A forest park is within about a 10-minute drive, and the beach is a short walk from the front door.

38 Glen Rd., Glenariff, Ballymena, Co. Antrim, BT44 0RF. ✆ **028/2177-1618.** www.lurigview.co.uk. 3 units. £60 double. Free parking. Breakfast included. **Amenities:** Wi-Fi (free).

The Meadows ★ This jovial guesthouse on the main Antrim coast road has a lovely view of the sea. You can even see Scotland on a (very) clear and sunny day. Bedrooms are basic but cozy, and the bathrooms are modern and well equipped. Most are doubles, but for families or groups, one room sleeps four and another is equipped for those with mobility problems. The hearty, tasty Ulster fry breakfasts are great fuel for a long drive ahead. Anne Carey is a thoughtful and friendly host, adept at making her guests feel welcome. She also accepts the euro, as well as British pounds—a helpful touch for those traveling on both sides of the border.

79 Coast Rd., Cushendall, Ballymena, Co. Antrim, BT44 0RX. ✆ **028/2177-2020.** www.themeadowscushendall.com. 6 units. £60 double. Free parking. Breakfast included. **Amenities:** Wi-Fi (free).

Whitepark House ★★ This fantastic little place is just a couple of miles from the Carrick-a-Rede Rope Bridge (see p. 481). It was built in the mid-1700s and still retains a traditional air. Beds are wrought iron framed; one is a four-poster, while the others have canopies. Heavy silk fabrics lift the design of the room. Views of the lovely garden are sweet, but it's worth asking for a room overlooking the sea for a spectacular vista to wake up to in the morning. Bob and Siobhan Isles are genuinely warm people; the fact that they've won awards for their hospitality comes as no surprise whatsoever. Breakfasts are delicious, and the full Ulster fry is the specialty, of course, but Bob also takes care of his vegetarian guests (he is one himself) with non-meaty options. What a lovely, idyllic find along the Antrim coast road.

150 Whitepark Rd., Ballintoy, Co. Antrim, BT54 6NH. ✆ **028/2073-1482.** www.whiteparkhouse.com. 3 units. £120 double. Free parking. Breakfast included. Children allowed, but must have own room (no discount). **Amenities:** Wi-Fi (free).

Where to Dine on the Antrim Coast

Red Door Tea Room ★★ CAFE This sweet little cottage tearoom is cozy and welcoming inside, with a turf burning stove and the day's menu chalked onto blackboards behind the counter. But you'll want to sit outside if the weather allows, because the view from the garden over lush green fields to Ballintoy Harbour is stunning. They serve tempting, fresh cakes and desserts, so dig into the delicious Victoria sponge cake (two layers, separated by jam and cream). They also serve good light lunches if you want something a little more substantial. Think salads, soups, bagels, sandwiches, or even a plate of tasty fresh fish. It all adds up to a welcome and idyllic rest stop along the Antrim coast road.

Ballintoy Harbour, Ballintoy, Co. Antrim, BT54 6NA. ✆ **028/2076-9048.** Main courses £4–£12. Easter week and June–Sept daily 11am–5pm; week after Easter–May weekends only 11am–5pm. Closed Oct–Mar.

Smuggler's Inn ★ IRISH/INTERNATIONAL A convenient lunch spot, right across from the Giant's Causeway, the Smuggler's Inn serves traditional pub lunches. Choose from a few sandwiches and light snack options, or go for the full works like hefty burgers, fish and chips, or Cajun chicken goujons (strips of meat, breaded and deep fried). There's also a separate children's menu. In the evening it's much the same kind of thing, but pushed up a notch in terms of choice when a couple of steaks join the menu, as well as the occasional dish with a bit more ambition, such as roast duck with fruity red cabbage and a sherry reduction. Like several places around here, euros are accepted as well as pounds. The Smuggler's also has rooms available for between £60 and £90 per night, depending on the season.

306 Whitepark Rd., Giants Causeway, Bushmills, Co. Antrim, BT57 8SL ✆ **028/2073-1577.** www.smugglersinnireland.com. Main courses £4–£12. Food served daily noon–2:30pm, 4–9pm.

Thyme & Co. ★ MODERN IRISH Another great little cafe on the Antrim coast drive, Thyme and Co. serves delicious, healthful lunches. The ingredients are locally sourced and the short menu is thoughtfully put together. Dine on fishcakes made from salmon and smoked haddock (something of a house specialty) or a tasty pie or quiche. The dining room is a pleasant kind of space, and the staff is always friendly and cheerful. On Fridays and Saturdays in summer they stay open into the evenings, when they serve thin-crust pizzas, a popular choice with locals. They do takeout too, which is a useful option to know about if you're staying nearby and your hotel doesn't provide dinner.

5 Quay Rd., Ballycastle, Co. Antrim, BT54 6BJ. ✆ **028/2076-9851.** www.thymeandco.co.uk. Main courses £4–£10. Pizzas £6–£10. Tues–Sat 8:30am–4:30pm; Sun 10am–3:30pm.

DERRY CITY

Northern Ireland's second city is a vibrant place, surrounded by 17th-century walls which you can climb and walk the ramparts all the way around the town center. Although they were the focus of attacks and sieges for centuries, the five-foot-thick fortifications are solid and unbroken to this day. Historians believe the city was modeled on the French Renaissance town of Vitry-Le-Francois, which in turn was based on a Roman military camp, with two main streets forming a central cross and ending in four city gates. It's made for walking, combining a medieval center with sprawling Georgian and Victorian neighborhoods.

Within Ireland, though, Derry is not known for its architecture, but for the fact that, in the 1960s and 1970s, the North's civil rights movement was born here, and baptized in blood on the streets. The "Bloody Sunday" massacre in 1972, in which British troops killed 14 peaceful civil rights protesters, shocked the world and led to years of violent unrest. In the **Bogside,** as the neighborhood at the bottom of the hill west of the walled section is known, the famed mural reading "You Are Now Entering Free Derry" remains as a symbol of those times.

Happily, much of that sectarian strife seems to be behind Derry now, and it is emerging as a promising center of culture and commerce. Symbolic of the changes in Derry is the ***Hands Across the Divide*** sculpture that you pass as you cross the Craigavon Bridge into town. Erected 20 years after Bloody Sunday, it is a bronze sculpture of two men reaching out toward one another.

A cannon on the medieval ramparts of Derry.

For travelers, Derry is strategically located at the edge of the picturesque Inishowen Peninsula, while the Giant's Causeway and the North Antrim Coast, the Northwest Passage and the Sperrins, and Glenveagh National Park in Donegal (see chapter 14) are all within an hour's drive. This makes the town an ideal base of operations from which to explore one of Ireland's most unspoiled regions.

Visitor Information

The **Derry Visitor and Convention Bureau** is at 44 Foyle St., Derry, B48 6AT (© **028/7126-7577;** www.derryvisitor.com). From July to September it's open Monday to Friday, 9am to 7pm; Saturday, 9am to 6pm; and Sunday from 10am to 6pm. The rest of the year it's open Monday to Saturday, 9am to 5:30pm, and Sunday, 10am to 5pm.

Getting There

BY PLANE Service to **City of Derry Airport** (© **02/7181-0784;** www.cityofderryairport.com) is provided by the budget airline **Ryanair** (© **0818/303030** in Ireland, 0871/246-0000 in the U.K.; www.ryanair.com) from London Stanstead, Birmingham, Liverpool and Glasgow, plus Alicante and Faro in summer only.

BY TRAIN **Northern Ireland Railways** (© **028/9066-6630;** www.translink.co.uk) operates frequent trains from Belfast, which arrive at the **Northern Ireland Railways** Londonderry/Derry Station—referred to everyone, somewhat more simply, as **Waterside Railway Station** (© **028/7134-2228**), on Duke Street, on the east side of the Foyle River. A free Linkline bus brings passengers from the train station to the city center. It's possible to travel by train from Dublin, but you'd have to take the train to Belfast and transfer. The whole journey costs about £40 one-way, and takes about 4 hours, depending on the transfers. For more information, contact **Irish Rail/Iarnród Éireann** (© **1850-366-222;** www.irishrail.ie).

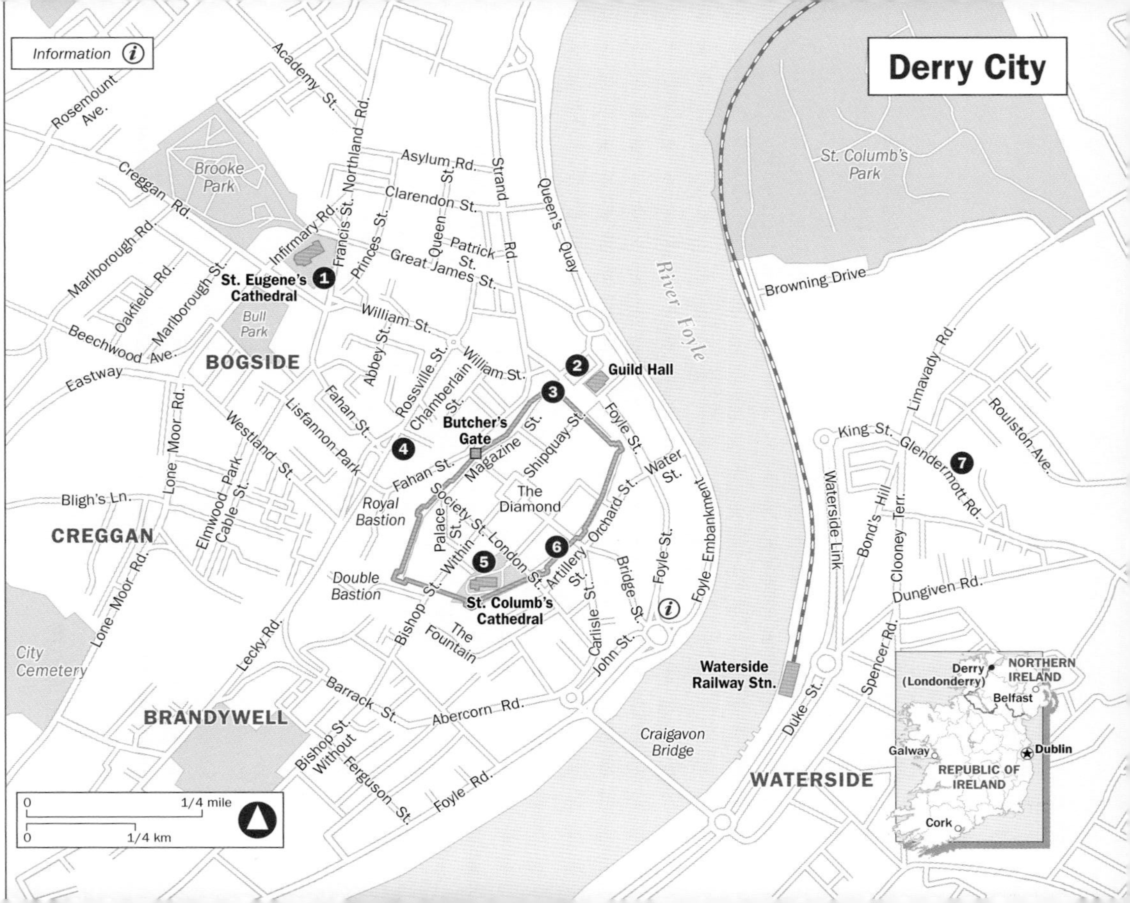

Bloody Sunday Monument & Bogside Murals **4**
Cathedral of St. Columb **5**
Centre for Contemporary Art **6**
Guildhall **2**
St. Eugene's Cathedral **1**
Tower Museum **3**
Workhouse Museum **7**

DERRY OR LONDONDERRY: what's in a name?

The short answer is: quite a lot.

Depending on which side of the border you're on, Northern Ireland's second city is called two different things. Road signs and maps in the Republic say **Derry;** in Northern Ireland they point to **Londonderry.**

This stubborn dispute dates to the Plantation of Ulster in the 1600s, when English settlers were given land in Ireland as an attempt to entrench Protestant rule. A new city was founded by the City of London trade guilds and named Londonderry in their honor. Nationalists have always objected to the term, preferring Derry, an Anglicization of *Daire Calgaich,* the name of the much older settlement that once stood on the same site.

During the Troubles, the dispute was a cause celebre. Many attempts have been made to change the name, including several unsuccessful court cases. Loyalists fiercely defend the name. But having a city with two names poses a knotty problem for residents and visitors alike—what to call it? The best advice is just to be tactful. If you're drinking in a pub with a big Irish tricolor on the side, it's probably best to use Derry; but if they're flying the Union Jack, opt for Londonderry. Of the two, Derry is probably the more commonly used in town, and certainly throughout the Republic, so we've chosen to call it Derry in this book.

Fed up with effectively being forced to make a political statement whenever they talk about their own city, residents have long since tried to find an acceptable solution to the Derry/Londonderry dilemma. In the '90s, local radio DJ Gerry Anderson suggested the wry compromise "Stroke City." (American readers: Stroke is a slash in the U.K.) Quick-witted locals swiftly nicknamed the DJ "Gerry/Londongerry."

To see further evidence of how far back this titular dispute goes, just look no further than a United States road atlas. Near Manchester, New Hampshire is a small old town called Derry. In the early 19th century there was a dispute over its name, so a group of residents set up a new town just to the south called—you guessed it—Londonderry.

BY BUS The fastest bus between Belfast and Derry, the no. 212, operated by **Ulsterbus** (✆ **028/9066-6630;** www.translink.co.uk), takes just under 2 hours. Ulsterbus also has service from Portrush and Portstewart. From the Republic, **Bus Éireann** (✆ **091/562000;** www.buseireann.ie) offers a few buses a day from Galway (about 5½ hours), Cork (between 7 and 9 hours) and Dublin (around 6 hours). Most of the long-distance routes involve changes.

City Layout

The focal point of Derry is the **Diamond,** a large square holding a war memorial in the center of the city. Four streets radiate out from the Diamond: Bishop, Ferryquay, Shipquay, and Butcher. Each extends for several blocks and ends at a gateway (Bishop's Gate, Ferryquay Gate, Shipquay Gate, and Butcher's Gate) cut into the thick city walls.

Two bridges connect the east and west banks of the River Foyle. The Craigavon Bridge, built in 1933, is one of the few examples of a double-decker bridge in the British Isles. The Foyle Bridge, Ireland's longest bridge, opened in 1984 and provides a dual-lane highway about 2 miles (3.2km) north of the Craigavon Bridge. West of the river are two major areas: the walled inner city and, beyond that, the area known as the Bogside. The streets near the waterfront are known as Waterside, and it's where most of the better hotels and many restaurants are located. Also in Waterside is a small grassy viewing point called the **"Top of the Hill,"** where you can enjoy spectacular eagle's-eye views of the city and its splendid environs. You'll never find your own way there, so take a taxi and bring your map. Short of a helicopter tour, this is the best way to get your initial bearings.

Exploring Derry

The Bogside Murals ★★ Just outside the walled city center, the Bogside was developed in the 19th and early 20th centuries as a home to Catholic workers. In the late 1960s, civil rights protests became regular events here, and the residents declared their neighborhood as "Free Derry," independent of local and British government. The situation came to a head on January 30th, 1972, later to be known as "Bloody Sunday," when British troops opened fire on a peaceful demonstration, killing 14. (The soldiers said they'd been fired upon first; eventually, in 2010, after a 12-year inquiry, the British government finally accepted this to be untrue and apologized.) Most of the Bogside has been redeveloped, but the Free Derry corner remains near the house painted with the mural reading "You Are Now Entering Free Derry." Since the 1990s, a group of local artists known as the **Bogside Artists** has painted further murals around the district, similar to those on the Falls Road in Belfast (see p. 449). Though some are overtly political in nature, many depict simple yet powerful messages of peace. Effectively this has turned parts of the Bogside into a free art museum, and together the murals have become known as the **People's Gallery.**

The Bogside, Derry.

St. Columb Cathedral ★ Within the city walls, near the Bishop's Gate, this cathedral, built by the Church of Ireland between 1628 and 1633, is a prime example of the so-called "Planters Gothic" style of architecture. It was the first cathedral built in Europe after the Reformation, although several sections were added afterward, including the impressive spire and stained-glass windows depicting scenes from the siege of 1688 and 1689. The chapter house contains a display of city relics such as the four massive original padlocks for the city gates. On the porch, a small stone inscribed *"In Templo Verus Deus Est Vereo Colendus"* ("The true God is in His temple and is to be truly worshipped") is part of the original church built on this site in 1164. An old mortar shell is on the porch as well. It was fired into the churchyard during the great siege; in its hollow core it held proposed terms of surrender. The flags around the chancel window were captured during the siege.

London St., Derry, BT48 6RQ. ✆ **028/7126-7313.** www.stcolumbscathedral.org. Requested donation £2 adults; £1.50 seniors, students and children. Mar–Oct Mon–Sat 9am–5pm; Nov–Feb Mon–Sat 9am–1pm, 2–4pm; also Sun at service times, year-round.

Centre for Contemporary Art ★ Drop in here to see new and touring works by contemporary artists from Ireland and further afield. Themed seasons include visual art, film screenings, performances, and public debates. The center builds strong international links too, and often hosts residencies for artists from across the globe. Recent seasons have included a retrospective of a pivotal, early 20th-century Dublin workers strike, as a springboard for cultural debate; art inspired by the Derry city landscape; and creative responses to revolution and unrest in Egypt. It's all serious and fascinating stuff for grown-up minds. Admission to the center and most events is free, but there may be a charge for some. Check the website for up-to-date listings.

10–12 Artillery St., Derry, BT48 6RG. ✆ **028/7137-3538.** www.cca-derry-londonderry.org. Free admission. Wed–Sat noon–6pm; Sun 1–3pm.

Guildhall ★ Just outside the city walls, between Shipquay Gate and the River Foyle, this Tudor Gothic-style building looks much like its counterpart in London. The site's original structure was built in 1890, but it was rebuilt after a fire in 1908 and again after a series of sectarian bombings in 1972. The hall is distinguished by its huge, four-faced clock (designed to resemble Big Ben) and its 23 stained-glass windows, made by Ulster craftsmen, which illustrate almost every episode of note in the city's history. The hall is used as a civic center for concerts, plays, and exhibitions. One nice bit of historical trivia: The Guildhall clock is designed not to strike between midnight and sunrise. This is because at the time it was finished in 1893, there was an expensive hotel nearby, and the management protested that a clock striking every hour through the night would disturb their sleeping guests.

Shipquay Place, Derry, BT48 6DQ. ✆ **028/7137-7335.** Free admission. Mon–Fri 9am–5pm; Sat–Sun by appointment. Free guided tours July–Aug; enquire at reception.

St. Eugene's Cathedral ★★ Designed in the Gothic Revival style, this is Derry's Catholic cathedral, in the heart of the Bogside district just beyond the city walls. The foundation was laid in 1851, but work continued until 1873. The spire was added in 1902. It's built of local sandstone and is known for stained-glass windows by the famed makers of stained glass, Meyer and Company of Munich, depicting the Crucifixion.

Francis St., Derry, BT48 9AP. ✆ **028/7126-2894.** www.steugenescathedral.com. Free admission. Mon–Sat 7am–9pm; Sun 7am–6:30pm.

The Tower Museum ★★ This engaging museum chronicles the history of Derry from the earliest times to the 21st century. It's located in **O'Doherty Tower,** a reconstructed medieval fortress originally built in the early 17th century (rather wonderfully to pay off a tax debt, rather than for any specific defensive purpose) before it was reconstructed later on. The **Story of Derry** exhibition presents a chronology of life in the city from the first Monastic settlers through the Plantation era, up to the turbulent 20th century, when the city was a focus of the civil rights movement driven by the Troubles. The main attraction, however, is the large, multi-floor exhibition devoted to an historic shipwreck that happened off the coast of Derry in the 16th century. **An Armada Shipwreck** tells the story of La Trinidad Valencera, part of the massive Spanish Armada that attempted to invade England in 1588. The ship was separated from the main fleet and sank during a storm. Four hundred years later the wreck was salvaged, together with an extraordinary hoard of treasure

CLIMBING THE walls

One of the best ways to explore Derry is via its 17th-century stonewalls, about 1 mile (1.6km) in circumference and more than 5m (16 ft.) thick. Climb the stairs to the top and you can circle the entire walled city in about 30 minutes. Steps off of the parapets are frequent, so you'll never get stuck up there. If you start at the **Diamond,** as the square in the center of the walled section is called, and walk down Butcher Street, you can climb the steps at **Butcher's Gate,** a security checkpoint between the Bogside and the city during the Troubles. Walk to the right across **Castle Gate,** which was built in 1865, and on to **Magazine Gate,** which was once near a powder magazine. Shortly afterward you'll pass **O'Doherty's Tower,** which houses the worthwhile Tower Museum (see p. 492). From there you can see the brick walls of the Guildhall (see p. 492).

Farther along, you'll pass **Shipquay Gate,** once located very near the port, back when the waters passed closer to the town center. The walls turn uphill from there, past the Millennium Forum concert hall, and up to **Ferryquay Gate.** Here in 1688, local apprentice boys saved the town from attacking forces, triggering the Great Siege of Derry (see p. 494).

Next you'll pass **Bishop's Gate,** where a tall brick tower just outside the gate is all that remains of the **Old Gaol.** The rebel Wolfe Tone was imprisoned here after the unsuccessful uprising in 1798. Farther along, the **Double Bastion** holds a military tower with elaborate equipment used to keep an eye on the Bogside—it's usually splashed by paint hurled at it by Republicans. From there you can easily access the serene churchyard of **St. Columb's Cathedral** (see p. 491). From the next stretch of wall, you have a good view over the political murals of the Bogside down the hill.

A bit farther along the wall, an empty plinth stands where once there was a statue of Rev. George Walker, a governor of the city during the siege of 1699. It was blown up by the IRA in 1973. The small chapel nearby is the **Chapel of St. Augustine** (1872), and the building across the street from it with metal grates over the windows is the **Apprentice Boys' Memorial Hall.** Walk but a short way farther, and you're back to Butcher's Gate.

including clothes, shoes, pottery, cannons, goblets, and other items that revealed tantalizing glimpses of life on board.

Union Hall Place, Derry, BT48 6LU. ✆ **028/7137-2411.** Admission £4.20 adults; £2.70 seniors, students, and children; £9.50 families. June–Aug Mon–Sat 10am–4:30pm; Sept–May Tues–Sat 10am–4:30pm.

The Workhouse Museum ★★ The building that this interesting museum currently occupies started out as that most feared of Victorian institutions: a workhouse. Ostensibly charitable homes for the destitute, in reality workhouses were little more than places of slave labor, where death from accidents and disease were common. Thoughtful exhibits tell that story in sober detail, broadening it out to cover the history of poverty, famine, and working class life in the 19th century. Other displays include the **Atlantic Memorial Exhibition,** which covers the significant role the City of Derry played in World War II (although the Republic of Ireland was neutral in the war, Northern Ireland, as part of the

THE GREAT siege OF DERRY

Changing Derry's name and planting it with Protestants didn't immediately end the city's troubles. In December 1688, after backing the English Parliament during the civil war, Derry was attacked by Catholic forces led by the Earl of Antrim. At one point in the battle, messengers from the earl were sent into the city, ostensibly for talks, but it was a trick to distract the city leaders as the earl's troops prepared to attack. At the last minute, some of the town's apprentice boys saw the ruse for what it was, and locked the city gates—thus saving the town, but setting off the Great Siege of Derry. For months, the town's population endured attacks, disease, and starvation as the earl's troops waited them out. By the time they were rescued, nearly a quarter of the city's residents had died.

The apprentice boys were seen as Protestant heroes, and have been celebrated by the town ever since in marches and parades held every summer, although these have been widely associated with conflict between Protestants and Catholics.

United Kingdom, was not). The most interesting items on display here include the remains of a Spitfire aircraft, downed during a practice dogfight in 1942. It was excavated from a bog in Moneydarragh, County Donegal in 2010, and is, to date, the only such aircraft lost in Ireland to have been recovered.

23 Glendermott Rd., Waterside, Derry, BT48 6BG. ✆ **028/7131-8328.** Free admission. Mon–Thurs, Sat 10am–4:30pm.

Where to Stay in Derry

Saddler's House & the Old Rectory ★★ Two charming buildings full of character with one pair of owners, these lovely B&Bs are among the best accommodations in Derry. Choose from the elegant Merchant's House, which was built in the mid-19th century (one of relatively few townhouses from the period left in the town), or Saddler's House, a slightly simpler, late-Victorian building. Both have been beautifully maintained and renovated with design-magazine interiors and antiques scattered about. Breakfast is served in whichever house you choose. The same owners also have three self-catering places in Derry, including a small terraced cottage opposite the cathedral, an apartment in the old pump house, within the walled part of the city, and a 1950s-style apartment. ***Tip:*** The Merchant's House family room sleeps up to five, and has its own kitchen, for just £100 to £135 per night.

36 Great James St., Derry, BT48 7DB. ✆ **028/7126-9691.** www.thesaddlershouse.com. 7 units. £60–£80 double. Limited free parking (on street); otherwise paid street parking nearby. Rates include breakfast. **Amenities:** Wi-Fi.

Troy Hall ★★ How delightfully unexpected to find this lavish Victorian mansion so close to the Derry city center. Troy Hall was built in 1897, complete with the Gothic flourishes that were so popular in the period. Turrets give the redbrick exterior an almost fairytale look, while the sweeping back lawn is a mere remnant of what was once a huge estate. The building suffered terribly over the years, until the current owners restored it to its now beautiful condition. The spacious guestrooms are individually designed but share a country-house-style chic, furnished with handmade wood or wrought iron beds and occasional antique pieces. Family rooms sleep up to five. Excellent breakfasts are served in the equally well-restored dining room, also known as the Turret. Central Derry is about 5 minutes by car or cab, and there's a bus stop nearby too.

9 Troy Park, Culmore Rd., Derry, BT48 7RL. ✆ **078/8436-1669.** www.troyhall.co.uk. 3 units. £80 double. Free parking. Rates include breakfast. **Amenities:** Wi-Fi (free).

Where to Dine in Derry

Badger's ★ IRISH A friendly, proper local pub, right in the center of Derry, Badger's serves hearty, traditional grub—stews, fish and chips, steak and Guinness pie, burgers, and the like, plus a few lighter options such as hot sandwiches and wraps. Plates are generous, and of course, you can wash it all down with a pint of the black stuff. The dining room is satisfyingly unreconstructed with plenty of polished wood and low hanging lamps. No matter what the time of day, there always seem to be a few locals propping up the bar, which helps keep the atmosphere authentic.

16–18 Orchard St., Derry, BT48 6EG. ✆ **028/7136-0763.** Main courses £5–£12. Mon–Sat 11:30am–1am; Sun 11:30am–midnight. (Food served about noon–9pm.) No children after 9pm.

Brown's Restaurant and Champagne Lounge ★★ BRASSERIE One of Derry's best restaurants, Brown's serves excellent Irish food with hints of an international accent. The menu uses plenty of local and regional ingredients, embracing traditional flavors with a touch of well-judged, modern innovation. Menus change frequently, but start with the local seafood tasting plate if it's on the menu—the turf-smoked salmon is particularly delicious. For main courses they have chargrilled beef served with celeriac and truffle puree, and sea bass filet with fennel, samphire, and citrus butter. The menu occasionally takes an unexpected turn. Moroccan style goat with couscous and apricot puree, anyone? But there's something to please everyone, and it's all beautifully prepared and presented. A six-course tasting menu is available for £40 (£65 with wines) and a three-course early bird special for £20.

1 Bonds Hill, Derry, BT47 6DW. ✆ **028/7134-5180.** www.brownsrestaurant.com. Main courses £17–£24. Tues–Fri noon–2:30pm, 5–9:30pm; Sat 5–9:30pm; Sun noon–3pm.

Primrose Café ★★ CAFE This lovely, cheerful cafe is nicely old fashioned without being remotely tired or stuffy. Drop in for a bowl of delicious soup, fresh sandwiches or a tasty pie (served with a side of excellent chips). Or you could just have a plate of homemade scones and some tea, served the proper way with a teapot and fine china. Service is cheery and prices are reasonable—just what you want from a casual lunch on the go.

15 Carlisle Rd., Derry, BT48 6JJ. ✆ **028/7126-4622.** Lunch £3–£8. Mon–Sat 8am–5pm; Sun 11am–3pm.

Derry After Dark

Derry pubs are an important part of the local fabric, and hanging out in one is a good way to meet locals. Boozers are tied into the local music scene, so you'll frequently find bands playing. The pub's even host debating contests, in the midst of which you'll hear Irish eloquence at its well-lubricated best. Here's a small sampling of Derry's more-than-ample pub options.

Along **Waterloo Street,** just outside the city walls, is a handful of Derry's most traditional and popular pubs, known for their live music and simply as the place to be. The **Dungloe,** the **Gweedore,** and **Peador O'Donnells** (see below) are three well-established hot spots. Walk from one end of Waterloo to the other—an act that will take you all of 2 minutes—and you'll likely find the bar for you.

The Clarendon ★ A laidback, traditional pub, the Clarendon is a good place for a pint and a chat. The attractive, redbrick building is on the corner of Strand Road and Lower Clarendon Street. 48 Strand Rd., Derry, BT48 7DL. ✆ **028/7126-3705.**

River Inn ★★ Allegedly Derry's oldest pub (the city walls form part of the building), the River Inn opened its doors in the 17th century. They also serve food, although people come for the atmosphere. 37 Shipquay St., Derry, BT48 6DW. ✆ **028/7137-1965.**

Peador O'Donnells ★★★ "Peadors" to the locals, this is one of the best places in Derry to hear traditional live music. Sessions are every night except Monday; generally they run from 10:30pm to about 1am weekdays, and start earlier in the evening on weekends—although spontaneous sessions have been known to start up anytime. The craic is lively and the atmosphere is buzzing. 59–63 Waterloo St., Derry, BT48 6HD. ✆ **028/7130-9297.** www.peadars.com.

THE SPERRIN MOUNTAINS

Southeast of Derry, the Sperrin Mountains rise up out of County Tyrone, reaching their highest point at Sawel. Here you can see as far as the Foyle Estuary and across the Northern Ireland countryside to Lough Neagh.

In the Sperrins, you won't find the tallest, oldest, or most famous anything. Even the highest peak in the range—Sawel, at 661m (2,168 ft.)—is an easy climb. This is Ireland in a minor key—but splendid, wide-open, walking country, home to golden plover, red grouse, and thousands upon thousands of fluffy white sheep. All the same, gold has been found in these mountains (literally) and poetry, too. The Nobel-winning poet Seamus Heaney grew up on the edge of the Sperrins and found words to suit their subtle splendor. There's also no shortage of standing stones (about 1,000 have been counted), high crosses, dolmens, and hill forts. More reminders that every last bit of bog on this island has its own slew of stories, if only we could hear them told.

Visitor Information

The **Sperrin Heritage Centre,** 274 Glenelly Rd., Cranagh, BT79 8LS (✆ **028/8164-8142**), is a good place to start, with tourist information and an interesting exhibition on the history the area. You can even pan for gold here (small amounts are found in the mountains). The center is east of Plumbridge, off B47.

In addition are four nationally networked tourist information centers in County Tyrone. The **Cookstown Centre,** Burn Road, Cookstown, BT80 8DN (✆ **028/8676-9949**), is open from October to May, Monday to Friday, 9am to 5:30pm, and Saturday, 10am to 4pm; June to September, Monday to Saturday, 10am to 5pm; and also Sunday 2 to 4pm in August. The **Killymaddy Centre,** Ballygawley Road (off A4), Dungannon, BT70 1AB (✆ **028/8772-8600**), is open Monday to Saturday from 9am to 5pm; from April to September it's also open Sunday from 1 to 5pm and until 9pm on weekdays. The **Omagh Centre,** Townhall Square, Omagh, BT78 1BL (✆ **028/8224-7831**), is open year-round,

Monday to Saturday, from 10am to 5:30pm. The **Strabane Centre,** 1A Railway St., Strabane, BT82 8EF (✆ **028/7188-4444**), is open Monday to Saturday 9am to 5pm (half an hour later in July and August).

Exploring the Sperrins

An Creagán Visitors' Centre ★ Beautifully designed to fit in with the craggy countryside around, this visitor center is an excellent place to get your bearings when you first arrive in the Sperrins. A small interpretive center has an interactive exhibition about the mountains and what the area has to offer. A few Bronze Age artifacts that have been excavated from nearby sites are also on display. The helpful staff will give you all the information you need on walking and cycling routes, as well as maps. The center even owns a few self-catering properties if you're interested in staying longer. Prices start at about £180 for a one-bedroom cottage in the low season. Call or visit the website for more details. The center is in the tiny village of Creggan, about 37 miles (60km) southeast of Derry. It's on a main road, but the back way is quicker and very scenic in places. See below for detailed directions.

Signposted off A505, Creggan, Omagh, Co. Tyrone. ✆ **028/8076-1112.** www.an-creagan.com. Free admission. Apr–Sept daily 11am–6:30pm; Oct–Mar Mon–Fri 11am–4:30pm. From Derry, take A6 heading east, then turn off onto B69 heading south. Turn left at the sign for Plumbridge, follow the road south to Ballynamallaght, then turn left again onto B48. At Gortin turn left onto B46 and follow this road until you reach the crossroads with A505 in Creggan (with a gas station on the corner). Turn right on A505; the visitor center is a short distance along this road, on the right—look out for the big stone gates.

Beaghmore Stone Circles ★ In 1945, seven stone circles and a complex assembly of cairns and alignments were uncovered here, in remote moorland north of Evishbrack Mountain and near Davagh Forest Park on the southern edge of the Sperrins. Arranged inside the largest circle are around 800 small stones, christened the "Dragon's Teeth". The precise function of this intriguing concentration of Bronze Age stonework is unknown, but it may have involved astronomical observation and calculation. The layout of the stones has also led archaeologists to believe that they surround unexcavated megalithic tombs.

11 miles (17km) northwest of Cookstown, signposted from A505 to Omagh, Co. Tyrone. No phone. Free admission (open site).

Drum Manor Forest Park ★ Once a private estate, this extensive park and woodland has numerous trails and three old walled gardens, one of which has been designed as a butterfly garden. Also on the grounds are a pond that attracts a variety of wildfowl, a heronry, and a visitor center.

2½ miles (4km) west of Cookstown on A505, Co. Tyrone. ✆ **028/8675-9311** (forest ranger). Admission £3 per car; pedestrians £1 adults, 50p children. Daily 8am–dusk.

Gortin Glen Forest Park ★★ Nearly 400 hectares (988 acres) of conifers make up this serene nature park. The woodlands are a habitat to a variety of wildlife, including a herd of Japanese sika deer. A forest drive offers splendid views of the Sperrins. Here you'll also find a nature center, wildlife enclosures, trails, and a cafe. The park has three separate marked walking trails; details can be found at the visitor center on the B48 road just south of Gortin. The long-distance **Ulster Way** hiking trail also passes through the park. 562 miles

(904km) in total, the Ulster Way follows the North Antrim Coast from Glenarm to Portstewart, before circling virtually the entirety of Northern Ireland. More information on the Ulster Way, including maps, can be found at www.walkni.com/ulsterway.

Vistor Center: On B48 (Glenpark Rd.), about 2½ miles (4km) south of Gortin, Co. Tyrone. ✆ **028/8167-0666.** Free admission; parking £4.50. Visitor Center: daily 10am–dusk.

Ulster American Folk Park ★★★ Another of the region's excellent "living history" style outdoor museums, this one celebrates and commemorates the links between Ulster and the New World. It chronicles the story of those 18th and 19th century emigrants who left their homes in the north of Ireland to seek a new life overseas. The park contains authentic structures from the period—some of them actual dwellings reconstructed from elsewhere—to give an accurate impression of what the life they left behind was really like. After looking around the humble thatched cottages, you can explore a small town street, complete with convincingly decked out shops, manned by costumed actors. Then you can see a full-size replica emigrant ship, before finally getting to see the kinds of frontier, log cabin-type homes the emigrants lived in when they settled in the United States. The park has an active schedule of special events, including a respected Bluegrass festival around the tail end of August or the beginning of September. Check the website for full listings.

2 Mellon Rd., Castletown, Omagh, Co Tyrone BT78 5QU. ✆ **028/8224-3292.** www.nmni.com. Admission £7.50 adults; £5 seniors and students; £4.50 children 5–17; £15.50–£21 families. Mar–Sept Tues–Sun 10am–5pm; Oct–Feb Tues–Fri 10am–4pm, Sat, Sun 11am–4pm. Closed Mon (except Bank Holidays).

Sports & Outdoor Pursuits

BIRD-WATCHING The Sperrins are home to golden plovers, peregrines, ravens, grouse, and hen harriers. **Sawel Mountain,** the highest of the Sperrins, is a great place to take out your binoculars and field guide.

CYCLING The Sperrin countryside is ideal for cycling. Bicycles can be rented by the day or week from the **An Creagán Visitors' Centre** (see p. 497). Bike rentals run roughly £10 a day, £35 a week.

FISHING The **Foyle System** of rivers, from Derry to Omagh and Limavady to Dungiven, makes this a promising area for brown and sea trout (April–early July and September) and a variety of salmon (Mar–Sept). Some good coarse fishing is also available north and west of Omagh, on the Baronscourt Lakes and on the Strule and Fairy Water rivers. The necessary permits, equipment, and good advice are available from **C. A. Anderson & Co.,** 64A Market St., Omagh, BT78 1EN (✆ **028/8224-2311**); and **Mourne Valley Tackle,** 50 Main St., Newtownstewart, BT78 4AA (✆ **028/8166-1543**).

GOLF Several 18-hole courses are located in County Tyrone, all within a modest drive from the heart of the Sperrins: **Strabane Golf Club,** 33 Ballycolman Rd., Strabane, BT82 9PH (✆ **028/7138-2271;** www.strabanegolfclub.co.uk), with green fees of £13 to £20; **Newtownstewart Golf Club,** 38 Golf Course Rd., Newtownstewart, BT78 4HU (✆ **028/8166-1466;** www.newtownstewart golfclub.com), with green fees of £18 to £25, dropping to £12 to £18 in winter; **Omagh Golf Club,** 83a Dublin Rd., Omagh, BT78 1HQ (✆ **028/8224-3160;** www.omaghgolf.co.uk), with greens fees of £20 to £25; and **Killymoon Golf**

Club, 200 Killymoon Rd., Cookstown (✆ **028/8676-3762;** www.killymoon golfclub.com), with green fees of £15 to £25.

HORSEBACK RIDING For private lessons or country trail rides, contact the magnificently named **Tullywhisker Riding School,** 51 Brocklis Rd., Strabane, BT82 9LZ (✆ **028/8165-8015**).

WALKING Whether you're on foot, wheels, or horseback, be sure to traverse the **Glenshane Pass** between Mullaghmore (545m/1,788 ft.) and Carntogher (455m/1,492 ft.), and the **Sawel Mountain Drive** along the east face of the mountain. The vistas along these routes through the Sperrins will remind you of why you've gone out of your way to spend time in Tyrone.

THE FERMANAGH LAKELANDS

In the extreme southwest corner of Northern Ireland, County Fermanagh is a resort area dominated by **Lough Erne,** a long, narrow lake with 154 islands and countless coves and inlets.

The **Shannon-Erne Waterway,** linking the lough to the Shannon system, enhances the lure of Lough Erne as a boating destination. Were you to cruise the whole length of the waterway between the village of Leitrim and Lough Erne, you'd travel 40 miles (65km), past 16 lochs, three lakes, and the Woodford River, all of which are ripe for aquatic exploration.

The hub of this lakeland paradise, wedged between the upper and lower branches of Lough Erne, is **Enniskillen,** a delightful resort town that was the medieval seat of the Maguire clan and a major crossroads between Ulster and Connaught. Both Oscar Wilde and Samuel Beckett were once students here at the royal school.

At the northern tip of the lake is **Belleek,** sitting right across the border in the Republic of Ireland, and known the world over for its trademark delicate bone chinaware. At the southern end of the lake is County Cavan and another slice of border with the Irish Republic. The surrounding countryside holds diverse attractions, from stately homes at Florence Court and Castle Coole to the Marble Arch Caves.

In medieval times, a chain of island monasteries stretched across the waters of Lough Erne, establishing it as a haven for contemplatives. Even allowing for less lofty minds, the Fermanagh Lakelands are still a peaceful place to get away from it all and to gaze, in a phrase from Hopkins, at the "pied beauty" of it all.

Visitor Information

The **Fermanagh Tourist Information Centre,** Wellington Road, Enniskillen, County Fermanagh, BT74 7EF (✆ **028/6632-3110**), is open weekdays year-round from 9am to 5:30pm (until 7pm July–Aug). From Easter to September, it's also open Saturday 10am to 6pm and Sunday 11am to 5pm. For an introduction to the Fermanagh Lakelands on the Web, take a look at **www.fermanaghlakelands.com**.

Exploring the Lakelands

Erne Tours Ltd., Enniskillen (✆ **028/6632-2882;** www.ernetoursltd.com), operates cruises on Lower Lough Erne. The MV *Kestrel,* a 56-seat cruiser, departs from the delightfully named Round "O" Jetty, Brook Park, Enniskillen,

County Fermanagh, BT74 7EU. Trips, including a stop at Devenish Island, last just under 2 hours. They also run a dinner cruise. Call for reservations and to confirm times. The fare starts at £9 for adults, £8 for seniors, £6 for children 11 and under, or £25 for a family of four. Saturday dinner cruises, including a three-course meal, cost £25 for adults, £23 for seniors, and £15 for children 11 and under.

The **Share Holiday Village,** Smith's Strand, Lisnaskea (✆ **028/6772-2122;** www.sharevillage.org), operates cruises on Upper Lough Erne. The 1½-hour trips are conducted onboard the *Inishcruiser,* a 57-passenger ship. The fares are about the same as those for Erne Tours, and the boat is fully wheelchair

BUYING belleek

Perhaps the most famous Irish homeware brand in the world after Waterford Crystal, Belleek Pottery has been making world-renowned fine china since 1864. The **Belleek Visitor Centre,** Belleek, County Fermanagh (✆ **028/6865-9300;** www.belleek.ie) is the world headquarters of the brand. You can look around their museum—which displays unique objects of Belleek pottery, such as the extraordinary International Centre Piece vase they created for the 1900 Paris Expo—and also take factory tours. But of course, the reason most people come is to visit the enormous gift shop.

If you're not a china expert, but you still want to bring back some Belleek pieces from your trip, here are a few tips to ensure that your purchases become heirlooms.

- The Belleek Heirloom Centre has the best selection of patterns from which to choose, giving you lots of options and a wide price range.
- At the center, all the china is displayed around the room. You walk around looking at all the pieces, then note the item numbers of those pieces you like. You take the numbers to the central counter, and they bring boxed china pieces to you.
- Make sure they pull the pieces out of the boxes so you can be sure they are what you expected.
- Take the pieces from the sales assistant and look at them closely. This is delicate china, and it can have tiny imperfections that you can only see by getting up close and personal.
- Be particularly conscious of the bottom of the piece—look for tiny hairline cracks. We bought a lovely Belleek vase once that looked perfect, but leaked through a nearly invisible crack.
- The center will ship internationally if you don't want to risk taking your purchases on a plane.
- If it looks good to you and you love it—buy it! You may not get the chance again.

The Belleek Centre is open from March to June, Monday to Friday, 9pm to 5:30pm, Saturday, 10am to 5:30pm and Sunday, 2 to 5:30pm; July to September, Monday to Friday, 9pm to 5:30pm, Saturday, 10am to 6pm, Sunday, noon to 5:30pm; October to December, Monday to Friday, 9am to 5:30pm, Saturday, 10am to 5:30pm, Sunday, noon to 5pm; January and February, Monday to Friday, 9am to 5:30pm (closed Sat and Sun). Tours are every half-hour on weekdays from 9:30am to 12:15pm and 1:45 to 4pm (last tour 3pm on Friday). From June to September there are also tours on Saturday from 10:30am to 12:15pm and 2 to 4pm. There are no tours on Sunday at any time of year.

accessible. Call for times and precise prices. Share Holiday Village also offers other watersports activities and self-catering, family-friendly cottages (called "chalets").

Numerous charter boat companies in the area will allow you to travel privately for a day or a week on narrow boats, barges, or yachts. Prices vary from a few hundred pounds to much more, for the more elegant options. For a good list of options, go to **www.fermanaghlakelands.com** and click on "Waterways," or call the tourist office to request a brochure.

Independent boatmen offer ferry crossings to some of the many islands in Lough Erne. White Island, Devenish Island, and Boa Island are all rich in archaeological and early Christian remains. Devenish Island has Lough Erne's most important island monastery, founded in the 6th century by St. Molaise. The extensive remains include a 12th-century round tower, which you can climb to take in the view and get a feel for the tiny space inside. From April to September, a ferry runs to Devenish Island from Trory Point, 3¾ miles (6km) from Enniskillen on A32; journey time is about 12 minutes.

On White Island, seven stone figures remain from a vanished 10th-century monastery inside a ruined 12th-century church. From April through August, a ferry runs to White Island, departing from **Castle Archdale Marina** in Irvinestown (✆ **028/6862-1156**); journey time is about 18 minutes. Departures are daily from 9am to 6pm in summer, weekends only from 10am to 6pm in winter. Call for schedule.

The round-trip fare is no more than a few euro. In the cemetery at the west end of Boa Island are two ancient Janus (looking both ways) idols, thought to date from the 1st century. Boa Island is connected to the shore by bridges.

Though it's possible to visit all three islands in a single day, it's a bit ambitious. Begin with Devenish, then visit White, and, if time permits, finish up with Boa.

Castle Coole ★ On the east bank of Lower Lough Erne, this quintessential neoclassical mansion was designed by James Wyatt for the Earl of Belmore and completed in 1796. Its rooms include a lavish state bedroom hung with crimson silk, said to have been prepared for George IV (1762–1830). Other features include a Chinese-style sitting room, magnificent woodwork, fireplaces, and furniture dating from the 1830s. A nearly 600-hectare (1,482-acre) woodland estate surrounds the house. A classical music series runs from May to October.

1½ miles (2.4km) southeast of Enniskillen on the main Belfast-Enniskillen Rd. (A4), Co. Fermanagh. ✆ **028/6632-2690.** http://www.nationaltrust.org.uk/castle-coole. House: £4.70 adults; £2. children; £11 families. Grounds only: £2.50 adults; £1.25 children; £5.25 families. House Mid-Mar–May, Sept Sat–Sun 11am–5pm (and all week during Easter week only); June–Aug daily 11am–5pm. Grounds Mar–Oct daily 10am–7pm; Nov–Feb daily 10am–4pm. Last admission 30 min. before closing.

Crom Estate ★★ This nearly 800-hectare (1,976-acre) nature reserve is a splendid National Trust property, with forest, parks, wetlands, fen meadows, and an award-winning lakeshore visitor center. The numerous trails have concealed places for observing birds and wildlife. You can rent a rowboat and row your way out to the islands. A 19th century castle is also on the estate, though sadly it's not open to visitors. The estate is also a great place to fish for bream and roach. Permits and day tickets are available at the gate lodge. During the summer, the weekends frequently feature special programs and guided nature walks. The estate has several cottages available for rent by the week (about £250–£800). Call or check the National Trust website for more information.

Upper Lough Erne, Newtownbutler, Co. Fermanagh, BT92 8AP. ✆ **028/6773-8118.** www.nationaltrust.org.uk/crom. Admission £3.50 adults; £1.50 children; £8.50 families. Mid-Mar–May, Sept–Oct daily 10am–6pm; June–Aug daily 10am–7pm. Visitor center Mid-Mar–Sept daily 11am–5pm; Oct Sat–Sun 11am–5pm. Last admission 1 hr. before closing. Closed Nov–mid-Mar. 21 miles (34km) south of Enniskillen. Take A4 and A34 from Enniskillen to Newtownbutler, then take the signposted right turn onto a minor road.

Devenish Island ★★ This is the most extensive of the ancient Christian sites in Lough Erne. In the 6th century, St. Molaise founded a monastic community here, to which the Augustinian Abbey of St. Mary was added in the 12th century. In other words, this is hallowed ground, hallowed all the more by the legend that the prophet Jeremiah is buried somewhere nearby—if you can figure that one out. The jewel of Devenish is the perfectly intact, 12th-century round tower, which was erected with Vikings in mind. The island is a marvelous mélange of remnants and ruins, providing a glimpse into the lake's mystical past. While you're in the spirit, be sure to explore Boa and White islands, with their extraordinary carved stone figures, and bring your camera (see the introduction to this section for details on island hopping).

1½ miles (2.4km) downstream from Enniskillen, Co. Fermanagh. ✆ **028/6862-1588.** Admission to round tower £2.50; £1.50 seniors and children. Ferry from Trory Point (4 miles/6.5km from Enniskillen on A32) Easter–mid-Sept at 10am, 1, 3, 5pm; other sailing times based on demand. Round-trip fare £3 adults; £2 seniors, students and children age 5–16, children 4 and under free. Closed mid-Sept to Easter.

Enniskillen Castle ★★ On the banks of Lough Erne in Enniskillen, this impressive castle was built sometime around the first half of the 14th century, but significantly remodeled in the 17th. It's unusual in that the design owes more to the Scottish Baronial style of castle, with its small round turrets, redolent of Gothic motifs, than the more solid, fortress-like English-French style that predominates throughout Ireland. Today its home to three different museums, each covering a different aspect of the Fermanagh area, including its history as an important center of clan power in the middle ages. The castle is on the west side of Enniskillen town center.

Castle Barracks, Enniskillen, Co. Fermanagh, BT74 7HL. ✆ **028/6632-5000.** www.enniskillencastle.co.uk. Admission £4 adults; £3 seniors, students, and children; £11 families. Apr–June, Sept–Oct Sat, Mon 2–5pm, Tues–Fri 10am–5pm; July–Aug Sat–Mon 2–5pm, Tues–Fri 10am–5pm; Nov–Mar Mon 2–5pm, Tues–Fri 10am–5pm. Closed last week of Dec.

Florence Court ★★ This 18th-century Palladian mansion is set among dramatic hills, 8 miles (13km) southwest of Upper Lough Erne and Enniskillen. Originally the seat of the earls of Enniskillen, its interior is rich in rococo plasterwork and antique Irish furniture, while outside is a fine walled garden, an icehouse, and a water-wheel-driven sawmill. The forest park offers a number of trails, one leading to the top of Mount Cuilcagh (nearly 660m/2,165 ft.). You can recover from the climb at the tearoom.

Florence Court, off A32, Enniskillen, Co. Fermanagh, BT92 1DB ✆ **028/6634-8249.** www.nationaltrust.org.uk/florence-court. House: £4.85 adults; £2 children; £11 families. Grounds only: £4.50 adults; £2 children; £11 families. House: mid-Mar–Apr, Oct Sat–Sun 11am–5pm; May, Sept Sun–Thurs 11am–5pm; June–Aug daily 11am–5pm. Last tour 4pm, year-round. Gardens and park Jan–Feb and Nov–Dec daily 10am–4pm; Mar–Oct daily 10am–7pm. Also open all public holidays. Last admission 1 hr. before closing.

Marble Arch Caves ★★★ West of Upper Lough Erne and 12 miles (19km) from Enniskillen near the Florence Court estate, these UNESCO-listed caves are among the finest in Europe for exploring underground rivers, winding passages, and hidden chambers. Electrically powered boat tours take visitors underground, and knowledgeable guides explain the origins of the amazing stalactites and stalagmites. Tours last 75 minutes and leave at 15-minute intervals. The caves are occasionally closed after heavy rains, so phone ahead before making the trip.

Marlbank Rd., Florence Court, off A32, Co. Fermanagh. ✆ **028/6634-8855.** www.marblearchcaves.net. Admission £8.75 adults; £6 seniors and students; £5.75 children; £20 families. Reservations recommended. Mid-Mar–June and Sept daily 10am–4:30pm (last tour); July–Aug daily 10am–5pm (last tour).

Sports & Outdoor Pursuits

BIRD-WATCHING These lakelands are prime bird-watching territory. To mention a few, you'll find whooper swans, great-crested grebes, golden plovers, curlews, corncrakes, kingfishers, herons, merlins, peregrines, kestrels, and sparrow hawks. On Upper Lough Erne, the primary habitats are the reed swamps, flooded drumlins, and fen; on the lower lake, the habitats of choice are the less visited islands and the hay meadows. Two important preserves are at the **Crom Estate** (see p. 501) and the **Castle Caldwell Forest and Islands** on Lower Lough Erne, near Belleek. The preserve includes a stretch of the lough's shoreline; the picturesque 17th century ruins of Castle Caldwell itself stand nearby.

BOATING Lough Erne is an explorer's dream, and you can take that dream all the way to the Atlantic if you want. The price range for fully equipped, four- to eight-berth cruisers is around £650 to £1,200 per week, including tax, depending on the season and the size of the boat. The many local cruiser-hire companies include **Erne Marine,** Bellanaleck (✆ **077/0812-7700**), and **Carrickcraft,** Lurgan (✆ **028/3834-4993** or 01/278-1666 from the Republic; www.cruiseireland.com).

On Lower Lough Erne, north of town, you can hire motorboats from **Manor House Marine,** Killadeas (✆ **028/6862-8100;** www.manormarine.com). Charges average £60 to £90 for a half-day, and £90 to £130 for a full-day, depending on the size of the boat (maximum eight people). You'll have to pay a refundable deposit before heading out.

CYCLING Several of the watersports and activity centers in the area, such as **One Great Adventure** (see "Watersports," below), also rent bicycles. Bicycles are also available from **Corralea Activity Centre,** Belcoo (✆ **028/6638-6123**), and **Belleek Bicycle Hire,** Belleek Cottages, Fermanagh (✆ **028/6865-8181**). Daily bike rental runs around £10.

FISHING If you can't catch a fish here, you will really have to question your technique. The best time for salmon is February to mid-June; for trout, mid-March to June or mid-August until late September. As for coarse fishing, about a dozen species await your line in the area's lakes and rivers. If you've left time for advance planning and consultation, contact the **Department for Culture, Arts and Leisure,** Bedford St., Belfast, BT2 7EG (✆ **028/9025-8825**). For on-the-spot info, tackle, and bait, try **Trevor Kingston,** 18 Church St., Enniskillen (✆ **028/6632-2114**). For locally arranged game fishing, call or drop in on **Melvin Tackle,** Main Street, Garrison, County Fermanagh (✆ **028/6865-8194**).

All necessary permits and licenses are available at the **Fermanagh Tourist Information Centre** (see p. 499).

GOLF The two 18-hole courses in the Lakelands are both in Enniskillen. The **Enniskillen Golf Club,** in the Castle Coole estate (✆ **028/6632-5250;** www.enniskillengolfclub.com), charges greens fees of £20 weekdays to £25. They sometimes have special offers that can drop the price by half midweek, especially off-season. The **Castle Hume Golf Club,** Castle Hume (✆ **028/6632-7077;** www.castlehumegolf.com), is 3 miles (5km) north of Enniskillen, with greens fees of £25 to £45, depending on the number of holes played.

HORSEBACK RIDING Pony trekking and riding lessons are available from **Drumhoney Stables,** Drumhoney, Irvinestown, BT91 1NB (✆ **028/6862-1892**).

WALKING The southwestern branch of the **Ulster Way** follows the western shores of Lough Erne, between the lake and the border. The area is full of great walks. One excellent 6.75-mile (11km; 3–7 hr.) hike is from a starting point near Florence Court and the Marble Arch Caves (see previous page) to the summit of **Mount Cuilcagh** (656m/2,152 ft.). For a detailed description of the route, and downloadable map, visit **www.walkni.com/walks/585/cuilcagh-mountain**.

WATERSPORTS **One Great Adventure,** The Grange Yard, Castlewellan Forest Park, Castlewellan, County Down, BT31 9BU (✆ **084/4770-5477;** www.onegreatadventure.com) is a watersports center based on an island west of downtown. They offer canoeing, sea kayaking, dinghy sailing, and a host of other sports. Prices start at around £25 adults, £15 children. The **Share Holiday Village,** Smith's Strand, Lisnaskea, BT92 0EQ (✆ **028/6772-2122;** www.sharevillage.org), offers sailing, canoeing, windsurfing, and banana skiing. Costs start at around £10 per person. They also offer artistic pursuits for children, such as pottery, balloon modeling, mosaic painting, filmmaking, and circus skills.

Where to Stay & Dine in the Fermanagh Lakelands

Belmore Court Motel ★ Don't be put off by the name—this is actually a good, quality budget option on the edge of Enniskillen. The basic rooms, which are laid out like a traditional American motel (virtually unheard of in Europe) are clean and modern, but, well, basic. Pay just a little more, however, and you get much more space, and nice little touches like free Wi-Fi, plus Nespresso machines and even little balconies in the executive rooms. The location, while not the most romantic spot in Enniskillen, isn't too far from the town center and nearby sights; **Enniskillen Castle** (see p. 502) is a mile in one direction, and **Castle Coole** (see p. 501), a mile in the other.

Tempo Rd., Enniskillen, Co. Fermanagh, BT74 6HX. ✆ **028/6632-6633.** www.motel.co.uk. 60 units. £65–£115 double. Free parking. Breakfast included. **Amenities:** Wi-Fi (free; some rooms).

Castle Leslie ★★★ This historic estate, surrounded by lush grounds that seem to go on forever, is one of the very best places to stay in the North. It's also one of the most historic places you could hope to lay your head in Ireland—it has welcomed a dazzling list of luminaries over the years, from historical figures (W. B. Yeats was a houseguest, and Winston Churchill was a cousin of the Leslie family); to celebrities (Paul McCartney and Heather Mills were married here in 2002). Because the owners were great collectors, it's a place of hidden treasures. Strolling around you'll wander past Wordsworth's harp, the Bechstein grand piano on which Wagner composed *Tristan and Isolde,* and Winston Churchill's baby clothes, among many other things. Guestrooms are individually designed, to varying degrees of grandeur; most are located in the converted hunting lodge, although guests with the deepest pockets can stay in the main house for the full *Downton Abbey* effect. **Snaffles Restaurant** is as outstanding as you'd expect from a place like this; classic and sophisticated dishes prepared with local ingredients, such as roast Silverhill duck served with orange marmalade and creamed sweet potato, or beef filet with a horseradish glaze, served with spinach and onion gnocchi. Less formal dining options are also available if you don't feel like sitting up quite so straight. Check the website for thoroughly reasonable dinner, bed and breakfast packages. In addition to several hundred acres of grounds to wander, where horseback riding, clay pigeon shooting, and other outdoors activities can be arranged, there's also an elegant spa to smooth away the few cares you have left.

Glaslough, Co. Monaghan. ✆ **047/88100.** www.castleleslie.com. 62 units. £132–£182 double. Free parking. Breakfast included. **Amenities:** Restaurant; bar; room service; spa.

The Enniskillen Hotel ★★ This stylish boutique hotel in central Enniskillen has a wonderfully *bon viveur* streak. Bedrooms are modern and chic, with subtle lighting and plenty of dark grays and oatmeal tones. The bar, Wilde's, specializes in whiskey, and sometimes hosts special tasting sessions. You can also take light meals here, or eat in the excellent **Beckett's Grill;** the relatively short menu focuses on barbecue, with a few fish options too. Dinner, bed and breakfast offers are outstandingly good value for money, at around £60 per person. The hotel is on the eastern side of the city, about a 20-minute walk from Enniskillen Castle (see p. 502).

72 Forthill St., Enniskillen, Co. Fermanagh, BT74 6AJ. ✆ **028/6632-1177.** www.enniskillenhotel.com. 35 units. £85–£95 double. Free parking. Breakfast included. **Amenities:** Wi-Fi (free); restaurant; bar; room service.

16

PLANNING YOUR TRIP TO IRELAND

The biggest decision most people will make when it comes to getting around Ireland is whether or not to hire a car. There are upsides and downsides, but if you don't go with a vehicle, then the sites available to you are severely curtailed—outside the major towns and cities, at least. This chapter gives an in-depth rundown of those issues, in addition to other information on getting to Ireland, guided tours, and a directory of other helpful things to get the most out of your Irish adventure.

GETTING THERE

By Plane

The Republic of Ireland has three major international airports. They are, in order of size, **Dublin (DUB)** (✆ **1/814-1111;** www.dublinairport.com), **Cork (ORK)** (✆ **021/413131;** www.cork-airport.com), and **Shannon** (✆ **061/712000;** www.shannonairport.com). Northern Ireland's main airport is **Belfast International Airport (BFS)** (✆ **028/9448-4848;** www.belfastairport.com).

The Republic of Ireland has seven smaller regional airports, all of which offer service to Dublin and several that receive some (very limited) European traffic. They are Donegal, Kerry, Knock, Sligo, and Waterford. In Northern Ireland, the secondary airports are Belfast City Airport and Derry City Airport. Airline service to these smaller airports changes frequently, so be sure to consult your preferred airline or travel agent as soon as you begin to sketch your itinerary.

By Ferry

If you're traveling to Ireland from Britain or the Continent, traveling by ferry is a good alternative to flying. Several car and passenger ferries offer reasonably comfortable furnishings, cabin berths (for longer crossings), restaurants, duty-free shopping, and lounges.

Prices fluctuate seasonally and depend on your route, time of travel, and whether you are on foot or in a car. It's best to check with your travel agent for up-to-date details, but just to give you an idea, the lowest one-way adult fare in high season on the cruise ferry from Holyhead to Dublin starts at around £30. A car usually costs about £80 including one adult passenger, £30 per extra adults, £15 per extra child.

Irish Ferries (✆ **0818/300-400** in the Republic of Ireland, or ✆ **353/818-300-400** in Northern Ireland/U.K.; www.irishferries.ie) operates from Holyhead, Wales, to Dublin, and to Rosslare from Pembroke, Wales, to Rosslare, County Wexford. They also sail from Cherbourg and Rosscoff in France.

Stena Line (✆ **01/204-7777;** www.stenaline.com) sails from Holyhead to Dun Laoghaire, 13km (8 miles) south of Dublin; from Fishguard, Wales, to

PREVIOUS PAGE: **Cliffs of Moher**

Rosslare; and from Cairnryan, Scotland, and Liverpool, England, to Belfast, Northern Ireland.

P&O Irish Sea Ferries (✆ **0871/664-2121** in Britain, ✆ **01/407-3434** in Ireland, or ✆ **352/3420-808-294** in the rest of the world; www.poferries.com) operates from Liverpool to Dublin and from Cairnryan, Scotland, to Larne, County Antrim, Northern Ireland.

SPECIAL INTEREST TRIPS & TOURS

Organized Tours

A limitless array of tour companies offer organized tours in Ireland, from Ghost Tours of Dublin to trips to the Aran Islands from Galway to horseback rides through the Burren. Some of the best of the best are noted here.

Dublin Bus (✆ **01/703-3028;** www.dublinsightseeing.ie) runs a good range of tours in Dublin and the southeast. They include a North Coast and Castle Tour, a South Coast and Gardens tour, as well as the extremely popular Ghost Bus. Most tours cost about €30.

Irish City Tours (✆ **01/898-0700;** www.irishcitytours.com) run hop-on, hop-off tours of Dublin and Belfast in addition to several day trips from Dublin. The destinations covered include **Powerscourt** (p. 171), the **Cliffs of Moher** (p. 329), and the **Giant's Causeway** (p. 482). Prices range from about €30 to €65.

A number of smaller tour companies are run by locals who lead excellent excursions to various regions. **Mary Gibbons Tours** (✆ **01/283-9973;** www.newgrangetours.com) leads absorbing, in-depth tours from Dublin to Newgrange and the Hill of Tara. And in Belfast, don't miss the extraordinary **Black Taxi Tours** (✆ **028/9064-2264;** www.belfasttours.com) that take you through the areas where the Troubles had the most impact and explain it all in compassionate, firsthand terms. See p. 448 for details

Package Tours

Package tours are simply a way to buy the airfare, accommodations, and other elements of your trip (such as car rentals, airport transfers, and even activities) at the same time and often at discounted prices.

One good source for package deals of all kinds is the airlines themselves. Most major airlines offer air/land packages, with surprisingly cheap hotel deals. Several big online travel agencies—such as **Expedia** (www.expedia.com), **Travelocity** (www.travelocity.com), **Orbitz** (www.orbitz.com), and **Lastminute** (www.lastminute.com)—also do a brisk business in packages

Fully escorted tours are where a travel company takes care of absolutely everything, including airfare, hotels, meals, tours, admission costs, and local transportation. Although we hope this book will help you to plan your trip independently and safely, many travelers still prefer the convenience and peace of mind that a fully escorted tour offers. They are particularly good for inexperienced travelers or people with limited mobility. They can also be a great way to make new friends. On the downside, you'll have little opportunity for serendipitous interactions with locals. The tours can be jam-packed with activities, leaving little room for individual sightseeing, whim, or adventure. Plus they often focus on heavily trafficked sites, so you miss out on many lesser-known gems.

Discover Ireland (www.discoverireland.com) can give advice on escorted tours and publishes up-to-the-minute deals on the front page of their website. If you prefer to speak to a person, the website has individual phone numbers for around 50 countries—and every region in the world—on the contact page of the website.

One highly recommended Irish company is **C.I.E. Tours** (✆ **020/8638-0715;** www.cietours.com). They offer fully escorted tours, help organize self-guided tours, and will even arrange individual, chauffeur-driven tours. Another, **Hidden Ireland Tours** (✆ **087/221-4002;** www.hiddenirelandtours.com), specializes in more off-the-beaten-path tours of Kerry, Galway, and Donegal.

A good company for travelers from the U.S. and Canada is **Authentic Ireland** (✆ **888/771-8350** or 065/293-3088; www.authenticireland.com). In addition to escorted, self-guided, and private tours, their range also covers themed tours such as castle and golfing vacations.

Those wanting to combine their trip with some serious learning opportunities might be interested in the **International Summer School** program at the National University of Ireland, Galway (University Rd., Galway, Co. Galway; www.nuigalway.ie/international-summer-school), which includes courses on Irish language and history. Contact the course administrator, Ms. Fiona Dwyer, on ✆ **091/495-442** for more information.

GETTING AROUND

By Car

Although Ireland has a reasonably extensive network of public transportation, there are many advantages to having your own car. Trains tend not to go to charming small towns and villages, and great houses and castles are usually miles from any major town. Buses are slow, and service to places off the beaten track can be infrequent.

In the summer, weekly rental rates on a manual-transmission compact vehicle begin at around €160 and ascend steeply. Rates are much cheaper out of season.

Unless your stay in Ireland extends beyond 6 months, your own valid driver's license (provided you've had it for at least 6 months) is all you need to drive in Ireland. Rules and restrictions for car rental vary slightly and correspond roughly to those in other European nations and the U.S., with two important distinctions: Most rental-car agencies in the Republic won't rent to you (1) if you're 24 and under or 75 and over (there's no upper age limit in the North) or (2) if your license has been valid for less than a year.

Driving Laws, Tips & Warnings

Highway safety has become a critical issue in Ireland during the past several years. The number of highway fatalities is high for such a small nation—Ireland regularly comes out near the bottom of European league tables for accident rates.

In an effort to rein in the Irish drivers, the Republic now uses a penalty "points" system similar to that in the U.K. and the U.S. While visitors won't have points added to their licenses, they may still be penalized with fines if they speed or commit driving infractions.

All distances and speed limits on road signs in the Republic of Ireland are in **kilometers,** while in Northern Ireland they are in **miles.** Take care if you're driving around the borderlands—the border is unmarked, so you can cross over from one side to the other without knowing it. It's easy to get confused and speed accidentally.

If you're not used to driving in rural areas on the left-hand side of the road, take precautions. Try to avoid driving after dark, and stay off the road when driving conditions are compromised by rain, fog, or heavy traffic. Getting used to left-side driving, left-handed stick shift, narrow roads, and a new landscape are enough for the driver alone to manage, so it's helpful if you can have somebody along to navigate. You can also rent a GPS navigation device with your car. Most major rental firms offer them.

Roundabouts (what Americans call traffic circles or rotaries) are found on most major roads and take a little getting used to. Remember always to yield to traffic coming from the right as you approach a roundabout and follow the traffic to the left, signaling before you exit the circle.

One signal that could be misleading to U.S. drivers is a flashing amber light at a pedestrian traffic light. This almost always follows a red light, and it means yield to pedestrians but proceed when the crossing is clear.

The Republic has relatively few types of roads. **Motorways (M)** are major highways, the equivalent of Interstates in the U.S. **National (N)** roads link major cities on the island. Though these are the equivalent highways in North America, they are rarely more than two lanes in each direction (and are sometimes as small as one American-sized lane). Most pass directly through towns, making cross-country trips longer than you'd expect. **Regional (R)** roads have one lane of traffic traveling in each direction and generally link smaller cities and towns. Last are the rural or unclassified roads, often the most scenic back roads. These can be poorly signposted, very narrow, and a bit rough, but they usually travel through beautiful countryside locations.

Both the Republic and Northern Ireland have severe laws against drunk driving. The legal limit for both is 35 micrograms of alcohol per 100 milliliters of breath. What that equates to varies by person, but even one pint of

road rules **IN A NUTSHELL**

1. Drive on the left side of the road.
2. Road signs are in kilometers, except in Northern Ireland, where they are in miles.
3. On motorways, the left lane is the traveling lane. The right lane is for passing.
4. Everyone must wear a seat belt by law. Children must be in age-appropriate child seats.
5. Children 11 and under are not allowed to sit in the front seat.
6. When entering a roundabout (traffic circle), give way to traffic coming from the right.
7. The speed limits are 50kmph (31 mph) in urban areas; 80kmph (50 mph) on regional and local roads, sometimes referred to as non-national roads; 100kmph (62 mph) on national roads, including divided highways (called dual carriageways); and 120kmph (75 mph) on freeways (called motorways)

beer can be enough to put you over the limit. The general rule is: Do not drink and drive.

Renting a Car

Try to make car-rental arrangements well in advance of your departure. Ireland is a small country, and in high season it can virtually run out of rental cars—but long before it does, it runs out of affordable rental cars. Major international car-rental firms are represented at airports and cities throughout Ireland and Northern Ireland.

If you rent with a credit card that claims to provide free protection, be sure to call your card's customer service line to make certain there are no restrictions on that coverage in Ireland. Not all cards do offer insurance protection for car rentals in Ireland.

By law, you must be between the ages of 25 and 75 to rent a car in Ireland. The only documentation you should need is your driving license and photographic I.D., such as a passport, plus a printout of your reservation if you have one.

By Train

Iarnród Éireann (Irish Rail) (✆ **1850/366222** or 01/836-6222; www.irishrail.ie) operates the train services in Ireland. Train travel is generally the fastest way to get around the country. Most lines radiate from Dublin to other principal cities and towns. From Dublin, the journey time to Cork is about 2½ hours; to Belfast, just over 2 hours; to Galway, just under 2½ hours; to Killarney, 3¼ hours; to Sligo, 3 hours; and to Waterford, about 2¼ hours.

In addition to the Irish Rail service between Dublin and Belfast, **Translink** (✆ **028/9066-6630;** www.nirailways.co.uk) operates routes from Belfast that include Coleraine and Derry, in addition to virtually all 21 localities in Northern Ireland.

One useful piece of lingo: when buying any sort of travel tickets—air, ferry, train or bus—a "single" means one-way, a "return" is round-trip.

By Bus

Bus Éireann (✆ **01/836-6111;** www.buseireann.ie) operates an extensive system of express bus services, as well as local service, to nearly every town in Ireland. The Bus Éireann website provides timetables and fares for bus service throughout the country. Similarly, **Translink** provides detailed information on services within Northern Ireland (✆ **028/9066-6630;** www.translink.co.uk). Bus travel in both countries is affordable, reliable, and comfortable—but also slow.

By Plane

Ireland is such a small country that there is very little point in flying from one end to the other. As it is, the options for internal flights seem to get more limited, year on year—partly because of improved roads and faster rail journey times. **Aer Lingus Regional** (✆ **081/836-5000;** hwww.aerarann.com), a joint operation between the national carrier and the smaller **Aer Arann,** still runs a couple of flights daily between Dublin and Kerry. The British budget airline **Flybe** (✆ **0044/139-268-3152;** www.flybe.com) has one or two daily flights between Dublin and Donegal.

Irish Rail Routes
North Channel
ATLANTIC OCEAN
Portrush
Ballycastle
Coleraine
Derry
Ballymoney
Larne Harbour
Larne
Whitehead
Carrickfergus
Antrim
Bangor
Belfast York Road
BELFAST CENTRAL
Lurgan
Portadown
Lisburn
Enniskillen
Newry
Dundalk
Ballina
Sligo
Collooney
Boyle
Carrick-on-Shannon
Ballymote
Foxford
MANULLA JUNCTION
Dromod
Castlebar
Westport
Claremorris
Ballyhaunis
Longford
Castlerea
Mostrim
Drogheda
Irish Sea
Mosney
Balbriggan
Skerries
Roscommon
Tuam
Mullingar
Enfield
Malahide
Dublin Connolly
Woodlawn
Athenry
Athlone
Galway
Maynooth
DUBLIN
Clara
Dublin Pearse
Ballinasloe
Kildare
Dublin Heuston
Dun Laoghaire
Tullamore
Attymon
PORTARLINGTON
Bray
Newbridge
ARAN ISLANDS
Portlaoise
Ennistymon
Roscrea
Greystones
Athy
Cloughjordan
Wicklow
Carlow
Ennis
Nenagh
BALLYBROPHY
Rathdrum
Birdhill
Templemore
Arklow
Muine Bheag
Kilkenny
Castleconnell
Limerick
Thurles
Gorey
Thomastown
Mouth of the Shannon
Listowel
LIMERICK JUNCTION
Enniscorthy
Clonmel
Tipperary
Campile
Charleville
Wexford
Cahir
Rosslare Strand
Tralee
Carrick-on-Suir
Rathmore
Farranfore
MALLOW
WATERFORD
Rosslare Harbour
Killarney
Banteer
Ballycullane
Millstreet
Bridgetown
Fota
Cork
Wellington Bridge
Cobh
St. George's Channel
ATLANTIC OCEAN
0 30 mi
0 30 km

Major Irish Bus Routes

TIPS ON ACCOMMODATIONS

In this guide, we use our own system of one to three stars for rating places to stay, based on quality of amenities, atmosphere, and the most subjective, overall value for money. Cost is only a factor inasmuch as it affects value. For example, an expensive hotel may rate only one star, while a moderately priced guesthouse rates two stars if it delivers an exceptional experience for the money. See the "Where to Stay" sections throughout this book for recommendations.

For even more information about staying in Ireland, *Be Our Guest* is a comprehensive guide to the hotels, country houses, castles, and inns of Ireland, published by the Irish Hotel Federation. It is available from the Irish Tourist Board. It's also online at **www.irelandhotels.com**, which is a handy, searchable site, with options to sort hotels by feature (TV in all rooms, elevators, babysitting, and so on).

Those looking for something exclusive should try **Ireland's Blue Book** (www.irelands-blue-book.ie), which lists a collection of upscale manor house hotels and castles.

Bed & Breakfasts

For anyone on a budget who is touring the country and spending only a night or two in each location, B&Bs are often hard to beat.

While most B&Bs are regulated and inspected by Ireland's Tourism Quality Services (look for the shamrock seal of approval), many operate outside the regulation system. Those without governmental supervision or approval are not necessarily worse than those stamped with the green shamrock. Approval involves an annual fee and some restrictions that some B&B owners choose not to accept.

In the high season it's a good idea to make your reservation weeks in advance. However, you can often find a room at a B&B when you arrive out of season. In a moderately priced B&B, the average cost for a room with private bathroom is roughly €85 per person per night. Obviously, some B&Bs charge less than this, and some charge more. While each year more and more small B&Bs accept credit cards, but many still do not—ask in advance.

In the North, the Northern Ireland Tourist Board inspects each of its recommended B&Bs annually. They also have a comprehensive accommodation rating system, with one to five stars given in various categories. More information about the system can be found online at **www.nidirect.gov.uk/where-to-stay-on-holiday-in-northern-ireland**.

Hidden Ireland

Hidden Ireland is essentially a collection of particularly elegant and unique B&Bs. These private houses offer you the opportunity to experience life in a castle or in a historic manor house, including some of Ireland's oldest and grandest buildings. Expect to pay anywhere from €150 to around €350 a night for a double room in one of these places. To explore this option, contact Hidden Ireland (✆ **01/662-7166,** 353/1662-7166 internationally; www.hiddenireland.com).

Farmhouse B&Bs

Many of Ireland's small, family-run farms offer an inexpensive alternative to hotels and guesthouses, especially for families with small children. **B&B Ireland** (✆ **071/982-2222;** www.irishfarmholidays.com) produces an annual guide to farmhouse accommodations, and we've included some of the best in this guide.

Self-Catering

If you want to stay awhile and establish a base, you might consider renting an apartment, townhouse, or cottage. Self-catering is a huge business in Ireland, and the range offered is impressive. The minimum rental period is usually 1 week, although shorter periods are negotiable in the off season. Families and small groups often find self-catering works out to be significantly less expensive than staying in hotels. However, in the high season, in both the Republic and the North, a cottage sleeping seven could cost anywhere from around €300 to more than €1,000 per week. Both Tourism Ireland and the Northern Ireland Tourist Board prepare helpful annual guides to self-catering cottages.

Among the self-catering companies worth checking out are **Cashelfean Holiday Houses** (✆ **027/62000;** www.cashelfean.com) for alluring seaside properties in west County Cork. **Rent an Irish Cottage** (✆ **061/411109;** www.rentacottage.ie) offer a selection of traditional Irish cottages all over Ireland, fully equipped to meet modern expectations.

Two companies specialize in self-catering accommodations in Ireland's historic and architecturally significant properties—including elegant Georgian manor houses, stately country mansions, lighthouses, towers, and castles. The **Irish Landmark Trust** (✆ **01/670-4733;** www.irishlandmark.com), rescues historic but neglected properties all over the island and restores them into fabulous hideaways, complete with period furnishings. It's a not-for-profit institution, so prices are lower than you might expect, given the unique properties they offer. Meanwhile, **Elegant Ireland** (✆ **01/473-2505;** www.elegant.ie), can put you up in anything from an upscale seaside bungalow to a medieval castle that sleeps 20. As most properties are privately owned, they are priced according to what the market will bear. Bargains are harder to come by, and deals are more likely in the off season.

Youth Hostels

Some Irish hostels are broadening their scope and redesigning to attract travelers of all ages, as well as families. Many have private rooms and, although they cost a fraction of even a modest bed-and-breakfast, quite a few are attractive and in extraordinarily beautiful locations. We've included the best of these in this guide.

AnÓige, the Irish Youth Hostel Association (✆ **01/830-4555;** www.anoige.ie), runs dozens of exquisitely located hostels in Ireland, many of them in buildings of real character.

In the North, **HINI** (Hostelling International Northern Ireland; ✆ **028/9032-4733;** www.hini.org.uk), runs similar hostels in often extraordinary locations.

The Bottom Line on Beds

RATES In recent years, there has generally been a downward trend in prices across the Republic and Northern Ireland. However, in the summer, prices can spike up and fall within the course of a week. We recommend booking well ahead to get the best prices. And please note that, especially in cities, if you book a month or two in advance, you can often get a better rate at a 4-star hotel than at a 2-star guesthouse. The most expensive hotels have been offering in-advance discounts of up to 50%. So before you book that cheap hotel with no services, just have a peek at your dream hotel's prices and see if it's not as cheap if not cheaper for at least some of your time in the country.

The price categories used throughout this guide indicate the cost of a double room for two per night, including tax but not service charges: Some hotels and B&Bs list their prices per person, but we find that confusing so in this guide we've used the price a double room would cost for two people spending 1 night. If you're traveling on your own, expect to play slightly more than half the price of a double. Children staying in their parent's room are usually charged at 20% to 50% of the adult rate.

TERMINOLOGY The Irish use the phrase "en suite" to indicate a room with private bathroom. A "double" has a double bed, and a "twin" has two single beds. (It's important to specify which you want). An "orthopedic" bed has an extra firm mattress. Queen- and king-size beds are not common except in large, deluxe hotels.

RESERVATIONS Foreign visitors to Ireland should always have at least their first night's room booked, as they will be required to give an address at Immigration when they arrive at the airport. If you need help finding accommodations for subsequent nights after you arrive in Ireland, contact the local tourism office as soon as possible.

QUALITY & VALUE Despite the various systems of approval, regulation, and ratings, accommodations in Ireland are quite uneven in quality and cost. Often these variations are due to location; a wonderful, budget B&B in an isolated area of countryside can be dirt-cheap, while a mediocre guesthouse in Dublin or Cork can cost much more.

In any given lodging, the size and quality of the rooms can vary considerably, often without any corresponding variation in cost. This is particularly true of single rooms, which can approach Victorian boarding-house standards in some guesthouses. Don't be discouraged by this, but know what you're getting into so you're not disappointed. If you have complaints, state them at once and unambiguously—doing so may bring an immediate resolution (ask for a lower rate or a better room).

Note: Many lodgings close for a few days or more on and around Christmas, even when they announce that they are open year-round. If you plan to visit Ireland during the Christmas holidays, double-check that the hotels, restaurants, and attractions you're counting on will be open.

[Fast FACTS] IRELAND

Area Codes Area codes in Ireland range from one number (the Dublin area code is "1") to three. Area codes are included in all listings in this guide. Within Ireland, you dial 0 before the area code. Outside of Ireland, however, you do not dial 0 before the area code.

Business Hours **Banks** are generally open 10am to 4pm Monday to Wednesday and Friday and 10am to 5pm on Thursday. Post offices (also known as An Post) are generally open from 9am to 5:30pm Monday to Friday and 9am to 1:30pm on Saturday. Some take an hour for lunch from 1 to 2pm, and small or rural branches may close on Saturday. **Museums and sights** are generally open 10am to 5pm Tuesday to Saturday and 2 to 5pm on Sunday. **Shops** generally open 9am to 6pm Monday to Saturday with late opening on Thursday until 7 or 8pm. Some shops in larger towns and cities will also open on Sundays (typically from late morning to late afternoon). Major shops, such as department stores, often stay open much later than other businesses.

Car Rental See "By Car" under "Getting Around," earlier in this chapter.

Cellphones See "Mobile Phones," below.

Crime See "Safety," later in this section.

Disabled Travelers For disabled travelers, Ireland is a mixed bag. Its modern buildings and cities are generally accessible, but many of its buildings are historic, and those often lack wheelchair access. Trains can be accessed by wheelchairs but only with assistance. If you plan to travel by train in Ireland, be sure to check out Iarnród Éireann's website (www.irishrail.ie), which includes services for travelers with disabilities.

If you're conducting research prior to your trip, one of the best Irish-based online resources is **www.disability.ie**.

For advice on travel to Northern Ireland, contact **Disability Action** (✆ **028/9029-7880;** www.disabilityaction.org). The Northern Ireland Tourist Board also publishes a helpful annual *Information Guide to Accessible Accommodation,* available from any of its offices worldwide.

Finding accessible lodging can be tricky in Ireland. Many of the buildings here are hundreds of years old, and older hotels, small guesthouses, and landmark buildings still have steps outside and in. The rule of thumb should be: Never assume that a B&B, hotel, or restaurant has accessible facilities and ask about your requirements before booking. Where there are serious mobility issues with a property, we've tried to mention them in this book.

Doctors Healthcare in Ireland is comparable to that in other European nations. In the Irish system, private doctors and hospitals provide care and patients purchase healthcare insurance. See the individual listings under "Fast Facts" in the other chapters of this book.

Electricity The Irish electric system operates on 220 volts with a large plug bearing three rectangular prongs. The Northern Irish system operates on 250 volts with a similar plug. To use standard American 110-volt appliances, you'll need both a transformer and a plug adapter. Most new laptops have built-in transformers, but some do not, so beware.

Embassies & Consulates The **American Embassy** is at 42 Elgin Rd., Ballsbridge, Dublin 4 (✆ **01/668-8777;** dublin.usembassy.gov); the **Canadian Embassy** is at 7–8 Wilton Terrace, Third Floor, Dublin 2 (✆ **01/234-4000;** www.canadainternational.gc.ca/ireland-irlande); the **British Embassy** is at 29 Merrion Rd., Dublin 2 (✆ **01/205-3700;** www.gov.uk/government/world/organisations/british-embassy-dublin); and the **Australian Embassy** is at Fitzwilton House, Seventh Floor, Wilton Terrace, Dublin 2 (✆ **01/664-5300;** www.ireland.embassy.gov.au). In addition, an **American Consulate** is at Danesfort House, 223 Stranmillis Rd., Belfast BT9 5GR (✆ **028/9038-6100;** belfast.usconsulate.gov).

Emergencies For the **Garda (police),** fire, ambulance, or other emergencies, dial ✆ **999.**

Family Travel Recommended family travel websites include **Family Travel Forum** (www.familytravelforum.com), **Family Travel Network** (www.familytravelnetwork.com), **Traveling Internationally with Your Kids** (www.travelwithyourkids.com), and **Family Travel Files** (www.thefamilytravelfiles.com).

Internet & Wi-Fi Wi-Fi is widespread in Irish hotels and B&Bs, even in rural areas. It's not universal, however. Most B&Bs and smaller hotels provide it free, but larger hotels sometimes charge for access.

Language Ireland has two official languages: English and Gaelic (which is also known as Irish). All native Irish can speak English. Gaelic is growing in popularity, and there is a strong national movement to preserve and expand the language. Areas of the country where Gaelic is protected and promoted are known as the **Gaeltacht** and include

Donegal, Galway, and parts of Kerry. In these regions signs are in Gaelic only (no English translation is provided). As Gaelic is a complex and ancient language that you will not be able to figure out on your own, don't hesitate to ask for help (in English) if you get lost—despite the government's best efforts, everybody in the Gaeltacht regions speaks English.

LGBT Travelers Ireland has come a long way since homosexuality was legalized in 1993 (1982 in the North), but gay and lesbian visitors should be aware that this is still a conservative country. Cities like Dublin and Galway are more liberal in their attitudes (particularly among the younger generation), and discrimination on the basis of sexuality is illegal throughout Ireland. Nonetheless, it's advisable to proceed with caution when traveling in rural areas. Recommended websites for gay and lesbian travelers include **Gay Ireland** (www.gay-ireland.com) and **Outhouse** (www.outhouse.ie).

Lost Property If your passport is lost or stolen, contact your country's embassy immediately. Be sure to tell all of your credit card companies the minute you discover that your wallet is gone and file a report at the nearest police station.

Mail In Ireland, mailboxes are painted green with the word post on top. In Northern Ireland, they usually look the same but are painted red with a royal coat of arms symbol. From the Republic, an airmail letter or postcard to any other part of the world, not exceeding 50 grams, costs €.90 (aside from Great Britain, when it costs €.60). From Northern Ireland to Europe, airmail letters not exceeding 20 grams cost £.88; to the rest of the world it's £1.28

Mobile Phones The Three letters that define much of the world's wireless capabilities are GSM (Global System for Mobiles), a big, seamless network that makes for easy cross-border cellphone use throughout Europe and dozens of other countries worldwide. If your cellphone is on a GSM system, and you have a world-capable multiband phone, you can make and receive calls while you're in Ireland.

Simply checking directly with your mobile phone provider is usually the best way to find out what you need to know; but do this before you leave your home country, as you sometimes have to ask for the "international roaming" capability to be switched on first—and that can't usually happen if you're already overseas.

Another way to check is to look up your phone on **www.gsmarena.com**, which handily lists all the makes models with GSM capability. The general rule of thumb is the older and more basic your phone is, the less likely you are to be able to use it abroad.

Unfortunately, using your own phone in Ireland could prove very expensive. Most mobile phone companies charge very large premiums on call charges made while abroad. If you use a smartphone, such as an iPhone or Android device, you should ensure that you turn off features such as location services and push notifications, or you could end up facing *enormous* charges for data roaming. Similarly, you should always use Wi-Fi if you need to download anything.

To avoid all of this hassle, many travelers simply prefer to **rent** a phone for their trip to Ireland. You can do this from any number of overseas sites; several Irish phone companies have kiosks at the main airports, and car-rental agencies can usually rent you a phone for the duration of your stay. Alternatively, **Rent-a-Phone Ireland** (**✆ 087/683-4563;** www.cell-phone-ireland.com) is a company that allows you to reserve a phone in advance and pick it up from the arrivals lounge at Dublin airport. They charge around €70 per week for a standard phone (including €5 worth of calls--enough for roughly a half hour call to North America), or €100 for a smartphone, including €20 of calls and a 150MB data allowance.

Another option is to purchase a disposable "pay as you go" phone. Disposable phones aren't quite as big here as in some countries, due to the relatively low cost of phone contracts; however, you can buy them quite cheaply from mobile phone stores (most airports and almost any town of reasonable size will have at least one), or even some supermarkets. You can also buy a SIM card from a phone shop and use that in your own phone, topping it up whenever you need to; ask for a "SIM only plan."

Call charges in Ireland, and across the European Union, are much lower than they are in many other parts of the world, including the U.S; on pay-as-you-go, expect to pay around €0.35 per minute. You are not charged for incoming calls.

Money The Republic of Ireland uses the single European currency known as the **euro** (€). Euro notes come in denominations of €5, €10, €20, €50, €100, €200, and €500. The euro is divided into 100 cents; coins come in denominations of €2, €1, 50¢, 20¢, 10¢, 5¢, 2¢, and 1¢. As part of the United Kingdom, Northern Ireland uses the British **pound sterling** (£). The British pound is not accepted in the Republic, and the euro is not accepted in the North—if you're traveling in both parts of Ireland you'll need some of both currencies, although shops on the border tend to accept both, as do some of the bigger tourist attractions in the North. For those traveling between Great Britain and Northern Ireland, although the pounds issued in Northern Ireland are legal tender in Great Britain and vice versa, the paper money actually *looks* different, and you may find that cabdrivers and small business owners in the North won't accept bills issued in Great Britain. In that case, you can change the money into locally issued versions at any large central bank, free of charge.

The British currency used in Northern Ireland has notes in denominations of £5, £10, £20, £50, and £100. Coins are issued in £2, £1, 50p, 20p, 10p, 5p, 2p, and 1p denominations.

Note for all international travelers: the values of most currencies have been fluctuating a great deal lately, so it is best to begin checking exchange rates well in advance of your visit to get a feel for where they will stand for your trip.

The easiest and best way to get cash away from home is from an ATM (automated teller machine), sometimes referred to as a "cash machine" or a "cashpoint." The **Cirrus** and **PLUS** ATM networks span the globe; look at the back of your bankcard to see which network you're on. Be sure you know your personal identification number (PIN) and daily withdrawal limit before you depart.

Passports See "Embassies & Consulates," above, for whom to contact if you lose yours while traveling in Ireland. For additional, country-specific information, please contact the following agencies:

For Residents of Australia Contact the **Australian Passport Information Service** at ✆ **131-232,** or visit the government website at www.passports.gov.au.

For Residents of Canada Contact the central **Passport Office,** Department of Foreign Affairs and International Trade, Ottawa, ON K1A 0G3 (✆ **800/567-6868;** www.ppt.gc.ca).

For Residents of New Zealand Contact the **Passports Office,** Department of Internal Affairs (✆ **0800/225-050** in New Zealand or 04/463-9360; www.passports.govt.nz).

For Residents of the United Kingdom Visit your nearest passport office, major post office, or travel agency or contact the **United Kingdom Passport Service** at ✆ **0300/222-0000** or visit its website at www.gov.uk/government/organisations/hm-passport-office.

For Residents of the United States To find your regional passport office, either check the U.S. State Department website (**www.state.gov**) or call the **National Passport Information Center** toll-free number (✆ **877/487-2778**) for automated information.

Pharmacies Drugstores are called "chemists" and are found in every city, town, and most villages of any size. See the individual listings under "Fast Facts" in the other chapters of this book.

Police In the Republic of Ireland, a law enforcement officer is called a **Garda,** a member of the *Garda Síochána* ("Guardian of the Peace"); in the plural, it's **Gardaí** (pronounced *Gar*-dee) or simply "the Guards." Dial ✆ **999** to reach the Gardaí in an emergency. Except for special detachments, Irish police are unarmed and wear dark blue uniforms. In Northern Ireland you can also reach the police by dialing ✆ **999.**

Safety By U.S. standards, Ireland is very safe, but, particularly in the cities, it's not safe enough to warrant carelessness. Be wary of the usual tourists' plagues: pickpockets, purse snatchers, and car thieves. Most advice is standard for travel anywhere. Do not leave cars unlocked or cameras and other expensive equipment unattended. Ask at your hotel which areas are safe and which are not. Take a taxi back to your hotel if you're out after about 11pm.

In Northern Ireland, safety has to be a somewhat greater concern, due to the long-running political tensions there. Violence is no longer commonplace; however, occasional flare-ups do happen, especially during the Orange marching season in the late summer. Still, visitors rarely have problems with this since they are simply not the targets of it. See chapter 15 for more information.

Senior Travel Seniors are sometimes called "O.A.P.'s" in Ireland (it rather unfortunately stands for "Old Age Pensioners"). People over the age of 60 often qualify for reduced admission to museums and other attractions. Always ask about an O.A.P. discount if special rates are not posted. Discover Ireland (p. 509) can offer advice on how to find the best discounts.

Smoking Ireland and Northern Ireland both have broad antismoking laws that ban smoking in all public places, including bars, restaurants, and hotel lobbies. However, most restaurants and pubs have covered outdoor smoking areas.

Taxes As in many European countries, sales tax is VAT (value-added tax) and is often already included in the price quoted to you or shown on price tags. In the Republic, VAT rates vary—for hotels, restaurants, and car rentals, it is 13½ percent; for souvenirs and gifts, it is 23 percent. In Northern Ireland, the VAT is 20 percent across-the-board. VAT charged on services such as hotel stays, meals, car rentals, and entertainment cannot be refunded to visitors, but the VAT on products such as souvenirs is refundable.

Telephones In the Republic, the telephone system is known as Eircom; in Northern Ireland, it's BT (British Telecom). Every effort has been made to ensure that the numbers and information in this guide are accurate at the time of writing. **Overseas calls** from Ireland can be quite costly, whether you use a local phone card or your own calling card.

To call Ireland from home:

1. **Dial the international access code:** 011 from the U.S., 00 from the U.K., 0011 from Australia, or 0170 from New Zealand.

2. **Dial the country code:** 353 for the Republic, 44 for the North.

3. **Dial the local number,** remembering to omit the initial 0, which is for use only within Ireland (for example, to call the County Kerry number 066/12345 from the United States, you'd dial 011-353-66/12345).

To make international calls: First dial 00 and then the country code (U.S. or Canada 1, U.K. 44, Australia 61, New Zealand 64). Next you dial the area code and local number. For example, to call the U.S. number 212/000-0000 you'd dial ✆ 00-1-212/000-0000. The toll-free international access code for AT&T is ✆ 1-800-550-000; for Sprint it's ✆ 1-800-552001; and for MCI it's ✆ 1-800-551-001.

To make local calls: To dial a local number within an area code, drop the initial 0. To dial a number within Ireland but in a different area code, use the initial 0. As in many parts of the world, phone booths are slowly disappearing; however, you will still find them. Calls from a phone booth usually require coin payment, but at some you need a calling card (in the Republic) or phone card (in the North). Both are prepaid computerized cards that you insert into the phone instead of coins. They can be purchased in post offices, grocery stores, and shops (such as newsstands).

Time Ireland follows Greenwich Mean Time (1 hr. earlier than Central European Time) from November to March, and British Summer Time (the same as Central European Time) from April to October. Ireland is 5 hours ahead of the eastern United States. Ireland's latitude makes for longer days and shorter nights in the summer and the reverse in the winter. In June, the sun doesn't fully set until around 11pm, but in December, it is dark by 4pm.

Tipping For taxi drivers, hairdressers, and other providers of service, tip an average of 10 to 15 percent. For restaurants, the policy is usually printed on the menu—either a gratuity of 10 to 15 percent is automatically added to your bill, or it's left up to you. As a rule, bartenders do not expect a tip, except when table service is provided.

Toilets Public toilets are usually simply called "toilets" or are marked with international symbols. In the Republic of Ireland, some of the older ones carry the Gaelic words FIR (men) and MNA (women). Check out malls and shopping centers for some of the newest and best-kept bathrooms in the country. Free restrooms are available to customers of sightseeing attractions, museums, hotels, restaurants, pubs, shops, and theaters. Many of the newer gas stations (called "petrol stations" in Ireland) have public toilets, and a few even have baby-changing facilities.

Visas Citizens of the United States, Canada, Australia, and New Zealand entering the Republic of Ireland or Northern Ireland for a stay of up to 3 months do not need a visa, but a valid **passport** is required.

For citizens of the United Kingdom, when traveling on flights originating in Britain, the same rules apply as they would for travel to any other member state of the European Union (E.U.).

Water Tap water throughout the island of Ireland is generally safe. However, some areas in the west of Ireland have been battling with out-of-date water-purification systems. Always carry a large bottle of water with you.

Wi-Fi See "Internet & Wi-Fi," earlier in this section.

Women Travelers Women should expect few if any problems traveling in Ireland. Women are accepted traveling alone or in groups in virtually every environment, and long gone are the days when women were expected to order half-pints of beer in pubs, while men were allowed to order the bigger, more cost-effective pints of ale. In fact, the only time you're likely to attract any attention at all is if you eat alone in a restaurant at night—a sight that is still relatively uncommon in Ireland outside of the major cities. Even then, you'll not be hassled.

If you drink in a pub on your own, though, expect all kinds of attention, as a woman drinking alone is still considered to be on the market—even if she's reading a book, talking on her cellphone to her fiancé, or doing a crossword puzzle. So be prepared to fend them off. Irish men almost always respond well to polite rejection, though.

In cities, as ever, take a cab home at night and follow all the usual advice of caution you get when you travel anywhere. Essentially, don't do anything in Ireland that you wouldn't do at home.

Index

C

D

T

Accommodations

Restaurants

Photo Credits

p. v, © Milosz_M; p. iii, © Gabriela Insuratelu; p. 1, © Captblack76; p. 2, © Ryan Simpson; p. 3, © Pierre Leclerc; p. 8, © Michael McLaughlin; p. 10, © Paul Krugman; p. 11, © Grianne Flynn; p. 13, © Matthi; p. 14, © Grianne Flynn; p. 15, © Lukasz Pajor; p. 16, © Lukasz Pajor; p. 18, © Eric70; p. 20, © James Horan; p. 25, © Michael McLaughlin; p. 26, © Michael McLaughlin; p. 28, © Laura Bittner; p. 30, © Rodrigo Bellizzi; p. 34, © Michael McLaughlin; p. 40, © Brooke Becker; p. 44, © Thomas Barrat; p. 49, © Victor Ginesi; p. 54, © Thierry Maffeis; p. 57, © Courtesy of the Merchant Hotel; p. 61, © James Horan; p. 63, © drserg; p. 69, © Morrison; p. 71, © Lumen-digital; p. 75, © Sean O' Dwyer; p. 76, © Sander van der Werf; p. 78, © Peter O'Toole; p. 80, © Madis Uudam; p. 81, © Morrison; p. 82, © Sander van der Werf; p. 85, © Milosz_M; p. 90, © James Horan; p. 91, © James Horan; p. 96, © Thomas Barrat; p. 100, © Lauren Orr; p. 101, © James Horan; p. 103, © littleny; p. 105, © Matthi; p. 108, © James Horan; p. 110, © James Horan; p. 113, © Semmick Photo; p. 114, © littleny; p. 116, © littleny; p. 127, © Courtesy of The Clarence Hotel; p. 161, © Courtesy Abbey Theater, Photo by Ros Kavanagh; p. 163, © Stephenkiernan; p. 167, © TheVectorminator; p. 169, © Derek Cullen/ Fáilte Ireland; p. 170, © Derek Cullen/ Fáilte Ireland; p. 172, © riganmc; p. 179, © Pecold; p. 189, © Irish National Stud/ Fáilte Ireland; p. 194, © Matthi; p. 202, © walshphotos; p. 203, © walshphotos; p. 215, © littleny; p. 216, © M Reel; p. 219, © M Reel; p. 220, © PHB.cz (Richard Semik); p. 223, © Artur Bogacki; p. 227, © Andrei Nekrassov; p. 223, left, 0803 © Peter O'Toole; p. 223, right, 0802 © Luis Santos; p. 238, © Sasapee; p. 239, © Andrei Nekrassov; p. 249, © Courtesy Ballyaloe Cookery School; p. 261, © Sean and Yvette Photography/ Fáilte Ireland; p. 274, © walshphotos; p. 283, © Courtesy Park Hotel Kenmare; p. 287, © Janelle Lugge; p. 298, © jordache; p. 305, © Greg Fellmann; p. 307, © Ambient Ideas; p. 319, © Marie Cloke; p. 324, © Michael Mc Lughlin; p. 327, © Courtesy AILLWEE CAVES; p. 332, © Michael Mc Laughlin; p. 333, © Courtesy Lahinch Surf School; p. 335, © Sean O'Dwyer; p. 338, © Rihardzz; p. 342, © Michael McLaughlin; p. 348, © Michael McLaughlin; p. 351, © Rihardzz; p. 356, © Michael McLaughlin; p. 367, © Lukasz Pajor; p. 371, © Gabriela Insuratelu; p. 373, © Grianne Flynn; p. 376, © Patryk Kosmider; p. 383, © LUKinMEDIA; p. 391, © Gabriela Insuratelu; p. 392, © Michael McLaughlin; p. 393, © Michael McLaughlin; p. 395, © Stefano Viola; p. 402, © Michael Mc Laughlin; p. 412, © PHB.cz (Richard Semik); p. 416, © Grianne Flynn; p. 420, © Michael McLaughlin; p. 421, © Grianne Flynn; p. 426, © Morrison; p. 428, © Grianne Flynn; p. 436, © Pecold; p. 446, © Victor Ginesi; p. 448, © Victor Ginesi; p. 450, © stenic56; p. 452, © Serg Zastavkin; p. 454, © Courtesy National Museums Northern Ireland; p. 455, © Stephen Lavery; p. 467, © Brendan Howard; p. 470, © Martin Heaney; p. 481, © PHB.cz (Richard Semik); p. 482, © PHB.cz (Richard Semik); p. 488, © Victor Ginesi; p. 506, © Meghan Lamb